RIDE THE THUNDER

RIDE THE THUNDER

A VIETNAM WAR STORY OF HONOR AND TRIUMPH

by Richard Botkin

WND BOOKS

RIDE THE THUNDER
A WND Books book
Published by WorldNetDaily
Los Angeles, CA
Copyright © 2009 by Richard Botkin

Jacket design by Douglas Miller, Mullerhaus Communications Group

WND Books are distributed to the trade by:
Midpoint Trade Books
27 West 20th Street, Suite 1102
New York, NY 10011

WND Books are available at special discounts for bulk purchases. WND Books, Inc. also publishes books in electronic formats. For more information call (310) 961-4170 or visit www.wndbooks.com.

First Edition

ISBN 10-Digit: 193507105X
ISBN 13-Digit: 9781935071051
E-Book ISBN 10-Digit: 1935071572
E-Book ISBN 13-Digit: 9781935071570

Library of Congress Control Number: 2008933752

Printed in the United States of America

10 9 8 7 6 5 4 3 2 1

*Dedicated to those who rode the thunder,
but especially to Cam Banh, Moline Ripley, Bunny Turley,
and the Marines of Ripley's Raiders and Binh's Third Battalion.*

As Ride the Thunder *was completed and going to initial publication, Colonel John Walter Ripley USMC, Ret. was taken from us. To all those who knew and loved him, to the Ripley family and the "greater family" of Marines he touched in ways too numerous and impossible to chronicle, his light will never dim. To his memory,* Ride the Thunder *is further dedicated.*

"…There is little use for the being whose tepid soul
knows nothing of the great and generous emotion,
of the high pride, the stern belief, the lofty enthusiasm,
*of the men who quell the storm and **ride the thunder**…"*[1]

—President Theodore Roosevelt

Ride the Thunder has captured the spirit and determination of an extraordinary "band of brothers"—a small group of U.S. Marine advisors and their Vietnamese Marine counterparts during a particularly desperate time.

Richard Botkin chronicles the exploits of the American Marines and their Vietnamese allies who were largely responsible for thwarting the North Vietnamese invasion of the northern portions of South Vietnam—known as the "Easter Offensive of 1972" in the West—that was intended to bring the nation to its knees.

Although everyone who was there during that period was personally locked in combat as or more intense as any experienced during previous tours, and individual acts of heroism and leadership abounded, Botkin focuses on three men in particular. Lieutenant Colonel Gerry Turley arrived in the area two days prior to the invasion to conduct what was supposed to have been a routine visit during a quiet time. As circumstances would have it, the unusual set of forces suddenly catapulted Gerry into the leadership role of his life. He would face annihilation from tenacious NVA hordes as well as challenges from an American and South Vietnamese military bureaucracy which initially failed to trust his judgment.

Excepting for those who already are familiar with the story of Captain John Ripley's actions at the Dong Ha Bridge, it is not possible to overstate the strategic impact his blowing of the bridge had on the remainder of all combat in Vietnam subsequent to that Easter Sunday afternoon.

Botkin highlights for the reader the special relationship American Marine advisors had with those Vietnamese Marines they served. The bond of genuine brotherhood and friendship between

Captain Ripley and Major Le Ba Binh—who commanded Third Battalion's seven hundred men facing more than twenty thousand NVA troops bent on their destruction at Dong Ha—transcended language and culture. The story of two great warriors serving together with a single purpose is evident. Had there been more men like Le Ba Binh the war's outcome would surely have been different.

In a departure from most books of this type, Botkin follows in some detail the families of each warrior, and tells the war's history through their personal experiences. In studying the history of war it is often easy to focus solely on the warrior—and get only half the story.

As someone who was there through these battles, as someone who witnessed many of the challenges chronicled during that particularly savage period, I was still largely unaware of what followed for our friends when the American portion of the war ended. For the officers of the Vietnamese Marine Corps, and their families, the seemingly unending nightmare of reeducation brutally imposed in the period after April of 1975—in the case of Le Ba Binh nearly twelve years—showcases the tenacity, resilience, and triumph of the human spirit.

America is blessed to have had at its service warriors like John Ripley and Gerry Turley. Our nation is doubly blessed to now count men like Binh among its citizens. *Ride the Thunder* is a fascinating, riveting read. It is history not yet told.

Brigadier General James Joy USMC, Ret.
Senior advisor to Vietnamese Marine Brigade 147 during 1971-1972

As I began research and uncovered the set of stories which have become *Ride the Thunder*, I was drawn in by the characters and how each of them, in their own unique circumstances, demonstrated implacable, unbending moral and physical courage. I was fascinated by how John Ripley, Le Ba Binh, Gerry Turley, and the others fought, suffered, bled, endured, and ultimately triumphed against what were often truly impossible odds.

In a world where most citizens celebrate the insipid and meaningless, where the traditional definition of hero and heroism has for years been utterly devalued and perverted, *Ride the Thunder* celebrates these men, and the women who stood by them, for their humanity, and most importantly for being the warriors they are.

Many people had a positive hand in the production of *Ride the Thunder*. I wish to thank my wife, our sons, my parents, and my sisters for their ongoing, unwavering encouragement and support. I also need to specifically thank Joseph Farah and Hugh Hewitt, without whose initial involvement the book never would have been written.

Among Marine friends, the list is too long to include them all, but recognition and thanks above the exceptional goes to Colonel Andrew R. Finlayson USMC, Ret.; Lieutenant Colonel John W. Bowman, Jr. USMC, Ret.; and Lieutenant Colonel George W.T. "Digger" O'Dell USMC, Ret.; who were three Marines with a special impact on the author. In addition, General Carl Mundy USMC, Ret.; General Walter Boomer USMC, Ret.; General Anthony Zinni USMC, Ret.; Major General John Grinalds USMC, Ret.; Brigadier General Jim Joy USMC, Ret.; Colonel Willard Buhl USMC; Colonel Geff Cooper USMCR, Ret.; Colonel Craig Huddleston USMC, Ret.; Colonel William Hutchison USMC, Ret.; Colonel J. Andrew Hutchison USMCR, Ret.; Colonel Clarke Lethin USMC, Ret.; Colonel William Wischmeyer USMC, Ret.; Lieutenant Colonel Andrew DeBona USMC, Ret.; Lieutenant Colonel David Randall USMC, Ret.; Lieutenant Colonel Robert Sheridan USMC, Ret.; Captain Ed "Machete Eddie" McCourt USMC, Ret.; First Sergeant Brad Norman USMCR, Ret.; Pete Andresen; Jim Angelis; Ken Crouse; Mike Etter; Ken Hendren; Frank Nowasell; O.D. Pinkerton; Tim Rickard; John Rivisto; Harry Warren; Alexandra Le; and the entire cast of U.S. Marine advisors who served with the Marines of the Republic of Vietnam all own a portion of the work. From the Navy side, thanks to Rear Admiral

Jeremiah Denton, USN, Ret.; Captain E. Chipman Higgins, SC, USN, Ret.; Captain George Oatis, Jr., DC, USN, Ret.; Captain B.L. Recher, SC, USN, Ret.; Commander Harry Heatley, USN, Ret.; and Jan Haldeman formerly of SEAL Team One and UDT 11. Hue Tan was always available to happily translate for me, Nguyen Luong, and the family of Le Ba Binh. Special thanks also to Colonel John G. Miller USMC, Ret., author of *The Bridge at Dong Ha*, for his friendship, guidance, and sage counsel. Kasey Pipes, my editor and friend, and Ami Naramor of WND Books gave more than expected to the project's success.

My large and informal "editorial staff" was likewise critical. Thanks to them all: Phil and Pat Bach, Craig Bertram, Ken Brooks, Jeremy Bruce, Bob and Candy Caskie, Dan Corbitt, Johnny Council, Kelly Crider, Dave Delihant, Connie Ferriman, George Gandre, Doug and Cathy Hemly, Jon Hemphill, Warren Hutson, Keith Johnson, Les Lyman, Joe Mauro, Ginny McClain, Marie Miller, George Oatis III, Tracy Rains, Lori Riffle, Joey Sanchez, Joseph Sanchez, Joseph Silveira, Kathy Slaughter, Neil Speth, Dan and Lori Van Hamersveld, Lee Wiggins, and Daniel Wilson. Randy Wilson, my dear friend and attorney, provided judicious guidance.

The folks at the Injured Marine Semper Fi Fund truly do God's work and it has been a privilege to partner with them for this project, in particular Karen Guenther and Wendy Lethin.

Thanks also to the entire *Ride the Thunder* family for opening up hearts and homes, for enduring the constant calls and interviews, and for helping to shape the story. Peggy Bell (Turley) was a faithful sounding board throughout. My intent is that the Marines and their families would be blessed by the proper chronicling of their stories, and that their children, grandchildren, and subsequent generations more fully appreciate the goodness, courage, character, and sacrifice of those who rode the thunder.

Richard Botkin
Granite Bay, California

The sweeping Communist victory in Southeast Asia in April 1975 and the ensuing tragedy which befell many of the people of South Vietnam was supposed to have occurred in 1972. In March of that year, the north launched a massive multi-division attack designed to overwhelm the Republic of Vietnam (RVN) Armed Forces and destroy the fledgling democracy. With the American military drawdown well underway and President Nixon's Vietnamization program limping along, the armed forces of South Vietnam were deployed in a thin line along the country's borders, committed to keeping the nation free from Communist domination. The tiny South Vietnamese Marine Corps and its American advisors were occupying a strategic avenue of approach in the northwest part of the country.

Few Americans are aware that the South Vietnamese even had a Marine Corps. The Vietnamese Marines (Thuy Quan Luc Chien or TQLC) never comprised more than eighteen thousand men or two percent of the RVN military forces. They were a curious blend of the best of Western and Eastern martial spirit. American Marine advisors played a key role in the founding of the TQLC in 1954 and for the next twenty-one years helped shape its training and foster its incredible fighting spirit. Without question, this tiny corps had a salutary impact far beyond its size in the Republic of Vietnam's struggle to survive. For those of us assigned to advise the various units of the TQLC, it was considered special duty; at times frustrating, but ultimately rewarding as we fought alongside them on the battlefield.

The much larger Army of the Republic of Vietnam (ARVN) was not always known for its battlefield prowess. The Vietnamese Marines continued to improve as the war progressed and with few exceptions were consistently outstanding. Many of its small but highly professional corps of officers were trained in the United States by American Marines. They attended our schools and lived with us, just as we did with them when assigned as advisors. The discipline and spirit of its troops was instilled in boot camp, which to a degree resembled U.S. Marine Corps recruit training at Parris Island and San Diego. Over time, the TQLC won the begrudging respect of their ARVN brothers and most certainly that of the North Vietnamese Army (NVA). The South Vietnamese Marines were different, just as the U.S. Marines from whom they sprang are different. That difference became readily apparent during the "Easter Offensive."

The so called "Tet Offensive" of 1968 still resonates in the minds of many Americans, particularly those old enough to remember the Vietnam War, yet, on March 30, 1972, the North Vietnamese Army launched an offensive which eclipsed "Tet" by a wide margin. Initially caught by the surprise and sheer scope of the Communist drive, ARVN forces everywhere were pushed to the limit, in some instances breaking completely under the overwhelming numbers and firepower of the attacking NVA. The Vietnamese Marine units were strategically located across the northern portion of South Vietnam close to the Demilitarized Zone, along with the newly formed Third ARVN Division. Generally oriented west, looking toward the old Khe Sanh battleground, were two brigades of TQLC, consisting of approximately five thousand men. The Third ARVN Division was defending to the north. Against this thin line, the NVA attacked with three infantry divisions, and the so called B5 front, which consisted of four additional infantry regiments, two artillery regiments, and two armored regiments. The 304th and 308th were two of the NVA divisions which participated in the attack. They had fought the French at Dien Bien Phu and were considered "Iron Divisions." The use of these divisions indicated it was a major offensive and the major NVA thrust of the "Easter Offensive." The North Vietnamese had a three to one numerical advantage over the RVN forces.

Sadly, by day four of the onslaught, much of the Third ARVN Division had fled in chaos or simply melted away. For the most part, the defense of the northern tier of the country was left to the Marines and a brigade of Army Airborne. It did not look good for those of us on the ground. The situation of the battalion advised by me and Captain Ray Smith (later Major General) was typical of what most of our advisor colleagues faced. After initially putting up a valiant defense and sustaining significant casualties we were simply overrun by the massive attack. We began a retreat to the east as the vastly superior NVA force pursued us. Our destination—the city of Quang Tri.

What most of us did not know was that at the same time an NVA armored column was driving south in an attempt to cut us off. Between us and probable destruction lay the Dong Ha Bridge which spanned the Cua Viet River. The river was a major obstacle, the bridge critical to NVA plans. Captain John Ripley (later Colonel), in what has become a legendary feat in the history of the U.S. Marine Corps, crawled beneath the bridge numerous times under intense fire planting explosives. He blew the bridge as lead elements of the NVA armored column were attempting to cross. For those of us escaping in an easterly direction and simply trying to stay alive, it was an act of courage for which we will be forever indebted to John Ripley. Had it not been for Ripley's destruction of the bridge, I am convinced that most of the Vietnamese Marine Corps and its American advisors would have been captured or killed. Trying to bring some order to chaos, and the person who gave the order to Ripley to blow the bridge, was Lieutenant Colonel Gerry Turley (later Colonel). Thrust into an almost surreal situation, his courage, calmness, and professionalism were the glue that kept the whole thing from unraveling. Botkin makes us understand the enormity of Turley's actions and appreciate how bizarre and crazy things can become in combat.

Despite the dire straits in which the TQLC found itself, the retreat was mostly orderly. Every Marine artillery piece was destroyed rather than left to fall into the hands of the enemy. Companies and battalions regrouped and remained intact with their American advisors by their side. This was in sharp contrast to units like the Third ARVN Artillery Group that opened its gates to the attacking NVA, rewarding them with dozens of artillery pieces in perfect working order and tons of ammunition. Why this difference in performance? I can only attribute it to the major investment in training based on the tried and true U.S. Marine Corps model and to a generation of advisors who valiantly endeavored to pass on their knowledge and beliefs to South Vietnamese counterparts.

The North Vietnamese almost succeeded. Generously supplied with practically unlimited quantities of armor and artillery and the latest Soviet anti-aircraft weapons, they came to the northern battlefields expecting to deliver the knockout punch. To capture the northernmost provinces which included Quang Tri and the old imperial capital of Hue would have been psychologically devastating to the RVN government. The north's pre-invasion intelligence, however, failed to account for the tenacity of the Vietnamese Marine Corps. Quang Tri did ultimately fall, only to be retaken by the TQLC on September 15, 1972. During the seven-week battle to recapture Quang Tri City, the TQLC suffered 3,658 casualties. It was vicious combat against a tenacious enemy, but the victory was ample testimony to the professionalism and courage of the Vietnamese Marines. The North Vietnamese ultimately succeeded in 1975. But at least the south was given a three year reprieve in which to try to bring their country together to withstand the north's determination to conquer them. Sadly, three years was not enough.

If you are inclined to believe the Communist victory was not sad, *Ride the Thunder* will help disabuse you of that notion. Woven into the narrative is the story of Lieutenant Colonel Le Ba Binh: Marine, patriot, husband, father. Binh was the commanding officer of the Vietnamese Marine battalion that John Ripley advised. His story will infuriate, inspire, and ultimately gladden your heart. The unsuccessful conclusion of the war and its tragic impact on millions of South Vietnamese is brought into clear perspective by Binh's saga. Also captured in *Ride the Thunder* are the family stories of several Marines, Vietnamese and American, whose sacrifice and courage were typical of military families past and present. For those of us who chose the profession of arms, their support, encouragement, and loyalty remain an inspiration.

The history of war is generally written by the victors and the Communists have aggressively expunged from the record any honorable mention of TQLC exploits. *Ride the Thunder* begins to write back into history the untold story of Vietnamese Marines and their families, who never surrendered, never gave up, and never lost faith. For those who fought, suffered, and overcame so much to attain the freedom that is theirs as new citizens of the United States, *Ride the Thunder* is a story that deserves to be shared with subsequent generations of Americans, but most especially young Vietnamese-Americans. I hope this book will help them understand the price their parents and grandparents paid to secure the freedom they now enjoy. And finally, while the title "Marine" holds a special place in the hearts and minds of most Americans, the chronicling of the exploits and service of Le Ba Binh and men like him will give the reader appreciation for the title in Vietnamese as well.

General Walter E. Boomer USMC, Ret.

The Marriage of Le Ba Binh and Cam Banh
Song Than Officers' Club
Saigon, Republic of Vietnam
Wednesday, January 19, 1972

M*en who stand for something*, upon whose shoulders, supple muscles, and dexterous minds ride the destinies of their nations, often have an edge in the competition for the finest women.

At the appointed place and time, Thieu Ta (Major) Le Ba Binh, commanding officer of the Third Battalion, known to friend and foe alike as the *Soi Bien* or "Wolves of the Sea," cut a rather dashing figure as a groom in the tropical dress uniform of the Marine Corps of the Republic of Vietnam. In another time, he might have ended up a lawyer, a doctor, a man of commerce or letters. These were not normal times and the cards dealt to Thieu Ta Binh's struggling country called forth men of action and determination because if there was no victory there would be no Vietnam. It was that hard. It was that simple.

Even though Vietnamese culture was long established before America had even been born, Binh could still have been best described, in his country's current cycle of life, as part of the first generation in the equation described two centuries prior by George Washington: "I am a soldier, so my son can be a farmer, so his son can be a poet." The men and women of the generation of Vietnamese born around the time of Binh and Cam had never known peace. Strife and tumult were thoroughly integrated into the patterns of everyday living. "Normal" was a relative, subjective term. As such, it was entirely normal in the face of war and struggle and death to press ahead because it was life's only option. And so it was not at all odd that Le Ba Binh and Cam Banh should come together as husband and wife in January of 1972.

Until his wedding, Le Ba Binh had served one continuous tour of duty. The Americans came and, if they survived, went home after a year or thirteen months. Binh had command of Third Battalion's First Company for nearly four years, this after commanding a platoon for two years. When that assignment was complete, there was no trip to Hawaii or Australia, no recuperative or educational tour to broaden him out or develop his *savoir-faire*. When Binh left First Company it was only to become Third Battalion's executive officer.

That a young man such as Thieu Ta Binh, who had gained position and power not because of his family's prestige or wealth but rather through continual personal exertion and exceptional leadership on the field of battle, should be bonded to a fair maiden like Cam Banh was a *fait accompli*. There had, in fact, been other men, a doctor and a lawyer among them, seeking the favor of this young woman with high purpose who was instead destined to marry her handsome Marine.

In traditional Vietnamese culture, selection of the most propitious time and date for a wedding is always cause for great concern and planning. Sages and family elders consult and deliberate to select *the* day that will yield greatest longevity and prosperity for the new husband and wife. After serious consideration and rumination, the decision that January 19, 1972, would be the day for Binh's and Cam's wedding was announced.

The Song Than Marine Officers' Club was located on some choice Saigon real estate. Erected in the mid-1960s and adjacent to the Saigon River, it was only six or so blocks from both the Presidential Palace and the American Embassy. Even though the Vietnamese Marine Corps represented less than two percent of its country's total military size, to view the club one would think their power and political influence was far greater than it really was. As opulent as it seemed to some, the club was also collocated with a supply depot for the TQLC (Thuy Quan Luc Chien—synonymous for Vietnamese Marine Corps) and the Marines made effective use of the space they were given. Smartly maintained and jealously guarded by the men assigned there, Marine officers had a right to be proud of this their service's impressive sanctuary of sorts, their clubby home away from home.

If they were not in the hospital recovering from combat wounds or in the field leading troops in direct action against the hated Communist foe, every officer who was anybody in the growing but still familial TQLC was that day in attendance at the wedding of Le Ba Binh and Cam Banh. Had the Viet Cong or NVA possessed the resources or capabilities, a terrorist strike on the wedding reception would have dealt the south a horrible strategic blow.

John Ripley, the only American in the gathered throng of TQLC leadership and multitudes of family and friends, marveled at the assemblage. Except for the *commandant*, Lieutenant General Le Nguyen Khang, who was down with a serious case of stomach flu and who was known to be extremely partial to the promising young officer he had personally recruited into the Soi Bien in 1962, every Vietnamese Marine officer "Dai Uy Ripp-lee" knew personally or by reputation was in attendance. As impressive a list of warriors as they were, their wives too had obvious presence and power. Many of the women were strikingly beautiful. At times John Ripley felt like genuflecting in their presence. For a man who possessed every bit as much of Virginia gentility as his wife and who less than a year before spent a tour with the British Royal Marines where ceremony and tradition were as important as their vaunted combat readiness, this day would forever be fondly recalled as noble and special and dignified.

Captain (Dai Uy) John Ripley had only returned to Vietnam two weeks before the wedding. The Christmas R&R he had concluded with his wife and children all the way back in Virginia had been harder to return from even than the magnificent honeymoon-like experience he and Moline had shared in Hawaii nearly five years earlier. That he had been given the opportunity to experience the magic of Christmas with his young children one more time, maybe for the last time, was something he would never forget.

Neither would Captain Ripley forget that in mid-December, one day prior to departure for R&R, when Third Battalion ended a particularly difficult operation near the DMZ outside of Gio Linh, Thieu Ta Binh had called his advisor, Dai Uy Ripley, into the humble abode that served as his field-expedient office. Gio Linh was pretty much the end of the line, as remote for Americans in late 1971 as the dark side of the moon was before astronauts flew around it. When Dai Uy Ripley reported in to the man he had increasingly grown to respect and deeply admire, he was without a clue as to the reason for the summons. Standing at ease once the proper greetings were exchanged, Thieu Ta Binh surprised his American friend: "Ripp-lee, I am familiar with your Christmas tradition."

In his typical reticent and understated way Thieu Ta Binh presented his *covan*—Vietnamese for "trusted advisor"—a Vietnamese princess doll, beautifully wrapped, in colored cellophane and ribbons, very traditional, and magnificently adorned. "Ripp-lee. For your daughter. From me." Dai Uy Ripley was stunned by the thought, the effort, the cost. To have arranged for such a gift would have required colossal planning. To present it in Gio Linh of all places demonstrated a level of respect and kindness, of acceptance and friendship, that moved John Ripley almost to tears.

John Ripley and Le Ba Binh, by the time of the wedding, had worked together for nearly five months—in combat conditions a virtual eternity. The advisor-commander relationship could not have been any better. Extremely like-minded in warrior spirit, aggressive combat styles, and concern for the welfare of their Marines, the monumental cultural differences between America and Vietnam were reduced to near insignificance by their appreciation for one another—just as the advisor-commander relationship was designed to work.

By early 1972 there had been nearly eighteen years' worth of USMC advisors who had rotated through duty with the TQLC. From its birth in 1954 the Vietnamese Marines had been in near-continuous combat. Most of the officer corps graduated from Basic School in Quantico. While they were not expected to be carbon copies of their American brothers due to an obvious combination of cultural differences and logistical constraints, no American who observed TQLC performance in the field questioned their *élan* or fighting spirit.

Outside of the opulence of the Song Than Marine Officers' Club, John Ripley had operated with Binh under the worst conditions. With his own history as a warrior, if anyone among the Americans could tell, Dai Uy Ripley could spot a gunfighter. Binh was a gunfighter. Not content to be limited by his own experiences and observations, Dai Uy Ripley had also overheard a senior American in serious conversation with a senior Vietnamese Marine who exclaimed to the *covan* that Third Battalion, Binh's battalion, was the "go-to battalion," *the* folks to call when the stuff really hit the fan.

Binh ran deep, extremely deep, and he did it without a hint of flamboyance or bravado. If Jimmy Dean had done a song for the Vietnamese, if there had been lyrics like those describing the large, quiet coal miner "Big John" on the good-guy side in Southeast Asia, he might have selected Thieu Ta Binh to sing about. His actions and those of the seven hundred men of the Soi Bien did the talking for him. Those in the know, those whose opinions were the most informed, revered and appreciated the fighting prowess of Third Battalion. It was all but impossible for Dai Uy Ripley not to love this man Binh like a brother.

Familiar enough with Vietnamese culture but not confident that he knew the ins and outs of what his actions should be at a Vietnamese wedding, Dai Uy Ripley maintained a low profile. To ensure that he would not offend and to show appropriate respect for his friend and his new bride, Dai Uy Ripley maintained a modified position of attention for a good portion of the afternoon. He munched with the others from the bounteous buffet of mixed traditional Vietnamese and Western food, joined in toasts, clapped at the proper time, laughed when it seemed right.

Instructive for Dai Uy Ripley were the conversations he was able to have with the Vietnamese Marines there. Always speaking English for his benefit so that he might not be embarrassed, and most importantly so that he might not lose face, they included him in every facet of the day's activities.

January 19, 1972, was a grand day, at least for those at the Song Than Marine Officers' Club. Binh had pulled out all the stops. The wedding and reception had cost a small fortune, a good portion of which was paid for by gifts. For reasons he did not quite comprehend Dai Uy Ripley was not allowed to give a gift; to have done so would have actually caused offense. His presence alone was more than enough for Binh. The others, the five hundred or so, more than made up for whatever the gentleman from Virginia was not allowed to give. Moline would have been horrified but, like her husband, would have understood in the end.

Even the music was superb. Playing for the union of Binh and Cam were not one, but two small orchestras. And Binh, with his own connections and notoriety as a warrior, had arranged for none other than Khanh Ly, the famous Vietnamese pop singer and a personal friend, to entertain the adoring crowd.

Yet there was still a war on and there was still no shortage of Communists left to fight. There would be no luxurious, romantic honeymoon to Bangkok or Hong Kong or Dalat or even Vung Tau. Due to the war and the rules of the TQLC, Thieu Ta Binh and his beautiful new bride were grateful to celebrate an abbreviated period of bliss aboard the base at Thu Duc.

Inside a week Binh was back in the fight, leading Third Battalion, as he always had: from the front ...with his faithful *covan* by his side.

INTO THE ABYSS

Republic of Vietnam
March 29, 1972

The entire cabin of the U.S. Air Force C-130 had been gutted of seats to allow maximum interior space for the one hundred-plus Vietnamese Marine replacement troops (and a few live pigs raised at the Thu Duc farm for the units up north to supplement their protein consumption) on the routine three-hundred-mile flight north from Tan Son Nhut in Saigon to Phu Bai. Having already learned well what fighting men in every military service in every country learn early on—to sleep in any and every position, wherever there is open space, whenever there is a spare moment— most of them hardly seemed to notice or be intimidated by the lone American Marine officer there among them.

In the very close and crowded quarters on the deck of the soon-to-depart C-130, the dozen or so enlisted Vietnamese Marines immediately adjacent to Lieutenant Colonel Gerry Turley were consumed by the oddity of his presence. In the rigid culture of deference and respect for status in Vietnam, and even more so its military, these men normally never would have dared to speak directly to or even physically touch a man of Gerry's rank—which was plainly clear as he now wore the same tiger-striped uniform they did along with Vietnamese rank insignia. There was the assumption on their part, which was correct in this case, that the American could not understand a single thing they said. It was as if because of that that he was not quite human or real like them. And so there were small groupings of men around the out-of-place American who discussed the incredibly strange things about him that were different from normal folks like them, things like the unusual amount of hair on his exposed forearms.

Like children quickly tiring of a new toy, the amusement soon subsided to the mere practical. Hardly corpulent, Gerry Turley was a man who was within five pounds of his high school weight. When he could he would still jump out of perfectly good airplanes, and would almost daily run three to five miles or take long, long swims. By American standards he was very much still a lean, mean fighting machine. Compared to most Vietnamese, and especially to the young, nearly cadaverous-looking troops around him, Lieutenant Colonel Turley might have been the model for the "before" picture for a diet advertisement in a Vietnamese magazine. Recognizing his relative plumpness when viewed against those around him, he became the pillow of choice for more than his share of the young Marines.

As the ramp door closed and the plane's engines spun up to maximum power for takeoff, Lieutenant Colonel Gerry Turley— who as an American Marine and ambassador of his country's goodwill had already accepted his temporary status as an inanimate object—was revisited by that old feeling. That old unsettling feeling that had visited him only twice before in his now forty-two years of life.

It was that unusual premonition of something strange about to happen, that extra-perceptive sense of foreboding and impending doom that had twice saved his life: once as a boy in Ogallala, Nebraska when he declined the invite from seven other buddies who later that day all drowned when they went swimming in the town's rock quarry, and again in Korea when, for no reason other than "that feeling," he pulled himself from the manifest of an R&R flight to Japan that crashed moments after takeoff, killing all aboard.

On March 29, 1972, that old feeling was just as disconcerting, just as mood-souring and bile-producing as it had been those two times before. On March 29, 1972, he did not know why, but Gerry Turley somehow sensed, with great conviction, that he was, at this very moment, headed into the abyss.

CHAPTER ONE

Red Tide

The map was turning Red. From Fortress America in late 1954, the world view was not encouraging. The cancer of Communism seemed inexcisable, popping up and spreading with creeping momentum. Russia, Eastern Europe, China, North Korea, and now a divided Vietnam with Communists controlling the north, hungrily eyeing the south and perhaps even Laos and Cambodia. The growing populations of enslaved peoples dimmed the brilliance of total victory from World War II.

While Old World colonialism crumbled and fell away, the political and economic vacuums created Third World climates hostile to the gradual or benign evolution of free markets and democratically elected governments. The perceived Soviet-Red Chinese monolith, from the American perspective an insatiable, amorphous *juggernaut* forever consuming whatever lay in its path, worked with vigor to expand its influence by freely exporting Marxist ideals, subversion, and assistance for People's War.

As Pearl Harbor had shaken America from its isolation, drawn it completely, if unwillingly, into the role of leader of the Free World, the climate that evolved after the conclusion of major hostilities in September 1945 was one that would require the reluctant giant to be continually vigilant, forever investing wealth, resources, and manpower at levels never before experienced or imagined necessary in times of peace.

The American experience in World War II, so complete and all-consuming, with every living citizen impacted in ways difficult to fully characterize or quantify, became the paradigm by which future military actions and the measure of victory or defeat would be considered.

The American experience in the Korean War, fought between June 1950 and a tenuous armistice reached in July 1953, was so unlike the total triumph of World War II that was still fresh in the national psyche. At a cost of more than fifty-four thousand men killed, more than eight thousand missing in action, and hundreds of thousands wounded, the inability to declare victory did not sit well with reasonable citizens. The optimists could at least say that the Republic of Korea still stood and the positioning of the Seventh Fleet in the Formosa Strait tempered Communist moves against Nationalist China and maybe even Japan. While the spread of Communism in northern Asia had been checked, at least temporarily, a similar cancer continued to fester further south.

LE BA BINH

Le Ba Binh's desire to be an officer in the newly formed Thuy Quan Luc Chien (TQLC)—the Vietnamese Marine Corps—was influenced mostly by his father.

Le Ba Sach, Binh's father, was born in 1910 near Hadong, a rural town slightly south and west of Hanoi. A bright young man, his family managed to secure his passage to France in the late 1920s where he attended technical college, earning a degree in engineering. Upon his return to Vietnam in the early 1930s he joined the French naval forces stationed in the Saigon area. As a Vietnamese, even though he was educated, his opportunities for rank were limited so he served as an over-qualified petty officer on the small boats and ships maintained there by the French navy.

In 1930 Sach's mother-in-law had moved to Saigon where she operated a restaurant near Cholon. Also joining him in Saigon was his new wife, Cat Thi Dan, who had come from the small town of Son Tay near Hanoi. Binh, who came into the world in 1937, was the first of four children born to this traditional Vietnamese Buddhist family.

The portion of French Indo-China that would become known to the world again as Vietnam was made up of three distinct regions. In the north, just below and abutting China, was Tonkin, its major geographical feature impacting the population being the Red River delta. In the extreme south was Cochinchina. As with Tonkin, its major physical feature is the larger and more productive rice bowl delta region of the mighty Mekong. In between the two, Annam could support far fewer people on its narrow coastal plains which rapidly transition to mountains and forests as one moves west into Laos and Cambodia.

Le Ba Binh's earliest recollections as a young boy would include memories of the Japanese occupation. The Greater East Asian Co-Prosperity Sphere brought anything but prosperity to the people of Indo-China. On more than one occasion, young Binh had seen Japanese soldiers swiftly, and for reasons he could not discern, cut the hands or arms off of ordinary citizens in Saigon street markets.

In his travels around the country, Le Ba Sach had personally observed a Japanese army officer use his sword to sever the legs of an elderly rickshaw driver who failed to demonstrate proper obeisance or move with appropriate energy and enthusiasm. In his hometown of Hadong, there was a woman who had sold rice to the Imperial Army for horse feed. When one of the pack animals died after eating some of the rice, the woman was taken and, still very much alive, brutally forced into the carved open carcass of the dead animal. Once she was stuffed inside, the soldiers sewed the animal shut and stood there laughing as they watched the lifeless horse's body writhe with ever weakening movements while the old woman slowly suffocated within. The people of Indo-China learned at a high price that their French colonial masters were not supermen. As the tide of war turned against the Japanese and as the U.S. Navy's submarine noose around the home islands grew ever tighter, the need for food imports soared. From the fertile rice bowls of the Red River and, to a lesser extent, from the Mekong, the Japanese extracted all the grain they could for export to Nippon. Accurate records do not exist, but reasonable estimates suggest that in 1944-1945, in Tonkin alone, as many as two million of the ten million residents may have died from this invader-imposed starvation that was exacerbated by an untimely regional drought. Relative to China, which also endured extreme suffering at the hands of the Japanese, the Vietnamese may have paid a higher price for their forced "membership" into the Greater East Asian Co-Prosperity Sphere. (Accepted estimates place Chinese deaths in World War II at between 10-12 million men, women, and children. With a total population at the time of probably 500 million, roughly two percent of Chinese died. Vietnam's population, estimated for Tonkin, Annam, and Cochinchina to be nearly 30 million, saw between one and two million deaths from the enemy-imposed famine, or between three and six percent of the entire Vietnamese population killed. Various sources.)

At the final meeting of the Big Three in Potsdam in July 1945, Truman, Stalin, Churchill, and their staffs did more than plot the ultimate outcome of the war in Europe and finalize strategy for the defeat of Japan. Among the issues minor to all excepting those who lived in Indo-China was the agreement that at the war's conclusion in the Pacific, Nationalist Chinese troops would accept the surrender of Japanese soldiers down to the area around the 16th Parallel. South of that, the Japanese surrender would be handled by units of the British army which included Indian troops.

Binh recalled the arrival of the Brits and their Indian allies into Saigon. So different were the two groups: the Tommies were jovial and friendly, comfortable in their interactions with Vietnamese kids. Though he knew no English, Binh could recognize a smile and certainly enjoyed what candy the young soldiers gave away to the throngs of children who followed without relent. Perhaps it was because they too were from such a poor country that the Indians, unlike their British allies, were all business, sparing, taciturn, unconcerned if they were liked by their humble hosts.

There was a certain constancy in the more than two thousand years of recorded Vietnamese history: struggle, strife, hardship, and sorrow so constant people seemed nearly inured to it. Whether waged against invading Cham from Cambodia, Chinese sweeping down from the north, or between battling clans of Nguyens and Trinhs in internecine combat, Vietnam seemed always at war. The history of its people was filled with two millennia worth of heroes and heroines in the nation's defense against foreign enemies. Beginning with sisters Trung Trac and

Trung Nhi who battled and established in AD 40 a kingdom that spread into southern China, to Trieu Au, the third century Vietnamese equivalent to Joan of Arc, and Tran Hung Dao, Le Loi, and Le Thanh Tong up through Phan Dinh Phung, the culture was replete with brave, intrepid men and women whose sacrifices were common knowledge to all Vietnamese children.

More recently the struggle had been with the French followed by the Japanese. With the Japanese set to depart, it was still uncertain which enemy would fill the vacuum created. Pain and hunger and death were as much a part of life's cycles in Vietnam as birth and joy and satisfaction. Could a person say that times were that much harder under the Japanese?

Perhaps they were. Those who had not completely succumbed outright to food shortages were made weak and vulnerable. In 1946, an outbreak of influenza claimed many victims. Among that group was Binh's mother who endured three days of sickness before she too died leaving her husband, Binh, and his brother and two sisters to a very uncertain future.

After having suffered humiliating defeat at the hands of the Germans in World War II, France was interested only in returning its colonies to their pre-war status. While the British shared similar intentions, the United States was not inclined to see Old World colonialism restored. As the Communist tide rose on the Asian continent, there appeared few easy options. Ho Chi Minh was seen as one more brick in the evolving Communist monolith. With the loss of China followed by war in Korea, American support for the French was the obvious, expeditious choice.

The movement among Vietnamese patriots anxious to shed the colonial yoke was well under way before the Japanese had assumed control of French Indo-China. Ho Chi Minh, who would ultimately emerge as the face of Vietnamese nationalism to the world, was the last man standing as his minions assassinated those viewed as a threat to his leadership in the north. In the north, especially after the war, incipient non-Communist nationalist movements were either brutally suppressed and eliminated by Ho's Viet Minh followers or co-opted and easily compromised by the French. Communists would do a masterful job with their propaganda in framing those Vietnamese who opposed them as somehow illegitimate and insincere in their patriotism, as lap dogs and puppets of the French, which in some cases proved correct. The same charge would be applied to the Americans and those receiving their support from 1954 onward.

The French invested little capital in training and raising up quality political and military leadership from the Vietnamese citizenry. Leadership development would be more Darwinian—survival of the most ruthless, cunning, or corrupt in both north and south.

Nationalist movements throughout Asia had gained inspiration from the 1905 Japanese victory over the Russians. Nowhere were native populations more anxious to gain independence than in Indo-China, and yet, except for their common goal of ousting the Europeans, there was often little else disparate nationalist groups could agree on. While Vietnamese comprised roughly 80 percent of the population of Tonkin, Annam, and Cochinchina, more than fifty minority groups were distributed throughout the long and narrow geography which constituted their incipient nation. Ethnic Chinese were the single largest minority group. Comprising nearly two percent of the population, their concentration in urban areas and dominance in commerce gave them influence out of proportion to their numbers. The Montagnards, Hmong, Nung, and others were more often found in the remote border and mountain areas.

Nationalist passions ran deep in Vietnam by the late 1920s. Vietnamese workers ranging from those in the textile industry to pedicab drivers staged massive strikes with some success. The Revolutionary Youth League, with decidedly Communist leanings, was formed by Ho Chi Minh in southern China in 1925. December of 1927 saw the establishment of the Vietnam Quoc Dan Dang (VNQDD). Known as the Vietnamese Nationalist Party, its members included mostly students, low-ranking government employees, soldiers, peasants, and even some landlords.[1] The VNQDD, modeled after the Kuomintang in China, was seen by the Communists as a direct rival. In June of 1929 came the official birth of the Indo-Chinese Communist Party (ICP). Along with Ho Chi Minh, others present at the party's inception included Le Duan and Pham Van Dong, men who would assume key roles in

Communist party issues in the coming struggle alongside the man once known as Nguyen Ai Quoc or "Nguyen the Patriot." (Ho Chi Minh was originally known by several names.)

The ICP came to life right at the time when the Great Depression began to wreak havoc across the globe. In French Indo-China the worldwide economic contraction would cut rice and rubber prices and exports, leaving countless citizens without jobs, income, or a way to feed their families. Communism's mass appeal gained momentum among those disenfranchised.

All this political activity drew the attention of French authorities, who invested considerable police and military resources in attempting to suppress these upstart nationalist groups. The ICP enjoyed its greatest influence in Tonkin. In Cochinchina the ICP did less well as other groups diluted their appeal. No less anti-French or pro-independence, the Hoa Hao and Cao Dai would absorb a high percentage of those seeking to put their patriotism into practice.*

When the Germans and Soviets entered into their Non-Aggression Pact in August of 1939, France outlawed the French Communist Party and all political parties in Indo-China. This move forced the ICP to a more rural effort which, in the longer run, bolstered their strength in Tonkin especially.[2]

Of the numerous challenges facing the budding nationalist forces in Indo-China, geography was among the cruelest obstacles. From the

---

* The Hoa Hao are a distinctly Vietnamese reformed Buddhist sect founded in southern Vietnam by Huynh Phu So in 1939. Viewed by the French as a political threat, the Hoa Hao were strongly anti-Communist, especially after Viet Minh assassins murdered Huynh Phu So in 1947.

Cao Dai, established in the 1920s, like Hoa Hao Buddhism, is uniquely Vietnamese. Originating in southern Vietnam as well, Cao Dai is an eclectic blend of Christianity, Islam, Taoism, Buddhism, Confucianism, and Hinduism. Adherents are expected to renounce materialism in order to cultivate spiritual growth. Because of the religious aspect, Cao Dai devotees, like Hoa Hao, have also traditionally been anti-Communist. Cao Dai employs spiritual mediums and channelers for use in *séances*. Important saints of Cao Dai include Trung Trinh, Sun Yat Sen, Joan of Arc, Rene Descartes, William Shakespeare, Victor Hugo, and Louis Pasteur.

northernmost tip of Tonkin on the border with China, to the southernmost spot in Cochinchina stretched nearly eleven hundred miles of changing, dissimilar, and regionalizing topography. Hanoi and Saigon, Indo-China's two major cities, were 750 miles apart and only marginally connected by a tiny railroad and Highway One which was, for most of the distance, little more than a well-traveled double-wide ox-cart path. The distance from Hanoi to Saigon is akin to that between Denver and St. Louis, Chicago and Charleston, Omaha and Tuscaloosa, Boston and Grand Rapids, Seattle and Santa Cruz, New York and Nashville, Des Moines and Atlanta, Minneapolis and Little Rock, and yet at the end of the war they may as well have been worlds apart. Geographic isolation presented opportunities for consolidation of local power to the Communists in the north and to a lesser extent to other nationalist groups in the south.

Tumult caused by the Japanese withdrawal and the relative weakness of returning French colonial forces gave Ho Chi Minh and the Viet Minh what they believed was an advantageous opportunity to strike. On August 28, 1945, they announced the formation of the provisional government of the Democratic Republic of Vietnam. Ho Chi Minh was declared its first president. To broaden its appeal, the Communists included Emperor Bao Dai in the government as well.[3] What followed was a series of moves and countermoves by the French and Viet Minh that would eventually lead to open warfare.

The Vietnam Quoc Dan Dang and the Dai Viet Quoc Dan Dang, which spun off from the VNQDD, were both eager for the establishment of a Vietnamese republic but were generally not sympathetic to Communism. Even though they had formed a loose alliance with the Viet Minh to oppose foreign control in Vietnam, in early 1946 the Communists systematically eliminated ranking party members and their families in a series of actions which ultimately removed them as a threat to Ho's leadership in the north; all this while keeping up the fight against the French.[4]

Political turmoil was the norm as the power vacuum left by Japanese surrender and withdrawal was closely followed by returning French forces attempting to reestablish colonial authority. In the face of squabbles among competing Vietnamese nationalist groups, the Viet Minh were more powerful in the north, less so in the south. The French had no intentions of giving in to Ho Chi Minh. Negotiations between the two sides proved futile while clashes between their military units gained frequency. By November of 1946 the ruse of a political settlement was finally set aside. What would become known as the First Indo-China War had begun. Complicating matters in the south was the April 1947 Viet Minh-organized assassination of Hoa Hao leader Huynh Phu So. Following his death both the Hoa Hao and Cao Dai formed alliances with the French.

As was tradition in Vietnamese culture, Le Ba Sach mourned the loss of his wife and mother of his four children for three years. Still a young man, he remarried in 1949. Binh and his brother and two sisters would have seven new siblings added to their family in the years following their father's second marriage. Theirs was a strong family and they all got on well with their new mother.

Among nearly all Asian cultures the pervasive impact of Confucius's teachings remained strong. Reverence for elders, the family, and education were particularly important. Boys were prized over girls and the oldest son always ranked first in each household. As the oldest son, Binh's sole mission as a young boy was to secure his education. From an early age Binh assumed his duty and studied hard.

Tan Dinh hamlet was home for Binh and his family. The area was about as "downtown" Saigon as one could get. Near the city's center, just a few blocks from the Saigon River, it provided a nurturing, secure environment for Le Ba Sach to house his new wife and raise their eleven children.

The home of Le Ba Sach was fairly typical by Vietnamese standards. For its time it would have been described as upper-middle class. On the level that opened to the narrow alley, the family's bicycles were parked just outside, off the lane and within their property line. Shoes or slippers were always left at the wide entrance, placed there in orderly fashion. The area where guests or friends were entertained and the kitchen took up most of the first floor. The family slept on levels two and three, but also kept a traditional shrine at the front side portion of the second floor, the kind common in most Vietnamese homes, whether humble or magnificent, where incense was burned and pictures deferentially arranged of important ancestors to be worshipped.

The narrow alleys that led back from the main drag and then forked onto other alleys were fairly dark but open to the sky above. Brightly lit only when the sun was directly overhead, these spaces constituted a large portion, however cramped, of the play area for the several dozens of children from the twenty-plus homes sharing this common-lane address. At its only entrance was a small, sturdy gate that was rarely closed but could be if needed. In their boyish games of warfare, Binh and his cohorts would often guard it from outside rivals. Little did they know that these sorts of gates, common to neighborhoods everywhere throughout the city, would take on great tactical importance in the real defense of Saigon from Viet Cong infiltrators during the Tet Offensive of 1968.

The invisible hand of the free market was as apparent on the streets of Tan Dinh as it was in Denver and Detroit or Paris and Amsterdam, and just as ruthlessly and efficiently applied. Vendors of every description hawked clothing, pots and pans, foodstuffs and spices, rice and noodles, locally grown fruits and vegetables, locally caught fish of every description, locally slaughtered pork and chicken. If a bicycle or small mechanical contraption was in need of repair there were men who could spot-weld them just down the sidewalk. A young boy was never far from refreshment or special treat if he had a few *piasters* in his pockets. Fruit peddlers continually roamed the streets pushing carts laden with fresh-cut mango, papaya, durian, and jackfruit. If thirsty, there were people to sell you fresh, cool coconut milk you could drink by a tiny straw directly from the husked shell. Children and indulgent adults could feast on tiny stalks of sugarcane cut, rolled, and pressed by street-side devices that concentrated the natural punch of its sweetness, further adding to the problem of tooth decay.

Commerce turned at the furiously pedaling pace of sinewy, muscular men, both young and old, who could move and maneuver incredible loads and irregularly shaped objects arranged somehow on bicycles or atop *cyclopousses*. While there were few people of girth, for those who were resourceful and willing to work hard, there was food to eat. The streets running through Tan Dinh were for all hours alive with this commerce. Even at night the city never slept but only seemed to slow down.

With all that was happening throughout Vietnam and in Saigon, politics and intrigue were lost on boys more concerned with schoolwork and playing with local chums. Binh's closest ally was brother An, younger by two years. An and Binh formed up with the other boys in their hamlet into one of two rival gangs. Established at that time and age more for fun than anything else, the gangs would compete in sport and mock battle, drawing blood only by mistake or over exuberance. Lacking material wealth or the availability of factory-produced toys in no way inhibited the creative play for the children in Tan Dinh.

Binh, An, and the Tan Dinh comrades in their younger years would spend countless hours kicking soccer balls made from locally produced rubber around the hamlet alleys and open spaces along the river. Like young boys everywhere, Vietnamese boys enjoyed the timeless game of marbles, the only difference being that the tiny glass spheroids were held against the fingerprint side of the middle finger and pulled back with the opposite hand to create flicking force.

Ever resourceful, the Tan Dinh boys would collect discarded cigarette packs made of thin but durable cardboard. Stacking their boxes one atop the other, the boys would stand back a ways and attempt to knock opposing columns over with small rocks or pebbles. As with marbles, the displaced tiny boxes became the personal wealth and property of ace shooters, serving as a measure of physical acuity and skill. For most of the group came the instinctive, inherent call to play games of war. Binh and his buddies were forever maneuvering about their hamlet armed with guns crafted from chunks of wood that could launch rubber bands a good distance with reasonable accuracy.

The pleasures of recorded music and broadcast radio were out of reach for most in Indo-China during the late 1940s and early 1950s. It was to the home of the richest family in Tan Dinh, where the man was employed in some manner by the French government, that the entire hamlet population would gravitate any time the Victorola was cranked up or the radio turned on. Whether the music was something new from France or America, or one of the old-fashioned, country-type, regional love songs unique to Tonkin, Annam, or Cochinchina, the elders especially never lost their sense of marvel at the squeaky sounds emitted from the turning black disks or the box of polished wood.

No holiday in Vietnam could approach the level of seriousness, significance, anticipation, and gaiety that Tet was for all citizens, even those who were not Buddhist. Tet Nguyen Dan—the Lunar New Year—begins on the first day of the first lunar month and is the first season of the new year. Usually taking place sometime in late January or early February, it is at once both secular and sacred; the holiday is too big not to be enjoyed by all Vietnamese. Tet is a period for families and friends to gather, for deceased ancestors to be worshipped, a time to set aside the past and to look expectantly to a bounteous future. For children especially it is a joyous time marked by games and gifts of money and new clothes, fireworks, and special delicacies served in abundance.

Binh particularly savored the food of Tet. His mother and the other women would cook for days in advance, shooing ravenous children away as they circled like vultures waiting for a morsel here, a tiny bite there, anxious to sample anything their elders might share. Aside from the candies, he was partial to the substantial *banh chung*—square-shaped cakes made of glutinous rice, pork, and green beans wrapped in the edible dong leaf, then boiled. *Banh tet*—a round-shaped rice cake which is more of a rice "waffle" was a favorite as well. Into his adult life, for Binh, Tet would always be a period of glad tidings.

Between 1946 and 1952, Le Ba Sach shepherded his young family north on half a dozen trips to visit his mother and remaining uncles and cousins who still lived in Hadong. Long before 1952 it was apparent that the Communists were becoming a force to be reckoned with. For Sach, the realization of Communist domination in the north was a bitter pill to swallow. It was painfully obvious to him that the war between the Viet Minh and the French would come at high cost to his family.

Even prior to the return of French forces after World War II, Binh's grandmother, a minor landowner in Hadong, had felt the increasingly bold wrath and pressure from Communist *cadres* and their insidious propaganda. A few years later, in their kindness and magnanimity, Ho's minions, when they finally appropriated her land for the people and the revolution in 1956, were nearly civil in their purging effort. As part of the hated class of capitalist, blood-sucking landowners, she and her family might have expected elimination: to be shot in the back of the head or tied up, weighted down, and politely pitched into a lake or deep river. Instead they were forced to suffer the indignity of eking out their survival on a portion of their property—which now belonged to the revolution—in a hovel that before was used as shelter for pigs and chickens.

CHAPTER TWO

Drawing the Bamboo Curtain

B*etween 1946 and the middle of 1954* Viet Minh and French forces waged war throughout Indo-China, with most of the serious fighting taking place in Tonkin. As the war continued on with no apparent end in sight and casualties mounted, French enthusiasm languished. The final climactic battle at Dien Bien Phu in northwestern Tonkin, near the Laotian border, was a resounding victory for Communist forces. Even with the ignominious defeat of the French, the transition from the battlefield to the peace table yielded little satisfaction to any of the parties involved.

The Geneva Agreements, begun in May of 1954, were attended by the four new countries of the former French Indo-China, France, Britain, the Soviet Union, the People's Republic of China, and the United States. When negotiations concluded in July a ceasefire agreement was reached. The 17th Parallel between Quanq Binh province to the north and Quang Tri province to the south with the Ben Hai River running through to the South China Sea was established as the east-west dividing line splitting the Democratic Republic of Vietnam (north and Communist) from the Republic of Vietnam (south and non-Communist). What would become known to the world as the Demilitarized Zone (DMZ) would become anything but demilitarized.

The ceasefire agreement provided a three-hundred-day period during which time freedom of movement between north and south was not to be inhibited by the new governments. By mid-1955 upward of one million citizens, the largest percentage of them Roman Catholics, opted to pick up all stakes, leaving the graves of ancestors and generations of village tradition behind in the north rather than live under Communism. While a small, indeterminate number of dedicated Marxist *cadres* from the Republic of Vietnam moved north, not one ordinary citizen is known to have made the same journey.[1]

By air, rail, and foot, but mostly by sealift they came south, these displaced northerners. Few on the outside were aware of the impact and consequence this *diaspora* had on the south. The culture and temperament of these generally more serious and fastidious Tonkinese used to eking out a living from the begrudging soil of the Red River delta, with their lighter skin color, different accents, dress, and traditions were at odds with their more laconic southern cousins who, with seemingly a lot less effort, could extract more sustenance from the teeming, bounteous Mekong Delta area.[2] In 1955 it would have been the same in America if 12 million New York City residents with all their hustle and bustle were suddenly relocated to rural Georgia or Mississippi, and all of it done with the thinnest assistance or safety net from a central government.

A portion of the Geneva Agreements which were accepted by all parties save the United States and the Republic of Vietnam called for national elections to be held throughout Vietnam in July of 1956. With an estimated population of 16 million in the north and 14 million in the south, and confident that they would be able to eliminate meaningful opposition and consolidate power north of the 17th Parallel, Ho Chi Minh and his forces gladly accepted these prospects.

Between 1953, prior to the end of hostilities, and into 1956 the Communists began a series of bloody purges in which identifiable vestiges of capitalism were ruthlessly eliminated. In a series of land-reform programs during that period the Communists figured that in each and every village the top five percent of the population represented landlords and it was these "rich" who were exploiting the remaining 95 percent. Their assets stripped from them and redistributed to those remaining, murders of this high-income five percent were carried out with precision by special teams of land-reform agents.[3]

No accurate details exist for the number of people disposed of during this period, nor was there a record of those eliminated during their attempts to leave or intimidated from moving to the south. As there was little in the way of press coverage, news of massive purges were only gathered by word of mouth when it reached the south and given scant attention in Western media.

Anything but benign and far from perfect, the government established in the south was preferable for those who had experienced the realities of Communism. While the obsolescent emperor Bao Dai was its titular head, the real power resided with Prime Minister Ngo Dinh Diem and his close *coterie* of family members. Facing greater challenges to his authority than were faced by his northern rivals, it was amazing that the welterweight government, even with support from the Eisenhower administration, managed to survive at all.

At once the Diem government was beset with challenges. A naturally hostile Western press gave little quarter when reporting the Diem regime's efforts to deal militarily with threats posed by Hoa Hao, Cao Dai, and other Buddhist forces who deeply mistrusted the Roman Catholic leanings of the prime minister and his group of displaced Annamites. In addition to religious and cultural strife, and the overwhelming burden of absorbing so many new citizens, the new government faced the financial and political clout of the Binh Xuyen. The Binh Xuyen were essentially pirates who preyed on shipping which transited the Saigon River in the 1930s and 1940s. After World War II, the Binh Xuyen had been left alone to run both the police and vice concessions in Cholon, the Chinese section of Saigon. Diem viewed the Binh Xuyen, like the Hoa Hao and Cao Dai, as a threat to his ability to lead the nation.

Communist gains throughout the world, particularly in Asia, effectively guaranteed American interest in Vietnam. As early as mid-1950, in reaction to the North Korean invasion, President Truman had ordered the establishment of a Military Assistance Advisory Group (MAAG) in French Indo-China. Serving largely as a funding vehicle through which aid could be funneled to the French in their efforts against the Viet Minh, the birth of the Republic of Vietnam gave it new purpose. The U.S. MAAG would begin to shoulder a heavy burden in the fight against the

Communists. One organization created in large part through the efforts of a single MAAG staff member was the tiny Corps of Marines for the new republic.

The American military would directly invest tremendous sums of blood and treasure in waging the Cold War. Of those things not noticed or fully appreciated by most was the training and assistance given to nations struggling to maintain their freedom in an increasingly hostile world. In the years immediately following World War II, another United States Marine Corps gift to the Free World was its part in birthing four new Corps of Marines in Asia.

For the new republics in Korea, Taiwan, and the Philippines, American Leathernecks generously sowed the seeds of expeditionary warfare to small groups of special men in their respective homelands. In each country the new Marine Corps would bear the imprint of their American elder brothers. Always the smallest service, as in the U.S., the title "Marine" in each of the local languages would come to be synonymous with all the best in martial spirit and soldierly virtue.

Of the four offspring Marine Corps, the relationship between the USMC and the TQLC would, by far, become the most personal, intense, and costly. For the Republic of Vietnam, only their army's Airborne division would stand as co-equal with a hard-earned reputation for fighting skill and reliance. The small group of men who were to serve as Vietnamese Marines from 1954 onward would demonstrate that characteristic institutional zeal which so obviously sets Marines apart in every culture.

The TQLC had its origins in a very small organization of far flung, commando-type units established with French assistance in 1946. These river-assault companies, known as "Dinassauts," were a conglomeration of specialized infantry units with amphibious capabilities. Their first actions were up north in the Red River Delta area. Of the Vietnamese fighting units begun with French assistance, the Dinassauts enjoyed a particularly strong reputation for their unit *élan* and *esprit de corps*.[4]

The partitioning of Vietnam in 1954 brought with it the effort to fully develop a national military force structure capable of defending the new republic from the obvious, imminent threat to the north. Along with the need for a modern army, air force, and navy came the tentative recognition for specialized units capable of conducting amphibious operations on Vietnam's many miles of sea coast and inland waterways.

The inter-service rivalries universal in every single nation's military structure were visited upon the Vietnamese as well. From its beginning the TQLC, like their American brothers, would be the smallest service, battling for resources at every turn. Months of debate among large groups of Vietnamese, French, and American military officers could not produce an acceptable organizational chart or develop the roles and missions this new amphibious force would operate by. It took the collective determination, grit, and sheer power of will of one Vietnamese major, one French army captain, and one USMC lieutenant colonel to turn the establishment of a separate Vietnamese Marine Corps into a reality.*

As the first son, Binh's primary job was to obtain his education. His father and stepmother were likewise committed to his success. Binh worked hard to that end.

Entering kindergarten at the tiny boy's school in Tan Dinh during the Japanese occupation, the normalcy of that chaos continued unabated through the contentious return of the French, the war with the Viet Minh, and into the tumultuous establishment of Binh's new country.

While those from the north most opposed to Communism had made their major exodus in 1954, there were still plenty of people in the south with little enthusiasm for the Diem regime. The allure of Communism, to many a choice superior to the oppressive yoke of French colonialism, had especially wide acceptance among first generation converts. Some were attracted by what amounted to the

---

* Lieutenant Colonel Victor Croizot USMC, like so many other Marine Corps officers, was a man of exceptional skills and accomplishments. His efforts on behalf of the TQLC are widely known. His leadership contribution in managing the exodus of the 807,000 Vietnamese citizens from north to south in 1954, while less known, cannot be overstated. Aside from being the American "father" to the TQLC, Lieutenant Colonel Croizot also served as the first official advisor— *covan*—to the Vietnamese Marines. He later retired as a colonel and authored the book *Across the Reef: The Amphibious Tracked Vehicle at War*.

Communists granting a virtual license to kill their landlords or any accused of exploiting the *proletariat*. Hard-core adherents of every background willingly accepted the party's call for sacrifice to overcome capitalism and foreign oppression. Those like Binh's family, who had lived under or been negatively impacted by the Viet Minh, were no less anxious to shed the vestiges of colonialism. Neither did they embrace the Communists' outright lies and half truths that they knew from bitter family experience.

A number of the instructors at Binh's *lycee*, his high school, may have been members of the covert group of Communist *cadre* left behind at the country's partitioning. They may simply have been part of that large minority in the south who were Communist sympathizers. Either way, they were unafraid to express what to young Binh was nothing more than propaganda. When able, he would respectfully challenge their world view on the greatness of China and the Soviet Union. While the students learned of the Chinese victory in the Korean War and of the Russian space triumph with the launching of Sputnik, little was said of the United States and when it was it was never positive. When Binh shared this with his father, the elder would fill in what he knew of historical facts the instructors conveniently left out.

In spite of the fighting, the uncertainty, and the never-ending political intrigue that constituted regular, everyday living in Vietnam, life's cycles continued on. The Japanese, the French, the Viet Minh, and even the uprising of the Binh Xuyen against Diem's regime in 1955 did not keep Binh from pressing ahead with the education his family craved so much for him. It was not until 1957, the year he finished high school at Petrus Truong Vinh Ky, that any of the unnamed, near-daily crises finally interrupted his schooling for a brief period of time. When he had graduated high school and was headed to university, Binh had had enough of the pernicious Communist threat, had heard the stories of how life in Hadong used to be before the Viet Minh had taken over, had heard a hundred times of the indignities foisted upon his grandmother and uncles and cousins. To right the wrong, to avenge his family's honor, to do what a reasonable young man must do, meant joining in the effort to rid his country of what he saw as the evil growing cancer of Communism. By 1957 Binh knew that his only option was to serve his country as an officer in its military forces.

Binh was an average student. Where he was headed, he was certain none of the troops he was to lead would ask him what his grades were. And while school did not come particularly easy for him, his graduation in 1961 with a degree in history and geography was a small measure of the mental toughness and self-discipline his professors and the exams they devised had no way of accurately assessing.

Between the establishment of the separate Vietnams in mid-1954 and 1959 both governments focused their efforts at domestic political consolidation. While little was reported on the forced communization of the entire population of the Democratic Republic of Vietnam and the murdering of thousands of citizens judged to be enemies of the state, challenges faced by the Diem regime and its many shortcomings were extensively aired.

Ngo Dinh Diem, an outsider to many and a Roman Catholic who had lived for a time in the United States, was initially viewed with favor in the anti-Communist West. In his own country, the more numerous Buddhists and various sects were deeply mistrustful of the Diem *clique*. Using the military to crush Hoa Hao, Cao Dai, and Binh Xuyen opponents only temporarily put off challenges to his regime's authority.

In 1958, with consolidation in the north complete, Ho Chi Minh ordered the movement of *cadre* back to the south and the following year they, along with those left behind or more recently recruited, began their people's war against the Saigon government in earnest. Between 1954 through the end of 1960, the Viet Cong had assassinated nearly seventeen hundred and kidnapped an additional two thousand pro-Saigon village leaders and elders.[5] From 1961 forward their efforts at terror would increase. As the Communist need for men and material surged, construction was initiated on what would become known to the world as the Ho Chi Minh Trail. By 1965 the trail system was capable of monthly handling the five to six thousand men and all of their supplies sent down to "liberate" their recalcitrant brothers.[6]

Major Buddhist protests began in 1961 that ultimately led to a series of spectacular, broadly reported events in 1963 during which time benign and harmless-looking monks in saffron robes and seated in the lotus position were doused with gasoline and lit on fire as a means to draw attention to the injustice of the Diem regime. Long before this, Communists had effectively infiltrated many of the groups opposed to the Saigon government. For many it was difficult not to sympathize with the opposition as the corruption of the Diem regime was easy to chronicle and the outright, egregiously amateurish leadership was not at all likable. While those in America may have wished for the second coming of the polished, genteel, Wellesley-educated Madame Chiang Kai-shek, Madame Nhu, Diem's near profane and anything-but-demure Dragon Lady sister-in-law, made the public comment after one of the immolations that they had just witnessed a "barbecue." Without a sense for how she would be perceived by those who might not identify with her point of view she told one interviewer, "Let them burn and we shall clap our hands."[7]

American political leadership in the 1950s and 1960s daily faced the prospect of nuclear war with the Soviet Union, and from its growing list of client states in Europe and across Asia, the risk of people's war, however defined. Fresh from what many Americans would describe as the unsettling armistice in Korea, both superpowers sought to minimize the chances of facing each other directly in combat that might quickly turn nuclear. Frustrations over the inability to secure complete victory were tempered by the belief that there could never again be that complete victory seen in 1945.

With Korea and not World War II as the age-appropriate guide, U.S. involvement in Southeast Asia was to be measured against that Cold War yardstick. The situation in the new Republic of Vietnam had many similarities to that on the Korean peninsula. Both Communist Korea and Vietnam shared a common border with and received significant aid from China. Both received similarly large amounts of aid from the Soviet Union. Both countries had recent experience with colonial occupiers, with the Japanese, by far, being the most brutally repressive.

The Korean War was a mostly conventional war fought on territory which, when both sides were not established in static positions, allowed for the maneuver of large units against a reasonably identifiable enemy. North and South Korea were divided at the 38th Parallel by the same arbitrary logic that had begun the division of Vietnam at Yalta in 1945. This 150-odd mile stretch of border territory was the only land avenue into or out of the south. Because there were few forests, enemy forces had difficulty hiding from prowling allied aircraft and isolating the battlefield was relatively easy. With limited naval capabilities, opportunities for Communist infiltration by sea were restricted to the movement of small units only.

It was the differences with Korea that would make defending Vietnam far more challenging for both American sponsors and those Vietnamese seeking to avoid Communist rule. Where the population of Korea, both North and South, was nearly homogeneous, Vietnam and its western neighbors shared porous, ill-defined borders and were home to a large population of disparate minority groups. With self-imposed rules of engagement and geographic limitations, the dense jungle and mountain areas of eastern Cambodia and Laos were havens for Communist sanctuaries and made the prevention of infiltration into Vietnam nearly impossible. Because of these geographic and political constraints, the battlefield initiative was ceded largely to the enemy.

Beginning with the Suez Crisis in the early summer of 1956, a series of aggressive acts from the Communists was unleashed: the brutal repression of Hungarian freedom fighters by Soviet troops, Communist Chinese aggression against Nationalist China during the Second Taiwan Strait Crisis in late 1958, the loss of Cuba to Castro's *guerillas* right at America's back door in 1959, the shooting down of Gary Power's U-2 over Russia, the debacle at the Bay of Pigs, the erection of the Berlin Wall, and challenges to the West in the Congo from Patrice Lamumba and his cohorts.

The situation on the ground in Southeast Asia by the early 1960s was no more promising than events elsewhere. Even though American military advisors had been actively employed in all manner of non-combat staff roles in Vietnam since 1954, the need to put Americans in the field to better observe and assist in fully developing their ally's capabilities was finally granted on a limited, restricted basis by 1960. American officers saw little that was encouraging in the early going.

The TQLC, which would never comprise more than two percent of Vietnam's total military effort, continually improved its fighting skills as the small size of the organization reflected its elite status among the Republic of Vietnam's (RVN) forces. The much larger Vietnamese army, usually referred to as ARVN, which had no shortage of brave men, was hamstrung by the problems typical in newly established military organizations in poor countries. Limited resources, limited training, and an officer corps comprised often, especially at the top, of men selected and judged more for political loyalty and connections than for demonstrated fighting and leadership abilities generally put the Saigon regime's units at a huge disadvantage against the sometimes more ably led and motivated Communist forces.

American military officers brought in to help create, shape, and guide the fledgling Vietnamese army were among the best and brightest men available. Successful in Korea with the establishment of that new republic's army, Lieutenant General John "Iron Mike" O'Daniel's assignment as chief of the U.S. MAAG represented the zenith in expectations by America's political and military leadership. The long, arduous process of building up the necessary military organizations and minimal support infrastructure was given over to hundreds of dedicated American officers, a decreasing number of French counterparts, and thousands of like-minded Vietnamese anxious to see their country prosper.

Initial performance by the RVN military in combat against *guerillas* was spotty. What victories they did achieve against the Communists, now referred to as Viet Cong, were often transitory events as policies of the Diem regime undermined their actions in the field. The decision to replace elected village officials with those appointed by the Saigon government alienated many in the rural population. Suppression campaigns against citizens even remotely believed to have Communist sympathies played further into the hands of the ubiquitous Hanoi-inspired propaganda. At the same time stay-behind agents were being activated, local recruitment for the VC was aggressively pursued and the infiltration of main-line NVA troops into the south added to the list of problems facing the republic. By 1961 and into 1962 it was estimated that Communists had *de facto* control of more than half the country.

At the highest levels of American leadership in Vietnam and Washington, a raging debate centered on what action to take and how best to handle Diem, whose own actions were often not in line with American intent. Diem's manner of governing and his regime's flagrant corruption were an embarrassment and hindered what Americans saw as their own magnanimous effort to stem Communist gains. Among Vietnamese civilians, Diem enjoyed minimal support, and from those in the military his popularity was even shakier.

By summer 1963, America had invested nearly nine years of political sweat equity in Vietnam's success. With the increasing advisory effort and near direct military support, there was a growing list of American casualties as well. For all the blood and treasure so far spent, there was little to show. Many senior Americans and more than a few top Vietnamese generals believed that Diem's continued leadership offered a future for Vietnam with little hope for victory.

To come this far having invested so much and have Vietnam fail and fall to its northern enemy would start the dominoes falling. The appearance of weak American resolve in Southeast Asia would embolden Soviet expansionism and aggression all over the world. Among Vietnamese military leadership was a growing circle of officers who believed that the only way to save their country was to get rid of Diem. American involvement in the *coup* to replace Diem, still controversial and the subject of heated debate, at least shows some level of accuracy in the earlier admonition outlined in the famous 1948 letter from George Kennan to fellow State Department official Chip Bohlen:

> This does not mean that all the governments we help to resist Soviet pressure will be enlightened, liberal governments, practicing democracy in ways which our people would find commendable. Many of these

25

governments may be corrupt or dictatorial. *But they will be preferable, from the standpoint of American interests, to Communist-dominated regimes; for they will not be aspiring to world domination, nor would they have the resources to permit them to dream of large-scale aggression"*(italics added).[8]

To the Vietnamese military leaders with the power to effect change it was obvious that Diem would have to go if the Republic of Vietnam was to have a chance at survival at all.

There was a reasonable, intuitive assumption among many patriotic Vietnamese in the South that, once the country gained its footing, a military effort to liberate their enslaved families from the transitory evil in the north would be undertaken. As someone familiar with military strategy, and naval strategy in particular, Le Ba Sach knew that at the vanguard of the eventual invasion would be the TQLC. Le Ba Sach loved his children, but so too did he love his country and harbor a bone-deep, visceral hatred for the Communists; a hatred strong enough that he was willing to invest his number one son toward that outcome. Le Ba Sach strongly counseled his oldest son to do his service as a Marine.

Following his graduation from university Binh immediately was accepted into the national officer candidates school (OCS) outside of Saigon for the ten-month course that would lead to his commissioning. Due to the relatively small size of Vietnam's military branches besides the army, the services shared their OCS to minimize costs and more effectively utilize scarce training resources. The ten-month school exposed the aspiring young officers to military leadership, customs, courtesies, culture, drill, and some very basic infantry tactics since the bulk of each class was headed for the army (ARVN) anyway. Binh's was an odd group in that of the several hundred officer candidates, sixty of them had selected duty with the now hungry-for-new-junior-leaders TQLC.

By 1962 the TQLC, in its brief eight-year existence, had just added its third battalion of infantry. With its own battalion of artillery, an amphibious support battalion, and a full-fledged recruit training section, the TQLC could now put an entire brigade in the field.[9] By the time Binh pinned on the gold bars of second lieutenant, nearly six thousand Vietnamese had likewise earned the right to wear the distinct tiger-striped uniform unique to their Corps and proclaim their service's motto: *"Danh Du To Quoc,"* which translates roughly as "To absolutely honor our country."

Following commissioning, the sixty new Marine second lieutenants were enrolled in a one-month course at Thu Duc designed to indoctrinate them further into the ways of the Corps. With an emphasis on infantry and amphibious tactics, it was meant to prepare them for combat leadership at the platoon and company level. Of the entire group, Binh graduated number one in his class.

The senior Marine of the TQLC, Lieutenant Colonel Le Nguyen Khang, had recently commanded Third Battalion, also known as the *"Soi Bien"* or "Wolves of the Sea." Proud of his former unit, the *commandant* was not at all above snatching up promising young officers to ensure the future success of his cherished Soi Bien. And that was how Binh got assigned to Third Battalion.

American Marine officers assigned to duty as *covans* with the TQLC would find a great deal of familiar culture. The Vietnamese Marine Corps quickly absorbed the same sort of toughness and organizational pride their American mentors had successfully sought to instill. Recognizing the extra value of their martial culture, the TQLC and the vaunted ARVN airborne brigade were designated as the general reserve force for the entire RVNAF in mid-1959.[10] These two small but reliable units became their nation's force in readiness, the "fire brigades" to use in case of extreme emergencies, the units to send in to handle the toughest assignments.

The primary unit of deployment and employment for the TQLC became the battalion. Organized very similarly to its USMC counterpart, there was also a touch of the British Regimental System in the way long-term business was to be conducted. As a small branch of the military without benefit of significant operational history, it made sense that officers and men remained with the same units for as long as practical. While none had yet served long enough to call their time a career, it seemed logical that a man might, if he lived through the combat, be assigned to the same battalion for the duration. Those opposed to this system argued that it stifled innovation and infusion of new blood. The *contra* argument was that even with the stratification of rank, a more familial environment was fostered which contributed to greater *élan* and *esprit de corps*.

The warrior culture within the TQLC was an eclectic blend of all that was uniquely Vietnamese with some room left for American influence. Just as there was no single profile for a young man who signed up for service as an American Leatherneck, there was no single Vietnamese profile. There were a number of groups in Vietnam who were represented disproportionately, though. As sects that had been particularly targeted by the Communists, young men with Hoa Hao and Cao Dai backgrounds saw service there as a way of seeking revenge. And while the American press would for years highlight those young Vietnamese men who sought to avoid service completely or, at most, serve in ways that would keep them out of harm's way, there was no shortage of new, young Vietnamese patriots who believed that Communism was not the answer and saw service in the TQLC as the best way to contribute to the south's freedom.

The TQLC was a volunteer organization. Regular enlistments, at least initially, were for three years. Boot camp was eight weeks long and organized very much along the same lines as those of the USMC. Many of the Vietnamese drill instructors had been schooled at San Diego and Parris Island.

Officers were saddled with greater time commitments. As the war progressed, if they were not killed or severely wounded, they were kept on active duty indefinitely. And like the enlisted ranks, the officers of the TQLC were not part of any one group in particular. The TQLC officer corps was a generous mix of southerners, displaced northerners, Buddhists, and Roman Catholics.

Nowhere was the Confucian respect for and stratification of authority more apparent than in the TQLC. Of the four American military services the Marine Corps is, by far, the most formal in terms of respect for and deference given those of higher rank. To the unknowing or uninitiated there is little appreciation for the deep feelings that most often are only just beneath the surface in officer-enlisted, senior-junior relations. While Marine Corps officers will rarely call their men by their first names and the men only refer to them as "sir" or by their rank, the bonds between groups are extremely strong even in marginally run units. And while rank and title somewhat separate officers and men, suffering and hardship are universal.

Within the American military, especially the Marine Corps, special emphasis is placed on initiative and training men to step up should a senior be killed or become incapacitated. It is something near unique to the American culture, perhaps a part of the "rugged individualist" mentality and second nature that allows units to continue fighting effectively even when those officially in charge are gone.

The stratification of rank in the TQLC was far less American, more Vietnamese or even European in practice. When addressing a senior it was common courtesy and respectful to never look a man squarely in the eyes. The notion of "face" and saving face was paramount. It could not be overemphasized. Ensuring that orders were obeyed and that all actions were first authorized before being executed was critical. The gulf between officers and enlisted was obvious even at the second lieutenant level. Platoon commanders each had a small section in their tiny headquarters, usually one to three men who acted as batmen, orderlies, messengers, runners for the young lieutenant. The higher an officer progressed, the larger the number of men assigned to take care of him. American officers would refer to these men as "cowboys." It was a job of honor and not a disgrace to serve as an officer's cowboy.

Second Lieutenant Le Ba Binh joined the Soi Bien in October of 1962, a month after the *Beverly Hillbillies* previewed on television, the same month "Monster Mash" by Bobby "Boris" Pickett became the number one pop song in the U.S., the same month the American Eagle and the Soviet Bear nearly came to nuclear blows over missiles in Cuba. Under a program named Operation Shufly, begun earlier in the year, USMC helicopters were now assisting with the transport of Vietnamese Marine and ARVN units into and out of combat.

The employment method for brand new lieutenants in the TQLC was mostly on-the-job training. Upon arrival with Third Battalion, Binh was assigned as a platoon leader with Second Company. (Unlike their American counterparts who gave companies letter designations, the Vietnamese numbered their companies.)

From the time Second Lieutenant Le Ba Binh reported aboard in October through early November of 1963, Third Battalion was deployed countless times engaging Viet Cong units from the central highlands well north of Saigon to the southern tip of the Ca Mau Peninsula.

Judged from the perspective of the Marines involved, especially those like Binh with combat experience, the enemy contact was significant. Viewed from the neutral, distant, global perspective, the engagements were of minor impact. In this two year "journeyman" period, Second Lieutenant Le Ba Binh was wounded three times leading his platoon against Communist forces and already recognized for his personal gallantry, learning lessons that would benefit him and those he would lead in the conflict ahead. Compared to what he would later face as a senior company commander and battalion commander, the slower, easier initiation into combat was a good way to break in as a junior leader.

It was simply a quirk of fate that in early November of 1963, with Saigon and nearly the entire senior Vietnamese military leadership involved in the intrigue and subterfuge that would end up with the *coup d'état* to replace Ngo Dinh Diem, the officers and men of Third Battalion were all on leave. Reporting back a few days after General Duong Van Minh—known as "Big Minh" by most Americans—had taken charge and was ultimately replaced in late January of 1964, after several more changes of government, by air force Marshall Nguyen Cao Ky, it was back to the business of fighting the VC, just as before, for the Marines of the Soi Bien.

While he was growing as a leader from his experiences as a platoon commander, Binh had already been selected and notified of his pending assignment to attend the U.S. Marine Corps' Basic School in Quantico, Virginia. The prospect of traveling to America, seeing it all for himself, and benefiting from the higher quality training he expected to receive was a challenge he eagerly looked forward to.

There is something irresistible and inevitable as to what most would describe as the omnipresent and all-consuming American culture. On that one subject there is little debate. The argument begins over whether its force is intentional, and proceeds to whether it has benefit.

Xenophobes in Europe and Asia, particularly those with a left- or Communist-leaning bent, would forever accuse Americans of cultural imperialism and subversion. Those less inclined to criticize would be more inclined to simply enjoy the movies and the music that were so much larger than the forty-eight contiguous states or even more with Alaska and Hawaii thrown in for good measure.

Was it possible to be a patriot in one's country of birth, to retain all the best of that culture, especially a new Third World nation, and yet marvel at the universal manliness of Burt Lancaster and Gary Cooper or the universal allure of Esther Williams and Deborah Kerr?

Could a reasonable person even entertain being a Communist once exposed to Gene Kelly seen and heard *Singin' in the Rain*? Could one avoid the body's natural rhythmic response to a Temptations or Four Tops song? Without any understanding of English at all, there was some inexplicable happiness and obvious joyful movement from such exposure that transcended every culture.

And so it was for Le Ba Binh, Vietnamese patriot and newly commissioned officer of Marines. As a young boy, without compromising his culture or his nationalism, absorbing Western influence without relinquishing the best of what was Vietnamese, he would mimic the tunes of Nat King Cole. Into the tiny Saigon movie theaters he would go, *piasters* in hand, to ponder the vastness of the Wild West through the likes of *High Noon* and *Veracruz*. Into early manhood he was only a few weeks behind counterpart American teenagers in exposure to the new sounds from Bill Haley, Danny and the Juniors, and all the others going forward. Let it further be known that the "British invasion" of 1964 and later did not stop in North America. The Beatles, the Animals, Herman's Hermits, the Yardbirds, the Rolling Stones; they had landed and conquered in Southeast Asia as well.

Binh managed the transition from university student to officer candidate to neophyte platoon leader to a man with the confidence which comes only after having survived constant combat. The on-the-job training as a new officer, far from the ideal way to learn about leading troops in battle, was the only option available in his country's circumstances. The opportunity for further learning in the United States was a gift from heaven. He dedicated himself to making the most of his upcoming Basic School experience.

The burden of constantly maintaining an American military at some level of war-fighting strength is given little thought by those born after World War II. Up until that time, from the nation's beginning through the start of the Cold War, America mobilized only for combat, never for deterrence. With its changing nature the cost of the Cold War in manpower, resources, and funds were far outside the national experience, and yet the vigilance required to blunt the Communist threat presented no other alternative.

Since World War II Americans came to expect that if a crisis were to erupt anywhere in the world there would very simply always be Marines to send in, an aircraft carrier task force nearby, or Strategic Air Command bombers lurking somewhere in the skies, awaiting only the president's order to strike.

World War II required so much of the nation's output and effort that no one was untouched. For four years it *was* the economy. In those days before victory was assured the national economic choice was "guns or butter." In general, people did without and suffered the shortages collectively. Even if they did not have a relative serving, Meatless Tuesdays and gas rationing allowed every citizen to share in the sacrifice for victory.

In the post-war environment, with America's economic growth on a strong path upward, there was a transition from "guns *or* butter" to "guns *and* butter." While military spending consumed far more of the national product than before World War II, economic growth and technological progress was such that the permanence of Cold War expenditures allowed citizens to enjoy freedom's material benefits without the same level of personal sacrifice required only a few years earlier.

The sheer enormity of the American military was difficult to fathom. From the draft or recruiting phase all the way through training of individuals to become soldiers, sailors, airmen, or Marines, many with follow-on training in critical specialties, to their assignment to units in which there would be further training, to the projection of American power wherever the need arose consumed resources only a truly rich nation could shoulder. In between the beginning and combat or deterrence there was the ongoing cost of provisioning, housing, and caring in every way for those who served the nation's military needs. Requirements for research and development added further expense to ensure American war fighters maintained a qualitative edge over potential foes who in no way could afford to train the way the Americans did. To place a wing of B-52s capable of delivering bombs on target or position an aircraft carrier task force where it could influence a situation with favorable outcome to U.S. interests was no simple task. The Russians were having a go of it as well except that they never reached the *"and"* part in "guns and butter."

A small country like the Republic of Vietnam surely did not have the resources or infrastructure capable of producing and training a military strong enough to do what it would eventually be tasked with doing. At the very earliest stages of its development, the decision to send all new officers in the TQLC to attend the Basic School in Quantico seemed prescient.[†] As a man progressed up the chain and if the situation permitted, that same officer might return to Quantico for schooling as a captain, major, and more.

Second Lieutenant Le Ba Binh's assignment to attend Basic School in Quantico, Virginia along with four other TQLC officers was perfectly timed. All five of the Vietnamese Marines were combat veterans. All the lieutenants had made dozens of combat flights on helicopter insertions or fixed-wing hops between in-country destinations aboard C-47s and other assorted military aircraft. All too familiar with danger, for them the long trip to America was a period of relief, education, and just plain fun. At least no one in the States, as far as they could figure, would be trying to kill them.

From Tan Son Nhut, the airport adjacent to Saigon, to Clark AFB in the Philippines to Guam, Seattle, and then to Travis AFB in California the flying was long and boring and cold. Somehow the logistics changed and the final three thousand miles was a

---

[†] The Basic School, commonly referred to as TBS.

three-day train ride. Three days from Fairfield, the town outside of Travis AFB, to Quantico; Binh was able to finally see and nearly touch much of the wide open spaces he had pondered as a boy during his afternoons at the movies right there in Tan Dinh not that long ago.

The Basic School class that commenced training in July of 1964, known by its letter designation—H Company or Hotel Company (also referred to simply as "Hotel")—was polyglot and polycultural. Among the fresh-faced, newly commissioned American college graduates were equally fresh-faced, newly commissioned young lieutenants from Korea, China, Indonesia, Venezuela, and Spain. Of the entire group, the Vietnamese were the only folks with significant combat experience.

While American youth were busy consuming Beatle Boots, music, and morphing hairstyles, Binh and his Hotel Company classmates settled into the Basic School routine learning all they could about infantry tactics, the exercise and coordination of all manner of American firepower, military customs and courtesies, and anything else the captain instructors could think of.

Binh and the four other Vietnamese second lieutenants of Hotel Company were all combat veterans. Their American brothers were fascinated by their stories and were often deferential in treatment. Expecting that they might soon be joining them in battle, the professional interest was sincere.

For the Vietnamese lieutenants the opportunities to share ideas with their instructors and fellow students was productive and pleasant. As the war was evolving, the formal introduction to tactics and the application of firepower in classroom and field exercise settings was something the TQLC simply had not, heretofore, had the resources or luxury to carry out. The group of Vietnamese would often discuss together the benefits of each lesson, down to the smallest details, and share thoughts on how best to implement what they had learned with their Marines when they went home.

As Hotel Company spent its days and most of its nights training in the Quantico woods, American involvement in Southeast Asia ratcheted higher. Just as Hotel finished its rifle range qualifications,

Congress passed the Gulf of Tonkin Resolution. Without officially declaring it, America had effectively gone to war.

As summer became fall, the TQLC officers would enjoy the change of colors. And while they had all known the bitter cold that could chill right down to the bone in the mountains of Vietnam, the first snowfall was a new experience that appeared as magic, calling forth the same delight any young child experiences with his first exposure to the stuff.

As rigorous as Basic School instruction was, it was far less stressful than getting shot at for real. Even if it did take a few weeks for the TBS mess hall cooks to figure out how to properly prepare simple rice, and even when they did it was the Americanized long-grain version, Binh had no problem with steak and hamburgers and hot dogs. Weekends were often times to travel and tour the numerous historic and cultural sites within driving distance of Quantico.

Graduating in December, Binh had time for a month's leave before returning home. There was no real rush. There would still be sufficient numbers of Communists left to fight. Binh had toured where he could on weekends off and then on the long, slow journey home. While he did not leave his heart there, it was San Francisco and its Chinatown especially he liked the best, expertly guided by a Basic School friend who had grown up just across the Bay.

In January 1965 he made it home, back to Vietnam, back to the Soi Bien now as a new first lieutenant in command of his own company, in plenty of time to be there before some of his American Basic School classmates hit the beach up north near Danang with the Ninth Marines.

CHAPTER THREE

Captain Ripley—Lima Six

When Captain John Ripley arrived in country in October 1966, he would be the third of three Ripley brothers there that year to visit destruction upon the Communist enemy. While brother Mike, older than John by one year but the last Ripley to enter the Corps, piloted A-4s and had actually concluded his combat tour in June, eldest brother George, the one who had poisoned his minor sibling with exposure to Leon Uris's *Battle Cry* and thus cemented his desire to be a Marine, was now a major and serving as the operations officer (S-3) for the Third Marine Regiment, parent unit to 3/3. Father Bud Ripley had actually penned an emotion-packed letter earlier in the year to the Secretary of the Navy pleading for the opportunity for all three of his sons to serve in the combat zone simultaneously. Concerned that laws meant to limit the losses one family might endure would also limit his sons' obligations to their country, Bud Ripley was willing to risk those he cherished most for the country he loved so much.

Captain John Ripley's appointment with destiny was not about to be interrupted by any law or man. John Ripley had bred, plotted, and willed himself into this exact situation. Lima Company, which had recently gone through two commanders in short order and was just another rifle company, was transformed within a matter of weeks of the new captain's arrival into the fightingest SOBs around. Before he had been in command for a full month the metamorphosis was complete.

Le Ba Binh
Saigon
February 1965

Judged from the outside, from the American point of view, it was odd that Le Ba Binh, recently promoted to first lieutenant and given command of the Soi Bien's First Company, was at once returning home *and* returning to war. Except for the American Civil War, there was nothing in the recent experience about fighting on home turf. Among the living, the collective memory was always of American boys going off to war or occupation duty—mostly to Europe but also to the Pacific or the Asian continent—somewhere, somewhere far from home. Even with the prospect of nuclear Armageddon never distant from the nation's consciousness, it was a possibility too horrible to seriously contemplate.

To its people, America was home, where the heart was, isolated and buffered by two oceans, a mighty fortress. American fighting men worried not that their towns and cities might be pillaged, that their women and children would be violated. Not so Le Ba Binh and the men of the TQLC. There was no such thing as Fortress Vietnam. At least not yet.

Binh's return to Vietnam was unremarkable. He had missed his family, the food, the familiar smells and sounds of his home. It was good to be back, satisfying to know that he would soon begin to return on the investment his country had made in him. He had enjoyed America, its bigness and its wide open spaces, the constant motion of its people.

Binh had learned a lot at Basic School, had made serious friends among the American Marines who would soon come alongside in his country's struggle. Binh was eager to apply the lessons learned which would, he knew, translate into lives saved among his men and, of greater importance, more dead Communists.

In the years following her marriage to Le Ba Sach, Binh's stepmother had managed to give birth to seven children, assist with the raising of her four older stepchildren, and run a combination grocery and food stall in the Tan Dinh Market. Specializing in many of the more common noodle and rice dishes from the north, she oversaw a profitable business with the assistance of her children who worked there after school.

For Binh, Tan Dinh was home, an oasis of calm, a refuge, a place to always come back to on weekends when Third Battalion was not deployed from its local base a mere fifteen kilometers away at Thu Duc. Daily life in Tan Dinh seemed relatively unaffected by the war being intermittently waged in villages and countryside not that far away. Outside of Saigon, evidence of Communist sympathy and VC control was not difficult to locate. Americans found it hard to fathom the plight of their Vietnamese allies. For Americans, going off to war meant a long ride in a plane or ship. For Binh and most in the TQLC, it was usually just a few minutes' jaunt on the back of a moto.

When they would saddle up for routine combat operations, the maneuver units of the TQLC would normally take along six days' worth of rations which included rice, dried fish, sausage, and soy sauce. American c-rations were brought along but were used as a last choice by those Vietnamese Marines with discerning palates. With a far less sophisticated or cumbersome system of supply, each battalion commander maintained his own cash allowance from which he could draw to supplement the rations of his men. Cash was easier to carry than tons of food. The ability to purchase fish, rice, produce, and whatever else his troops may need from local sources gave units commercial clout in the areas in which they operated. The lighter load also simplified the logistical effort.

Water was drawn from local sources, usually wells or streams. The TQLC, whether city or country boys, generally had constitutions suited to the adequate but less-than-pure-by-American-standards liquid. The Viet Cong were known to poison wells when they could. A crude but effective test for such tampering involved dipping fresh-cut chili peppers into the newly drawn water. A resulting color change determined whether or not it was safe to drink.

One of the greater challenges, when operating in or around populated areas, was identifying those Vietnamese sympathetic to the Communist cause. Unlike the North Vietnamese Army (NVA), the Viet Cong did not wear uniforms. Stealth and deception, the ability to blend back into the population from which they came, were advantages they always sought to exploit.

Americans especially had difficulty separating neutral civilians from enemy combatants. Huge differences in both language and culture together combined to make effective communication and understanding the subtleties of this way of life, so completely outside of what the typical G.I. had ever known, a major hindrance to American attempts to clearly defeat an enemy overmatched in firepower but not in cunning or dedication. With neither cultural nor language barriers, Vietnamese Marines were generally able to locate areas where the VC operated.

A broad range of techniques and indicators determined Viet Cong presence. Simple conversations with villagers would usually reveal their sympathies or intentions. It was particularly evident if a person was anti-Communist by his or her willingness to tell what was going on since aiding the government often came at high price to civilians caught in the middle. VC retaliation for such disloyalty was swift and brutal.

In areas of VC control or intimidation the population was more often silent, reluctant to answer the most basic questions. The silence alone was harbinger enough for Marines to be extra vigilant. Villages and adjacent rice paddies with only skeleton populations of working adults during regular daylight farming hours typically meant they were attending required classes of propaganda and indoctrination. Sometimes the Marines would ask suspected VC villages to keep their lanterns on at night so that movement could be easily observed. Lights out told the Marines there was something to hide.

Separately and together there were a range of obvious and not-so-obvious patterns to determine the level of threat in any particular area. The best source of intel, however, the sure-fire way to find out if there were Communists around was to engage children, young children, in conversation. Culling them out from the crowd, plying them with kindness and candy, it was far easier to gain the truth from youthful innocence that no amount of training or admonishment by the most hardcore VC parents could completely eliminate.

That Binh and the growing number of TQLC junior officers had been further educated at Quantico was good. As their fighting prowess was improving and the size of the Vietnamese Marine Corps was growing to meet the increasing demands of the war in 1965, so too was the ferocity of the battles being waged. When Binh was a second lieutenant the preponderance of the combat had been closer to Saigon against smaller units of Viet Cong. Immediately after his promotion to first lieutenant and assuming command of Third Battalion's First Company, Binh found himself involved in fighting further north against larger VC units and even the NVA.

From his initiation into combat, well before his days at Quantico, Binh had gained appreciation for the presence of the American Marine *covans* whose participation in action alongside their Vietnamese brothers assured delivery of healthy amounts of firepower. Rapidly responsive and reasonably accurate air support from both Vietnamese and American pilots and artillery support from the TQLC's own artillery battalion often spelled the difference between victory and defeat, living or dying, especially against the often numerically superior enemy forces up north.

First Company's actions in 1965 took place mostly in the area that would become known to servicemen and the American public as I Corps (pronounced "Eye Corps"). South Vietnam had been divided into four regions for military purposes. I Corps was the northernmost corps region in the country. As it was the corps region that included the border with North Vietnam (the DMZ) as well as territory adjacent to Laos where the NVA maintained the Ho Chi Minh Trail and significant base camps from which they could infiltrate South Vietnam at numerous locations, I Corps would, of the four corps regions, be the area of the most desperate fighting and highest casualties for the duration of the war.

Nineteen sixty-five was the bloodiest year yet for the Marines of the Soi Bien. Of necessity, Binh's acumen as an infantry company commander grew exponentially. Major engagements against much larger units of Viet Cong at places like Tam Ky in Quang Nam Province, adjacent to Highway One, sixty kilometers south of Danang, 570 kilometers north of Saigon, and only six kilometers from the coast, was the place where Binh's First Company participated in a major victory over several VC regiments. Other clashes, like the one forty kilometers south of Tam Ky at Ba Gia and further inland, was a costly lesson in avoiding deception. At Ba Gia the VC had done a masterful job at preparing the battlefield prior to combat. Though First Company drew a fair amount of Communist blood, when contact was finally broken off, it was the enemy who had inflicted greater casualties. This time.

Wounded a fourth time while up north leading First Company, and again recognized for his personal heroics, Binh's professional reputation as a thinker *and* a warrior unafraid to do battle with a tenacious enemy was becoming widely known in the tiny but growing brotherhood of the TQLC. His brothers, sisters, parents, and old friends marveled at his stoicism as he seemed forever on the mend from some shrapnel wound or jungle crud.

Between operations the Soi Bien replenished, repaired, replaced, relaxed, and trained at Thu Duc. There was always time for Binh to spend with family and friends in nearby Tan Dinh. With nothing strategic in their urban hamlet except a police station of limited size, the risk of a Viet Cong terror attack was remote. For Binh the near constant transition between combat in whatever location he might be sent to and the solace of Tan Dinh was by now routine. Once the Communists were defeated and peace was restored, they would all go back to living lives that none of them had ever really experienced but all were eagerly looking forward to. In the meantime they would make the needed sacrifices.

Nowhere was the expectancy of the sacrifices needed today for a better tomorrow more evident than in the music of the times. Contemporary Vietnamese music by the early and mid-1960s was a most unusual blend of some modern American and French influence, but more often a reflection of the times locally tempered by more than two millennia of culture within the country.

Modern Vietnamese music could actually be divided into rough time periods. From 1954 up until around 1962, while the collective effort was on building the country internally, songs chronicled recent struggles and pride in the republic's possibilities. "Chien Do Vi Tuyen" was dedicated to those eight hundred thousand-plus citizens who had given up so much to come from the north by boat. "Nang Dep Mien Nam," translated roughly as "The Rising Sun of the South," was a tune that enjoyed wide popularity as the title said it all, and was just one of many similarly themed songs typical for the time.

From 1962 forward, as the conflict intensified, the music followed. Hoang Oanh's maudlin and chivalrous rendition of "Tinh Anh Linh Chien"—"The Love of a Fighting Man"—was known to all and tugged at the heart of every man in uniform as well as the women who waited for them. In the song the soldier is at the front and his lover back at home. In the night time he spies the full moon and wonders, like soldiers everywhere, if his girl is seeing the same moon at the same time and thinking of him.

Other songs, while not quite as heart-rending, appealed to patriotism and sacrifice. "Ai Di Chinh Chien" asked and answered the question, "Who are those joining the army to build for a peaceful future?" Many of the songs were patriotic and anti-Communist, but not all. The south was large enough and secure enough even to tolerate Pham Duy's popular anti-war music.

As early as 1962 the American footprint in Vietnam was significant and pervasive enough, and most men's tours short enough, to impose its culture in country so that there was little incentive or reason to go outside of what was easy to enjoy. Going from speaking English to Vietnamese was not like learning high school Spanish or French. You could not add an "o" at the end of each word and fake it, although a few words of French still made some difference. American soldiers and Marines would speak of "boocoo VC," "boocoo this," and "boocoo that." The sing-songy subtle intonations of the local language were lost on Americans who struggled even with chopsticks, and found Vietnamese culture indirect and incongruous to what they believed were their superior and straight-forward Occidental business methods.

Among the Vietnamese merchant class were those rapacious and ultra-capitalistic men and women only too anxious to latch onto American *largesse* and compound the lack of meaningful exchange. Within the confines of the dozens of "Little Americas" which were omnipresent wherever American military personnel operated, was all the exotic and erotic that most of these young men cared to experience. Few would ever really get to know the people or the culture in a friendly way beyond what was available in the honky-tonks, brothels, and bars.

Where American cultural imperialism apparently left little room for that which could not be understood in American terms, Binh would enjoy, along with many of his friends and family, the colorful potpourri of music forever on the airwaves. Everyone knew by heart the upbeat "C'est Ci Bon" and most, because of the French legacy there, truly understood the words. With his command of English, Binh even comprehended the words to Beatles songs like "I Saw Her Standing There." And yet he certainly enjoyed them no more than the hundreds of thousands of Vietnamese youngsters unconcerned and unfamiliar with the lyrics' meanings but completely taken in by the sound of the music. At least Vietnamese and Americans together could find a bit of something to share in the universality of rock-n-roll. For those old-fashioned patriots who appreciated Sergeant Barry Sadler and his "Ballad of the Green Berets," had there been interest or perception, the Americans might have found common ground, and "Tinh Anh Lien Chinh" would have seemed more appealing and familiar.

As a young infantry lieutenant Binh was much more focused on prosecuting his portion of the war and looking out for the men of First Company than anything else. While he enjoyed what music there was, he spent little time in serious contemplation over the meaning of any song in particular. Fortunately for him, there was a special young woman with a deeper sense of the art and the poetry and the romance of these times and this unique period. Binh would have a personal reason to later be grateful for Hoang Oanh's having sung "Tinh Anh Linh Chien" as its constant playing would serve to be the final determinant in Cam Banh's ultimate agreement to marry him.

LIMA SIX

When John Ripley showed up in Vietnam he had only one professional goal in mind. As much as he loved his wife Moline and their son Stephen, John Ripley was a Marine Corps infantry officer. He was a Marine Corps captain. Marine Corps infantry officer captains, by design, commanded rifle companies—in combat when possible. Any skipper with reasonable testosterone levels, any skipper with one or more functioning testicles would crawl naked over broken glass for the opportunity to lead Marines in combat. Any skipper lacking that level of enthusiasm was not likely to succeed in his leadership endeavors.[*]

Few people outside the military understand or appreciate the absolute power and god-like decision-making authority given over to males during combat who are barely out of their teens. The history of war is replete with examples of these only recently former boys and their rapid metamorphosis. Because of the nature of the ground fighting in Vietnam, an overwhelming amount of non-nuclear firepower was concentrated in the hands of those twenty-four-, twenty-five-, twenty-six-year-old captains who routinely ran their companies through the rice paddies and jungles and up and down the torturous trails.

For the infantry officer who relished the *ultimate* challenge, for that man who absolutely had to know if he had the requisite blend of brains and brawn to lead men in desperate struggle, the job of rifle company commander was the singular test.

Several factors combined to make the war in Vietnam what some would refer to as a "company commander's war." Terrain and topography most often inhibited the use of larger units and the implementation of sweeping maneuver. With so much of the fighting done in jungles or mountains, visibility was limited, communications were a challenge, and contact with the enemy was

---

[*] The term "skipper" is not lightly bestowed. In the U.S. Navy, a skipper is the commanding officer of a ship of any size; from lifeboat to aircraft carrier. In the U.S. Marine Corps, the term refers to a man in command of a company—in this case a rifle company. In all cases, it is a term of respect and endearment.

very up close and personal. This meant units larger than companies could not often be employed to optimal effect. Because of these geographic limitations, the generals who commanded divisions, the colonels in charge of regiments, and even the lieutenant colonels running battalions were sometimes relegated to overseeing battles from command posts in the rear or in helicopters above, but only rarely from the front. The war in Vietnam, strategized and meticulously planned at the high and middle levels, was executed largely from the captain level on down.

The role of skipper for a rifle company has unique appeal. It is the fulcrum point, the absolute center of the Marine Corps universe around which revolves a perfect blend of hands-on leadership. The CO, without contention, who represents and becomes both "management" and "labor," can still be as close as an older brother to his platoon commanders and men, see the immediate results—the fruits of his unit's abilities—and at the same time employ the full measure of his intellectual skills coordinating and directing all of the supporting arms his thought processes can manage.

In combat there is no greater challenge than engaging the awesome firepower of naval guns, artillery, and air support and integrating them successfully, correctly with the men on the ground. When it all worked together, as it often did, victory was a near certainty. Sometimes not everything worked out right. Even then, it was *always* the collective actions of well-trained and properly led individual Marines in the fire teams, squads, and platoons that were constituent parts of the companies who would overcome mistakes in judgment, faulty communications, "friendly fire," odd circumstances, or an equally determined enemy who made the difference between success and failure.

At his beck and call, using his fully authorized but still maturing judgment, awaited the full array of destructive force, everything short of nuclear weapons, put up by the best scientists from the biggest companies of the mighty American military-industrial complex. All a skipper had to do was ask for, and then tell where the destruction needed to be placed. It was all there for him and his Marines, sort of like a huge buffet table with unlimited seconds. Very heady stuff; destructive firepower that would rip and tear the earth apart, destructive firepower that would turn a man to mist, erase all evidence of his ever having existed—all of this force in the hands of a young man, the weight, the responsibility for the lives of two hundred men and unlimited firepower dependent on the thought processes of a fellow barely shaving, who only a year or two earlier may have considered his most immediate concern passing a college exam, the bedding of some promising young woman, or pondering nothing more than "Who Wrote the Book of Love?" or "Who Put the Bomp in the Bomp Bah Bomp Bah Bomp?"

No other organization offers the same thrills, emotional highs and lows, responsibilities, or opportunities for personal risk and psychic reward or loss. After the job of company commander, a man would never again have that completely personal level of god-like power. If he moved back to the civilian world, no amount of accumulated wealth would ever equal that level of responsibility and authority earlier granted. Even if he rose to command larger units, that experience would be minus the same personal attachments to his men at the tip of the spear. Nearly every Marine Corps general, it was said, would gladly trade his stars for another shot at commanding a company in combat.

It took a bit of doing after arriving in Vietnam, but John Ripley was ultimately given the command of the company he so strongly craved. Assignment as commanding officer of Lima Company came rather quickly. The company had, for various not too terribly unusual reasons, been through several COs in short order. Even with a few remaining veterans from recent campaigns, that duty had been quite different. Earlier deployed to an area around Danang, 3/3's action had been primarily against Viet Cong guerrillas in intermittent, fleeting engagements. The war they would soon be part of in northern I Corps would be far more rigorous, conventional, and incessant than prior experience. Daily contact with the better trained (than the Viet Cong) and more formidable main force NVA units in even less hospitable terrain would make this combat orders of magnitude bloodier.

When Captain Ripley assumed command of Lima Company he brought no personal combat experience with him. Neither did he bring any bad habits. An open mind coupled with the desire to be the best he could be was a good start. His Force Recon background coupled with his Ranger training, his personal zeal for stealth and patrolling, strong land navigation skills, and a solid grasp on how to maximize available fire support were intangible assets he would soon employ with tangible effect.

Training Lima Company beginning with the most basic infantry tactics, Captain Ripley was a strict taskmaster. Movement of a rifle company at full strength plus attachments, upwards of 225 Marines, and Navy corpsmen, was no simple matter, especially in northern I Corps. Inside of two weeks Lima Company was routinely able to execute movement to contact with 100 percent nonverbal communication.

There was no grab ass, no fooling around. All senses were fully engaged. Every Marine and corpsman knew his job, knew what to do when the stuff hit the fan. The men became like bloodhounds, sleuthing for any hint of enemy presence before the NVA would find them. In the months following, Lima was never caught unawares, never ambushed by the enemy. Lima Company initiated all contact. They found plenty. Ripley friend and disciple Ed "Machete Eddie" McCourt, then a lieutenant with 3/3's India Company, was quick to observe: "Rip was an NVA magnet. My Marines and I used to request to be assigned to one of Lima Company's flanks because we were always sure to see a lot of action."

CHAPTER FOUR

Suicide Squeeze

First Platoon, Lima Company, Third Battalion, Third Marine Regiment (3/3)
Northern I Corps, Republic of Vietnam
Thursday March 2, 1967
1630 hours

For the Marines of Lima 3/3 who would survive the unnamed battle that could be described only by an obscure grid coordinate somewhere in the jungle northwest of Dong Ha up near the DMZ that took place during the daylight hours of March 2, 1967, that day would be *the* point in time that defined them, *the* day that marked them, *the* day that tested, above all other days, whether or not they had what it took to endure all that war could dish out, its gravest horrors, and rise to overcome them.

By about 1500 on March 2, 1967, Chuck Goggin, only two days a corporal, had, of necessity, assumed command of what remained of Lima Company's First Platoon. It was not quite thirteen months earlier that Corporal Goggin had been a civilian, a promising young athlete doing what he could to make it as a big league baseball player. As one of the relatively small group of Marines actually drafted into service during the Vietnam War, he had been meritoriously promoted to private first class during his abbreviated eight-week boot camp experience made shorter by the demands of the conflict. His only official school following the rigors of Parris Island had been ITR (Infantry Training Regiment), a four-week infantry training program given to all Marines headed for service with line units. And now he was in command, had life or death authority of what was left of Lima's First Platoon in the fight of his life.

From July through the early part of December 1966, Chuck served as a rifleman in one of the three squads of Lima Company's First Platoon. That period was more than long enough for him to transition from tenderfoot to experienced jungle warrior. Those five months gave him more combat time than he cared to have, opportunities to observe too many comrades killed or wounded, and develop levels of friendship with other Marines that exceeded anything he had known anywhere else.

Recognizing his initiative and leadership, Second Lieutenant John Bledsoe selected Chuck Goggin, now a lance corporal, to serve as the platoon radio operator in early December. The job of radio operator was a curious one. It was said that the enemy always targeted a unit's leadership, its corpsmen, and its radio operators first. Along with becoming a more lucrative target came the increased physical challenge of humping the additional weight of the AN/PRC-25's (called a "Prick 25" by the troops) thirty or so pounds, including extra battery.

Radio operators were required to be figuratively joined at the hip with the commander they were serving. Wherever he went, they went. When they were not preparing to relay a request for artillery or air support or emergency medevac, they needed to be listening in for direction from the next higher unit—in Lance Corporal Goggin's case orders and requests for info from the company commander. Platoon commanders and company commanders would live, eat, fight, and sleep next to the men who became, by default, their alter egos. The intensity of combat developed bonds quickly and survival requirements were such that a good radio operator could get inside the mind of his boss, would anticipate and almost know in advance what to do, what to ask for, when to get the fire support requests going.

The ability to continually observe the actions of their school-trained officers, to witness the coordination with supporting units required for success, to see how the parts fit in together gave a broader appreciation and bigger picture than was available solely at the rifleman level. A particularly perspicacious radio operator might even learn by watching and experiencing how to land navigate, what it took to maneuver a unit in contact, how to adjust artillery onto a moving target. If the first five months of Lance Corporal Goggin's tour in Vietnam were his undergraduate degree in war fighting, he began work on a master's degree, no thesis required, the day he strapped on the PRC-25. Fortunately for the men of First Platoon, Lance Corporal Chuck Goggin would prove to be, time and again, a very quick study.

It was not at all uncommon, given the way individuals were rotated in and out, wounded or killed, to have units commanded by men of rank lower than was designed for. Second Lieutenant Bledsoe's regular tour with Lima 3/3 ended in December 1966. Without another lieutenant immediately available to take over the platoon, the job fell to First Platoon's platoon sergeant. Staff Sergeant Gerald Witkowski—called, naturally, "Staff Sergeant 'Ski" by his Marines—assumed the duties for the next nine to ten weeks, until a new lieutenant arrived. Second Lieutenant Terry Heekin, fresh from Basic School in Quantico, and the man finally slated to replace the last lieutenant, had been with First Platoon only a day or two prior to Lima Company's action on March 1, 1967.

In an earlier life, Chuck Goggin had been a baseball player. Relative to a fair number of his mates in First Platoon and the rest of Lima Company, Chuck was practically an old man. Nearly twenty-two, the 1963 Pompano Beach Senior High School grad and baseball star had done some time in junior college in Florida before being picked up by the Los Angeles Dodgers organization in 1964. For two years he played on Dodgers Class A teams, first as a shortstop with the Salisbury Dodgers of the West Carolina League and then as an outfielder with the St. Petersburg Saints of the Florida State League. An injury during his first season, torn ligaments in his left knee, the kind that required surgery which left a train-track scar, might have exempted him from military service had he pushed it. But that was not the way Chuck Goggin did business.

Between the countless hours of radio watch and digging fighting holes and tramping the jungle trails, of battling the NVA and the elements, Lance Corporal Goggin sometimes had the rare luxury of a few moments to ponder the world of baseball and in a painful way imagine it all moving forward without him.

At about the same time that Lima Company was in and out of contact with NVA units desperate to annihilate them, Chuck's old teammates, oblivious to what was going on in northern I Corps, were commencing their spring training, suffering the anxieties of making the cut or not. While Lima Company baked and became near desiccated in Vietnam's humid jungle ovens and endured a marginal system of water resupply, his old baseball buddies, he knew, were every night tipping a few and partaking of the amply available young lovelies there in sunny Florida.

In its continuing efforts to indoctrinate and train leaders at every level, the Marine Corps did a decent job with the inculcation of leadership principles, especially for combat. Where classroom instruction focused on the most basic notions which could be reduced to mnemonics and acronyms for easy regurgitation and testing, the real world was a bit more daunting. When all the leadership maxims, which often seemed like a page stolen from the Boy Scouts, were boiled down to the practical—there is a timeless USMC-deprecating quip which joked that the only difference between the Boy Scouts and the Marine Corps was that at least the Scouts had adult leadership—it could fairly well be summed up that the successful leader took care of both his assigned mission and his Marines. If a leader could string together the myriad constituent components he needed to execute his mission while selflessly looking after his men, his chances of success were high. As Napoleon famously opined: "There are no bad regiments, only bad colonels." And fellow Frenchman Dutourd years later offered corollary observation with his memorable comment that: "Men are neither lions nor sheep. It is the man who leads them who turns them into lions or sheep." Captain John Walter Ripley meant to ensure that his Marines went to the field as lions. It was his overriding intent that Lima Company would be king of its very literal jungle experience.

The building of Lima Company in the image of its young captain included far more than was obvious even to the well-trained military man. It was not just the combat stuff, it was the other things too that built them up. Little things. Lots of them. Added together, bit by bit, the synergies began to become real. Things like bringing the company's cook to the field at the "company hill" in Ca Lu rather than keeping him in the rear area so the men might have hot water to shave and for making soup and coffee.[1] Things that showed a level of concern others had not considered possible or practical. If someone in the rear told Captain Ripley "no" he would find a way to get to "yes."

In training his Marines, many of them with far more combat time than he then possessed, he brought the knowledge of Ranger School, of his patrolling expertise from his Force Recon days. He stuck with the basics. In football they call it "blocking and tackling." In the Corps they call it "move, shoot, communicate." Master the basics and you master the battlefield.

Everything was rehearsed. All Marines knew their jobs and most knew the jobs of others if comrades fell and positions needed to be filled. When they conducted movement to contact the two hundred-plus Marines and corpsmen of Lima Company moved stealthily and communicated 100 percent non-verbally. When contact was made, a certain level of order was evident in the guaranteed bedlam and roar of combat.

All Marines in combat want to have confidence in their leaders. That yearning springs not from sentimentality but more from self-preservation. Competent leaders do not foolishly get their men killed. Added to the mix was the confidence the men of Lima Company had in their skipper's ability to deliver precision supporting arms. Aside from managing the list of things a combat leader needed to be and do, perhaps even more important than the Marine Corps equivalent of the thrifty, clean, and reverent stuff, was the ability to execute effective land navigation. To bring in that emergency medevac, to call in and properly adjust artillery, and, if they were operating closer to the coast, naval gunfire, meant knowing close to exactly where Lima was at all times.

Much of the instruction at Basic School was dedicated to mastering all aspects of land navigation. The young lieutenants would spend hours and hours and hours in the classroom going over the fundamentals and the fine points in the proper use of map and compass. From the classroom to the outdoors the lieutenants would sweat out the time attempting to correctly move from point to point, using all their faculties and developing their terrain associating skills. While some men were naturally better than others, like everything else, the mastery of land nav required focus and major intellectual effort. Among the gravest sins a young officer could commit, a sure-fire way to destroy a platoon or company's morale and confidence, was to get them lost, especially if that place was northern I Corps.

One of the popular television shows at the time was *F Troop*. Poking fun at both sides in the Wild West equation, bumbling U.S. Cavalry soldiers were pitted against equally innocuous Indians. The tribe's name—the Hekawi—was a forever subtle one liner as Sergeant O'Rourke or Corporal Agarn always asked "Where're the Hekawi?"—who were always lost. Being the cultured fellows that they usually were, whenever Marines got lost they would, if the situation had not yet gotten too critical, ask a slightly less subtle question: "Where're the Fukawi?" A Marine officer never wanted, and could not afford to be, the butt of that joke or accused of being the leader of that "tribe."

Seven weeks shy of his twenty-third birthday, Second Lieutenant Terry Gene Heekin of Covina, California was fresh from Basic School in Quantico when he reported for duty in Vietnam. Assigned to Lima Company's First Platoon in late February, his first significant action was to be the operation kicked off on March 1, 1967.

The pressure on new lieutenants was huge. With no second chance for a first impression, neophyte officers were only too aware of the leadership microscope their Marines had them under. In an instant these untried and untested platoon commanders needed to establish credibility and respect while making rapid ascent on the steeply inclined combat learning curve. Some young officers, in an honest attempt to prove themselves, might come off as overbearing or as too well school-trained. Most of the time the transition from unknown quantity to battle-tested was pulled off with only minor, acceptable challenges. Lieutenant Heekin, very early on, seemed to be a part of the latter group. Smart enough, perceptive enough, and secure enough in his manhood, he asked the right questions, relying on the judgment of his veteran platoon sergeant and radio operator as he began to learn the ropes. Terry Heekin's learning curve would be steeper than most.

"MY BAYONET'S NOT BROKE!"

When Lima Company saddled up and moved out the early morning of March 1, 1967, Captain Ripley had placed his First Platoon at the point position. On movement to contact, especially in a jungle environment, the folks walking point are the ones who almost always, by design, initiate contact or trigger an ambush before the rest of the unit moving in trace of the point gets to the action. Point men and point units have a special responsibility to be on guard for signs of enemy activity, presence, land mines, booby traps, etc. Walking point requires a man, a fire team, a squad, a platoon to operate with all senses fully engaged to ensure that an enemy is not able to exercise any element of surprise against the larger unit they are serving.

Captain Ripley had placed First Platoon on point for a number of reasons. Aside from it being their turn and that the threat level was high, walking point would be a learning experience for Lieutenant Heekin, a way for him to break in more quickly. And even with an untested platoon commander, Captain Ripley had confidence in Heekin's platoon sergeant and squad leaders, and knew their experience and judgment were some compensation for their lieutenant's newness.

The proper, effective movement along jungle trails of a full strength Marine rifle company expecting to make contact with the enemy was no easy task. Even when everything went as planned, as it seldom did, maintaining focus and orientation required maximum leadership input from Captain Ripley on down to the last rifleman.

Lima Company had actually been transported east by truck on Route 9 from a fire support base known as the Rockpile to a dismount point between there and Dong Ha where they then began to conduct the day's operation. Most of the men were already sweating profusely when Lima had begun to move with any speed and the rhythm of the march was established. The day was going to be another ball-buster, they could tell, and it was still hours until maximum heat.

As the morning wore on and they inched further north, the jungle began to thicken and the hills grew gradually steeper. A few hours before noon Lima Company had experienced one minor contact with an NVA unit of undetermined size at a trail junction that resulted oddly in absolutely no action or casualties. It was about an hour later, with First Platoon still on point, with Lance Corporal Taylor twenty or so meters out front of the rest of the unit, just after he had crested a hill that had some open areas on the slope and was beginning to work his way down the trail to the bottom of a thickly wooded ravine, that he began receiving fire. Caught in the initial fusillade, Taylor was hit in the leg and went down.

The rest of First Platoon had yet to make it to the top of the hill. Immediately, without a word spoken or direction from the platoon commander or the squad leaders, the men spread out, on line, perpendicular to the direction of march, half to the left of the trail, half to the right. Corporal Goggin had run over the hill after Taylor and had brought him back into the new defensive position set up by the quick acting Marines of First Platoon.

Even before Corporal Goggin had pulled Lance Corporal Taylor to safety, the Marines began returning fire, still unable to get a good view of where exactly the enemy fire originated from. The jungle scrub and grass were almost knee high and the prone Marines could only fire at the sounds as their view of the target area was obscured. By the volume of fire it appeared the enemy had at least two machine guns firing up at them. The enemy fire had little effect other than to keep the Marines from moving forward.

Behind First Platoon's line of fire, the rest of Lima Company was spread out back down the trail; the men hunkered down in defensive positions with weapons pointing outward and at the ready. Within seconds of the first enemy machine gun burst Captain Ripley was on the company radio net calling forward to First Platoon wanting a situation report (SitRep). As he came back over the hill with Lance Corporal Taylor in tow, Corporal Goggin resumed his radio operator duties and responded to his skipper.

A Marine rifle company goes to the field with three infantry platoons and a weapons platoon. About the same size as an infantry platoon, the weapons platoon is the company commander's own "personal artillery," the unit's organic heavy firepower. The two primary weapons of a weapons platoon in Vietnam were a number of M-60 machine gun teams and a section of 60mm mortars, usually three tubes. A bear to hump in the field, the mortars, base plates, *accoutrements*, and all the rounds sure came in handy in situations like the one Lima Company now faced. With a maximum effective range of approximately eighteen hundred meters, the ability to fire them indirectly (without eyeballing the target) at high angle also allowed for bringing them in close as well if the enemy was just outside the perimeter. The mortars would often serve as a lifesaver until more serious fire support could be brought on station.

As soon as the fire to the front had been heard, without an order being given, the men in the mortar section began to set up. Instinctively, they knew what was coming next. Rounds were passed forward and back from those men glad to be shedding the extra weight they had been packing. (Mortar rounds and extra ammo for machine guns were routinely distributed and packed by all the men of the company.)

There is a definite protocol and procedure for Marine Corps radio communications. In combat that procedure was generally followed with proper effect. Each unit with a radio changed frequencies and call signs daily in attempt to keep the enemy from eavesdropping or identifying who was communicating. To minimize time spent broadcasting, messages were brief. Marines had good motivation to minimize broadcast time. The NVA possessed exceptional direction finding (DF) capabilities that allowed them to, in a relatively short time, direct artillery in on the broadcasting position. By 1967 Marines had gained enough respect to assume that a high percentage of their comm was being listened in on.

In the normal back and forth on the radio within a unit, the senior man was called "the Six." Captain Ripley was "Lima Six." When Captain Ripley himself was being referred to or was doing the talking he was identified as "Lima Six Actual" or "Six Actual" for short. Each platoon was identified by its number and the platoon commander by the number along with "actual." First Platoon was "Lima One," its platoon commander "Lima One Actual," Second Platoon was "Lima Two," its platoon commander "Lima Two Actual," etc. It is doubtful that the NVA were fooled by this but it was still a better procedure than using names.

First Platoon continued to pour fire in the general direction of the brush line at the bottom of the hill. Getting the basic picture from Corporal Goggin, Captain Ripley gave his mortars a fire mission, hoping a single three-tube volley would silence the enemy's guns. In the meantime one of the First Platoon Marines, frustrated by his inability to see his target, stood up part way to get off some rounds. Known to the others as Baby Huey for his prodigious size and strength, Baby Huey got off only a few rounds before himself being drilled in the chest. It may have been his size that ultimately saved him that day, but he became First Platoon's second WIA of the early afternoon.

After the initial mortar barrage, the men of First Platoon were disappointed when the NVA resumed their relatively inaccurate but reasonably high volume of fire. For the next few minutes First Platoon continued to more selectively return fire in an effort to preserve ammunition.

Back down the trail, Captain John Walter Ripley, with the rest of Lima Company, was growing impatient. Supremely confident, and perhaps a bit anachronistic, he continued to monitor the radio himself. The NVA was starting to piss him off as was this delay in his movement. With the medevac helicopter already inbound to extract Taylor and Baby Huey, his next decision required a double take by First Platoon's incredulous radio operator.

Captain Ripley called his First Platoon on the company net: "Put One Actual on the phone." Lieutenant Heekin was busy directing the action, just like he was supposed to be doing. The volume of fire made the noise, as always during contact, near deafening.

Corporal Goggin told his captain: "One Actual is pretty busy, Skipper." It was really hard to even make out the radio transmissions.

"I want you to pass this on to One Actual." Pause. "I want you to fix bayonets."

Corporal Goggin could not believe what he thought he had just heard. He hoped it was some sort of mistake in transmission, some sort of garbling. He hoped he had misunderstood. Shocked by the order, he came back with: "Six Actual, say again your last."

Captain Ripley was firm: "I want you to fix bayonets. We are going to give you a multi-round mortar barrage. After the last round goes off I want you to stand up and charge the position. Fix bayonets."

Still dazed by the order, Corporal Goggin crawled over to where Lieutenant Heekin was directing the action. Lieutenant Heekin rightly figured the company commander had an order to be passed to him. As Goggin got close enough so that they could shout louder than the noise of the weapons he asked: "What did he say?"

"Lieutenant, he wants us to fix bayonets and charge."

Without hesitation Lieutenant Heekin demanded: "Ask him to repeat that."

"I already did, sir."

Corporal Goggin then explained the plan as directed by Captain Ripley. Corporal Goggin suggested to the lieutenant: "Sir, why don't you pass the word to the left and I'll pass the word to the right?" Both the lieutenant and his radio operator were armed only with .45s.

With the continuing noise and roar and confusion it was difficult to deliver the order. It needed to be passed down the line, from man to man. To Corporal Goggin's immediate right was a young lad from Louisiana who was fully engaged in the battle, focused on the enemy down the hill. While he had probably not come from Harvard nor would he be going there after his tour, he was a fighting son of a gun. He did not hear Goggin at first shouting out the orders to him as he kept firing out rounds. Finally Corporal Goggin took the butt of his .45 and tapped him on the helmet to get his attention. With their faces inches apart so he could give him the order, Corporal Goggin shouted, "Fix bayonets!"

Stunned for a moment the young Marine pondered the order, trying to make sense of what made no sense at all to him, and replied with deep sincerity: "My bayonet's not broke!" Pause.

"Put your bayonet on the end of your rifle!!!" and Corporal Goggin showed him with a hand motion.

The word was passed initially from Marine to Marine and then the remaining groups saw what was happening and followed suit. There was no romance in the order. No Hollywood-seeming aura or fanfare, no sound of trumpets. The signature click of metal on metal as the bayonets were seated at the rifles' barrel tips could not be heard above the din of the weapons' reports. No one timed it. Maybe it was a full minute before all of First Platoon had fixed bayonets. Lieutenant Heekin looked at his radio operator. As the new guy he genuinely queried him: "Corporal Goggin, have we ever done this before?"

"Sir, I don't think *anyone* has done this since the Civil War."

About that time Captain Ripley called over the radio: "Is everybody ready?"

"Yessir!"

"Stand by." Almost immediately came the rapid thumping and crumping sounds of multiple volleys being fired from the 60s a hundred meters to the rear.

In what seemed too short a period of time Captain Ripley was back on the net: "Charge."

And First Platoon stood up, every single one of them. The forty or so remaining Marines stood up on line. All men scared spitless but somehow emboldened by the sheer brazenness of this act, they began to move with purpose and speed. And they began to yell and scream and curse like mad men. Rebel yells. Blood curdling rebel yells. Just like the men who followed Stonewall Jackson and Jeb Stuart. Here in the godforsaken jungles of Vietnam one hundred years later another crazy-like-a-fox Virginian was ordering men to fix bayonets and charge. They advanced into what could have been the murderous fire of NVA machine guns. When they reached the bottom of the hill not a shot had been loosed at them. Practically falling into the well-camouflaged trench left by fleeing NVA, all they found were hundreds and hundreds of spent shell casings. And a few splotches of blood. With adrenaline flowing at levels even the toughest and longest serving veterans had rarely experienced, it felt good to be alive. Very good.

ON TO THE NEXT OBJECTIVE

There was little time for celebration. This was not a movie. The rest of Lima Company came forward. Captain Ripley and the others assessed the results. The splotches of blood at least signaled that the Marines had "got some." The march was resumed.

Lima Company had not gotten too far on the trail when the bodies of several recently killed NVA were discovered, obviously dead from the earlier action. It was evident that Lima was moving into, not away from, the heart of Indian country. They had not gone much more than one click (kilometer) before Captain Ripley decided to circle the wagons and set in for the evening. In a location that he believed offered good cover and concealment and could be reasonably well defended, the Marines of Lima Company began to dig in.

When Marines in the bush set up for the night, the first thing they always did concurrently was assign a few fellows to man security outposts, begin to dig their evening fighting holes, and commence close-in local patrolling of the area around the company harbor site to ensure that the NVA would not surprise them. There was never ever a chance to let down one's guard. The evening of March 1, 1967 was relatively uneventful, the proverbial calm before the storm. The men at least had opportunity to fill canteens from nearby streams and consume what rations they had with them. Since kicking off the operation earlier in the day, Lima Company had not yet been resupplied. Captain Ripley ordered that ammunition from the other platoons be redistributed and given to men of First Platoon who had expended a fair amount in the day's earlier firefight.

With the lives of more than two hundred Marines in the balance, young John Ripley, in deepest darkest Indian country, felt the pressure. With Lima Company spread out in a tight perimeter all around, with his platoon commanders and platoon sergeants and squad leaders all doing their jobs, with his position radioed in to higher headquarters and a fair amount of artillery now at his disposal awaiting only the order to shoot, John Ripley was ready for the night. As ready as he could be.

For any man in combat it was difficult to believe the world outside his world continued to press on and yet each man knew that it did and was probably grateful that it did. For Captain Ripley the world outside his world was Moline and Stephen. With all the planning that he could possibly do concluded, he could steal away into his mind and heart and think about Wednesday, March 1, 1967, that really had not yet been lived back in Alexandria, Virginia.

Eleven hours behind Vietnam time, as one squad from each of Lima's platoons quietly crept about the darkened jungle on patrol outside the company position, Moline was no doubt tending to young Stephen, cleaning, feeding, bathing, walking him in a stroller, or playing at a park, whatever. Also reassuring was the knowledge that big brother George's wife Maureen with her three daughters, all older than Stephen, lived in the same apartment complex in Alexandria, just south of DC. With both of their husbands in Vietnam, Maureen and Moline had grown closer than they already were. And it was not too far a drive, only a couple of hours, for Moline to pack up and head down to Radford where both Moline's parents, the Blaylocks, and the senior Ripleys lived. On the Blaylock side of things Stephen was the first and only grandchild so far. When he was in town he was center stage, the main attraction. And even at the Ripley home, where there were already other grandchildren older than Stephen, he and his momma were always warmly welcomed. John Ripley did not have to worry about their welfare too much. He just missed them terribly.

As pleasant as it was to ponder Moline and Stephen, the closer reality was that within his own several-square-kilometer world were at least hundreds, maybe even thousands of NVA regulars, flesh-and-blood men like those of Lima, just as anxious to destroy him as he was them. He needed to keep that perspective, that warrior's edge. He needed to focus on survival.

Somewhere north of Route 9, west of Dong Ha
Thursday, March 2, 1967
Sometime after sunrise

Even though the calendar revealed a new day verified by the rising sun, there was little that suggested an advance of time. Waking up on Thursday, March the Second for the Marines of Lima Company, if they had been able to sleep at all, was not like it would have been anywhere else except in northern I Corps.

Living in Bad Guy Country allowed no clean break from the day before, no expectation of an end to combat operations until Lima would retire from the field, whenever that might be. Out where they were, they were either in the action, recovering from prior action, or prepping for imminent action. Aside from always being dirty, aside from always being tired, aside from always being hungry and thirsty and sweaty, the only other thing that was continuous was fear—a monotony of fear. In the bush there were no time outs, no commercial breaks, no instant replays, no happy hour, no weekends; only death or survival.

As intense as events had been for Lima Company 3/3 on Wednesday, Captain Ripley and his Marines were but a small cog in a much larger ongoing effort all over Vietnam. In northern I Corps alone, Lima's parent battalion was joined in the field by four other USMC infantry battalions. In direct support of those five battalions was the entire 12th Marine Artillery Regiment along with several squadrons of helicopter and fixed-wing attack aircraft. Analysts in the intelligence community were convinced that the NVA had at least four divisions operating in the vicinity. If correct in that assessment, the American Marines would have all the action they could handle.

In general the Americans usually enjoyed local fire superiority, especially when airpower could be fully exploited and, if close enough to the coast, they could add naval gunfire to the mix. The use of helicopters to move men and material gave commanders unprecedented flexibility. The system of fairly rapid resupply gave those consigned to ground combat duty some level of confidence in knowing that if they were wounded, heaven and earth would be moved so that they would be expeditiously transported to nearby medical care, and when beans and bullets ran low there would shortly be more coming. Still, the outcome of infantry combat was in the hands of a bunch of young men on both sides who usually were nothing more than teenagers led by men only slightly older.

The NVA were not without local advantages as well. Operating within close proximity to North Vietnam and eastern Laos where the expansive tentacles of the Ho Chi Minh Trail kept them amply provisioned, even if that supply effort was far more manpower and man-packed dependent than U.S. reliance on technology, the NVA were usually unhampered by logistical limitations in northern I Corps.

Perhaps the greatest advantage enjoyed by the NVA was the publicly stated U.S. policy that its ground forces would not cross into Laos or North Vietnam. Freeing up countless soldiers who might otherwise have been required to defend sanctuaries, supply depots, and artillery positions if there had been concern that U.S. or ARVN forces might invade, this politically imposed limitation ceded the strategic initiative on the battlefield largely to the enemy.

PURPLE HEARTS AND VALOR AWARDS

The standards for the awarding of valor medals—the Congressional Medal of Honor, the Navy Cross (in the Army they award the Distinguished Service Cross, and the Air Force Cross in the USAF), the Silver Star, and the Bronze Star—did come with Marine Corps-generated guidelines.

With the write-up for awards initiated and first processed at the battalion level, the granting of awards for combat heroism was largely contingent upon a number of subjective inputs. The normal and relatively rapid rotation of battalion commanders, the men with the major and primary impetus to get things started, meant that the standards were always changing as these men often had widely divergent opinions concerning valor recognition. Other issues factoring into the award equation included the ability of the person writing up the award to properly articulate the events and craft them into a compelling story. The quality and quantity of witnesses also had impact. Among senior and mid-level Marine Corps officers there was a substantial number who believed that simply wearing the uniform along with being kept in critical positions of leadership during the most trying times was recognition enough. When it came down to it the Marine Corps in general, and 3/3 in particular, was downright niggardly, completely illiberal in the awarding of valor medals to officers and enlisted men who survived their time in combat.

The criteria for the awarding of Purple Hearts, a bit less parsimonious and far less subjective, were also conditioned upon rigorous standards. It was encouraging to note that a very high percentage of those men wounded would often refuse their Purple Hearts due to the rule that if a man was hit three times he was automatically sent home. Unit loyalty and personal camaraderie more often than not kept Marines in the fight. With that said, the standard for Third Battalion, Third Marines included three key points. First, a wound had to be the result of enemy action. Second, the Marine had to be "knocked down." And finally, there had to be penetration. Purple Hearts were not to be awarded to those Marines injured while "seeking rapid cover." Injuries resulting from jumping in a ditch or fighting hole during a mortar attack, forgetting to duck while running into or out of a building and banging one's head on a low-hanging edge of metal roofing did not meet the 3/3 standard for a combat wound.

In Captain Ripley's case, after assuming command of Lima Company he had admonished his senior corpsman that he was never to "tag" the skipper for medevac without his consent or unless he was effectively dead. The events of March 2, 1967 would demonstrate the prescience of that order.

CHAPTER FIVE

Lima Company Moves Out

Captain Ripley, *ever judicious*, always meticulous, prior to any possible contact had prepared for the day just like before, or maybe just a little bit more. Before stepping off, he and his attached artillery forward observer (FO) had stacked up the air requests and radioed in all the preplanned potential artillery targets. When Lima Company made contact, air strikes would be there in a New York minute, rounds of artillery even sooner.

Dubbed "Prince Henry the Navigator" by his approving skipper, the arty FO had earned the respect of his company commander and enjoyed the confidence of all of Lima's Marines for his land navigational prowess. When there was a moment to bicker, Prince Henry and Captain Ripley, who usually could agree on a six-digit grid coordinate (which had a wiggle factor of plus or minus one hundred meters in any direction), would lock horns in a friendly way and argue over the last ten meters in an eight-digit grid coordinate (an eight-digit grid coordinate described a location to within ten meters). With Prince Henry as backup on navigation and completely dialed in for calling in artillery and air strikes, Captain Ripley could focus more effort on maneuver and the bigger picture.

As Lima Company prepared to move out, the unit was as ready for combat as it could be. Saddled with the same challenges facing every Marine Corps infantry company—a broad spectrum of experience levels among its officers and men—the strength, wisdom, and skill of its leaders and veterans would have to carry the day.

While the folks back in the World were starting to hear stories of problems with discipline and drugs in Vietnam, they were *not* a problem in Lima 3/3. The notion of a Lima Company Marine smoking dope or using heroin in the bush was *anathema* to any man concerned about his or his comrade's survival. All of the recent learning and training and fighting experience was about to be put to severe test.

With the ongoing action in and around where Lima was currently operating, Captain Ripley's first order on March 2, 1967 was to proceed from his overnight position to a trail junction several kilometers away and establish an ambush or blocking position. As intense as it all was, as concerned in executing everything as flawlessly as he was able to influence, Captain Ripley still had a fleeting moment or two to muse and be prideful of his Marines. Lima Company, with all its attachments, with approximately 215 officers and men, was a sight to behold. All these men, young men by most measures still boys really, here together, primed, senses acute, leaning forward in the hunt, moving with stealth and calm determination like the Marines they were. No one needed to be told what to do, they all knew. There was no extraneous noise. All communication was by hand and arm signals. The sound of boots on soil, very muffled, was diffused by the time it reached knee high. Everything that was done was deliberate. It was as if one very long, green centipede-type insect with hundreds of legs was moving rather gracefully down the uneven jungle trail.

Within moments of stepping off, the Marines ran into a lone sniper whom they shortly dispatched and pressed on down the trail. Spying evidence of recent enemy presence—blood and rice—they all knew they were on to something, and knew they would be onto it sooner rather than later.

The NVA were exceptionally fastidious in removing their dead and wounded from the battlefield in an effort to deny the body-count-crazy Americans satisfaction in knowing the real score. Many of the NVA soldiers would come into battle with thick jungle vines wrapped around their ankles. At first the Marines believed the vines to be part of some elaborate camouflage scheme when, in fact, the vines were meant to serve as handles which comrades could grab onto to drag the dead or seriously wounded from the battlefield. While the practice served the purpose of denying immediate body count, signs of dragging often left a trail by which even a marginal point man could track his foe.

Along the trail of rice and blood Lima Company Marines soon discovered a number of fresh graves. One of Captain Ripley's men, a fellow with a bit of an odd, *macabre* sense of humor, presented to his skipper an NVA boot he had found…with the foot still in it.

Second Lieutenant Terry Heekin, Lima One Actual, still a neophyte, was a little bit less of one after the action of the last twenty-four hours. With typical second lieutenant alacrity he took in what lessons he could from that action and was moving ahead just as designed and expected. The Wednesday action was the only on-the-job training he would receive for what would take place Thursday.

Arriving at the position designated by the battalion commander, Lima Company set up a hasty defense at the trail junction. Captain Ripley decided that he would leave Third Platoon along with the mortar section from Weapons Platoon in place. From First and Second Platoons he dispatched a squad from each to recon the two trails that forked from the direction of Lima's original approach.

At about the time Lima Company had been ordered to the position it was approaching, the battalion commander had admonished Lima Six Actual not to engage the enemy until the remainder of the battalion would arrive. In the battalion's operations (S-3) officer's estimate, that would be eight hours or so. Captain Ripley replied that, "I will deploy to protect the company."

Corporal Hobbs was a First Platoon squad leader and it was his Marines Captain Ripley sent north to have a look-see in that direction. Hobbs, another one of Lima's solid performers, and his squad had not traveled far when he radioed back in barely muffled tones to his skipper that they had stumbled onto what he thought was something big and that the captain might want to come up and have a look. All was quiet within the group of Lima Company Leathernecks. The only sounds were the radios being keyed by those communicating in hushed voices.

Moving forward to Corporal Hobbs's position, Captain Ripley brought the rest of First Platoon. Second Platoon would follow shortly once they recovered the patrol they had sent in the opposite direction. As Captain Ripley and First Platoon approached for link up, there was no talking. Corporal Hobbs communicated quite effectively with hand and arm signals. With the recovery of Second Platoon to their position only moments later, Captain Ripley had Hobbs push ahead. Moving into a jungle clearing Corporal Hobbs spotted what looked to be a setup almost exactly like the one they had stumbled upon, in precisely the same manner, not two weeks earlier twenty kilometers west out near Khe Sanh.

Since the NVA members were masters at camouflage and using terrain to maximum advantage, this hidden, capacious base camp Corporal Hobbs and his under-strength squad crept up to required the greatest discernment and visual acuity to make out. Even Captain Ripley, once he was called forward to eyeball the find, required a long look before the evidence of NVA presence became apparent. Enemy fighting holes, more than he cared to count, were properly dug and all were connected with comm wire. Hidden artfully in the tree line, just yonder, the Marines were able to make out a number of large radio antennas, the kind that could only belong to a unit much larger than Lima Company. Captain Ripley and the Marines who had been with Lima two weeks earlier had, because of their ability to move stealthily, walked right into an NVA regimental headquarters. Just like today, they had done it so that the bad guys only had time to immediately bug out. Apparently not everyone had gotten the word.

More remarkable was what the eagle-eyed Hobbs spotted fifty meters or so to his front. Having given the order to freeze, Lima's two platoons silently and instantaneously assumed defensive positions with nearly all eyes on Hobbs. In slow, deliberate, exaggerated movements Hobbs, a rather tall and well-built Marine, advanced into the clearing toward what looked like nothing more than nothing in particular. It took concentration and focus, sort of like trying to read the lowest line on one of those visual testing charts, but Captain Ripley finally saw it—or him—too. In a perfectly dug fighting hole the upper torso and head of an NVA soldier could be partially made out. He was hunched over, engaged in something requiring his full attention. The NVA soldier had no clue of his foe's approach.

Once Corporal Hobbs was practically on top of his hapless victim, he reached down and in one sweeping grab, unceremoniously snatched him from his hole, like a cartoon character cat seizing a cartoon baby bird from its cartoon nest. The only thing different was that Corporal Hobbs did not try to eat him. If this had not been northern I Corps in 1967 it might have passed for comedy, this particularly large American Marine holding on for dear life to this particularly diminutive NVA soldier, a proper Son of the Revolution, the kind of specialized and well-trained radio operator to be found only in *large* units, who had faithfully been listening in on his radio (he had earphones over both ears) and tapping out Morse Code on his kneepad to somebody further up the food chain when he was so rudely disturbed by this imperialist running dog. Kicking and flailing, his strength was no match for Corporal Hobbs who had by then gained assistance from squad mates in subduing their prisoner.

With the captured NVA radio operator secured and sent back to Third Platoon's location for further transport to the rear for interrogation, the men of Lima Company made a second discovery. In another clearing adjacent to the area with the fighting holes were piled extremely high what had to have been five hundred NVA rucksacks. At least five hundred, probably more. To the too few Marines of Lima the pile looked like a mini-Mt. Suribachi. To the too few Marines of Lima the pile seemed so big that had it been permanent it would have qualified as a legitimate terrain feature were new maps to be crafted. Corporal Goggin's thoughts were far from unique: "*Where are all those sons-of-bitches who belong to all those rucksacks? And how many of us are there...?*" The collective Lima pucker factor was ratcheted ever higher. Every man, no matter how tired, no matter how scared, was switched on.

Once again good training took over. Without a word being spoken or having to order it, the Marines intuitively knew to fix bayonets, then got on line and began to move through this amazing landscape chock-full of enemy booty but with no NVA

71

currently in Lima's crosshairs. The Marines sensed they were being observed. The only sounds were the muffled noises of professional warriors walking gingerly and yet with some amount of purpose toward certain contact. Each man knew it was a silence that would not last, that every advancing step brought these paltry few Marines closer to a precipice they knew was out there somewhere, somewhere they could not see. They would only know they had crossed it when the fight was on.

With just two platoons, with fully one-third of his combat power, including the mortar section, well back at that trail junction Captain Ripley had been told to hold, Lima Company had advanced no more than twenty-five meters when all hell broke loose. The fight was definitely on, and in a very big way.

The NVA were switched on as well, and in the briefest moment it seemed that all manner of their firepower had erupted along Lima's front. Everything but airpower; small arms, machine guns, mortars, rockets, hand grenades. Close enough to throw grenades, Lima Six Actual had never seen this volume of Chinese-Communist (Chi-com) grenades employed. Different than the American high-explosive hand grenades which were spherically shaped and either thrown like baseballs or lobbed because of their weight, Chi-coms were more like the old "potato-masher" grenades employed by the Germans in World Wars I and II. Using a wooden handle atop which explosives were affixed, Chi-coms were probably easier to throw than the American version. Spinning through the air—and the air was currently full of them—they looked a bit like twirling batons except that this was no football game halftime show.

Lima Company's volume of fire was impressive. Even with the number of friendly casualties immediately taken, the Marines kept the pressure on, advancing into or towards the NVA positions. Covering a fair amount of ground early on, Lima Company initially appeared to be routing whomever it was they were fighting.

Captain Ripley did not have to ask, nor did he have to say a thing to his FO. As soon as the battle was joined, the earlier requests for air support were immediately activated. Fully engaged, all of Lima Company had no spare brain capacity to worry about where the A-4 Skyhawks came from. All that mattered was that they were somehow magically on station and overhead. Prince Henry the Navigator, with Captain Ripley's oversight and approval, worked them in close. Very close.

The fight was on and there was no way, no way that Lima could break contact. To break contact and attempt to move back to where Third Platoon was would have meant certain annihilation. The best way to handle this situation was to try and destroy the NVA before they could destroy Lima Company.

Almost as soon as the air and artillery requests went in, folks in the rear, especially 3/3's battalion commander, were anxious to know what was going on. Lima Six Actual complied when he could but he had his company to fight and had no time yet to count dead NVA. This action was anything but close to being over.

The thunderous attack jets' approach was evident only briefly but was longer than the split-second flash view of their passing just above the jungle canopy. More distinctive than the jet noise, and evident above all the furor, was the horrifically violent and unique multiple snapping and cracking sounds when metal locked on metal as the Mk-82 "Snake Eye" bombs were released from their under-wing pylons and the four retardant stabilizing fins of each munition were sprung near instantaneously to slow the 241-kg bombs' descent long enough for the low-flying fast movers to get ahead of their impact.

The volume of fire from the NVA side was surprisingly intense. With the estimated five-hundred-odd rucksacks in the pile that Corporal Hobbs had just discovered, there had to be boocoo NVA around. And if this was, like the unit they had discovered up at Khe Sanh awhile back, an NVA regiment, there would be the quantity of weapons a regiment would rate—more and larger mortars, more and larger machine guns, and lots, lots more men. Angry, pissed off men. There was no question that Lima was outnumbered locally. Whether they would be outfought was still to be determined.

Ground combat in Vietnam was subject to its own barely perceptible rhythms and cycles once the action was initiated. Rarely did American troops get full-on views of their enemy in the open. Whether they did or not, initial contact was usually accompanied by extremely high volumes of outgoing fire triggered by both nervous reaction and the need to establish fire superiority. As the situation might stabilize, as more of the enemy's disposition became known to the leaders at the small-unit level, and as the realization for conserving ammunition crept back into people's thought processes, a steadier, measured response was re-established.

Along with coordinating the necessary artillery and air strikes, maneuvering his two forward platoons, and concerning himself with extricating from the fight only those men who absolutely required medevac, Captain Ripley had also to be wary of Lima's dwindling stocks of ammunition. The material fecundity of American industrial power, the production of Detroit and Pittsburgh and Youngstown, mattered not one bit if that fruitfulness was sitting on a dock at Cam Ranh Bay or some supply depot in Phu Bai. It would cause Lima's skipper no end of gall this day that as a member of his nation's proudest military force, a nation with resources and material abundance second to none, that he was about to be forced to strip the bodies of the dead and severely wounded for the supplies needed to stay in the fight.

The initial fighting, Lima's casualties notwithstanding, was moderately encouraging for Captain Ripley. Artillery and air support were quite effective. The NVA appeared to have been forced to pull back before the American firepower. What the Lima Company Marines were about to learn was that their enemy had simply fallen back to secondary positions from which they would soon deliver more of their own supporting arms and launch their counterattack.

Lima Company, with its Third Platoon well back at the trail junction, was arranged on line to attack toward the direction of Hobbs's find. Second Platoon just happened to be in the line of fire, to its immediate front, of two well-placed NVA machine guns. Heavy enough to require wheels and built with an actual seat for the man firing it, these Chinese or Soviet knock-offs of the Maxim gun began to deliver effective fire into the Marines of Second Platoon.

Corporal Richard Strahl of Glendale, Arizona was of the same cut as those Marines who would get hit and then refuse evacuation. The Second Platoon radio operator had already extended for three months after finishing his normal thirteen-month tour. His extra three months were now also past, but he felt the need to assist his still-not-completely-snapped-in platoon commander. One more operation would do it for sure. After this stretch in the bush he would depart Second Platoon with a clear conscience knowing he had done all he could to pass on the lessons he had learned to "his lieutenant." With that work done, he could go home and marry the young woman who had waited faithfully for him and live happily ever after.

Lieutenant Heekin and crew in First Platoon had managed to turn the enemy on its flank. As the fighting inched forward from clearing to jungle cover and then again to small clearing, Second Platoon broke into the open as all of Lima pursued the enemy. Unfortunately for Lieutenant Butch Goodwin, Second Platoon's commanding officer, and his loyal, seasoned radio operator, they moved smack dab into the sights of one of those Maxim-type guns. A well-aimed long burst of fire caught them both as they stepped out of the jungle into the open. First Lieutenant Goodwin and Corporal Strahl were killed instantly. At very close range, the fighting continued without interruption.

Meanwhile, the folks back at the regimental and division command posts (CP) were able to listen in on the chatter among and between the Marines in contact, as well as the myriad fire support requests liberally being sent in. Lima's action was currently the only major battle going in northern I Corps. There was no vicarious thrill listening in. Real Marines were already KIA. Real Marines were still duking it out, obviously with an enemy force several times Lima's size. The men listening in back in the rear could tell something big was up and they began working with even more determination to bring the necessary resupply and fire support resources to where they would be needed. Medevac helicopters were already inbound to Lima's position. The Direct Air Support Center (DASC) was diverting all the available A-4 and F-4 aircraft over to where Lima was engaged.

The sudden appearance of Brigadier General Michael Patrick Ryan on the battlefield late on the morning of March 2, 1967 was a mixed blessing for the Marines. As the Assistant Division Commander for the Third Marine Division and the senior Marine in northern I Corps, General Ryan was part of that select *coterie* of senior Marine Corps officers with significant personal combat experience from both World War II and Korea. There was no question that among this group, General Ryan was both Old Corps and hard core. As part of that old school of Marines who believed in leadership that was very hands on, up front, and personal, General Ryan knew he could understand the action best not by listening to snippets of it in the rear over the radio or by flying above it in his command helicopter, but by walking around the center of it where his companies and platoons and squads were in direct contact with the enemy.

As a twenty-seven-year-old major with the Second Marine Division in November 1943, Michael Patrick Ryan's personal leadership and courage were recognized constituents in the particularly bloody victory at Tarawa. Forming a composite battalion from the decimated companies that came ashore under murderous, withering Japanese fire, Major Ryan's actions helped relieve sufficient pressure on Colonel Shoup's Second Marine Regiment and helped the Americans to gain the initiative. There were those who believed that had it not been for Major Ryan's leadership, victory at Tarawa would have come at a much higher cost. For his contributions during those seventy-six hours of hell, Major Ryan was awarded the Navy Cross. At fifty-one years of age, a veritable dinosaur compared to the Marines in Lima Company, it was no exaggeration at all to say that General Ryan, for the Marines who knew him or about him, was one of the larger than life personalities of the USMC in 1967.

Captain Ripley's plate was already overflowing before General Ryan flew in unannounced to have a personal look at the battlefield. Ripley's First and Second Platoons had been in heavy contact with the NVA for a considerable period. Friendly casualties were already numerous and waiting for medevac as the general moved through Lima's very tentative positions. While rounds were still being exchanged, the general, with Captain Ripley in tow, walked among the Marines and the dead NVA who were intermingled on the terrain currently in American hands.

Perhaps the most grisly spectacle on this tiny piece of newly acquired Marine Corps real estate was the Maxim-type, wheeled machine gun, the exact one that had earlier killed Lieutenant Goodwin and Corporal Strahl. Destroyed less than an hour ago by a white phosphorous (called "willy-peter" or "willy-pete" by the grunts) hand grenade, the NVA gunner was still at his appointed place of duty, facing the direction from which the Marines had attacked, suspended forever at his seat as if he was, even in death, still trying to get rounds off. That the machine gun had been taken out in close quarters by a hand grenade was testament to the brutality and extreme cost of the battle so far.

As tough as the day had so far been, as stressed as all the Lima Company Marines already were, the presence among them of this former human being, his body still smoldering and the stink of burning flesh mixed together with whatever chemicals constituted a willy-peter round was most disconcerting. This further assaulted the senses and underscored just how unreal and surreal the entire action had been. The site of the dead gunner also gave the Marines some bizarre yet tangible sense of retribution and satisfaction, some very personal sense of payback, especially for the men of Second Platoon.

Vast quantities of enemy equipment were strewn about the landscape, much of it churned up and displaced haphazardly by the heavy air and artillery strikes Ripley had earlier ordered in. The general instructed Marines from his helicopter crew to secure the more significant items, like the large Chinese radio set captured intact by the advancing Lima Marines, for extract back to the rear so the intel folks might have a look.

As the general and the company commander moved about the position, Captain Ripley was continually advising and encouraging his Marines, ensuring the lines were maintained, that ammunition was redistributed and taken from men who were either KIA or too severely wounded to continue fighting. Men with non-debilitating wounds, which by this time was a high percentage of all the men of Lima Company, were still fully employed and few, if any, even contemplated being medevaced.

General Ryan took in the entire scene. Familiar with extreme combat, he had been in similar predicaments before. As the two officers continued their rounds, slowly working their way toward the general's helicopter in the tiny LZ at the center of the position, conversation centered on how best to fight the company and what the general might do in the way of securing further fire support and reinforcements. He knew this was a significant contact and could tell that Lima Company was up against a much larger unit. While the general saw the cost to the Marines, he also saw opportunity to fix and destroy what appeared to be this NVA regimental headquarters.

The area currently controlled by the Marines was a treasure trove of NVA gear, much of it still boxed in original factory packaging awaiting initial use. Unopened crates and boxes were everywhere along with stacks of weapons, medical supplies, rucksacks, all manner of things except living, breathing NVA.

As they drew closer to the waiting helicopter where the engine still ran, the pilot, spying the general and anxious to get the heck out of Dodge, began his prep for departure and the engine rpms were spun up. Above the straining whines of the warbird about to lift off, General Ryan and Captain Ripley shared their final exchange:

"Can you hold on here, Captain Ripley?"

"Yes sir. Yes sir, we can."

"I'm going to direct all the available fire support assets in northern I Corps to support Lima Company. I'll get you ALL the support I can."

"Thank you, sir."

"Carry on, Captain Ripley. You're doing a helluva job, Skipper. A helluva job."

"Yes, sir."

The helo was turning at full throttle before the general was aboard. Once he stepped onto the landing skid and before he was even seated, the anxious crew chief gave the pilot thumbs up. Within seconds they had lifted off and it was only a few seconds more before they had cleared the tiny landing zone and then the jungle canopy. Lima Company was alone again. The day was far from over.

As much as he appreciated General Ryan's personal involvement in the action, Lima Six Actual was glad to be rid of the high value target the general presented to the NVA. Certain they were being observed by enemy soldiers in the surrounding jungle, Captain Ripley wanted to draw no more attention to his Marines than possible. A large green UH-1 command helicopter with rotors turning was a siren call to his nemesis, like posting a "kick me" sign right on his forehead. That he did not need.

Once airborne, General Ryan must have instantaneously come up on his command net to turn whatever wheels he could with as much force as he had available; fire support, resupply, reinforcements, medevac. Lima Company needed all of it, and right now.

The exchange between Lima Company and the NVA continued on; brutal, without quarter and unabated, but at a pace reduced from that at initial contact. Part of the reason for lulls in battle, aside from ammunition constraints, which by now may have impacted the enemy as well, was sheer exhaustion.

It was not that long until General Ryan's helicopter was back, immediately overhead. Hovering above the old LZ, John Ripley ran over to wave him off, certain the NVA would not blow the second chance to take out the helicopter and what had to be a bunch of Marines in the immediate vicinity.

Over in First Platoon the adrenalin and ammunition stores, as they were for everyone else, probably to include the NVA, were close to empty. No one, not even these fittest of fighting men, could carry on forever at the pace they had been operating. Just before the general's helicopter had re-approached the landing zone, word was passed that battalion (3/3) had already helicoptered in a number of replacements, men scraped together from the admin sections and supporting units in the rear. Deposited into an LZ back a way from where Lima was now engaged, Captain Ripley radioed over to First Platoon to send a man back down the trail to guide the fresh troops in.

First Platoon was spread out pretty much on line. Tied in and to its left, Second Platoon continued on down another hundred meters or so. Second Lieutenant Heekin, Staff Sergeant Witkowsky, and Corporal Goggin, constituting the First Platoon's "command element," had established themselves right where they could best control the situation, about ten meters behind and in the center of the platoon's position. Like their men, these three were basically running on fumes. For a brief period the fighting had died down and First Platoon's command element simply collapsed in place for a moment's rest.

Cobbled together by the stretched-thin sinew of its grit and collective will, Lima Company's precarious status was about to spiral nearly out of control, and almost all at once. When the word had been passed to bring up the replacements, Captain Ripley and one of his radio operators were moving to where the general's helicopter was about to land so that they could wave him off. At precisely the same time, Corporal Goggin's magnanimity would save his life.

The "old man" of First Platoon, Staff Sergeant Witkowsky was thirty, maybe thirty-two tops. Corporal Goggin could see that both Staff Sergeant 'Ski and the lieutenant were wiped out, exhausted. While the platoon sergeant would have been the logical choice to send back for the link up, Corporal Goggin volunteered: "Don't worry, Staff Sergeant 'Ski. I'll get 'em…"

Lieutenant Heekin and Staff Sergeant 'Ski were prostrate on the ground. Corporal Goggin, still carrying the Prick 25, had leaned back against a small tree to reduce the pressure of the radio's weight on his shoulders. Slipping off the pack as he stepped to the rear with the headset still clipped to his helmet, Chuck Goggin had not completed that first step before the all too familiar crumping thunder sound of many enemy mortar rounds was heard even above the *whop-whop-whop* of the helicopter the skipper at that very moment was attempting to wave off.

Believing himself, along with those in his immediate vicinity, to be caught in the crosshairs of whatever artillery observers the NVA had nearby, Corporal Goggin dove for cover. To his front in this tiny clearing where he and Lieutenant Heekin and Staff Sergeant 'Ski had plopped down were a number of five-gallon water cans which must have been brought forward from some unnoticed earlier resupply effort. Praying that they were still filled so that the water might absorb most of the shrapnel as he dove for the ground on the other side of where they were, Corporal Goggin hit the deck only a split second prior to rounds impacting all around. The water cans were in fact empty, but he had moved far enough away from where the mortar rounds struck the earth. A burning sensation in his left ankle told him he had been hit. He was wounded but not gravely. Recovering from the shock and trauma, he spied Lieutenant Heekin and Staff Sergeant 'Ski. They had not been so lucky.

The volley of mortar rounds had impacted much closer to Heekin and 'Ski. By the time he got to the lieutenant, less than a minute later, Corporal Goggin knew he was gone. Staff Sergeant 'Ski appeared headed for the same outcome.

The volley that nailed First Platoon had been well executed. No one ever accused the NVA of not being superior mortar men. During that very same volley, a volley launched at such close range that Captain Ripley could see the enemy mortar rounds with their distinctive color scheme almost lazily reach the apex of their trajectory and then begin what seemed to be their almost casual return to earth and Ripley's position, he was certain one of the rounds miraculously passed between the rapidly turning main rotor blade of General Ryan's helicopter. Having loaded the helicopter with vital medical supplies back in the rear, the helicopter's crew chief was busy kicking the stuff out the door as it hovered several feet above the ground. Fortunately, the pilot was of sufficient altitude that when the mortar round impacted he was not blown out of the air, but instead realized the bad situation he was in, applied power immediately, and departed this increasingly unfriendly area.

Captain Ripley and his radio operator, engaged in trying to get the helicopter away from his men so that the enemy did not have such a giant point of reference to aim at, were not as lucky as the men in the general's chopper. The NVA mortar round which managed to pass between the turning rotor blades seemed to have its point of detonation atop one of the boxes of medical supplies beneath the hovering helo. The helicopter pilot had the good sense to rapidly depart the area.

There must have been other rounds as well. One of them caught Captain Ripley and his radio operator with enough force and blast to toss them into the air, head over heels, his radio operator with hand set to his ear as if still broadcasting, before each landed a good distance away. The initial shock of the blast was disorienting, to say the least. For Lima Six Actual, his first thought was that he had been badly wounded. Blown through the air, Captain Ripley, hit with shrapnel on his left side, landed on his right side with the butt of his pistol between him and northern I Corps.

Several ribs were immediately broken. The instantaneous pain on both sides caused John Ripley to initially believe he had been shot clean through. His radio operator was covered in blood. Shaking off the disorientation and realizing that his death was not yet imminent he had not regained composure or control of Lima Company in time to keep a second radio operator, who had run up to check on the situation, from blurting out over the radio that, "The skipper's hit! The skipper's hit!"

Corporal Goggin had heard the broadcast announcing his skipper's demise, and without corroborating evidence assumed it to be true. With Lieutenant Goodwin killed earlier, with Lieutenant Heekin and Staff Sergeant Witkowsky now KIA, all the main leaders were gone. With the world exploding around him, Chuck Goggin—ever the optimist, ever the confident Marine—for a brief moment began to think. Then he spoke: "Jesus Christ! They're all gone. We may not make it. We may not make it…" And then he looked up. And could see down the line that Lima Six Actual was up, up and back in the saddle. And that small cloud of doubt began to recede.

Within moments of that ill-advised broadcast, incoming fire seemed to increase. The NVA *had* to be listening. Even though the skipper had quite literally been blown up and was now functioning quite fully, the damage was already done. The NVA gunners were like sharks circling for a kill.

Every Marine in Lima Company still breathing and capable of pulling a trigger was involved in the fight of his life, completely consumed by events which took place within his world now defined by the five-meter bursting radius of a Chi-com or American high explosive (HE) grenade. For squad leaders their world was maybe three or four times that, platoon commanders larger still. Lima Six Actual had an unfathomable responsibility, a virtual universe of 150–200 meters to concern himself with. Having just been hit, and hit hard, Captain Ripley was, by some miracle, still very much in command.

Chuck Goggin, two days a corporal, junior to the three squad leaders in First Platoon, had the good sense to presume that the bad guys were listening in on all radio traffic. That the volume of incoming fire had seemed to increase after the earlier broadcast transmitted that the skipper was hit was too coincidental. The last thing Corporal Goggin wanted the NVA to know was that they had killed Lieutenant Heekin as well. But Captain Ripley needed to know. And he needed to know that Chuck would take over. For now.

Given the circumstances, Lima Company's front was rather straight and remarkably intact. Through the clearing and dislocated jungle and dust created by all the explosive force Corporal Goggin could actually spy his skipper a hundred or so meters down the line, directing the action, coordinating the fire support. Leaving the radio behind, Chuck Goggin took off running. He ran as if his life depended on it only because it did. The exchange between the two was brief. "Skipper, the lieutenant and Staff Sergeant 'Ski are dead. I can handle it for now…"

"Goggin, it's yours. You got it! Watch your flank. Don't let them turn your flank!" That was it. He ran back and took over.

Captain Ripley did not need to remind Corporal Goggin to watch his flank. That much was evident to all. Corporal Charles Francis Goggin USMC, only thirteen months a Marine, had command of what was left of First Platoon. He had just become Lima One Actual.

Chuck Goggin, now Lima One Actual, knew that his duties and responsibilities were greatly expanded. Understanding his former role well and the importance of a good radio operator for the proper functioning of his platoon, he called down into the forward tree line where what remained of his platoon could engage the enemy from maximum cover and concealment. Lance Corporal George Petri, a

Brooklyn Marine, was his intended victim. Corporal Goggin knew Petri to be a cool hand, very steady when the going was roughest. Their exchange was only slightly longer than the one Lima One Actual had just concluded with Captain Ripley.

Corporal Goggin ordered: "Petri, get out here!"

"Why?"

"Lieutenant Heekin is dead. The skipper has made me platoon commander and I need a radio operator."

"I don't know how to talk on the radio."

"Don't worry about that. You carry it. I'll talk on it."

And that was that.

As radio operator for First Platoon, Corporal Goggin had always been, of his platoon mates, the fellow most in the know. He was the man who did the transmitting and he was the man who did the receiving. He was the man from First Platoon who listened in on all of Lima's intra-company radio traffic.

Over a short period of time a radio operator—even if he was only mildly intelligent—could adequately assess the actions and temperament of those he listened in on. Over time it was near impossible to bamboozle a competent radio operator. A commander's level of fear or frustration, when he transmitted, was an open book to a discerning radio operator. Being a radio operator involved being part of a relationship akin to some funky, communal marriage. As such, as one of the participants, the radio operator saw and slept with all the "brides," observed them in the morning without makeup, warts and all, all the time. He knew every strength and every quirk of every other commander and radio operator who shared the same radio net with him. The constant, unending stresses of combat were nowhere more evident than in the way a man communicated over the radio. Sharing the net, especially in extreme situations, quite literally was opportunity to peer into the souls of every man broadcasting.

Of the many things Corporal Goggin respected in Lima Six Actual, as he could personally observe or listen in on over the radio, was that when the heat was on, and it was as hot as he had ever experienced today, Lima Six Actual was one cool customer. Chuck Goggin, only thirteen months a Marine, was seasoned enough to appreciate that his skipper's level of confidence or fear had impact on the battle's outcome. Late in the day on March 2, 1967, wounded, exhausted, his company bled white, Captain Ripley was showing no signs yet of folding, at least none that were obvious to the man who had just been promoted to command First Platoon.

There was no time to beef about Corporal Goggin being "junior" to the other squad leaders he now commanded. Circumstances were what they were and no one had the luxury of time to quibble or bicker. The fighting continued on between periods of little or no action—probably the times that coincided with some sort of resupply, attempts to move wounded, or again, sheer exhaustion—and intense, full-blown bedlam. At one instance Captain Ripley had the presence of mind to time how long it took for his company to run out of its own ammunition after re-provisioning. The time he timed it, Lima's ammo stores were empty in less than five minutes.

On the American side the major ground relief effort was India Company, one of 3/3's other rifle companies that was force-marching its way through the jungle. At the initiation of contact in the morning 3/3's operations officer had told Captain Ripley that India would have to march eight hours to get to them. In the meantime Lima would utilize as replacements all the men available back in the battalion who could be spared—truck drivers, clerks, cooks, any man who had graduated from San Diego or Parris Island.

Of the multiple helicopter lifts into that LZ several hundred meters behind the action where all replacements and ammunition were brought in and the wounded flown out, Chuck Goggin got his one laugh for the day. On the third or fourth or fifth sortie into that LZ, Corporal Goggin watched a young lad emerge from a helicopter with still un-sunbleached and dark clean green sateen trousers and jacket. Eyes wide with fear and skin unblemished by duty in the bush, he was an old pal from boot camp way back when who had ended up a clerk. He was about to earn his combat pay, about to live out the old USMC adage "Every Marine a rifleman." Chuckling to himself but sensitive to the fear of a man's first combat—and what an initiation he was about to receive—the new Lima One Actual passed on what sage wisdom he could in their brief reunion before sending him forward to the point of contact.

CHAPTER SIX

Ripley's Raiders

The fighting raged on from mid-afternoon to late afternoon; still personal, still brutal, often at between bayonet and hand grenade range. Marine air and artillery were a godsend, keeping the much larger enemy force at bay, dulling but still not eliminating completely their enthusiasm to regain all the gear they had left behind.

Replacement Marines were worked into the various squads of First and Second Platoon along with all the ammunition they could shoot. Medevacs took out only the most critically wounded. The rest of the wounded—nearly everyone else—stayed in the fight.

Meanwhile, India Company, Lima's relief, continued inbound throughout the day. At around 1730 or a bit later, a platoon from India made contact with Lima's perimeter. What a joy for all the men of Lima to know that the "cavalry," however late, had made the scene. A collective, heartfelt "God bless India" was on the lips of all Lima Company Marines.

Fully expecting to have his position reinforced and consolidated in order to keep all the NVA gear from falling back into their control, after paying such a high price to conquer this piece of jungle hell now consecrated with so much Lima Company blood, it came as brutal affront and outright shock to Captain Ripley when Gunnery Sergeant Mack, the platoon commander from India Company who had made the linkup, delivered orders to abandon this locale and pull back for the night to the junction where Lima's Third Platoon had been forced to sit out the battle.

Captain Ripley was livid. Even if they had not paid the huge price to appropriate all the NVA gear they now controlled, Lima Six Actual was not about to leave it for them to come back and repossess. Even if all of Lima Company's walking wounded had been at full strength and maximum health, even if this was not a tactical situation and even if he could have checked the Yellow Pages for a moving company to pack this stuff out of there, Captain Ripley would have needed a fleet of trucks, all the elephants in Hannibal's supply train.

There was no textbook method or typical manner by which to break contact. The fighting on this position just sort of petered out on its own as night approached, both sides experiencing near complete physical, mental, and material exhaustion.

Prior to departure from this ground now drenched in Lima blood and littered with NVA dead and their equipment, Captain Ripley and Prince Henry the Navigator, who like his skipper had been dinged but was still very much alive, worked up an even greater volume of air and artillery strike requests to continuously blanket the position they were about to vacate. Like a stubborn, selfish child the Marine attitude was that if they were not sticking around then neither could the NVA. From the air strikes it was "snakes and nape" (Snake-Eye bombs were five hundred-plus pounds of high explosives, napalm the gelatinous substance that burned everything it touched), from arty came multiple volleys of high explosives. By the time those missions were "rounds complete" there would be little that the NVA could use of the supplies which had been left behind.

Policing the site to ensure that all Marines were accounted for, Captain Ripley spoke briefly with his company gunnery sergeant. Surveying the diminished and dramatically rotated roster of Lima Company personnel, this very prototypical Marine Corps SNCO, in prototypical Marine Corps SNCO eloquence, gave Lima Six Actual a partial, horrific score for the day: "Skipper, there's only fifteen motherfuckers left in this outfit who ain't been killed or wounded today...an' you ain't one of 'em, sir." With that, Lima Company, what was left of it, moved out together and headed down the trail.

THE GRIM REAPER COMETH

Captain Ripley's emphatic, official, but probably illegal, order to his senior corpsman—"Don't you ever tag me!"—was never disobeyed. The ill-advised broadcasting over an uncovered net that "The skipper's hit! The skipper's hit!" by one of the reasonably flustered company radio operators was heard by everyone back at the Division G-3 where all comm was monitored. That very same transmission was no doubt listened in on by prying NVA radio operators as well.

Mindful that the regimental operations officer for the Third Marines, parent regiment to 3/3, Major George Ripley, was big brother to the skipper in question, an unnamed but concerned fellow monitoring the broadcast in the rear had the presence of mind to record the info on one of those official U.S. government three-colored, carbon-between-the-copies message pads. Major George Ripley received the yellow copy of the semi-official and still inconclusive news: "Skipper L 3/3 hit. Still breathing…" Major George Ripley, the same man who by allowing his baby brother to read, against the counsel of his parents, Leon Uris's *Battle Cry* way back when that helped set the hook in the tender-hearted youngster to a life that now seemed just about to be snuffed out, with a heavy heart partially folded and then in a mix of grief and anger balled up the yellow paper and placed it in his pocket.

Once the word was out that Captain Ripley was a casualty, whatever the status, the ironclad, no-nonsense process for notification to next of kin was inexorably begun. With Ripley still in the field, there was no way he could preempt the casualty-call process.

The fighting that had taken place on March 2 had long concluded, to be replaced by other skirmishes in subsequent days by the time the Casualty Call Officer (CACO) tasked with delivering the news to Moline Ripley arrived. Still in the field, in command and very much in the fight, Captain Ripley was unaware that his wife and folks were soon to be notified of the wound he received but had claimed no credit for.

As much as she feared what might be shown or broadcast, Moline Ripley was drawn to every news report concerning

Vietnam. With senses acute, she could be in another room tending to young Stephen or doing other chores but still alert for key words like "Marines" or "casualties" or "northern I Corps." No news, no mention of action involving Marines; that was good news.

By the late morning of March 3, 1967 Moline Ripley had already read where Senator Robert Kennedy the day before had announced a three-point plan to end the war. His plan included a suspension of U.S. bombing of the north, withdrawal of both American and North Vietnamese ground forces from the south, and a replacement with some sort of neutral international force. The senator's good intentions had certainly not trickled down to either side currently locked in mortal combat in northern I Corps.

There was also continual coverage of growing opposition to the war on the American college scene. It had not been two weeks since a major demonstration had taken place at the University of Wisconsin where students protested the presence of Dow Chemical representatives on campus. Dow, manufacturer of the very napalm Captain Ripley and Prince Henry the Navigator had only hours before adroitly applied in order to save the lives of Lima Company Marines and terminate those of their enemy, had come to recruit promising young scientists. The protests garnered national attention. At their conclusion, those who had joined in, except for the organizers, were able to return to the more serious college pursuits of getting laid and loaded. For the Marines spared thanks to the scientific genius of Dow engineers, life or death in the jungle was all they could continue to look forward to.

Networked with and well supported by her slightly older sister-in-law Maureen, whose husband Major George Ripley had been the first family member to hear the bad news, the two women were as close as they could be. Living in the same apartment complex in Alexandria, Virginia while their husbands were at war, they were within shouting distance of one another. George and Maureen had three daughters, all older than Stephen. Both of the young mothers could spell the other for a break when the need arose.

Maureen's kitchen window looked out onto the main lot where visitors to this section of the complex were forced to park. She was the very first to spot the approach of the official USMC vehicle that might as well have been replaced by a skeleton riding a horse. As she and Moline were the only military wives in this portion of the development, unless the Marine officer was lost, her day was instantly ruined; she knew she was either minus a husband or a brother-in-law.

Maureen Ripley gathered up her youngest daughter, the other two at school, and rushed out to intercept the young Marine captain who had just parked his sedan. Recognizing from a distance the extreme fear in her eyes as the distance between them closed, the captain spoke a split second before she did, both speaking over the other. "I'm looking for the Ripley family, please."

"Which Ripley is it you want, Captain?"

When Maureen learned that it was John and not George, she was grateful for the briefest moment, thankful that her husband was alright. That relief was immediately replaced by her own survivor's guilt and then sadness and empathy for Moline and sweet little Stephen. "I'll take you to Captain Ripley's wife…"

Maureen Ripley accompanied him to her sister-in-law's apartment. As pleasant and professional as he appeared, there was simply no way to make friendly conversation on the walk. And it was a long walk that seemed to last forever. When they got to the door, the captain politely rapped on the door's frame with Maureen standing behind him.

Expecting no one in particular, Moline Ripley was quick to respond; her sister-in-law would not have knocked. Opening the door her demeanor changed with the speed of sight from the natural smile she almost always wore to what could only be described as shock and fear and extreme sadness. While still not used to this, the young captain had experienced the broad range of outcomes—none of them good, some only less bad than others—to the responses his presence always evoked. He would rather have faced the same enemy John Ripley currently faced than serve as a CACO, but duty called.

Moline moaned, then emphatically said, "No…?" Somehow able to maintain her composure and dignity, she managed to find the words to invite him in. The shock of the moment consumed her, so much so that she blindly closed the door on Maureen as if she were not even there.

Such bizarre and horrible duty it was to serve as a Casualty Call Officer. In the cases where the Marine involved was KIA, there was never a positive outcome from the visit, no joy at all. With a family, especially that of a professional officer or long-serving SNCO, folks became almost giddy when they would learn that their Marine was "only" wounded.

Once the CACO had assured Moline that her husband was very much alive and expected to recover, the mood changed dramatically. Thanking him profusely, Moline noted his kindness and professionalism. She took great comfort in knowing that her Marine had not been killed. At least not yet.

The process for notifying primary next of kin—a wife if a man was married or parents generally if a man was single—was far more personal than notification for secondary next of kin. In Captain John Ripley's case, his folks received the typical, timeless, and without-any-compassion-at-all telegram. (By 1967 telegrams were used by fewer and fewer people as long-distance phone calls had displaced their need except for the odd method of communication such as the need for a government agency to inform a family member of their relative's death in combat.)

Further south and west in tiny Radford where Bud and Verna Ripley were widely known, it was common knowledge that all three of their sons had been, for a period of time, in Vietnam together. It was also common knowledge all across small-town America in 1967 that the man who delivered telegrams for Western Union, as innocuous as he might look in that silly uniform, more times than not, especially as the war intensified, became the Grim Reaper himself. Unless someone was sending a telegram announcing the birth of a child—which would have been worth the expense of a long-distance call—and there were currently no pregnant women in the greater Ripley family circle anyway, whatever message he might bring would not be joyful news.

When the message arrived and before it was delivered, even without its contents being disclosed to anyone, the news that there was a telegram for the Ripleys traveled with amazing haste in tiny Radford, so quickly that a fair number of folks presumed to know its portending doom before Bud and Verna Ripley ever took delivery of it.

Verna Ripley spied the approach of the hapless Western Union man well before he reached the door. Assuming instantly the news was bad, she took off in the opposite direction, crying hysterically, as if not knowing for sure might deny the reality of what she was about to learn. Bud was left to initially deal with news that was inconclusive but still, by God, confirmed that their youngest son was alive.

The notion that Captain John Ripley had, at last report anyway, been seen alive, was reasonably healthy, and still fit enough to command his rifle company served as elixir to his lovely young bride. Moline Ripley's ability to isolate and then extrapolate that news, and hang on to it as if he was somehow safe and sound was the only reasonable way to cope with not knowing a lot of details, details that would have sickened her with worry. At least he was alive. That was comforting to know, something that would allow her to keep focused on the one good thing in her life that she did have some control over which was the mothering and nurturing of sweet little Stephen.

But Captain Ripley wasn't safe and sound. While he would have wanted his wife and folks not to worry, the real truth was that the action in northern I Corps had never really stopped, had never really de-escalated at all...

It was probably not at all ironic that as the clock was again about to advance one more twenty-four-hour period to check off on the service calendars of everybody left alive after the day's fighting—both of Ripley's platoon commanders had been killed and every squad leader from First and Second Platoon was either KIA or WIA—that the final contact with the enemy would be initiated and concluded by the squad of the very man who had sniffed out the NVA regimental headquarters a dozen or so hours earlier.

Captain Ripley, along with his few remaining stalwarts plus all those who had joined as replacements throughout the day, had finally linked up with Third Platoon at the original trail junction. In addition to the ersatz collection of Lima Marines were most of India Company and a smattering of others from the battalion.

Just because they had fought a major engagement and lost and replaced a large number of their comrades was no reason to kick back. This was not a football game. The clock had not run out of time even though Lima had nearly run out of men. This was the USMC and here in northern I Corps the war was still definitely on.

Once the disparate units had linked up for the night, the normal tactical routines were reestablished. Placed on 50 percent alert, with two men to each fighting hole where one man slept and the other kept watch, each platoon also sent out a security or ambush patrol to protect the greater harbor site. As tired as he was, Captain Ripley monitored the comm with his radio operator. Corporal Hobbs had been sent out with his squad to a general location selected by his skipper. Figuring that if the NVA were to come calling they would pass a certain spot on the trail, they selected a proper ambush position. Corporal Hobbs and crew did not have to wait long for visitors.

It was a slaughter. Perhaps the NVA expected the Americans to lay low, to expect no pressure from an enemy who had lost many times the number of men they did, to be as tired as they were. The volume of fire shattered the night's stillness. The ambush site was distant but close enough for the entire company to hear the screams of the enemy shouting, seeming to plead, "*Chieu hoi! Chieu hoi!*" "Same to you. Assholes. Whatever '*chieu hoi*' means."

It was only later the Marines learned that the men caught in Hobbs's ambush, once discovered, had decided to surrender. ("*Chieu hoi*" means "I surrender.") No prisoners were taken that night. Had there been understanding of what they said, after the experience of the earlier combat, it was still doubtful there would have been prisoners taken that night.

The action that followed on March 3 was little different than that of March 2. March 3 was followed by the fourth, the fifth, the sixth. Lima Company remained in the field, humping from place to place, in contact with the NVA every single day. Machete Eddie was correct in his assessment; John Ripley had some kind of magnet that attracted action. Lima Company would remain in the bush for the rest of March. Chuck Goggin was still in charge of First Platoon, was even promoted to sergeant by his skipper who had no real authority to do so. General Ryan, a day or two later, came out and made it all legal.

Every single new day was nearly the same as the day before, and the one before that. Marines knew it was Sunday only because it was the day the corpsmen would pass out malaria pills. The fighting, the continual contact with the enemy went on and on. Without relent. Men were routinely killed or wounded every single day. Without relent.

The action involving Lima 3/3 in early March of 1967 was not unique. In northern I Corps, the rest of I Corps and throughout all of South Vietnam, the first week of the month saw the greatest casualty toll for the war so far with 1,617 Americans killed, wounded, or missing.

As much as they were ground down and exhausted, those who remained were by now pretty confident in their abilities and those of the man who led them. The Lima Marines who remained had a right to be proud. In every single engagement they had taken their fair share of hits but they had always bested the NVA. Always.

It must have been at least two weeks after that first major action of March 2 when one of the Lima Company vets received in his letters from home news clippings about the exploits of an outfit the *Boston Globe* or some other East Coast newspaper was now referring to as "Ripley's Raiders."

Oddly enough, throughout the course of that day that seemed never to end, during one of the countless resupply/medevac runs to the position Lima Company attacked into and then defended on March 2, a gaggle of print and broadcast journalists were transported out to have a look-see at the hornet's nest Lima had stirred up. With Captain Ripley and every one of his Marines focused on the battle, camera crews and men with tape recorders haphazardly surveyed Lima Company's positions, almost as if they were not part of or subject to the fighting taking place all around. More than anything else, their presence was an annoyance and a distraction for Marines trying to get to the business at hand. As if these men were completely neutral about the outcome, one camera crew even filmed a group of Marines transporting a wounded comrade to a waiting helicopter using a poncho as a stretcher. When an incoming mortar barrage caused the stretcher bearers to drop their buddy as they sought cover, the camera crew filmed the episode. The parents of the fellow in the poncho learned of their son's wounding when they saw all the action on the evening news. This particular news report caused them no end of sadness and grief.

Long before this incident occurred, the popularity of media types for most Marines in contact was only slightly higher than their love of the NVA. As the attack progressed and intensified, with members of the press also standing in harm's way, the desire for self-preservation caused one of them to charge a CH-46 which was just about to lift off with its ramp nearly up. Running at a speed rivaling Jesse Owens, the man in question threw his equipment up and into the helicopter, where it landed on several of the wounded Marines being medevaced. With his gear aboard he then attempted to scale the closed aft ramp of the helicopter. The Marines witnessing this egregious display of cowardice and self-preservation were enraged. At least one of the Lima Marines wanted to shoot the man.

Of the group of journalists who made it out and were able to file reports, at least one was impressed by the pluck and determination of Lima Company's exploits. In writing about what he was able to personally observe and learn from the Marines in contact, he described this seemingly august and increasingly smaller-by-the-hour group of Leathernecks as "Ripley's Raiders."

The name stuck. For those who were a part of it, it was a title of honor, a proud thing to describe oneself as a member in that now too small group of men known, as long as their skipper led them in combat, as "Ripley's Raiders."

Whether the NVA had access to the *Boston Globe* or not mattered little. They poured their finest troops into the action at an increasing rate to do battle with Marine units all across I Corps. The constant contact and intensity of combat for all USMC units from late February 1967 onward was a reality few at home could appreciate.

In any other military organization, return to Ca Lu could only be described as extreme hardship duty. Compared to where Lima Company had spent the last four weeks, compared to the brutal action they routinely engaged in every single day as they battled NVA units across the width and breadth of their tiny section of northern I Corps, return to the "company hill" that was Ca Lu, a veritable Ft. Apache in the wilderness, was as close as mud Marines would get to heaven without dying first in early April 1967.

Strategically located along Route 9 adjacent to the Thach Han River, Ca Lu was the furthest west fortified position occupied by Marines before Khe Sanh, some twenty or so kilometers closer to the Laotian border.

To give Lima Company a small break from the action another rifle company was helicoptered in to man the perimeter at Ca Lu. When the last Lima Marine was inside the wire sometime around 1730, the quality festivities and classiness of Marine Corps goodness were revealed. With unlimited quantities of steaks and cheap beer magically made available to the men who looked more like participants in some crazy mass experiment in sleep deprivation, stress, and starvation than the battle-hardened warriors they had become, a whole host of those aboard had grown sufficiently sick to their stomachs from gorging on steaks or blotto from the beer by 2200 when the word came that a battalion from Ninth Marines had gotten into some big-time action. Reinforcement was required. By 2230 Ripley's Raiders were formed up, on the road, good to go. They were back in it...all the way...again.

CHAPTER SEVEN

Little Bit of Heaven...and Then Straight Back to Hell

R&R in Hawaii
Summer 1967

P*rosecution of operations in Vietnam* placed an incredible strain on the 15 percent of the total forces doing the actual fighting with the enemy and the 85 percent of the support forces keeping them supplied, fed, housed, and healthy. Units assigned to duty in Southeast Asia, once there, did not leave. Rather than rotate entire battalions or squadrons, and maintaining the cohesive bond of the organization, the decision early on to rotate individuals was most controversial. In every single fighting unit were men just arrived in country, fresh-faced and well-trained but untested in real combat. Among their mates were the veterans, many anxious to leave and awaiting imminent departure. This mix of old and new was a significant challenge to leadership at every level.

One of the benefits to the twelve- or thirteen-month regular tour of duty was every man's opportunity to take, at least once during his Vietnam time, maybe twice if he was extremely lucky, a five-day period of rest and relaxation (R&R) in havens far from the combat zone. The allowable R&R destinations did not make provision for return to the continental United States. Primary stops included Hong Kong, Bangkok, Taipei, Penang, Australia, and Hawaii.

Asian destinations were favored mostly by the single men where the strength of the dollar and the availability of companionship for hire would satisfy their most basic and prurient needs. Stories of drunkenness and debauchery were legion, and there was no shortage of young men anxious for the experience. For those married or engaged in more serious relationships, Hawaii was the destination of choice.

As America's Gibraltar of the Pacific, Hawaii with its near-perfect climate and virtual year-round summer was the ideal location for the country's sons to restore themselves briefly with wives or girlfriends in tow.

Logistics for a Hawaii R&R were a simple 50-50 proposition. The military was responsible for bringing the men east; the women made their own arrangements to head west. By design, the women would usually arrive ahead of their men.

Incoming wives and girlfriends were not difficult to identify. They were the ones with the properly coiffed hairdos, the still un-sunburned skin and the modern yet bland-by-Hawaiian-fashion-standards attire. Faces showing hopefulness and excitement, their eyes searching out into the distance eager for a glimpse of their inbound soldier or Marine in the off chance that he had arrived early and expectant of a pleasant surprise, they were a stark contrast to those who had already seen their men depart.

The timer was about to begin ticking off 120 hours and they were determined to extract every moment of life and meaning, to forge tender memories in the unthinkable chance that when they said goodbye as the clock struck twelve, there might not be another homecoming, at least not the kind with a fairy tale ending.

Ft. DeRussy's reception center in the heart of Honolulu, at the Ewa end of Kalakaua Avenue where Waikiki begins was Ground Zero, the start and finish for all R&R. On those few acres of hallowed real estate the world revolved, and when it had turned five revolutions each man and woman was spent, strung out from the gut-wrenching emotional highs and lows crammed into not enough time.

In a period not quite extending from sundown to sundown a combat soldier or Marine might find himself plucked from a firefight in the rice paddies or jungles, on a jet, and sipping *mai tais* with his wife or girlfriend while listening to the real Don Ho there in the International Marketplace. A man's ability to process the transition and incongruity of it all taxed his sense of what was rational.

If a soldier or Marine had come directly from a unit in combat, the ability to come down, to drop one's guard, to be the empathetic listener and loving spouse required the rigid compartmentalization of experiences and emotions. Rarely was it possible to put it all behind in such a short time, to act as if it were just some extended business trip he was on, especially if he knew he was headed right back into the meat grinder.

For the wives and girlfriends, especially those who were moms, was the pressure of putting up a bold, cheerful front: to be the glue keeping the family knit during these times of extreme separation. The erstwhile attempt to minimize the challenges of being a single mom, the daily praying that the Grim Reaper would steer a path far from her door, could be put on hold for these too few days. No cloying, no complaining, this was a time to be perfect. They had made it to this point. The rest of the tour was to be downhill from here, please God!

Arriving in dribs and drabs from the West Coast and origins further east, armed with dittoed transportation instructions and shepherded by military liaison personnel there at the Honolulu International Airport, the wives and girlfriends would ultimately coalesce in Waikiki. Usually there was time to check into their hotel, plan a little romance, square things away, ensure that everything would be just so when the bus carrying their men pulled up.

In the receiving area where the busses delivering the men arrived, the fresh aroma of flower *leis* mixed well with the scents of each woman's liberally applied best perfume and the uncommon-for-most humidity of the islands. Hawaiian music in the background, if heard and noticed at all, was light and gay, upbeat, and signaled anticipation of good things about to happen.

Military planners had demonstrated proper foresight in logistical issues surrounding the players involved with R&R. Those just beginning their period of bliss were kept away in time and space from those undergoing the heaviness of the abrupt and painful goodbye. Still the arriving women could see them as they left the airport or if they had too much time to wait in Waikiki.

They were the sullen, morose ones, the long faces with eyes showing an abundance of recent tears. By now sunburned and peeling, as not all R&R was taken indoors, they were the ones who had traded in their mainland duds after a visit to Hilo Hattie's or the Ala Moana Center. For them the clock had already struck twelve and the fairy princess stuff was over, the club coach now a pumpkin and all attending folks turned to mice. For them all that was left was memory and prayerful hopes that part two of their man's tour would see him come home, with all parts functioning the same as when he left.

Hawaii-bound flights from Vietnam were civilian charters mostly. Upon arrival the men were rapidly placed aboard waiting military busses and sped off to Ft. DeRussy for the much anticipated reunions.

As each bus pulled up, a rush of female humanity greeted it. Anticipation and tension were ultimately tempered by squeals of joy and kisses long and passionate. Once the initial greeting ended, every participant became acutely aware of the time. The invisible elephant had just entered the room, and no matter where they were in the next 120 or fewer hours, it managed to make itself felt, sucking an ever-increasing amount of oxygen from whatever remaining pleasure each couple could share.

Aside from the obvious things for long-separated couples to catch up on, there were the obligatory events for all tourists to the islands. Awash with fine restaurants and clubs, the hours not spent loving or eating would find many at places like the Kodak Hula Show, the Polynesian Cultural Center, snorkeling at Hanauma Bay, visiting the North Shore, and shopping in the hundreds of retail establishments happy to cater to these eager *malihinis*. Those on R&R were easy to distinguish from the other "regular" tourists who were usually older, less fit, and if they had hair, kept it a bit longer.

Beginning with a common goal, John and Moline Ripley may as well have initiated their journeys to Hawaii from different planets. Certainly the world in which each existed was not the same one.

Twenty-one-month-old Stephen Ripley was safely in the care of his doting Grandmother Blaylock, way down in Radford, Virginia so that his momma could focus on her upcoming time with his father.

Moline Ripley might well have walked right off the pages of the current issue of *Ladies Home Journal* or *Good Housekeeping*. So finely turned out was the young Marine Corps wife as she boarded her first-ever flight that she was invited to take a place in first class for the duration—a good omen and a perfect way to begin a perfect experience.

The ditch at the end of the expeditionary airstrip at Dong Ha offered no overhead cover from incoming rocket and artillery fire, let alone any sort of reasonable accommodations to freshen up prior to departure. Huddled there with several others from disparate Marine units hoping to catch their Freedom Bird to Hawaii, Captain Ripley and the other outgoing warriors waited anxiously in the muck for the C-130 to touch down at the opposite end of the single landing strip. Once on the ground the large, always-moving target would turn around, taxiing with its tail ramp down just slowly enough so that the expectant passengers had to sprint to get aboard, all the while praying that some NVA artillery observer did not have time to get a round or two off on them. Given the thumbs up by the slowest man aboard, the plane's crew chief raised and sealed the ramp, the pilot applied max power, and they were off to Danang for further connection to all points east. Time on the ground rarely exceeded sixty seconds. A heck of a way to run an airline.

The spectrum of issues, experiences, emotions, and stresses dealt with during five days in sunny Hawaii was enough to challenge the sanity and stability of any reasonably sound marriage or relationship.

Coming right from the combat zones of Vietnam, stress was compounded by the lack of decompression time, the guilt associated with having left buddies in the fight, the now painful countdown of 120 hours, and the issue of how much a man could or would tell his wife about what he was really experiencing.

For women, the inability to truly empathize, the tug between wanting to know or not know all their men were experiencing, and ultimately the prospect of saying goodbye again, perhaps for the last time, shredded their emotions. As they were usually the last ones to depart, they were left again, usually alone, there in paradise to begin the long journey home.

Bittersweet at best, the experience was a joy only if one had strength enough to focus solely on the immediate moment. The memories would only be fond and pleasant if they could be part of a happy ending and recalled twenty years hence.

Moline Ripley had survived the emotional trauma of her husband's first reported wound. Her concern was now for his well-being, both emotional and physical. As he stepped off the bus she noticed the changes immediately. Always fit, and again borrowing from the song which shared his name, he looked "broad in the shoulder and narrow in the hip." Captain Ripley looked amazingly good; a little raw-boned perhaps, and more tanned than before.

When Moline put her arms around John for the first hug she could feel the wider spread of his back, the even-harder-than-before muscles. It was, except for a tiny bit of fleshiness, like hugging a refrigerator with cords of rope or steel cable wrapped around it. Even his facial features appeared sharper, more chiseled, just a few pounds above gaunt. She could tell without being told that he had been through a lot.

FIVE DAYS — 120 HOURS AND COUNTING DOWN

Stretching their meager captain's pay to the very limit, John and Moline enjoyed the relative splendor and romance of the Princess Kaiulani Hotel. At the Diamond Head end of Waikiki, filled with the receding charm of old Hawaii and the slowly ebbing *aloha* spirit, it was ideally suited to their needs. From the hotel they could take a short walk and experience dinner by candlelight at world-class restaurants. Later they would stroll along the beach at night arm in arm, oblivious to all that was around them.

The adjustment back to civilization and to feeling clean for Captain Ripley was a challenge. Even though he had shown up in Honolulu in an only moderately soiled uniform, even though the sheets on their hotel room bed were washed and tidy, even though by day two he had showered numerous times, he still had

Vietnam's earth in him and on him. Intellectually he was certain there were no NVA on Oahu but the lack of threat and incoming artillery seemed odd.

To Moline it did not matter. For both of them it was a wonderful five days. Between the beaching and touring and eating and everything else they even found time to take in a movie. *The Sand Pebbles* starring Steve McQueen had recently been released and was playing a way down the beach from their hotel at the venerable and somewhat antiquated but elegant Waikiki Theater. Having enjoyed the book while on sea duty, and now as a seasoned "Asia hand," John Ripley related well to the issues faced by the gunboat sailors dealing with situations their own upbringings did not teach them to deal with. Aside from that, it was just nice to enjoy air conditioning, sit in the soft, crushed-velvet seats, eat popcorn, and hold Moline's hand.

For John Ripley, the R&R period could only have been made more perfect had son Stephen been able to be there. He physically ached to hug and nuzzle the little boy who by now had probably forgotten who Daddy was.

Moline had done her best to plan for this one missing part to the reunion. In her bag she carried what seemed like hundreds of photos of Stephen. In every conceivable situation, time of day, and stage of his young life she had pictures and regaled John with stories of his every antic. They spoke of him incessantly.

For a man of John Ripley's temperament, the visit to what the old Hawaiians called Pu'owaina and everybody else called the Punchbowl was predestined, unavoidable. Occupying an old volcano crater in Honolulu midway between Diamond Head and Pearl Harbor, the National Cemetery of the Pacific is a sacred shrine to American valor and the blood price paid in battles against the nation's foes. In a *macabre* sense the notion that because of where Captain Ripley was shortly headed back to would make him a prime candidate for entrance there was not lost on either of them. That bothered him little. He and Moline simply needed to see it, to pay their respects, to marvel at the shrines and tile mosaics to the great Pacific war battles, and reverently weep together in awe of the collective sacrifices of so many forever-young men. Mixed in with those tears of pride and sorrow for those unknowns lost long ago were more than a few for the men he had personally known in his own recent experience.

The road to the Punchbowl, to Vietnam, and wherever else he might serve, surely began at the railroad station back in Radford in what must have been late 1942 or early 1943. At breakfast one morning Bud Ripley had asked both John and older brother Mike if they would like to go with their dad to the train station. A special train was passing through. Thrilled to spend time with him, a chance to be around the rail yard was also an opportunity the boys would never want to miss.

Bud Ripley was a man of some position with the railroad. The Ripley name was accorded as much respect in town as any other. John and Mike were always treated kindly by those familiar with Bud and Verna. Arriving well before the train, the boys were allowed to run about without being disruptive, and so they did. The station platforms were crowded with onlookers, mostly well-dressed as if headed for church on a weekday.

The young Ripleys gave little thought to anything until a train's whistle announced its slow approach. When it finally came into view they could see the red, white, and blue bunting, the extra cars that stretched beyond the bend in the track. Slowing but not stopping as it inched through Radford, the crowd of citizens, men mostly, all stood ramrod-straight at the position of attention. Men with hats removed them and placed them over their hearts, others put their right hands there. It was all so natural, so solemn, so automatic, so deeply respectful. Many had tears in their eyes as they watched the train slowly rumble by. In the dozens and dozens and dozens of cars was the cream of American youth, headed for war. Most appeared jubilant and certainly reflected the crowd's appreciation. John and Mike were the only kids present, and as such somehow drew the attention of the soldiers, sailors, airmen, and Marines.

What began as a trickle turned into a torrent as the passengers began gently tossing candy and coins to the Brothers Ripley. It was a fun time. More than anything, though, from that one moment in time, John Ripley remembered his father; the tears in his eyes and the deep respect he exuded as he watched these young men going off to war. Even after his own combat experience, John Ripley could never recall that morning and his father's lesson in patriotism without losing composure.

As John Ripley held his wife's hand, unable to speak, pondering the battles at Guadalcanal, Tarawa, Peleliu, Guam, Iwo Jima, Okinawa, he thought of those men and his own Marines, all mixed together in equal sacrifice.

CHAPTER EIGHT

The End of the Beginning

Late Summer 1967

Captain *John Ripley's decision* to leave newly promoted Sergeant Chuck Goggin as Lima One Actual after the early March action that killed his platoon commander, for what amounted to the remainder of his combat tour, was not a decision based upon fiscal parsimony or prudence. Even though American taxpayers, and the Marine Corps in particular, were spared the $109.50 monthly differential (in 1967 dollars) between what was paid to a sergeant and what was due a second lieutenant for five months, the discerning rifle company skipper made the call because he could recognize value.

BACK FROM HAWAII

As much as there was genuine joy and fun and romance in the first 115 of their 120-hour respite from the prospect of John Ripley's horrible death in the hell of northern I Corps, those few last hours in Honolulu served to bring the very much in love young couple back to pending unfortunate reality. When they arrived back at the Ft. DeRussy Reception Center for the final goodbye, the concluding embrace, John and Moline Ripley together and individually knew—as did every other couple there doing the same thing—that this might well be the *last* kiss or hug or "I love you." In the end the pain of departure almost seemed to cancel out or even outweigh the earlier period of bliss and happiness.

Looking healthier than when they had arrived, with sunburns crossing over to tans, and a bit less awkward and almost at home in their gaudy *aloha* attire, the sorrow of goodbye was evident for all who could see. The tears and sobbing were only partial relief for the deep physical gut-wrenching angst.

By design the men left first, boarding the same busses at Ft. DeRussy that had only moments before delivered fresh-faced soldiers and Marines to begin the exact process these unfortunate souls were now concluding. In virtually the same spot where five days prior *"aloha"* meant welcome, where the scent of plumeria *leis*, liberally applied special perfume, and Hawaiian music all joined together to signify expectation of a pleasant experience, those same sounds and smells now mixed together to show that *"aloha"* also meant goodbye.

From Waikiki they would return to the airport, enroute passing—alone—spots that only days before were places where fond memories were forged, and board the charter flights that hours earlier had come from Vietnam. The mood once airborne on the westbound flights was anything but festive. Captain Ripley could at least commiserate with friends he had made on the flight from Vietnam to Honolulu. The three other Marine infantry officers, a captain and two lieutenants, had called themselves the "Four Musketeers."

Moline Ripley was essentially left there by herself. With little choice in the matter she would endure and press on. Loneliness in paradise was an especially painful experience but that was a price to be paid and so she paid it. Like all the other women in the exact same boat, she too would do what had to be done, endure what had to be endured.

The painful goodbyes experienced by the husbands and wives in John Ripley's informal group, those Four Musketeers, were not the expression of farcical, school-girl sentimentality. For two of the four wives, the Hawaii R&R would turn out to be the end of the line. Within the next six weeks, two of those four Marine officers would be KIA.

The return to action for John Ripley, except for all the great R&R memories that he would suppress during the rest of his tour to maintain his focus, was seamless. There was never a break in the intensity and outright brutality of the fighting Lima Company participated in. The March battle on the day Chuck Goggin became Lima One Actual could have been a single frame of film spliced from nearly anywhere in a nonfiction movie climax scene that continued to run without end. It was the same for any man, every man from the skipper on down to the last rifleman, who survived every action. Unless a man was killed or gravely wounded he had only more combat to look forward to before his tour was complete.

The rate of turnover in personnel in the fifty-plus rifle companies from the eighteen infantry battalions of the First and Third Marine Divisions operating throughout I Corps by mid 1967 was mind-numbing. Every week more Leathernecks were killed and wounded. The war's appetite for small unit leaders seemed insatiable. In the leadership slots at the company and platoon levels especially there was a virtual revolving door with healthy, whole men going in and fully or partially broken men coming out.

In the normal course of events Lima Company was given its fair share of replacement lieutenants and SNCOs. Curiously Captain Ripley directed them all over to his Second, Third, or Weapons Platoons. Sergeant Goggin was left in place as Lima One Actual, and no one complained.

Sergeant Goggin's tenure as the CO of First Platoon was anything but uneventful. Coming up on his six-week anniversary as platoon commander, the entire company was conducting a long-range patrol and sweep out west on the Ho Chi Minh Trail. Enduring a foot march of between twenty-five and thirty miles in a one-day period, Lima Company was near the limit of its advance on April 13, 1967, deep in Indian Country. First Platoon had been at the point position for the company all morning; in fact the platoon point man had been killed earlier the same day. Four at a time, as they continued their sweep of the trail area, Marines from First Platoon rotated the duty of carrying their comrade's corpse along with them inside a doubled-up poncho.

With the jungle canopy too thick for a routine medevac, they would carry their dead friend all the way back from their mission, as best and respectfully as they could. When it was time to again switch off the "pallbearers," it was not clear as to exactly how it happened or who set it off but in the process of changing positions and passing off their dead Marine buddy a mine adjacent to the trail was triggered. Four Marines absorbed blast and shrapnel. Lima One Actual received the brunt of it. With miles to go from the planned extract point and still under canopy that would not allow for a helicopter medevac, Chuck's only option was to walk. So he walked. In pain. For three or four miles.

Servicing the wounded in this particular episode was not like all the television news clips the folks at home were routinely viewing. There was no waiting helicopter to whisk Sergeant Goggin or the others away to the healing hands of qualified naval surgeons somewhere in the rear.

After Lima Company had walked the final three or four miles to their pickup point, the dead and wounded were put on trucks headed back down Route 9 to Ca Lu. The unwounded Marines walked on.

For Sergeant Goggin—with fourteen pieces of shrapnel in both legs, his back, and a portion of his left shoulder, mercifully spared from being crippled because his pack took the brunt of the hit—the ride to Ca Lu was followed by yet another bumpy truck ride further east on Route 9 to Dong Ha. There he was taken to a very basic navy field hospital where the shrapnel was plucked, pulled, and dissected from his body.

From the field unit Sergeant Goggin was finally flown down to the naval hospital in Danang where the more serious concern with infection was addressed. As the biggest long-term health risk, doctors decided not to sew him up just yet. Twice daily for the next week and a half Chuck was forced to endure the physical scrubbing, cleansing, and washing of every one of the fourteen punctures in his body. The cure was many times worse than the pain of the original injury.

While a patient at the naval hospital in Danang, Chuck was one day visited by a Marine general who presented him his Purple

Heart. Unfortunately the senior Marine's time on the ward occurred while Chuck was only semi-conscious and he learned of the visit later when he awoke to find the medal pinned to his blanket.

When the doctors were satisfied that the risk of infection had passed, he was at last stitched up and helicoptered out to the hospital ship USS *Repose* (AH-16) for final convalescence and recuperation. As much as he appreciated the stress-free environment, the clean sheets, and decent chow, Sergeant Goggin was deathly bored. While he was lying around doing very little he was also witness to the arrival of many of his Lima Company comrades who had gotten into more big action in his absence. He knew he had to go back. Now. Somehow he managed to get discharged early.

While Sergeant Goggin was away, Lima Company had received a new lieutenant who was assigned to First Platoon. Chuck had no problem with that. When he returned he automatically picked up as platoon sergeant and was content to offer insight to the new Lima One Actual.

The new officer lasted just barely a month before going down hard with malaria. Sergeant Goggin, by late May, was platoon commander once again.

Captain Ripley had not been the only officer to recognize Sergeant Goggin's value to the Corps. Upon his return to duty Chuck was offered a direct commission. As much as he appreciated the honor and the confidence in which he was held, Chuck Goggin was still clinging to the dream of returning to baseball if he was not killed or maimed too badly. Respectfully, he declined the offer. It would have kept him on active duty for an additional year—a virtual lifetime in professional sports.

THE END OF RIPLEY'S RAIDERS

Most places in Vietnam, certainly the entire area of northern I Corps where Lima Company had fought throughout the period of Captain Ripley's tenure, would fall into the category of "the middle of nowhere." Even the relative splendor of the company hill at Ca Lu, which would not have been nice enough to even be called a slum back home but was a near oasis for Lima's Marines, would certainly have qualified in any reasonable person's description of "…nowhere."

For twelve of the thirteen months he was in Vietnam, John Ripley had been skipper, Six Actual, the Old Man of Lima Company, Third Battalion, Third Marines. Like his younger, now stateside, friend Chuck Goggin, Captain Ripley wanted to live and to leave. More than anything he missed his bride, wanted to hold the son who by now would certainly no longer remember his daddy. And yet the intensity of the daily combat, the need for focused leadership and 100 percent of his attention 100 percent of the time kept him, for both personal and professional reasons, from even pondering the notion of leaving. For Lima Company to survive, and to win, required everything John Ripley could possibly give.

The typical rifle company command time for a captain was six months maximum, if a man was not killed or severely wounded first. As fast as the war was consuming young infantry officers, lieutenants especially, there were only so many rifle companies to go around. Command of one in combat was the single most coveted job in the Corps and the organization was reasonably good about getting eligible captains in touch with that opportunity.

Captain John Ripley would be among a small number of young officers left alone to do what they did so well until it was absolutely necessary to send them home. During the twelve months that he skippered Lima, especially since the beginning of March all the way through to November, the combat was nonstop. Few people at home, even with the growing casualty numbers, could understand or appreciate the level of brutality and intensity Marines and soldiers were routinely experiencing in I Corps especially.

By early 1967 Captain Ripley was beginning to personally observe the bias in what was and was not being reported by the Western press. The routine terrorizing of Vietnamese villagers by Viet Cong and NVA forces was regularly deemed not newsworthy. When the American press refused to cover the story of how several Marines had been captured and then, nearly like Christ, staked alive with bridging spikes to trees just outside friendly positions near Con Thien for their comrades to listen to their cries of pain and ultimate death, it soured him completely on reporters.

In the one-year period that John Ripley had served as Lima Six Actual there had been greater than 300 percent turnover in personnel. His unit had suffered more than 300 percent casualties. Most of the wounded were, like him and Chuck Goggin, men who had been hit, sent to the rear for some period of time, and then returned for further duty. Many of Lima's Marines repeated this process more than once. Captain Ripley, given only one Purple Heart for this tour, had been wounded three times. In addition to the combat casualties, Lima Company lost sixty men to malaria during that same period.

From the time John Ripley became Lima Six Actual to the time of his departure the combat in northern I Corps had gone from hot to super-heated. Every time they went to the field they made contact. Every time they made contact with the NVA they took casualties, but every time they engaged the enemy they defeated them. The NVA were good soldiers. No one disputed that. But they were no match for the American Marines. When John Ripley left to come home, the Americans were winning.

As hard as it had been to turn over the reins of Lima Company, he recognized its inevitability. Coming home to his wife and son lived up to every fairy-tale expectation he allowed himself to indulge in only after he had left the field. Once his thirty days of family leave was concluded, and the father-son relationship was successfully re-established with Stephen, John Ripley did a quick six-month tour as a student at Quantico's Amphibious Warfare School, a class the Corps sent its most promising captains to attend. From there he was further assigned to duty at Headquarters Marine Corps in Washington, DC. as the monitor for infantry lieutenants. Monitors serve as *de facto* career counselors and go-betweens for professional Marines and the institution. Their job is to try to match up the needs of the Corps with the professional desires for postings of its members. During Captain Ripley's time as the monitor, the job was somewhat less than intellectually stimulating; nearly every man needing assignment was destined for Vietnam.

CHAPTER NINE

1968: Beginning of the End

January 1968 saw the United States entering its thirty-fourth month of major ground combat operations in Vietnam. With the almost fondly recalled experience of World War II as the yardstick, there were few reasonable indicators aside from assurances given by President Johnson and senior military officers that progress was being made toward victory.

By the thirty-fourth month of American involvement in World War II there was an unbroken string of victories and conquests by which folks at home with *National Geographic* maps could follow the advance. In the Pacific bloody wins at places like Midway, Guadalcanal, Tarawa, Guam, and the Philippines showed the continual shrinking of the Japanese Empire.

By the thirty-fourth month of American involvement in World War II, in the European Theater of Operations, the Germans had been removed from northern Africa, the Italians had been removed from the war, the Allies had broken out of their D-Day beachheads, liberated Paris, and were advancing on Berlin. The Russians were steadily advancing from the east. Stalin, Churchill, and Roosevelt were already talking publicly about the post-war world. Americans, who were willing to suffer further, could at least sense that victory was somewhere out on an approaching horizon.

By the thirty-fourth month of American involvement in World War II the folks at home had been thoroughly indoctrinated and made part of the war experience. With 12 million men and women under arms out of a population of 140 million, few families did not have at least a son or husband or nephew or cousin serving. The economic effort required to support total war virtually guaranteed that even if a family did not have a relative or dear friend in uniform, they were somehow involved or significantly impacted through their own civilian employment.

Culturally, by the thirty-fourth month of World War II Americans had grown used to seeing weekly newsreels chronicling the victories Allied forces were chalking up across the globe, were used to watching their celluloid heroes—those who had not themselves gone off to participate for real—righteously dispatching their perfidiously portrayed enemies in great and not-so-great movies like *Corregidor, Fighting Seabees, Air Force, Guadalcanal Diary, Wake Island, Behind the Rising Sun, Five Graves to Cairo, Destination Tokyo,* and *Foreign Correspondent.*

Neither was the music quite the same by January of 1968, evolving or devolving—depending on one's view of things—from "Rum & Coca Cola" to "Purple Haze" and "Eight Miles High." The perceived sweetness and sincerity of songs like "Don't Sit Under the Apple Tree" and "The White Cliffs of Dover" had morphed into incongruity and chaos with "White Rabbit" that would soon to be followed by the likes of "The Fish Cheer." From the Andrews Sisters and Dinah Shore, the leap to the raw sexuality of Grace Slick and Janis Joplin simply did not spell wholesomeness, certainty, or confidence of victory in any familiar way.

Even using the more recent Korean War as a measure of progress yielded few encouraging parallels. Aside from the fact that the conflict in Vietnam to date had cost fewer lives than had the war in Korea, and had not drawn in direct Soviet or Chinese participation—at least none that was made public—by the thirty-fourth month of ground combat operations on the Korean peninsula, the armistice was close to being signed.

The beginnings of 1968 brought with it no bond or scrap metal drives, no Meatless Tuesdays, no gas or sugar rationing. The average American manufacturing worker was not producing bombers or bullets or battleships. There were no admonishments that "Loose lips sink ships" and Rosie the Riveter had split the scene. While in World War II collective suffering and shared sacrifice had one in twelve Americans wearing a uniform with perhaps half of those folks serving somewhere overseas, by the time of the Vietnam

War maybe one in one hundred were serving, and only one in four hundred was in Southeast Asia. By the late 1960s, if a family did not directly have a son, brother, husband, or dear friend serving in Vietnam, and if that man was not directly participating in the out-in-the-bush combat, American involvement was little more than an inconvenience or nuisance to most, something to be upset about until the evening television news ended and *Batman, Dragnet, Laugh-In,* or *The Monkees* came on instead.

MARKING TIME

By the time Gerry Turley, John Ripley, Chuck Goggin, and hundreds of thousands of other American fighting men had concluded their first—and for most last—tours of duty, by the time Second Lieutenant George Philip's, U.S. Naval Academy Class of 1967, was set to begin, Captain Le Ba Binh was still nebulously in the middle of his.

Fighting men throughout the four corps regions anxiously ticked off days remaining on their Vietnam time. When a man got down to ninety-nine days or less he became "short," a "double-digit midget." With less than ten days he became "extremely short" and a "single-digit midget." In Lima Company, Ripley's Raiders had their own tradition and would give a deck of cards to every man when he had fifty-two days remaining on his tour. Saving the Ace of Spades for the final day, a man would mark his time by randomly pulling a card from the deck each and every day. The days for him became known by the card he pulled. The only other recognition of days were Sundays when the corpsmen would pass out malaria pills for all to take.

For Le Ba Binh, the men of the Soi Bien, and the entire TQLC there was no moving on, no baseball, or anything else for that matter, to go back to. To be sure, there were loving wives, mothers, girlfriends, and families, but they were all right there or reasonably close by. For the Vietnamese there was no bigger picture to consider. While America's strategic concerns and commitments spanned the globe from Asia to Europe and all the oceans in between, while America possessed manpower and industrial prowess to meet disparate obligations, and Vietnam was only one of those obligations—although currently the bloodiest, it was still just one of many dominos needing support. For the Vietnamese the battle with the Communists was all-consuming. There were no other considerations. This was it.

The American military had wisely decided that if a man was wounded three times during his tour and still breathing, it was best to get him home. There was no need to tempt fate too greatly. How much more could one person give short of his own life? Captain Le Ba Binh, by January 1968, had already been wounded five times since his commissioning in 1962. But his country did not have the luxury of excess manpower to promise such things.

By January 1968 growing numbers of Americans were questioning the nation's willingness to continue following President Kennedy's promise to "pay any price and bear any burden..." With little to tangibly show the folks at home for the blood and material prices paid so far, it was sounding more reasonable to challenge that line of thinking. For American men ages eighteen to twenty-five, the prospect of fighting and dying in a war many had not been convinced was their fight to begin with held little appeal.

Americans could politely or not so politely debate and protest the war without significant consequence. The direct NVA and Viet Cong threat to Hollywood or Berkeley or Madison or Ann Arbor was minimal. For Vietnamese who wished not to live under the yoke of Communism, the options were limited. They did not enjoy the same security of space and time and position as did their American benefactors. The threats to them were far more real and immediate. Events outside of Vietnam, to a large degree, mattered to the Vietnamese only to the extent that they impacted America's ability or willingness to support and supply their own efforts to remain free.

THE RUN-UP TO KHE SANH AND TET '68

Whether physically present or not, correspondents covering the war in Vietnam over time left American readers and television viewers solidly with the impression that the length and breadth of the country was laced with enemy tunnels and safe havens, with cleverly cloaked VC operatives controlling the jungles and lurking in every hamlet, village, and town. There was the sense that no one and nowhere was safe. That was simply not true.

Communist propaganda and a generally harsh, unsympathetic Western press aside, the new Republic of Vietnam's fledgling democracy was beginning, by 1966, to show real progress and promise. Compared to their former colonial masters in post-World War II Europe and the very difficult-to-keep-track-of changes in governments the French had experienced, the situation in Vietnam, if held to a similar standard, did not appear terribly critical. Following the elimination of Diem in 1963 and the successive *coups* and counter *coups*, after Nguyen Cao Ky became prime minister, a semblance of stability was established, in spite of the nation being at war. In 1966 85 percent of those citizens eligible to vote actually made the effort to register.[1]

The Vietnamese national elections held in November 1967 and the general integrity of the voting process was no small miracle. While the American and European media quickly pointed out that candidates with avowedly Communist leanings were not allowed to run, even though their sworn objective was the violent overthrow of any non-Communist government, dozens of outside religious and political organizations sent in election observers who found little in the way of irregularities. That Nguyen Van Thieu won was expected, but that he won with only 35 percent of the vote did not validate the Communist charge that the elections were rigged. No such expression of freedom took place in the Democratic Republic of Vietnam.

On the American home front, many were still expectant of victory and believed what they were being told by the conflict's optimists and lingering political supporters. General Westmoreland, the senior American officer in Vietnam, during a speech given in Washington, DC to the National Press Club on November 21, 1967, referring to the coming New Year, continued with the positive outlook he was well noted for when he said that, "the end begins to come into view." He also went on to state that within the next two years or less Americans would likely be turning over a greater burden of the work to South Vietnamese forces.[2]

President Johnson's State of the Union address from early January of 1968 was resolute and to the point. Within the first moment he was into discussion on Vietnam and stated:

> Since I reported to you last January: Three elections have been held in Vietnam in the midst of war and under the constant threat of violence. A president, a vice president, a House and Senate, and village officials have been chosen by popular, contested ballot. The enemy has been defeated in battle after battle. The number of South Vietnamese living in areas under government protection tonight has grown by more than a million since January of last year.
>
> These are all marks of progress, yet: The enemy continues to pour men and material across frontiers and into battle, despite his continuous heavy losses. He continues to hope that America's will to persevere can be broken. Well, he is wrong. America will persevere. Our patience and our perseverance will match our power. Aggression will not prevail. But our goal is peace—and peace at the earliest possible moment..."[3]

The president went on further to outline briefly his goals for some form of peace with the Communists in Hanoi. Beyond that, the bulk of the speech was more concerned with his illusive pursuit of the Great Society.

At the same time, American military planners were looking for opportunities to engage and destroy large elements of NVA. Khe Sanh, a remote village in northwest I Corps on Route 9 just shy of the Laotian border, looked to Americans like a proper staging area from which to interdict the Ho Chi Minh Trail and perhaps later initiate ground action into Laos or possibly even North Vietnam.

The benefit to Americans fighting out away from populated areas, in spite of massive logistical constraints, was the ability to employ the full measure of airpower without risk of killing innocent civilians.

For several years there had been significant debate between Army and Marine generals on how best to prosecute the war in Vietnam. Marines favored attempts at pacification, controlling coastal towns and villages, and trying to deny the Communists access to the civilian populations—as Marines had done during the Banana Wars against bandits with some success. General Westmoreland and his MACV staff of Army generals preferred efforts to engage the enemy away from populated areas where superior American firepower and rapid resupply might prevail. That the Third Marine Division found itself, by late 1967, fairly well-established in near static positions across the area adjacent to the DMZ and out near Khe Sanh, was mostly a result of General Westmoreland's strategic vision.

Nineteen sixty-seven had been the year of greatest challenge and sacrifice yet for American ground and air forces in Vietnam. The nearly ten thousand men killed in those twelve months was more than had been lost there in all the prior years combined. In northernmost I Corps just south of the DMZ and where combat had been especially intense, Marines labored and battled under conditions not to their liking.

The Leatherneck proclivity for offensive operations was hamstrung by the additional responsibilities of constructing and defending the building effort of what would become known derisively as the "McNamara Line"—named after then Secretary of Defense Robert Strange McNamara. The concept for some sort of physical barrier that would discourage infiltration from the north had been given strong consideration for several years, even briefly by senior Marines.

Known to many as Dyemarker, the strongpoint or barrier system was to be a cleared and bulldozed six-hundred-to-one thousand-meter-wide swath of real estate extending roughly east to west across portions of the DMZ on which mines, sensors, and barbed wire would be emplaced to prohibit enemy infiltration or to channel them into areas where allied forces could more easily kill them. Additionally Dyemarker would include intermittent concrete blockhouses so that units of Marines or ARVN could observe and defend the line.

Unhappily tasked with its construction by MACV, Marines at all levels saw the futility of the effort, considering it a rehash of the Maginot Line. The need to direct resources to clear the area, emplace mines and sensors, erect the concrete structures, and all the while defend that huge construction effort stretched already thin resources of units assigned to this duty.

As early as July 1967 Lieutenant General Victor Krulak, serving as the senior Marine general in the Pacific theater and an early proponent of denying the civilian population to the enemy—winning "Hearts and Minds"—rather than fighting a defensive war in remote areas, voiced his opinion about waging war in the DMZ. His assessment of NVA goals was that they wanted: "…to get us as near to his weapons and to his forces as possible, drench us with high angle fire weapons, engage us in close and violent combat, accept willingly a substantial loss of life for the opportunity to kill a lesser number of our men, and to withdraw into his North Vietnam sanctuary to refurbish."[4]

Fighting Marines and soldiers at the point of contact with the enemy had long been exasperated by incredibly bizarre and counterintuitive rules of engagement. Disallowed from physically pursuing retreating NVA units into Cambodian, Laotian, and North Vietnamese sanctuaries, the anachronistic and falsely chivalrous notions of holiday ceasefires were equally farcical. During the Christmas 1967 and New Year's truce the following week enemy ceasefire violations were legion. Major Gary Todd, an intelligence officer with the Third Marine Division, described what everyone already knew to be true when he opined that "the last shot fired before the 'ceasefire' took effect was like a starter's pistol to the North Vietnamese, crouched down and tensed to explode into a sprint" to resupply their forces in the south.[5]

General Giap and his North Vietnamese colleagues were said to view the pending, seemingly inevitable battles for Khe Sanh as an opportunity to repeat their 1954 Dien Bien Phu victory over French forces. If sufficient numbers of American troops could be lured there, isolated somehow, and then destroyed, the American public might finally lose its stomach for a war in which it appeared that the Communists would never surrender, no matter what the cost.

The North Vietnamese had moved considerable resources and troops into the area in and around Khe Sanh. Intermittent but intense contact in the hills surrounding the soon-to-be-expanded combat base in the months before year-end 1967 confirmed to American intelligence sources that there were likely at least three full divisions of NVA present and anxious to engage the Marines.

From the White House President Johnson paid particular attention to the looming battle and the fortunes of the Marine regiment placed there like bait in a trap. Comparisons to Dien Bien Phu had already been made by the press. The president would make sure there would be no repeat of the shameful mistakes made by French generals whose cavalier disregard for the ingenuity of their enemy and failure to adhere to basic war fighting principles had cost the lives of so many brave men.

At Dien Bien Phu the French had occupied positions in a valley and ceded the high ground to the Viet Minh, believing them incapable of placing long-range artillery in the surrounding mountains. Logistically Dien Bien Phu was a resupply nightmare as it was located far from friendly bases. Fighter aircraft had short loiter times once they arrived on station. Clever positioning by the Viet Minh of effective anti-aircraft guns kept bombers from making more accurate, lower level bombing runs. Lumbering C-119 cargo planes used for aerial resupply were forced to drop gear from altitudes that, because of wind conditions aloft, often caused ammunition, food, and medicine to land inside of the enemy's continually expanding lines.

American forces had several advantages unavailable to the French. Khe Sanh itself was on high ground and the Marines effectively controlled a number of key adjacent mountaintops. Even though the NVA would position large quantities of long-range artillery in the Laotian mountains to the west and would be able to fire near continuously, and even though they had effectively cut Route 9 between Khe Sanh and Dong Ha which all but eliminated the American ability to reprovision or reinforce by truck convoys, American air power along with abundant helicopter and fixed-wing resupply would keep Marines in the fight indefinitely. The big guns at Camp Carroll—the 175s—had the range and punch required to help protect the combat base from approaching NVA infantry. In the meantime operations throughout I Corps and the rest of Vietnam continued apace.

CAM BANH

In late 1967 Cam Banh was a twenty-one-year-old clerk in the purchasing department at the U.S. Navy Exchange, the PX, in downtown Saigon near Cholon. Her life story and family experiences to this point very much reflected and chronicled the tumult and change that had gone on in her country since the end of World War II.

Born in Hanoi in 1946, the second child and the second girl, Cam had moved to Saigon in 1952 with her mother, older sister, and two younger brothers. In Vietnamese culture it was not at all uncommon for a man to carry on or have a second family with another woman. There was little recourse for the wife and children pushed to the disadvantaged position. There were few options for Cam's mother when her father chose this course for himself. With four young children in tow, Cam's mother picked up and moved south, two years prior to the major exodus that would bring a million more northerners to freedom from Communist oppression in 1954. She was fortunate because she was quickly able to secure a position working as a secretary in the equivalent of Saigon's city hall.

While Cam's older sister had married and moved away, Cam quit school in 1962 to assist her mother with the expenses associated with the raising of her two younger brothers. Prior to working at the U.S. Navy PX in 1966, she worked a series of different jobs.

The impact on the Vietnamese economy from local American spending was significant. Benefits accrued disproportionately to those directly employed or aided immediately from the results of that spending. Paying significantly more for whatever services they used than was typical prior to their arrival, that spending would ultimately have long-term, deleterious consequences on inflation and the allocation of scarce wartime resources.

For Cam Banh and her family, the job at the Navy Exchange instantly made her the primary breadwinner and afforded them a standard of living significantly better than they could possibly have enjoyed were she not in the employ of the Americans. The combination of her income from her job and that from her mother's municipal job ensured that Cam's brothers could continue their education without interruption.

Life for the young and attractive Cam in late 1967 was reasonably good by Vietnamese standards and in many ways differed only slightly from what women her age might experience elsewhere.

Every weekday morning Cam became a part of the mass of humanity that to any outsider seemed a riot of movement but to the citizens of a free and thriving Saigon was business as usual. Traveling from her mother's home in Phu Nhuan to the PX by *cyclopousse*, she would enjoy the sights and smells and sounds of her adopted hometown. On the ten-kilometer ride she would see all the life she knew as normal; children in uniforms heading off to school, shopkeepers and sidewalk merchants setting up but willing to sell their wares to any passersby at any hour, policemen directing traffic, occasional Vietnamese or American soldiers driving by in jeeps looking back, transfixed, at her and all the other pretty young women going about in their *ao dai*.

Vietnamese cultural superiority had been absolutely established with the invention of the *ao dai*. The outfit does, for virtually all women, what nothing else can in any other language or culture.

Simple in design, sensual beyond measure, it accentuates all that is best and all that is feminine. Unlike so much of what is Western and boorish, exposed and leaving little to the mind, the *ao dai* exposes nothing, but challenges a man's appreciation for lines and geometric proportions, and a suggestion of that which is beneath the fabric is left fully to anticipation and imagination. With so much beauty on the streets, sidewalks, and boulevards it was a wonder that soldiers and Marines could find the strength or focus to fight a war.

Saigon traffic flowed—bicycles mostly with a small but growing number of motorbikes and cars. Saigon was always moving. Its population required all manner of things to live and to eat. What was not produced within the city for consumption was moved mostly in tiny, tiny increments, one bicycle load at a time, whether it was chickens or pigs, bananas or breadfruit, sacks of rice, or bunches of green vegetables. There was little refrigeration. What was sold on Monday was consumed on Monday. For Tuesday the process began all over again. The cycle was without end.

The omnipresent street-side noodle vendors—the authentic and original purveyors of fast food—with their tiny, portable "restaurants" that could be set up or taken down in a flash just about anywhere for anyone, and were carried from point to point in two large cauldrons that balanced on shoulder-borne poles or slightly larger contraptions on tiny pushcarts fed a hungry city just coming to life. It all may have seemed loud and disorganized to Americans doing whatever it was they were involved with, but the regularity and constancy of this routine was business as usual and an indication for the citizens of the new Republic of Vietnam that there might very well be hope for a bright and certain tomorrow.

As traditional and strict as Cam's mother and most of Vietnamese society still was about dating and courtship, the environment was safe enough so that Cam was allowed during the evenings, when there were no family obligations, to go to clubs and *cabarets* with her young lady friends. They enjoyed the active Saigon night life, dancing, and music.

While there was a paucity of locally produced movies to view, there was no shortage of foreign films subtitled or dubbed in Vietnamese. She very much enjoyed Sophia Loren and Gina Lollobrigida, glamorous and beautiful in any language. Cam's absolute favorite, though, the one she referred to as her "angel," was Elizabeth Taylor.

CADET NGUYEN LUONG

Cadet Nguyen Luong had begun his education to become a professional military officer when he joined Class 24 of the National Military Academy in the fall of 1967. Known by their class number, this group of three hundred-plus patriotic young men, if things went according to plan, would graduate as new second lieutenants and ensigns in December of 1971.

The Vietnamese National Military Academy was originally established by the French in 1948 as l'Ecole Inter-Armes in Hue. Programmed somewhat after St. Cyr, the French equivalent to West Point, the mission was to provide a trained and educated *cadre* of reliable, professional officers.[6] Among the Academy's distinguished graduates, President Ngyuen Van Thieu had been a member of Class One.

Situated now in the balmy mountain resort town of Dalat, approximately 140 miles northeast of Saigon, the academy's curriculum had, for the greatest portion of its existence, been two years in length. With French and American assistance the curriculum was expanded to three and then four years in the late 1950s. By 1960 however, real world constraints, service needs to combat the escalating Communist threat, and the war's insatiable appetite for junior officers caused a move back to a two-year education.

With increasing American involvement, the Vietnamese were encouraged to adopt the four-year West Point model in the mid-1960s. Class 22 was actually divided into two parts; 22A would graduate in two years and 22B in four. Classes 23 and 24 were both four-year programs. The plan was to continue in this manner indefinitely.

Admission to the National Military Academy, like its American counterparts, was extremely competitive. From a pool of many thousands of qualified applicants anxious to fight for their country, Class 24 had been culled to the three hundred or so candidates with the highest academic and physical qualifications. As Vietnam was not yet established or prosperous enough to afford separate academies for each service, the air force, navy, and Marine Corps would be apportioned a few young officers from every class with the highest percentage going to the army which was, by far, the largest service. It was quite common for the top graduates, reflecting the *élan* and fighting spirit of the school and the times, to request service with the Airborne or Marines.[7]

Born in 1947 in Bien Hoa, twenty miles northeast of Saigon, Nguyen Luong was the oldest of five brothers and one sister. His father had initially worked as an officer in the local *gendarmes* prior to the country's division in 1954. Once the Republic of

Vietnam was established, Luong's father transferred to the postal service where he was part of a highly covert group that labored in secret inspecting correspondence for coded messages between Communists in the north and their agents in the south. Often such mail was routed through Europe or other perceived-to-be-benign addresses in hopes of avoiding the discerning eyes of men like Luong's father.

Growing up, Luong enjoyed playing the guitar, classical guitar especially. Like young boys everywhere, the fantasy and excitement of movies captured his imagination. Action films, Westerns, science fiction; he enjoyed them all. Movies like Jules Verne's *Twenty Thousands Leagues under the Sea* were among the stories he would always recall fondly.

As a member of the local Boy Scout troop, he and his companions went camping when they could in surrounding remote areas near Nha Trang, Thu Duc, and Binh Duong. They even camped out at the Giac Lam pagoda in Saigon. Often the teenaged scouts were tagged with real missions of assistance or mercy as their young country faced its challenges. It was not at all unusual for them to assist at fires, new construction projects, or the reconstruction of combat-damaged roads and bridges; anything to lend a helping hand in time of need.

Luong's education prior to coming to the National Military Academy had included the American equivalent of two years of technical college. In Vietnam, studies at such institutions were engineering-oriented so they naturally tilted toward math and science. This was important preparation for Luong as the military academy curriculum, in following the West Point model, was similarly filled with engineering coursework.

By 1967, in America, being in the military—and looking like you were in the military in particular—did not necessarily improve a young man's odds with the greater population of eligible young women. In Vietnam, a country fighting for its very survival, aspiring officers were viewed far more favorably—as the saviors of their country—by female contemporaries than at Annapolis, West Point, or the Air Force Academy. The pickings for cadets from the academy were generally quite good.

When not involved in studies or field exercises, Luong maintained a steady relationship with a young woman from his hometown of Bien Hoa. From the beginning their courtship was strong and she happily and dutifully attended all the disparate functions required of his formal social calendar.

SECOND LIEUTENANT GEORGE PHILIP III USMC

Second Lieutenant George Philip III, U.S. Naval Academy Class of 1967, was worried that his opportunity to look squarely into the elephant's eye might evaporate before he was able to get to Vietnam and personally win the war. On his own, he cut short his period of graduation leave and reported in to Quantico having used less than half the time allotted to join an earlier forming Basic School class. To his surprise and delight there were eight or nine other former middies who showed up early, similarly anxious to begin the training process.

George reported into TBS and Alpha Company 1-68 (the first class scheduled to graduate in fiscal year 1968—sometime in mid- to late October) in late June of 1967 fully intending to get his 0302–Infantry Officer—MOS. The Corps was all about the infantry. If you were not in the infantry as a Marine, then you worked to support those who were. It was that simple, at least from the perspective of a new second lieutenant.

The road to Annapolis, Quantico, and Vietnam for Second Lieutenant Philip had begun just a bit differently than it had for the bulk of his midshipmen and soon to be new lieutenant friends. For most, their education as professional military officers and inculcation into the warrior culture began the day they had arrived at the Academy or OCS. Certainly they had all been directly and indirectly influenced by American society and history, by fathers, brothers, uncles, and friends; men who had served and had tales to tell. The uniqueness of that service, the obvious pride and satisfaction displayed by men who, because of their military experience seemed unusually wise and insightful, drew in young boys eager to absorb the lessons shared. The intensity of the stories appealed to their youthful sense of daring and romance, to be a part of something that had deep meaning. There was no other calling that gave a young man the opportunity for special challenge, risk, and potential for personal satisfaction and psychic reward.

The road to a military life for George Philip had begun long before conception. On his mother's side, the Taussig family, since the Civil War, had put forth an unbroken line of men who had gone down to the sea in ships and served with great distinction. Aside from losing her first husband, George's father—and being his father's only living male heir made George a legitimate "sole surviving son"—his mother's younger brother, Joe Taussig, USNA '41, had simultaneously earned a Navy Cross and lost a leg as a junior ensign aboard the USS *Nevada* at Pearl Harbor on December 7, 1941.

In every house they would move to during his stepfather's own Marine Corps career George's mother always displayed, on the longest hallway wall, portrait after portrait of Taussig men: stern, serious-looking fellows, many whose names were in books of naval history, men whose bravery and faithful service had helped transform the U.S. Navy from fledgling coastal force to absolute global preeminence.

On the Philip side, the service to country and sacrifice had been at least as significant. George's grandmother, Alice Waldron Philip, was one-quarter Sioux Indian. Her younger brother, John Waldron, U.S. Naval Academy Class of 1924, was the first man from his half of the family to pursue a naval career. As a pilot and commanding officer of Torpedo Squadron Eight (VT-8) aboard the USS *Hornet* (CV-8) in early June of 1942 during the opening engagement to the Battle of Midway, Lieutenant Commander Waldron led his fifteen technologically outclassed and obsolete TBD-1 Douglas Devastators into impossible odds as they sacrificially attacked the aircraft carriers of the Imperial Japanese Navy. The first unit to locate and engage the enemy that June 4th day, their actions, which cost the squadron all of its planes, all of its men save young Ensign George Gay, and inflicted no damage upon the enemy ships, served the purpose of drawing down to lower altitudes most of the available Japanese fighters aloft as fleet protection. Moments later, remaining American forces were able to press home the attack largely unopposed, because of what Torpedo Eight had done. This one battle, and the events that transpired in the next four to eight minutes, forever turned the tide of war in the Pacific in America's favor. For his selfless leadership and valor that day, John Waldron was posthumously awarded the Navy Cross.

Three years later, during the Battle of Okinawa, Grandmother Philip's son, Commander George Philip, Jr., USNA Class of 1935, after having seen extensive naval action in the Solomons, Philippines, and at Iwo Jima, was commanding the USS *Twiggs* (DD-521) when his ship was attacked by *kamikazes* while serving picket duty. While many of the crew were saved, there was great loss of life. Commander Philip was among the 174 sailors who paid the ultimate price. Like his uncle John Waldron, Commander Philip was also posthumously awarded the Navy Cross.

World War II had created many young widows and children without fathers. Margaret Taussig Philip was twenty-six when her husband was killed. George Philip III, U.S. Naval Academy Class of 1967 was nine months old, big sister Snow three years old when their father was lost.

Wilbur Helmer, a young Marine Corps artillery major, had survived hellish action on Bougainville, Guam, Iwo Jima, and was ashore on Okinawa battling Japanese when the USS *Twiggs* was lost. George's mom and Major Helmer met after the war and were married in 1947. In the years following, three more children were added to the family.

Even with their mother remarried to now Colonel Helmer, George and older sister Snow would spend summers at Grandma Philip's in South Dakota who ensured they were steeped in that side of the family history. Grandma Philip reintroduced them to their Sioux heritage. Long before it became fashionable she took young George and Snow to places like Wounded Knee. They were made acutely aware that they had descended from the *first* Americans.

The Philip-Taussig union gave young George *entrée* into a military-patrician familial blend that was uncommon but not unique. They were patrician not in the sense of incredible material wealth but patrician in the sense that for generations the family's men seemed bred to serve and had an inordinate proclivity to rise to the top in the profession of arms. They had not necessarily been captains of industry but they had certainly been captains of ships and commanders of men going into harm's way. That was the family culture George Philip was born into.

George's decision to become a Marine and not a sailor had not been a hard one. With his father's immediate legacy as a destroyer skipper, there was never pressure to join the Navy. Nor had his Marine stepfather pushed him. George Philip was, quite simply, meant to be a Marine.

FROM BASIC SCHOOL TO FT. SILL

Never known for frivolity or excess, by the middle of 1967 the curriculum at The Basic School had been further distilled down to the barest essentials. The ever increasing need for infantry platoon commanders in Vietnam had forced Quantico planners to cut what they could from the program that did not directly benefit an officer's combat leadership skills. Time at TBS was now less than five months. The last two classes of fiscal year 1967, Companies N and O, had been combined into one company and nearly 80 percent of those lieutenants were assigned to Vietnam as infantry officers. The balance was used to fill all the remaining specialties like artillery, armor, supply, communications, etc.

A second lieutenant's education at The Basic School was something the Marine Corps invested in and emphasized. The resources employed to produce junior officers who would leave Quantico and go immediately onto the field of battle were truly impressive. Instructors at TBS were nearly all captains, men recently returned from Vietnam with direct experience doing all manner of things these lieutenants would soon be tasked with doing themselves. The Corps paid particular attention to the quality of officers it sent to instruct at TBS which manifested in the quality of lieutenants graduating.

Training five and a half days a week, the student lieutenants needed no reminding as to the seriousness of instruction and where they would soon be heading. Classroom lectures followed by extensive field training and practical application on subjects starting with infantry fire team and squad tactics progressed to the platoon and company levels. Within that framework the lieutenants would spend countless hours on land navigation, patrolling, offensive tactics, defensive tactics, ambushes, the proper employment of all manner of available firepower, and on and on. Nothing was insignificant. If something seemed superfluous or ridiculous there was a captain instructor with a real-world combat story as to why whatever the subject was, was important. Introductory phrases like "Lieutenants, this could be the most important class you'll ever take," or the admonishment to "Pay attention, gents, this could save your life or the lives of your men," were heard all day every day.

Second Lieutenant George Philip had come to The Basic School fully intending to go to Vietnam as an infantry officer. That his stepfather was a career artilleryman may have had an subconscious impact that George had not pondered greatly. As much as the Marine Corps is an infantry organization, tremendous assets are required to support that infantry effort. The Corps had need for other officers in a host of MOSs (Military Occupational Specialties) to make that support reality. From artillery to armor to air to communications and supply along with countless needs in between, the student officers at Quantico, about midway through their schooling, were either drafted—as they were in classes when the need for infantry officers was great which had happened with the two classes prior to Alpha Company 1-68—or allowed to compete and apply for slots in the various specialties.

No one would argue in the bars, pubs, or classrooms, whether in jest or complete sobriety, that the United States Marine Corps was first and foremost an organization focused on its infantry roots. Among gentlemen there was allowed friendly discussion as to who had the greatest impact, who was smarter, handsomest, etc. Pilots would taunt their ground-pounding friends and remind them that the reason their flight suits had so many pockets was to store all the extra money they earned in flight pay. Infantry officers would counter with questions about their status as true warriors since pilots rarely slept in the bush or ate c-rations like "real Marines." Between the infantry and the artillery was the worn out but still appreciated by every new generation of lieutenants discussion of which of the two had greater impact on any battle's outcome. Artillery officers would boldly and brashly claim that their military specialty was the "King of Battle." Every infantry officer's trained response to that remark was something like "You may be the King of Battle but the Queen (infantry) always tells you where to put the BALLS." And so it went.

Second Lieutenant George Philip probably made his final decision on MOS selection in less than completely intellectual fashion. Always certain that he would serve, at a minimum, in the ground combat arms—infantry, artillery, or armor—it was the day on one of Quantico's numerous ranges that his fate was sealed. With the entire Alpha 1-68 assembled in the humblest of bleachers to witness a firepower demonstration, the captain in charge of this particular period of instruction, an artillery officer back from Vietnam, called the lieutenants' attention to a piece of ground several hundred meters to their front. With an open microphone and over the radio he very precisely and professionally called in an artillery fire mission, exactly as they had been taught to do in class. Directing their attention to the target area, the students listened and watched. With the fire mission requested, the radio exchange of "Shot, over" followed by "Shot, out" meant that destruction was immediately to follow.

For most, this was the first time they had witnessed up close the firing of real, live artillery. The impact of the firing battery's rounds tore the earth apart. Far enough away from the explosions to be safe, they were close enough so that every sense was still fully engaged. The visual display with soil churned, rocketing upwards and outwards almost as if in slow motion, was shortly followed by the thunderous roar that was actually a rapid fire *clump, clump, clump* as the rounds hit milliseconds apart while the ground betrayed a slight tremble. The overpressure from the displaced atmosphere was the final sensation to hit the lieutenants. It was evident to all, in the case of artillery, that it was always more blessed to give than to receive. George said audibly and emphatically, but only to himself, "That's for me."

The Marine Corps relied heavily on its sister services to assist with certain initial MOS training of its junior officers. Aside from taking its medical, dental, and chaplain support entirely from the Navy, all Marine Corps pilots were trained naval aviators and earned their wings alongside young ensigns at Pensacola, Florida.

While the Corps rightly decided to handle every aspect of infantry training to ensure the proper culture and Marine brand of war fighting was infused into its lieutenants, the Corps did not have the resources or infrastructure to fully develop its new armor or artillery officers. Would-be tankers were sent to Ft. Knox in Kentucky and artillerymen were assigned to school at Ft. Sill in Oklahoma.

As "guests," especially at an army school, it was made abundantly clear to student Marine lieutenants that they were expected, at all times, to demonstrate proper comportment, to always remember *who* they were, to do absolutely nothing to sully their Corps' hard-earned good name and reputation.

MEANWHILE...BACK AT THE WAR...

From the sham holiday truces and the return to "normal" combat operations early in January 1968, especially for soldiers and Marines on the ground, and aircrews flying support missions, it was simply the "same war, different day." For those at home able to focus on things other than the war, the Green Bay Packers, under Vince Lombardi's leadership, had won their third NFL championship and second Super Bowl victory. In the meantime, the Communists had been covertly putting in place forces and the logistical support to spring both the massive effort at Khe Sanh and the even more sophisticated pending countrywide Tet Offensive. Allied intelligence analysts were certain something was afoot. Whatever their interpretation, effective response to intercepted enemy communications data was insufficient to counter the magnitude of Hanoi's clandestine efforts.

Vindication of intelligence expectations about the anticipated action at Khe Sanh was quick in coming. On January 20, fierce battles between American Marines and main force NVA units signaled that the long-awaited fight had been joined. Escalation was near instantaneous with both sides committing huge resources to prosecute the now major engagement that had so much political gravity. For the coming days Khe Sanh maintained America's undivided media attention.

The ongoing struggle to win American hearts and minds through television in the country's living rooms was not going well. Reporting on the Khe Sanh battles, scores of reporters would fly into the combat base just long enough to film Marines being shelled and ducking for cover before flying out again to nightly post their stories and sip beer in safe rear areas.

Constantly replaying rather dramatic footage of the NVA artillery strike that destroyed Khe Sanh's substantial ammunition dump gave folks at home a view of Marines contrary to what they were used to. Seeing the nation's most storied warriors on the receiving end of the punishment, night after night, left a distorted impression at home as to how the war was being prosecuted. Those impressions, however inaccurate, would only be exacerbated with the initial attacks and reported enemy successes of the Tet Offensive.[8]

On January 23, America was rudely reminded that its strategic interests stretched beyond the narrow scope of Southeast Asia. The unprovoked seizure of the intelligence vessel USS *Pueblo* by North Korean forces was, at a minimum, an egregious act of war. The world braced for the anticipated American response—massive air strikes, invasion, whatever.[*]

---

[*] The seizure of the *Pueblo* netted the Soviets a huge intelligence prize. The traitor John Walker had earlier given them American naval codes, now they had the equipment to read those messages. This was unknown to Americans at the time.

CHAPTER TEN

Tet Offensive: Opening Rounds

If the United States had considered using military force to spring the *Pueblo's* crew or simply punish North Korea, the attacks begun all across the Republic of Vietnam early on January 31 certainly refocused Washington's attention on Southeast Asia and demonstrated its limitations or unwillingness to use multiple conventional military options in response to multiple crises.

The sanctity of Tet for most Vietnamese was difficult to overstate. As much as the holiday had religious significance, like Christmas to secular-minded Americans, it was a holiday that transcended its Buddhist origins to include all Vietnamese. And if Christmas was a measure secular Americans might understand, the Tet holiday period was Christmas, Easter, Thanksgiving, and then some to its celebrants.

More cultural than religious, the celebration of the lunar New Year was a tradition practiced throughout Asia. Tet was the uniquely Vietnamese version and celebrated by all citizens. Reasonable adult Vietnamese would assume that since Tet was enjoyed by Buddhists, Catholics, and everyone else, and since there was a ten-year history of the Viet Cong minimally honoring the holiday, the tradition of Tet seemed even to transcend Communism as well.

The North Vietnamese and Viet Cong had invested incredible resources in planning, provisioning, and moving forces into place to spring the pending, too-numerous-to-count countrywide Tet attacks. Relying on initial overwhelming shock and terror, Hanoi planners hoped that the presence of eighty thousand highly dedicated liberators would be catalyst enough for enslaved southerners to rise up against their American puppet government and welcome their northern brothers as the rightful inheritors or torch bearers of true Vietnamese nationalism.

Action at Khe Sanh aside, American intelligence analysts believed there was more combat on a much larger scale still to come. With another holiday truce approaching, and privy to information he for some reason did not share with his Vietnamese allies, General Westmoreland placed all U.S. forces on full alert just one day prior to the beginning of the scheduled Tet holiday period.

For most Vietnamese the lunar New Year would stretch over a weeklong period of celebration. Preparations in every household were significant. It was a widely held belief and common practice right before Tet, in cleaning, to sweep from the outside in so as to ensure all the good luck stayed within a home. Great quantities of special foods were prepared over several days as friends and relatives were expected to visit and share each others' good fortunes and exchange gifts.

While regular civilians, even during wartime, might coax a full week of family fun and enjoyment out of the Tet festivities, members of the Republic of Vietnam's military, if not part of the 50 percent assigned to remain on duty, were officially given four days of leave. Those who remained at their posts could probably be partially forgiven, if not directly in contact with enemy forces, from focusing their full attention on anything but what they were missing out on.

Vietnamese children and probably a high percentage of adults went to bed the evening of January 30 in joyful anticipation of welcoming in the Year of the Monkey with the cultural equivalent of "sugarplums dancing in their heads..." Even the din of gunfire and explosions, unless extremely close by, was mistaken for the normal, reassuring sounds of fireworks which signaled happiness and glad tidings.

The ferocity, boldness, and quantity of the attacks that began the Tet Offensive in the very early morning on January 31, 1968 were truly impressive. At once all of South Vietnam, especially its cities and larger towns, seemed aflame. The Communists seemed to appear out of nowhere and suddenly seemed to be everywhere.

In the opening hours of the Tet Offensive Communist forces initiated attacks against thirty-nine of South Vietnam's forty-four provincial capitals, sixty-four district capitals, and numerous hamlets, as well as nearly every allied airfield, base, or installation of any significance. In Saigon proper the Communists attacked the U.S. embassy, the Presidential Palace, the Joint General Staff Headquarters, Tan Son Nhut airport, RVN naval headquarters, and the main radio station.[1] The cities of Hue, Dalat, Kontum, and Quang Tri would, in the first few days, be overrun by the enemy. It was similar to what the Japanese had pulled off on December 7, 1941 with their pan-Pacific surprise assaults on Pearl Harbor, Malaya, Hong Kong, Guam, the Philippines, and Wake Island, except the Communists did it in the middle of a war already well underway.

Even though it was the same country, for the moment it was an entirely different war. Heretofore having battled elusive enemies in mostly remote rural or jungle and mountain terrain, Communist soldiers and attackers disguised as civilians now massed for assaults in comparatively urban environments under comparatively conventional circumstances.

Only hours after the initial shock was sustained and stabilized, RVN and American forces re-organized and began to counterattack and regain the combat initiative. Friendly casualties, especially among innocent civilians, were high. Among the attacking forces they were higher. Far higher.

The initial chaos of the Tet Offensive made for interesting news reporting. Activity at the U.S. embassy was particularly compelling. Even though the nineteen man platoon of sappers who had blasted their way into the embassy compound were all killed within hours, television viewers at home in America were given the mistaken impression that the Viet Cong were generally in control at the embassy as well as other key installations throughout the country.

As much as the Tet Offensive was a series of major conventional attacks by the Communists that gave allied forces tremendous opportunities to locate, close with, and destroy in conventional combat an enemy that nearly always before had refused to engage in a manner that favored American firepower, the media circus created by the intensity and shock continued to favor the enemy.

Almost from the beginning, events seemed to cartwheel out of control from the media's perspective. For those opposed to American involvement, the most enduring photos of the Vietnam War through year-end 1967 were probably those from a few years earlier depicting various self-immolating Buddhist monks protesting the evils of Ngo Dinh Diem's regime. That was soon to change.

For the vast population of Vietnamese citizens, especially those living in towns and cities, until the attacks on January 31, war and terror was something they mostly had read or heard about secondhand. That situation was forever altered that day. Western media chronicled the deliberateness and ubiquitous nature of the Communist attacks. On the formerly-bustling-with-commerce avenues of Saigon the streets now ran red with the blood of innocents and Communists disguised as such.

On February 1, Vietnamese President Nguyen Van Thieu declared martial law and U.S. and ARVN forces regained control of Tan Son Nhut.

Journalists were given ample opportunity to observe American and South Vietnamese forces engage and battle back against the enemy. In World War II at Iwo Jima an intrepid Joe Rosenthal chronicled on film for eternity the moment that would forever encapsulate Marine Corps culture with the historic flag raising atop Mt. Suribachi. What Associated Press photographer Eddie Adams captured in filming the actions of General Nguyen Ngoc Loan on February 1, 1968 was anything but a Joe Rosenthal experience for South Vietnamese forces locked in mortal combat against a foe every bit as vicious and hell-bent on their destruction as the Japanese holed up in Iwo Jima's caves.

By late 1967, Nguyen Ngoc Loan had been selected to serve as the chief of the RVN National Police. Known for his intelligence, bravery, competence, and integrity, this qualified combat pilot led his men from the front. Already a veteran of many actions, both in the air and on the ground, during the morning of February 1, General Loan was again personally on the streets of Saigon, this time in Cholon, the Chinese section of town, observing and directing the action of those in his charge.

Police and ARVN soldiers were battling Communist forces, most of whom were dressed as civilians or even police officers so as to blend in with the hapless, terrified masses. Having personally witnessed the murder of one of his officers along with that man's wife and three small children by a Viet Cong captain disguised as a civilian, General Loan took the recently captured Communist aside to administer appropriate situational justice. Aware that *saboteurs* and terrorists did not enjoy traditional rights as prisoners and certain of the man's guilt, the general operated within accepted rules of land warfare in meting out his on-the-spot execution.[2]

Unfortunately for General Loan and the RVN cause, the Pulitzer Prize-winning still photo that captured the visceral reality of the prisoner's brains being blown out of the side of his head did not come with adequate printed preamble or explanation. The man who, only moments before without the slightest remorse had brutally murdered an entire family was instantly and incorrectly transformed into helpless lynch mob victim. In addition to Adams's still photo, another film crew videoed the entire execution. Without audio explanation to the situational context, this added to the incorrect perception of General Loan's actions. With this picture published and video broadcast and rebroadcast around the free and Communist worlds, General Loan immediately became the personification of all that was corrupt and diabolical with the American puppet government.

With his picture plastered across the front pages of the world's newspapers and the video of his kangaroo court execution replayed *ad nauseum*, General Loan would continue to lead his men in brutal, close quarter house-to-house urban fighting and sustain wounds serious enough to require the amputation of one of his legs.[3]

HUE

Action at Hue came more slowly. Closer to Hanoi than Saigon, the city's historical and cultural significance to all Vietnamese had so far largely spared it from serious action in this the

American War. Among the Communist leadership Vo Nguyen Giap, Le Duan, Pham Van Dong, and Ho Chi Minh, before he was Ho Chi Minh, had matriculated at the elite Quoc Hoc secondary school in the center of the city. Oddly and ironically, Ngo Dinh Diem was among the school's alumni as well.

For the four thousand to six thousand unfortunate men, women, and children identified by Communists and their agents as reactionary or sympathetic to the RVN government who were shot, bludgeoned, or bayoneted before being buried in mass graves—some while still alive—at the battle's beginning, there was little mention in the American media. If anyone in Hollywood, Berkeley, Madison, or Ann Arbor shed a tear for these particular victims, it went unnoticed in the press.

The battle for Hue City that began a day after the Tet Offensive had started everywhere else in South Vietnam would be particularly bloody and protracted, egregious NVA atrocities aside. The NVA and VC ultimately committed fourteen battalions of infantry to a twenty-seven-day battle that resulted in roughly 85 percent of the six thousand Communist troops involved being KIA. ARVN dead approached four hundred and American Marines lost 147 men killed.[4]

At Khe Sanh the siege would continue for an incredible seventy-seven days. The synergies of Marine tenacity and the endless, near limitless application of American airpower eviscerated the NVA divisions arrayed against them. Including those men killed in the March 6 crash of a C-123 aircraft on the Khe Sanh airstrip, 248 defenders were lost in the action the Marine Corps had designated as Operation Scotland. While it was impossible to gain accurate numbers, intelligence estimates placed NVA losses in the same period in and around Khe Sanh at ten thousand to fifteen thousand killed.[5]

The major siege at Khe Sanh, recorded as Operation Scotland and chronicled by the military and press as lasting seventy-seven days, did not really end after eleven weeks. Followed almost concurrently by Operations Pegasus and Scotland II, fighting continued for several more months with major Army and Marine Corps units involved. As surviving NVA units withdrew piecemeal back into their sanctuaries in Laos, action in and around Khe Sanh eventually dissipated into incongruous calm, almost as if both sides had finally lost interest.

The tremendous ground and air effort had cost the NVA dearly and yet, even with round-the-clock B-52 strikes, American forces had been unable to destroy the artillery positions carved into the caves of the Co Roc Mountains west of the combat base, just barely inside the Laotian border. Debate would continue indefinitely and inconclusively as to whether the Khe Sanh battles had been an elaborate strategic ruse by the enemy to focus attention away from the Tet attacks, or an honest effort to spring a second Dien Bien Phu-type victory against the Americans, or both.

Except for the fighting at Khe Sanh and Hue, the massive Tet Offensive was largely spent and defeated within two weeks. South Vietnamese civilian, ARVN, and American military casualties soared to levels not yet experienced in this war, but with Communist losses estimated to be forty-five thousand to fifty thousand men killed and thousands taken prisoner, American military and ARVN political and military leadership were calling these series of actions a major allied victory.

Fighting across the rural and jungle landscape of South Vietnam continued. While achieving a measure of surprise, Communist forces failed miserably in their objective to encourage southerners to rise up, *en masse*, against the Americans and their lackeys. Likewise, ARVN forces generally held their ground and, along with massive U.S. response and support, decimated the now exposed in every location local Viet Cong infrastructure. In addition to enemy losses, Communist perfidy and treachery observed and experienced for the first time by so many in the south was catalyst for a huge surge in the number of men now volunteering to serve their country. The TQLC would benefit greatly from this the South Vietnamese psychological equivalent of Pearl Harbor.

Body counts aside, the sheer brutality of the Tet Offensive did not play well on the nightly news viewed in American living rooms. While General Westmoreland may have wanted more troops and a follow-up counterstrike into Laos or southern North Vietnam to deliver the *coup de grace*, which was turned down, the

Communist offensive did achieve a major public relations *coup* with the American public well beyond what a militarily defeated Vo Nguyen Giap could have possibly dreamed.

THE CRIMSON PIRATE

By the time the Soi Bien's First Company had been given the assignment to help defend the Binh Loi Bridge, Le Ba Binh had served as a Marine for nearly six years and had more combat experience than he cared to think about. He and his men knew how to patrol, how to establish ambushes, how to sweep through jungle, rice paddies, villages, and, more recently, urban terrain. They could execute amphibious landings and helicopter assaults as seasoned professionals. There were few things that they had not yet done.

Saigon and its surrounding area was ringed by rivers, canals, and estuaries. There were dozens of bridges, all critical to the orderly flow of routine traffic and commerce. The loss of any one of them, for the most part, would have been an inconvenience to the city and nation, but not a body blow. In most places, for most purposes, if a bridge was destroyed, an alternate route could be found.

The Binh Loi Bridge was a structure that would likely draw attraction with the enemy focused on attacking and destroying targets of strategic value. As a key railroad bridge—for the train that still ran between Saigon and Hue—its defense was critical both logistically and psychologically. Spanning the meandering Dong Nai River, which ultimately joined with the Saigon River, it was barely five kilometers east of the runways at Tan Son Nhut. Binh's parents' home in Tan Dinh was well within mortar range, to the southwest of where he now operated.

Originally designed by the French and built with Vietnamese labor, the bridge was greater than three hundred meters in length not including the approaches. Built to support the narrower than American gauge track, there was also room for what was the equivalent of one lane of traffic used mostly by civilians on foot or bicycle, but more and more by light vehicles as well. Its proper defense, because of sheer size and the slight bend of the river, required the deployment of three of Third Battalion's rifle companies, with a fourth company always held in reserve.

Senior and mid-level officers of the ARVN and TQLC believed, by this late in the Tet Offensive, that the enemy no longer possessed the local manpower to stage any sort of conventional attack on the bridge. The perceived threat was from terrorists and sappers who might sneakily attempt to place demolitions in hopes of closing this critical avenue of commerce.

For Le Ba Binh it would be ironic that between his nearly two thousand days of combat and personal leadership experience, and all the fancy training he had received at Quantico, the ideas that ended up saving the Binh Loi Bridge from destruction came not from a military manual or lecture but were borrowed from the laws of physics he saw loosely applied in a barely third-rate, hardly-remembered Burt Lancaster movie produced in the early 1950s.

In the lead-up to the Tet Offensive, and prior to moving over to defend the Binh Loi Bridge, the Marines of Third Battalion had seen more than their fair share of combat action. Among their most publicized exploits was the joint effort undertaken in July of 1967 in the Mekong Delta with the TQLC's Fourth Battalion—known to all as the *"Kinh-Ngu"*—which translated roughly as "Killer Fish"—and the U.S. Army's Ninth Infantry Division. Officially designated as Operation Coronado II, Vietnamese and American troops battled for several days against significant Communist opposition.

During the prosecution of the battle, the senior American, Lieutenant General Fred Weyand, USA, flew in to advise the commanders of both VNMC battalions to pull back from close contact with the enemy so that U.S. airpower might be more effectively employed. The universal Marine response was that to break such contact might allow the enemy to escape. The two battalion commanders instead ordered their men to directly assault VC positions. Enemy killed in this particular engagement totaled 145.[6]

These guys were different than most ARVN units—they could fight. In fact, they were eager to fight. These guys would never back down from a fight. The martial spirit and capable leadership of the Tuy Quan Luc Chien was at last becoming known to Americans outside of the small group of U.S. Marine

Corps officers who had been rotating through as advisors with them for years.

Prior to Tet, the entire Soi Bien, minus the few men who had actually been granted holiday leave, was deployed to Vinh Loc. Vinh Loc was a nondescript flat, open, and relatively under-populated village area seven kilometers directly west and slightly south of Tan Son Nhut. Due to its level topography, it was an ideal spot from which to fire rockets and mortar rounds into the airfield. The Viet Cong had developed a nasty habit of occasionally sneaking into the area to get off a few rounds and disrupt flight operations. Folks higher up the TQLC's chain of command had decided to routinely rotate a battalion, if one was currently local and in a semi-stand down mode, out to Vinh Loc whenever one was available. In late January 1968 the Soi Bien just happened to be around to take the mission.

Familiar with the terrain, the battalion commander carefully positioned his four companies across a broad landscape of several square kilometers to maximize his presence and his unit's organic firepower. In doing this the intent was to discourage the VC from attempting anything, at least while Third Battalion was on the job. All of Third Battalion's rifle companies were in place in and around Vinh Loc by the evening of January 30, 1968, as they too awaited the birth of the Year of the Monkey.

When the world, including and adjacent to Saigon, erupted into pandemonium in the early morning hours of January 31, Third Battalion Marines were firmly in control of Vinh Loc. Five kilometers from the closest combat, all of the men were awake and braced for action well before sunrise. Vinh Loc itself was oddly quiet. Rather than attempt to launch mortars from its environs, the VC had attacked, in force, directly into Tan Son Nhut—and dozens of other places apparently at the same time.

Quality news and information at the individual grunt level in the early hours of the first day of this new action was hard to come by. At the battalion commander's tiny headquarters area radio operators monitored frantic transmissions of other units in contact. What was heard initially did not reassure or paint a picture of confidence. The natural concern for the officers and men was for their families, most of them either in Saigon or living at the nearby

TQLC base in Thu Duc. Reasonable men might have attempted to bolt, to get home and help out, especially since Thu Duc was not that far away. There was, however, no leadership challenge. They were Marines. They stuck to their assigned mission—to guard Vinh Loc—but hungered to move into the attack and deliver some payback to their now massed and brazen foe.

In the first twenty-four hours of the Tet Offensive the men of the Soi Bien essentially sat and waited, the action seeming to pass them by. Receiving only a few randomly fired mortar rounds into their area, which caused no casualties, the battalion was finally relieved of its duties to defend Vinh Loc when a company of U.S. Army M-48 tanks was sent to take over their positions.

From Vinh Loc they were immediately dispatched into downtown Saigon where each of the four rifle companies paired with local forces and elements of the national police now operating aggressively in what were the Vietnamese equivalent of police precincts.

Binh and his First Company were assigned to work in Quan 1, in south-central Saigon, not three kilometers from his parents' home. Local forces had a better sense for the urban situation so the Marines were used mostly to block or seal off areas while the police went into homes and buildings to flush out the enemy.

Initially taken by surprise, the local forces were quickly able to regain the combat initiative. It was relatively easy to identify the bad guys. With skin color just a shade lighter than the southern brothers they came to liberate, the misplaced northerners also often donned clothing that was different enough to mark them as targets. Many of the VC wore adequate disguises but then had on things like distinctive scarves which immediately gave them away. Running up and down the streets carrying AK-47s was also a sure sign that the person in question was a worthy target. In some cases, if it had not been combat, it might have been funny; so many of the VC flailing about as if each one was festooned with a very large "Shoot Me" sign. The local forces and men of the Soi Bien killed these red devils with great enthusiasm.

Along with the apparent Viet Cong lack of Saigon fashion consciousness, defending forces were also aided by the local ability to close off virtually every alleyway and narrow lane that led into or out of every tiny neighborhood in the city. Fifteen years earlier, Binh, his brother An, and all their young pals had defended their territory in games of war by denying access through the very gates that were now locked tight and used to keep real intruders from entering. Most regular civilians remained indoors and locked down from the outside violence that touched so many areas. By their very presence on city streets and avenues, especially during periods of curfew, Viet Cong terrorists were essentially forced, with nowhere to seek shelter, into the kill zones of angry, vengeful Saigon police, ARVN soldiers, and Marines.

In addition to the locking down of entire neighborhoods, thousands of Saigon homes and small business locations also sealed and boarded up tight from easy outside intrusion were made secure by the quick thinking and decision making of General Loan. By Loan's liberally distributing great quantities of ammunition and small arms to regular civilians within days of the initial terror attacks, the VC became reluctant to attempt home or business break-ins as a means to escape aggressively pursuing police and ARVN military forces. This newly armed citizenry of Saigon, by itself an incipient force to be reckoned with, made a difference in the defense of the city. The government's decision, born of necessity, to entrust its citizens with their own protection—an experiment not likely to have been allowed in the north—proved a wise one. The resurgent sense of self-reliance that came from that one move would go a long way in ultimately re-establishing calm and order.

Throughout the period of urban fighting, Binh dared not risk a personal visit even though he was within walking distance of his parents' home. While a high percentage of the attackers and terrorists were from up north and easily identified, it was also widely known that there were local spies and traitors who assisted the enemy. If someone was able to inform the Communists that Binh was a captain in the TQLC and see him visiting with his parents, his family might well have been targeted by the VC who thought nothing of terrorizing civilians, especially those viewed as actively opposed to the revolution. Binh would have to wait a few weeks before he could physically return home. In the meantime he would communicate with his folks through intermediaries.

During a period of several days in Quan 1 and across Saigon, local forces, the national police, and RVN military units continued to take back areas initially seized by the enemy and root out remaining pockets of resistance. At first week's end, the city was secure enough from the terror threat to post Third Battalion to a more strategic role in the defense of the Binh Loi Bridge.

Perhaps it was because the dozens and dozens of motion pictures he had seen in the crowded theatres in and around Tan Dinh had been so completely outside of what was reality in Vietnam that a tender-hearted Le Ba Binh would remember, in uncanny detail, the plots and story lines of the great and not-so-great movies he had enjoyed watching in what now seemed a lifetime ago.

Each of the Third Battalion's rifle companies would, to stay sharp, rotate the areas assigned to them as they guarded the Binh Loi Bridge. One company would take up position on and immediately adjacent to the bridge. A second company would take up position on the Saigon side of the river and a third company would be responsible for the farther side. There would be a fourth rifle company held, by the battalion commander, in reserve in the event that one of the other three companies needed to be reinforced or there was some unrelated situation to respond to. The threat was very real and all of the Marines braced for action.

Dai Uy Binh took his job seriously. Every day, several times a day, he personally walked the terrain in his company's sector of responsibility. He knew the surrounding landscape; the peculiarities of the shoreline in his sector, the minor bend of the river, understood how the water flowed and where it eddied. What ground he did not personally tour, he covered with extensive visual observation. He and the men of First Company were always watching, on guard for some hint of how the enemy might attempt to destroy the bridge.

Like a detective viewing a crime scene for clues, Binh looked for the obvious and the not so obvious, for changes in patterns that might signal something was amiss. He respected the cunning of his foe and knew the VC was capable of using limited resources to initiate major attacks. As the breadth and sophistication of their Tet

Offensive had demonstrated, and their willingness to egregiously violate the sanctity of the Tet tradition had proven, there was nothing the red devils would not do.

A few hundred meters east and downstream of the bridge, of the countless things to observe, Binh had noted for two days two barrels sitting on a dock. On the third day as he placed his binoculars to his eyes for the first look of the morning, he noticed everything just as it had been the evening before, except that the barrels on display were gone.

For no apparent reason he recalled a scene from the old Burt Lancaster movie *The Crimson Pirate* where, in comedic fashion, Lancaster and two sidekicks had used the trapped air in a submerged and inverted rowboat to escape from a bad situation undetected. If the turned-over rowboat had held enough oxygen for the movie's heroes to make good their underwater getaway, Binh wondered if his local enemies might have used the same idea with the now missing barrels. Could the VC have placed them up against the bridge structure beneath the waterline and used the same principle to plant explosives?

The disappearance of those barrels troubled the young captain enough for him to order his men to seek out and borrow a generator from a local merchant. Within an hour Marines of First Company had returned with the largest gas-powered electric generator they could find. Within another hour they had rigged the generator to send an electric charge into the slow-flowing waters immediately beneath the Binh Loi Bridge near its columns. Binh's men fired up the generator in an irregular pattern every so many minutes as a defense measure against underwater demolition attempts. Some of his Marines thought this was absolutely crazy. *What was Dai Uy Binh up to now?*

It worked. Early the next morning the very dead bodies of two Viet Cong combat swimmers, along with quantities of explosives, were discovered by Third Battalion Marines from a different company several hundred meters down river in the tall weeds. Their bodies displayed no bullet holes, no puncture wounds, nothing. The two had obviously drowned, drowned while trying to blow up the Binh Loi Bridge. Later in the day some of Third Battalion's own combat swimmers dove beneath the bridge's columns and found drums similar to those Binh had observed as missing attached below the water line just as he thought they might be.

In the middle of all the carnage and craziness Binh had to laugh. His Marines could only be amazed. In Le Ba Binh's own real-life movie, *sans* Burt Lancaster, he had himself just outfoxed and outfought these real-life Crimson Pirates. At least this time. At least in this scene. *Thank you, Burt Lancaster. Thank you, Hollywood.*

CHAPTER ELEVEN

Hearts and Minds At Home

The Basic Artillery Officers' course that George Philip had been a part of graduated from Ft. Sill in early March 1968. By the time of graduation, he had learned of more friends killed in Vietnam; one of them an infantry lieutenant he had recently spent a portion of his Christmas leave with at Disneyland. That particular friend was killed within one week of arriving in country.

Beginning now to believe in his own mortality and realizing that there would probably be no shortage of targets to plot no matter when he arrived in I Corps, Second Lieutenant George Philip took full advantage of the one-month leave granted to all service members before heading overseas. The parting sage but almost ordinary-seeming counsel of his stepfather would turn out to be brilliantly insightful: "Keep your head and ass down, son."

The months of February, March, and April had witnessed an ever-increasing tempo of major, major events, mostly but not all related to issues surrounding the war in Vietnam. The continued fighting in Southeast Asia shared time on the nightly news broadcasts and front pages of all the newspapers with stories of swelling racial tensions in America's cities and increasing public dissatisfaction with the war in general, especially on the nation's college campuses. The political landscape was undergoing radical change.

The massive casualties inflicted on the Viet Cong and to its infrastructure in particular along with the North Vietnamese assuaged few who focused on the record number of Americans killed and wounded in February. If this was victory, it was a Pyrrhic one at best. On the last day of the month Robert Strange McNamara resigned as secretary of defense.

Given more political weight and gravity than he might have deserved, Walter Cronkite's nightly pronouncements about the war daily grew darker. Advertised as the most trusted man in America, his broadcast on February 27 included observations from a recent trip to Vietnam and his own prediction that it seemed "more certain than ever that the bloody experience of Vietnam is to end in a stalemate."[1] His assessment of action at Khe Sanh was fortunately not played live for the Marines currently engaged there: "Another standoff may be coming in the big battle expected south of the Demilitarized Zone. Khe Sanh could well fall with terrible loss of American lives, prestige, and morale and this is a tragedy of our stubbornness there." President Johnson was alleged to have been deeply disturbed by the newsman's remarks and confessed to his advisors that, "If I've lost Cronkite, I've lost the country."

Meanwhile, the *Pueblo* incident remained unresolved with her crew suffering continued torture and abuse, and American ability to respond appearing weak and *effete*. On March 7, a Soviet Golf class missile submarine, the *K-129*, mysteriously exploded and sank in ten thousand feet of water approximately four hundred miles north of Pearl Harbor. Kept secret from the American public, even the Soviets were unaware that U.S. anti-submarine resources had tracked the *K-129*; the issues surrounding the boat's loss only complicated the morass of Soviet-American relations. At the same time tensions between the Chinese and Soviets were increasing without any apparent American ability to extract battlefield gain in Vietnam or in the court of international public opinion.

Effective use of spies and controlled assets in the foreign media by the KGB allowed misinformation and disinformation to cause expanding damage to American prestige. One such example included a Soviet-inspired fabrication of a letter from the U.S. Office of Naval Research "revealing the existence of (in reality non-existent) American bacteriological weapons in Vietnam and Thailand."[2] Originally published in the *Bombay Free Press Journal* and later reported in the *London Times* on March 7, it was happily and widely accepted as fact by America's enemies and those opposed to the war.

On the American political home front the situation was becoming particularly acute for Lyndon Johnson. With the first presidential primary in New Hampshire, LBJ barely eked out a victory against the strongly anti-war candidate Eugene McCarthy on March 16. As the incumbent Democrat things only went downhill when Senator Robert Kennedy of New York, the charismatic younger brother of John Kennedy, announced his entry into the race later the same day.

On March 25, the results of a recent Harris Poll showed that in the last six weeks "basic" support for the war among Americans went from 74 percent to 54 percent. A whopping 60 percent of those polled believed that the Tet Offensive was a defeat for U.S. objectives in Southeast Asia.[3]

From the very beginning of major American involvement, from the time of the first retaliatory air strikes against North Vietnam in late 1964, the decisions of when, where, and how much to bomb various targets inside the Democratic Republic of Vietnam were meant by President Johnson and his close *coterie* of advisors to send esoteric but discernible messages to Ho Chi Minh and his close *coterie* of advisors. On the evening of March 31 the president addressed the nation in a bold speech that ended with a shock. Making his most publicly aggressive call for some form of peace in Southeast Asia, he called for a unilateral halt to all bombing above the 20th Parallel, an area that included about 90 percent of North Vietnam. The long speech ended with his removing himself from the presidential race, ostensibly so that he could focus his energies solely on pursuing the peace.

Whatever the interpretation of a halt in bombing this time meant, the Communists never dwelt on the falsely chivalrous notions of good faith the *naïve* Americans seemed wedded to. Publicly announced bombing halts simply gave the Communists opportunities to redeploy scarce resources to some other point where they might be utilized to help win the war.

What came as a shock to the nation and the world in the March 31 presidential address mattered little to George Philip. He was not a fan of the way LBJ had been prosecuting the war, and whether the president would seek re-election or not had little immediate impact on the things George was about to participate in.

Three days prior to his scheduled departure for Vietnam, on April 4, a sniper shot and killed civil rights leader Martin Luther

King in Memphis, Tennessee. Within hours rioting had spread across the country and within a few days at least sixty American cities were enveloped by violence and bedlam. The nation's capitol was among the cities hardest hit.

While watching the television news and waiting at Travis AFB in the outbound passenger lounge for the flight that would take him to Okinawa so that he might be processed into Vietnam, George Philip, along with hundreds of other Marines and sailors also headed to The Rock, watched in horror as the newscasts rolled film after film, in city after city, of the violence.* Not lost on him was the irony that here he was preparing to go off to war and older sister Snow, currently a graduate student at George Washington University in DC, was herself now living in a combat zone. Able to speak prior to his departure, she assured him that the National Guard had the situation under control and not to worry about her. For Second Lieutenant George Philip USMC, it was a very strange way to go. This was certainly not his father's war.

There was absolutely no letup in the strangeness. Time spent in and around the honkytonks and bars of Lawton (the small town adjacent to Ft. Sill in Oklahoma) while a student at Ft. Sill was small cultural preparation for what Second Lieutenant George Philip would experience during the four-day period in early April between his arrival on Okinawa, the processing for further shipment to Vietnam, and actually finally flying south into Danang.

If Lawton or Tijuana were, to George Philip, the Wild West, Okinawa was Dodge City times twenty. If the young officer had been forced to write scripture for a new Old Testament, the action outside of every Marine camp and air force base on the tiny island would have been chronicled as a modern-day Sodom and Gomorrah. If America's grandmothers, mothers, wives, girlfriends, aunts, and great aunts only knew what went on...

Taken from the Japanese at massive cost in the final land battle of World War II, in 1968 Okinawa was still under American control and served as a Cold War fortress in the western Pacific.

---

* The island of Okinawa, once World War II concluded, became an important forward U.S. base in the western Pacific, especially for the Air Force and Marine Corps. To those who passed through, the island became known as "the Rock."

The Marine Corps and Air Force in particular had significant installations spread across the island. With all the infrastructure and support facilities developed and in place for the Third Marine Division located there, it was a logical place from which to feed men into, or retrieve them back from, Southeast Asia. As such, Okinawa was awash in virile young men, thousands and thousands of virile young men with raging hormones and emotions, coming and going, all mixed together; men on the way to war convinced they were about to die or at least for a very long period not be able to partake of all the delights that were now available in great quantities at low prices at all hours, and men on the way home who had recently survived long hellish periods without any of the delights that were now available in great quantities at low prices at all hours.

Okinawa was at once a nightmare and a fantasy. It was raucous and evil. Okinawa must have been the Japanese word for "debauchery." Okinawa was a commander's conundrum. If a man on the way over to Vietnam broke the rules and stayed out late or got into a drunken brawl, what could they do to him? Send him *home*? That hundreds of Marines were not killed in bar fights and all the other goings on that took place was no small tribute to plain good luck and superior small unit leadership.

Having stretched what probably could have been done in one or two days into four, but not to the disappointment of most of the men having to endure their ninety-six-hour interlude on The Rock, from there it was onto the combat zone. If a man was not yet sobered up by the time he boarded the flight south, those few hours left gave him opportunity to ponder what was about to take place.

In Vietnam the unofficial measure of a man's value to his unit depended greatly on his time in country. Men new to the fighting, regardless of rank, were viewed with suspicion as untested, unproven, and probably dangerous. Terms like "Cherry," "Boot," "F---ing New Guy," or "FNG" for short, were titles no one wanted to be known by, at least not for very long.

The Marine Corps bureaucracy that processed Second Lieutenant George Philip from his initial in country point of entry all the way out to the tip of the spear at whatever godforsaken location Leathernecks were engaging the enemy and were in need of the skills a new artillery officer might bring, or any other combat-trained man for that matter, was about as efficient and effective as it could be after three years of continuous hard combat. For George Philip that meant a few days of paperwork and acclimatization right there in the rear in Danang. Taking care of various administrative odds and ends and being issued the appropriate uniforms and all that allowed for time to get used to the heat and humidity of Vietnam. Fully aware that wherever he went his rank and the newness of his uniforms would betray his "cherry" status, there was little he could do.

From Danang the small group of artillery lieutenants George had arrived with, on their own, hitched a short ride on a C-130 north to Dong Ha where they were further processed, drew their pistols, (officers were issued the venerable .45 pistol and were not expected to act as riflemen) flak jackets, and other equipment for the bush. From there they all got on a truck that was headed out Route 9 east to Camp Carroll and the 12th Marines—the artillery regiment that supported the Third Marine Division. It was Camp Carroll's 175 mm guns that had fired tens of thousands of rounds in defense of the base at Khe Sanh, and were still mostly oriented in that direction.

The major in admin to whom they reported at the 12th Marines would determine exactly how the great needs of the Marine Corps would be best served in assigning the recently arrived lieutenants. Taking hold of each man's individual record book, the still familial smallness of the Corps was again made evident. Scanning George's personal information and the sheet entitled "Notification of Next of Kin," the major looked up in minor surprise: "You Will Helmer's boy?"

"Yessir."

A few pleasantries were exchanged. That was it. A moment later he declared: "Lieutenant Philip, I see by your personal data that you are single. You're going to Khe Sanh."

As if being single or married mattered at all, George Philip dutifully responded: "Yessir."

The aerial view during George Philip's helicopter ride into Khe Sanh Combat Base seemed a combination of Dante's *Inferno* and *All Quiet on the Western Front*. The military population of Khe Sanh itself had been drastically reduced by the time of his assignment there. From his own vantage point all that he could see were a few grunt companies, his artillery battery, and the cats and dogs of support units remaining to help close the place down.

From the air he could see it all: the random shell craters everywhere scarring the earth, the already moldering bunkers and disintegrating layers of sand bags, the multiple strings of concertina wire on the perimeter now highlighted by snagged, wind-blown litter, the meticulously engineered approach trenches dug by the NVA as they had steadily come closer to the Marine perimeter almost until the end of the siege, the burned out hulk of the one C-123 the world had seen aflame a thousand times on the nightly news sitting just off the airstrip, the endless quantities of spent shell casings strewn about the place, and all the other countless signs of recent activity. Except for the faraway green of the jungle and mountains, he thought he was looking at a black and white newsreel of hell or the dark side of the moon.

Everywhere the war's debris lay exposed. Prominent and ubiquitous were the tiny parachutes and spent canisters from the many thousands of illumination flares that had been fired by artillery or dropped by U.S. aircraft during the long siege. Their miniature canopies dotted the landscape and many were continually twisting and turning as if trying to break free of Khe Sanh's hold in the occasional breeze that swept the area.

The broad hilltop that was the Khe Sanh Combat Base that he had seen so many news clips and photos of, had heard and read so much about, was now like an abandoned gold claim, a ghost town in which the miners had lost interest and moved on to more promising diggings. How odd it all looked as the CH-46 Sea Knight helicopter, with Second Lieutenant George Philip as its only passenger, made the rapid descent into an area that only weeks before had been the primary focus of world media attention.

The battle for Khe Sanh had officially ended about a week prior to George's arrival. As silly as it would later seem to him, and among the many things he was now pondering as he was about to finally make his entrance into the war, was that he had somehow missed out on the action again by getting there too late.

Alpha Battery, First Battalion 13th Marines—a unit of the 13th Marine Regiment (also artillery) and known to all as "Alpha 1/13"—was under the operational control of the 12th Marines. Alpha 1/13 was the last arty unit still at Khe Sanh Combat Base and was in need of a new lieutenant.

The CH-46 that deposited George Philip into the landing zone near Alpha 1/13's position sat down only long enough for its passenger to run down the already depressed and extended aft ramp with all his gear. The crew chief was actually in the process of retracting the ramp even before George Philip had stepped onto *terra firma,* and before he could clear the tail rotor wash had told the pilots to get the hell out of there. In an instant the helo, which closely resembled a giant, metallic grasshopper that could have been part of a low-budget 1950s B-movie with nuclear holocaust, large-breasted women, and monster-sized insects, was out of the zone and jinking away from Khe Sanh.

Alone in the LZ, Second Lieutenant Philip noticed the strange quiet, except for the quickly receding sound of the outbound helicopter and the hint of a minor breeze evidenced by the gentle, random flapping of the tiny parachutes still attached to the spent illumination rounds and stuck in the barbed wire cluttering the landscape.

The solitude was quickly broken. In a moment it was evident that his arrival had been expected when a young lance corporal named Brown ran up to the zone. A well-muscled black Marine, Lance Corporal Brown was bare-chested except for his buttoned-up flak vest. "Welcome to Khe Sanh, Lieutenant. Follow me, sir." Lance Corporal Brown, obviously senior in combat experience to this new officer counseled: "Sir, if you hear a rumblin' sound, it's Gook rockets. Hit the deck just like me, or if we're near our bunkers, get into one."

On the several hundred meter trek from the LZ to A 1/13's main bunker there were no Gook rocket attacks. Alpha Battery's commanding officer was currently down in Dong Ha. The XO was left in charge but for all intents and purposes, especially since they had not been firing any missions recently, the routine running of the battery was in the capable hands of its senior enlisted Marine, First

Sergeant Bauerman. After Lance Corporal Brown, First Sergeant Bauerman was the second man Lieutenant Philip met at his new unit.

First Sergeant Bauerman was the kind of Marine new lieutenants at TBS had been lectured about. They were the senior SNCOs; the backbone, skeleton, and nervous system of Mother Corps; the corporate knowledge, the unofficial official deliverers of Old Breed justice. Feared and revered, proud and usually profane, they were the lubricant that kept the Marine Corps a well-oiled machine, maintaining sacred tradition and high standards.

At this time in USMC history it was not at all uncommon for these Old Corps warriors to be three-war veterans. First Sergeant Bauerman fit the mold perfectly. A private at Iwo Jima with additional combat service in Korea, he was close to concluding his career by the time he was at Khe Sanh. During the in-between years of tenuous peace he had done and seen everything else — "in every clime and place" — there possibly was to do.

George Philip showed great deference to First Sergeant Bauerman, even though he had literally grown up in the Corps, even though one of his boyhood chums was Chesty Puller's son, even though his own stepfather and all of the men Colonel Helmer was close to had served at all the places any person remotely familiar with American military history might consider significant.

Even though he was a military brat and so many things about the Corps that were new to those young officers who had grown up in civilian communities were second nature to him, George Philip held this man in high regard. First Sergeant Bauerman, and Marines like him, were worshipped — especially by the young enlisted Marines, warts and all, quite simply because they were worthy of being worshipped.

George was five months shy of his twenty-fourth birthday when he stepped foot on the LZ at Khe Sanh. To Second Lieutenant Philip his new first sergeant seemed old and sage-like, discerning and wise. By the time he had turned twenty-four, First Sergeant Bauerman was probably already a veteran of his second war. Now probably in his early forties, he was a veritable dinosaur, or so it seemed to the young Marine officer just starting out.

George could not remember ever learning or hearing First Sergeant Bauerman's Christian name. As the senior enlisted man in the battery he had no peer equals. To the skipper he worked for, to the lieutenants it was his job to tolerate and nurture, to the troops he was both big brother and hammer to, his first name really was "First Sergeant." That was just the way it was, Corps wide, in every single unit of battery and company size.

In the week or so after Lieutenant Philip's assignment to Alpha 1/13 at Khe Sanh, the battery was tasked with very few fire missions. In late April the entire battery, along with several infantry companies and some combat engineers, became part of a fairly large convoy out. It was George's impression at the time that Khe Sanh Combat Base was being abandoned. He had personally watched the engineers demo and bulldoze anything of value so that if the NVA returned there would be little they could salvage.

The convoy traveled Route 9 from Khe Sanh east all the way to Dong Ha, past Ca Lu—recently built up by army engineers and known to many now as "LZ Stud," the Rockpile, Camp Carroll, and Cam Lo—locations where as recently as weeks ago ambush and enemy contact for every single vehicle transiting the road was as certain as the I Corps morning mist. The NVA, as intelligence had surmised, maybe really had largely skulked back into Laos to regroup and reprovision because the entire movement was conducted without incident. For the time being Route 9 was just another crummy, winding, bumpy road in the middle of nowhere that connected a few disparate dots.

At Dong Ha George was finally detailed to the duty he had actively sought. Assigned as the artillery forward observer (FO) to Bravo Company, First Battalion 26th Marines—B 1/26—he replaced the company's former FO who had been KIA several weeks earlier.

During the siege at Khe Sanh, B 1/26 had been one of the infantry companies that endured some of the most grueling combat. Often at the center of the action, they had both generously dished it out to the NVA, and suffered high casualties. By the time 1/26 had rotated out of Khe Sanh Combat Base, the surviving Marines in the various rifle companies were savvy, battle-hardened veterans.

CHAPTER TWELVE

Forward Observer
with Bravo 1/26

From *the beginning of the fighting* American forces were involved in during World War II, reliance on the material prowess of its civilian industries to turn out massive quantities of armaments significantly impacted their style of warfighting. The application of high-quality and precision firepower whenever it might replace extra manpower was liberally employed at every opportunity. The Marine Corps had been on the cutting edge in attempting to integrate and coordinate the various destructive assets available—naval gunfire, air power, and artillery—and direct the use of those resources down to as low a level as they could manage effectively.

All Marine Corps officers who attended TBS were schooled in the theory of integrating supporting arms. When new infantry platoon commanders showed up for combat duty in Vietnam they were expected to be able to call in and adjust fire from mortars and artillery, and have a working knowledge of close-air support.

By the time a man took command of a rifle company he was expected to have mastered the ability to call in and coordinate every destructive asset he had available to him. A skipper's dexterity to adroitly employ and manage these assets was among the two or three skills he could not fail his men in. The entire company's survival would often depend on them.

To be a good artillery FO, a young lieutenant had to do several things well and simultaneously. An astute FO needed to understand and get inside the thought processes of the commander he was working for. In terms of what a developing combat scenario or situation might present, the lieutenant needed to understand the commander's intent when formulating a plan or issuing an order.

He needed to be perceptive to the company commander's own style of combat leadership. He needed to thoroughly comprehend the mission—day or night—and consider various contingencies. He needed to have a keen sense for terrain, the lay of the land in which his unit would operate and maneuver, and how that would impact the employment of available fire support assets. He needed to be a skilled navigator and know, at all times, his unit's precise location so that when it was time to summon up critical support, the rounds landed on the bad guys and not on friendlies. He needed to stay two or three steps ahead of his skipper so that if the Marines were taken by surprise, friendly response would be rapid, accurate, and overwhelming.

When a company set up for the evening in a defensive position, the FO needed to establish a *de facto* steel curtain—called his "night defensive fires"—around the company's position in the event of an enemy assault.

Often it helped to preplan and register—to shoot at—targets in advance. When artillerymen back in the gun positions had the technical target data for specific locations beforehand, it was much easier to expeditiously get rounds on those targets when they were later requested. It was also much easier to shift aim to nearby targets when locations had already been registered before the action began.

In terms of managing people, an FO needed to ensure that his assigned radio operator was a skilled, competent communicator. A forward-thinking FO would also take the time to ensure that his radio operator knew as much about calling in fire support as was possible, in the event that if the FO got hit the radio operator could continue the mission. (On this count George was extremely lucky in that he inherited a radio operator who had served at Khe Sanh with the FO who was earlier killed. It was Lance Corporal Tom O'Grady who would ensure that his new FO was locked on and good to go. The two soon became as close as rank would allow, and an effective team.)

A good FO was a skilled technician in the science of artillery. The more competent he was at every facet of his destructive art, the less his commanding officer needed to worry once the fight was on.

By design, every Marine Corps rifle company that took to the field in Vietnam was supposed to have with it an artillery forward observer, a Ft. Sill-trained artillery forward observer. That was not always the case. By design also, every Marine Corps rifle company that took to the field in Vietnam was supposed to have as its commander a man completely dialed in and competent in every way. That was not always the case either.

Bravo Company, at Khe Sanh, had been led by Captain Ken Pipes. Similar to John Ripley, Kenny Pipes was the consummate warrior and was likewise utterly passionate in the loyalty he had for those he commanded. His Marines revered and adored him. Captain Pipes, under almost any conceivable circumstance, in war or peace, would have been an extremely tough leadership act to follow. He had already relinquished command of Bravo Company by the time George Philip reported aboard, although the legend of Kenny Pipes lived on through the stories told by the remaining troops and lieutenants.

The skipper who replaced Captain Pipes proved to George Philip that even the Marine Corps had in it leaders who did not walk on water. A former enlisted man, a mustang, he was certainly no Kenny Pipes.* Superfluous and critical remarks made while addressing the entire company or while talking with his men in smaller groups succeeded in alienating his Marines, mustang or not. Fortunately the small circle of remaining platoon commanders, all Pipes trained, were able to balance and make up for what was no longer available from the top. Bravo Company would carry on.

Second Lieutenant Philip actually joined Bravo Company at Thon My Thuy on the coast near the mouth of the Cua Viet River. The Army, Navy, and Marine Corps together had developed a LOTS (Logistics over the Shore) facility to process support being

---

* A "mustang" in the naval services is an officer with prior service as an enlisted man. Both the Navy and the Marine Corps draw a fair number of officers from their enlisted ranks. Gerry Turley and John Ripley were both mustangs.

further transshipped mostly by landing craft upriver to Dong Ha. With a name like Thon My Thuy it was not long before Vietnamese-language-challenged Americans came up with something easier to pronounce.

Lieutenant Colonel Charles Sunder was in command of the army's 159th Transportation Battalion, the primary unit initially running operations there. His men called themselves "Sunder's Wonders." "Wunder Beach" became the somewhat illogical, not-so-obvious result. It stuck.[1]

The NVA and VC did not hesitate to establish themselves in places where American interest was keenest. The strategic location coupled with the river and ocean traffic where the Cua Viet River joined the South China Sea made Wunder Beach a contested area. For the Marines of 1/26, pulling security duty at Wunder Beach, while not a cakewalk, was orders of magnitude less intense than the battle they had just left.

Bravo Company, currently assigned to duty in the Wunder Beach area, had been blessed with a group of lieutenants who, by simply surviving their duty at Khe Sanh, was in short order a crusty, combat-savvy bunch. George Philip was immediately made to feel at home by John "Matt" Dillon, Pete Weiss, and Charlie Sharples. All three of them were capable, professional, tactically proficient, aggressive Marine officers who also, at the appropriate times, had raucous senses of humor. Of the three "Matt" Dillon, just like the *Gunsmoke* character for whom he was nicknamed, really was the sheriff of the bunch, and whenever the skipper was away he would lead Bravo Company in a manner that their idol and mentor Captain Pipes would have been proud of.

The introduction to combat operations in B 1/26 was immediate. It helped that Lance Corporal O'Grady, his radio operator, already had significant action under his belt, and that the other lieutenants seemed to size George up favorably. Along with the quantity of technical training he had received, the simple admonition from his stepfather just prior to departure to, "Keep your head and ass down, Son" would be driven home very early on.

During the first week of duty with his new unit, while still operating within the Wunder Beach area, George and Lance

Corporal O'Grady were one afternoon perched atop an old French bunker, exposed to the world in the belief that there were no bad guys around. In an almost casual, peace-time mode they were registering targets like an FO was supposed to be doing, except that they were not being very tactical about it. Focused on a potential target a thousand meters to his front, Second Lieutenant Philip, without a shirt on, taking in a few rays while getting the job done, at first did not see the lone black-pajama-clad fellow who stepped from a distant tree line well outside of his peripheral view. Lance Corporal O'Grady just happened to be looking that way.

Fortunately, the lone VC was probably armed with something other than a high-powered sniper rifle. The enemy soldier quickly squeezed off a few shots before Lance Corporal O'Grady returned fire in his direction. Whether the bullets missed him by an inch or a few feet, George Philip felt the pressure change and a brush of displaced air as the rounds seemed to nearly crease his ear. Upset with himself for being so casual, and more importantly for knowing better, he was immediately grateful for this one pass, this first invaluable real-life combat lesson. Never again would he make this same mistake. "I get it, Dad. I get it," he said to himself. In a flash the VC vanished back into the thicket from which he had appeared, almost as if none of this had ever happened.

The school of combat reality was always in session, day and night, throughout a man's tour in Vietnam. A few days after the incident atop the old French bunker, still in the vicinity of Wunder Beach, Bravo Company was setting up in a night position. Just as he had been trained to do, and just as they did it for real in the bush in Vietnam, George Philip, Forward Observer, made up his list of pre-planned targets for the night. Like a good FO he called several of them in to the artillery battery that would support Bravo for this particular evening for registration. Target selection for night defensive fires, unlike so much of artillery which is literally almost rocket science, is plain old common sense. You figure where an enemy is most likely to stage an attack from, where he might cache his gear, etc., and then blow him up before he does the same to you, if you can. The identification of obvious and not so obvious targets was discussed in class and field work at Ft. Sill. There were no right or wrong answers in target selection in the planning of night defensive fires. After ensuring that one did not target innocent civilians, all that really mattered was that you kill bad guys and keep them from killing good guys.

As George and his radio operator set about planning their target list for the evening there was one obvious geographic feature they could not miss. A dirt road that stretched straight across a few thousand meters of open paddy land before dead-ending into a tree line was a perfect spot to locate mortars. Of the three or four targets they together identified, they even had the arty battery prep fire and zero in on the targets in daylight. All that was required now, if they really needed to hit those areas, was to call back to the folks controlling the guns on the radio and tell them to fire target number such-and-such. They were good to go.

Later that very evening, George saw something he thought he would never see, and after seeing it once was certain it would never happen again. Just as he was watching from his fighting hole in the dark, he saw the indistinguishable flashes followed a few seconds later by the whumping sounds of mortar rounds leaving a tube…right where he and Lance Corporal O'Grady had predicted. Right where they predicted…and had planned for.

Within seconds the FO was on the radio to the supporting battery with the request for the fire mission: "Fire mission…fire target Alpha Tango blah-blah-blah…" A perfect request for fire. George was near euphoric as he, like the school-trained FO he was, expected near immediate response and an opportunity to smoke a few bad guys. But this was Vietnam. And they were not out at Khe Sanh any longer. Wunder Beach was near populated areas. There were real civilians out there the U.S. did not want to kill.

Instead of acknowledging the request for fire and then notifying the FO that rounds were being fired, all he heard was: "Wait one, over…" "Wait one" turned into a lot longer than "one." In the meantime, during the "wait one," the FO was given his first dose of cold reality on rules of engagement in areas where civilians were in fairly close proximity or where political exigencies trumped the ability to engage targets of opportunity.

Informed by someone else that prior to firing the mission they would first need to get permission from the local hamlet chief, "Wait one" became a half hour. By the time the mission was finally approved to shoot, the enemy mortar team was, no doubt, long gone. As George would lament to Lance Corporal O'Grady: "Old Luke the Gook is probably already back in the rack with *mamasan*." In disgust he cancelled the fire mission. *Welcome aboard. Welcome to Vietnam. Keep your head and ass down, son…*

What sane men describe as normal, or horrible, or funny, translates into something very different when described within the confines of brutal combat. For the men who fought out in the bush of Vietnam, death and dismemberment, whether one's own or that of a friend, was always a close companion. The way in which each man chose to respond, or that his personal temperament allowed him to respond, to the war's horrors and situations of *macabre* humor was always a measure of a man's personal resilience and coping skills.

It was not a full week after the nighttime mortar in the tree line incident that Bravo Company was performing other missions in the *hinterlands*. Forced by terrain, as they often were, to move single file down a jungle trail, the company had halted briefly for a ten-minute water break, the common thing to do every hour. Lieutenant Philip's constitution had still not made the adjustment to his new diet of c-rations and marginal stream water, and he trudged along plagued with intermittent bouts of diarrhea.

Deep in Indian country, the men of Bravo Company dropped down for the too-short period of rest while keeping aware that security needed to be maintained. Near the front of the company column, George walked past the point man on the trail, silently letting him know where he was going and what he was about to do. From the trail he turned fifteen or so degrees into the jungle, walked ten meters and then dropped his trousers. Fumbling for the buttons, anxious to relieve himself, he had no sooner assumed the proper position for relief when he heard several distinctive voices that were definitely not Marines.

Able to see them briefly through the brush from his squatting position, George counted four NVA soldiers. They had to be a mortar team or something.

Instantly his diarrhea was temporarily cured. Drawing his .45 but not taking the time to pull up his pants from around his knees, he frantically duck-walked the short distance back to Bravo's position. His lily-white butt hanging out and down, calling out in an excited, strained whisper, just like Paul Revere only different, trying to be loud enough to be heard by the good guys but quiet enough not to be heard by the others, he alerted the point position: "Gooks! Gooks!"

Among the Marines near the point the word was quickly passed down the line. Just as George had rejoined them, and had gotten his pants up and buttoned, in pure American fashion, the Marines let loose with everything they had. The four NVA soldiers beat a path up the trail in hopes of fleeing what had to be thousands and thousands of M-16 rifle and M-60 machine gun rounds, and the four or five well-aimed pistol rounds Second Lieutenant Philip put down range.

Bravo Company, with all the rounds expended, did manage to kill one NVA for sure. His body was left by the others as they fled. Whether any of the other three had been hit was not determined. There were no blood trails.

Later that evening, with Bravo dug into its night defensive position, as the lieutenants informally huddled up for a briefing at the company command post, the conversation ultimately shifted to the one enemy KIA. Without ever looking at George but certain that he was listening, it was Matt Dillon who spoke to Lieutenants Weiss and Sharples with as straight a face as he could muster: "Hey, did you guys see that dead gook? He had three or four .45 holes in him sure as shit!" They collectively turned to face their new FO, their serious faces now contorted in muffled and restrained—because of where they presently were— gut laughs. He had been accepted into the fraternity now for sure.

Kidding and snippets of odd humor aside, there soon began for George Philip the period of ceaseless, interminable field operations without serious meaning, at least from his rapidly maturing combat and tactical perspective. While Bravo Company would be moved around to fight in different areas with different terrain, every day in the bush became, for every man there, just another opportunity to get killed or maimed. Enemy contact was not terribly common. When contact was made they rarely eyeballed the bad guys. It was the same war, different day; go out for two weeks, come back in for a few days, and then do it again. And again, unless they became part of some larger, "named" operation, in which case they might stay out even longer. No weekends off, no happy hour, no overtime. Through May, June, July, August, and into September it was simply one day after another of combat drudgery. Just like in Ripley's Raiders, the only day that marked the week was Sunday when the corpsmen passed out malaria pills.

Mail and mail call was a big, big deal. Younger sisters Jody and Betsy were faithful correspondents, keeping oldest brother George apprised of family issues and all the things that young teenage girls were interested in, along with admonishments to, in their sweet and innocent, teeny-bopper fashion, keep his head and ass down. In addition, they kept him fairly well supplied with chocolate chip cookies which, once they arrived, were shared and instantly consumed.

George's own letters home were sanitized and innocuous, never mentioning danger or death or combat. Will Helmer knew the drill. The others need not know. His sisters were too young, and he did not want to worry his mother who would have read the letters also, looking for any reason to worry.

CHAPTER THIRTEEN

My Lai

T*he massacre* of more than three hundred innocent civilians at the tiny village of My Lai, the worst such action perpetrated by an American Army unit since the wars against the Indians nearly one hundred years earlier, occurred on March 16, 1968. It happened in an area within the confines of I Corps a few weeks prior to George Philip's arrival. While it would not be made known to the American public until 1969, it would become the *cause célèbre* for all who opposed American involvement in the Vietnam War.

To the misinformed, and the intentionally uninformed, the term "My Lai" became a descriptive adjective, the perceived measure by which the military routinely did business or conducted operations. The massacre at My Lai was, in fact, the result of extremely poor leadership within certain units of the army's Americal Division and was an aberration, completely *anathema* to the way combat operations were being run.

The action at My Lai was more a page out of the Viet Cong playbook, a repeat—on a much smaller scale—of recent NVA conduct at Hue, or what would follow routinely in the Communist offensives of 1972 and 1975 that would make My Lai seem almost inconsequential in terms of sheer numbers and cold-blooded brutality.

The national and international news, even without the revelations of My Lai being made yet, was not at all encouraging from the American political perspective. Continued racial strife and anti-war protests at so many of the nation's college campuses diverted, diluted, and dissipated whatever national resolve there had earlier been to finish this war with some sort of traditional recognizable victory.

The mysterious sinking of the USS *Scorpion* (SSN-589)—a nuclear attack submarine—on May 22 was a major embarrassment for the Navy in general and to its elite Silent Service in particular. Following barely more than five years after the loss of the USS *Thresher* (SSN-593) and very closely on the heels of the capture of the USS *Pueblo*, the loss of the *Scorpion* was just one more event that chipped away at the public's faith in the quality of its military services.

At the very highest levels of government and military the sinking of the USS *Scorpion* had to be cause for major concern. Following only ten weeks after the loss of the Soviet *K-129*, something the American public was unaware of, there were questions as to whether *Scorpion* had been sunk by hostile action or suffered some as yet to be identified mechanical or systems failure. Could the Russians, under the mistaken impression that *K-129* had been attacked by a U.S. submarine or other anti-submarine forces, gone after *Scorpion* as retribution? It was a question that would not be publicly considered but had to have been pondered by the president and his advisors.

Even with the tremendous number of NVA and Viet Cong killed and captured during the Tet Offensive, Americans who had earlier believed stories their leaders had told about there being light at the end of the tunnel now saw it more and more as the proverbial oncoming train. The national willingness to continue investing blood and treasure *carte blanche* into Southeast Asia was waning. President Johnson's decision to turn down General Westmoreland's request for an additional two hundred thousand troops and his unwillingness to call up the reserves were signs of declining resolve that did not go unnoticed by the leadership in Hanoi, Peking, or Moscow.

The shooting of Robert Kennedy after winning the California Democratic presidential primary late on the evening of June 5 and his death early the next morning ended forever the relentless, nostalgic wish by many Americans, particularly those opposed to the war, to return to the seemingly magical days of his brother's presidency.

In late June Khe Sanh Combat Base was finally, officially closed and abandoned. On July 1, General Westmoreland turned over the duties as MACV to General Creighton Abrams. General Westmoreland went on to the top job in the army as Chief of Staff. With his departure from Southeast Asia, after four years in command, also—at least for the time being—went any serious plans for launching ground operations into North Vietnam itself, against Communist sanctuaries in Laos, or the formidable infrastructure of the Ho Chi Minh Trail system.

FEEDING THE BEAST

When Gerry Turley successfully concluded his first Vietnam tour—his eclectic tour as a regimental staff officer and then as the operations officer and executive officer for Third Battalion, Seventh Marines, when John Ripley turned over command of Lima Company, they were winning—at least Turley and Ripley, and all the Marines they had been partnered with—thought they were. By any reasonable measure their American minds and Western-influenced thought processes could conjure, they were winning. Over the days that became months many comrades had been killed. Many more had been grievously wounded. But in those same days and months, in mostly nameless battles, they had stood firm, sometimes bent but never buckled, and in every single engagement prevailed. Every single engagement. They had at least left for home knowing they were doing good, certain that the sacrifices had value, knowing that the tide was in their favor.

PRAGUE SPRING

The summer of 1968 would not be "the Summer of Love, Part Two."* By this stage in the war, with widespread race riots and creeping societal upheaval that seemed mostly tied to the

---

* The summer of 1967, dubbed "the Summer of Love," was most closely associated with hippies and the San Francisco scene and was immortalized by the Monterey Pop Festival of 1967 and songs such as Scott McKenzie's "San Francisco—Be Sure to Wear Some Flowers in Your Hair."

perceived rottenness of American foreign and domestic policy, it was difficult to remember that the United States was not the sole source of evil in the world. Missing from the front pages and television news were stories of real repression in real police states.

Underreported also were the incremental yet incessant, inevitable gains for freedom and free markets being made nearly everywhere in Asia except in Red China and North Korea. Nationalist China, Hong Kong, Singapore, South Korea, Indonesia, Malaysia, Thailand, the Philippines, and especially Japan; none were free of problems but all were showing signs of economic ascendancy and growth as countries free of Communism's yoke. Most of the population in Japan had already passed from the era of the "Three Sacred Treasures" (washing machine, refrigerator, and black & white television) and was progressing to that of the "Three Cs" (car, color television, and cooler—air conditioner).[1] The other smaller economies would attempt to follow close behind. Once exposed to the benefits of freedom and higher living standards, there was little chance of going back the other way.

At the same time and lost to most in the West was the growing enmity between North Vietnam's two major benefactors. By April of 1968 the Soviet Union had already begun to deploy what would eventually amount to a third of its ground combat forces against a similar number of Mao's legions along their four-thousand-mile contiguous border.[2] Unfortunately for Le Ba Binh, George Philip, and all their comrades similarly engaged, American politicians lacked in ability to tangibly exploit the rift between the two red behemoths.

For more than twenty years the freedom *genie* had been forcefully and routinely kept inside her bottle by Warsaw Pact forces—read USSR—in places like Hungary, Poland, and East Germany. Attempts to break out were always met with crushing, overwhelming police and military power. Now in the summer of 1968, college students in Czechoslovakia were similarly infected with the freedom bug that seemed to be passed to others in the population who also began to demand change. To crush the epidemic, Soviet medicine prescribed a massive dose of six hundred thousand troops and thousands of tanks—more men than the United States had at the same time, *or ever*, in Vietnam — to cure the patient.[3]

It took three weeks of Soviet-style medicine to administer the "cure" to the patient. Untold, undocumented thousands of mostly innocent, mostly unarmed — if they were armed at all, they were very lightly armed — Czech civilians were killed without a prying press to chronicle events. Similar to the murderous actions perpetrated by the NVA in Hue only six months earlier, there was likewise no uproar in Hollywood or demonstration against Soviet action on a single American college campus.

MEANWHILE, BACK AT THE WAR — SEPTEMBER 1968

Bravo Company and the rest of 1/26 continued to see action throughout I Corps, moving around in checkerboard fashion to wherever those higher up who made those decisions deemed their presence most critical. As before, their operations were without end. Unlike most of the troops who knew exactly how many days remained on their tours, George Philip had not yet begun the countdown to going home.

The type and intensity of combat experienced ranged from minor contact of fire teams to major engagements where the entire battalion might get involved. It was during those periods when George witnessed how, in most cases, everything really did seem to work together — combined arms — air and artillery (and naval gunfire if they were close to the coast) doing all they could to support the infantry, just as has been advertised at Basic School.

As much as Bravo Company was in the field, it was often the brief respite periods that became most memorable. With the constancy and drudgery of bush time, except for those instances of major contact or something bad happening to a close comrade, what became burned into a man's recollections were those small things, good things sometimes, that broke routine.

For reasons unknown to Second Lieutenant George Philip, and just like those days when they would be moved by the gods of operations from one place to another, there was a day when they had been working somewhere south of Danang and had been, without explanation, taken from the field by truck back to the "rear" in Danang.

It was always a shock to come in from the field; to be back among the living, the breathing, the Marines who did not go to the bush, the folks who got their mail every day, who got to move their bowels at sit-down facilities, who showered regularly, could shop at the PX or go out into town for a little companionship for hire, slept on cots and who, without fail, daily ate at least two hot meals with real fruit and bread and fresh milk. The bush Marines, the *real* Marines, called these men REMFs. REMFs (Rear Echelon Mother F---ers) were easy to spot. They had shiny boots and clean-pressed uniforms that were not faded or torn. REMFs were close-shaved and were heavier than their brothers in the bush who were denied all that milk and good chow. Real Marines at once both actively hated and secretly envied REMFs.

On the day that George and most of the other Bravo officers came in, their very first stop was some Danang mess facility for officers. Arriving like they had just come from a few weeks in the field—which they had; smelling of the bush and body odors that had become a part of their flesh and their uniforms, they stuck out like black folk at a Klan meeting, and were just about as welcome.

After going through the line and piling each of their plates with far more food than they could possibly consume, after drinking several glasses of cold, fresh, whole milk and "Bug Juice" while still in line, and then refilling the glasses before looking for a place, away from the REMFs, to sit, George Philip and company spied something special.[†]

Of the countless basic things missed by virile young men who spent weeks on end in dark jungles and fetid rice paddies all over

---

[†] Bug Juice—the name used to describe the flavored, Kool-Aid type drink often dispensed aboard ship, in mess halls, and even prepared for troops in the field, before technology allowed for the introduction of carbonated drinks. Bug Juice was basically sugar water with artificial coloring. Bug Juice was also a name used for mosquito repellant which was often carried in tiny plastic bottles held in place by the large rubber-band-like devices Marines and soldiers wore on their helmets.

Vietnam was the simple pleasure of looking at and speaking with a real American woman.

What was available to soldiers and Marines in line units in the way of female interaction in Vietnam, if available at all it was to REMFs mostly, was usually an impersonal business transaction with some old *mamasan* cleaning a hooch or doing laundry, or an intensely personal business transaction that included an opportunity to contract some virulent strain of social disease. The ability to interact with an American woman, or women; nurses, stewardesses, correspondents, whatever, was always a noteworthy experience because it rarely happened.

Just as George and the other Bravo Company officers had staked out their table, he looked up and was stunned to see three women. American women. The women were "Donut Dollies," probably in the employ of the USO, and they seemed to be moving towards where the Bravo Company officers were seated.

Carrying their plates, and following politely in trace, were three clean-shaven, starched, and pressed REMF lieutenants who had not yet observed George and crew. Giving the signal to his buddies to hold on, desist from eating, and take a look at the miracle about to occur, the Bravo officers, as one, straightened up, braced themselves for intelligent conversation, any conversation. Aware that their appearance and hygiene were far from *kosher*, they were counting on the overriding compassion of these latter-day Florence Nightingales. At this stage of their tours they would take female attention any way they could get it. Ann-Margret look-alikes the Donut Dollies were not, but significant bush time had a way of degrading a man's standards. Possessing all the necessary *accoutrements* and appendages, at least they were women.

The momentary anticipation was sublime. George Philip felt like a seventh-grade boy with a crush on a high school cheerleader—all in the space of a few seconds—until reality was rudely re-imposed by the REMF lieutenants who, once they observed the Bravo Company officers' presence, abruptly steered the Donut Dollies away and towards the more genteel section of the mess hall. What a letdown. Amongst themselves the Bravo officers resumed eating, instantly and collectively murmuring varying statements which all had as their root theme "…f---ing REMFs…"

Even though there was little discussion about the seniority of second lieutenants, by the time George was beginning his sixth month as an FO with B 1/26 he was a pretty seasoned Marine, at least by American standards. By virtue of his having survived this long, to the newer troops he was a sage. With many dozens of fire missions under his belt, there were few things that now really rattled his cage. He could order up a fair amount of death and destruction with precision in the wink of an eye. He had taken Colonel Helmer's advice, applied it, and now shared it with others.

In September 1968 George Philip, his friend Matt Dillon, and many others of the long-serving Bravo Company Marines were afflicted with jungle crud—some unknown nasty stuff that attacked the skin, especially in critical, sensitive areas. The only real cure was to get out of Vietnam to a more hospitable place, like home.

Even with the occasional gorging at places like the Danang officers' mess, George now weighed in at between 120–125 pounds, down from his earlier already lean weight of 150 pounds. George had the look of one of the chubbier folks coming out of Auschwitz or Buchenwald in mid-1945. Body painted yellow with some questionable lotion the corpsmen treated all skin problems with, if his mother could have seen how he looked she might have had a stroke.

TRANSITION BACK TO ALPHA BATTERY 1/13

At about midway through his thirteen-month tour, it was time for George to transition back to service with an artillery battery, as was the routine for all artillery lieutenants. That duty, while not easy, was nowhere near as rigorous or dangerous as the first half of his tour humping the trails and rice paddies with the grunts.

December of 1968 marked the forty-fifth month since Marines had come ashore in Vietnam and America's major combat effort in Southeast Asia had begun.

By the forty-fifth month of ground combat in the American Civil War, the Confederacy was teetering on the brink of collapse.

General William Tecumseh Sherman, the scourge of the South and a name still reviled a hundred years later below the Mason-Dixon Line, along with his troops was having his way in Georgia and would shortly move into the Carolinas, destroying everything in his path.

Forty-five months after the United States had declared war on Germany in April of 1917, the "War to End All Wars" had been over for more than two years. Americans were set to begin enjoying unparalleled prosperity and would be Jitterbugging and Charlestoning their way through the Roaring Twenties.

Forty-five months after the Japanese had attacked Pearl Harbor, the United States was preparing to deliver the atomic *coupe de grace* by dropping Fat Man on Hiroshima and Little Boy on Nagasaki. War-weary Americans were again looking forward to enjoying the peace—which would prove to be illusive and illusory—and spending all the money they had saved during the conflict on things that were soon to be manufactured by the nation's freed up wartime industrial capacity.

Forty-five months after Soviet-supplied T-34 tanks for the first time rolled through Seoul, the cease-fire agreement had been in effect for nine months. Forty-five months after the initiation of action there in northern Asia, Bill Haley and the Comets recorded "Rock Around the Clock."

As 1968 rolled to a close, even with NVA and VC dead stacked like cordwood, there was limited tangible evidence for Americans at home to show that the good guys had made much progress in what was now the bloodiest, costliest year of the conflict. From the Herculean effort throughout those twelve months, a look at the map revealed little that appeared to have changed for the better. There was still fighting all over the Republic of Vietnam. The nation was outwardly growing tired of its commitment that seemed only to be yielding a bitter harvest. If the NVA and remaining Viet Cong had lost the will to fight, it was not apparent at the level George Philip and his comrades operated.

LIFE GOES ON/BINH MEETS CAM/NOT HIS FATHER'S WAR

In the months following duty at the Binh Loi Bridge, Third Battalion and all of the other maneuver units of the TQLC continued to serve wherever those higher up the chain of command decided their services were most critically needed. As hectic as the pace of operations was, there was method and routine to their employment.

During the brief periods of refurbishment and reorganization when Third Battalion would rotate through Thu Duc, Dai Uy Binh was able to come home to his family and friends for quick visits. As before, he always arrived with the mandatory retinue of bodyguards and cowboys who, after the experience of the Tet Offensive, were more attuned to potential danger. His presence and his comings and goings were both sobering and reassuring to the greater neighborhood which also had many families whose sons were away serving.

For Americans who only saw the war on television or read about it in magazines and newspapers, the perception of regular life in Vietnam was near impossible to comprehend. To most, the country seemed awash in VC and NVA, thick with Buddhist monks just looking for an excuse to touch a match to their saffron robes, its main city streets teeming with hucksters and harlots. That life went on as before was known only to those who could see it happen. And life, in every way and in every cycle, proceeded on with minor interruption.

The marriage of Binh's younger sister Yen on November 17, 1968 was especially noteworthy for the combat-seasoned Marine captain. Yen Le had worked in the accounting office of the U.S. Army PX since 1966. Among her closest friends, Cam Banh was part of the small group of attractive, eligible young women in attendance. Advocating on behalf of her brother, Yen had continually extolled his goodness and greatness, like any proud sister, to Cam in the many months leading up to her wedding celebration. Between Binh's nearly always being gone fighting somewhere and Cam's mother's particularly traditional ways, there had been no earlier opportunities for a proper, formal filial introduction. The marriage of Yen Le provided such an occasion. The rest, as they would all say, would be history.

Elusive though victory in Southeast Asia appeared, not everything in December of 1968 pointed to the eminent demise of Western Civilization. There was genuine national joy in the return of the crew of the USS *Pueblo* who had endured eleven months of torture and torment at the hands of the North Koreans.

As much as American military might appeared mired in Vietnam's swamps and rice paddies, the launching of Apollo 8, the first manned-mission to orbit the moon, showcased the nation's technological superiority. George Philip listened in with a few other Marines on Christmas Day—Christmas Eve at home—to the Armed Forces Radio Network broadcast of the surprise yuletide greeting from the three Apollo 8 astronauts hundreds of thousands of miles away in their tiny spaceship.

In what was then the most listened to broadcast ever, astronauts William Anders, Jim Lovell, and Frank Borman each read a short passage from the book of Genesis. Anders began:

> For all the people of Earth the crew of Apollo 8 has a message we would like to send to you: In the beginning God created heaven and earth. And the earth was without form, and void; and darkness was upon the face of the deep. And the spirit of God moved upon the face of the waters. And God said, let there be light. And there was light. And God saw the light, that it was good, and God divided the light from the darkness.

Lovell continued:

> And God called the light Day, and the darkness he called Night. And the evening and the morning were the first day. And God said, let there be a firmament in the midst of the waters, and let it divide the waters from the waters. And God made the firmament, and divided the waters which were under the firmament from the waters which were above the firmament, and it was so. And God called the firmament Heaven. And the evening and the morning were the second day.

Borman concluded with:

> And God said, let the waters under the heavens be gathered together unto one place, and let the dry land appear. And it was so. And God called the dry land Earth; and the gathering together of the waters he called Seas. And God saw that it was good. (Genesis 1:1-1:10)
>
> And from the crew of Apollo 8, we close with good night, good luck, a Merry Christmas, and God bless all of you ...all of you on the good Earth." (NASA sources, Wikipedia)

Later that Christmas evening, George sat outside the FDC bunker looking up at the near full moon, musing as only a young man often does. He thought about his folks, his brother and sisters, the war, the friends he had seen killed and wounded. He thought about how odd it was that a half million American men were in Vietnam fighting in the most primitive circumstances while three men were up there circling the moon. It made little sense to him to try and understand what could not be made sense of. He thought some more. He thought some more, and then he went back inside the bunker.

Just like the Marines who were too busy fighting the NVA to hear Walter Cronkite's February prediction of their expected demise in the battle for Khe Sanh, it was probably a good thing that the men in Vietnam were mostly spared the news about a poll taken near year end which showed that, among American college students, the person they chose to identify with most was Che Guevara.[4] As the year 1968 drew to a close, as George Philip, recently promoted to first lieutenant, reflected on all that had gone on and was about to come, he kept returning back to what he had early on surmised—"this was not his father's war."

CHAPTER FOURTEEN

Back to Vietnam

Well *into the year 1971,* American college students continued to protest the war along with other perceived and real injustices. From peak strength of 543,400 reached in April of 1969, President Nixon's zeal to disengage from Southeast Asia had taken the number of troops in country down to 430,000 by the end of 1969. Twelve months later 280,000 remained. Somewhat more encouraging, at least from the limited perspective of trying to "Vietnamize" the war was the ever-diminishing number of Americans being killed. Marine Corps dead had gone from 4,634 in 1968 to less than half that in 1969. In 1971 a total of forty-one Marines were KIA in Vietnam.[1] To everybody who was not engaged in the fight or stuck in enemy prison camps, Vietnam was becoming just a painful memory, however recent.

By July of 1971 the last regular USMC ground combat units had left Vietnam. By late December fewer than 160,000 Americans remained in country, and of those, less than a thousand of them were Marines.

With President Nixon's widely publicized Vietnamization program well underway, the Marine Corps was attempting its return to "normalcy" and to focus attention back on its other global commitments—the "every clime and place" stuff. For Marines prior to 1965 and after 1971 "normalcy" meant duty at some point again on Okinawa—both lovingly and derisively referred to as "the Rock." As a junior lieutenant colonel, Gerry Turley's time had come up once more, for another one year unaccompanied tour to the Rock.

Discussing job opportunities currently available for a man of his skills and rank, Gerry's monitor also made him aware of a job in Vietnam. The Marine Advisory Unit, the organization whose main mission was to provide all of the infantry and artillery officer advisors to the various battalions of the TQLC, was in need of a number two man, sort of an executive officer role with the title "Assistant Senior Marine Advisor." If Gerry wanted it, the job was his.

In his mind, Gerry assembled a mental balance sheet for each location. For both Vietnam and the Rock, he would be away from Bunny and the kids for a year no matter what.

Duty on Okinawa would have its modern conveniences: he could eat good chow, sleep in clean quarters, have decent fellowship with Marines he already knew and develop new friendships with others. He would be reasonably safe. He would probably have, relative to his earlier duty in Vietnam, a job without much physical danger. When he was not working he could work out or read or relax or involve himself further in his job since there was no one to go home to at night.

Duty on Okinawa would be no cakewalk, either. By late 1971 the Marine Corps, along with all the services, was plagued with virulent race and drug problems. The cultural revolution that began years earlier had manifested in the Corps as well with horrible, ongoing, and unresolved consequences. Serious leadership issues had developed that Gerry and all his Old Corps friends could never have imagined only a few years ago. Well-respected historian and commentator, Colonel Robert Heinl, Jr. USMC (Ret.), in June of 1971 had observed the ongoing challenges in all of the services and stated that the current situation demonstrated "the lowest state of military morale in the history of the country."[2]

On Okinawa he would be in the thick of it, and as was his style, he knew he would have volunteered for the toughest assignment. If something was broken Gerry Turley would do all he could, by God, to fix it. If there was a job titled "Third Marine Division Race Riot and Drug Control Officer" Lieutenant Colonel Turley would have raised his hand to take it not because he wanted to do it but because it would be the right thing to do.

The Marine Advisory Unit in Vietnam was a reasonably small organization; fewer than sixty men with most of them assigned out to support nine infantry and three artillery battalions. Duty as the second in command would probably involve lots of logistics and paperwork, maybe a little exposure to combat; probably not too much, possibly just a little indirect enemy fire from time to time.

It was also well-known among Marine officers that the men who served as advisors to the various battalions of the TQLC were typically among the best, brightest and most accomplished infantry and artillery captains and majors in the Corps. In Vietnam there would be no time for drug and race problems. Even though American units were not fighting, "Vietnamization" meant the South Vietnamese were fighting that much more, and so too were their advisors. As the number two man he certainly would not be expected to lead troops into or out of harm's way, but his leadership, administrative skills, and experience could at least be of value to those doing the heavy lifting. Like the tiny Force Reconnaissance community he had spent his early years in, he knew instinctively that his association with this particular *coterie* of warriors would be the more rewarding job. He had just to convince his wife Bunny that it was the right move. Whether she believed him or not, she would quietly accede to his decision, he was certain.

THE RIPLEY FAMILY BETWEEN VIETNAM TOURS

There might have been something in the water back in Radford, Virginia. Maybe it was Verna Ripley's special home cooking or just Bud Ripley's style of fathering. While it was not unique, it certainly had not been every American family that proudly and emphatically put three sons in Vietnam, in combat, at one time. That they had all survived their tours was no minor miracle.

After completing his time as a student at Amphibious Warfare School (AWS) in Quantico and the obligatory, sobering duty too often serving on funeral details at Headquarters Marine Corps, good fortune smiled again on the young, serious captain and his expanding family. Selected to serve as an exchange officer with the British Royal Marines, John Ripley's career was indeed firing on all cylinders.

The relationship between the much larger American Marine Corps and the world's oldest and even more tradition-bound tiny corps of Royal Marines is arguably the most special and genuinely fraternal relationship enjoyed by any two military services of different nations in modern history. As a much smaller service, the Royal Marines are a more specialized infantry outfit akin to USMC Recon and Force Recon units or U.S. Army Rangers.

For an American Marine officer to be selected for this duty demands impeccable leadership credentials as well as physical toughness bordering on the extreme. Service with the Royal Marines requires that the exchange officer complete the very rigorous and physically dangerous Commando Course. Even though those selected to attend are thoroughly screened beforehand, nothing other than guts, keen intellect, refusal to quit under horrific training conditions, and a little bit of good fortune assure one's success in passing.

While many of the technical skills John was exposed to throughout his time with the Commandos were new, most of them simply reinforced and underscored the valuable lessons he had learned at Ranger School and in the school of real life in Vietnam. Little did he know that many of those skills would again soon come in handy.

As physically and mentally challenging as the initial training and all of the follow-on postings were—the British majored heavily in the same "every clime and place" stuff as did their American brothers—the duty, when he was not deployed, was also incredibly ceremonial and required an enormous amount of entertainment. While John was off doing cold-weather training up in Norway, desert training in Aden, or jungle-warfare training in Malaya, sometimes under real combat conditions, Moline was nearly always doing something to advance or maintain friendly foreign relations with their British hosts.

The Ripleys had expected the birth of their third child when they arrived; second son Thomas was born in England and bookended his slightly older sister Mary. John and Moline could not have been happier during this posting. Together they already knew that, if he survived long enough, the friends they would make on this particular tour would be lifelong ones.

John Ripley was typical of many Marine Corps officers who, as young men, did not require long periods of down time between tough assignments and who, in fact, might have been stifled when not being continuously stretched and challenged. Contacted by his monitor while serving with the British, he was made aware of an opportunity to get back into Vietnam as an infantry advisor with the TQLC. Now that the redeployment of all USMC ground combat units out of Southeast Asia was nearly complete, he eagerly accepted the challenge as advisory duty was the only real action still available.

From jolly old England, it was back to Virginia just long enough to establish Moline and the children near grandparents while he would be away. It was during that in-between time that tragedy struck the greater Ripley family.

Thirty-three-year-old Major Mike Ripley, one year and a few months older than baby brother John, had entered the Marine Corps through the Aviation Officer Candidate (AOC) program while John was a midshipman at the Naval Academy. Like his two brothers, Mike was a man of exceptional physical prowess, and had the eye-hand coordination and myriad other skills needed to pilot high-performance aircraft.

Initially assigned to flying A-4s—the Navy and Marine Corps' souped-up, single-seat attack jet used mostly for close-air support; upon returning from flying combat missions in Vietnam he was selected to enter the Navy/Marine Corps test pilot program located at Patuxent River in Maryland.

Test pilots are generally considered, in the aviation community, to be the best of the best. Not only are they required to be tough physical specimens, their continued employment and very breathing often depends on their abilities to instantaneously process complex issues and translate extraneous information into critical responses. Besides, being a test pilot is just plain dangerous work which, of course, adds to the allure of the job.

Major Mike Ripley, married and the father of three young children under the age of six, would go on to become the first Marine test pilot in the program that was developing the AV-8A Harrier VSTOL attack aircraft for the Corps. VSTOL—which stands for "Vertical/Short Take-Off and Landing"—technology was brand new in the early 1970s and the airplane was initially plagued with major operational problems that could be worked out only by lots and lots of hands on flying done by the most competent, intrepid test pilots.

The Harrier concept itself, if it could live up to program goals, was ideally suited to the Marine Corps' mission of expeditionary warfare. Because the plane could take off or land from a hover, the need for large aircraft carrier decks with steam catapults or long concrete runways was minimized. Theoretically Harriers would be deployable from any ship with sufficient deck space to launch and recover a helicopter. Ashore the planes could be hidden amongst the trees and then launched to deliver all sorts of death and destruction upon an enemy from reasonably small, flat open areas.

If the Harrier could be employed to maximum potential, reliance on a fleet to protect assaulting Marines on some contested beachhead could be greatly reduced. American carrier admirals appreciated the notion of not being tied to landing beaches to defend Marines going ashore in future conflicts, especially in light of the burgeoning Soviet naval threat. Marine planners were glad to have the added local punch the Harrier would deliver to ground forces whether the plane was to be used in a close-air support or a deep-strike role.

The AV-8A Harrier held a great deal of promise. Prior to realizing all of those benefits there was still a long, long list of issues needing to be fixed in order to make the plane live up to its billing. At this point in its development the Harrier was unfortunately a greater threat to the men who flew it than to the enemies it would ultimately be deployed against.

The initial investigation, which would later be corroborated by a more formal and detailed investigation, into the crash that killed Major Mike Ripley showed that while making a rocket run on a target right there in the Chesapeake Bay next to Patuxent

River, his AV-8A Harrier failed to respond as he attempted to pull out of the attack dive he had been in. The only merciful thing was that the young husband and father of three was killed the moment his plane hit the water on the morning of June 18, 1971.

As fate would have it, the funeral with full military honors for Major Mike Ripley was held within twenty-four hours of Captain John Ripley's scheduled departure for Vietnam. The entire Ripley family, but most especially Bud and Verna, were troubled with having to say their final goodbyes to one son and then potential final goodbyes to a second in such a short period of time. All that was before them, with John's assignment to Vietnam, was another twelve months of uncertainty. But the call to duty would always be answered.

BINH IN BETWEEN

Hue Tan, seven years younger than Le Ba Binh, had finished high school in 1964 and immediately enlisted in the Vietnamese Air Force (VNAF). The rapid expansion of all military services was a factor in combination with his English-language skills that had seen his rapid promotion to staff sergeant by 1968. Tan worked in a liaison role for the Defense Attaché Office (DAO).

Tan's family lived right next door to Binh's just off the tiny alleyway perpendicular to Hai Ba Trung, the main street that ran through Tan Dinh. As a boy he had chummed around with one of Binh's younger half brothers doing all the same things, playing all the same games Binh had only a few years prior.

By late 1968 and into 1969 Tan would often be home at his parents' place when his "elder brother" friend would return to visit. As was neighborly and customary, they would sit for hours in the first floor parlor of either home sipping cool tea, talking of the things young men everywhere speak of.

In his work at the DAO Tan had opportunity to interact with Americans, and would also see them everywhere his air force duties took him. Like Binh, who had enjoyed his time in Quantico, Tan had developed a particular fondness and curiosity for the Americans. Both young men could overlook the negative impact American presence often brought with it. While not all Vietnamese felt the same, Tan and Binh could not quite understand why America would send its own sons to fight and die to keep the Communists out of Vietnam.

Tan loved to tease his elder brother that the new woman in his life—and it was evident to all by early 1969 that Binh would eventually, if he was not killed first, marry Cam Banh—was far too pretty for him. And yet Tan understood the dynamics; he understood that powerful men get first dibs on the most desirable women. It was as obvious as the sunrise well before 1968 to anyone who knew him or knew of him that Dai Uy (Captain) Binh was a powerful man.

Whenever Binh came home he was driven in his own jeep crowded in the back with at least two, sometimes three cowboys or bodyguards. And it seemed that Binh was always recovering from some sort of combat wound that he would not discuss or give much recognition to. Binh would never talk about himself or what he did. It was when he would walk alone down the alley to visit other neighbors that his cowboys or his jeep driver would reveal stories to family and friends of their commander's amazing skills and bravery. All the folks in Tan Dinh, but especially those cloistered nearest his boyhood home, shared and retold the tales of the combat exploits of their own local hero and favorite son Le Ba Binh.

Unlike his American counterparts there was no short-timer calendar, no end of tour, no in between, no true R&R for Le Ba Binh or any of his long-serving mates. When Gerry Turley, John Ripley, George Philip, and every other American who would serve a second tour in Vietnam had time and duty in between, Binh was still somewhere in the undefined middle of his effort to help his country win its war.

Sure, the military of the Republic of Vietnam by the late 1960s was nearly large enough and increasingly professional enough to send a few officers to mid and senior level schools in the United States. There were even a number of TQLC officers who made it back to Quantico as captains and majors. Binh was not one of them. Essentially trapped by his own success, his skills and leadership were such that he remained with Third Battalion for the duration.

Richard Nixon's election in November 1968 and his assumption of duties early the next year brought with it his promise to "Vietnamize" the war. While the entire TQLC and certain units of the RVN army could certainly take issue with the idea that to this point they had not borne their fair share of the fight, the American electorate was increasingly weary of the investment that had, so far, yielded little in the way of tangible benefit.

For nearly five years Vietnam had consumed most of the foreign policy focus of the United States. In every other area of the world America's strategic interests had been sorely neglected. The evolving Nixon Doctrine would seek to refocus the nation's resources in a way that would more appropriately reflect those global requirements, while at the same time physically disengaging from Southeast Asia by provisioning and training the forces of South Vietnam to fully handle the northern invaders on their own.

For Binh, and for every Vietnamese citizen with a stake in the outcome of the battle for their country, there was no bigger picture, no concern about Soviet influence in Europe or Latin America or northern Asia. Everything that mattered, except for the political decisions made in Washington that would directly impact the flow of material assistance to his country, was taking place within the four corps regions of the Republic of Vietnam.

From day one Cam would grow used to the long periods of separation from Binh that were punctuated by his sporadic, occasional unannounced returns from Vietnam's farthest corners. There would be few surprises in the relationship that, from the very first moment, seemed destined for marriage...if Binh lived long enough.

The developing association between Binh and Cam was at once both modern and traditional, but mostly traditional. Binh was a dutiful, deferential son and also a respecter of the woman who would be his mother-in-law. Cam was a dutiful, solicitous daughter. Their dates and his visits were always properly supervised and chaperoned. With all the combat and ugliness that he had seen and experienced, for Binh maintaining the filial traditions was reassuring and calming.

GEORGE PHILIP IN BETWEEN

For the men who were professionals, respectfully and sometimes not-so respectfully referred to as "Lifers," coming back from Vietnam was far different than it was for those who were the more traditional-in-American-history citizen soldiers. The draftees and single-term volunteers who joined the military, went to Vietnam, came home, and then tried to take up life from there generally had homecoming experiences far different.

Men like Gerry Turley and John Ripley, when they returned from Vietnam, were immediately re-assimilated into a culture that affirmed them, moved them along, and to a certain extent shielded them from the harsher realities of the greater societal changes then taking place. There was still great pride in service, even an unspoken but very real hierarchy among warriors delineated by difficulty and duration of combat endured.

In the civilian world, in this war, there were no homecoming parades, no warm hugs or slaps on the back to say thank you, no one asking about how it was in ways that demonstrated awe or respect for having served. For many who answered their nation's call, the Vietnam experience was something to put behind, to put away, compartmentalize, forget about.

For men like George Philip, bred to serve but still too junior to be called a lifer, and without a wife to ground him as a man in the culture he had grown up from as a boy, there was some sense of disconcertment, a slight gnawing about where exactly he was supposed to fit in back here in "the World."

After a month's leave it was back east to Quantico for duty at Officer Candidates School (OCS). It was not difficult to sense the overall national *malaise* and antipathy towards the war in Vietnam and those perceived as professional military men in particular.

In spite of the broader national mood, service as a platoon commander at OCS running officer candidates through the ten-week program was actually rather rewarding for George. In spite of the fact that in the late summer of 1969 five hundred thousand young people attended the festivities at Woodstock in White Lake, New York—most of them strongly opposed to the war—from his perspective in Quantico he was encouraged that there was still a large number of young men eager to serve as Marine officers in a war that daily grew more controversial. With the still-great need for second lieutenants, OCS was operating at full tilt. In a one-year period George would help process four separate classes through OCS.

Prior to graduating from Annapolis in 1967 George had spent considerable time with his midshipmen buddies in and around the Washington area in college bars and pubs joyfully pursuing the favors of local coeds. Returning to the same establishments in the late summer of 1969 and looking for outcomes similar to those experienced only two years earlier yielded a bitter harvest.

The very first bar George and one lieutenant comrade went into on their initial foray back to DC was a rude reminder of all the change that had taken place since those earlier, now seemingly halcyon times. As the only two with military haircuts, they stuck out. While no one had the courage to say anything directly to them, the hostility was palpable. After quickly consuming just one beer each, George turned to his friend, admonishing him: "Come on. Let's go. We don't belong here anymore…"

ACTION WITH THIRD BATTALION …

When the Americans essentially took over the main role of prosecuting the war in Vietnam in 1965, they changed completely the way business was being done. The American way of war was, from the view of their South Vietnamese allies, sort of like Texas was to the rest of the United States: everything was bigger and somehow grander. The American way of war fighting sought near epic, decisive engagements with large units using massed firepower, relying on an unending supply of material. The employment of American fighting men, and its battalion through division level leaders in particular, reinforced the desire to seek and gain victory expeditiously. With Vietnam tours lasting twelve months for the Army and thirteen months for Marines,

197

and with most officers only given combat commands for half of their time in Vietnam, there was a natural proclivity for those in combat leadership positions to aggressively seek to engage the enemy, to gain some sort of knock-out blow, to make their mark, as soon as they could.

For the Vietnamese it would not be entirely fair to say that the RVN military leadership did not aggressively, and in American terms, seek to "locate, close with, and destroy" the enemy at every opportunity. Cultural dissimilarities along with logistical and material constraints made the Vietnamese method for prosecuting the war different from methods taught and favored by Occidentals.

At the same time Americans were concerned with the marginal aggressiveness of their South Vietnamese allies, RVN political and military leadership were flummoxed as the Americans became increasingly wedded to accepting the strategic defense as a way to properly conduct the war. Even Binh's father, who had counseled his eldest son to become a Marine so that he might one day take part in the liberation of their old family home near Hanoi, expected that at some point, in the not-too distant future there would be ground attacks against and an invasion to deliver the north from Communist oppression.

Remembering that one million Red Chinese had crossed the Yalu River in November of 1950 when MacArthur's forces had gotten too far into North Korea, American political leadership convinced itself that, to keep the Soviets and Chinese from considering the introduction of their own troops, they would limit ground combat to areas within the borders of South Vietnam. The Soviets and Chinese Communists were only too happy to encourage and exploit that line of thinking.

Where the Vietnamese Communists saw all of what was formerly French Indo-China as one giant, legitimate battlefield, the U.S. chose to confine its ground efforts to within the borders of the Republic of Vietnam. Americans further convinced themselves that their overwhelming mobility and firepower would more than make up for the self-imposed geographical limitations, and that the Communists would ultimately either quit or be driven to the bargaining table after having lost so many men.

The myriad challenges facing the armed forces of the Republic of Vietnam from 1954 forward had always been significant. With the Americans, by late 1968, now wanting to turn over the bulk of the war fighting responsibilities to their junior ally, those issues were further amplified. One unintended consequence with the American takeover of the main fighting from 1965 forward was that ARVN leadership, in many cases, grew too reliant on their American benefactors. The development of intangible yet critical-for-command leadership qualities like initiative, innovation, and professional competence were arguably reduced when they should have been enhanced and encouraged. Dependence on fire support that could only be supplied by American forces was another resource many became sorely predisposed to.

Along with the technical problems facing ARVN were the even greater issues of outright corruption, political reliability and overall fighting proficiency. The portrayal of ARVN in the Western media was mostly as an agglomeration of *effete*, ineffective, and at times even treasonous units being run by and for the benefit of mandarin-like generals who were no more than modern-day warlords.

From the country's birth in 1954, the blood of young soldiers and Marines in South Vietnamese units had been liberally shed in the nation's defense.

Bravery and competent leadership were never in short supply among the elite units; Marines, Airborne, Rangers, and Special Forces. For the remaining regular infantry divisions which comprised the other 90 percent of ARVN, quality was far from uniform. To be sure, there were those generals who infused their formations with fighting spirit and gung ho. All too often however, nepotism, corruption, insufficient training, and weak leadership led to poor morale and poor performance.

A SHORT HISTORY OF THE TQLC

From its very beginnings, the Vietnamese Marine Corps was an organization that would be largely free of scandal and corruption. Forced after its birth to evolve and adapt or perish, the TQLC became an eclectic blend of Oriental and Occidental martial excellence. Within five years of being formed, its junior officers were routinely being sent to Quantico for training at the Basic School with fresh-faced American second lieutenant counterparts. Its most promising young corporals and sergeants went to the United States to learn the art and science of becoming drill instructors.

By June of 1959 the TQLC and the equally elite and politically reliable airborne division (both organizations at the time were then still of brigade size) were designated as their country's national strategic reserve. With the increasing pressures of the Communist insurgency the TQLC almost naturally grew in both size and stature. Forming its first infantry battalion in 1954, by 1960 there were four battalions. The following year the TQLC, with the assistance of its American Marine advisors, formed a brigade that included a battalion of artillery and smaller support units to handle the various command, control, and logistical requirements.

As 1968 drew to a close the TQLC had eight infantry battalions formed into three brigades. With this three-regiment equivalent the TQLC was officially designated to be at division strength. The support infrastructure had also been beefed up to sustain the increasing demands of combat. Plans were on the books to add a ninth battalion of infantry to flesh out the third brigade as soon as personnel could be recruited and trained.[3] (A brigade is essentially a regiment with additional units attached to make it a more effective fighting unit. A regiment generally has three battalions. In the case of the TQLC, each brigade had three infantry battalions, an artillery battalion, and a host of other smaller units for support. Initially when the TQLC fielded three brigades, they numbered them Brigades 147, 258, and 369. Brigade 147 originally consisted of the First, Fourth, and Seventh Battalions, etc. As time went one, the battalions would rotate between the three brigade headquarters so that First Battalion at various times was in the other two brigades, etc. but the brigade titles remained unchanged.)

As much as the TQLC resembled its American Marine Corps mentors in terms of aggressive fighting spirit, high standards, discipline and leadership, the differences were equally noteworthy. The USMC was known to the American people to be the most tradition-bound, demanding, and ascetic of the four military services, an austerity that was seemingly anachronistic in the face of the societal changes then taking place. The Bushido-like implicit and explicit code of conduct widely practiced and accepted within the tiny corps of Vietnamese Marines made their American brothers seem not quite so serious.

Issues involving criminal and less than honorable acts were sternly dealt with in the TQLC, particularly if committed under combat conditions. Corporal punishment for various crimes or rules infractions was meted out almost exclusively at the battalion level or lower. If a crime was serious enough, capital punishment was administered directly by the battalion commander himself with all of the unit's Marines looking on. The near unlimited authority given to military leaders allowed the swift execution of justice for those crimes deemed as capital offenses.

More than any other man, the temperament, warrior culture, and scandal-free reputation of the TQLC was infused, instilled, imbued, and encouraged most by one young forward-thinking officer who had been in the delivery room when the TQLC was born and became its first *commandant* in 1960. Having served first as a brand new lieutenant in the riverine forces that would ultimately constitute the incipient corps of Vietnamese Marines, Le Nguyen Khang was the right man at the right time for the right job. As with a number of displaced northerners who would rise to positions of power in the new Republic of Vietnam, Major General Khang's brilliance for leadership and vision for what the TQLC needed to become was compounded by a hatred for the Communists that ran soul deep.[4]

The many challenges facing General Khang and his Vietnamese Marine Corps, while truly monumental, were less significant than those facing ARVN which, because of its much greater size, did not have the same uniform quality of officers and men. The greatest obstacle to the improvement of overall organizational success for all RVN forces on the field of battle was the cultural predisposition towards the rigid respect of and for authority.

Those long-engrained Confucian concepts of respect for elders and those in positions above one's station greatly retarded individual initiative and the free-flow of ideas. The "cult of the commander" could be depended upon only when things were going in a unit's favor and rested greatly upon the combat genius of the single man in charge. Changing battlefield conditions nearly always required a deviation from the plans established and rehearsed prior to initiation of contact. Once the "fog of war" set in, fluidity of action was often hampered by the need to gain overt, specific approval from those in charge before making needed changes and critical decisions. In those all too frequent instances that consumed too much time, precious lives, and resources were often compromised.[5] Coincidental to rigid chains of command were the problems of "face" and "saving face," a concept difficult for American advisors to place much value in when mission accomplishment hung in the balance.

Another significant weakness that became more acute as the TQLC continued to assume a greater portion of the tactical responsibilities from departing American units in I Corps, and they transitioned from fighting as separate battalions in favor of brigades (three battalions), was the need to properly exercise and implement the staff functions required of more sophisticated military operations. Things that were routine and second nature to perennially-schooled professional military officers like the importance of effective equipment maintenance programs were not necessarily obvious under the old "cult of the commander" system. The criticality of developing integrated, functioning staffs and standard operating procedures so that administration (S-1), intelligence (S-2), operations (S-3), and logistics (S-4) could effectively coordinate their efforts and maximize their commander's chances of battlefield success was something the American advisors had a particularly difficult time selling to their Vietnamese counterparts.[6]

CHAPTER FIFTEEN

Back in the States

A*djusting back to life in America* had its challenges. For so many returning Vietnam combat veterans the most gut-wrenching, angst-producing aspect of their service was not having to deal with the gruesomeness they had experienced so very far away that sometimes returned to them in vivid distortions when they slept. It was not that every single one of them who served and survived had lost friends in the most unforgiving, unkind ways, or that others had been maimed and would forever be both physically changed and emotionally damaged for having answered their nation's call to serve. What bothered George Philip more than anything else, what stumped him and most of his comrades working there at OCS, was the way they were treated when they came home by those who had not served.

In the spring of 1970, after having pushed through four series of officer candidates as a platoon commander, George was reassigned as an instructor at OCS. As much as anyone could enjoy that duty, he did.

At about the same time that American and ARVN forces invaded Cambodia to go after the vast Ho Chi Minh Trail network and system of sanctuaries NVA forces had, up until this time, been allowed to use with complete impunity, First Lieutenant George Philip was feeling restless and not quite comfortable teaching classes at OCS. There had to be something more that he could do.

Bored with the safe, routine work now assigned to him at OCS, George was looking for something else, something more than shuffling papers that would have action and meaning. He had heard from others of opportunities for already commissioned officers in different military occupational specialties to transition over to the aviation community. The prospect of flying helicopters in combat appealed to his still unsated sense of adventure.

George had ridden in his fair share of helicopters in Vietnam, had personally seen both army and Marine pilots pull off extremely hairy, brave stuff going into and out of hot landing zones. Flying helicopters certainly beat teaching classes in field sanitation to officer candidates there in Quantico. Flying helicopters would get him back into the action. Flying helicopters would not be boring.

First Lieutenant George Philip submitted all the necessary paperwork. He had the eyesight. He passed the written tests. He passed the flight physical. He had the recommendations. He was accepted. He was good to go. He was headed to Ft. Rucker in Alabama to be trained by the Army.

Within days of being accepted, the Marine Corps pulled the plug. The big push for more pilots all of a sudden simply and mysteriously ended. Disappointed, he took a ride up to Washington, D.C. to visit his monitor and explore other opportunities.

Seated respectfully across from the gentleman who was the monitor for junior artillery officers, George was initially a bit nervous. Scrupulously reviewing the detailed official file that the Marine Corps had on First Lieutenant Philip, the monitor sensed opportunity. Seeing as how George's various scores on aptitude tests administered over the years suggested a proclivity for foreign languages, would he not have interest in attending seven months of school in Monterey, California studying Vietnamese so that he might become an artillery advisor to the Vietnamese Marine Corps? Chagrined, George suppressed a smile. In high school he had had to take two years of Spanish I. Now the Corps was telling him he had a thing for languages. Who was George Philip to question the wisdom of the United States Marine Corps? And besides, seven months in Monterey he could suffer through somehow. The advisory stuff, and the Vietnamese Marine Corps, he knew nothing about; at least not yet. But he had an open mind. The major told him to think it over for a few days. The following morning George called the monitor. He took the orders.

THE CAMBODIAN INVASION AND ITS AFTERMATH

The incredible punishment inflicted on the NVA by striking the heretofore inviolate sanctuaries in Cambodia was significant. American and ARVN forces had conducted, according to President Nixon, "the most successful military operation of the Vietnam War."[1] From April 29 to June 30, 1970 the allied forces, at a combined cost of twelve hundred men KIA, killed more than ten times that number of enemy troops. In addition, and perhaps of greater importance, the supply and logistical disruption to enemy operating capabilities was huge. Thousands of tons of rice, millions of rounds of various kinds of ammunition, and all other sorts of vital supplies were captured or destroyed. The NVA/VC war-making and fighting capabilities were dramatically impacted.

Diminished NVA and VC activities, particularly in both the III and IV Corps regions of South Vietnam (III Corps was the corps region that included Saigon and IV Corps was the area south of the city) gave U.S. forces greater breathing room for orderly withdrawal from the country, allowing for "Vietnamization" to take place under significantly lighter enemy pressure. Reduction in Communist capabilities also bought time for ARVN to develop further their improving combat skills and now burgeoning confidence.

Third Battalion, with Dai Uy (Captain) Binh as XO, participated as part of Brigade 147 in the Cambodia operation. While not a cakewalk, the terrain they worked was entirely to their advantage against an enemy who had done little to prepare the battlefield. From his perspective as XO, the mission they were given was a good one. With only minor losses, the men of the Soi Bien were able to kill many, many Communists.

GEORGE IN MONTEREY

George Philip's assignment to the Defense Language Institute (DLI), located within shouting distance of the U.S. Navy's well regarded Post Graduate School (NPGS), would be for seven months.

There was an old joke that was actually more revealing and mildly disturbing than funny:

"What do you call a person who speaks three languages?
Tri-lingual.

"What do you call a person who speaks two languages?
Bi-lingual.

"What do you call a person who speaks only one language?
American."

DLI's mission was, in a very small way, to ameliorate that specific problem. On its campus men and women serving in the nation's military and other governmental agencies were schooled in languages critical to the conduct of foreign policy and intelligence gathering. Training in languages ranging from the more obvious Russian, Mandarin, and Spanish to the more esoteric like Swahili, Farsi, and Hindi, the school also taught students in languages the average American citizen had never even heard of. Instructors, especially those who taught the courses vital to Cold War defense, were often displaced refugees from countries recently subjected to Communist oppression. The Monterey experience, in the same place that Eric Burdon had captured in song describing events at the 1967 Pop Festival, was completely agreeable. As Burdon had exclaimed: "Even the cops grooved with us..."

At times it was near impossible to recall that there was a war on. Several of George's Annapolis classmates, naval officers mostly, were students over at NPGS. During the period that he was there, he played for their championship softball team.

Class routine was rigorous but not impossible. Taught by a group of instructors who had all been born in what was now North Vietnam and then made the 1954 exodus to South Vietnam, each of them had stories of property confiscated and close family members brutally and barbarically murdered by the Communists. Every day was total classroom immersion for six hours with two or three hours of required homework.

As a single officer, George had the financial resources to purchase a motorcycle. During breaks and weekends he would often head south on Highway One, enjoying the magnificent coastal beauty of places like Big Sur. Shortly after arriving he met up with and became attached to an attractive young lady who taught elementary school in Carmel.

That George Philip, as a language student at DLI and even after having served a full tour in Southeast Asia, for the first time was really learning something of Vietnamese culture and interacting with Vietnamese people was an ironic and sad commentary on the way America was prosecuting the war. Like 90 percent of the other Americans who went to Vietnam after 1964 but essentially remained inside the amorphous cocoon of American culture, he had had no real interaction with regular Vietnamese folks, had formed no ties or friendships outside his circle of Marine comrades. Most GIs dealt with Vietnamese only if and when they had to, and from those limited perspectives the experiences were rarely positive.

"TIN SOLDIERS AND NIXON COMING..."

Lost in the press reporting of the actions surrounding the Cambodian incursion and its aftermath was the direct positive impact the invasion had on the morale of the men who fought there. While no American soldier wanted to be the last man killed as the Vietnamization process continued on, there was great relief amongst those who had battled on the ground at the appearance of finally shucking the completely ridiculous Byzantine rules of engagement that prohibited Americans from doing a complete and thorough job in attempting to destroy their enemy and his base areas.

Prior to crossing over into the Cambodian sanctuaries, American forces were, for those five long years, like cartoon guard dogs chained down and able to defend and dominate, however imperfectly, only as far as the chain could reach. Until late April in 1970, those chains kept them inside the borders of the Republic of Vietnam. Communist forces, like Bugs Bunny or Daffy Duck opposite the hapless guard dog, were home free once they crossed the magical borders of Laos or Cambodia, and would routinely and figuratively thumb their noses at their American adversaries who, like the angry celluloid canine above mentioned, could do little more than bark and snarl and be pissed off.

The twelve thousand-plus NVA soldiers killed in Cambodia by American and ARVN forces did not necessarily die in vain. The swift blowback from the actions ordered by President Nixon came at tremendous domestic political expense. With the new perception that the war was being widened there was a near instantaneous uproar across the country. On hundreds and hundreds of college campuses thousands and thousands of students rose up in violent protest.

The drama at Kent State University immortalized in song by Crosby, Stills, Nash, and Young, became the *cause célèbre* for the reinvigorated anti-war movement. Whatever their motivations, the anti-war protesters became witting and unwitting allies to the Vietnamese Communist leadership who had, with acute perspicacity, astutely observed after the events of Tet 1968 that the war's center of gravity had shifted from the jungles and rice paddies of Southeast Asia to the American political arena.

The war and everything about it, from a domestic political perspective, was cartwheeling out of control. That National Guard troops would kill unarmed college students simply confirmed to many of the war's opponents that every single thing about Vietnam that was questionable, no matter how nefarious or evil or corrupt, was all true.

Rather than being a single, egregious, unspeakable blotch that sullied the honor of the U.S. Army, many now believed that the actions at My Lai were the way American forces routinely conducted operations. At home, no matter how outrageous the story—and the source might be someone who knew someone who knew someone who knew someone who had a cousin's son's friend working in supply in Bing Bang Bong—there were embellished tales, repeated and accepted as factual, told over and over, of atrocities and fraggings and dope and on and on. Because it was Vietnam nothing was too unbelievable, if it was bad, to be believed.*

---

* Many are familiar with the permutations of the CIA story about the agency allegedly running dope which was very widely believed, and perpetrated also by the foreign media with the aid of hostile intelligence services but when accurately researched it could never be corroborated—(Peebles, *Twilight Warriors*, 254, 255).

In Washington, the direct political response to the Cambodian incursion was an attempt to limit the president's power to prosecute a war without explicit congressional approval. Many believed that the executive branch, beginning with Franklin Roosevelt, had been gradually usurping Congress's constitutionally granted war-making authority. The Cooper-Church Amendment was the first amendment to limit presidential powers during a war. Its intent was to deny funding for any American ground forces being used in Laos or Cambodia after June 30, 1970.

The original amendment did not pass. In the meantime American forces had pulled back into the borders of South Vietnam anyway. A revised and watered-down version did pass both houses in late December and became law in early January of 1971. Placing minimal restrictions on the future use of air power, the subsequent use of American ground forces anywhere in Southeast Asia outside of the Republic of Vietnam, even for those in the advisory role to the South Vietnamese military was specifically proscribed.

The follow-up RVN operation designed to capitalize on the successes of the April-June 1970 Cambodian interdiction of enemy sanctuaries was called *Lam Son 719*. Khe Sanh, the same place U.S. Marines had battled the NVA in the famous seventy-seven-day siege in 1968, would be used as the primary staging area for RVN forces. In *Lam Son 719*, RVN units would finally be utilizing Khe Sanh in the way that General Westmoreland had earlier envisioned using the old combat base.

The goal of *Lam Son 719* was to attack NVA sanctuaries and seize vital portions of the Ho Chi Minh Trail system in Laos as far west as Tchepone, blunting the enemy's abilities to conduct the war inside of South Vietnam. For RVN, the massive operation would be at least as critical and ambitious to the war effort as the earlier Cambodia foray.

By late January of 1971, the time of *Lam Son 719's* kick off, the Cooper-Church Amendment was in full effect. RVN ground forces would still rely heavily on all manner of American air support. From massive B-52 ARCLIGHT strikes down to countless sorties of tactical aircraft dropping iron bombs and napalm in close proximity of infantry operations, American airpower was crucial. More important even than the bomber and fighter-bomber support was the dependence upon the hundreds and hundreds of U.S. Army helicopters required for insertion, extraction, resupply, medevac, reconnaissance, command and control and fire support. The American ground officers who served as advisors to the various ARVN and TQLC units to be engaged, the folks who were the critical extra eyes and brains to assist in the organization for battle and, most especially, who often coordinated the use of all the American-supplied firepower, would have to remain in Khe Sanh and listen in on the action over the radios while they sat it out in reconstituted bunkers.

By any measure, *Lam Son 719* was a massive undertaking. The ARVN general given command of the operation was the same fellow who had been in charge of all South Vietnamese forces in Military Region One (MR 1), known to Americans as I Corps, since 1965.[2] Lieutenant General Hoang Xuan Lam had a reasonably good reputation with Americans. Among senior officers of the TQLC however, there was little love lost for General Lam.

To execute the ambitious goals of *Lam Son 719*, General Lam had available to him an impressive assemblage of ARVN units. Along with the First Infantry Division, extensive artillery and armor assets, and several ranger battalions, General Lam had at his disposal nearly the entire National Strategic Reserve; both the Airborne and the TQLC. *Lam Son 719* would be the very first time the TQLC went to the field to be employed as a division.[3]

The sixty-four-day series of running battles went on from January 30 through March 24, 1971. While the South Vietnamese took significant casualties, it was generally accepted that they had killed a greater number of NVA who had likewise committed some of their best units and tremendous resources to counter the ARVN and TQLC forces. When the operation was complete there was some debate about just how much benefit had been gained. In actuality, and with little press fanfare, a great deal of damage had been, like the earlier Cambodian foray, inflicted upon the NVA.

From the Nixonian viewpoint with a goal toward Vietnamization, *Lam Son 719* was a public relations disaster. Every South Vietnamese weakness and foible was chronicled and highlighted by the western media. Problems for ARVN began with interference in the conduct of the operation by President Nguyen Van Thieu who, as an elected official in a fledgling democracy, was hypersensitive to the political fallout of taking excessive casualties. The Communist leadership in Hanoi suffered no such pressure.

What command, control and coordination challenges there were that existed were made known by an unsympathetic press. The lingering, recurring presentation of *Lam Son 719* in the Western media was film of ARVN troops attempting to forcefully board extract or resupply helicopters. These shots were given repeated play in the U.S. as had many of the shocking film clips from Tet '68. Most people back home had difficulty empathizing with soldiers who appeared unwilling to fight for their own country while Americans had already bled so much to help, and were still doing so by providing all of the helicopter support for the entire operation during which time many of those crews were shot down and killed.

The upside to *Lam Son 719* would go completely unnoticed once the correspondents filed their reports. As with the Cambodian incursion, NVA forces and their resources had been deleteriously impacted. This was widely noted by allied intelligence which saw declines in infiltration on the Ho Chi Minh Trail and enemy initiated actions on the battlefields throughout all of South Vietnam in the months following.[4]

TQLC performance during *Lam Son 719*, on balance, was recognized as quite good. The bravery and sacrifices of the individual Marines were, however, largely compromised by their egregious organizational misuse from higher ARVN headquarters. The bitter inter-service and internecine rivalries among senior officers, particularly General Lam's well-known hatred for the Vietnamese Marine Corps, and the reflected dislike for him by Lieutenant General Khang (recently promoted from Major General) and his top lieutenants, grew only more intense.

Lam Son 719 was anything but a repeat of the relatively easy go TQLC forces had had with their hated enemy just months earlier in

Cambodia. Fighting this time on more challenging terrain, the Marines paid a far higher price for the pain they inflicted.

With Binh still as XO, Third Battalion was operating as one of Brigade 258's constituent units. Most of the Marine action was centered near a place named Co Roc. The thickly jungled mountainous terrain was as much an enemy as were the determined NVA. The heaviest contact for the Soi Bien was when the First Battalion had been attacked by a regiment of NVA and Third Battalion assaulted into the NVA flank to relieve pressure on their brother Marines. As the fighting wound down and ARVN and TQLC forces withdrew back into South Vietnam, Binh and the command group he controlled were among the last to depart the field of battle by helicopter to Khe Sanh.

Extensive logistical assistance and planning was increasingly required as the TQLC continued to grow in size. (The ninth battalion of infantry had been added in 1970.) Sustaining fully two-thirds of its units in the field, in I Corps, in action, all the time, placed an incredible strain on the evolving support infrastructure. Together senior Vietnamese and American officers planned and plotted the myriad requirements to take care of the combat Marines *and* their families housed in and around Thu Duc. Engineering resources were dedicated to building increased family housing facilities, medical support, and on and on.

Keeping fighting men and their families properly fed was another issue planners attempted to tackle. Military families were encouraged to grow their own vegetables and rice on plots of land controlled by the TQLC to supplement the meager pay and resources available. As an interesting aside, it was noted during Operation Vu Ninh XII, which took place prior to *Lam Son 719,* that many Marines who had been in the field in northern I Corps for extended periods were ultimately being medevaced with malaria-like symptoms. It turned out that the men were, in fact, suffering from protein deficiencies in their diets which was an easier battle to win than the one with mosquitoes.

The protein solution was in part delivered by a resourceful *covan* named Gene Harrison. Prior to gaining his commission, Major Harrison had been a farmer and a county agent in Florida.

His answer to improving the meat consumption for the TQLC was to go to the Philippines and seek out a better, more substantial breed of pig that would yield more meat. Major Harrison became a very popular man with the men, but was even more appreciated by the families in Thu Duc.[5] Subsequent to the introduction of the heartier, more prolific breed of pig, it was a rare resupply flight north from Tan Son Nhut that did not have a hog or two or three aboard for the various battalions to supplement what rations they would locally procure.

CHAPTER SIXTEEN

Going Back Over

*I*t *was impossible, war or no war,* not to have a good tour as a student at DLI and a grand time in Carmel and Monterey, and yet George Philip was looking forward to leaving. He had already seen more than his share of death and destruction, had satisfied adequately that curiosity all fighting men have prior to their first action; *Do I have what it takes?* and *Will I stand up in the breech?* George did and he had.

This late in the war George did not have to be going back over to Vietnam. For most American military professionals, the war was all but finished. The opportunities to serve, except for pilots and air crews, had been greatly reduced. For Marine officers, advisory duty was the only serious action the Corps had going on except for a few other esoteric postings. But this was his chosen profession and going back was simply the honorable thing to do. Along with that, the national mood was thick with anti-military sentiment that disturbed him a great deal. Neil Young, Joan Baez, their fellow travelers, and all the others would not likely be visiting northern I Corps or anywhere else he might serve with his soon-to-be new friends of the Vietnamese Marine Corps. Duty as an advisor would have all the meaning and intensity he could handle.

Promoted to captain just prior to graduation from his course at the Defense Language Institute, George took full advantage of the one-month leave he was again granted before going back to Southeast Asia.

The trip over the second time was far less raucous, far less intense than the first. With very few Americans now involved, he was essentially alone for the entire flight and could consider all things in private. He silently laughed at himself, recalling how when he had first gone to Vietnam in early 1968 he was concerned that he would not get there in time to be part of it. Now, nearly four years later, he was going back to a war that still, at least from his own perspective, had no reasonable end in sight.

NORTH TO I CORPS...AGAIN

Life for American Marines and soldiers in Vietnam had been a constant struggle with the elements. This was especially true for those in infantry units as they had to contend with heat and rust and humidity and filth and thirst and hunger and fear. Time was as much an enemy as the NVA and it seemed to pass at glacial speed while events at home moved ahead at a breakneck pace, certainly beyond where the warriors may have seen themselves.

A major risk from the grunt perspective was that back in "the world" girlfriends or young wives might move beyond or outside of the orbits these men were wedded to and revolved in. There was a fear for some, maybe also a bit of anger, that loved ones would simply be unable to understand the uniqueness of the stresses of combat in Vietnam.

More unusual was life for the people upon whose real estate the war was being prosecuted. For those in the cities but mostly for those in the villages, the absolute constituent component of Vietnamese culture, life managed to continue on. Whether their sympathies were with the RVN government, the Communists, or they simply wished to be left alone, people still required food and shelter and whatever else comprised the necessities of life.

The great Russian author Fyodor Dostoevsky had observed that man is a being who can get used to anything. He might well have been describing the regular folks of the Vietnamese *hinterlands*. For generations they had endured. They would continue to endure.

In the villages and tiny, tiny towns of northern South Vietnam, the day's routine centered on eking out a living from a grudging and parsimonious earth. Rice was the staff of life. Planting, tending, harvesting, and processing rice was central to every person's existence. Along with rice, non-city dwellers would raise chickens and ducks, an occasional pig, catch fish where they could—fish from the sea, the rivers, the streams, from flooded rice paddies, tiny pools created by monsoon rains, wherever. Fish was the most ubiquitous protein source.

To the Americans unable to pierce the veil of reticence, of inscrutable Orientalness, the Vietnamese people appeared as merely another inanimate part of the inhospitable landscape, outwardly inured and used to the horrors of war all around them. When an American Marine or soldier survived his tour and went home, those others, the locals, would remain in place, living in the same bad dream that to Americans was the entire Vietnam experience. For nearly all Americans, the view from the RVN side, those with the greatest stake in the outcome, received scant attention or consideration.

It was not so unusual that, as a lieutenant, George Philip was unaware of the close relationship the American Marine Corps had had with the Vietnamese Marines since 1954, when he himself had been in fourth grade. Very few Americans, especially those closest to the fighting between 1965-1971, experienced anything but the "American experience" in Vietnam in which meaningful interaction with ARVN or TQLC forces was limited.

By the time he arrived in Tan Son Nhut outside of Saigon to begin his second tour, Captain Philip had necessarily been brought up to speed by the language and cultural training he had this time been given. Of the nearly four hundred thousand American Leathernecks who had, by mid-1971 come and gone from Vietnam, fewer than six hundred had been tasked with advisory duty.

Advisory duty with the Vietnamese Marine Corps was a curious assignment, particularly this late in the war. By 1971 the men in command of the nine infantry and three artillery battalions of the TQLC were typically majors. (The American practice was to place lieutenant colonels in command of battalions.) While nearly all of the American officers assigned to serve with the TQLC were folks with at least one prior tour of combat action, virtually all the men commanding Vietnamese battalions had entered service as second lieutenants and, because they had not yet been killed or wounded too severely, and the war was not yet won, were still effectively on their one and only, continuous tour of duty.

Because of the way the TQLC conducted operations, each infantry battalion, by design, usually had two American advisors. When in the field, TQLC battalions would divide their command element into two groups. The primary element, the Alpha Command Group, contained the battalion commander and the senior American advisor, usually a senior captain or a major. The second element was headed by the battalion executive officer (XO). Known as the Bravo Command Group, it was established with the intent that if the Alpha Command Group was hit or incapacitated, the XO's could take over. Spreading out the leadership this way ensured that the enemy could not easily neutralize the entire command structure of a battalion. If a battalion had a second American advisor he usually traveled with the XO and was typically a captain junior to the other American advisor.

One of the great spiritual and psychological boosts to any fighting man is the notion that he is literally part of a family or group to which each man closely relates and on which each man completely relies. Comradeship and friendship are taken to levels experienced nowhere else. Nearly all men who do brave things do so not because they are thinking of mom and apple pie, but because they are trying to save their buddies. *Covan* duty complicated this concept ever so slightly.

As advisors, American officers were at least partially removed from the close bonds they had earlier established with the men they had served with, had led and were led by.

As advisors they technically had no command authority, and as Americans, even after language training, few had the verbal skills to converse in complex, deep ways with those whom they now shared life's most intimate ordeals. It was impossible to not experience at least some isolation, especially in the beginning as the *covan's* skills and value was being coldly assessed by the men they were advising and by the troops who surrounded the headquarters element and observed in fascination the differences of these hairy, usually much larger Americans.

Every single TQLC battalion commander had, at a minimum, eight to ten years more combat time than the most senior, erudite American advisor. Combat experience was *not* the main asset the Americans brought to the equation.

Having grown up in a culture that lived and breathed the concepts and realities of the integration and effective use of fire support, and even as comparative neophytes, the American Marine officers were in high demand. Even if the Vietnamese officers did not personally like the Americans paired with them, which happened on rare occasions, they always appreciated the resources that were represented.

In addition to being able to effectively deliver the needed fire support when requested or required, *covans* had to remember, just like they did when they commanded platoons and companies, that their actions were always on display for those around them to observe. The fishbowl existence as advisors was magnified because of their being the relative oddity compared to the Vietnamese troops they served and lived with.

The TQLC had, by 1971, artillery resources in increasing amounts. What they did not have, and likely never would have, was a navy with unlimited rounds to fire from destroyers and cruisers like the U.S. Navy did. Neither were they ever likely to have an air force that could put the amount of bombs on a target that a B-52 ARCLIGHT strike or a strike delivered by any type of fighter-bombers the U.S. Air Force maintained in abundance could.

As much as an American advisor might be forgiven his foreign quirks, especially if he was good, especially if he got on well with the men he was in immediate daily contact with—the radio operators and the cowboys—those whose positive or negative gossip would filter over to the other men in the rest of the battalion, he still had to remember at all times who and where he was.

Covans really were required to be, aside from unflappable warriors and master practitioners of fire-support coordination, American ambassadors in tiger-striped uniforms. At all times a *covan* needed to be empathetic to the cultural nuances and differences between what he was used to doing as an American Marine and how things needed to be done with the Vietnamese Marine Corps. Above all else he needed to be aware of "face" and "saving face."

The American proclivity to attempt to solve problems in the most direct, expeditious manner often ran counter to maintaining Confucian decorum. Flagrant, egregious breaches of cultural sensitivities could be a huge problem. An astute *covan* needed to juggle these issues all the time, every day.

All U.S. Marine officers who served with the TQLC had varying periods of adjustment that included isolation and loneliness, no matter how close they usually became with their Vietnamese comrades. This made relationships with other *covans*, especially in the world of Vietnamization as there were fewer and fewer Americans in country with whom to have fellowship, incredibly important. When units would have periods of refurbishment or R&R back at Thu Duc near Saigon, American officers would often spend their off-duty hours in the company of brother *covans*. This was the environment in Saigon in which Captain George Philip first met a few of his soon-to-be best friends.

George had known intuitively and by listening to various war stories and scuttlebutt before coming over that a large percentage of the already in-country *covans* were big-time gunfighters, legitimate legends throughout the USMC infantry community. In World Wars I and II, men like John Ripley, Ray Smith, Walt Boomer, and others who had reputations as serious, hard-core warriors acquired during earlier tours, would have been celebrated and known to the greater American public. This war was different. While many could identify Lieutenant Calley and the ignominious actions at My Lai, it was only in the tiny community of professionals that the real leaders and their brave deeds were known.

George Philip knew he had been on the varsity team as a Marine fighting up in I Corps during his prior tour. Now as a *covan* he was certain he had joined the all-star team. The deep bench of talent the Marine Corps had assembled for this particular mission was a "Who's who" of some of the best junior officers anywhere. It was at once humbling and exhilarating.

MOVING ON

By the summer of 1971 there were more than 200 million Americans who had never spent a day sweating or bleeding anywhere close to Southeast Asia. For nearly all of them, Vietnam was mostly a vicarious inconvenience, a nightly television nuisance, an issue maybe to be upset or frustrated about.

For those who stayed at home, the Vietnam experience was still something that impacted them, which moved them in ways impossible to fully describe, quantify, or even understand. The concurrent societal changes and upheaval, the civil rights movement, the drug culture, the sexual revolution, the denigration of respect for most forms of authority; all these things were somehow inextricably linked to and were part of the greater Vietnam phenomenon which included every person old enough to remember having watched *Leave it to Beaver* or *The Adventures of Ozzie and Harriet* before they were relegated to reruns.

By the summer of 1971, America was beginning to move on. The number of men left in theater belied their levels of risk as very few of the more than one hundred thousand still in Vietnam were assigned to hazardous duties. The draft was still going but was winding down. The numbers of casualties were a far cry from levels of 1968 and 1969. Even the music was getting past the war as fewer and fewer songs directly protested American participation.

By the summer of 1971 it was evident that the future was being looked to with Vietnam not in it. Memories of Vietnam did, however, still crowd the picture from the rearview mirror, especially for those young men who had been there, returned, and were now involved in taking up again life's normal pursuits, whatever those were.

Of the forty-three thousand or so other men drafted into the Marine Corps during the Vietnam War, few of them, if any, ever commanded an infantry platoon in combat. While no one was then tracking these things specifically, Chuck Goggin may well have owned the record for the length of time a corporal, promoted to sergeant after two months, held combat command.

The single Purple Heart he had been given, even though he was hit on three separate occasions by enemy shrapnel, was typical for the men he served with who often refused evacuation or recognition for their wounds, choosing instead to remain with their buddies in the bush who needed them.

Put in for a Silver Star by his skipper, John Ripley, the award was downgraded to a Bronze Star that was granted during a time when the leadership of Third Battalion, Third Marines, had been downright niggardly in the dispensation of valor medals.

Released from active duty on February 10, 1968—nearly two years to the day from his time of induction—Chuck Goggin was in Vero Beach, Florida nine days later for baseball spring training with the Dodgers organization. While his former comrades who remained in Vietnam fought a hundred firefights during the Tet Offensive, Chuck now existed outside and apart from that, this time instead battling figuratively to make the team.

Among his baseball teammates there was little or no discussion at all about the war in Vietnam, let alone any serious questions concerning Chuck's participation in it. The only thing most of them cared about was that they did not have to go. In fact, many of the ball players he knew had actually joined reserve and National Guard units with the express intent of avoiding Vietnam service. "Purple Heart" or "Purple Haze," it was all the same to those more interested in pursuing whatever there was to pursue in the taking up of life.

From spring training in 1968 all the way through to the summer of 1971, while not quite as tumultuous as action in northern I Corps, Chuck's life was a blur of non-stop movement in a world that turned around baseball. Following his first spring training it was AA ball in Albuquerque for summer league, winter league in Arizona where he was managed by a gentleman he particularly liked named Tommy Lasorda. Next year, still with the Dodgers organization and still managed by Lasorda, it was AAA ball in Spokane. From there he was traded to the Pirates organization for a young pitcher named Jim Bunning.

Playing for AA and AAA teams in Columbus, Charleston, and Waterbury in Connecticut, there was even time carved out to play

Mexican winter ball. Through it all, through the numerous injuries which included a severe ankle break, Chuck Goggin endured and pressed ahead, clawing his way up. Hopefully, he was about to make it into the majors.

By the summer of 1971 there was still not a day that went by that Chuck did not think about his Vietnam time. By the summer of 1971 it was a rare day indeed that he ever spoke of his Vietnam experience at all.

By the summer of 1971 Chuck Goggin was married to both baseball and a new bride. He was moving on. Vietnam had been an experience he would never have traded for anything. But he was glad it was, for him, history and no longer a current event.

IN COUNTRY...PART TWO

The flight into Tan Son Nhut was uneventful. Captain George Philip had never made it down to Saigon before on his first tour. His entire Vietnam experience was just as it had been for most Marines; the coming, the fighting, the going had all taken place up north through and in I Corps.

Upon arrival, George was met by two brother *covans* who spirited him through whatever were the incoming processes at the airport. Except for occasional sandbagged positions along the route into town and the presence of Vietnamese army and police, it was difficult to tell in August of 1971 that there was a war on.

Saigon was abuzz with life and commerce. Enjoying the scenery and the activity, but aghast at the way folks drove, George Philip was certain he would become KIA on the ride in from the airport on day one.

From the airport they drove directly to the headquarters of the Vietnamese Marine Corps, a place called the Bo Tu Linh, in the center of Saigon. Welcomed aboard by the American XO of the advisory command, he was also given the tiger-striped uniforms (George had sent his measurements over in advance so that the tailor-made uniforms all *covans* wore would be ready for him upon arrival.) and the distinctive beret he would wear during his one-year tour. As it was late in the day and the in-processing and familiarization issues would take several days anyway, George was dismissed so that he could get over to the Hotel Splendid, also in the center of Saigon, where most *covans* maintained a room.

Though he was dead tired, he joined the group of majors and captains, all senior to him, who were back from the field that evening at the Hoa Binh, the Saigon club of choice for discerning *covans*. It was apparent from the moment he sat down, before he could tip his first beer, that this odd collection of American Marine officers really was special. He knew immediately he was in the company of greatness. It was as if he had fallen in with a twentieth century version of Robin Hood. This group of Merry Men was unique to his experience.

Hoping to cure or recover from his jet lag and retire early to make up for the sleep he had been unable to have on his flight over, he tried to excuse himself. Major Andy DeBona, one of the merriest of the Merry Men and who could have passed for Little John himself, disabused the young captain of the idea of not spending the entire evening in revelry with all the others.* As George respectfully attempted to leave, the major asked him: "And where do you think you're going?"

George tried to explain.

"The hell you are. You are going to stay here and drink with us!"

George was stuck. All the very junior captain could say, with as much enthusiasm as any Naval Academy midshipman might, was "Aye, aye sir!"

---

* As the commanding officer of Company M, Third Battalion, 26th Marines in September of 1967 Andy DeBona had been awarded the Navy Cross for extraordinary heroism during a particularly bloody battle with the NVA in the vicinity of Con Thien. DeBona was already a legend among infantry Marines. His actions as an advisor with the TQLC's Seventh Battalion during the Easter Offensive would only enhance his reputation as a warrior.

CHAPTER SEVENTEEN

King Kong Lives!

The process that brought young Captain George Philip up to speed and into the relatively small world of the advisory group of American Marines took about five days in Saigon. The pace of operations there in the rear, in the vaunted "Pearl of the Orient," during the late summer of 1971, was far different than he had recalled from his frenzied, earlier arrival in 1968 up in Danang.

In those leisurely few days George met all the *covans* who happened to be in Saigon, was briefed on TQLC operations, squared his paperwork and personal affairs away, and listened in to routine daily radio exchanges between headquarters there at the Bo Tu Linh and units in the field nearly three hundred miles away. In those unhurried few evenings at the Hoa Binh, George continued to drink beer and marvel at the crew he had thrown in with. It was also made plain to him by the particularly cordial relations he had with civilians and observations he made that the regular Vietnamese showed great deference for the American officers clad in the tiger-striped uniforms of the TQLC.

Once he was sufficiently snapped in, George was given the mail bag for delivery to the *covans* up north, grabbed his gear and motored back out to Tan Son Nhut. By now he was used to Saigon traffic. The jeep ride out was far less traumatic than the ride in only days before.

Thumbing a hop on a C-123 cargo plane that was filled with Vietnamese Marines, a few female dependents going to visit their men, along with a mix of chickens, ducks and pigs, he was again going off to war up yonder in I Corps, this time *covan* style.

By the summer of 1971, the defense of the northernmost part of I Corps had been given over to the ARVN Third Division and the three rotating brigades of the TQLC. This included the portions adjacent to both the Demilitarized Zone (DMZ) and the eastern border areas of Laos which included Khe Sanh, an area formerly defended by the Americans of the Third Marine Division (the First Marine Division's tactical area of responsibility was to the south of the Third Marine Division's).

The Third Division, a division created in the aftermath of *Lam Son 719*, was comprised of soldiers who were largely from the surrounding northern provinces. The ARVN Third Division was also understood to be the institutional receptacle for malcontents and deserters.[1] As the most remote major unit from Saigon, the purgatory existence was thought to be the perfect cure for marginal soldiers who would have a difficult time deserting from there with defection to the north being the only alternative to honorable service.

The Marine brigades (each one consisting of three battalions of infantry, an artillery battalion, various supporting units, and a brigade staff which was small by American standards) balanced the marginal proficiency of local ARVN units and became the defensive pillars for the government and civilians reliant on support to keep the Communists at bay and on their side of the DMZ. Vietnamese Marine brigades would typically spend three months up north before rotating back through Saigon and Thu Duc for a month of maintenance, refurbishment, and R&R. The intent was to have two of the three brigades, or at least two of those brigades' three battalions, forward at all times.

The Vietnamese Marine Corps' First Artillery Battalion was currently the fire support component to their Brigade 369. It was also the unit to which Captain George Philip had been assigned as a *covan*. With not a lot of heavy action then taking place, it was decided to break him in by farming him out to B Battery where he could observe and also handle fire support coordination planning if things suddenly got hot.

B Battery was occupying the northernmost firebase in all of South Vietnam. Several kilometers north of Dong Ha, the last town on Highway 1 as one approached the DMZ; Gio Linh was the absolute end of the line, the farthest place one could be from Saigon and not be in enemy territory. Known also by its military designation A-2, or Alpha 2, on the map it was a fraction of an inch inside the friendly side of the border, just short of the DMZ. From the moment his jeep headed north out of Dong Ha going to A-2 it was evident to George that, even without shots being exchanged, he was definitely back in Indian Country. Saigon and its relatively provincial living seemed a million miles away.

From their positions in fortified old bunkers—with one dating back to the time of the French—and observation posts, located on high ground just east of Highway 1, the Vietnamese Marines and their American advisors could look straight across the Ben Hai River, the official boundary between the two Vietnams, and see the NVA flag flying defiantly in the stultifying humidity. When they were not shooting at each other, and after *Lam Son 719* the level of activity had dropped off precipitously, sometimes there seemed to be an uneasy, unofficial, awkward truce in effect.

A separate, five-man Naval Gunfire Team was collocated with B Battery. Equipped with a state-of-the-art night vision device and laser range finder that probably weighed fifty pounds and was of questionable value, the team's presence gave added lethality as Alpha 2 and the surrounding area was within range of guns from U.S. warships prowling the northern coast just offshore. For George, it was also nice to have these other Americans to talk with.

By early September, George had established a routine of sorts; he had learned and now understood his function as a *covan*, and how things operated. He was a veteran...again. As designed, pretty much on schedule and as expected, he had bonded with his Vietnamese contemporaries, enjoyed working with his Vietnamese cowboy, and was making a tangible contribution to his ally's fire support effort. It still seemed an odd thing that they could be this close to the DMZ, in range and in view of enemy positions, and not be in constant contact. Whenever George had this or other unusual ideas he would simply remind himself that he was in Vietnam.

The American experience and expectations in Vietnam were limited by the American experience in everything else. Made safe from physical invasion by two ocean buffers, by the summer of 1971 there was no one alive in Fortress America who could recall the horrors of their own Civil War. Since then the nation's warriors had all gone off to fight for democracy on foreign territory. Those who had remained at home, especially during World War II, had been thoroughly indoctrinated into the need to make the world safe for democracy. As civilians they worked overtime, making good wages, as part of the great Arsenal of Democracy, safely cranking out all the bombers and tanks and ships that would overwhelm the Axis.

It was always all about democracy. Painter Norman Rockwell's famous and widely published *Four Freedoms*, a stroke of propaganda genius, (inspired by a 1941 speech given by FDR and published first in the *Saturday Evening Post* in 1943) captured the national consciousness, sense of justice and the chivalrous, patriotic hearts of the American people in a way no one else could or had done since. Even in the darkest days immediately after December 7, 1941—before the Doolittle Raid, before the battle at Midway and the invasion of northern Africa—few Americans except maybe those in Hawaii for a brief time, believed a ground war or an enemy invasion would be in their future. Rarely was there ever, for the folks at home, a collective fear for their direct physical security.

Americans at home, who all throughout the Cold War lived under the threat of Mutually Assured Destruction (MAD) from the Soviets, did not live with the serious prospect of the Red Horde showing up on their doorsteps in Detroit or Denver or Duluth. The fathers and mothers and sons and daughters living in the Republic of Vietnam had no such assurance.

What Americans continually failed to recognize as they righteously preached the gospel of democracy and free markets, what Americans could not truly appreciate because they had mercifully been spared as a nation, was that man's need for physical security superseded all the fancy talk about individual rights and personal liberties. The Communist enemy was not so limited. They, who in the Communist north had not in this current war experienced invasion and only limited impact from

American strategic bombing, understood well the value of terror in keeping the contested population outside the grip of the Americans and their perceived puppets in Saigon. The very good news was that by the summer of 1971, the Communist effort or ability to terrorize had been dramatically reduced. Confidence in the RVN government and its improving military forces were not lost on the politically attuned leadership in Hanoi.

ROUTINE AT ALPHA 2

Life as an American officer with the Vietnamese Marine Corps took some adjusting. While there were the obvious cultural and language differences and challenges, there were also unusual benefits. As formal as the American Marine Corps was with its structure of rank, where the USMC had drilled into recruits from the moment they first stepped aboard at the recruit depots at Parris Island and San Diego a tremendous respect for those senior to one's position, the Marine Corps was equally forceful in instilling the notion of responsibility for those who were under one's command. Ensuring the needs and welfare of the troops were met was always a very close second to the goal of mission accomplishment. Marine officers were expected to be the first on the field of battle and the last to leave. They were to conspicuously lead from the front at all times. That concept carried over into every aspect of leadership, including things like ensuring the troops were fed and cared for before their seniors, etc. Officers had people to assist them to the extent that it led to mission accomplishment. That was it. That assistance did not include personal servitude. Personal servitude was simply *anathema* to American military culture.

Doing business with the TQLC was slightly different. Asian culture, inspired and influenced by things outside of what Americans were familiar with, along with the omnipresent cult of the commander at nearly every level, was far less egalitarian.

All officers, even junior officers, in the Vietnamese military had their attendants. To be assigned to assist an officer, to be his radio operator, his body guard or his personal aid—called a "cowboy" by the Americans—was not viewed as a job for obsequious, apple-polishing types. To be any part of the leadership entourage was to become a part of the leadership. It was to become a part of the inner circle. No matter what it was, it was important, dignified duty.

George Philip did not rate a radio operator in his current job. Those things he could handle quite easily by himself. He did, however, rate having an attendant. Ha Si (Corporal) Tuong was a relatively old man for his rank (He had a son who was a soldier in the ARVN serving somewhere else in Vietnam.) but discharged his duties as Dai Uy (Captain) Philip's cowboy in a typically TQLC fastidious, professional manner. Tuong never asked his captain for favors and was always grateful for the things George did like buying him cartons of American cigarettes. They got along extremely well, each looking out for the other with genuine respect and appreciation.

Every morning when he awoke Dai Uy Philip could be certain that, as sure as the sun would rise, there was a bowl of hot soup and another of heated water for shaving waiting for him. If his boots had been judged marginally dirty by the doting Tuong the night before, they would be cleaned and ready to go at the foot of his cot no matter when he got up. Whether there was intense artillery fire going out to the units they supported or things were sublimely peaceful, Tuong discharged his duties without fail.

BREAKS IN A-2 ROUTINE...

Every human being who could string together two consecutive, critical thoughts knew intuitively that war was hell and that war was strange. Certainly anyone able to read or hear knew that the war in Vietnam was something outside most folks' range of what might be called normal. One thing that made the war even more unusual, nearly surreal by the summer of 1971 for Americans still involved, was that by that time, with the rapidly diminishing number of men serving in Southeast Asia, those men who were still serving there would go to even more extreme lengths to assist one another in very odd circumstances that never failed to amuse.

As young and strapping as he was, barely twenty-seven-year-old Captain George Philip had developed a mild case of hemorrhoids. While certainly not life threatening or dramatically impacting his ability to coordinate all the fire support that he had so far coordinated, they were still a problem. Whether it was from the stresses of combat or the continued digestion of a less than ideal diet, George Philip had hemorrhoids. They were a pain, literally and figuratively. Unashamedly, he got right on the horn and called back to brigade headquarters, asking if anyone in the rear had anything he could take for it. What a surprise he had when not one hour later a U.S. Army Huey from an Air Cavalry unit called in with a request for permission to land in the A-2 landing zone with a small package for Captain Philip. Running out to meet the bird as it touched down, but did not shut down; George was bent over to avoid the turning rotor blades and approached the helicopter at the co-pilot's window. Approaching the bird, still bent over, the smiling pilot with his eyes covered up by the helmet shades reached out his small portal and handed him an Air Cavalry business card and a small tube of Preparation H, saluted his new Marine friend, applied power and then quickly lifted off. George wondered what would have happened if Senator William Proxmire, the man known for making a big deal about government fraud, waste and abuse, was to learn of this new attempt of inter-service cooperation.

Captain Philip was like most Marines of his grade and station in his genuine respect for bravery, whether it was demonstrated by Marines, American or Vietnamese, or by folks from the services most Leathernecks considered not quite equal to the USMC. George Philip was certain that the absolute craziest and bravest bastards in all of Vietnam, as a group, were the army warrant officers who flew Hueys. On too many occasions he had seen these guys fly into situations any reasonable, sane person would have refused. To him and all the others, it was always a tremendous comfort to know that there were army helicopters nearby in case there was need for an emergency medevac or gunships or resupply, hemorrhoid problems notwithstanding.

Captain Philip had great appreciation for the Navy as well. In the first months at Alpha 2 he and the Naval Gunfire Team had called in more than their share of support missions from the various cruisers and destroyers just off the coast. Perhaps it was because his father had been a destroyer skipper in World War II when he was killed that George gave extra thought to the ships he could not see from his bunkered positions there, just shy of the DMZ, but could always count on to deliver the goods when called to that he jumped at the chance for a visit.

From the time American Marines first went ashore in Vietnam in early 1965, the extra layer of protective firepower afforded those units operating within range of the guns from the dozens of Seventh Fleet men-of-war was a critical aspect to American success against Communist forces. When most American combat forces had been sent home by mid-1971, ships of the Seventh Fleet remained on station to provide the same support to Vietnamese Marine units operating close to the coast. With so few Americans now calling in that support, the relationships between those ashore and those at sea became even more acute and personal.

It was not at all uncommon one sunny day when not a whole lot was going on that the Naval Gunfire Liaison officer aboard the USS *Rupertus* (DD-851) called ashore and asked George Philip if he would like to fly out to visit the ship that had been recently providing a good share of their gunfire support. Captain Philip jumped at the opportunity. Cajoling another army Huey crew into flying him out to the ship, it was that crew's first ever attempt to land aboard an underway ship which was no easy feat. Knowing no fear, the army pilots braved the landing and became part of the tour group in the *Rupertus* wardroom for lunch.

What impressed George most that day after having grown used to Ha Si Tuong's meals was being able to sit down to real linen table cloths, eating with real silverware, and—as if he had finally died and gone to heaven—eating as much ice cream as he could consume for dessert. When it was time to fly back, the ship's captain gave each of his visitors a cigarette lighter with the *Rupertus* logo emblazoned on the side and a box of frozen steaks.

Returning the favor in true Marine Corps fashion, George invited the ship's captain to send an officer ashore to Alpha 2 for a day to see how the war was conducted on the ground and live as Marines did. When that particular ensign returned to the ship he would no doubt have war stories to tell, maybe something even for the grandchildren someday. Those things happened during the good days when not a whole lot of bad things were taking place.

Not everything was fun and games even when fun and games were involved. Even when there was no contact with the NVA there were constant reminders of how serious life ashore could be.

There was the incident in one of the TQLC infantry battalions that had come up near Alpha 2 in which one of the young Marines had lost a considerable sum gambling with his comrades. When the fellow refused to honor his debts, his platoon commander ordered him to pay. In a rage that evening, the offender had thrown a hand grenade into the platoon commander's hooch killing one officer and wounding several others.

The next morning, with the entire battalion in attendance, the guilty, soon-to-be-dead ex-Marine was ordered to dig his own grave so that when he stood before the firing squad, his soon-to-be-lifeless body would collapse into the hole he just dug when they shot him, making it easier to bury him. The American *covans* made it a habit of not being present and of not observing the meting out of TQLC justice, remembering again at all times that they were in Vietnam.

JOHN RIPLEY ARRIVES

As long as Brigade 369 had the duty up near the DMZ, the First Artillery Battalion, with B Battery at A-2, would remain in place to provide support for any of the brigade's three infantry battalions or any other friendly unit operating in the area. While the artillery units would usually remain in fixed positions, positions that were also known and dialed in by NVA gunners, the infantry battalions would, to keep their Marines fresh and alert, rotate their operation areas across northern I Corps.

When a TQLC infantry battalion would get posted to the area north of Dong Ha, it was common for them to send their one or two *covans* up to the outpost position George Philip and the Naval Gunfire Team occupied with the Vietnamese Marine artillerymen for a period of time.

That the Marine Corps had failed to send Captain John Ripley to any formal language school prior to sending him back to Vietnam as an advisor in no way limited the demand for his services. Arriving nearly two months prior to Captain Philip, John Ripley went through the same process in Saigon before heading back to his old stomping grounds in northern I Corps.

By the time he rotated into Alpha 2 in late September 1971 with his host TQLC battalion, John Ripley had only recently been attached to work with his new friend, counterpart, and kindred spirit Thieu Ta (Major) Binh and the Soi Bien as their senior *covan*. In the two months prior to joining Third Battalion, John had served, in what he described in letters home to Moline and his folks as a "free agent"; first as an assistant brigade advisor to Brigade 258 and then as a regular infantry advisor for a short period with the TQLC's Fifth Battalion.

By the time Third Battalion again, along with *covan* John Ripley for the first time, arrived in the area of Alpha-2/Gio Linh, they had seen a fair amount of recent, hard action. What a peculiar experience it was for Captain Ripley to spend a day or two with his new friend George Philip in the observation bunker with no shots being exchanged and tons of enemy activity out in front of them in the DMZ. Had it been up to Ripley he would have called in all the B-52s he could and turned the area humming with activity into a parking lot. The oversized NVA flag that flew night and day just across the Ben Hai River would have been his initial aiming point. But it was not his call to make. When all else failed, like his friend George Philip and every other right-thinking man, he would remind himself that he was in Vietnam and everything about that was crazy. And while it still made no sense to him, he could at least continue to tolerate the incongruity of life as he was living it.

Most combat for anyone was typified by short periods of intense action followed by long stretches of eerie quiet, boredom, inactivity, and waiting for the next surge and opportunity to kill or be killed. Life at Alpha 2 was no different except that they were always in plain view of the bad guys.

No one thought it was the least bit strange that the two senior men in the bunker, John Ripley and George Philip, both combat savvy, battle-hardened, and college-trained engineers from the U.S. Naval Academy, would spend the better part of a reasonably quiet afternoon engrossed in the construction of a jigsaw puzzle. Putting the skills of their taxpayer-funded educations to maximum effort, they built it with a precision that would have made any of their old engineering professors proud.

Life in combat had a way of reducing things to their most basic wants and needs. As much as their physical security could be assured by sound bunker construction and the enemy deterred by the threat of rapid retribution from nearby artillery or offshore naval gunfire if attacked, the next level of need to be satisfied — for the average American or Vietnamese Marine there was zero opportunity for female companionship at Alpha 2 — was food and intellectual stimulation.

Mail and news from home were super critical. Letters were always read and reread, and then stored away to be reread again later. Care packages with, by the time they arrived in Vietnam, reasonably stale cookies or brownies were widely shared and rapidly consumed. Other food items like Tabasco sauce and dried fruit or canned whatever would be later added into the regular diet to spice things up. Newspapers from home, no matter how out of date, were always popular as were paperback books that could be perused during those long, slow periods between those short, intense bouts of pandemonium.

In one of the more recent packages he had received, stuffed with the obligatory food and news items, George's girlfriend had cleverly included a thousand-piece jigsaw puzzle of the original King Kong. The box cover showed the finished product that was the 1933 poster that had to have adorned the lobbies and window displays in the theaters way back when with the stern but sentimental and love-struck-looking behemoth clutching the sweet and vulnerable-appearing Fay Wray in his hairy grip.

Like the engineers they were, they found the corners and all the straight pieces first, looked for color concentrations and patterns, and then built it from the outside in. The American and Vietnamese Marines around them hardly noticed, going about their duties and routines as always. The puzzle was actually constructed over a period of hours during times of complete concentration mixed with others when duty called. When it was finished, it was finished. Someone took a picture of the two captains and their masterpiece. The two friends admired, very briefly, their finished product as did passersby. From then, it was on to something else.

There was nothing particularly special about the King Kong puzzle or any action that took place while it was being put together, piece by piece, that made the day unique. What would become unique to that single, odd episode was that on every subsequent meeting between the two *covans*, whenever their paths would cross, whether at Alpha 2 or Dong Ha or Saigon, the two warriors would greet each other in their own personal, private way. "King Kong lives!!!" was the secret-handshake equivalent into the two-man Ripley-Philip fraternity. If they both lived past the war it would be something to try and explain to children and grandchildren. Few on the outside knew the meaning but every man who had been through scary times could understand this special language between warriors.

CHAPTER EIGHTEEN

"Talk, Fight. Talk, Fight."

Northern I Corps
Fall 1971

The number of Americans left in South Vietnam by the end of the year would be fewer than 160,000. Of those, nearly all were men serving in support or combat support roles. By year-end 1971 every single Marine ground combat unit was gone from Southeast Asia and the U.S. Army had very few actual trigger-pulling soldiers still there. Those who remained really were in support roles, there to help the Vietnamese "Vietnamize."

The only thing more unusual than the rules of engagement imposed upon American ground and air forces in Vietnam was attempting to understand the Rube Goldberg workings of the politics shaping whatever action there was. Between April and October of 1968 the U.S. had, in a number of *naïve* goodwill gestures towards the Communists, essentially ceased the bombing of North Vietnam above the 20th Parallel. This left roughly 90 percent of the country untouched. The more practical and focused-on-victory North Vietnamese correctly used the opportunity to strategically reposition critical war assets and to build a much improved, ultra-modern Soviet-supplied air defense system around Hanoi and Haiphong.

Movement to the peace talks in Paris with the inscrutable, intractable Communists was an especially painful process for the results-oriented and anxious-to-work-out-a-deal Americans. That it took nine months to agree on the shape of the actual table around which negotiations would take place was a not so subtle harbinger of things to come. In the meantime both sides, with the Communists arguably demonstrating greater cunning and political acumen, engaged in the very typical Maoist notion of "talk, fight…talk, fight"—the practice of simultaneously fighting as if not involved in negotiations and negotiating as if not involved in fighting.

Of central importance to the American people, aside from a general withdrawal from Southeast Asia, was the repatriation of the increasing number of POWs known to be held under crude and torturous conditions in ironically-named places like the "Hanoi Hilton."

Although the November 1970 American raid at Son Tay, twenty miles west of Hanoi, by highly trained and extremely motivated forces led by army colonel Arthur "Bull" Simons failed in its attempt to spring the POWs held there—they had earlier been moved because of the threat of flood to a different location— the action had significant upside. That a large group of American special operations forces had so brazenly penetrated into the heart of North Vietnam sent a strong political message which all parties understood. Where the Americans would bend or yield on certain things, the treatment of men confirmed as prisoners was something the enemy, at some later time, might be made to account for. The treatment of POWs improved subsequent to the Son Tay raid as did morale among the prisoners. The raiding force also had opportunity, during their brief moments inside the Son Tay compound, to happily dispatch a fair number of bad guys. No Americans were lost in the rescue attempt.

The negotiating and bickering at the interminable Paris peace talks continued. From the very earliest when the talks first began in May of 1968, the Communist position had multiple aims: to gain recognition from the U.S. and RVN for the National Liberation Front (NLF) of South Vietnam (which the southern Communists were known by in their own circles), to drive a wedge between the American imperialists and their illegitimate South Vietnamese lackey allies, to get Americans to accept responsibility for everything that was bad and then to have them leave and grant no further aid to the RVN side.

For more than three years all parties had futilely engaged. In May of 1969 President Nixon had proposed the withdrawal of all forces not indigenous to South Vietnam. This meant both American and North Vietnamese troops. In October of 1971, not much further along, the Americans again put forth a similar proposal.[1] Unfortunately for Nixon, the northern Communists were nowhere near as anxious to leave as were the Americans, who seemed to be on the way home anyway, with or without negotiations. The Communists remained focused on victory; victory at some unknown, unquantifiable price above which Americans were willing to pay or to outwait their enemies for.

In July of 1971 President Nixon surprised the nation and the world with the announcement that he would soon travel to Peking with the express intent of normalizing relations with the world's most populous country. The strategic benefits to be gained were significant. The Soviets and the Chinese had, within the last two years, fought a number of bloody territorial skirmishes at several spots on their long contiguous border. To expedite the breaking up of the great Red monolith and to exploit their visceral mistrust for each other might leverage and rebuild American power perceived to have been spent for questionable gain in Southeast Asia. Whether the president could turn that into political or battlefield advantage in Vietnam remained to be seen. The men who ran North Vietnam were justifiably concerned. They did understand that, especially after learning the lessons from the Son Tay raid, the American Achilles' heel was the prisoner issue. They would continually play that card in all further negotiations. In the meantime, the withdrawal of American forces went on without interruption.

Vietnamese National Military Academy
Graduation Ceremony
Da Lat, Republic of Vietnam
December 27, 1971

It was a balmy, typically perfect Da Lat day with families, friends, and well wishers gathered to celebrate the graduation of their young men as second lieutenants and ensigns in the service of their battle-born country. That the Republic of Vietnam and Class 24 of the National Military Academy had, so far, together survived was no minor miracle. That there were, by late December of 1971, incipient signs of promise, and even victory, was something all could be proud of.

With the year about to conclude, the future, while nowhere near assured, was showing definite patterns of brightness. The Saigon government controlled more of the countryside than it had since the nation's birth nearly eighteen years earlier. Genuine reforms were being implemented and while they would never occur at a pace to assuage the government's critics at home or in the Western press and American universities, they were blunting Communist appeal. The Viet Cong infrastructure, so badly damaged during Tet 1968, still had not been able to reinvent or reconstitute itself. The withdrawal of American ground forces was being balanced by the pledge for access to their ally's deep pockets and continuing air support.

About to be commissioned a second lieutenant (Thieu Uy pronounced "two—wee"), Nguyen Luong was graduating high enough in his class to be among the fourteen men allowed the honor to wear the tiger-striped uniform and select the Marine Corps as their service of choice. While the average American citizen still might have been shocked to learn that the Vietnamese even had a Marine Corps, there would have been twice the surprise to learn that only the top graduates, the best and the brightest, were selected to serve as junior officers in the TQLC and other elite units like the Airborne and Rangers. The competition for placement was intense.

The parade ground for the ceremony was a slightly reduced version of the one at West Point. Smaller in size than the American model, there was no diminution in dignity, pride or passion for the ceremony itself here in Da Lat. Of the 311 young men who had started out with Class 24 back in 1967, 245 had endured and would shortly cross the graduation dais to receive their degrees and commissions as officers in front of the gathered throng of adoring friends and relatives. The excitement and promise that exists at every graduation was tempered for these young men about to enter into the brotherhood of arms by the near certainty that they all, each and every one of them, would soon be leading men in action against the hated Communist foe.

December 27, 1971, was to be the very last day that Class 24 would all be together as one body of men. In every subsequent reunion they might now ponder, whether in five or ten or thirty years, there were those comrades among them, most likely a fair number of them, who would long before then, have made the ultimate sacrifice for their country in its current struggle to survive.

TO DUTY WITH THIRD BATTALION

Following graduation, Thieu Uy (Second Lieutenant) Luong took the full fifteen days of leave he was authorized to spend time with his family and his long-time girlfriend and also to mentally transition from student officer to real, live Marine.

Even though the Vietnamese Marine Corps continued its rapid expansion, by January of 1972 it was still small enough to maintain the strong familial feel it had always had.

Throughout the war, the TQLC had managed to maintain high standards for its officers and men, and was free of the political intrigue that seemed to continually plague ARVN senior officers and their units like so many military forces in developing countries. Neither was the TQLC "over generaled." Lieutenant General Khang, the TQLC's *commandant*, was the only flag officer serving in early 1972.

The fourteen new lieutenants graduated from the National Military Academy in December would be appropriately parceled out to the various battalions. With nine infantry battalions, some would get two. As Third Battalion had always done more than its share of hard fighting, there was always need for new officers. Major Binh would, this go round, be apportioned two platoon leaders.

Luong's assignment to service with Third Battalion was as much a function of the sense of humor of the man who would later become the TQLC's next general officer as it was the genuine needs of the Corps. Colonel Bui The Lan, who would shortly become the next *commandant*, was in charge of officer assignments. Along with Luong went his close friend from school, Second Lieutenant Nhai. As with all languages, words or names often have more than one meaning. In Vietnamese, the second meaning of "Luong" was "eel." In Vietnamese, the second meaning for "Nhai" was something akin to what most in America might term "frog" or an indigenous-to-Vietnam reasonable facsimile. So to the Soi Bien went animal Lieutenants Eel and Frog. Luong went to Fourth Company, Nhai to Second Company. Everyone had a brief, good-natured laugh. That both "animals" were amphibious and marine in nature was a favorable omen not lost on their new battalion commander. Thieu Ta Binh would accept all the good fortune there was available. After that it was back to the serious business of killing Communists.

In All the Way
Northern I Corps, Republic of Vietnam
March 29, 1972

As the new assistant senior Marine advisor, the checking-in process for Lieutenant Colonel Gerry Turley was a bit more involved than it had been for Captains Ripley and Philip. Like John Ripley and a few of the others, Gerry Turley had come to this tour without benefit of language training but very much in possession of an advanced degree in leadership and planning and logistics and fire support coordination and all the other things Marine infantry officers willed themselves to master.

As the number two man in this select group of men, he knew he might, at some odd moment, need to fill in for or replace his boss, Colonel Josh Dorsey, the senior Marine advisor. Without having to read a formal job description, Gerry knew he needed to learn all he could about everything, understand the unusual command relationships the Marines operated under, and get to know the key men of the Vietnamese Marine Corps. Like a studious boxing manager, he needed to meet and get inside the thought processes of his—or his colonel's—fighters, the advisors attached out to the various brigades and battalions, and through them discern the various strengths and weaknesses of the units they served with. Because this was a USMC operation it was no real surprise that he already knew a fair number of the *covans* personally, and nearly all the others by reputation.

As the Assistant Senior Marine Advisor, Lieutenant Colonel Turley had access to higher level intelligence reports than he had heretofore not been allowed to see. In his new job he was directly involved in every aspect of material planning and logistical support not only for the *covans* in the field but for the American Marine support going to the TQLC as well. Lieutenant Colonel Gerry Turley was a busy man. His plate was full.

While there were many things about his new job that he could not or would not reveal in the reestablished routine of regular daily letters to Bunny and the kids, the excitement of simply being in Saigon and appreciating its uniqueness gave him ample subject matter to write about. Saigon was nice enough, exotic enough, peaceful enough even to ponder having Bunny join him there for a visit later in his tour.

The dynamics at home for Bunny Turley and her smaller-by-one brood had evolved significantly since Gerry's first Vietnam tour now more than five years earlier. Oldest daughter and close *confidant* Anne was out of the home and finishing her third year of nursing school in St. Louis. No longer requiring the complete hands-on physical supervision of managing the two small boys and their two slightly older but still sweet and innocent sisters, the job of motherhood had necessarily become more emotionally intense and cerebral.

Chris and Bob, ten and eleven years old respectively, were typical boys, doing scouting and sports and neighborhood stuff that boys their age did. Jeri was now the oldest at home and in three months would graduate from high school. Her father would deal in his own way with the guilt associated with missing that event. Peg was doing nicely as an eighth grader. That two of them were normal, blossoming high school-aged girls added to their mother's daily excitement. All of the Turley children, just like all the children of their parent's friends were "Marine

Kids"—tough as nails, used to the constant moves and making do without Dad around.

At least this time Bunny Turley could take some comfort in knowing the risks in Southeast Asia were low, that the war was almost over, that Gerry was probably safe. As it had been during his first Vietnam tour, finances were a struggle; there was always more month than money. Feeding them all hamburger was a stretch, forget about eating steak.

Gerry Turley took two weeks in Saigon to get up to speed on his new duties. In that period he met with TQLC *commandant* Lieutenant General Khang and toured the various local TQLC training facilities and hospital at Thu Duc. Daily he listened in on operational briefings concerning the disposition of Vietnamese Marine units. He also made numerous trips to MACV, the center of American activities, where he was also routinely briefed on all manner of things.

Colonel Josh Dorsey, the Senior Marine Advisor, who had earlier commanded Third Battalion, Third Marines up north, was of the mindset that the war was winding down. On more than one occasion he shared with his new assistant that he believed they very well might close up the unit during their tour. The action in I Corps, while not completely stopped, certainly was not at a level they had earlier experienced. Things were looking good.

For Gerry, after learning all he could in Saigon, it was time to do what Marine officers do and take a run up to see his *covans*, to get a personal sense for what was going on. It was supposed to be a milk run, completely routine. No big deal. While Gerry was to head north, Colonel Dorsey was scheduled for a brief, well-deserved Easter R&R with his family in the Philippines. Just like it was for every *covan* going to I Corps, he was admonished to remember to take along the mail bag. With his boss out of the country, Gerry would be in charge.

GOING NORTH AND INTO THE UNKNOWN

The scientific evidence was overwhelming. In his own life experiment Gerry Turley was two for two with these death-dealing premonitions. As a young boy he had mustered the sense to stay home that day back in Ogallala, Nebraska when all his buddies had gone swimming at the rock quarry and drowned, and then again as a junior Marine in the Korean War he had somehow declined the R&R flight to Japan and missed the plane crash.

This time there was no getting off. Even if he had not been virtually pinned down on the C-130 deck serving as pillow to those young Vietnamese Marines around him, there was no way out. No way out.

By March 1972 Gerry was too senior, too professional to back out now, no matter what. As young as he still was—especially with Colonel Dorsey gone—he was "the Man," "the Old Man." When troops at the point of contact talked about the organization making it all happen, the "them" in every conversation, Gerry Turley was now one of "them." No, Lieutenant Colonel Gerry Turley USMCR, husband to Bunny, father to Anne, Jeri, Peggy, Bob, and Chris, friend to so many, would dutifully ride this train right over the cliff if he had to. And he would do it with a brave heart. The thing that kept him sane, kept him from taking counsel of his fear was that in his position, with the responsibilities he now shouldered, the pace of things allowed him to block those thoughts out. At least partially.

The flight north from Tan Son Nhut to Phu Bai, except for the very unpleasant personal belief that something horrible was going to happen, was without incident. Gerry was amazed when he landed to see the changes in places that only one or two years earlier were hotly contested with the NVA.

The airfield at Phu Bai, once a beehive of activity and considered to be among the busiest airports in the world, now had tall weeds sprouting between the runway matting that had been placed there by U.S. Navy Seabees. Where once hundreds of helicopters and fighter bombers were in constant motion, the lone USAF C-130 that dropped Gerry and his new TQLC friends off seemed strangely out of place.

It was not just at Phu Bai. As he helicoptered north following Route One it was the same everywhere. And while Gerry could recall dozens of men he had known who fought, bled, and died in the areas that now seemed oddly peaceful, he was also pleased to see the obvious evidences of commerce and progress where before there had only been strife. As indifferent as the locals appeared to him, he was still happy to see some sort of return to normalcy, however defined. Maybe, just maybe, the war really was about to end.

1972: AN ELECTION YEAR

By late March 1972, Vietnam was rarely on the front pages of American newspapers anymore. With Vietnamization progressing at a rapid clip, fewer and fewer Americans were in harm's way. On March 27, UPI reported that, for the first time in more than six years, not including sailors on ships off the coast or air force units in Thailand, there were fewer than one hundred thousand American troops in Vietnam. Sticking with a plan that was routinely withdrawing eleven hundred men per day, the U.S. would reach its goal of sixty-nine thousand troops remaining by May 1.

Capitalizing on his Vietnam withdrawal promises, Richard Nixon was looking especially presidential by March of 1972. Engagement with the People's Republic of China was a political *coup* of major proportions that began to put Southeast Asia in a perspective more appropriate for American global interests. So too did the increasing public cooperation with the Soviets regarding the joint, peaceful exploration of outer space. It was "talk, fight…talk, fight" on the maximum scale.

Back in Saigon, American intelligence analysts and their Vietnamese counterparts had puzzled for months over the recall of several key NVA divisions home from the field. There was healthy debate as to the enemy's intentions. Since as far back as 1970, the North Vietnamese had been receiving increasing quantities of war fighting material from both the Chinese and the Soviets. Many believed the relative calm they were now experiencing did not presage peace but that Hanoi was husbanding resources for another major offensive. The belief, even made public to members of the press, was that the NVA would strike first and hardest from the west out of Laos and Cambodia at the Central Highlands and

Kontum Province with the key town of Pleiku, in order to split the country in half as well as destroy the growing confidence Vietnamese civilians were showing in their government along with Nixon's entire Vietnamization program.

BRIEF MUSINGS

For nearly twenty-three years now Gerry Turley had been a Marine. Like any seasoned Leatherneck, he knew the Corps to be far from perfect. And yet, it never failed to amaze him—after combat and unaccompanied tours and all the unusual assignments that were routine for Marines but extraordinary for most regular folks—to affirm him and nurture his faith in the goodness of the institution when he stopped to think of the concentration of truly good men who always seemed gathered together, voluntarily, under the most horrid conditions. More than counterbalancing his earlier dark premonitions was the reminder that these *covans* who were sparingly sprinkled in among the operating units of the Vietnamese Marine Corps were good men, the very best men America had. At every rank they were uniformly magnificent even though they were each unique and special individuals. The thought of these men gave Gerry Turley comfort and confidence, gave him true joy. If bad times were about to be set upon them, this was the crew to head into the storm's center with.

IN ALL THE WAY

Major Jim Joy USMC, senior advisor to Brigade 147 of the TQLC, was slated as Gerry Turley's official tour guide and handler for the first portion of his four day I Corps visit. From Phu Bai they flew north and west by Huey to Fire Support Base (FSB) Mai Loc which served as Brigade 147's headquarters. Gerry would observe operations there and remain overnight with Major Joy. The plan was to spend his second night, with several other visits in between, at Fire Base (FB) Sarge as Major Walt Boomer's guest. Major Boomer was senior advisor to the TQLC's Fourth Battalion and was, like most senior battalion advisors, collocated with their Alpha Command Group.

During his brief four days up north, Lieutenant Colonel Turley hoped he would be able to personally meet with as many of the American Marine advisors as possible. With Brigade 369 back in Saigon participating in the normal rotation of rest, refurbishment and retraining, Gerry would visit most of the battalions constituting Brigades 147 and 258, the two TQLC brigades currently on station and poised for action in northern I Corps.

That there existed a deep bench of *covan* talent could not be overstated. Beginning with the senior brigade advisors—Jim Joy at Brigade 147, Jon Easley at Brigade 258, and Bob Sheridan at Brigade 369—the excellence continued down into each of the battalions. Starting with Fourth Battalion and its senior advisor Walt Boomer, a former rifle company commander on his earlier Vietnam tour during which time he was awarded the Silver Star, the junior American at Fourth Battalion was Captain Ray Smith. On his prior Vietnam tour Smith had twice been recommended for the Navy Cross and was twice awarded Silver Stars instead. Aside from his reputation as a warrior, Captain Smith was also recognized as the strongest Vietnamese linguist among the current crop of *covans*. At the time of Gerry's visit to FSB Mai Loc, Captain Smith was with Fourth Battalion's Bravo Command Group on Nui Ba Ho.

In the Sixth Battalion, Major Bill Warren and Captain Bill Wischmeyer were an especially strong team, operating under all the same bad conditions every other *covan* did. The dynamic Warren-Wischmeyer duo faced the additional challenge of serving under a Vietnamese battalion commander whose open dislike for Americans was no secret. The genuinely good-natured Warren and Wischmeyer had their patience and rapidly improving political skills tried daily in addition to performing all their routine warfighting duties.

At FB Barbara, John Ripley was solo as the senior advisor over in Third Battalion with his friend and partner Le Ba Binh. Vietnamization and the planned drawdown of American forces were impacting the *covans* as well. By early 1972, as they were concluding their tours in the field, advisors rotating home were simply not being replaced.*

And so it was with the other TQLC infantry battalions, appropriately positioned to defend the areas adjacent to the DMZ and the RVN's northwestern border area with Laos. Upon arrival with Jim Joy at the Brigade 147 headquarters, Gerry was duly briefed by Joy's staff. He also listened in on radio reports coming from *covans* out with the various battalions. Even though Mai Loc had not received an incoming artillery round in more than two years, the recent activity now being reported by those closer to territory more contested was suggesting something big was about to happen.

Except for the routine, almost normal outgoing artillery from ARVN guns over at Camp Carroll, the night of March 29 passed uneventfully. That Jim Joy believed it safe enough and gave no thought to going by motor vehicle, rather than by helicopter, all the way along Route Nine to their Thursday morning meeting at Ai Tu and Quang Tri City with the ARVN Third Division's senior staff, was encouraging. Major Joy had arranged for Gerry to visit with the senior American army colonel who directly advised the commanding general for the ARVN Third Division. This was not just a friendly visit. The Third Division also had operational control over the two TQLC brigades currently deployed to I Corps. Gerry's group and the American soldiers on the staff of Advisory Team 155 would compare notes, have a quick lunch together, and then he would be flown out to FB Sarge for his scheduled time with Walt Boomer.

As he rode in the front, right seat of the M151 Jeep, Lieutenant Colonel Turley suddenly noticed that it was absolutely quiet. From the ARVN guns at Camp Carroll there were no outgoing rounds and, mercifully, from the enemy side there was nothing either. Nothing. In all the time he had spent in I Corps, in 1966 and 1967 and now in 1972, Gerry Turley could never recall such stillness. The quiet had some unreal quality he could not quite define. And just as before, intermittent conversation with Jim Joy shook him from those thoughts.

---

* John Ripley was the senior advisor to the Soi Bien. Captain Jim Johnson, who was out of the country, was the junior advisor.

The Turley entourage arrived at the Team 155 position at about 0930. With a few hours to go before his scheduled departure to FB Sarge, Gerry was introduced to the key Americans on Team 155 and briefed in on the disposition of the Third Division's three regiments. While the briefing was underway, the rumbling sound of distant impacting enemy artillery instantly became an indicator the situation was changing. Within seconds, incoming radio traffic picked up as well. As seasoned warriors they all took it in stride, continuing to listen in on the action. Something was definitely up. How much was yet to be determined.

Retiring to the chow hall for a quick meal before he was scheduled to take the short helicopter hop out to FB Sarge, Lieutenant Colonel Gerry Turley USMCR had finished his main course when the closer sounds of incoming artillery rounds, directed to impact on the Third Division's headquarters area, disturbed the local quiet. Those Communist bastards had timed it just right for Gerry to have to miss dessert. As they all headed for the bunkers, and though they did not yet know it, the Easter Offensive was on.

CHAPTER NINETEEN

The Easter Offensive

W*hat the Communists* in the Democratic Republic of Vietnam (DRV) would refer to as the Nguyen Hue Offensive of March 1972, became known to those in the West by its Occidental title. The Easter Offensive, like the Tet Offensive of 1968, was a bold stroke meant to deliver both the military and political *coup-de-grace* against the perceived minions of American imperialism in the south. At once northern planners hoped to appropriately mass all available fighting power to maximum effort and, hopefully, cause panic and chaos in the south. Because the threat, by now, of the Americans or the Republic of Vietnam attempting an invasion anywhere north of the 17th Parallel was extremely remote, it was believed safe to essentially go for broke again. Except for those who manned air-defense systems, there was little need to maintain regular ground forces at home; although the NVA would keep some units in reserve for an inordinately long period north of the DMZ during this invasion.

Using the massive shock effect of combined infantry, armor and artillery resources, supplemented by generous use of the most modern Soviet-supplied anti-aircraft missile defense systems brought all the way into the forward operating areas, the ultimate goal again was total victory.

While the regular citizens of the DRV did not have outlet for their frustrations in the cost of so many of their young and not-so-young men being consumed for the greater glory of the revolution, the leadership was acutely aware of the war's cost in manpower. To date, the men who comprised and held the power in the north had not yet reached a measurable point of capitulation.

The effort toward Vietnamization was clearly well underway. The Communist leadership was aware that, as a nation, the United States had been strongly influenced by its free press and the widespread expression of hostility towards the war at nearly all college campuses. While similar behavior would have been enthusiastically smashed in Hanoi or Haiphong, or anywhere else north of the 17th Parallel, the Politburo was happily eye to eye with so many of those Americans possessing or creating influence on the war's conduct.

The outcome of Tet '68 had seen a complete rout of Communist forces by allied troops. The civilian population in the south did not, as planned, rise up even a bit to welcome their liberating brothers. Victory instead, at very high price, had come by breaking the American national resolve to fight further. The blood costs, with so little to show for the investment, were judged as simply too high. The value America placed on life, and also the tangible concern it placed on the repatriation of its POWs, only served to corroborate the observations made by those in power in the north.

Actions at My Lai became like a national badge of shame, sackcloth and ashes, a horse-hair shirt Americans seemed to draw perverse pleasure in feeling guilty about. Communist atrocities and routine brutality, far in excess of anything perpetrated by the U.S., were rarely fair game for serious discussion or press coverage.

Of major concern for the DRV planners was whether the Americans could or would turn around the huge withdrawal effort that was now like a snowball halfway down the hill, growing larger and gathering ever increasing momentum. Not likely. The South Vietnamese had no friendly political constituency inside the United States. There were no strong lobbies to advocate for them, to effectively counter or blunt the impact of angry college students and small groups of bitter, increasingly vocal veterans opposed to the war. There also was no grand tradition, as there had been with China, of American missionary work or long-term association with those freedom-loving citizens of Vietnam. President Kennedy's famous 1961 inaugural address in which he stated that Americans would "pay any price, bear any burden, meet any hardship, support any friend, oppose any foe, in order to assure the survival and success of liberty" no longer applied to Vietnam.

The effective utilization of airpower and its application in frequency on a scale not yet seen had to have been a consideration. The latest Soviet air defenses would at least mitigate or neutralize some of the American retaliatory punch. So too would weather assist in the first few days. Perhaps if NVA forces could secure enough territory before the weather turned back against them, they might have inflicted enough pain to claim victory or somehow force an ouster of the hated Thieu regime.

No, the Americans would not reintroduce their soldiers or Marines. The media and the war's opponents in Congress would never allow it. If Nixon was foolish enough to make such a move the nation's college campuses would erupt in a fury that would make the Kent State response pale in comparison. As for airpower, the NVA would take their chances on this effort, betting it "all on Red" so to speak.

The preparations for the massive offensive and the bold NVA actions simply confirmed what the most pessimistic allied intelligence analysts had feared all along. It would be several days more before the initial fog of battle had cleared enough for the very slow to respond joint U.S.-ARVN command structure to develop any sort of coordinated defensive, and then counter-offensive plans.

The gods of war certainly seemed to favor the invaders. In the days and weeks prior to the offensive's initiation, NVA anti-aircraft artillery and surface-to-air missiles had claimed a number of U.S. aircraft flying routine support missions in the area of the DMZ. With the greater enemy defensive capabilities and a deteriorating weather situation, the ability for aerial reconnaissance on enemy movement was seriously degraded.

The use of an array of Soviet- and Chinese-supplied long-range artillery pieces, which had heretofore only been used against allied forces when fired from the Co Roc area in Laos against targets like Khe Sanh, across the entire length of the DMZ and portions of the border with Laos revealed far greater enemy capabilities than previously experienced. All at once it seemed that every occupied position held by ARVN and TQLC units, along with any notable civilian population within range, came under extremely intense and accurate artillery fire.

FROM THE BUNKER INTO THE FRYING PAN

If there had been a more propitious time for the Communists to spring the gargantuan sets of attacks all across the DMZ and out of the northwest from Laos, it would have been difficult to identify. One did not need to be a Sun Tzu or a Clausewitz or a MacArthur or even at the bottom of the class at any mid-level war college in the West or Soviet Union to see that the Communists had selected an ideal time to go for broke.

Whether intentional or not, the allies may have been lulled into a false sense of security as no one had even pondered the prospect of an attack across the full width of the DMZ. The Communists had never done it before, and of course they were obligated by treaty not to do so. At the moment, the weather aided the enemy as cloud cover down to around one thousand to fifteen hundred feet in all of northern I Corps virtually precluded the use of tactical air support.

Adding to the confusion, chaos, and especially to the question of perfidious and treasonous actions at senior ARVN levels, was that, at precisely the time of the NVA attack, two of the three regiments constituting the ARVN Third Division's infantry strength were executing what is called a passage of lines. During a passage of lines, two units, usually of similar size, essentially swap positions with the intent that the enemy in front of them is unaware of the switch. Under training conditions such a move is a leadership and logistical headache. Under combat conditions it can be a nightmare. For the Third Division the passage of lines would be disastrous.

The Third Division was created in the aftermath of *Lam Son 719*, and had not yet celebrated its first anniversary as a division. Made up of three infantry regiments—the Second, the 56th, and the 57th—only the Second Regiment had a history older than its parent division and was judged marginally combat effective by U.S. Army officers who had recently served there in the advisory role. The 56th and 57th, even though they were legitimate army units, could be likened more to a militia in that most of the men were from right there in Quang Tri or other nearby provinces. With poorly trained soldiers, the leadership at most every level was likewise inexperienced and inadequately trained. There were also a fair number of soldiers in the regiments who had been sent there as punishment for deserting from other ARVN outfits.[1]

The ARVN/U.S. Army relationship in many ways mirrored the TQLC/USMC relationship. Where the U.S. Army was quite a bit larger than the USMC, the size of ARVN completely dwarfed the TQLC. With its small size and limited, but always seeming to expand missions, the TQLC even this late in the war, was able to maintain high standards. ARVN units had their share of brave men and bold small unit leaders. The unfortunate issue for them was that most were lost among a greater number of poorly led and poorly motivated comrades. While the U.S. Army had, for years, similarly employed advisors with ARVN, size was also an issue. With Vietnamization and the continuing drawdown of American forces, few ARVN units had combat savvy American army officers to lean on for critical assistance. On March 30, 1972, the Second Regiment was without any direct American advisory input. Both the 56th and the 57th had advisors, but only at the regimental levels.

Beginning at noon local time on March 30, 1972 the twelve static firebase positions spanning the full east-west length of the DMZ and then roughly twenty kilometers north to south on the adjacent border with Laos at once came under ruthless, relentless artillery and rocket fire on a scale no one there had before experienced. Again, as defenders, ARVN and TQLC units operated out of established, well-observed positions that were easily zeroed in on by NVA forward observers. Except for the four ARVN 175mm guns at Camp Carroll, ARVN and TQLC units in contact had only 105 and 155 artillery support to call on. With maximum range exceeding both the 105s and 155s, NVA 130mm guns and 122mm rockets would comfortably position themselves outside the ARVN artillery fans, and then pound them with impunity.

NVA planning was such that their initial strikes included all known ARVN artillery positions. Counter-battery fire by ARVN was slow to respond at best. The men manning the guns were not at all used to being on the receiving end of the equation. Once the ARVN batteries were silenced—by either obliteration or complete intimidation—the enemy could shift to other targets at will. As it happened, the initial barrages had also taken out a great deal of ARVN communication capabilities, adding to the sense of chaos, isolation, and the loss of local command and control.

Behind the artillery strikes, upward of thirty thousand NVA infantry and, for the first time in Vietnam on any scale, hundreds of Soviet-supplied T-54 and PT-76 tanks rolled forward like an unstoppable *juggernaut*. The conventional war the Americans had always spoiled to fight in Vietnam—after having won it once in Tet '68—was being launched again on an even grander scale.

The NVA offensive was in no way limited to military targets. Having been naturally lulled back into a sense of peace and normalcy in recent years, Vietnamese civilians were not expecting to be intentionally attacked by any invaders. The shelling of populated areas with the southward creeping NVA artillery fires was a critical part of the plan to spread panic and block critical road networks, further degrading ARVN/TQLC ability to respond.

From the perspective of the most cynical of the war's opponents in the U.S., ARVN fighting response, or lack thereof, was predictable. While many ARVN units attempted to hold and fight, a number of infantry, artillery, and support units simply melted away; some ceasing to exist altogether. In the opening hours of the Communist assault, the roads running south and away from the action were choked with thousands and thousands of civilians walking, running, crawling, shuffling, or riding any sort of animal or wheeled contrivance that would allow them escape from the northern firestorm. Liberally mixed in with the disparate population of displaced civilians were more thousands of young men still clad in ARVN uniforms but which no longer displayed name tags, rank insignia, or unit patches. Many of those men seen traveling on Highway One were soldiers from the 57th Regiment who had dropped their arms to quickly return home and move their nearby families south and away from the carnage. From almost anywhere in northern Quang Tri Province, the world looked to be coming apart. There was no good news.

Along with there being no good news to report, in the first hours of the Communist assault the flow of information down south to Saigon was only begrudgingly given over ARVN tactical radio nets. Perhaps because the attack had caught them by surprise, there was a sense of embarrassment—that ever critical loss of face—among senior ARVN officers which slowed the transmission and acceptance of bad news.[2]

Not as hampered by issues of saving face, Americans in the Third Division Tactical Operations Center (TOC) bunker, where Gerry Turley now stood taking in the situation initially as nothing more than an interested but un-empowered observer, instantly began to send situation reports to Saigon. (The communication between the Third Division TOC and MACV in Saigon was conducted over an obsolete, single-line, hand-cranked field telephone that was hard-wired into the bunker. Whether that line went all the way to Saigon or was boosted by some sort of intermediary radio relay, Gerry did not know. All that he was concerned with was the quality of that comm, which was to be spotty at best throughout the battle.) Those at MACV were, like their ARVN friends, slow to respond but for different reasons. Wedded to the belief that if a major offensive was to be launched it would be against targets further south and certainly not out of the DMZ; the action was thought to be some sort of feint. As it was difficult to empathize and feel the dampness of San Francisco fog when one was experiencing warmth and sunshine in Los Angeles, so too was it a challenge to fathom all-out combat in Quang Tri Province while Saigon was business as usual. There was certainly no indication yet of MACV's deep concern.

The view from and the action at the Third Division TOC in Ai Tu was in some ways surreal. In addition to receiving its share of incoming artillery and rocket fire, it was the place where data and radio reports from all the subordinate units were received and monitored, and then plotted on big map boards so that those with responsibility for making decisions about where to apply scarce resources; where to inject fresh blood, where to apply the tourniquet or perform amputation, could be made. Neither the U.S. Army personnel serving in the support roles nor the ARVN staff they were assisting were prepared for the scope and enormity of these attacks.

Being in the TOC was the closest thing to being in contact—in the way that the front-line units were in contact—without being in contact. The ever-changing situation as evidenced by the always moving plotting now going on, and it was all headed in the wrong direction, painted a grim picture at every spot on the map where friendly positions looked to be overrun. For the operations personnel it was like being at a college wrestling tournament where multiple bouts were continually ongoing, except that in this competition there were no time limits or referees. On every separate mat opponents were consumed by the world immediately around them as they grappled for life and death, unaware of what took place on adjacent territory. Only the folks in the TOC had the minor luxury of seeing the bigger picture. As daylight was fading on March 30, 1972, that bigger picture showed very little promise.

CHAPTER TWENTY

One Link in the Chain

"To each there comes in their lifetime a special moment when they are figuratively tapped on the shoulder and offered a chance to do a very special thing, unique to them and fitted to their talents. What a tragedy if that moment finds them unprepared or unqualified for that which could have been their finest hour."

—Winston Churchill

Third ARVN Division Tactical Operations Center (TOC)
Ai Tu, Northern I Corps
Republic of Vietnam
Evening of March 31, 1972

The American army colonel serving as the principal advisor to Brigadier General Vu Van Giai, commanding general of the Third ARVN Division, had his hands completely full. Tethered to a man whose leadership style was widely regarded by most Americans as competent, switched on, brave and up front, the colonel went everywhere his general went. With all of Third Division's units fully engaged in the opening hours and days of the Easter Offensive, the general's intent, by personally visiting each of those units, was to infuse his subordinate leaders and troops with a fighting spirit that was so far not being too greatly evidenced.

At the same time the colonel was charged with advising General Giai, the proper functioning of the American staff advising their Vietnamese counterparts in the Third Division

Tactical Operations Center in Ai Tu, known also as Team 155, was likewise his direct responsibility. In the first day and a half of coming and going with his general, the colonel could not help but observe the increasingly greater challenges and strains being placed on the folks attempting to run operations there.

Lieutenant Colonel Gerry Turley gradually took charge of operations in the Third Division TOC and Team 155. He did it without usurping or co-opting the others. He did it without consciously thinking about what he was doing; instead focusing solely on a mission to begin to bring order out of chaos. From the imposition and restoration of what order he and Captain J.D. Murray could come up with for matters relating to the Vietnamese Marines, their influence and impact gradually and naturally spread to issues for the Third Division as well.

At this stage of the war, the American ground presence in northern I Corps was mostly limited to advisory and support staff work. The greatest value added by Americans was in the coordination and application of fire power, which at this very moment was becoming increasingly critical. As it would turn out, Gerry's skills at fire support coordination would soon be put to severe test for him and the ersatz collection of folks he was in the process of bringing together. This massive undertaking, now the responsibility of a junior lieutenant colonel rather than some general officer along with a fully functioning staff, was indicative of the serious nature and changing, deteriorating combat situation.

That Gerry would be put in charge of what was essentially an army operation, a Vietnamese army operation no less, was so far outside his thought processes as to be considered an impossibility. Anyone even remotely familiar with the way military operations were properly and routinely conducted, or the way staffs functioned, would have given little thought to turning the entire show, even temporarily, over to a visiting, interloping Marine.

This was simply supposed to be a long weekend trip, a milk run; four days in I Corps and back to Saigon to his as yet un-established routine of duties as the Assistant Senior Marine Advisor. Gerry Turley was only there to check things out; to eyeball, shake hands with and encourage his guys, deliver the all-important mail bag, get a sense of what was happening out where the rubber met the road. Turley was nothing more than an unofficial, official observer, almost a tourist by military standards.

Gerry Turley—the same fellow who only twenty-three years earlier joined the Marine Corps Reserves so he might play basketball and earn some extra spending money—had by now become as much a part of the institution as was humanly possible. When he landed in northern I Corps it was as if, unknown to him, he had walked into the stadium where a surprise Super Bowl that only the opposing side knew about was was set to kick off.

With coaching staff for the friendly team all around the TOC, it was as if the team owner, only seconds into the first quarter and with a fairly large pool of known talent to select from, decided to change his offensive coordinator by picking from outside the group and infuse new, unknown blood into a game that this soon into it looked to be lost already.

Within hours of the Easter Offensive's initiation, the army officer charged with running things in the TOC was showing disturbing signs of stress and constantly excused himself for breaks while all the others remained at their posts. Taken aside less than eighteen hours into the battle by the senior colonel, there was a private discussion Gerry had not been privy to. When the colonel emerged from that brief meeting, he came straight to Lieutenant Colonel Turley and asked him, effectively ordered him actually, to temporarily take charge completely over operations in the TOC; at least until a qualified senior army officer could be helicoptered up from Danang or Saigon or materialized from the ether. What else could he say? He did not have the luxury of time or position to negotiate his options. The NVA, like the Big Bad Wolf, were out there aggressively huffing and puffing. The house was about to come down.

From the first moment that soon stretched into hours and hours of continuous action at points all across the DMZ; from the coast where the Ben Hai River emptied into the South China Sea over to Alpha 2, and out west to the border with Laos and then south all the way down to Fire Base (FB) Sarge and a dozen-odd points in between, thousands and thousands of rounds from rockets, artillery, and mortars had fallen with great precision on every target the NVA judged to have military or civilian terror value.

Exacerbating problems and magnifying the fog of war was the attendant chaos which stymied communication. Low cloud ceilings limited tactical air response. Issues of embarrassment and saving face for ARVN leaders slowed the reporting of events. On the receiving end of those slow-to-be-generated reports were men, both Vietnamese and American, who appeared to be willingly incredulous to the catastrophe unfolding.

Inside that split-second metamorphosis from relative innocent bystander to the man with whatever power and responsibility there was left to muster in a military situation that seemed to be rapidly deteriorating, there was no time for self-pity or doubt. Gerry Turley recognized the moment for what it was. All he could do was all he could do. He did not step into the arena. The arena had rather simply sprung up around him, and he was now both literally and figuratively at its center. With the fighting going on all over northern I Corps, every American and Vietnamese then serving was likewise at Ground Zero in his own personal arena and battle to survive.

It was at once obvious to Gerry that he and all the others were in all the way, whether they wanted it or not, in what would be the fight of their lives. There would be no more time to prepare. There was no time to rest or freshen up, not even time for a last meal like the ones given Marines before they had made those murderous amphibious assaults in World War II. For Gerry, everything that had shaped his will and character in his forty-two-year life, and all that taken place in his Marine Corps career from 1949 until now would have to be enough, he prayed, to meet whatever challenges he was immediately facing. It was exactly the same for every other American and Vietnamese now involuntarily involved in the battle.

Inside of that split-second eternity, Gerry recalled a stanza from a poem that Naval Academy midshipmen, for a very long time, had routinely been required to memorize. Shared with him by an Annapolis graduate friend on Okinawa back when they had both been captains in 1959, he now recalled its simple, haunting admonishment:

"On the strength of one link in the cable,
Dependeth the might of the chain.
Who knows when thou may'st be tested?
So live that thou bearest the strain!"[*]

Lieutenant Colonel Gerry Turley would concentrate and focus his entire mental and physical processes to ensure that the link he was about to become would not be the one to fail.

After the opening day and a quarter of the Easter Offensive, there was little for Lieutenant Colonel Gerry Turley, as the new operations officer at the Ai Tu TOC, to be optimistic about. The South Vietnamese forces were beginning to crack under the unrelenting enemy assaults. At every location where ARVN and TQLC forces were being engaged across a fifteen-mile front, they were receiving incoming artillery barrages of intensity never before experienced. Behind the seemingly inexhaustible curtain of steel, every major friendly position within spitting distance of the DMZ was undergoing well-planned, large-scale infantry assaults of overwhelming force. The lack of effective ARVN counter-battery artillery fire and, because of poor weather, tactical air response, gave NVA forces a free pass to continue their invasion with minimal resistance. The only reliable source of help had been naval gunfire which was of value only to those units nearest the coast. On March 30, 1972 the USS *Buchanan* (DDG-14) was the sole American man-of-war available for support. The *Buchanan's* skipper, in an attempt to provide maximum punch and protection, pulled his ship dangerously close to shore to extend the limits of the gunfire support further inland. The *Buchanan* was even taken under fire by shore-based NVA batteries attempting to silence the only currently effective fire support the South Vietnamese could rely on. The *Buchanan* never wavered and, as long as her guns were up and she had ammunition to shoot, provided uninterrupted support. More ships would be added to the gun line in the next several days.

---

[*] From the poem "The Laws of the Navy" by Admiral R.A. Hopwood, Royal Navy.

ACTION WITH THE SOI BIEN

When the Easter Offensive began, Major Binh, Captain Ripley, and the Marines of the TQLC's Third Battalion found themselves in the unfamiliar position of being out of the direct line of fire. Having just returned a few days earlier from their scheduled three-week R&R rotation down in Thu Duc near Saigon, the Soi Bien's four rifle companies were now providing security for Brigade 258 somewhere between Firebases Barbara and Nancy, near the My Chanh River. Several kilometers beyond the range of the NVA heavy artillery that was now continually pummeling the entire breadth of the DMZ and the ARVN/TQLC western flanks, it seemed strange to so far be sitting out the major action.

When Third Battalion had been sent back to northern I Corps, prior to the Easter Offensive's initiation, John Ripley noticed a number of odd things. All of a sudden, and seemingly out of nowhere, an ARVN battalion of tanks had been moved north. Never before, at least in both Ripley's and Binh's collective experiences, had an ARVN armor unit of this size been this close to the DMZ. At the same time it seemed very unusual to John Ripley that Third Battalion was operating this far south. Ever since he and Binh had worked together it had always been right up close to the bad guys where there was always action. And while the action near Barbara and Nancy still included daily incoming mortar fire and the essential requirement to continue platoon and company-sized patrols, the lack of aggressive NVA activity suggested change was afoot. While there were those who might have earlier wistfully believed the reduction in enemy actions was a sign things were improving, Binh and Ripley had never believed that peace was at hand.

John Ripley had not attended any formal language training prior to making his *covan* tour. Of necessity he had picked up what Vietnamese he was able to, daily adding to his *repertoire*, and by this late in his tour was actually rather conversant. Dai Uy Ripley was so well regarded by Binh, Nha, his radio operator, and the few others in Third Battalion he had regular interaction with, they were able to make sense of his sincere attempts at communication, Virginia-accented Vietnamese notwithstanding. And of course,

Binh's English was better than Ripley's Vietnamese. Between the two there was more than enough understanding to make them a serious threat to the NVA.

Service as a *covan* had its extra blessings and special challenges. Like all the others so assigned, John Ripley recognized the unique responsibilities put upon those American officers attached to the various fighting units of the Vietnamese Marine Corps. Unlike nearly all Americans, even including most who had come and fought and bled in the battle to blunt the spread of Communism, the *covans* really were among a select group given opportunity to view the war from outside the American perspective.

With the ongoing drawdown of forces from Southeast Asia, with what seemed to be the irreversible withdrawal of combat troops that did not appear to be conditioned on any serious Communist concessions, all that was important to the American side now—win, lose, or draw—was complete extrication from the quagmire that the war had become.

As much as Dai Uy Ripley appreciated the significance and critical nature of the job he performed as senior advisor to what he believed was the best infantry battalion in the TQLC, he missed leading his Marines. Even though the Vietnamese Marine Corps had their own Chuck Goggins, and so many things were basically the same; it was not the same. Aside from Binh and Nha, John's opportunities to seriously bond, on a daily basis, with other Marines, whether American or Vietnamese, was nothing close to what he had enjoyed when he was Lima Six Actual with Third Battalion, Third Marines back in 1967.

Daily gaining more appreciation for the Vietnamese perspective and position on the war, even the *covans* came to Vietnam for their second tours handicapped to the extent that they were possessed of a "grudge deficit." The earlier Americans, especially those who came for their first combat tours, arrived as well-trained as their stateside instructors could make them and yet the cause for which they would be expected to possibly die for was, for nearly all of them, still amorphous and ill defined.

The motivations for the Americans were simply different than those for the Vietnamese on both sides. With Henry Kissinger, at

President Nixon's behest, now attempting to position America's strategic interests as beyond Vietnam only, the Americans by now could just as well have been fighting in eastern Europe or northern Asia; anywhere to prop up a domino threatened by Communist oppression.

For the men of the TQLC there were no other dominos to consider. By 1972 the loss of Quang Tri Province, to Americans was no big deal, did not at all suggest that the enemy would soon be marching down Hollywood Boulevard or Pennsylvania Avenue. To Binh, Luong, Nha and patriotic citizens of the Republic of Vietnam, what happened in Quang Tri Province *really* mattered. For them, victory was the only option.

In addition to the near brother-like relationship Ripley enjoyed with Binh, he had grown particularly close to his young radio operator Nha. It was not at all uncommon, given the exigencies of war that friendships, even cross-cultural ones, ran extremely deep. In spite of the tremendous language, cultural, and formal barriers of protocol meant to separate them, Dai Uy Ripley and his trusted radio operator Nha developed a strong mutual respect and affection for one another. Nha's awe and fascination with this kind, jovial American officer whose bravery seemed to match that of his beloved battalion commander, even after several months, had not diminished. Nha marveled also at the way Americans were different; especially that the culture of the U.S. Marine Corps allowed for closer interaction between officers and enlisted men that was simply not considered possible or appropriate in the Vietnamese Marines.

Nha was a special young man. In so many ways he reminded his "Big Brother" *covan* Dai Uy Ripley of the best of the young Marines he had served with in the USMC. (As a term of respect and endearment it is common in Vietnamese culture, which is heavily influenced by Confucian ideals, to address a person who is not family but very well liked and considered worthy of deference as "Big Brother" or more properly "Elder Brother." The person showing that respect, if a male, is always "Little Brother" or more properly "Younger Brother.")

To be assigned to the headquarters element of the battalion meant that Nha was already recognized as being a squared-away Marine; a cut above the rest. Daily his routine actions, down to the most mundane, reflected his dedication and professionalism.

Dai Uy Ripley was "Elder Brother" to Nha every bit as much as Nha was "Younger Brother" to Ripley. There were many things that endeared Nha to his "Elder Brother." From the very beginning, from before Dai Uy Ripley had personally established, among the Marines of the Soi Bien, his reputation as a warrior worthy of deference and respect, Nha demonstrated his professionalism and loyalty to the new *covan*.

Nha was obviously bright and had a tremendous sense of initiative and tactical intuition. He seemed to know, in every situation, what to do almost before it needed to be done. Even though he was "only" Ripley's radio operator, he looked after his *covan* as if he were personally responsible for his safety, health and well-being. Between Nha's pidgin English, Ripley's hackneyed and Virginia-accented Vietnamese, a generous use of hand-and-arm signals, and true empathy between them, the two warriors were able to communicate quite effectively. Together they were a powerful team.

The day-in, day-out existence Third Battalion endured as it fought throughout the greater northern I Corps area saw the relationship between the two develop to some depth. As Ripley's stature within the Soi Bien grew, Nha, who was partially responsible through his own actions for the successes of his *covan*, refused any recognition at all for his skill and bravery.

What touched Dai Uy Ripley the most was the genuine humility Nha displayed. It was none of this phony, false modesty "Aw, shucks..." type stuff. It was a complete shunning of any recognition for the very obvious things, whether ordinary or extraordinary, that the young radio operator did as he served Third Battalion and his admiring *covan*. In any culture, Nha was an extraordinary young man. He seemed to draw great satisfaction from selfless service.

CHAPTER TWENTY-ONE

Their Finest Hour

*S*econd Lieutenant *(Thieu Uy) Nguyen Luong* was anxious to get his first action behind him. He was anxious to prove himself. He was anxious to prove himself to the thirty-six Marines of Fourth Company's First Platoon which he now led, to his company commander, and to his storied, near-legendary battalion commander. Mostly Luong was anxious to prove himself to himself; to see if he was worthy of the title "Marine" and membership in the Soi Bien. Second Lieutenant Nguyen Luong, like his battalion commander and their *covan*, was also perplexed as to why Third Battalion was being used in what seemed almost to be an insulting role down at the firebases so far from the serious action.

The contrast between recently graduated, shave-tail Second Lieutenant Luong, who was eager to do good as second lieutenants are in every military organization the world over, and so many of the young and not-so-young enlisted Marines in his platoon was greater than that which was experienced by most American officers. New infantry lieutenants, fresh from Quantico and Ft. Benning, would benefit by relying on young NCOs and troops who had been in country awhile and, because they had survived however long it took for their lieutenants to get there, were bush savvy and may have even developed a genuine hatred for their capable, cunning, ruthless enemy.

Americans were culturally predisposed towards magnanimity and, out of sentimentality, naturally favored the notion of freedom and all the other wholesome-sounding stuff. Except for those new young American men whose families might have escaped to freedom from behind the Iron Curtain or Cuba, few native-born citizens had experienced what living under Communism really meant.

Among the enlisted men in Luong's platoon, a platoon typical of all the others in Third Battalion and the rest of the TQLC, were long-serving Marines mixed in with battle-hardened fellows who had previously served hitches with ARVN Airborne and Special Forces, even a few former Rangers. A decent percentage had been born in the north and had come south with their families in the 1954 *diaspora*. In that group, every one of them had personal experiences with the Communists and special reasons for wanting to serve. These men did not keep short-timer calendars but craved only to settle old scores and personal or family grudges; something completely outside the American ken.

The seven hundred-odd Marines of Third Battalion, with the Alpha Command Group that included Thieu Ta Binh, Dai Uy Ripley, Nha and two of the battalion's four rifle companies along with the weapons company at Firebase Nancy, and the Bravo Command Group with the remaining two rifle companies at Firebase Barbara, were standing by. From the top all the way down to the most junior or newest fellow, like Second Lieutenant (Thieu Uy) Luong, it was obvious that action, heavy action, was imminent. From their positions near the My Chanh River, on the afternoon of March 30 they were ordered to assume the role as Division Reserve and move by the most expeditious means immediately to the town of Dong Ha. That night they made a rather hasty, non-tactical motor march to their new position.

Except for their periods of stand down and refurbishment at Thu Duc, at least during John Ripley's time with the Soi Bien, Third Battalion had never been held back from the central action. Being expeditiously assigned as the Third ARVN Division reserve force was certainly not meant to be a slight. When sunlight on March 31 revealed the systematic, ongoing destruction it was immediately apparent that major action was forthcoming.

Dong Ha, now under near-constant rocket and artillery assault, was about twelve miles south of the DMZ. NVA ground forces were still at least eight or nine miles north up near Alpha 2, but it was obvious to all that the enemy soon would be heading this way.

Dong Ha itself was utterly unremarkable. What made the town important to the Marines defending it and the NVA about to begin their assault was that it sat astride the major bridge that crossed the Cua Viet River over which ran Highway 1, the road built years earlier under French supervision that ran the entire length of both Vietnams. (A second bridge which also crossed the Cua Viet and could support armor was approximately ten miles west out at Cam Lo. Of the two, the bridge at Dong Ha was far more critical to commerce and military traffic. Fewer than one hundred meters upstream from the Dong Ha Bridge was an older, much smaller crossing everyone simply called the "Old French Bridge." It was capable of mostly pedestrian traffic and was wide enough only for a single jeep to travel it as long as there was no contra traffic. Another kilometer or so further west was an old railroad bridge for the train that no longer ran between Hanoi and Saigon. That particular bridge was known to have one of its spans down in the water and was believed to be currently impassable.) If the NVA could gain control of Dong Ha's bridge, they would have a virtual gateway into all of Quang Tri Province. With the weather limiting allied airpower's ability to interdict the enemy advance, the NVA were hoping they could get sufficient forces on the south side before the weather cleared. If they were able to pull this off it would have a severely deleterious impact on the Thieu regime. The only obvious advantage the allies currently enjoyed at Dong Ha was that it was well within gunfire range of the growing number of U.S. Navy destroyers patrolling the coast.

Dong Ha was also the eastern terminus for Route 9 that ran west past many of the critical firebases, past Khe Sanh and ultimately into Laos. On his earlier tour with Lima 3/3, John Ripley had run convoy duty numerous times over this perilous route. From Dong Ha the Soi Bien were ideally positioned to reinforce the Third Division at any location General Giai desired.

Third Battalion, like their sister TQLC battalions, was divided into their Alpha and Bravo Command Groups and took up separate positions in town awaiting further orders. As Good Friday mercifully came to a close, Binh's Marines were unable to sleep from the constant barrages but did what they could to husband their strength and resources for action that was certain to come.

BACK TO TURLEY AND ACTION AT THE TOC…

The Team 155 bunker in Ai Tu (approximately five miles south of Dong Ha), which not so long ago had served as the tactical operations center for the U.S. Army's vaunted 101st Airborne Division up until the time Vietnamization forced its retirement from the field of battle, was a hornet's nest of activity. Outside the bunker, large sections of the Ai Tu fire base was ablaze under the continual and deadly accurate NVA artillery fire.

Lieutenant Colonel Gerry Turley had responsibility for a number of disparate issues, every one of them requiring tremendous focus and attention. Until they were overrun by the NVA and he was killed at his post or he was somehow properly relieved from this duty which had been improperly foisted upon him, he would do his best to keep all tactical and logistical balls in the air.

Hours into the fight of his life, Gerry had no reasonable idea yet who the thirty-odd men were that he was now responsible for leading, or where all of them were physically located. He began to make a list of all American advisors in northern I Corps. There needed to be some way to account for these men in the event they were overrun, captured, or killed. Of those he was actually able to eyeball, his confidence in the non-Marine personnel was, for the moment, negatively tempered by the performance of the man he had just replaced. Fortunately most of the others would avail themselves in the days ahead and prove to be of sterner stuff as the battle unfolded.

Among the Marines in the TOC, Gerry had already been leaning heavily on Captain J.D. Murray, a true professional and recipient of the Navy Cross for earlier actions. Also serving in the bunker was a two-man Naval Gunfire Spot Team run by a sharp, unflappable first lieutenant named Joel Eisenstein.

First Lieutenant Joel Eisenstein, who would turn out to be a critical player in the prosecution of key events in the coming days, was a tough, articulate, tactically sound, twenty-six-year-old officer from Missouri. With three semesters of law school under his belt, Eisenstein had chosen to volunteer for Marine OCS after receiving his draft notice. Passionate in his beliefs, he already had the cool precision of a senior prosecuting attorney when advocating what needed advocating. He was not at all afraid to lock horns with others senior to him in the pursuit of mission accomplishment and taking care of the Marines he was currently responsible for out at Alpha 2 who were, by the minute, appearing more isolated and about to be surrounded by the advancing NVA. He and the lieutenant out at Alpha 2 running the team there had already begun preliminary planning for an emergency extract of their tiny, unattached-to-any ARVN or TQLC unit group of American Marines.*

The action faced by Turley, Murray, Eisenstein, and all the others in the TOC bunker seemed to be without letup. It was intense at every ARVN and TQLC position known by the NVA. Some positions had it worse than others, and none within range of any kind of enemy artillery was going unscathed.

Team 155 Bunker
Ai Tu, Quang Tri Province
0400 1 April, 1972

It was early Friday afternoon back home and Gerry Turley forced himself to take the very transitory luxury of imagining Bunny and their kids, who this week would have been out of school for

---

* First Lieutenants Joel Eisenstein and David Bruggeman, along with the enlisted members of the Naval Gunfire Spot Team were not a part of the same advisory effort that Gerry Turley, John Ripley, George Philip, and the others were. They were not *covans*. They were, however, a part of the ANGLICO (Air & Naval Gunfire LIasison Company) effort that remained, like the *covans*, long after the main ground forces had departed. ANGLICO personnel were vital in their assistance, like the *covans*, at delivering fire support to the South Vietnamese. Unlike the *covans* who, at the battalion and regimental levels, advised on a whole host of issues, the ANGLICO folks were not attached to TQLC units and they were used solely for fire support coordination. It should also be noted that ANGLICO had a chain of command separate from the U.S. Marine advisors.

Easter vacation, doing whatever it was they would be doing about now. At home it was fifteen hours earlier, early Friday afternoon—payday—and she probably would have already joined the countless other Marine wives at the Camp Pendleton commissary shopping for their families. Aside from the normal shopping cart full of food items, this time there would be a few Easter treats. Chris and Bob were almost old enough now where they might not want to color eggs too much longer, but not yet. And then she would purchase for all the obligatory spread of yellow, sugar-coated marshmallow Peeps, Robin Eggs, and jelly beans. They would all attend Easter Sunday services with her folks down in San Diego and have as good a celebration as they could with Dad in Vietnam and Anne away at nursing school.

As it was only Friday afternoon at home, Gerry was certain that if MACV in Saigon did not yet seem to be too concerned with what was taking place in northern I Corps, the *San Diego Union*, which Bunny dutifully read each morning for any hint of news that might give her a clue about her husband's comings and goings, would likely have nothing on the action he was now smack dab in the middle of.

Gerry could laugh at himself briefly for the unintended prescience he had shown in the last letter home written before departing Saigon for his scheduled four-day tour up north. He had told her: "Don't be concerned if you don't hear from me for a few days..." If current trends were not reversed he could very well be killed or a POW before she even received that letter, probably still a day or two out.

BACK INSIDE THE BUNKER

Gerry Turley had not experienced a wink of sleep since the attacks began, now almost forty-eight hours ago. He was surprised actually at how strong and lucid he felt given these very odd circumstances.

At about 0400 on Saturday April 1, for some reason unknown to anyone on the allied side, there was a genuine lull in the fighting; a lull sufficient for Gerry to really take stock of all that had gone on since the Communist offensive had begun.

There was nothing in the bunker other than the few clocks on the wall and each man's wristwatch to tell any of the folks there that it was a new day. There was no new news that was positive or cheery. It was difficult to remain optimistic, and yet Lieutenant Colonel Turley shouldered the unprecedented responsibility so uniquely thrust upon him. He was a professional, much was at stake, and with all eyes upon him, he could ill afford to appear anything but focused on salvaging this continuing-to-deteriorate situation.

As the day began, he had to take stock, run an inventory of all that had transpired since he had been forced to miss dessert nearly three lunchtimes ago. There was time only for cold calculation; no luxury to muse or ponder or casually consider all options. Most decisions were life and death, and like a single surgeon with too many patients requiring attention, Gerry was forced to triage his judgments.

From out of the DMZ in the north and out of Laos in the west the NVA continued to relentlessly apply pressure at every point ARVN and TQLC units were positioned. Up until this time the weather was such that there had been no ability to call in air strikes to relieve embattled defenders. ARVN counter-battery artillery fire was, at best, ineffectual, in most cases nonexistent. The sole reliable source of fire support was increasingly naval gunfire as the number of ships off the mouth of the Cua Viet River had now grown to four.

Unknown to Gerry, the *Buchanan's* captain began sending periodic combat reports back to his superiors at CINCPAC in Pearl Harbor, five thousand miles away. These reports, which painted a picture of an increasingly desperate situation up north, would cause no end of frustration, confusion, and later embarrassment to the MACV staff in Saigon. Up until this time, and only three hundred miles away, MACV and ARVN staffs had refused to acknowledge the seriousness of the situation from their own folks or ARVN personnel involved in the action.

Additionally, the constant mentioning of a Marine lieutenant colonel named Turley, who seemed to be running Army Advisory

Team 155 in the Third ARVN Division TOC, was drawing some attention. As a courtesy to their military brethren, CINCPAC (which had no way of knowing that there had been little communication between the people in I Corps and Saigon) began forwarding the *Buchanan's* messages to General Abrams and his people at MACV. It was only through these strange reports that the MACV folks first learned of some Marine they had never even heard of seeming to be mysteriously in charge of a situation they had no idea had gotten so far out of hand. The senior MACV and ARVN officers in Saigon were finally being forced to recognize, against their closely-held preconceived beliefs, that the situation up north was probably more than a minor action or strategic feint. The repercussions of that reality would soon fall heavily upon Gerry Turley.

None of the troops could yet know that they were witnessing the opening salvos in the largest enemy offensive of the entire Vietnam War. This was bigger even than Tet '68 when Walter Cronkite—billed as the most trusted man in America—had pronounced the Marines at Khe Sanh defeated in advance.

From Turley's informed, over-stimulated perch in the action, the intentional slow reporting of bad news through ARVN channels, which he attributed to significant loss of face for their being caught off guard, along with what was probably a pervasive pre-Easter holiday laxness, was so far assisting the enemy in meeting their strategic objectives. (It would later become known that several of the key U.S. and ARVN officers in Saigon had already taken off for a long weekend before the attacks began.)

In the moments between considering all of these issues, Gerry still had difficulty processing the reality of what was taking place. Less than forty-eight hours ago he was just the Assistant Senior Marine Advisor up to see his dozen or so advisors, deliver them their mail, and see how the war was winding down. Now he was at what seemed to be Ground Zero to an impending Armageddon with implicit authority for all kinds of decision making he was certain there was no explicit authorization for. As crazy as it seemed, and he knew that only other Marine officers would empathize, the thing he feared most was not his own death. His concern, with his ever-increasing amount of responsibility, was how his own actions and leadership would be judged—especially if he were killed and the battle lost—by those who remained. The last thing Gerry Turley wanted was to besmirch the honor of the Corps. It was said that victory had a thousand fathers but defeat was an illegitimate child. Fortunately or unfortunately, with all that was going on, there was little time to ponder that issue. Win or lose, Gerry was like the man in the arena in the famous Teddy Roosevelt quote. He would focus on those things he could influence, leave the rest to the critics, and worry about the other stuff later. If he survived. Right now he had a war to fight.

The lull soon ended. All across the now contracting northern and western I Corps borders the destruction of the fortified allied firebases continued; at some spots more rapidly than others. At no point on the map were the good guys winning. The best any friendly unit was doing was losing more slowly.

As bad as it had so far been for the allies, it was about to get a whole lot worse. Round two was set to begin. The full force of the NVA's four divisions along with many hundreds of artillery pieces had just about moved into their most forward battle positions. As intense as the earlier actions had thus far been, the initial ground combat was like the junior varsity game being played before the seniors took to the field.

Up at Alpha 2 the ground situation was growing particularly acute. Unlike the American Marine officers assigned as regimental and battalion advisors with specific TQLC units, who were essentially members of those units and would live, fight, and die with them, the five-man Naval Gunfire Spot Team at Alpha 2 was on its own. There were no TQLC units at Alpha 2 and the ARVN forces there were showing little enthusiasm to aggressively defend their ground.

The tenuous position at Alpha 2 had not been lost on First Lieutenant Joel Eisenstein. The American Marines up there were *his* guys. The officer in charge of this small group, First Lieutenant David Bruggeman, kept Eisenstein apprised of what the situation was and on the evening of March 31 the two had already, over a secure radio net, discussed the possibility of a need for an emergency extract.

On early Saturday morning, Eisenstein had gone to the army colonel who at the time just happened to be back in the bunker with General Giai. The colonel told him to begin planning but not to launch without his approval. Eisenstein went to work.

The key aspect to this particular extract would be coordinating the helicopter and naval gunfire assets. The risks were huge. Typical of the American way of war fighting, many men and valuable resources would be put at risk to save a smaller force. Joel Eisenstein would serve as the extract officer, leading the mission from both the air as they approached and on the ground when they landed. Even with the incredibly bad enemy situation expected on the way into and on the ground at Alpha 2 the U.S. Army helicopter pilots needed no prodding to serve on this mission. The debate among peers was how best to execute the extract. Having hashed out the basic plan by the early morning of April 1, all Eisenstein needed was the authorization to go.

It was particularly tense inside the Team 155 bunker on early Saturday morning. Even though Turley had effectively been running things since he had been drafted by General Giai's American advisor, the army colonel still maintained nominal control—though he never once questioned or countermanded anything Gerry did—over the staff when they were there, especially with the ARVN staff. The biggest problem, from the American perspective, created with the attempted blend of American and Vietnamese officers was the Asian reluctance to make decisions without their commander's explicit approval. With General Giai's long absences as he visited units in contact, reaching key decisions was often slowed for fear of making a decision contrary to what the general would have wanted and therefore losing face. Gerry Turley was well aware of this and the frustration it caused him was significant. With these awkward, unspecified command relationships, Gerry, even after effectively running things and coordinating all the personnel and resources for the last two days, still saw himself as a helper, a facilitator; *ad hoc*—a Band-Aid waiting to soon be replaced by more serious surgery. If this was a bad dream, he was hoping he would momentarily wake up.

The initial call from Dave Bruggeman requesting immediate extract came in at 0840. Eisenstein had gone immediately to the army colonel with the idea. The colonel told him to plan the mission but to launch only with his approval. Coordinating the naval gunfire and helicopter support took more time than Eisenstein had hoped to spend. By the time he had assembled the intrepid pilots and locked on the necessary naval gunfire support, General Giai and the Team 155 army colonel had gone back into the field. Having been told, ordered effectively, to get approval to execute from the Team 155 army colonel who was not there, the decision to launch this epic undertaking, probably also without real legal authority, now fell to Gerry Turley.

There was some unique indescribable quality to the whole process of authorizing the final go-ahead for the emergency rescue mission that changed the bearing and countenance of Gerry Turley. When taking the call from Joel Eisenstein to approve the mission, in the absence of the army colonel, time once more slowed to a crawl. Just as he had done two days before when given charge of the tactical operations center, in the space of several seconds his mind, with amazing clarity and lucidity; he mentally drilled into all aspects of the issues at hand. There was no question that attempting the rescue was the right thing, the honorable thing. If it succeeded those Marines and the army helicopter crews would walk away from it. If the extract force was destroyed or Eisenstein's Marines were captured or killed, it would be "Gerry Turley's Folly."

In that span of seconds, Gerry Turley was changed. Not in a physical sense. Something about the launch decision moved Lieutenant Colonel Turley from facilitator to the man in charge. The metamorphosis from being the substitute teacher tenuous with his students to confident headmaster, in that brief moment, was now complete. Something he did not understand had changed. Whatever it was was good. Gerry Turley had tapped into an inner peace and strength, a strange sense of relaxation with his new position that until this precise moment had so far eluded him. It was a very good thing. He would need that edge, that confidence, that certainty of purpose in the long hours and days ahead. And for Lieutenant Colonel Gerry Turley, the day was just getting started …

CHAPTER TWENTY-TWO

"No Place for a Nice Jewish Boy..."

During his Vietnam tour Joel Eisenstein had spent more than his fair share of time out at Alpha 2. He knew the surrounding topography well, had called countless naval gunfire and artillery missions from the very spot Dave Bruggeman and his four Marines were now in dire need of being rescued from. The helicopter pilots he was briefing who would fly the extract mission had never been there. With one Huey to serve as the extract bird and two Cobra gunships flying support, it was Eisenstein's counsel that they make a low approach from the south, taking advantage of the terrain's sloping away from Alpha 2 to minimize the enemy's view of their ingress.

The Cobras would fly top cover with guns and rockets blazing once they reached the target area while the Huey would land as close as possible to where Bruggeman and his Marines were located. Naval gunfire, firing from the front (north) and east of their positions would cover their approach, their time on the ground which was not expected to be more than a few minutes, and finally their departure; again at low level and heading back south toward Dong Ha and Ai Tu.

Eisenstein was grateful, as were all Marine advisors in the know who had benefited from their heroics, that these army helicopter pilots and crews almost routinely stepped into near-impossible situations without complaint. He knew the Huey crew would have to sit in the landing zone for some undetermined time with rounds crashing all around until the Marines were aboard. Sitting in a hot LZ, as nothing but a big, juicy target waiting to be blown away like a clay pigeon, was something that confounded even the bravest man's notion of sanity.

Eisenstein had briefed the pilots and the key folks on board the two Navy ships that would provide the gunfire support to cover them. The plan was as good as he could make it. At this point of the battle they were assuming, based upon how ARVN forces had reportedly abandoned so much of their critical equipment, that the NVA were now able to listen in on their communications, even secure communications. Because of this Eisenstein did not give Bruggeman too much detailed information other than to be ready to go.

By late morning of April 1, in the middle of a difficult fight, Lieutenant Colonel Turley was trying to sweat through the Eisenstein-planned-and-led rescue attempt of the five-man Naval Gunfire Spot Team at Alpha 2. At the exact same time Turley was worrying how that operation would turn out, he was also concerned about bigger issues.

From the field the TOC began receiving snippets of information; inconclusive reports over the tactical radio nets that General Giai, who was somewhere on the front lines with one of his subordinate units and without bothering to inform his own staff in the bunker, had ordered the withdrawal of all ARVN forces currently north of the Cua Viet River. If this was the case, the Second and 57th Regiments would have to retreat—*en masse* and with blinding speed—back across the river immediately and form up somewhere near both Cam Lo and Dong Ha. The idea made tactical sense. If all friendly units were south of the river, everything north of it was a legitimate target as most civilians were now in exodus as well; also moving south, away from the intentional, indiscriminate NVA shelling.

The reality part of the retrograde was the hard part. Attempting to establish order to such a move for units which, heretofore, had shown only marginal combat proficiency and élan was a pipe dream. This retrograde could quickly turn into a rout and all control would be lost. But General Giai had few options. As frustrating as it was to observe, Turley saw the practicality of the decision. He was also seeing just how critical the two major bridges capable of sustaining major traffic, the one at Cam Lo and the other at Dong Ha, were becoming to the NVA plan of attack. Both bridges needed to remain intact if the enemy hoped to get into Quang Tri and ultimately places further south with forces sufficient to seize, defeat, hold, and then finally defend against ARVN counterattacks.

The manner in which ARVN units displaced their positions and began their shameful retreat could have been a war college textbook example of how not to fight a war. Artillery pieces were left in place without being permanently disabled and might later be used against friendly forces. Even more critical, radios and their accompanying lists of call signs and frequencies, including crypto gear, were not destroyed. It would have to be assumed from now on that the enemy would be able to listen in on all communications.

Everything was happening so fast. Life for Turley and his men seemed like a 33 rpm record being played at 78 speed without letup. As they attempted to process the parsimoniously reported incoming news from various units in contact, as they made every attempt to keep their map boards current and deliver what limited resources they could, it was evident that there was little to stop the NVA *juggernaut*. The two bridges, Turley could see, would be critical. Of the two, the bridge at Dong Ha was obviously the more important one.

Joel Eisenstein had still not returned from his rescue mission when things in the bunker for Lieutenant Colonel Turley took an even stranger turn. At the same time, all ARVN fire base positions that fronted the enemy were under continued, constant assault. The TOC and the adjacent area in Ai Tu was also receiving steady artillery fire, albeit at a rate reduced from the estimated seven hundred to one thousand it had endured in the first twenty-four hours of the offensive. So far the ten feet of sandbags and overhead timbers, probably not as deep as it had been forty-eight hours ago, were still protecting those inside the bunker. Later on in the day, when Turley would emerge for the first time to move his bowels, he would be shocked at the level of devastation and destruction. Nothing in his Korean War experience or earlier Vietnam tour would compare to the now moonscape appearance of the surrounding area.

It must have been just prior to the noon hour when they arrived. Out of nowhere. Into the cacophony of action at the TOC that had now settled into some semblance of order and odd routine in spite of the dire situation, and unannounced to Turley or any of the others present, six U.S. Army colonels seemed to materialize out of the very ether.

Unsure at first if he was dreaming or hallucinating, these six might well have been apparitions. They all looked the same. Six Saigon colonels. Not lieutenant colonels but colonels; full-bird colonels with the big eagles on their collars. Armed with official-looking clipboards and fully clad in disgustingly clean uniforms, helmets worn with chin straps snapped just so and shiny boots; Turley knew that nothing good would come of the encounter unless he could wake up from this nightmare. He could not get over it. They all really did look the same, as if they had been manufactured in some Hong Kong colonel factory, moving together as one jerky body, like recruits on a drill field who were not yet quite fluid in their marching skills.

The first one who spoke to Gerry was obviously the leader and said, with all seriousness and complete solemnity, "We're here to see what your building requirements are ..." "Could you say that again, Colonel?"

Gerry was incredulous. He was thinking *"This is not happening. Are these guys nuts? Am I going nuts? Are these guys, if they are for real, serious? Do they even have a clue what is going on?"*

The colonel went on, unaffected by the random but continual thumping of artillery rounds impacting outside, "Now Colonel So-and-So here wants to know what your plywood needs are, and Colonel So-and-So there wants to know your ..." Turley was beside himself in complete and utter frustration. For a moment he thought maybe this was some cruel hoax and that Allen Funt would pop out of the shadows announcing to all that they should smile because they were on *Candid Camera.*

In the meantime the war and its demands continued. Staff in the TOC were moving about, doing whatever it was they did. The six Saigon colonels in a row created a bit of a traffic jam for folks needing to get from one place to another within the bunker.

Gerry suggested they move aside. Gathering them, out of the way, in a semicircle he said: "Now gentlemen, I am a Marine. Just a lieutenant colonel. This is an army operation. Forty-eight hours ago I had never even heard of Team 155. All of you are senior to me and I want to know, which one of you are here to replace me? Which one of you is here to take over?..."

They all stood there looking down at their clipboards. By this time Gerry was getting so angry that he actually then, starting with the man he had earlier believed to be the senior man, asked the exact same question but to each one individually. The first man replied "Well, I'm a logistician..." The others answered similarly: "I'm an engineer," "I'm here to look at electrical systems..." and down it went.

Gerry was nearly blind with frustration bordering on rage. He began to repeat himself. "Forty-eight hours ago I was just a f--ing visitor up here. I'm a Marine. One of your generals told me he would send up an army colonel to relieve me. One of you guys ought to take over."

And then, regaining a small amount of composure, pointing at the TOC in general and the system of map boards in particular, he continued. "Gentlemen, take a look at the map. We have lost nearly everything. We're losing our butts. We're about to make a stand at the Dong Ha Bridge ..." He kept going a little longer, admonishing these six colonels to step up, and they all sort of collectively mumbled at Gerry and, with each one of them still looking down at his clipboard, said something like "thank you very much" and just as mysteriously as they had shown up, sort of skulked from the bunker between moments when Lieutenant Colonel Turley was tending to issues needing tending to. Except for the others stuck in the bunker with Turley who also saw the six Saigon colonels, there was no record of their having been present at all. Gerry had never thought to ask for names or to see IDs. It was as if they had never been. And the war went on. He would never hear from or see them again.

Once he was given Lieutenant Colonel Turley's authorization to launch, Joel Eisenstein and his courageous assortment of army helicopter crews were up and gone. The approach to Alpha 2 was most likely not unobserved by the NVA who were aware that Americans were on the ground there. The NVA probably also hoped to exploit the sentimental leanings of the Americans who would, by their very nature, be certain to make at least one attempt to keep their men from becoming prisoners.

As the three helicopters approached—the Huey flying at treetop level and the Cobras taking up positions slightly higher to provide the covering fire—and just as the Huey was about to set down where Eisenstein directed, NVA artillery delivered a massive barrage all across the face of Alpha 2. The Huey pilot pressed on as if nothing had happened. On Eisenstein's cue, naval gunfire had already begun pounding the areas earlier outlined and the Cobras attacked the most obvious, provocative targets.

Under withering enemy fire, the Huey landed within thirty to thirty-five meters of the bunker where Eisenstein expected Bruggeman and his Marines to be. Before the helicopter's skids touched the deck, he was on the ground sprinting towards his comrades with the door gunner following close behind. Near the bunker they came upon the body of a wounded man who turned out to be Dave Bruggeman. The two quickly scooped him up to get him back in the bird for extract. Eisenstein could see that his friend had taken what looked to be some sort of serious wound to the skull. His body was limp and heavy in their arms. Simultaneously, Eisenstein made contact with Sergeant Newton, who for the moment had been around the bunker's corner gathering up his other men. Together they all beat it back to the helicopter that was just sitting there amid the conflagration.

Anxious to depart the area, in the excitement to account for his Marines, Eisenstein had even thrown a few wounded ARVN soldiers into the waiting Huey. As he counted his men, he realized there were only four. "Where is Corporal Worth?" he screamed at Newton and began a mad dash to some nearby bunkers. In what seemed an eternity he quickly ran, shouting, pleading for Corporal Worth to answer. Unable to find him in the bunkers and certain the other Marines did not know where he was, he made the toughest decision he had ever made, even though it was the right decision. With rounds continuing to impact all around him and the Huey with its turning prop wanting to depart this certain graveyard if they remained much longer, he ran back to the bird and—after doing a Mexican standoff with an ARVN soldier who nearly shot them down with a grenade launcher for not allowing him to board—they quickly departed the area.

The horror for Joel Eisenstein could not have been greater. *Where was Corporal Worth?* That question would continue to plague him. At the same time he was wrestling with that grief and guilt, he had the limp but still barely-breathing body of Dave Bruggeman in one arm while he held on for dear life to a strap in the madly jinking Huey with the other.

Only after they landed and Dave Bruggeman was pronounced dead by a corpsman, did Eisenstein learn the circumstances that got his friend killed. The day before, one of the enlisted Marines at Alpha 2 had had his helmet stolen by an ARVN soldier. As all Marine leaders are schooled to do, First Lieutenant Dave Bruggeman insisted that the young Marine take his. During the NVA shelling Bruggeman had taken shrapnel to his head. If he had been wearing his helmet perhaps the wound would not have been fatal. They would never know for sure. They were all certain of one thing though. First Lieutenant Bruggeman's selflessness and example of leadership cost him his life.

When he returned to the bunker area Eisenstein was completely spent physically and emotionally. Having done all he could have, way more than most men would have to get his men out, it was small consolation that the team made it at the cost of his friend Dave Bruggeman being killed and Corporal Worth's status now as missing in action. Calling down on the ANGLICO radio net to his commanding officer in Danang, Joel Eisenstein, trying to maintain a bold front with his boss who knew him well, declared with serious reflection way beyond his twenty-six years: "This is no place for a nice Jewish boy, over..."

Saturday Afternoon April 1, 1972
Team 155 Bunker TOC
Ai Tu

Fortunately or unfortunately for First Lieutenant Eisenstein, once he had concluded the quick debrief of those who were rescued from Alpha 2, it was back to work in the Tactical Operations Center (TOC). Requests for naval gunfire were on the rise and the young ANGLICO lieutenant was the man best qualified to handle that critical coordination. There was no time for him to feel the pain or process the loss. At least not yet. The North Vietnamese Army had other plans.

As much as it bothered Lieutenant Colonel Turley that Marines were lost at Alpha 2, he was relieved that Eisenstein's mission had succeeded to the extent that it did, that all the helicopters made it back, and that the survivors were now inside friendly lines, at least as long as Ai Tu could be held. Eisenstein had impressed Turley with his genuine bravery and leadership skills; his willingness to personally risk everything to save his Marines.

While the rescue was taking place out at Alpha 2 and Eisenstein was attempting to save his small portion of the world, the rest of the northern I Corps universe was looking pretty bleak. At about the same time Joel Eisenstein and the intrepid army helicopter crews were pulling his Marines off of their untenable position, the entire fire base was being decimated. The other three major fire bases just south of the DMZ, Alphas 1, 3, and 4, were likewise facing assault by overwhelming infantry and artillery forces.

At approximately 1045 Alpha 4, known also to American veterans of I Corps as Con Thien, was evacuated under General Giai's orders. As much as the general's intent was to free up and move his forces back to the south side of the Cam Lo-Cua Viet River, with so much enemy pressure and the full force of all these NVA divisions and their supporting artillery now fully engaged, the withdrawal from Alpha 4 as Turley could make out from the TOC, became the initial domino that triggered the others to fall.

By mid afternoon on April 1, the withdrawals from Alphas 1, 2, 3, and 4 had become a rout. On Alpha 2 it was observed that an

ARVN artillery battalion had abandoned their six 105mm Howitzers without disabling them. Things were little better out west with the losses of FB Fuller and Khe Gio, after earlier losing Nui Ba Ho and FB Sarge.

By late afternoon on April 1, the Third ARVN Division had given up all seven major fire bases north of the Cam Lo-Cua Viet River. Lieutenant Colonel Turley had one of the men there in the bunker duly check each fire base off as it was reported lost. The battle that would be known to the North Vietnamese and Communist world as the Nguyen-Hue Offensive was now well into its third full day. During that time Lieutenant Colonel Gerry Turley had gone from officially being the Assistant Senior Marine Advisor on an unofficial trip up north to see his people, to the drafted-without-any-legal-authority unofficial/official operations officer for Team 155. In less than forty-eight hours he had gone from a man with zero operational responsibilities to coordinating the supporting fire power and what movement he could for the entire Third ARVN Division and their two attached brigades of Vietnamese Marines, and was fighting against what his intel officer now told him were three full infantry divisions of NVA along with a few extra regiments, perhaps a thousand pieces of artillery and possibly enemy armor; lots of armor. Between the willfully poor reporting of and not believing in the seriousness of activity up in northern I Corps by both U.S. Army and ARVN senior officers down south and the genuine chaos that currently existed to cloud reality in an already poor system of communications with the powers that be in Saigon, no one knew who the heck Gerry Turley was, or what the heck he was doing now seeming to be running the show; making decisions and pronouncements way beyond what a lieutenant colonel—an interloping U.S. Marine lieutenant colonel no less—should be making.

During that entire period that was now beginning to be day three of the Nguyen-Hue Offensive, Gerry Turley had not slept a wink, had not eaten a thing, and had only needed to urinate a few times. The stress and strain were significant. Even with a fair number of genuinely competent officers and troops assisting there in the bunker, the issues were such that he was needed at nearly every moment. In those opening two days Turley had only left the bunker briefly to relieve himself, just outside, within a few feet of the bunker entrance because of the continual shelling, and then went right back to his duties. The stress and strain, by day three were finally beginning to catch up to him. After the visit from the mysterious six Saigon colonels, after the return of Eisenstein, after dealing with a hundred other things that all added up to life and death for those soldiers and Marines at the different fire bases, it finally hit him. Gerry Turley had diarrhea.

Feeling the urge, he excused himself, turning things over to J.D. Murray and smiling at the troops in the bunker who happened to observe him; giving a reassuring thumbs up to encourage and bolster them as he made his way to the bunker's only hatch. In the few times he had come out to urinate he had never really taken in the view, never really observed the level of destruction all around Ai Tu. This time it was just a bit different. With the sun still far from going down there was sufficient light to see all there was, or what no longer existed. He was awed by the spectacle and sheer destruction.

Even though Gerry Turley had figuratively been alone since the moment he was thrust into a position of authority, he had not been physically by himself since this entire mess was improperly and allegedly temporarily foisted upon him. Now walking outside to find a spot to move his bowels, he really was alone; literally.

The devastation of the entire surrounding area was something he was not quite prepared for. There was not a spot of ground, within his view, that had been spared the destruction of the unrelenting NVA shelling. The terrain had ceased to look like anything resembling anything he had ever seen. It really was, at least to Turley, otherworldly.

At the same time that he was consumed with the look of things, he also needed to *go*. What small amount of privacy he hoped for was minimized by the immediacy of the physical urge. Well outside the bunker, he did manage to cozy up next to the hulk of a now burned out jeep. Gerry Turley was tired, he was hungry, and he now finally had a spare moment to begin to feel sorry for himself. Squatting next to the jeep, doing his business, having left the bunker without his flak jacket, he actually found himself slipping into modified prayer…. He began, "Dear Lord…if You are gonna take me, please take me now. Don't hurt me. Just take me quick…" Gerry was thinking that a simple, relatively painless way out might be to be at or near the point of impact for one of those Soviet-supplied rocket or artillery rounds that for the last three days had impacted all around the area. A few moments passed. Nothing happened. As he finished going, and began to pull up his trousers, he had already determined that he and God were not currently on the same frequency and that this prayer would probably not be answered. At least not now.

Taking in the scenery, something caught Gerry's eye. Looking up as he buttoned his trousers, he saw a familiar-looking sign that shook him from his lethargy. All during his career he had seen these signs on every military base he had ever been aboard. The small red signs with a star or two or three or four on them signifying the presence of a general officer. Marines anywhere close to these were taught to beware, to practically genuflect when near one, to respect and stay off of anything that might be considered holy ground.

This particular sign had a single star and below it was the name of Brigadier General Vu Van Giai, Commanding General Third ARVN Division. Adjacent to the slightly tilting sign was a small patch of remaining lawn—actual green grass—that only a direct hit would now remove from Ai Tu. Less than seventy-two hours earlier this area, now officially marked by Gerry Turley, had been General Giai's capacious and liberally cared for front lawn to his headquarters bunker, his pride and joy, the very place Marines and dogs were supposed to stay off of. Lieutenant Colonel Gerry Turley USMCR had just committed a major sin.

As strange and crazy as everything was, every single thing from the moment he stepped into the Team 155 TOC bunker at Ai Tu after the shelling began at lunch on March 30 up through whatever issues he had dealt with right before exiting to take a dump, there was not one iota of humor to anything that happened. For Turley, as drained and tired as he was—both literally and figuratively "pooped"—this was the action that gave him an edge. Crapping in the middle of what used to be the general's yard made him laugh. Seriously laugh. He was now anxious to get back inside the TOC and tell the others, confess to the others, brag and boast to the others, what he just did. The Marines, at least, would get the joke. If nothing else, they would laugh at it because he was senior.

When he stepped back inside the TOC and J.D. Murray acknowledged that Turley was again in charge, he was smiling. Smiling and laughing. Lieutenant Colonel Gerry Turley, operations officer in "temporary" charge of Team 155, called his subordinate officers into a huddle. They were a bit apprehensive coming together. As intimate as they had all been in the last three days, they had never seen Turley this way. "Gentlemen, Gentlemen, come on over here for a moment if you would. I've got something to tell you about ..." They got it. All of them; they got it. The mood in the bunker had, at that moment, suddenly improved just a bit.

The fog of war was still thick, perhaps a bit less thick than before, as Turley returned to his duties. The increasing number of calls he was receiving from staff and watch officers continually phoning or radioing in from Danang and Saigon was at least an indication that MACV was finally getting a sense that things were serious in northern I Corps.

It had not been Turley's job to inform the world that he was given temporary charge of operations for Team 155. Had he even had the time to think about it, he would have assumed that the army colonel working for General Giai might have told Saigon. From the genuine hostility Turley was receiving by those calling in, it was very apparent that no one in MACV or Danang or anywhere else had been informed. Now that it was beginning to sink in down south that the problems up north were serious, that the folks in the bunker had all been operating on zero sleep and under less than ideal conditions, tempers flared. When calls would come in to speak to the "Ops O" — operations officer — and they went to Gerry Turley, someone unknown and not of the Army, the average response was something like "Let me speak to the senior army officer."

Turley now had to increasingly defend his backside against constant carping and pettiness from the folks in Danang and

Saigon. He hated having to invest time that should have been focused on fighting the NVA to dealing with a hostile group from down south. It seemed to him that he simultaneously had to fight two battles at once.

The MACV staff in Saigon appeared genuinely miffed that they had to actually speak to a Marine. Having fielded that same request for what were now hours on end, Turley had begun to tire of the seemingly uncritical to the battle, internecine service squabbling. When he came back into the bunker he began receiving the same calls, but this time was speaking to whoever was on the other end and was laughing out loud at them. Even on the horribly poor telephone landlines the people in Saigon could recognize the slight. They were of course, incensed. It did them no good. Turley had no time for games. He was still running the war and would, both politely and impolitely, tell these guys "F--- you..." and press on. Some of these guys began to believe that Turley had flipped his lid.

Lieutenant Colonel Turley's momentarily improved psychological state had minor impact on the war's course. Across the approaching northern front that ran east to west, ARVN forces continued their broad, ignominious retreat at varying speeds. Units in flight from the Second and 57th Regiments, for the most part, had simply up and left their equipment, including all communications gear, in the face of the advancing enemy. Now the communicators in the Team 155 bunker were actually receiving calls from brazen, confident-in-victory NVA on the remaining landlines that connected the former friendly positions with the rear or over radios they had captured with all the accompanying call signs and frequencies. The effect of those calls did not bolster morale.

Out on the western flanks, under equal or greater pressure, the Marine brigades were also being beaten back, albeit at a much slower pace. The story was basically the same everywhere: the enemy advance was continuing without reasonable expectation that it would be stopped anytime soon. Every passing moment brought the NVA closer to Dong Ha, Ai Tu and all critical points further south.

The increasingly untenable situation in northern I Corps had created many challenges for the ARVN-U.S. team that was trying to at least stabilize the battlefield.

Included among the obvious tactical and strategic issues were the extra political issues created by the ongoing Vietnamization of the ground war. With that effort well under way, it was critical that American involvement, except perhaps for air power and support, appear to be minimized at points closest to the action.

At about 1900 on April 1, General Giai's American army colonel, the one who had earlier drafted Turley for the temporary duty as the Team 155 operations officer, had returned to the bunker. In the last several days he and Turley had not spent ten minutes together. The colonel called Turley aside. In the prior three days there had been absolutely no tactical guidance given from the senior man to the junior. Not once had he offered insight or overridden anything Turley ordered. The colonel now had instruction for Lieutenant Colonel Turley.

With the ongoing deterioration of the battle situation all over northern I Corps, General Giai was ordering the Americans out at Ai Tu, and would relocate most of the Third Division headquarters people back south several miles to Quang Tri City which was at the moment still out of range of NVA artillery. In the meantime Turley, as the senior American, would remain in the current TOC and handle operations with a skeleton crew and continue to run all the fire support until the new headquarters was established.

Immediately the two men were in spirited disagreement. While Turley could see that there really were no other options, it was maddening to split the resources. The two men were both speaking at once, neither of them listening to the other, neither of them able to make the critical points needed to win an argument. In his frustration, Gerry continued to point out that this was an Army show and that as a visiting Marine officer he really had no authority or business running the operation. The colonel countered with the issue of operational emergencies and all that. He again promised to get a man up to properly relieve Turley "as soon as possible." Turley did not believe him. As with most arguments between men of dissimilar rank, the army colonel's orders stood. There was, however, some compromise.

The American Marines stayed. So too did the Vietnamese Marines. With all the USMC *covans* out at the TQLC brigade and battalion levels currently locked in mortal combat, there was no other honorable option. The army colonel also allowed Turley to keep a relatively small staff of operations and critically needed communications folks there at Ai Tu to keep the TOC fully operational for executing fire support missions for as long as was needed.

Angry and upset, Turley still recognized that what was being done was probably the only thing they could do. What absolutely drove him, again, to near rage was the manner in which this new retrograde movement was conducted.

The retrograde movement of personnel from the Ai Tu TOC was done without order, certainly without positive leadership or dignity. ARVN personnel there in the bunker with Turley and his remaining crew simply stood up from the desks, radios, and switchboards they were manning and walked out. Among the Americans who were also leaving, behavior was often little better.

When the American army CH-47 helicopters came in to the Ai Tu landing zone to lift out those going back to Quang Tri City, senior ARVN officers were seen as the first to board. It was looking more and more like it was every man for himself.

Of the original eighty or so Americans assigned to duty as part of Team 155, only about thirty would remain. Turley did not have a sense for how many people Third ARVN Division still had in Ai Tu. It seemed to him that the only folks from the Vietnamese side who remained were Marines.

To say that those who remained in the Ai Tu TOC with Gerry Turley were there because they felt duty bound was not correct. Most who stood by were there because they were ordered to be. Every man was scared. Even Gerry Turley. No one knew what the battle's outcome would be. Certainly as Saturday, April 1 was drawing to a close things were not looking good for the South Vietnamese and their allies.

Turley was relatively comfortable with most of those who remained. He had his rock, J.D. Murray, to lean on. His incredibly well informed and insightful Marine intel officer, Captain Tom O'Toole, was also there to give good guidance. Major Dave Brookbank of the Air Force, serving as his air liaison officer and who would coordinate all air strikes had already proven to Turley that he was someone to have around in tough situations, would soon be of even greater value as the weather improved and air power could once again be fully employed. And finally, the army officer in charge of all communications, Major Wilson, was a tireless, unflappable gent whose tenacity and attention to detail kept their comm going. Joel Eisenstein continued as the man coordinating all naval gunfire requests. The senior Vietnamese officer now present was Colonel Ngo Van Dinh, commanding officer of Marine Brigade 258. Known only to Turley by reputation, he was said to be a real warrior. Providing security for the area was the TQLC's Sixth Battalion.

As good a crew as remained with Turley, they still had their challenges. Among the Americans was an officer who twice attempted to leave the bunker even after being informed he was part of the group to remain. It was an ugly situation on the second go-round when Turley, with Captain O'Toole as his witness, took the American officer aside. In words the man would understand Turley assured him that when it was time to leave the bunker the two of them would be the last out. And, oh, yes, if he tried to leave again, Turley "would blow your f---ing brains out."

With the shift of personnel, life in the TOC turned back to what those there would have described as routine. What units remained from the Second and 57th Regiments who were north of the Cam Lo-Cua Viet Rivers continued their full retreat. The 56th Regiment out west at Camp Carroll was still intact but was now isolated and under increasingly heavy enemy siege. TQLC units at Mai Loc were also facing increasing enemy pressure. Turley's crew kept track of the ever-devolving situation and attempted to apply what meager firepower there was available. They were doing all they could do. And the battle continued.

Gerry Turley was now making near regular trips back out to his special spot on General Giai's former front lawn. Perhaps it was the third or fourth foray after the initial one, he had lost track now, but the humor had diminished completely. On this visit he happened to look down the road, or what used to be the road, away towards Highway 1 which ran north and south less than two hundred meters from the

TOC bunker. Right there in front of him was a spectacle he could have never imagined or adequately described. It might have been the staging for a Cecil B. DeMille epic film, except this was not Hollywood, there would be no Moses or Charlton Heston to part the Red Sea or lead these people to the Promised Land, and worst of all, the suffering he had a front-row seat to was for real.

Right in front of him, and part of the very same experience that all military personnel there were a part of was a massive, unending, amoeba-like line of hapless, nearly hopeless refugees, thousands upon thousands of people, perhaps tens of thousands of people, coming from somewhere up north and all heading somewhere, anywhere to the south, as long as it was out of range of the intentional and indiscriminate NVA artillery fire. Gerry Turley had never seen anything like it. It disturbed him greatly. For a few moments he stood at the bunker entrance, mesmerized, taking in what he could, trying to imagine what was happening for these now-homeless legions of Vietnamese peasants.

The group was mostly civilians with lots of young women carrying or attempting to hustle crying children along, small boys leading water buffalo, old bent-over *mamasans* with what had to be either grandchildren or their meager belongings strapped to their backs. There was every combination of family imaginable. Mixed in with the civilians Gerry could see young soldiers still in uniform but none were carrying weapons or their equipment other than canteens maybe. Even though he could not see well enough, he knew those men had stripped their uniforms of unit patches and rank insignia. Some of these men, perhaps many of them, had fled their units to get their families out of the indiscriminate NVA shelling if they were from the local area. Others, those who were alone or with other young men, were simply, and obviously, deserters.

As he stood there watching something that was so real, yet unreal-seeming, he witnessed the impact of what he thought, because he recognized enemy artillery shells and their impact, was an NVA 130mm round right in the center of a group of regular folks on the road. That the enemy were intentionally targeting civilians could not have been more obvious.

Just as a body of water would only instantaneously displace when an object of any size was dropped into it, and then close back up erasing all signs of the object's having been there anyway, so it was with these long-suffering Vietnamese civilians. He saw the effect of the artillery round impact followed by a temporary flailing about by those affected, and then an informal closing back of ranks by those not killed or maimed. Those who were killed or turned back into only particles of DNA were grieved over if a family member survived; otherwise the now newly-created empty space was filled in by other nameless, anonymous folks. The long march south continued, no matter what; it seemed to Turley, essentially uninterrupted.

This mass exodus of Vietnamese humanity had its own energy, its own constant drumbeat of sound, all mixed together; sounds of tough life going on. Gerry could pick out, even at the distance he was from them, mothers castigating children, aside from the crying of little ones, the wailing of those who must have just lost loved ones, the bickering between people who were under pressures few could truly appreciate. And yet, the suffering, the movement, the whole thing continued on almost as if there was a certain inevitability to it and acceptance of it.

Turley was relieved that he knew none of these folks, that the empathy he felt could be a bit impersonal. The notion that these were mostly women and children saddened him greatly. For the briefest moment he thought of Bunny and their five children. Except for an accident of birth it might have been his family on the road, enduring the worst of life's nightmares. As he had heard more Americans than he could remember say—"There but for the grace of God go I..." and as trite as that now seemed, he thought that thought anyway.

The personalization of these losses and thinking of his own family were possibilities that, for the moment, were too oppressive for Gerry Turley to entertain. He forced them from his mind. The only thing he could do to assist was to help defeat the people responsible for the carnage. And so he went back inside the bunker.

What was the Big Picture for Lieutenant Colonel Gerry Turley and his crew in the Team 155 bunker at Ai Tu was just one of several smaller screens to the Americans in MACV and the Vietnamese Joint General Staff (JGS) in Saigon. Having convinced themselves before the invasion's beginning on March 30 that if action started up north, it would merely be a feint, they were still waiting to be proven correct on the late evening of April 1. The JGS, remaining confident of its earlier beliefs, was sending reinforcements to the Central Highlands in advance of any enemy action there yet.

After the new, reduced crew in the Ai Tu TOC had briefed the staff of Brigade 258 late Saturday evening, a semblance of order was regained. With that, the ground situation all across northern I Corps still continued to worsen. At least those who remained, especially on the Vietnamese side for a change, were resolute in developing and working a plan to stop the Communists at the Cam Lo-Cua Viet River and not at locations further south. As these not insignificant changes were being made from the allied side, positive attention was slowly beginning to come from senior American officers in both Danang and Saigon.

Shortly after midnight on Easter Sunday in Vietnam, Turley spoke directly with an American army brigadier general in Danang who informed him that "All restrictions are off on U.S. air. Continue to request targets for B-52s." Their further conversation revealed to Turley that the targeting decisions for these massive strikes, known as ARCLIGHT strikes, were now entirely at his discretion. Turley had not yet attended War College but knew what he needed to about planning and coordinating all manner of the use of firepower. That the U.S. Air Force, a service known for its extremely legalistic, formal methods for selecting and then bombing targets, had essentially just thrown away the book in turning over targeting authority to a lowly, unknown Marine lieutenant colonel was no small matter. Less than two hours later, one of the American Marines serving now as a watch officer in the bunker took a call from Saigon from the senior air force general at MACV. The general told the Marine major that Turley now had control over *all* air assets in northern I Corps. *Happy Easter*.

CHAPTER TWENTY-THREE

Easter Morning at Dong Ha

Early Easter Sunday in Northern I Corps
Ripley Home
Blacksburg, Virginia

*I*t *was easy for Moline Ripley*, in her own way, to mentally keep track of her husband. Vietnam time was twelve hours ahead of Virginia. As her day would wind down, his was just beginning; or so she reasonably imagined.

As much as she was unable—mercifully—to fully know what a typical or atypical day was like wherever he was, especially these last few days, John Ripley was able to experience a sense of peace and comfort knowing, at least, that his bride and kids were safe and sound and loved and in a routine twelve hours out from his, and a million miles away.

When John Ripley had gone back to Vietnam for his second tour immediately following the death of his brother Mike, he had set Moline and the three children—by Easter 1972, Stephen now age six, Mary a month shy of three, and Thomas just turned two—up in a rented home in Blacksburg, in large part because there were no suitable homes available in Radford. Home to Virginia Polytechnic University and barely ten miles northeast of Radford, Blacksburg was a cute little college town that was perfectly situated to give Moline space and privacy when needed, but close enough so that both sets of doting grandparents could help out and enjoy the pleasures of having the Ripley grandchildren nearby.

Moline's twin sister Marcella, also married with children of her own, lived in Nashville, which was hours away. For Moline's parents, grandchildren Stephen, Mary, and Thomas were the only regular show in town. Grandmother Blaylock daily drove from Radford to Blacksburg to take one of the children; a different one each day, for several hours so that she might spell her daughter and lighten her logistical load a bit, but more importantly so that she might love and spoil and indulge her grandchildren.

More experienced in the grandparenting arts and with older grandchildren in the area, Bud and Verna Ripley demonstrated no less enthusiasm for John and Moline's children. Whenever they were together, the Ripley grandchildren were the center of Bud and Verna's universe. Except for their father being gone again after the near idyllic Christmas 1971 home visit, their young lives, to them, were filled with love and nurturing and picnics and bedtime stories; and a pending visit from the Easter Bunny.

Stephen, at age six, had the Easter egg thing down cold, and knew what to look forward to. This Easter would be the first one Mary would truly be able to comprehend the aspect of near-unlimited goodies and searching for special treasure. Thomas would follow, finding things his mother, grandparents, and cousins would ensure he might stumble upon even after the older kids had picked an area clean.

Both Ripley boys would look sharp with their momma reminding them, admonishing Stephen especially because he was the oldest, that they should mind their manners and not roughhouse too much. Mary, of course, would look the sweetest with her special Easter dress, lacy socks, and black patent-leather shoes that every little girl wore to look special and melt the hearts of the adult men in her life. This Easter it would just be her two grandpas. Moline would dutifully take pictures to later show John.

With three children to be responsible for, Moline had little down time. It was only during those infrequent moments throughout the day, usually when Stephen was off to school and the two younger ones were napping, late at night or early in the morning when she prayed, that she had time to miss her husband to the point of aching.

During the day, even while attending to the children, she often left the radio on for any news about Vietnam. Along with

Gerry and Bunny Turley's wedding, May 2, 1950, seven weeks before Communists invaded South Korea (photo courtesy of Gerry Turley).

Korea, 1951 (photo courtesy of Gerry Turley).

Sergeant and Mrs. Turley with Anne, a happy homecoming from Korea, January 1952 (photo courtesy of Gerry Turley).

Newly commissioned Second Lieutenant Gerry Turley in San Diego, bound for Quantico (photo courtesy of Gerry Turley).

Gerry Turley on a troop transport to relieve forces in Korea, February 1952 (photo courtesy of Gerry Turley).

First Lieutenant Gerry Turley on Viegas Island, July 1954 (photo courtesy of Gerry Turley).

Trung Ta (Lieutenant Colonel) Le Ba Binh in Saigon,
late 1972 (photo courtesy of Le Ba Binh).

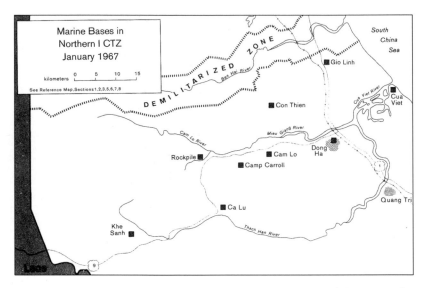

Map courtesy of Gerry Turley

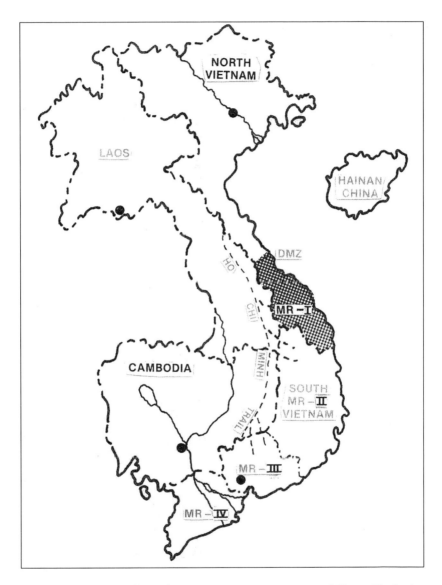

Military regions of South Vietnam (map courtesy of Gerry Turley).

"Lima Six Actual" with "Lima One Actual"—Skipper John Ripley and Sergeant Chuck Goggin after the action in which Lima Company became known as Ripley's Raiders, Ca Lu, March 1967 (photo courtesy of Chuck Goggin).

"King Kong Lives!" Captains George Philip and John Ripley display their jigsaw puzzle construction skills at Alpha-2, just south of the DMZ, fall 1971 (photo courtesy of George Philip).

Allies: Captain George Philip with Dai Uy Tam V. Nguyen at Alpha-2 in northern I Corps, fall 1971. Dai Uy Tam was captured during the ARVN surrender of Camp Carroll and spent eight years in reeducation (photo courtesy of George Philip).

Second Lieutenant Nguyen Luong (at extreme right) with comrades in Saigon, fall 1971 (photo courtesy of Nguyen Luong).

The wedding of Le Ba Binh and Cam Banh at the Song Than Officers'
Club in Saigon, January 1972 (photo courtesy of Le Ba Binh).

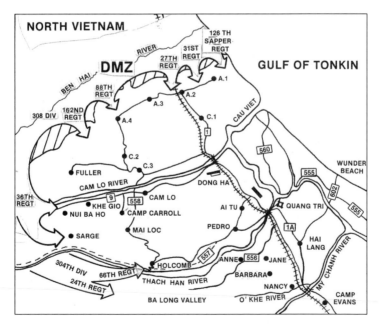

The initial thrust of the NVN offensive (map courtesy of
Gerry Turley).

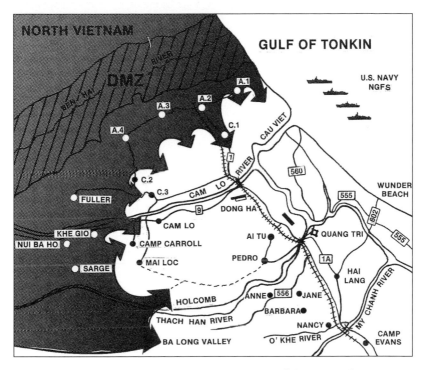

Situation April 2, 1972 (map courtesy of Gerry Turley).

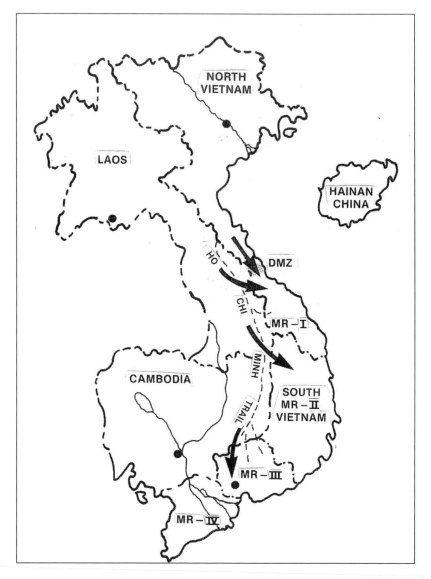

The Nguyen Hue Offensive (1972 North Vietnamese invasion of MR-1) (map courtesy of Gerry Turley).

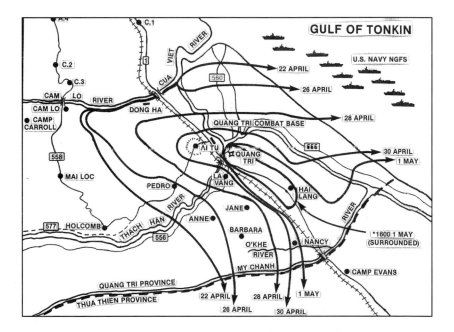

The encirclement of Quang Tri City, May 1972,
surrounded May 1, 1972 (map courtesy of Gerry Turley).

Captain George Philip's official Marine Corps photo, summer 1972 (photo courtesy of George Philip).

Recently promoted to Trung Ta (Lieutenant Colonel), Binh stands in Quang Tri as the commanding officer of Third Battalion just prior to being wounded for the ninth time, August 1972 (photo courtesy of Le Ba Binh).

Gerry Turley as the assistant senior Marine advisor, 1972 (photos courtesy of Gerry Turley).

Roberto Clemente and Chuck Goggin in the locker room
after Chuck's first hit as a major leaguer. In the same
game, played on September 30, 1972, Clemente hit his
three thousandth and, tragically, last hit. He was
subsequently killed in a plane crash while delivering aid
to Nicaraguan earthquake victims on December 31, 1972
(photo courtesy of Chuck Goggin).

"Thanks for the memories!" Gerry and Bunny Turley outside the Vietnamese Marine Corps Officers' Club at Song Than, December 1972 (photo courtesy of Gerry Turley).

Binh and Cam at Song Than base camp in Saigon, 1973 (photo courtesy of Le Ba Binh).

A proud father with his precious daughter. Binh and Le Mong Ngoc on the beach in Vung Tau, 1974 (photo courtesy of Le Ba Binh).

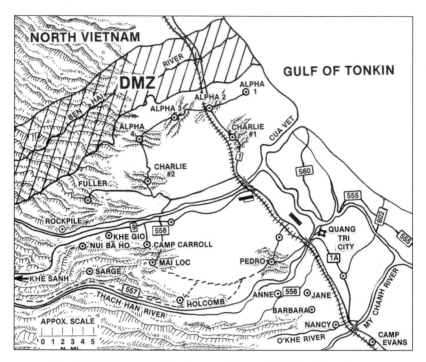

South Vietnamese fire bases, Quang Tri Province (map
courtesy of Gerry Turley).

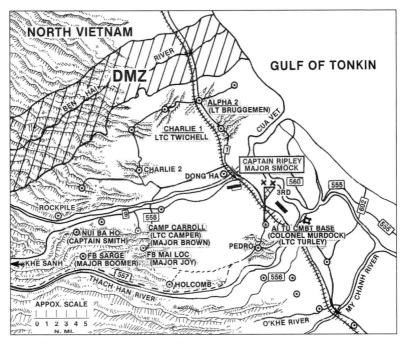

U.S. advisors and their fire base locations (map courtesy
of Gerry Turley).

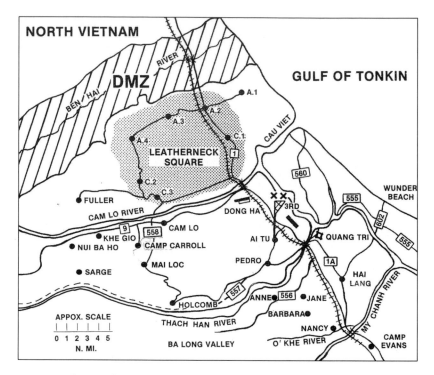

Leatherneck Square in northern Quang Tri Province (map
courtesy of Gerry Turley).

Captain John W. Bowman, Jr., right, piloted an AH-1J, and First
Lieutenant David L. Androskaut was his co-pilot when they
crashed off the Vietnamese coast while providing cover and
support for American forces during the evacuation of Saigon on
April 30, 1975. The crew of the USS *Kirk* rescued them moments
later (photo courtesy of Captain Russell R. Thurman USMC, Ret.).

Le Mong Ngoc on her fifth birthday in Saigon, July 4, 1979. Her father was away in a "reeducation camp" (photo courtesy of Le Ba Binh).

Caroline Le graduates from California State University with a degree in information technology, June 1999. Left to right: Fiancé Steven Nguyen, Caroline, and proud parents (photo courtesy of Le Ba Binh).

Trung Ta Le Ba Binh receives the Silver Star, the highest
award authorized for non-U.S. allies. Left to right:
unidentified Vietnamese Marine, General Walter Boomer,
Trung Ta Le Ba Binh, and Colonel John Ripley, Washington,
DC, summer 2003 (photo courtesy of Le Ba Binh).

At the USMC-TQLC reunion in Washington, DC, summer 2003.
Left to right: Cam Banh, Madame Le Nguyen Khang (wife of
former TQLC *commandant* Le Nguyen Khang), John Ripley,
Moline Ripley, Le Ba Binh, and Brigadier General Bui The Lan,
final *commandant* of the TQLC (photo courtesy of Le Ba Binh).

Comrades forever. Le Ba Binh and Nguyen Luong at
Binh's home, 2006 (photo courtesy of Le Ba Binh).

Filming an episode of Oliver North's *War Stories* in San
Francisco, summer 2006. Left to right: Oliver North, Nguyen
Luong, Hue Tan (translator), Le Ba Binh, and John Ripley
(photo courtesy of Le Ba Binh).

Author Richard Botkin with Gerry Turley, 2008 (photo courtesy of Richard Botkin).

her mommy radar always keyed for signs of pain or irregularity from the little ones, she was also tuned in to pick up any key word or phrase that, if spoken during a news broadcast, would tell her something she might need to know about her husband.

Moline and the children, although they had now been fairly regularly attending services in Blacksburg, for Easter Sunday would join the Ripleys at St. Jude's in Radford, the same church in which she and John had been married eight years ago, before she had ever even heard of Vietnam.

TURLEY AND CREW IN THE BUNKER

Early Easter morning
Ai Tu

If he had not been so concerned about ensuring the survival of the remaining allied forces in northern I Corps, especially those still on the wrong side of the Cam Lo-Cua Viet River, if he had not been so consumed with keeping track of the three NVA infantry divisions, several independent regiments and the untold numbers of artillery pieces and suspected tanks Captain O'Toole continued to not so gently remind him were arrayed against them and poised to deliver even greater punishment, Lieutenant Colonel Turley might have had time to be intimidated by the amount of firepower and additional responsibility that had just been squarely added to everything else resting on his men's size medium shoulders.

Even with all that was going on, and all that was weighing in upon him, Gerry Turley really did consider the gravity of his new responsibilities. The B-52 targeting authority; that was a big deal. It was a huge deal. Briefly he even wondered if anyone of his rank had ever, even under these unusual circumstances, had this charge. At this very moment, Lieutenant Colonel Gerry Turley was about to exercise, coordinate and implement more military firepower than any one man in the entire world.

Gerry Turley had the full measure of the great American military-industrial complex at *his* disposal. B-52s, like the Polaris nuclear submarines and the Minute Man ICBMs that together made up the three components of the nation's nuclear triad, were considered national strategic assets. The decision to employ B-52s, even in a non-nuclear role, was always made at the very highest levels. Gerry Turley had just become, by the nature of his position, an instrument of American national military strategy.

Used in a role in the Vietnam War other than which it was primarily designed for, the non-nuclear capabilities of the B-52 were still formidable. The ARCLIGHT strikes, with their unending strings of bombs that seemed to come from the heavens unannounced, had tremendous deleterious impact on the NVA, especially their morale, when the targeting information was accurate.

Turley wasted little time in designating where he wished, what he described to the folks in Saigon as the "center of impact," for the thousands and thousands of bombs he would shortly be able to unleash should land once the giant bombers were on station. To the chagrin of his intel officer, Turley's first impact area was the Ba Long Valley out west and south of FB Sarge and Nui Ba Ho. He and Captain O'Toole debated briefly. Tom O'Toole thought it wise to nail the NVA to their front first. Turley wanted two-thirds of his initial B-52 strikes used to eliminate the under-appreciated but significant pincer threat from the west. The remaining strikes would be for securing his northern front. It was the first time since he had arrived in the bunker that Turley now believed they had a small chance of success. It was payback time.

The NVA had not come unprepared for this potentiality. As much as the weather had been assisting the offensive so far, when the weather cleared and allied airpower was able to scramble to full strength again, the American and South Vietnamese air forces would face incredibly daunting anti-air defense systems the NVA had brought along to the forward-most portions of the areas of the land battle.

The tempo of operations in the always-shrinking area under the control of friendly forces in northern I Corps showed no signs of slowing. Turley and crew continued to process information at a rate suggesting the tactical situation was growing ever more acute. With the ongoing fallback of what few friendly forces remained on the north side of the Cam Lo-Cua Viet River, it was obvious to Turley that the strategic value of the bridge at Dong Ha was increasing by the minute.

It was difficult to take accurate inventory. It seemed that every few moments the ground situation was being altered ever so slightly. By 0400 on Easter morning Turley was able to tell that the quality of communication for what remained of the forward elements of Third ARVN Division and its attached Marine brigades had actually improved. Every American advisor known to be in the field with ARVN and TQLC units could be reached over the radio. So far this morning that and the ability to soon apply B-52s would have to be the goodies in his Easter basket to satisfy him.

Up through 0400 Turley could now count off ten major firebases overrun and lost to the NVA. He couldn't know accurately how much of the gear that ARVN forces had abandoned had been destroyed or was now being used against the good guys. Only Mai Loc and Camp Carroll remained unconquered by the advancing NVA. Out at Camp Carroll, with its twenty-two artillery pieces that included the four precious 175s, the 56th Regiment was taking an incredible pounding but was still alleged to be holding on—barely.

Back in the TOC the news continued from every source to over-stimulate but not quite overwhelm those who were almost routinely dealing with the volume of critical information coming in nonstop. Turley, still afflicted with diarrhea and now nearly dehydrated by it, continued to make frequent trips outside to relieve himself. No matter when he emerged from the bunker there was always a crush of Vietnamese humanity heading south on Highway One in a line of livestock, people and what meager resources they could carry that seemed never to end.

At 0630, while monitoring the naval gunfire net, First Lieutenant Eisenstein picked up an unusual report. A USMC Special Landing Force (SLF) of three thousand Marines was allegedly somewhere offshore within two hours steaming time. While the news cheered the crew in the TOC, Turley had no illusions of their being brought into the battle. The reintroduction of American fighting men back into Vietnam would be a presidential decision that would not be made without very serious consideration. From his own perspective Turley saw the probability as low. Knowing the SLF was somewhere out there over the horizon made him feel better but it was like having an insurance policy that would never be used except in the strangest of circumstances; and things had not yet gotten that strange.

Sometime in the early Easter morning, Dave Brookbank delivered to Turley news that the weather was soon expected to break in their favor. Before the day was out, he predicted, TAC air would again be available. In any event, the battle continued.

At precisely 0854 a call came in over both American and Vietnamese tactical radio nets from elements of the still-in-retreat 57th Regiment. Enemy tanks had been spotted on the high ground at Alpha 2. This was the first actual confirmation of enemy armor after days of rumors and lots of guessing. Sixteen minutes later observers aboard U.S. Navy ships just off the coast were able to eyeball tanks in the open at locations north of the Cua Viet River. The immediate requests for naval gunfire to suppress the armor threat were responded to rapidly.

As if he did not have enough to concern himself with, at 0915 Gerry Turley received a personal call from the American colonel with General Giai who was now way down south in Danang. With the briefest exchange of pleasantries the colonel informed the lieutenant colonel: "This telephone call is to order you to take over as Chief Advisor, Third ARVN Division (Forward). The commanding general, FRAC, directed that I make this call directly to you. This is an operational emergency. Do you understand my order?"

"Yessir, Colonel, I do."

Just as it had been the first time the colonel had prevailed upon him three days earlier, what else could Turley do? There was but one option. To protect himself, though, in the only way he thought possible and as if this might keep the army officers from later denying the order at all, Turley asked the colonel for his social security number, wrote it down on a piece of scrap paper, and put it in his front trouser pocket.

The new order from higher up changed very little. Now that it was somehow all more official, Turley's duties did not change one bit. He did take another moment to indulge himself; a half moment to ask the rhetorical "Why me, Lord?" question and the second half of the moment to resurrect the earlier suppressed consideration of doom from when he had been on the flight up to Phu Bai. Turley again recalled that day as a boy when he had had "that feeling" that kept him from swimming in the quarry when all the other boys drowned, and then again in Korea when he stayed off the R&R flight that crashed right after takeoff, killing all aboard. The train he was now charged with engineering was probably, if his batting average was to remain the same, about to go right over the cliff, and this time there was not a blessed thing he could do to save himself from complete and utter destruction.

The irony was not lost on Gerry Turley. Easter Sunday. With the situation in northern I Corps growing worse by the minute, those in authority over him certainly seemed to be in the Pontius Pilate mode—trying to wash their hands of responsibility for what looked more and more like something that would end in an unfavorable outcome.

They had forced him into taking a job that no one else could or would accept. The personal risks to Turley were great; extending far beyond the obvious ones of physical danger. He also knew that because of the national implications to the Nixon Vietnamization policy and the massive size and broadening scope of the NVA offensive, that if he survived this duty he would someday have to stand before his seniors, quite possibly even the *commandant* of the Marine Corps, and explain his actions. But that was if he survived, and if he did that would be a long time from now. There was really no time for personal thoughts although for the briefest moment he felt empathy for and identified with the Old Testament character Job; isolated, ostracized, alone, suffering pain that could not be relieved, without friend or support, without anyone to affirm him.

As much as Gerry Turley might have enjoyed spending a little more time being angry or upset about his unfavorable circumstances, the inopportune set of cards dealt to him these last few days, the hot knife that was the North Vietnamese Army moving through ARVN butter afforded no such opportunity. The substantial presence of armor changed the complexion of the entire fifteen-mile wide and shrinking battlefront. For all the damage tanks could do on the north side of the Cam Lo-Cua Viet River, there were by now few local targets left still worthy of their commitment. It was immediately apparent to Turley that the NVA's main armor and infantry thrust was headed straight to Dong Ha, to cross the bridge that would give them *entrée* into all of Quang Tri Province. If they could get that far, who knew what might happen? Dong Ha was the key. The enemy would have to be stopped there. If not, the psychological shock of enemy armor against forces mostly unprepared to defeat tanks would totally collapse what frail ARVN defenses were holding the line.

With so much at stake, it did not take him but another moment to decide his only option was to blow the bridge at Dong Ha.

EASTER MORNING AT DONG HA

The town of Dong Ha would likely not have been on any tourist's list of must-see places in the extreme north of the Republic of Vietnam if Americans had never come to fight in Southeast Asia. Adjacent to Highway One, it was the last, reasonably large concentration of humanity that anyone might have described as a town before crossing the DMZ, twenty-one kilometers to the north, and entering the Democratic Republic of Vietnam. With its location astride both the Cua Viet River and Highway One, as well as being the eastern *terminus* or the western beginning, depending on one's view, for Route Nine that ran into Laos, Dong Ha was a natural gathering place for farmers and fishermen to transact commerce in northern Quang Tri Province. Its markets were daily stocked with produce from the surrounding areas and the men who fished the South China Sea, thirteen kilometers downstream, kept nearby residents amply supplied with quantities of protein from the Gulf of Tonkin.

Since the beginning of the American involvement in Vietnam and because of its proximity to the DMZ, Dong Ha garnered the attention of American forces bent on defending the country at points closest to the enemy border. From 1965 until the American Marines had been sent home in 1971, Dong Ha was also home to the headquarters elements of the Third Marine Division. With the advent of Vietnamization, combat activity in Quang Tri Province had decreased significantly; until noon on March 30, 1972. As testament to the resiliency of the Vietnamese citizens, until the artillery assaults had begun, life was not that bad at all with a relatively vibrant market economy naturally reasserting itself; just as Gerry Turley had observed in other places to the immediate south when he and Jim Joy had flown up by helicopter from Phu Bai less than a week ago.

Due to Dong Ha's proximity to the South China Sea, there had always been industry in waterborne travel to move people and products up and down the river which happened to run reasonably fast and deep where the bridge crossed it and it flowed east to the Gulf of Tonkin. There had been a bridge spanning the Cua Viet River at Dong Ha for quite some time. In fact, there were now two bridges; the second one was the "Old French Bridge" referred to earlier and was less than one hundred meters upstream from the newer and more capable bridge. The original, larger bridge built for foot and vehicular traffic had been rebuilt by a U.S. Navy Construction Battalion (known to the world as "SeaBees") in 1967.

The newer bridge represented the very best of American intentions and engineering acumen. Built to last, the concrete, steel and wood, mostly steel, leviathan had America, especially the industrial might of Pittsburgh and Youngstown, at its very core. Nearly two hundred meters in length, its great strength came from the six longitudinal I-beams that served as its hulking skeleton which was over-laid with substantial, thick-cut wooden timbers. The five columns upon which the massive structure rested were made of steel-reinforced concrete. To defend against sappers, on both the northern and southern banks, the SeaBees had erected significant chain link and razor-wire barriers to the bridge's underside. Destroying this monstrosity in the best of circumstances would be no easy task. Destroying the bridge before the NVA could secure it would be all but impossible.

If the man in charge of the NVA armor thrust, allegedly now concentrated near Alpha 2, was halfway inclined, if he had studied a little bit of Patton or Rommel or Guderian, he might be an exceptionally dangerous adversary, aside from simply having all that shock and firepower available to him. Turley was hoping his education as a good Communist had kept him from such exposure and that, if he was a genuine son of the revolution, he might be even more concerned about criticism and losing face than his southern adversaries seemed to be. If the man in charge of the NVA armor had just an ounce of gumption and initiative, and given the current paucity of ARVN resistance, he might have his tanks and supporting infantry already on the road and on the northern banks of the Cua Viet River in less than an hour. If he was not so inclined; if he was the cautious, plodding type, his units could still cover the eleven kilometers between Alpha 2 and Dong Ha in no more than two or three hours maximum. Turley had no time to waste.

Turley understood armor's terror and shock value. He knew that if just one of the Soviet-supplied T-54s was able to cross onto the south side of the river, its forty-odd tons of hulking, menacing steel would create disproportionate fear and chaos among fleeing civilians and the ARVN forces ill-equipped to defend against tanks.

Lieutenant Colonel Turley's options for response were actually rather limited. Realizing the strategic value of the bridge, among his first thoughts were the efforts to seize the critical bridge at Remagen as allied forces entered western Germany in early 1945. Decisions to destroy or defend bridges that crossed significant bodies of water were not made by lieutenant colonels. But this time things were a bit different than when American forces had been trying to cross the only remaining bridge across the Rhine twenty-seven years earlier. Turley was not seeking authority. There was no time. He had to take it and he had to execute that decision expeditiously.

There was only one way to blow the Dong Ha Bridge. Airpower was out. As optimistic as Major Brookbank had earlier been about improving weather, there was no time to call in TAC air to do the job. The NVA would be across before the cloud ceilings allowed their employment. Even with targeting authority now for B-52s, Turley never even considered their use. ARCLIGHT strikes were only reasonably accurate, and if he could have concentrated that destructive power all right on the bridge, that might have done the trick. ARCLIGHT strikes really were good for areas not requiring pinpoint accuracy. There were no guarantees though that they could strike only the bridge. With Major Le Ba Binh's Third Battalion and attached *covan* John Ripley currently assigned to defend Dong Ha, and thousands of refugees still in the area, Turley, who would have happily dropped anything and everything he could on the advancing NVA, would have called a strike in on himself before knowingly putting bombs on fleeing civilians; unlike the NVA who continued to intentionally target innocent civilians with their artillery.

The growing number of naval gunfire ships offshore likewise was insufficient to take down the bridge. As valuable as they had already been in taking out concentrations of troops and would soon prove against approaching armor, the relatively small caliber rounds they fired could not destroy the bridge. If Turley had had the battleships USS *Iowa, New Jersey, Wisconsin*, and *Missouri* all firing in direct support it might have been a different story. But they were not. It did him no good to fantasize now. No. Turley knew that the only way to take down the bridge was the good old-fashioned way. He would have to have someone go under it with explosives, someone who knew what the heck he was doing, and do it that way. That was the only way.

The two-front battle Gerry Turley was fighting was never more obvious, and the Job-like isolation of his leadership position was never more evident than when he happened to inform those in the rear that he intended to blow the bridge at Dong Ha. For days he had made decision after decision about the employment of firepower, about the movement and disposition of forces; all of them critical. All of them life and death. Over the last several days a number of American and Vietnamese general officers aside from General Giai and his American army colonel had been in and out of the Team 155 bunker. Not once had anyone senior to Turley ever countermanded anything he had done or even offered tactical guidance. It seemed that a full minute did not pass after Turley had told whoever it was that was on the other end of the radio or telephone line in Saigon or Danang of his decision to drop the bridge that word came back specifically ordering him not to. "We have to save it for our counterattack north. Don't destroy the bridge. This is an order, Colonel Turley."[1]

Turley understood that if the NVA crossed the bridge with tanks there might never be a counterattack. If the NVA got their forces across the river in sufficient numbers in the next couple of hours, at some point in the not too distant future there might not be a Republic of Vietnam. It was that critical. He knew that. He believed that. The staff people in Danang or Saigon, wherever they were, whoever they were, still had no clear picture of how tenuous the ground situation was up here. The exchanges were far from friendly ones. Turley, as angry as he was, could understand that those down south were incredulous, nearly incapable of empathizing with the rate of decay of the ground situation. It was hard for *him* to process, and he was in it. In a bit of restrained rage, he set the radio handset aside and for the moment refused further conversation. He knew what to do. Turley and crew would stop the NVA or die trying. The bridge was coming down.

CHAPTER TWENTY-FOUR

Easter Morning in Saigon

Saigon
Easter morning
The home of Le Ba Sach—Binh's parents

W*hen Cam Banh married Le Ba Binh* three months earlier, she
gave up her long-time job at the U.S. Navy Exchange in
Saigon. Her life would subsequently be divided into two parts.
When her husband was not up north fighting the hated
Communists, she lived with him at Song Than, the TQLC base in
Saigon where they had been married. During that time she also
performed what ceremonial duties were required of the wife of
the Soi Bien's commanding officer.

When Binh was away, which was most of the time, Cam lived
with his parents over in Tan Dinh as the number one daughter-
in-law. She was fortunate that she and her mother-in-law (Binh's
step-mother but the woman who had loved and raised him like a
real mother) got on so well. Cam assisted in duties with the
household and with raising the children who still remained at
home. She was adored by all. When there was time, she would
often take a cyclo over to visit her mother living not too far away.
(Both brothers were by now serving in the military.) If there were
wounded Marines to call on in the TQLC hospital at Thu Duc, she
would go there also to help.

On the late afternoon of Saturday, April 1, even among wives
and dependents, there was little news still regarding the disposition
of ARVN and TQLC forces now engaged up north. In the network

of wives though, there was incipient chatter that something was beginning to brew.

Everyone was well aware of the process for keeping two of the TQLC's three brigades forward at all times. With the word out that Brigade 369, the unit currently at Thu Duc for routine stand down, R&R, refit, etc., was heading north as soon as possible, well in advance of its scheduled rotation date, tongues began to wag. Something serious was up. Cam, who had over the years already seen her man return from wherever it was he was frequently sent with wound upon wound, would endure the wait and try to be a dutiful wife.

BACK IN DONG HA WITH THIRD BATTALION

When Major Binh, Captain Ripley and the men of Third Battalion were sent to Dong Ha late the evening of March 30 to assume the role of division reserve, they by no means went into a stand down posture. While the lead infantry elements of the NVA invasion had yet to reach Dong Ha, Third Battalion's presence had not gone unnoticed. NVA artillery forward observers on the north side of the river, the same ones who were routinely calling in fire on the columns of refugees heading south on Highway One, were also calling missions on the Soi Bien when they could. No one in Third Battalion, including both Binh and Ripley, had ever experienced the intensity of the artillery shelling that had gone on since before their arrival. Sleep was all but impossible. Rest was difficult even when they were well dug in and the incoming rounds were impacting a safe distance away. The best the Marines could do, as Binh, Ripley, and all the others in the command group would try to do, was to simply relax, attempt to ratchet lower the intensity as the situation briefly allowed— power down with heads back while still able to listen in on radio traffic, etc.—as best they could when the shelling was not close by. This they did with a reasonably fair amount of success since arriving in Dong Ha. It was the same in the rifle companies also. And while no one could physically operate in this manner indefinitely, there were no other options in the short run.

Major Binh kept the Soi Bien at the ready at all times; always prepared to transition from the defense over into the assault. As was standard operating procedure with all TQLC battalions, the entire unit rarely came together as one. Functioning separately as Alpha and Bravo Command Groups, currently the Alpha Command Group which included Binh, Ripley, their headquarters troops, the First and Fourth Companies, along with most of the firepower from Third Battalion's Weapons Company, was operating in and around Dong Ha. The Bravo Command Group with the XO in charge and the remainder of the battalion, Second and Third Companies and everyone else, were several kilometers west of town, on Route Nine, out toward Cam Lo working in conjunction with the ARVN 20th Tank Battalion.

To minimize his men's exposure to the incessant NVA shelling, Binh would constantly reposition his companies, often moving into dummy positions just prior to darkness to ensure that they had been observed by enemy forward observers, and then surreptitiously abandoning those positions after dark. To make the deception more complete, Binh would have his Marines camouflage the area to be departed, set up remote antennas for his radios, and continue to remotely broadcast from those areas after leaving. When the NVA artillery would fall on the empty position, Binh's radio operators would broadcast false messages they assumed were being listened in on by the enemy, telling of damage inflicted and requesting fake medevacs. Binh did all he could to have the enemy expend its ammunition on worthless targets. These actions required the men of the Soi Bien to be constantly vigilant and on the move. Even though they were not yet physically engaged with enemy infantry, the moving around and active defense used up significant energy.

John Ripley's observations of the helpless Vietnamese refugees were similar to Gerry Turley's, if not even more personal. As he was about ten kilometers closer to the advancing enemy than Turley was at Ai Tu, he was also witness to greater death and destruction. His hatred for the Communists had been taken to new levels after having seen the intentional, indiscriminate wholesale killing of so many innocents. He wondered how it was for the men of the Soi Bien; if some of them could hate any more than they already did. Ripley had sat quietly, listening to story after story over the months as Binh's Marines revealed to him, as they came to know and trust him, how many of their families had endured pain, suffering, and indignities at the hands of the Communists that most Americans could not even imagine. In the end, he was simply grateful that he did not have to deal with those issues. Like Turley, with whom he had never discussed this subject, he was thankful that his wife and children were far, far away.

Major Binh's Third Battalion assignment as the division reserve was proving to be a propitious move. It was evident now that the Dong Ha Bridge was a strategic target for the enemy. The poor showing of ARVN units in general, and in the area around Dong Ha the near disintegration of the 57th Regiment in particular, left much of what defense there was going to be in the hands of the Vietnamese Marine units which refused to give ground without a fight.

The Soi Bien had been in Dong Ha since late on the evening of March 30 and the infantry companies were positioned where Major Binh thought they were best deployed for both current defense and to be ready for later offensive operations. After deciding to destroy the bridge, Lieutenant Colonel Turley phoned down to the new Third ARVN Division headquarters in Quang Tri City. It should be reiterated that with all the authority to engage U.S.-supplied firepower, when it came to the actual directing of ARVN and TQLC units, the Americans were *advisors*. All troop movement and decisions to employ those troops were made by the Vietnamese. Americans often made recommendations but all authority was properly with those they advised.

Turley called down to Third ARVN Division with the intent of recommending that General Giai finally "commit the reserves"—in this case Third Battalion for the specific defense of the Dong Ha Bridge—to prevent the NVA from crossing it until it could be destroyed.

Committing the reserves is significant. It means that the situation is grave. It is a measure of last resort. Commanders are usually reluctant to take this action because it represents the final option, the last arrow has been fired; the quiver is essentially empty. Sometimes it is all a commander can do. Gerry Turley certainly believed that the ground situation warranted this move, and right now.

When Turley called back to Third Division headquarters, both General Giai and his American colonel—the same colonel who had been responsible for Advisory Team 155 and who had also drafted Gerry into this current assignment—were not there. Speaking instead with the general's chief of staff, Turley ran into a cultural brick wall. The ARVN colonel in question, with the world around him crumbling to the ground, simply refused the decision out of fear of losing face and all the other stuff that moved Turley's blood pressure further into the red zone. "We must wait for General Giai to return. I can take no action now. We wait." It was a cultural thing again.[1]

Growing wiser in his massive frustration, Turley in desperation turned to Colonel Dinh, the Brigade 258 commander, located there with him in the TOC bunker.

Turley had just opened his third battlefront. To his north and west were three or four divisions of NVA infantry, five regiments of artillery, what now appeared like a large but still undetermined number of tanks, and who knew what else. The kitchen sink could not be that far behind. To his south Turley faced an increasingly inhospitable chain of command in Danang and Saigon which was continually sniping at his authority and challenging his decisions.

Expecting more from Colonel Dinh, because he was a Marine, Turley got the same exact response given only moments earlier by the chief of staff. Initially stunned, Turley did not give up. Turley made his case. He pleaded his case with a passion that he did not know he had, in every logical way, imploring Colonel Dinh to commit Third Battalion to the Dong Ha Bridge. Time and again Turley explained the need for immediate action, and still Dinh deferred to higher authority. "I cannot" was his stock, repetitive answer. Crestfallen, Turley knew that without committing the Soi Bien there was absolutely no hope of stopping the NVA.

The exchange between Turley and Dinh had appropriately taken place away from the others in the G-3 area. When Turley came back into view of his folks, especially the close group of officers who had now been working with him for three days, they could see by his facial expression and body language that he had failed to convince Colonel Dinh. Knowing he somehow had to remain positive for the others, he had not yet come up with what he would recommend.

Fortunately, he did not have to. Just a minute or two later, Colonel Dinh came up behind him and announced "The Third Battalion will take the Dong Ha Bridge. I will give the battalion commander the order to hold Dong Ha. You radio your advisor and tell him my decision."[2] With unexpected joy and uncharacteristic emotion, Lieutenant Colonel Turley actually hugged the Vietnamese Marine colonel.

AFTER THE RADIO CALL

Reassembling Third Battalion under current conditions for the express purpose of defending the area immediately adjacent to the Dong Ha Bridge, essentially to the last man, was no easy task. Binh, Ripley, and the security element that was forever around them, once they received Colonel Dinh's orders, left the First and Fourth Companies at the bridge and then headed west toward Cam Lo to link up with and retrieve the Bravo Command Group along with the ARVN 20th Tank Battalion back to the bridge area.

Up until this time Binh and Ripley had not been thrilled with their assignment as the division reserve force. With the world all around them appearing to come apart, it was incredibly frustrating to have no offensive role in what was going on. For several days now they had endured continual shelling and all those stresses without opportunity to strike back. That was very soon to change.

Binh and Ripley both knew they would need the firepower of 20th Tank Battalion and every spare rifleman from the Soi Bien to maximize their chances of survival if they intended to hold Dong Ha against what, as every passing moment suggested, were increasingly frightful odds. What they did not yet know was that "as many as twenty enemy tanks" would really be more like two hundred enemy tanks. Linking up with and bringing back to the bridge area the Third Battalion's Bravo Command Group and 20th

Tanks was critical if they expected to keep the enemy on the river's north side.

It was rather counterintuitive that, of all the players in the command elements of both the Third Battalion and the ARVN 20th Tank Battalion, John Ripley, who was the only American in the group, had far more operating experience than any of his Vietnamese hosts, was the one most familiar with the geography in and around Dong Ha. As the two units linked up finally on the west side of town and Binh made physical contact with the ARVN lieutenant colonel in charge of 20th Tanks, the NVA just happened to unleash an especially punishing artillery barrage of the entire Dong Ha area. Ripley was certain that during the forty-five-minute fusillade as many as one thousand rounds may have impacted. Fortunately where they were now positioned was outside of that impact area, but the injurious psychological effect on those who observed the raw display of enemy firepower, specifically the commanding officer of 20th Tanks, was considerable.

Meeting under extreme combat conditions was rarely the best way to establish cordial, professional, business-type relationships. Meeting under harsh conditions did however, allow people to skip all pleasantries, all the fluff, and get right down to business. Ripley's initial impression of the ARVN officer in command of the 20th Tank Battalion, which may have been tempered by his overall reduced regard for how most ARVN units in the area had been performing of late, was not favorable. It was evident to any person within view that the man responsible for this collection of nearly fifty M-48A3 tanks was not at all enthusiastic about committing them to the defense of Dong Ha. Unlike so many of the most serious, dedicated, and professional TQLC officers, and a smaller portion of ARVN officers Ripley had observed, who would rather die than lose face or be seen as weak and cowardly, this particular ARVN officer seemed to care little for the issue of face at the moment. It was clear to John Ripley that this man, even though senior to Binh in rank, was in no way any sort of kindred spirit.

The commanding officer of the 20th Tank Battalion was fortunate the set of rules apportioning U.S. Army infantry officers as advisors only at the regimental level for infantry units, as forced by the ongoing Vietnamization of all operations, had somehow not yet been applied to his unit. John Ripley met Major Jim Smock, the American Army armor advisor to the 20th Tank Battalion, at the same time he made the acquaintance of the ARVN tank battalion commander. Leery in the opening moments of their relationship, and, again, he could probably be forgiven those feelings since none of the ARVN units at the time seemed to be doing anything but retreating *en masse*, Captain Ripley considered Major Smock's bold, positive comments about the quality of the 20th Tank Battalion to be, at best, questionable. On his own, Ripley believed the armor edge on the current battlefield would likely go to the NVA anyway.

Ripley's logic was simple and straight forward. The ARVN tanks, the M-48, were fine tanks but the T-54 had two advantages which he expected the enemy to fully exploit. The T-54 had a bigger gun—100mm versus 90mm for the M-48—and in most cases size really did make a difference. The other critical advantage was the T-54's much lower profile. It presented a smaller and therefore harder to hit target than did the larger, noisier, maintenance heavy, albeit more finely engineered M-48. Those issues aside, the real deciding factor, as in any battle, would be in the quality of the leadership and the *élan* of the men doing the fighting.

How odd it was that tanks were being employed at all. Everyone knew Vietnam was hardly the ideal environment for the modern tank. They were meant to be used in massive, sweeping formations on Europe's central plain or on the vast, trackless deserts of the Middle East; not in Vietnam where fetid jungles and rice paddies dominated the landscape. And that was precisely the reason for their employment. NVA planners had been correct in believing their southern cousins, along with their American puppet masters, would not expect the introduction of armor on the scale they would soon witness.

A number of the tank's inherent battlefield advantages were neutralized by ground that kept the hulking behemoths wedded to the few hard-packed roads and trails that could actually support them. Still, against ARVN and TQLC troops who possessed little or no anti-tank weaponry at the moment, the mobile firepower and shock effect tanks could bring to whatever action they were able to influence with their direct-fire weapons was significant.

As much as Major Smock conceded that the battalion commander he was advising needed lots of advising, he promised his new Marine friend that the young lads in the tanks were combat ready and itching to mix it up with the enemy. Thieu Ta Binh was, at the moment, seriously engaged in berating his ARVN senior, admonishing him to act like a man and order his unit to do the right thing in defending Dong Ha. During the near one-sided exchange between the lion and the lamb, Binh held nothing back in his attempt to infuse a bit of spine into the ARVN tank battalion commander. Fortunately for Binh, he was not constrained in the ways Gerry Turley was constrained. It took some time and the judicious employment of every trick Binh had in his leadership repertoire but it somehow worked. Shame and guilt were powerful motivators.

Ripley's intricate knowledge of the local area was a big plus, as was Binh's continuing to admonish the ARVN lieutenant colonel, while he guided the Marines and their reluctant tanker allies through Dong Ha's back roads away from the incessant artillery barrages and ultimately to the area directly south of the bridge.

At the Dong Ha Bridge the Soi Bien's First and Fourth Companies had already engaged in furious gun fights with NVA forces that had recently arrived on the river's north side. Once the enemy armor could be seen Ripley got to work calling in naval gunfire. His first naval gunfire mission awhile earlier and out west of town had resulted in four PT-76 tanks being destroyed. As they worked back towards Dong Ha he continued to employ naval gunfire. Subsequent missions were killing mostly T-54s.

The arrival of lead elements of the 20th Tank Battalion further bolstered the situation as the ARVN M-48s actually drew first blood against the enemy who seemed unaware that they would face any allied armor. For the time being the Communists showed no indication that their attempt at crossing would be in the next few moments. But everyone knew they would come; sooner or later.

MEANWHILE, BACK AT THE TOC...

Where the limit of the universe currently and for the immediate future for John Ripley, Le Ba Binh, and the men of the Soi Bien was the maximum effective range of whatever weapons they could employ and visually witness a round's impact, Gerry Turley's in the Ai Tu TOC was just slightly larger. For anyone able to read a map it was entirely obvious that Dong Ha and its bridge would be the key to battlefield success or failure in the next few hours. As much as he and the others recognized that fact, Turley and his crew still had to fret and coordinate issues at the other points on the northern I Corps geography where ARVN and TQLC forces were enduring increasingly difficult situations.

In the continuing triage for applying time, effort, worry and resources, what was expected to soon take place at Dong Ha made it the primary focus of most, but not all, of the allied effort. There were other places still in need of attention which would also negatively impact the strategic picture if left untended.

Roughly thirteen kilometers to the west of the Dong Ha Bridge, the smaller bridge spanning the river at Cam Lo was also capable of supporting heavy tanks. That bridge, it was obvious to everyone, was the NVA's second choice for their armor columns if they could not seize the one at Dong Ha. Turley would want to destroy this one as well. One advantage the allies had at Dong Ha was that naval gunfire, although not powerful enough to put the bridge in the water, had so far been used to good effect against the initial armor thrusts thanks to the coordination and earlier planning of Joel Eisenstein's crew matched up with the quick work of John Ripley as he called in and adjusted fire on the enemy. Cam Lo was too far inland for naval gunfire to be of any help and, until the weather improved, airpower was unavailable to assist.

At the moment the ARVN Third Division's Second Regiment was retreating back down to Cam Lo in a fashion far more orderly than had the 57th over at Dong Ha. With the NVA close behind however, it was nearly impossible for ARVN combat engineers to properly place demolitions and blow the Cam Lo Bridge.

Five kilometers southwest of Cam Lo at Camp Carroll, the 56th Regiment and their critical twenty-two artillery pieces, which included the four prized 175mm guns, was likewise under huge pressure from the NVA. Turley and his crew in the TOC could not know it, but covert and perfidious forces were at work in the local ARVN leadership there which would soon see the abject surrender of the entire firebase with all its men, weapons, and material. At the moment all Turley knew was the situation at Camp Carroll was desperate and calls for artillery support from its batteries were not being answered.

The only positive thing about the situation at Fire Support Base (FSB) Mai Loc, less than four kilometers south of Camp Carroll where Vietnamese Marine Brigade 147 was positioned, was that the TQLC forces, while heavily outnumbered and outgunned, were putting up a ferocious defense. They could not hold on forever.

Since the Easter Offensive's initiation naval gunfire had proven to be the only reliable fire support to forces within range. By Easter morning there were five ships just offshore: USS *Buchanan* (DDG-14), USS *Strauss* (DDG-16), USS *Waddell* (DDG-24), USS *Anderson* (DD-786), and USS *Hamner* (DD-718). All of the ships provided aggressive and accurate suppressive fires. The ships' skippers ran their men-of-war as close to shore as possible to milk every last yard of range from their guns.

The use of so much naval power required tremendous coordination and communication between the ships themselves and with forces ashore. Along with that effort the afloat commanders also sent copies of all message traffic to both Pearl Harbor and Saigon. That communication took on a momentum and inertia of its own with consequences and impact Turley and the others there in the TOC with him could not have imagined and were completely unaware of.

By Easter morning folks in the TOC began to hear more regularly from their navy brothers just off the coast who referred to the Marine forces afloat and strongly inferred that they were there simply waiting to be invited in. Turley dismissed that idea completely, giving it little thought as he instead focused on maximizing the resources he knew he could count on for sure.

What no one in the TOC could have any appreciation for was the momentum many of the miscommunications were gaining. It was as if Turley and crew were unwitting participants in a very adult version of the kids game "Telephone" and with each transmission and retransmission, the facts being reported higher up the chain grew more distorted. As much as the people in Saigon were gaining slow appreciation that all was not well in northern I Corps, they unfortunately seemed almost more concerned that there was some rogue Marine lieutenant colonel run amok in the Ai Tu TOC.

CHAPTER TWENTY-FIVE

High Noon at Dong Ha

By *early Easter Sunday*, the Nguyen Hue Offensive's nearly four-day momentum continued to compound for both parties involved: positively for the NVA and not so positively for the RVN side. With the 57th Regiment's withdrawal having long ago turned to rout, the chaos and fog which surrounded that particular portion of the I Corps geography had its own increasingly negative consequences. Without order there was no confidence, and without confidence rumors, very negative rumors, filled the informational void.

It was unclear whether the news that the NVA, along with their accompanying armor, was already across the bridge and in control of portions of Dong Ha was spread by soldiers and radio operators of the utterly defeated 57th Regiment, perhaps as excuse for their universal and wholesale cowardice, or not. As sophisticated as the NVA were in some ways proving to be, it might have been their people who infiltrated friendly radio nets by using left-behind equipment to spread rumors and falsehoods that could only benefit their side. With the intensity of the recent artillery barrages it was not at all too farfetched to assume the NVA had physically arrived in Dong Ha. But it was not true. At least not yet.

Binh and Ripley both understood the pernicious impact rumors were having on friendly forces and remaining civilians; even their Marines. The Marines had to be just as scared as the ignominiously retreating ARVN troops, although not one of the men of the Soi Bien bolted from the scene. The difference was in their superior discipline and professionalism and leadership. Bold, dramatic action and words were needed to begin to stem the tide, to infuse RVN forces with a sense of hope and purpose, to let them know that the battle was not yet lost.

Americans, and Westerners in general, would have recognized the character and nature of the very public, bordering on flamboyant and necessary for the situation, remarks Le Ba Binh was about to make. Those with a sense of history might have been reminded of an abbreviated Winston Churchill "This was their finest hour"-type speech or John Paul Jones "I have not yet begun to fight"-style utterance.

To quell the storm, Binh spoke first to his friend John Ripley, telling him that he wanted his *covan* to broadcast the very same message he would deliver as well. His broadcast was for the world to hear. It was as much for any NVA listening as it was for friendly forces tuned to his frequency. If there were Communists listening they were being told there was a new sheriff in town. There would be no doubt, no equivocation. There would be no more retreating, no ground given without heavy payment exacted. From when he was a young boy in Tan Dinh, Binh was a huge fan and had seen what Gary Cooper movies there were, most of them several times. Today was Binh's own "High Noon" and he was sticking around to endure odds far greater than Cooper ever faced.

In the much longer history of Vietnam, Binh's comments might compare favorably to anything put forth by any of the greater-known Vietnamese heroes familiar to every school boy and girl. If the Soi Bien could hold here and somehow help turn the tide, their part in the two-thousand-year continuum of Vietnamese history in fighting invasion and oppression would be assured.

Binh had no time at the present to consider his position in history on Easter morning 1972. His only focus was to carry out his orders and stop the Communists; to hold Dong Ha at "all costs." Binh understood perfectly and completely what those orders entailed. He was personally and passionately committed to carrying them out.

Whether the actions of Binh and the seven hundred men of the Soi Bien he commanded, against what would turn out to be more than twenty thousand invaders, would put them in the same category as the Trung Sisters from two thousand years ago or Emperor Le Loi in the 1400s remained to be seen. It would depend on how well they fought but even more importantly on who would write the accounts of the battle now about to be fully joined in Dong Ha.

The men of the Soi Bien felt a mixture of emotions as they watched, from their freshly dug fighting positions adjacent to both the bridge and the river, those who only hours ago had been members of the now-in-full-flight 57th Regiment mixed in with the ill-fated civilians for whom they felt nothing but sorrow and compassion. Few of Binh's men experienced anything other than pure contempt for those now ex-ARVN soldiers. As disciplined as they all were in staying in Dong Ha as ordered, for some of his men it took even greater discipline to keep from turning their weapons on those men who were, until recently, their unequally yoked brothers-in-arms. To have wasted precious ammunition in that way would have only limited their options with the approaching NVA as resupply was at this moment a growing concern. While the men of the 57th Regiment should have been carrying a portion of the area's defensive burden, the defense of this portion of Quang Tri Province, which for the moment hinged solely on holding the Dong Ha Bridge, now fell to four companies of Vietnamese Marines reinforced by an untested and untried ARVN tank battalion.

Binh and Ripley were riding shotgun, holding on for dear life to one of the M-48 tanks belonging to the 20th Tank Battalion, headed back towards Dong Ha when they heard the erroneous news that the NVA had crossed the river. Ordering the tank to a brief halt, Binh and Ripley jumped off and made the broadcast. The message was sent out over two nets. As was his manner, Binh calmly turned to his *covan*, his genuinely "trusted advisor," and said:

> Captain Ripp-lee, if you please, I am going to send a message on my command net and I want you to send it on your advisor net so there will be no possible opportunity for misunderstanding.

> Message follows:

> It is rumored that Dong Ha has fallen. There are Vietnamese Marines in Dong Ha. My orders are to hold the enemy in Dong Ha. We will fight in Dong Ha. We will

die in Dong Ha. We will not leave. As long as one Marine
draws a breath of life, Dong Ha will belong to us.[1]

DAVID VERSUS GOLIATH—TQLC STYLE

Ha Si (Corporal) Luom was the anti-tank rocket team leader for
Team A from First Company's Weapons Platoon. Prior to assuming
command of Third Battalion, and prior to assuming duties as
executive officer for Third Battalion, Binh had commanded First
Company. Binh knew Luom quite well. He knew him to be a good
Marine, a strong leader, diligent, steadfast, brave. Being in charge of
the rocket team did not mean a whole lot in terms of rockets. It was
more of an additional infantry duty. There were not too many
rockets, or in this case the M-72 LAAW, pronounced "law," devices
to go around. According to what others in the unit had told both
Binh and Ripley, there were only ten of them in the entire battalion
at this stage of the battle.

THE M-72

As the follow-on weapon for infantry troops to use as replacement
for the venerable yet marginally effective bazooka of World War II
and some Korean War fame, the M-72 LAAW (Light Anti-Armor
Weapon)—referred to most commonly as "the LAAW"—would
never be loved enough to have a piece of candy named after it.
Entering service in the mid-1960s with American and NATO
troops, the new weapon had a reasonably sixties feel to it: light,
disposable and a warhead that was supposed to be able to burn
through lots of steel. For NATO forces it was the Western
equivalent to the Warsaw Pact-produced Rocket Propelled
Grenade (RPG). It was meant to be carried, like everything else
American troops carried—and they arguably carried far too much
gear with them—into battle to be used against enemy armor and
fortified positions. In Vietnam, which for the most part was hardly
tank country, the LAAW was seen as something for use against
omnipresent and well-camouflaged bunkers utilized everywhere
by the wily NVA and VC.

Billed as a weapon that would "penetrate twelve inches of homogeneous steel," stateside instructors cheerfully trumpeted that fact over and over as if they really knew what "homogeneous steel" was. Maybe it reminded them of fresh, cold milk. No matter. If properly employed, the LAAW's warhead could allegedly penetrate the armor of all known Warsaw Pact tanks, and do a decent fry job on the crew inside.

The greatest challenge was its range. Like the bazooka, the advertised maximum effective range was in the two hundred to two hundred and fifty meter area. Whoever the fellow was to stick around until a forty- to sixty-ton tank got that close would be a fellow with huge stones which were both fully operational and producing extra doses of testosterone, or simply a young man with a death wish. At two hundred fifty meters a man with a LAAW was well within range of everything mounted on a tank; its main gun and all of the machine guns stuck to it. The sites used for the LAAW had twenty-five-meter increments to them, suggesting to any reasonable gent that Kentucky windage along with prayer might factor into one's ability to actually hit a threatening target. Thoughts of and analogies to "David versus Goliath" were not at all inappropriate.

Even after firing a LAAW in training and seeing the damage it might cause, it was hard to really have confidence that the one you carried would do the trick. With the weapon's casing constructed of some sort of plastic and fiberglass, it would not even serve as a very decent bludgeon if the fighting got in close enough, and would probably crumple when used as a baseball bat against any reasonably thick skull. Its light weight—it weighed in at slightly more than five pounds including the warhead inside—made it seem almost insubstantial relative to the destruction it was supposed to inflict. As a weapon for use against bunkers and fortified positions, if there were no other direct fire weapons available, the LAAW was alright. To score any kind of catastrophic kill on a tank was asking a great deal; for all the cards to be perfectly dealt, for all the planets to be perfectly aligned.

Corporal (Ha Si) Luom and one of his rocket team members approached the south entrance to the Dong Ha Bridge in a crouch and a crawl. As they did there were still civilian refugees crossing although the numbers had been drastically reduced by now. With the arrival of the NVA on the north side of the Cam Lo-Cua Viet River and the bridge, traffic was obviously reduced. There were no more soldiers, at least none in defrocked uniforms, from the disgraced 57th ARVN Regiment mixed in with the stragglers.

For protection more psychological than anything else, Corporal Luom and his junior mate pushed in front of them, as they crept towards a firing position at the south side of the bridge that would allow them a shot straight across to the north side of the bridge's approach, two dirt-filled wooden ammunition crates. Civilians were still crossing the bridge, although at a much reduced rate from before the NVA's arrival. The two Vietnamese Marines slowly got into firing position two hundred meters or so from the lone green-painted NVA T-54 tank that was about to come onto the bridge from the northern side of the river.

There was action going on all around as all of this was taking place. Binh had positioned First Company on the river's edge to the immediate east of the bridge with responsibility for covering the bridge itself. Fourth Company was given tactical responsibility for the real estate west of the Dong Ha Bridge. The Alpha Command Group, with Ripley, the radio operators including Nha and all of Binh's security force, along with members of the ARVN 20th Tank Battalion headquarters element were back fifty or so meters from the action to better control and observe. From their vantage point Binh and Ripley, and Smock and his Vietnamese boss, could see well up and down both sides of the river.

Ripley watched Ha Si Luom, whom he had met, with rapt amazement. He watched Luom and the other Marine slowly, deliberately maneuver into position pushing and pulling the ammo crates and two as yet unarmed LAAWs. One did not require great insight to understand what was about to unfold. If Luom and the other man each weighed one hundred pounds soaking wet, John Ripley was Santa Claus. Unsure if Binh was watching, he called over: "Thieu Ta!" and pointed. Binh had not missed a thing. Familiar enough with the Old Testament even though he was a practicing Buddhist, his reply in perfect English to his *covan* friend did not surprise. "Ripp-lee. David and Goliath!" Binh was smiling; genuinely smiling almost to the point of laughter as he said that. Ripley had not seen Thieu Ta smile since before they had come up to Dong Ha late the night of the 30th.

Le Ba Binh had spent his entire career as a Marine officer in Third Battalion—nearly two and a half times as long as the American involvement in World War II, and four times longer than *Batman* had aired on primetime television. Except for the not quite one year when he, as a member of Third Battalion, had been assigned as a student to The Basic School in Quantico, he had served with the Soi Bien, in action, for the entire period.

To frame things from the American perspective, Binh had come aboard with Third Battalion at about the same time the *Beverly Hillbillies* came into America's living rooms. By Easter morning 1972, Jed, Grannie, Ellie Mae, and Jethro had already done a year of reruns. Binh was still doing prime time.

By now Binh had been wounded eight times according to the exacting Purple Heart standards his friend John Ripley had applied as a company commander with Lima Company back in 1967: to be "knocked down," for penetration to have occurred, and that the wound be the result of direct enemy action. Using a lesser standard which, unfortunately, not a small number of Americans had used to gain their Purple Hearts, Binh's wounds would have been too numerous to count.

Binh's personal decorations included nearly every award for bravery and exceptional leadership possible from his young country, many of them given several times. Now familiar with the awards of the South Vietnamese military, when they had been down in Saigon at functions like Binh's wedding, Ripley was able—as he was when around American military men—to look at a man in uniform and from the decorations on his chest sort of "read" or effectively interpret his career story as a warrior. Binh had even been given four American Bronze Star medals for earlier joint actions with the U.S. Army. It was evident to all, from that limited perspective, that Binh had few equals in the war-fighting profession.

The medals he had been awarded, as they are for all true warriors, did not fully measure the man, his bravery, commitment to his country or the true depth of his sacrifice. Of far greater importance was Binh's reputation within the relatively small fraternity of Vietnamese Marine officers who collectively and disproportionately carried so much of the burden of defense for their struggling country. Within that group of resolute, trusted souls Binh was at home and widely recognized as one of the best. His leadership was critical. His insights were trusted and valued. He was a man who made a difference for the TQLC and for the Republic of Vietnam.

For Americans the notion of ten hard years of combat service seemed a virtual eternity. In the twenty-century expanse of Vietnamese history punctuated with so much struggle and strife, invasion and conquest, the greater than three thousand days of combat Binh had so far served and all the blood he had personally shed did not seem so extraordinary; would have hardly been a blip on any graph attempting to chart that much time in the grander scheme of things.

As a member of Third Battalion, Binh had served as a platoon commander, company commander, battalion executive officer, and now as commanding officer. As much as any man could come to embody the organization he led, Binh *was* Third Battalion. Given the nature and cultural peculiarities of the Vietnamese military, but most especially its Marine Corps, where the unit commander really did have authority to mold his forces to his exact persona, it was no surprise that the Soi Bien grew to reflect the aggressive fighting style of its revered leader. As much as any commander could infuse a combat organization with the principals he valued most, Third Battalion reflected those of its current commanding officer. In a military force where the "cult of the commander" was a normal way of conducting business, it was fortunate for the Republic of Vietnam that it was Binh's influence that would be doing so much of the influencing at Dong Ha.

Even though he was not one hundred meters from the Dong Ha Bridge, and hardly safe, John Ripley felt as if he was somehow not part of what was about to take place. Rarely in his experience, both as a rifle company commander and now as a *covan*, had he ever felt like a spectator in this war. For the moment, though, he and Binh and Smock and Nha and all the others, the entire Alpha Command Group, were watching Corporal Luom and his assistant, as if they were at some strange sporting event, inject themselves into the path of the lead T-54 tank about to cross the bridge. The men of the TQLC and their two American advisors were nearly mesmerized by Luom's calm, almost casual manner as he set himself up for his two, and only two, LAAW shots.

More puzzling was the way the tank commander aboard the NVA's lead T-54 dealt with this minimal threat. Although he did not need to use them, Ripley watched the tank through his binoculars. North Vietnamese tanks were painted the most hideous, revolting, meretricious, pale green color. The Communists clearly had no sense of style, that was obvious. Dai Uy (Captain) Ripley could see the tank commander's head and torso above the open hatch in the T-54's turret. He noted the cosmonaut-like but anachronistic appearing tanker's leather ribbed helmet. In some strange way it reminded him of Knute Rockne and old-time Notre Dame football. The only real similarity to that thought was that soon he and Smock would attempt to likewise "win one for the Gipper."

Through his binoculars John Ripley was certain he saw a look of indifference or even mild disgust on the NVA tank commander's face. Why he simply did not squeeze off a short burst from his coaxial machine gun and do away with the rocket team and then proceed across the bridge to crush the reasonably defenseless-against-armor Marines was a mystery to all, especially Ripley.

Corporal Luom's first LAAW shot was wide of the mark; arcing above and exploding harmlessly behind the T-54 on ground where there were, unfortunately, no Communist troops milling around. Unphased, Luom readied his second shot. The tank had not moved and so it was easier for Luom to adjust for his final round. Ripley and Binh, and probably every other man of the TQLC who saw the entire episode could not believe that the enemy tanker simply sat there. They were all waiting for the inevitable machinegun burst to end it all. It never came.

Luom's second shot had been properly tweaked. The round impacted the T-54 right at where the turret met the chassis. There was no catastrophic explosion like in the movies, only wisps of smoke from the commander's hatch and perhaps from the point of impact itself. Whether any of the crew inside were killed or injured could not be determined from where Ripley was observing. The tank commander appeared dazed but unhurt, almost more annoyed than anything else.

What he did next convinced Ripley and the others that this might not have been the best man to lead the NVA armor spearhead across the Dong Ha Bridge. He backed the tank off the structure a few meters and stopped in a shallow culvert. In another moment it was also apparent that the LAAW had damaged the tank so that it could no longer fully rotate its turret. And that was that; at least for the immediate time being. Time sort of stood still; again. It was long enough for both Ripley and Smock, with Nha humping his radio in close pursuit, to make their mad dash for the southern underside of the Dong Ha Bridge.

Turley's decision to blow the Dong Ha Bridge was almost academic. Ordering its destruction, from a command perspective, in spite of the problems it caused for him—further isolation from every single other person up the chain of command in Danang and Saigon who would at some point in the future, if he survived the battle, happily send him to the gallows when he failed—was the easy part. The actual physical destruction of the bridge, that was an entirely different subject. It was mid to late morning on Easter Sunday when Gerry Turley radioed John Ripley with orders to "somehow destroy the bridge." In ordering Ripley to take down the bridge, Gerry Turley was certain he was signing the younger man's own death warrant. Turley, as the man in charge, faced horrible odds; sort of heads the NVA wins, tails the good guys lose type odds. No one in Las Vegas would have logically bet on Turley's decision to win, place, or even show. Turley knew that also, and so he immediately set about developing a backup plan in case Ripley failed.

John Ripley's attempt at blowing the Dong Ha Bridge was Gerry Turley's "Plan A." As a seasoned, professional military officer, he knew he needed a backup plan. With the as yet unchanged weather, TAC air was out, as were naval gunfire and B-52 strikes. Turley's best idea for "Plan B" was to call on Captain John Thiesen USMC, there in the bunker with him and in country now for a whopping two weeks. "John, I want you to go find yourself a six-by and a driver. (The ubiquitous six-wheeled military truck which was standard transport for both U.S. and RVN forces and could carry a dozen or so troops or two and a half tons of cargo—and because of that cargo capacity also known as a "deuce-and-a-half.") Load it up with all the explosives you can find and be prepared to drive it on to the Dong Ha Bridge and detonate it, if necessary."

Like the good Marine officer that he was, Captain Thiesen replied "Aye, aye sir." He then set off to carry out his new orders.

If the odds against Turley's order looked grim, the chances of Ripley actually succeeding somehow were even worse. There was simply no way, no way at all, that John Walter Ripley could personally destroy the Dong Ha Bridge in time to halt the inevitable NVA armor advance.

CHAPTER TWENTY-SIX

Ripley at the Bridge

There had been little time so far during the battle for Binh or Ripley to take serious pause and consider what thought processes were running through the minds of the enemy leaders arrayed against them at the point of contact or those slightly back up the chain of command. When Corporal Luom had disabled the first T-54 with his second and final LAAW, the Marines were shocked, pleasantly shocked, that there had been no serious attempt to follow through. That seemingly miniscule dulling of NVA momentum was all Ripley, along with Major Jim Smock, needed to get going under the bridge.

How odd. The roles of the adversaries, in some respects, had been completely reversed. Having always been seen as manpower-rich and relatively resource-poor, NVA forces now had, at least for the time being, a decided material edge as well in Quang Tri Province. That and the continued bad weather that kept allied airpower neutralized since the offensive's beginning had given them huge advantage. Why would they not seek to continue to exploit that advantage?

There was the oft told anecdote that spoke of Communist resourcefulness, will, and focus on victory: After however many months of walking from northern North Vietnam through snake and disease-infested jungles, after hiking over hundreds of kilometers of treacherous mountain trails in Laos and Cambodia, after enduring countless ARCLIGHT strikes, a porter arrives at his assigned destination faithfully carrying the two mortar rounds he was given to deliver. He reports into the supply sergeant at the remote cache site somewhere in southwestern

South Vietnam who blandly tells him, "Put those two rounds there in the corner. Now go back and get two more."[1]

What was it that kept the NVA tankers in check that afternoon? Maybe it was that they had already lost a number of tanks to naval gunfire and, unused to all the *largesse* they now were privileged with, were afraid to lose more. Maybe it was the old Asian proclivity for hording riches, of seeing value in having all those tanks without somehow really having to use and therefore risk losing them. Where Americans did place value on human life and would think little of material losses or expenses, to the Communists that was a luxury they could ill afford. And where Americans would invest lives to save others, often more than were being saved, to the Communists that was simply *bourgeois* sentimentality. Something did not make sense to Ripley or Binh or anybody else who witnessed the heretofore unstoppable NVA *juggernaut* all of a sudden come to a, however temporary, screeching halt.

Maybe someday in the future, when tourists might come to Dong Ha to study this battle, there would be some bright, informed docent-like chap to explain the foibles of the NVA armor commander, just as there were people at Pearl Harbor to tell you of the strategic blunders Admiral Nagumo and his strike forces made when attacking the Hawaiian Islands on December 7, 1941. Even the most amateur historians understood that the Japanese had missed the American aircraft carriers, had failed to destroy critical fuel storage and dry-dock facilities, had chosen to retire too early when follow-on attacks would have finished Hawaii as a forward Pacific base for a much greater period. Just as there were questions about the quality of aggressiveness of the Japanese naval leadership in the attack on Pearl Harbor, on April 2, 1972, those NVA leaders controlling the operations failed to exploit their very obvious advantages that, had they been just a bit more tenacious, might have swept them to more immediate victory.

The at-first unappreciated gift to RVN forces on Easter Sunday was the timidity of the local commander of the NVA armor column. Just as Turley had hoped, maybe the Communists were even more concerned about face and all the more subtle issues of their style of leadership than were the RVN commanders. Whatever it was, it was the first serious break RVN forces were unintentionally given in the Nguyen Hue Offensive. The Communist momentum had just degenerated, ever so slightly. If only one platoon of tanks had been able to cross the Dong Ha Bridge, the day would have turned out far differently. The allies could thank Corporal Luom for the initial break and the time that it bought them. Now it was up to Ripley and Smock to extend those gains.

Ripley, Binh and Third Battalion at the Bridge

Rarely does history turn on the actions of one or two or three men who literally change or significantly alter the course of events. And it is only afterwards that there is the luxury to ponder what might have happened—in this case in northern I Corps—had Gerry Turley not stepped up as a leader demonstrating unflappable moral courage in refusing to back down when condemned by nearly everyone senior to him, had Corporal Luom missed the lead NVA T-54 tank with his second and final LAAW shot, had a lesser man than Le Ba Binh commanded Third Battalion, and had John Ripley failed in his attempt to blow the Dong Ha Bridge. Had these men individually and collectively not participated in the action on Easter Sunday 1972, the remaining history of the entire Vietnam War, and so much of what came afterwards, would have been completely different, impossible to project or surmise.

Serious and amateur historians love to discuss historical "What ifs?" "What if the Japanese had caught the American aircraft carriers at Pearl Harbor on the morning of December 7, 1941?" "What might have happened at Midway had the Japanese found the American naval forces first?" "How would the war have changed if the Japanese had learned that their codes had been compromised?"The Vietnam War would receive far less of that same kind of scrutiny, in part mostly because of its unfavorable outcome for the American side. With America on the way out anyway, few at home personally cared what was going on in Southeast Asia by 1972.

UNDER THE BRIDGE

John Ripley's world had quite suddenly and necessarily gotten very small. While all of northern I Corps that was above the underside of the Dong Ha Bridge was being overrun, his only concern was the proper placement of the explosives abandoned and left for him and Jim Smock by the ARVN combat engineers earlier sent to do the job.

John Ripley's world was reduced to only two thousand to three thousand square feet of disconcerting, incongruous-to-the-surrounding-area steel spaces between the six channels created by the seven massive I-beams which constituted the steel-skeletal frame of the Dong Ha Bridge. During a roughly four-hour period he would focus his entire physical and spiritual energies on placing five hundred pounds of explosives at the appropriate points so that he might blow the bridge to smithereens.

Not that it would have mattered to Ripley in the ultimate course of carrying out his duties, but the interior spaces and crevices beneath the Dong Ha Bridge were surprisingly free of the debris one might expect in such strange, perennially semi-dark and dank surroundings. It was not because enterprising local businessmen or farmers paid young boys to go up and under the bridge to scrape away *guano* from bats and birds or whatever else might nest there to use as fertilizer in nearby fields that there was not the expected filth. It was rather that directly above the massive I-beams he was now crawling and pulling and pushing himself between, like some mad contortionist one might watch on the *Ed Sullivan Show*, was the actual wood surface of the bridge. The thick-cut timbers covering the I-beams were right there and Ripley could tell that, as tight together as they were, they would rumble and shake and displace just a bit whenever vehicles or heavily laden, animal-drawn carts moved across them. The constant traffic and vibration of commerce in normal times would provide no peaceful habitat for any creature seeking refuge there.

Thieu Ta Binh had positioned Third Battalion's four rifle companies, its Weapons Company and the various elements of Headquarters Company in close proximity to the Dong Ha Bridge so that the Communist hordes on the far side would pay the maximum price for attempting to cross the Cua Viet River there. Up from the shoreline First Company was occupying and covering, from freshly dug fighting positions, the terrain several hundred meters to the east of the bridge. First Company also had tactical responsibility for the bridge itself. Tied in to their left as they faced the NVA, Fourth Company had control of the shoreline in their fighting positions which extended west and upriver another one hundred to two hundred meters. In the off chance that the NVA had sent forces across the river at some point further inland with the intent of attacking from the west, Binh had placed Second Company to protect his western flank. Third Company he held in reserve back near his battalion headquarters position so that he might inject them if and when he needed to plug his rather thin front line. He also kept the 81mm mortars and 75mm recoilless rifles of his Weapons Company about eight hundred meters south of the bridge to maximize their coverage across the tiny two-company front and take advantage of what little cover there was. Binh himself, along with his radio operators and several men of his security detail were actually only a hundred or so meters back from the bridge where he believed he could best direct as much of the entire battalion's action as possible.

Mixed in with Binh's First and Fourth Companies and providing needed additional firepower across the four-hundred-meter front were six tanks of the ARVN 20th Tank Battalion. Major Smock's claims that the ARVN tankers really were itching to kill enemy tanks was early on proving an accurate assessment, at least initially and in spite of the less than enthusiastic leadership of their battalion commander.

The Marines of both First and Fourth Companies understood their mission well. Maintaining a restrained but measured, steady rate of fire, they were hoping to keep NVA attention on them rather than on Dai Uy Ripley whose dangling legs would every so often appear under the bridge as he shimmied up and back on the I-beams moving demolitions and attempting to rig them for detonation.

The exchange between defenders and invaders went on without relent; at most times the rate of fire was steady but not overwhelming. By this time in the battle at the bridge civilians had mostly departed the area. Unable to expend ammunition at the same rate as the NVA now seemed capable of doing, the fire discipline of the Soi Bien and reasonable resupply kept them in the fight. Wounded Marines were periodically being evacuated by military ambulance back down Highway One to the south.

For Binh the ongoing leadership challenges were not so much with the men of the Soi Bien. His officers and his men were professionals. They would perform as ordered; of that he was certain. Binh's worries, for the moment and aside from what appeared to be at least several thousand NVA soldiers and their supporting armor just on the other side of the bridge, were with the ARVN tank battalion. What he had so far seen of their unit performance had encouraged him. Binh still was not feeling good about their commander, though, and felt the need for continued haranguing and cajoling and shaming him into performing the job he needed to perform.

The Roman Legion-style strict discipline and enforcement of it within the Vietnamese Marine Corps was legendary, at least in Vietnam. The average American citizen would have been surprised, horrified probably, by how seriously, how jealously the Vietnamese guarded the honor of their small corps of Marines. Commanders at the company level and higher had implicit capital authority over their troops. If a man committed a crime or somehow sullied the honor of the Corps, retribution would be swift, certain, and *expected*. From Lieutenant General Khang, *commandant* of the TQLC, on down, Marines were held to extremely high standards of behavior and performance. Proper, respectful treatment of civilians and private property was a given, as was attention to duty in combat.

Particularly troubling to Thieu Ta (Major) Binh, and all of his Marines, by the afternoon of April 2, 1972 was the utterly shameful and, to them, pusillanimous bugging out by those soldiers, now ex-soldiers, of the 57th Regiment who streamed by their hold-or-die fighting positions. For every ARVN soldier who threw down his weapon and self-servingly retreated from the advancing NVA, the burden of defending Dong Ha fell increasingly to the very small number of men in the Soi Bien.

Before the Ripley group's dash to the Dong Ha Bridge's underside, and in between the one-sided leadership exchange between the TQLC's Third Battalion commander and the ARVN's 20th Tank Battalion commander, a very frustrated Thieu Ta Binh had personally confronted a small group of fleeing ARVN soldiers. With drawn .45 pistol Binh actually executed one of the ex-soldiers right on the roadside, without fanfare and, unfortunately, with little or no effect on his utterly disheartened comrades who simply continued their aimless retreat from Dong Ha. None of Binh's Marines batted an eye during the exchange other than to be ready to protect their battalion commander if the need arose; which it did not.

In full view of the ARVN tank battalion commander, perhaps the shock value of Binh's actions were to, unintentionally but beneficially, create fear in the mind of the wavering man who still appeared inclined to extricate his tanks from the battle area. Knowing that Binh or any of his Marines would have no trouble doing the same to him was some motivation to remain engaged at the point of contact with the NVA.

If Ripley somehow managed to live through and succeed in his current undertaking, he would happily supply all the liquid refreshment for the party he would put on in Ha Si Luom's honor. It was Luom's second LAAW shot that stopped the NVA armor advance for a period, and bought the time needed for Ripley, Smock, and Nha to make their spirited dash for the base of the Dong Ha Bridge's southern underside.

What the intrepid trio did not see once they had made it, under fire all the way, to the bridge and began the arduous process of emplacing demolitions—with Nha positioned in a small culvert back from the advisors so that he could observe their actions and report on them to higher headquarters via radio, with Major Smock on the friendly side of the anti-sapper fence and razor wire shoving the boxes of explosives and all the accoutrements through to Ripley, and with Ripley then breaking down the explosives into manageable packages he could carry as he crawled into the bridge's underside—were the actions of the second anti-tank rocket team as they engaged a second T-54 in the near-exact same manner Ha Si Luom just had.

Sergeant Phuoc was also part of First Company's Weapons Platoon. He was the Team B anti-tank rocket team leader; and like Luom had extensive combat experience. He and his partner had moved into place about the same time as Luom and his mate. Roughly twenty meters east of Luom, Phuoc engaged his LAAW and hit a second T-54 only a moment after Luom's hit. He scored what was called a "mobility kill" as the partially destroyed behemoth became an impediment to vehicles that might now attempt to cross the bridge. In the meantime, the exchange of small arms fire continued unabated.

BACK IN THE TOC

Lieutenant Colonel Gerry Turley could only try to imagine what Ripley was doing as he too plodded on and continued to fight the war with the few reliable assets he had available to him. Turley had to assume that, in the absence of news to the contrary, Ripley was alive and still somehow trying to carry out his orders. Concurrently, Captain Thiesen was assembling and scrounging explosives to load onto the six-by truck he would eventually drive onto the Dong Ha Bridge if Ripley was killed or failed to blow the bridge himself.

The world beyond and outside of Dong Ha continued to dissolve into chaos and what looked like certain defeat for the good guys. Where John Ripley's immediate world had gone from the area within M-16/AK-47 range of the Dong Ha Bridge to the confines of the structure's most southern underside, Gerry Turley's had diminished only to whatever extent the NVA now controlled even more of northern Quang Tri Province than they had a few hours earlier. As concerned as he was with the developing actions of Captain Ripley, he also had other things to worry about.

There was no good news. The best Turley could do, because he had heard nothing yet to the contrary, was assume Ripley to be still alive and somehow pressing forward with his effort to destroy the Dong Ha Bridge. At every other major allied position things had changed only to the extent that they had gotten worse.

Out west of Dong Ha at Cam Lo, the ARVN Third Division's Second Regiment had successfully retreated across the bridge there with NVA units in close pursuit. It was made known to Turley and crew in the TOC that, with the enemy at their heels, there was no opportunity to destroy the Cam Lo Bridge; the other bridge over the Cua Viet River capable of supporting armor.

The 56th Regiment, five kilometers south of Cam Lo at Camp Carroll, had earlier been ordered by General Giai to hold at all costs. Communications with the TOC were sporadic at best. There was still no indication Turley could see that any of the twenty-two artillery pieces located there were answering calls for fire support.

The improvement in the weather was not yet sufficient to bring in TAC air. There were still five U.S. Navy ships offshore providing gunfire support. Prior to his going under the bridge, John Ripley, who had to communicate with the ships through Joel Eisenstein anyway, had arranged with the ANGLICO personnel back in the TOC to continuously deliver fire on a number of "fireboxes" the two had earlier worked on together. Ripley had asked Eisenstein to maintain a steady rate of fire into the boxes. Even without the ability to actively adjust the naval gunfire, the destruction rained down on obvious targets such as troop concentrations north of the bridge and the long axis of Route One further up the road where they could not observe, but were confident there were aggregations of enemy troops and material, it was reasonable to assume they were killing bad guys. If nothing else, the ongoing fire would hamper and slow their efforts; or so Ripley surmised.

As much as people outside of Quang Tri Province were gaining growing, grudging appreciation that the battles there were becoming increasingly acute, the volume and sheer weirdness of these naval messages was causing no end of apoplexy in Saigon. Even though he had now been running operations for several days, the most senior U.S. Army officers at MACV still had no real clue who Gerry Turley was, where he came from, who gave him authority to do what he was doing, and on and on. If this had not been during wartime it might have been good material for a modern, military-oriented version of Abbott and Costello's "Who's on First?" or more appropriately tailored to the culture and geography for the area "Hu's on First?"

What finally pushed General Abrams, the senior American commander at MACV in Saigon, over the edge was the communication Turley and the others who would later see it called the "Land the Landing Force Message." Composed entirely aboard one of the U.S. Navy ships off the coast and then broadcast to a list of important recipients, the missive certainly appeared genuine and legitimate. Reporting the ground situation in Quang Tri Province as extremely dire, it requested immediate relief and reinforcement by the American Marine forces allegedly afloat just offshore. No matter how authentic it appeared, the people in the TOC had other issues they were focused on. They had absolutely no idea this message had been composed and sent out as if Turley had written or authorized it. The problem however, and the damage done, was that the people further up the chain of command had no way of knowing the message was *not* issued by Turley. General Abrams' terse response to subordinates was what one might expect given all that had so far taken place. "I need to meet this fellow Turley. Get him down here as soon as possible."

The unique set of combat skills John Ripley specifically brought to battle at the Dong Ha Bridge on Easter Sunday 1972 would only later, if he was successful in his effort to bring the massive structure down, be judged as a near miracle of circumstances or extremely unusual quirk of fate. Throughout all of northern Quang Tri Province there was certainly, at that very moment, no shortage of fully committed, brave men at every level locked in the most personal, mortal combat against vastly superior NVA forces. There was, on that Sunday afternoon, no lack of courage among remaining Vietnamese Marine and ARVN forces along with the Americans who stood by to support a situation looking more like what had taken place at Custer's Last Stand, than anything smelling remotely of victory.

Of the American Marine officers sparingly sprinkled in with the TQLC battalions and brigades, not one of them had so far demonstrated anything but complete support for the units they advised.

Major Binh's earlier radio broadcast to the world was the Vietnamese Marine Corps' institutional public commitment to hold on against what so far appeared to be impossible odds and fight to the last man if necessary. No one considered his remarks as puffery or flamboyance. They were taken as completely sincere; completely literal.

John Ripley and his critical new ally Jim Smock would claim no corner on bravery or sacrifice that day. Far from it. What made Ripley the round peg in the round hole at precisely the right moment was that he was the *only* man available with both the physical abilities *and*, of far greater importance, the technical skills and know-how to blow the Dong Ha Bridge.

It had been seven years, going on eight, since First Lieutenant Ripley was a student at the U.S. Army's Ranger School. As much as Ranger School was, in the grand scheme of things, an existential exercise in discovering one's physical and mental limitations, and then finding ways to press beyond exhaustion to carry on with missions most regular folks would simply judge as impossible, for those men who really excelled there, it was also a laboratory to master the art and science of patrolling; "rangering" if you will. Including demolitions.

Blowing demo was not like learning to ride a bicycle or speak Spanish. You did not instinctively remember or intuitively know how to safely and effectively rig explosives for maximum impact; let alone rig them at the critical places to destroy a bridge as daunting and formidable as the one Ripley was now matched against. With demolitions you could not figuratively add an "o" to every word and expect a positive outcome. There were specific rules and procedures to follow which could not be violated. There were no short cuts. It was not like the movies or television shows.

For some reason even he could not swear by or identify, on the afternoon of Easter Sunday 1972, Ripley could well recall that very late night, or was it early morning, in the Georgia woods in mid-December 1964, as his Ranger class trudged to an open-air classroom, halfway frozen and all the way wet, sleep and food deprived, to take a few hours instruction in explosives. Maybe it was as simple as understanding that any small error might cost a man a few fingers, a hand, his private parts. Maybe it was that he simply learned and remembered best *in extremis*. Whatever.

For some other unknown reason, in the same period which had seen America commit and then dispatch hundreds of thousands of its very best and not so very best men to a war the nation now only marginally supported, in the same timeframe that took the world from James Bond's *Goldfinger* and the incomparable Honor Blackman as Pussy Galore all the way past *Diamonds Are Forever*, in the same period that had seen the rise and fall of Janis Joplin, Jim Morrison, and Jimi Hendrix, John Ripley had probably forgotten a hundred other things the Ranger *cadre* assiduously imparted; he should not have remembered this stuff. No way. But he did. All of it.

AT THE SOUTH SIDE OF THE BRIDGE

With all that he had experienced as skipper of Lima 3/3 in 1967 and the more recent duty with the Soi Bien, John Ripley had never observed civilians being intentionally targeted in the manner in which they were now being targeted by the NVA. To say that things were strange, even more strange than they earlier were or had been was not description enough. Nothing was normal and yet everything in Dong Ha that had taken place, was currently taking place, and was probably about to take place was, relative to everything else, normal. It was war; full-scale war. To say that war was hell or give some other description of all that was going on seemed insufficient, glib, *clichéd*. Ripley had been around long enough, had survived countless close calls, had witnessed too many good men killed and maimed, acts of evil, feats of bravery and courage to know what war was all about, or mostly what it encompassed. Whoever said it first was right; war *was* hell. Today in Dong Ha he saw it confirmed with devastating truth that now included innocent women, children, and the very old. Could things become any more unreal, surreal, any more horrific than they already were at Dong Ha? All that seemed to continue was the ongoing incongruity and sensory overloading they were—every one of them—experiencing.

After positioning Nha at a nearby vantage point roughly twenty to thirty meters back from the bridge where he could view the advisors' actions, and from relative safety report their progress or demise via radio to higher headquarters, Ripley and Smock arrived at the southern underside of the massive structure. Already spent, already depleted, already way past empty, the two Americans discovered upon their arrival at the base of the bridge five very pitiable, defeated-looking ARVN combat engineers. Surprised that they were even there, and more surprised by the small mountain of explosives on hand to do the job, Ripley and Smock stepped under the bridge itself to have a look, make a proper assessment for the work at hand. As much as the combat engineers had a collective deer-in-the-headlights look to them, they had at least performed the critical duty of delivering to the base of the bridge enough explosives to get the job done. While the two Americans had gone from their view to survey the underside of the Dong Ha Bridge, the ARVN soldiers bolted and when Ripley and Smock returned they realized they were now alone.

Ripley understood enough about bridge construction and engineering to know that he had his work ahead cut out for him. In order to do the job right he would need to get over the significant anti-sapper fence and razor-wire barrier, and up into the channels created between the seven massive I-beams. Had Ripley had the luxury of time to ponder his situation he might have realized that the work he intended to complete was not only dangerous, it was physically impossible. With no time to spare, he did not think to talk himself out of it as any sane, reasonable man might have done.

Together Ripley and Smock quickly discussed the ground situation and what needed to be done. With Ripley as the local expert—the only local expert—on demolitions, Smock wisely deferred to his junior mate and assumed a support role. Keeping all of his combat equipment affixed and attached, Ripley swung himself up onto the razor wire atop the fence. There was no other way. In the process he cut his already tattering uniform and sliced his skin in too many places to count; instantly drawing blood. He had no time to worry if his tetanus shot was current.

Once Ripley was on the inside of the barrier it was Smock's duty to lift up and push through the wire the explosives and other gear to his crazy Marine captain pal. Like his new friend, each time he pushed equipment through the wire Smock cut his hands and arms to shreds.

The physical requirements were daunting. From the shore Ripley would hand walk out a good ways, carrying thirty to forty pounds of explosives or equipment to rig the explosives along with all his warfighting gear. As a thoroughly trained infantry Marine it was completely outside of his thought processes, near heretical, to not always have his weapon and accompanying gear with him. In addition to the explosives and his rifle loosely slung around his neck, he also carried his modified web belt, or "kit" as he now referred to it after his time with the British Royal Marines. In all he would hand walk carrying, in addition to his own body weight, probably seventy pounds of gear with him. Once he got far enough out he would, with the deftness of an Olympic gymnast, swing his body and somehow hoist himself up into the relative safety of the channel created by two adjacent I-beams and crawl to where he needed to go; all the while sweating and bleeding and continually chanting to himself a prayer or exhortation to somehow keep going. (As he hand walked out to the place where he would swing into the I-beam channels, his body, at least his legs, were visible and exposed to those NVA soldiers on the far side who would occasionally crank off a few rounds at him.) If Ripley's grip failed or he was to slip and fall into the moderately rapid running waters of the Cua Viet River fifteen feet below him he would have sunk to the bottom like a stone.

After the division of labor between Ripley and Smock was established, and the work begun at what could crudely be described as the routine was set, John Ripley's *raison d'être* became the transport and appropriate placement of the five hundred pounds of TNT left by the ARVN combat engineers. By his own calculations Ripley would have to make a dozen trips into the belly of the bridge; two for each of the six channels. The first trip into each channel was for placing the explosives. The second trip was to rig, wire, and set the charges.

The boxes of TNT, once he hoisted them into the channels, were of perfect length to sit between the inboard edges of each channel. Because of this, he could crawl on his knees on the lips of the channels created by the I-beams and push the boxes along to where he wanted them. Ripley positioned the boxes of demolitions in a staggered and diagonal pattern so that when they eventually blew, their explosive force would magnify and twist the I-beams from the shore abutment and the concrete columns upon which they rested.

Most of the time while under the bridge Ripley was in his own little world. Even with the hordes of NVA less than two hundred meters away from him on the north side and Binh's First and Fourth Companies stretched to the limit on the south side of the river who continued to keep the enemy occupied with their steady, measured fire, he was essentially isolated and alone with nothing but the physical challenge of getting the job done. When he would return to the fence and wire near the southern side for more explosives or other equipment, Smock would, each time cutting and slicing his skin and uniform while pushing through the razor wire, lift the material to him and act like an exuberant boxing manager in the corner after every round; doing what he could to encourage, entreat, beseech, incite, enjoin, humor, and cajole his prizefighter to do what needed to be done.

Occasionally the NVA tank Ha Si Luom had earlier disabled, which was sitting just off the road in a small culvert on the western side of the bridge, would fire a round or two from its fully depressed 100mm gun. Fortunately it could not get good aim or drop its barrel lower. At nearly point-blank range, the round would slam into the upstream, outboard stringer of the bridge. Although the rounds were unable to penetrate the heavy steel or cause any fragmentation, the concussive effect and indescribably loud sound of impact always managed to clear his ears and hurry Ripley along.

For Ripley there really was no thought of or concern for time. His sole focus once he began the emplacement of the TNT, the wiring, and the plastic explosives was to get everything in its proper place and blow the bridge. While the work itself did not really require complex thought, because of his already utter and complete exhaustion, it did require 100 percent of his mental faculties to ensure that his body would respond to his demands of it and summon 100 percent of what physical strength and reserves he had left.

At the very beginning of the endeavor, as he and Smock unpacked the TNT, the plastic explosives, and other sundry items for rigging, Ripley had the most unusual recollection. The plastic explosives and the way they were packaged reminded him of a toy wagon his son Thomas had received at Christmas. The plastic explosives were shaped and packed tightly, exactly as the little wooden blocks that came as part of the gift on the interior of the red wagon. In that passing moment he allowed himself the luxury of thinking about Moline and their three children. In a few more hours they would be waking up for Easter Sunday services and all the family fun and hoopla. By the time their day was set to begin he might very well be dead. At least the casualty notification process would be such that the Grim Reaper would likely not get to Blacksburg until after most of the Easter candy had been consumed. Fleetingly pondering the worst, he quickly forced himself to shut everything outside of the bridge, the mission and his immediate surroundings from his mind and went back to work.

John Ripley probably knew it but at the time gave little thought that he had stepped onto the field to engage in the Super Bowl game of his life. Like the underdog New York Jets against the Baltimore Colts in the famous 1969 matchup, Ripley faced horrible odds. With an enemy, two enemies—the NVA *and* the bridge—he was like a single Joe Namath lined up against the life-or-death military equivalent of several thousand Bubba Smiths. Unlike Broadway Joe who came to the game tanned, rested, ready, pampered, and adored, Ripley had not slept or eaten a decent meal for going on four days along with having operated at maximum effort during that time. There were no adoring crowds although the odd mix of folks constituting his cheering section, including every one of the Soi Bien and Major Jim Smock, U.S. Army (Armor) would have to suffice.

If a sports analogy could begin to describe the long-term physical demands and endurance necessary for what John Ripley was up against and what he had to accomplish in terms of moving all of the demolitions out to where they needed to go, if he ever hoped to destroy the Dong Ha Bridge, it might have been likened to a marathon. He had long ago hit what marathon runners call, in their own parlance, "the wall." Every single movement, every single effort of physical exertion now had to be willed and deliberate. His marathon was different in that it needed to be divided into at least twelve increments: one for each trip out to where he was placing and rigging the explosives. Each increment, even though part of his greater marathon effort, would require his running it at full-sprint speed. Every step, every hand placement as he pulled himself along, with all that extra weight a part of his fully depleted body, required maximum mental and physical effort only because it required maximum mental and physical effort.

No one would have faulted John Ripley had he failed. Any objective observer who might later come to Dong Ha, study the bridge and its underside would clearly see the complete impossibility of Ripley's task. He would become the modern example of Teddy Roosevelt's "Man in the Arena"—"whose face is marred by dust and sweat and blood; who strives valiantly; who errs, who comes up short again and again, ... who spends himself in a worthy cause...and who at the worst, if he fails, at least fails while doing greatly..." Ripley's noble, quixotic effort would have been noted by his comrades who survived him. He would have been remembered for trying to accomplish what few others could or would have even attempted. But John Ripley was not thinking about any of that stuff. He was certainly not interested in failing while doing greatly. All he wanted to do was blow the damn bridge.

CHAPTER TWENTY-SEVEN

A Four-Hour Eternity

F*ocused completely* on trying to stabilize the ever-shrinking amount of real estate under the control of friendly forces, Gerry Turley could never have imagined on this mid-Sunday afternoon that he had personally raised the ire of General Abrams himself. Concerned more about the intentions of General Vo Nguyen Giap, the architect of the French defeat at Dien Bien Phu and the current senior military commander of the North Vietnamese Army, than those of the MACV leadership, Turley had no time to consider whose feelings were ruffled, let alone "Hu was on first?" All he cared about, all any of those with him in the Ai Tu TOC cared about was trying to stop what had so far been a near unstoppable enemy invasion.

It was nearly 1500 on Sunday afternoon when Gerry received his first friendly phone call of the entire offensive. It came from *covan* headquarters down in Saigon. By this time John Ripley had been doing whatever it was he was doing for probably more than two hours. At Camp Carroll the 56th Regiment, as best as he could discern, was still receiving an incredible artillery pounding. Communications with the two U.S. Army officers serving as advisors to the 56th's regimental commander were negligible. Over at Cam Lo the NVA had not yet attempted to cross the bridge now minimally defended by elements of the Second Regiment. It was early Easter Sunday morning on the American East Coast. In California and in a few more hours Bunny and the kids would be up and headed to church. He knew he could count on their prayers.

Major Bob Sheridan was the senior Marine advisor to Brigade 369, and currently the senior *covan* remaining in Saigon. On

Easter Sunday the unit he advised, which included the artillery battalion Captain George Philip was assigned to, was still in Saigon but was rapidly preparing to head back north far sooner than originally planned. The exchange between Turley and Sheridan lasted for a fairly long time; maybe fifteen minutes. In their dialogue Sheridan explained to Turley that he had become a pariah, his name was a curse word among the MACV staff, and that General Abrams now wanted to see him. Turley reciprocated by attempting to explain all that had gone on in those few days; the ten firebases lost to advancing infantry forces, the unrelenting volume of enemy artillery, the introduction of an as yet undetermined number of enemy tanks, the incredibly poor showing by ARVN units, the uncountable thousands of civilian casualties and the challenges their massive exodus was creating, and on and on. Fifteen minutes worth of bad news, talking at an excited clip. Even though he had been up there a few weeks prior, it was difficult for Bob Sheridan to fully process or comprehend the scope of what Turley was telling him.

Meanwhile, the volume of information to chronicle exceeded the abilities of whoever was attempting to record events in the journal being kept in the TOC.

Just as Turley and his crew in the bunker had been oblivious to the stir created by the naval messages received in Saigon, they were likewise completely blindsided by developments at Camp Carroll which no one, American or Vietnamese, would have rationally contemplated before they were first reported.

THE SURRENDER OF CAMP CARROLL

If ARVN regiments could be judged solely by the histories of the men commanding them or in the same way as were battalions in the Vietnamese Marine Corps, the Third Division's 56th Regiment should have been among the better fighting outfits. Lieutenant Colonel Pham Van Dinh, the 56th Regiment's current commanding officer, was a national hero, a name known to nearly all informed citizens of the Republic of Vietnam.

As a captain during the Tet Offensive four years earlier, Dinh had led his elite reconnaissance company in the same brutal fighting in Hue that American Marines experienced. While the actions of his Black Panther Company—the Hac Bao—had been essentially missed by the American media focused on chronicling instead what the Leathernecks were up against, it was his unit that was first to raise the flag of the Republic of Vietnam once again on Hue's Citadel. Their exploits and heroics captured the hearts of patriotic Vietnamese. That flag raising was significant. It was the ARVN equivalent of the USMC flag raising atop Mt. Suribachi on Iwo Jima in 1945. If there was a small group of South Vietnamese warrior *glitterati*, Pham Van Dinh would have been among them. His seemingly out of character, stark, and abject treason in the surrendering of all Vietnamese forces at Camp Carroll to the NVA that afternoon was a tremendous blow; a horrible, unspeakable blow to the ARVN side.[1]

The ignominious surrender of the 56th Regiment was so shocking and outrageous, that it was denied by nearly everyone who received the news when they heard it for the first time. It would have been the American equivalent of Sergeant York throwing in with the Huns or Patton surrendering to Rommel in the north African desert. It was a big deal; a very big, bad deal.

The forces at work against American army advisors Lieutenant Colonel Bill Camper and Major Joe Brown were likely even more unfavorable than they were for most of the other Americans in northern Quang Tri Province currently attempting to assist their Vietnamese allies. In comparison, for example, to the relatively long-term relationship John Ripley enjoyed with his close friend and associate Le Ba Binh, Camper and Brown were relative babes in the woods. Even though both men were seasoned, experienced combat veterans with distinguished records, and Camper had served an earlier tour as an ARVN advisor, their three weeks with the 56th Regiment did not allow for the critical, intangible bonding needed to maximize the advisory relationship.

The two American army advisors assigned to the 56th Regiment out at Camp Carroll were known to Gerry Turley only by their good reputations. The initial radio contact Turley had with Camper, however, was anything but positive. With the situation appearing grim at best, and with so many things in complete disarray, the constant stress and need to make bold, critical decisions left Turley little time for sensitivity, the ability to parse words or discern messages meant to be somewhat cryptic. In attempting to communicate what was not really possible to communicate about how crazy the ground situation was at Camp Carroll and that Dinh was planning to surrender the entire position, the full meaning of his message to the TOC, logged in at 1502, was initially lost on Turley:

Camper: "Yeoman Echo (Camper's call sign) requests to leave this position. He and his assistant are no longer needed. He has reasons but cannot explain now."

Turley: "No, Colonel. Stay there and do your damn job."

Just as Turley knew the northern I Corps ground combat situation better than the MACV people in Saigon trying to keep him from blowing the Dong Ha Bridge, Bill Camper was astute enough not to argue, but to carry on with what he knew he had to do. Turley recognized his own error at the near moment he made it and instantly began to suffer the guilt even before Camper concluded the exchange a moment later with his respectful, almost doleful "Roger, out."[2]

Less than twenty minutes later, with the situation even more serious, Camper sent his next message. This time there was no need to disguise a thing. "The base commander wants to surrender. The white flag is going up in ten minutes."

It was another near miracle and testament to the bravery of the American army helicopter pilots that Camper, Brown, their ARVN radio operators who stayed loyal to them, and a few other Vietnamese were actually able to be extracted and flown back to the Third Division headquarters in Quang Tri. Reporting immediately to General Giai, they described events as they had experienced them and what Dinh had done. The general was beside himself and could not believe such an incredible story. At first, in his anger, he accused the American officers of lying to him.

In the Ai Tu TOC, Turley and crew, as exhausted as they already were from the unrelenting battle, were stunned by the loss of Camp Carroll and were immediately trying to understand what that loss would mean to the overall allied situation. As the lone extract helicopter was returning Camper and Brown to Quang Tri, Turley personally made the call to higher authorities to report the fire base's surrender.

Gerry Turley could not have imagined relations with those down south becoming any more poisoned than they now were. But he was wrong. As fate seemed to continue to work against him, at least with the people at MACV in Saigon and wherever else those mistrusting him were located, Turley's *other* battle continued unremittingly.

On the line to receive the report of Camp Carroll's demise was the same fellow he had earlier sworn at when arguing about what to do at the Dong Ha Bridge. It was a lucky thing for whoever he was that there were three hundred miles of Vietnamese real estate to separate them, otherwise Turley might have gladly walked or even low-crawled to his position for a personal counseling session had he been anywhere close by.

Still feeling as angry or angrier than he was from the first encounter, Turley simply hung up the phone before the urge to resort to profanity overcame his good judgment. Focusing instead on what he and the remaining Vietnamese Marine forces needed to do, he immediately got with the Dinh who was not the traitor, the Dinh who was the Brigade 258 commander. Himself a displaced northerner, Colonel Dinh took the news of Camp Carroll's demise hard. Referring to the enemy only as "Communists" and not Vietnamese, the normally taciturn Brigade 258 commander simply said to Turley, and probably to himself as well: "We must destroy the Communists."

The Vietnamese and their American advisors continued to work together, doing what they could, applying what limited resources there were, monitoring what there was to monitor and reporting to higher headquarters what they believed needed to be passed on.

It was not too many minutes more after Turley's exchange with the army officer who accused him of having flipped his lid that he received another call. This time the call was from Danang; from another Marine officer of similar rank but slightly senior to Turley. He had obviously been enlisted in the effort to not so cryptically communicate MACV's displeasure and deep concern with Turley. The message was clear, and clearly insulting. What Turley got from the brief exchange was "Cool it, and return to Saigon as soon as possible and practical." General Abrams really did want to see him.

Though he was worn down, he recognized the not-so-subtle castigation that came across the wires and over the airwaves. He had only done, to the best of his abilities, what he had been told to do by army officers not really in his legal chain of command. Now he was going to fry for all sorts of things he had zero control over or input on. He was immediately resigned to take his medicine like a man; but he would make his case first. He still did not have a clue about the apparent crimes he had committed or awareness for the disarray that existed in the system for communications behind the scenes.

At this time of the afternoon there was no practical means to begin the extract process to Saigon. There was no way that he would get to MACV today and so, even though everyone in the TOC was instantly aware that something was up with Lieutenant Colonel Turley, he had no choice but to continue to run things as before, and fight the NVA with the same focus he had earlier been fighting them with. He would leave for Saigon in the morning.

Gerry Turley forced himself to steal a moment to reflect again on all that had taken place since lunchtime on March 30, a near lifetime ago. In his mind a tape of events flashed at rapid speed as he looked around the TOC. These men, Americans and Vietnamese of every military branch, were a genuinely disparate bunch. They were tired, drained, and filthy beyond regular description but continuing to function like the professionals they were. As spent as he now was, he continued to gaze at these young men who looked older than they were, who collectively carried the weight of the world on their tired frames, and simply smiled to himself. God alone knew how proud Turley was of these men. And the battle continued on ...

BINH IN THE OVERWATCH POSITION

While Ripley, Smock, and Nha were dealing with the issues of attempting to destroy the Dong Ha Bridge, Binh had a battalion to lead and fight. Blessed with aggressive, competent company commanders, there was no need to micromanage their efforts. In fact Binh had personally trained all of them; several of them had been his platoon commanders when he had command of First Company. All of them bore *his* mark. All of them were as committed to their country's survival as was their battalion commander. In the familial, collegial brotherhood that was the tiny officer corps of the Vietnamese Marines, Binh was also recognized for his zeal in teaching and mentoring the officers and staff non-commissioned officers he worked with. If Third Battalion was to be beaten at Dong Ha, it would not be due to poor or weak leadership. And besides, the ground situation was, for the moment, relatively stable. Constantly on the radio with his brigade commander, Colonel Dinh, who was back in the TOC with Gerry Turley, Dinh would always conclude Binh's situation reports with the unnecessary reminder to honor their uniform; to fight on.

Thieu Uy (Second Lieutenant) Luong had not even been in combat command of his platoon for a full week by Easter Sunday. As junior as he was, as much as he was a "cherry" by American standards, he understood the significance of Dong Ha, Third Battalion's role in defending it, and Dai Uy Ripley's mad attempt at trying to blow up the bridge.

Luong's only experience with Americans had been limited to his education at the Vietnamese National Military Academy and with the one USMC *covan* he had encountered during his time as a platoon commander with Fourth Company. Within his circle of family, friends, comrades, and acquaintances those people could roughly be divided into three groups in terms of attitudes towards Americans in general. There were those, a small group, who simply hated Americans. There were those who recognized that American support was essential even though it had deleterious impact on Vietnamese society; but accepted those things as a price necessary to pay when compared to the alternative of Communist domination. And finally there were those who could not quite figure out why another country with so little to gain would magnanimously sacrifice its young men in the fight for someone else's freedom. Luong and most of his friends from the National Military Academy were in this group.

Luong, even prior to his arrival with Third Battalion, was well familiar with the special relationship between the TQLC and the American Marines. When he had taken over his platoon he heard his men speak of Dai Uy Ripley, whom he had observed only briefly and always in the presence of Thieu Ta Binh, with a reverence approaching that accorded their beloved battalion commander. On this Sunday afternoon as he and the men of his platoon watched, from one hundred meters south of the bridge, what the American *dai uy* was attempting, he understood the reason for that deference and regard.

Luong's platoon was given the reserve mission by Fourth Company's company commander. Like all the other platoons in all of Third Battalion's companies (and throughout the entire Vietnamese Marine Corps actually), Luong was blessed to have serving under him a small *coterie* of strong, professional sergeants and corporals. (Luong, as commander of First Platoon, was also doubly blessed to have not one, but two staff sergeants to assist him with the proper running of his unit.) Their individual and collective zeal to kill the hated Communists matched or exceeded anything their officers brought to the battle, and like the USMC, the TQLC counted heavily on the criticality of their small-unit leadership. The TQLC had also followed the American example by investing significant resources in training and additional schooling for their non-commissioned officers.

With the rest of his company securing the battalion's left front as they faced north across the Cua Viet River, Luong and his thirty-six Marines were just a ways back from the closest action. A hundred or so meters down from the southern entrance to the bridge, Luong's platoon was stretched across Highway One itself, also facing north. To his platoon's immediate east were the remnants of some sort of tire shop which only days ago had, no doubt, been a reasonably viable business tending to the hundreds of two-, three-, and four-wheeled vehicles daily passing in either direction. Under the constant NVA artillery barrages all that remained was rubble along with indestructible piles and groupings of tires spread here and there. With very little interest in digging fighting positions any deeper than they had to, the resourceful Marines of Fourth Company's First Platoon immediately appropriated all the tires there were to use as extra barricade and cover to their front. Until they would be called to reinforce the extremely narrow and crowded battle line two of Third Battalion's companies were currently covering, they would await orders behind the tires.

While Ripley was under the bridge the U.S. Navy men-of-war just offshore continued to fire the missions he had earlier planned and coordinated with Joel Eisenstein. Naval gunfire remained the only reliable fire support available. With the weather slowly improving it was reasonable to expect air support before the day was out.

FROM HERE TO A FOUR-HOUR ETERNITY

How long was the four hour period John Ripley was under the Dong Ha Bridge? Four hours was long enough to watch Audie Murphy morph from poverty-stricken, orphaned, gangly, undernourished, sharp-shooting backwoods Texas farm boy to the most decorated soldier of World War II in *To Hell and Back*. Twice. Ripley had now visited that same place in those four hours, only he hadn't yet returned.

Four hours was long enough to listen to Iron Butterfly's "In-A-Gadda-Da-Vida," the 17:05 long version, fourteen times; or to "Come Go With Me" by the Del Vikings—the song that collectively framed John and Moline's fondest memories—nearly ninety-three times.

Four hours was long enough for former Ripley's Raider Chuck Goggin to play a major league baseball game with several extra innings.

Four hours was not quite long enough to fly from Los Angeles to Honolulu, but it was sufficient time—with a tailwind—so that the pilot was, by then, giving passengers the landing brief and pointing out that the large land mass off the starboard wing was the island of Hawaii.

Four hours doing what Captain John Walter Ripley was doing was a very long time...especially since what he was doing was not humanly possible.

After twelve trips into the belly of the incredible beast that was the Dong Ha Bridge, Ripley and Smock could rejoice for just a moment. All the demo was in place. After twelve trips out and back emplacing explosives and all the requisite wiring though, they still needed to be detonated. All the demolitions in the world were like bullets on the outside of a weapon; completely worthless until they could be fired. John Ripley would need to make one more trip out under the bridge to set the charges.

In a perfect world, if Ripley could do it all by the book like they did at Ranger School—which was the safest and best way anyway— he would have used crimpers and electric blasting caps and it all would have been pretty and slick and clean, and in one fell swoop the bridge would be down and in the river. But Easter Sunday afternoon at Dong Ha was far from Camp Darby and the Georgia woods. This was far from ideal, but Ranger School had also reinforced the notion of field expedience and improvisation. Reflecting well his Ranger training, Ripley would explode the demolitions with what gear the ARVN combat engineers had left for them.

In the small mountain of demolitions earlier abandoned by the ARVN combat engineers, neither Ripley nor Smock were initially able to locate electric blasting caps or the crimpers that would have made the job of affixing the caps to the detonation cord (aka det cord) far simpler. Crimpers are a sort of unique pliers-type tool that are used specifically to squeeze the relatively soft, ultra-thin sheet metal that makes up the Lucky Strike cigarette-sized and slightly thinner shaped blasting cap's housing so that, after being squeezed at its open end, the blasting cap remains permanently in place, until a charge is applied through the det cord and...*blammo*. In the absence of having a pair of crimpers, the next best "tool" is a man's teeth; biting down hard on the metal to ensure the blasting cap remains in place. Aside from the creepy, shocking feeling of biting down on cold metal, there is also a good chance that when "jaw-boning," as it is called, the blasting cap might prematurely explode in one's mouth thus ruining one's day completely.

Instead of locating electric detonators, Ripley found only time-fuse detonators. Time-fuse detonators were far less sexy, far less precise, and therefore far more dangerous than electric detonators. But that was all there was, and Ripley had come too far to stop now or to be concerned about issues of safety. He was not interested in failing while doing greatly. Ripley would rig his explosives using method number two, the field expedient way, taught to him all those years ago at Ranger School.

Using time-fuse detonators to do the job increased Ripley's chances of failure or of blowing himself up before he might clear the bridge. It was like using a shotgun instead of a long-range hunting rifle to take down a big-game target requiring the latter. Time-fuse detonators required a fair amount of luck and prayer and guess work. At the moment though, those were his workable options. Ripley prepared his detonators and, under fire once more, returned to the underside of the bridge where he affixed them to the explosives. He lit the fuses and moved with a speed he did not think he had left in him to get back once again to the relative safety of Jim Smock's position.

Forever in Ripley's mind was a third option, most likely his final option. He knew enough about field expedient demolitions to understand that he could always unscrew one of the hand grenades he still kept affixed to his H-harness or magazine pouches and simply insert the grenade's detonator into the TNT. The only problem with that choice was, once the grenade's pin was pulled, he would have four seconds maximum to clear the area before it would all blow. It was, realistically, simply a suicide option. Very early into the endeavor Ripley had taken stock and figured his chances for survival were slim to begin with. He decided that if the NVA had dinged him or he knew the end was certain, even if the bridge was only partially rigged, he would employ this "other" option and take out what he could. John Ripley was not interested in failing while doing greatly.

Completely exhausted, he had done his best. If the lit fuses would not somehow burn out or be snuffed out or be displaced by the NVA the bridge would blow. Eventually. As he lay there, used up and spent, with Smock, the two enjoyed another brief moment of gallows dialogue humor. The banter between officers of rival services and different MOSs (Ripley the infantry officer and Smock the tanker) could have taken place at the bar in any officers' club anywhere rather than on the recessed underside of a bridge about to blow with thousands of enemy troops anxious to kill them just two hundred meters away.

As the banter continued, Ripley spied, almost by accident off to the side, a box he had somehow missed in the earlier excitement. Electric detonators. By God and by golly; electric detonators. Even as the volume of small arms fire from the enemy side seemed to be increasing, Ripley was gripped with some indescribable sense of foreboding, some unquantifiable, completely irrational notion that the only way to do this right, to be ninety-nine and forty-four one-hundredths sure that the bridge would blow, would be to go out—again—and rig these additional detonators. He was a man completely consumed by his impossible mission. Ripley was not at all interested in failing while doing greatly.

Going back out a second time was sheer lunacy. If John Ripley had been a cat he had easily used up all nine lives as Lima Six Actual back in 1967. On Easter Sunday 1972 he was into a whole new level of tempting fate; several orders of magnitude or lifetimes of blessing and luck beyond what most men are dealt. Going back out that one extra time to rig the detonators for the first time was bad enough. Discovering these other, more appropriate detonators drove him beyond reason. Surely he would collapse from exhaustion. Surely the NVA would finally find their range or mark and blow his tired behind away; relieve him of the incredible physical and spiritual burden he was carrying. That first rig would probably do the job anyway. *Probably.* Probably was not good enough. It drove him to distraction. With all the effort, with the literal blood and sweat equity he had invested, he would make certain the bridge would blow. John Ripley was not at all interested in failing while doing greatly.

It was as if he was in one of those very strange but common dreams in which a person finds himself somehow striving to do something utterly impossible, attempting some deed over and over and over; forever coming up short. The only reasonable solution is to wake up. If this was a bad dream it was time for the alarm clock to ring. There was no physical explanation for what he was about to do. It was like having Jim Ryun, the master miler most famous for his final lap kick, go out and immediately run another, faster mile after already turning in a barn-burning, world-record performance. How many more final laps could one man run? Ripley had been running this final lap longer than he had hoped to. He had been "kicking" for a long, long time. What he needed to do—again—simply could not be done. But it was.

He did it. He had continually chanted and prayed aloud to himself as he crawled and scraped and hand walked out and back. With the time fuses still burning, Ripley placed the electric detonators and ran a wire back to the position where he and Smock again huddled. In the meantime Smock, under enemy fire, had also rigged the much smaller and far less formidable Old French Bridge just upstream for destruction. If their electric detonation system would work, both would blow together.

The next and final step was supposed to be simple. All Ripley needed to do was take the communication (comm) wire that he had the explosives connected to and run a sufficient charge of electricity into them and it would all be over. Why should they have assumed that that process would work on Easter Sunday? Nothing else had been easy. It was like they were part of another evil *Candid Camera* gimmick. Ripley and Smock had sprinted back to another position away from the bridge; trailing comm wire.

If this had been one of those Hollywood serial cliffhangers, Ripley, as "Don Winslow of the Navy" or "Cowboy Tom Mix," had taken his audience to extra episodes. He had run the snack bar out of popcorn and Milk Duds long ago. It was beyond time for the climax. Everyone on the good guy side was ready, praying, expecting the sensational, the breathtaking apogee of action to be followed by some sort of happy ending, except he could not get it.

Ripley needed a "hellbox"—that tiny or not so tiny contraption, depending on the type one used—either with a plunger that, once the wires are properly connected, is pulled up, and with great fanfare pushed down or the other, smaller kind with the half-crank handle, sending the electric charge through the wire to the expertly rigged explosives and it is game over. Neither Ripley nor Smock had been able to locate one. No matter. He was Ranger-trained and he knew that any reasonable electrical source would do.

Nearby was an abandoned jeep that had obviously been hit in the recent shelling. Turned on its side, it was relatively easy for Ripley to access the vehicle battery which was under the driver's seat. The vehicle's tires were actually on fire and as he worked to get to the battery's terminals the acrid smell of burning, melting rubber assaulted his senses.

He had already prepared the wires attached to the demo by stripping away insulation with his K-Bar knife so that they might receive the electric charge. Quickly, expeditiously, in a frenzy and like a madman he placed the wires against the battery's terminals, hoping for the reaction required. Nothing. Touching the wires to the leads on the battery, then reversing them one, two…five, six…nine, ten times…nothing. This time he really could not go back out there, even if he had to run yet another sub-four minute mile. There was too much fire coming from the north bank. The NVA had finally figured him out. And then…it happened.

Victory, for the moment, was a relative, transitory term. The detonation of the explosives Ripley had with Herculean, near superhuman effort painstakingly emplaced over the near eternity of four hours came to him as both a figurative and literal shock. The explosion's initial wave of overpressure reached him just ahead of the deadening roar of the bridge going up, and lifted him bicycling into the air as if plucked by the giant, invisible hand of God.

Ripley had not been facing the bridge when the explosives blew. He was instead in the process of attempting to shield and hurry along a young Vietnamese girl who was still in the area and had been separated from her mother who was twenty or more meters ahead of her heading away from the combat area. Seeing this mother and daughter in the middle of the hell going on all around them tugged hard at his heart. It forced him to think of his own children for the first time since he began placing the demolitions.³ This particular girl, like nearly all Vietnamese children, was, for her age, quite small by American standards. She was, he guessed, older than his oldest son Steven but was not much larger, and probably lighter, than his youngest son Thomas.

For Ripley, it was an incredible, strangely beautiful sight. As if taking place in slow motion so that he could witness this bad dream now turned positive reach its final conclusion, he watched while chunks of concrete and twisted steel cart wheeled through the air. The deck timbers on the bridge adjacent to the portions that had just blown up, he could see, were already on fire. The new open space between the bridge spans was a reassuring picture. The Old French Bridge was now down as well. NVA armor and support vehicles would not be crossing the Cua Viet River at Dong Ha anytime soon.

For a brief moment, the war within their immediate vicinity, within small-arms range anyway, came to a halt. A complete halt. On the north side of the Cua Viet River the NVA likely had figured out too late that they should have paid more attention to the curious fellow whose legs had periodically dangled in the open while moving about the bridge's underside. The men of the Soi Bien—all of them Ripley fans—erupted in thunderous cheers once the bridge blew and the gunfire stopped completely.

In the instantaneous, near festive resulting melee Ripley took the radio handset from an ecstatic Nha and phoned in the message to Lieutenant Colonel Turley in the TOC. Turley immediately rogered Ripley's initial broadcast. "The Dong Ha Bridge is down. I say again...the bridge is down. Over..." And that was that.⁴

Turley, acknowledging the call, could feel the enervation and total exhaustion in Ripley's voice. While he certainly was grateful the bridge was burning and in the river, he really had no full sense for what Ripley had to overcome in destroying the bridge. Turley had never seen the Dong Ha Bridge, nor could he fully understand the challenge this young American captain faced. He instructed one of the captains standing watch with him there in the TOC to log the message in at 1630.⁵

Finally allowing himself the luxury of recognizing his exhaustion, Ripley leaned against a bunker a ways back from the bridge. He was suddenly surrounded by dozens of men from both First and Fourth Companies, all of them patting him, touching him as if somehow his good fortune would go into them, like he was Jesus healing the leper. Enthusiastically they shouted over and over *"Cam on, Dai Uy."* ("Thank you, Captain.") *"Bac-Viet het roi."* ("The NVA are through.")[6] Their own culture and strict protocol would never have allowed the men of the Soi Bien to so informally and personally express themselves to their own officers. But again, Dai Uy Ripp-lee was *their covan*.

Binh's senior bodyguard surprised Ripley the most at this moment of maximum exhaustion and effort. The position as senior bodyguard to the battalion commander, at least in Third Battalion, was reserved for the fiercest and most respected warrior of the group. Known to Ripley as "Jack," or "Three Finger Jack" because the thumb did not count and he had personally cut off the last two knuckles of his own smallest finger on his left hand as a demonstration of loyalty to his battalion commander, this knightly or *samurai*-like warrior was clearly an anachronism in the twentieth century.

More venerated even than the most senior, crusty, all-knowing and all-seeing SNCOs who were the "Old Corps" to junior officers and troops in Ripley's experience, Binh's current senior body guard enjoyed unique stature within Third Battalion. To Ripley, Jack was as mysterious and unknowable, enigmatic and unfathomable as all of Asia was to most Occidentals. To Ripley, Jack was the Vietnamese Marine Corps' poster child for steadfast devotion and sacrifice. Wherever Binh went, Jack went. Wherever Binh positioned himself, Jack always assumed a place between whatever danger there might be and the man he was pledged to sacrifice himself for. Even without trying, although Ripley was certain he cultivated the image, Jack had a fierce, gladiator look to him. On his own Ripley was convinced that Jack was a direct descendant of Genghis Khan. All of the Marines, including Binh's captains and lieutenants, demonstrated near obeisance to Jack.

Like Nha but in a far more ferocious way, Jack was utterly selfless in his devotion; and he was everywhere Binh was. As little as Binh slept, it seemed that Jack was there when they hit the rack and was always up before his Thieu Ta. He was omnipresent with never a hint of exhaustion or emotion. He just was. As devoid of the emotions Americans liked to see with their back-slapping, gregarious ways, Jack was taciturn and formal. He made Charles Bronson seem animated. If Sergio Leone had come east to shoot an Asian equivalent to his spaghetti Westerns and was looking for an Oriental version of the so-called Man with No Name, Jack could have outdone Clint Eastwood; and he was for real.

He had grown to regard Ripley with favor and esteem. Over time Jack had really become Ripley's bodyguard as well; not because he was ordered to but because he seemed driven to out of deference and a genuine concern for the American *dai uy*. This was most unusual even for the close relationship between the Vietnamese Marines and the USMC. Ripley's respect for Jack was more than mutual. These two warriors from completely different cultures and with little ability to verbally communicate were able to transcend those minor challenges.

It frustrated John Ripley that the American evening television news at home was forever full of film depicting things like the 57th Regiment's ignominious retreat, of ARVN soldiers acting in ways that were anything but soldierly. If only the folks at home could witness the dedication and fealty of men like Binh and Nha and Jack, along with the rest of the men of Third Battalion, they would understand the depth of their commitment to defeating the Communists.

As much as Ripley knew that he and Smock had pulled off something significant, and even though, for the moment the war really did seem to stop, it certainly was not victory with any sense of finality. There were no champagne bottles, no victory laps; he was not quite ready to head to Disneyland. No one had told the NVA the battle was over. But with the destruction of the bridge Ripley could finally take a moment to rest, however brief. If he had ever been this exhausted as Lima Six Actual he could not recall. That was five whole years, an entire lifetime, ago. He was so tired he felt himself on the verge of hallucinating.

With the crush of Marines all around him, congratulating him, Jack appeared. Without fanfare or clamor the crowd of Marines present simply parted, and like Moses with the Red Sea, a path opened for Jack to approach their *covan*. Ripley was on the ground, leaning back against the bunker when Jack presented himself before him. In his hand, the hand with the missing digit, he held a can, of all things, of condensed milk. In his other hand Jack had his unsheathed fighting knife and before he sat down next to Dai Uy Ripley he had jammed the blade into the top, carving out a hole large enough to fit his one remaining pinky finger into it.

Not quite sure of what Jack intended, Ripley remained in the supine position. With the tenderness a father might show a young child, the fiercest warrior of the entire Soi Bien removed Dai Uy Ripley's helmet, cradled his head in his lap and began to rub his neck and shoulders in a firm and soothing manner. Over and over, like a parent attempting to calm or settle a distraught youngster, Jack spoke words that Ripley had never heard but could discern their meaning by the gentle, soothing intonations; "Suuuuaah Dai Uy, suuuuah..." Over and over, without rushing and as if they had all the time in the world, Jack rubbed the circulation back into Ripley's spent and wearied body. As he massaged his American friend he would simultaneously dip his pinky into the can of condensed milk, a finger that had probably last been washed and clean long before the battle had begun, and each time would scoop out a glob of coagulated, congealed sweetness and essentially force feed it to his *covan*. "Suuuuaaah Dai Uy, suuuaah..." Ripley, his body desperate for nourishment, could feel the life coming back into him but was still not sure that he was not hallucinating...."Suuuaaah Dai Uy, suuuaah..."

BACK IN THE TOC

What Ripley and Smock had pulled off was nothing short of miraculous. The mood in the TOC had improved just a bit. The ground situation was still grim, but just a bit less than it was before. The destruction of the Dong Ha Bridge was an event that had strategic impact and implications. Everyone there knew that. They could all read the map.

There was insufficient intelligence on enemy capabilities at or near the point of contact in Dong Ha to know if they had come with significant engineering and expeditionary bridging resources to attempt to repair the bridge. The NVA had shown that they had near limitless artillery and a greater number of troops and tanks than originally expected. Even with as much equipment and manpower as the NVA brought to the battle, it was unlikely they would have planned on Turley's resolve, Luom's lucky shot, Ripley's mental toughness, physical endurance and bravery, or Binh's tenacity.

Prior to the initiation of this offensive it was noted that the NVA anti-aircraft effort had been beefed up. More likely they did not have local ability to repair the bridge so that T-54s could get across. Naval gunfire would make such an effort costly. But what about the PT-76s? They were known to have amphibious capability. No, Turley and his crew of tired Americans and Vietnamese believed the most probable next move for the enemy would be to shift their focus towards Cam Lo. The bad guys had maps too; and good battlefield intelligence. At Cam Lo was the one remaining bridge which crossed the Cua Viet River capable of holding T-54s; and there would be no threat from naval gunfire. There were no Vietnamese Marines at Cam Lo. With Camp Carroll's artillery silenced for sure, the only significant threat to the NVA would be from allied airpower when it could be brought on station.

Gerry Turley was getting briefed routinely by his air liaison officer. As promised earlier, the weather was improving and Major Brookbank was talking to the appropriate people charged with coordinating all air assets to be used in this extremely target-rich environment. The allies believed the enemy to have brought significant anti-aircraft resources to the most forward edge of the battle area. They would soon find out how deadly the threat was; and there were still a good seven hours left of Easter Sunday during which they would continue to have to fight the war. The day and the day's action was far from over.

CHAPTER TWENTY-EIGHT

The Ongoing View
from Dong Ha

John Ripley was not yet aware of Camp Carroll's demise. Gerry Turley had purposely kept that information from him during the period that he was under the bridge. Turley had wisely surmised that Ripley's focus needed to remain on Dong Ha. Had he heard of allied setbacks elsewhere it might have somehow impacted the motivation to act as expeditiously as he did.

For all intents and purposes the war in the immediate vicinity of the Dong Ha Bridge, or what was left of it, really did come to a halt. That odd circumstance was made even more evident when only moments after the structure had been destroyed and Jack was tending to Ripley's speedy recovery, two Vietnamese Air Force (VNAF) T-28 Trojan aircraft came on station. In the U.S. Air Force, T-28s were used almost exclusively for training pilots. In the VNAF they were used expeditiously to both train in and fight from. Binh's Marines were happy to get the support, however late.

The scene became reminiscent of the one Ripley had found himself in prior to going under the bridge when he and the others had watched, like spectators at a sporting event, Ha Si Luom stalk and kill the first T-54. The difference was that *everyone* was watching. On both sides of the river, but especially on the friendly side, the troops were up and out of their fighting holes pointing and cheering (the NVA were not cheering) as the lead T-28 made its run in on targets the Marines mostly could not see as they were just beyond the wood line north of the river. Ripley assumed they were targets, tanks and other pickings probably backed up on Highway One, stopped and waiting to cross the bridge that was no longer there for them.

The first T-28 made several very predictable low-level passes over enemy positions strafing and loosing ordnance. Binh's Marines roared with exuberance similar to that shown Ripley when they had congratulated him after blowing the bridge. It felt good, really good, to be giving some back to the enemy.

The actions of the men of the Soi Bien made Ripley think of similar times in Lima Company in 1967. His own Marines, his Raiders, would once in a while lose all sense of tactical propriety, sometimes even when fully locked on with the NVA, when close air support aircraft—especially the A-1 Skyraiders which were in many ways similar to the T-28s except they were larger, far more muscular, carried more armament, and could remain on station for what seemed like an eternity—rode in like the cavalry to the rescue and saved the day. Ripley could recall how he, his company gunny, his platoon commanders along with all the platoon sergeants and squad leaders would almost have to crack heads among their men who, for the moment, were up out of their fighting positions waving and yelling, a whoopin' and a hollerin', acting more like they were at a high school football game cheering rather than in the middle of a life-and-death struggle in the godforsaken jungles of northern South Vietnam.

After the first aircraft completed its run, "Dash-Two" as Ripley called him, began his relatively predictable, slow approach on some target yonder across the river. As he pickled iron from his bomb racks and began to climb out for the purpose of coming round again for another run, the Marines were shocked by something they had never before seen.

In the twinkling of an eye, they heard and saw an audible crush of hissing that followed the trail of a tiny wisp of smoke right up towards the T-28 attempting to gain altitude. There was a pronounced but muffled whoosh, a streak of something tracking the airplane and then, suddenly the T-28 was turned into a close and massive orange ball of flame.

John Ripley was taken aback by the size of the explosion. The bird must still have had a fair amount of ordnance on board. More incredible was that there was, in another instant, a blossoming parachute that appeared. How that pilot survived was beyond belief. His initial escape from death was a miracle, at least for the moment. His wildly oscillating parachute signaled to Ripley, a veteran of many dozens of jumps from his Force Recon and Royal Marine days, that this intrepid but instantaneously hapless pilot, who was probably just now experiencing his first parachute jump, had no idea on how to control his descent. The moderate northward-blowing winds aloft were slowly carrying him to the far side of the river. If only he knew to "slip" and dump air like all basic airborne students were taught. It was too late to learn now.*

The temporary victory's joy concluded in barely audible hushed remarks as the pilot and his chute were seen to come down on the wrong side of the river and he was taken prisoner. After that too short interlude, the men of the Soi Bien quietly and solemnly got back into the war.

Binh, even after Ripley blew the bridge, did not relent or relax. With two radio handsets, one in either hand, he was at once talking with Colonel Dinh in the TOC and his rifle company commanders. When directing his attention to his brigade commander he was giving situation reports, arranging additional fire support, or requesting medevac and resupply. (With the attachment of 20th Tank Battalion the resupply effort in Dong Ha was given far more priority than if there had only been Vietnamese Marines present.) When the communication was meant for his captains he was making sure his rifle companies were dug in, redistributing ammunition, medevacing only the most critically wounded, and preparing for the inevitable follow-on attacks the NVA were sure to mount.

Binh and Ripley together would momentarily assume that the enemy might still attempt to cross the river close to Dong Ha. Just upstream from the bridge, a few hundred meters west, was a small island not quite midway between each bank. Not much

---

* What Ripley and all the others present had just witnessed was the first observed-by-the allies use of the Soviet-built SA-7 or *Strela* shoulder-fired anti-aircraft missile.

more than an overgrown sandbar really, it was oblong in shape and on its one or two acres was a fair amount of heavy vegetation; some of it quite tall. Looking across the Cua Viet from the south side to the north from the banks immediately adjacent to the island, it was difficult to see what was going on. This might well be a spot to defend in case the enemy tried, under the cover of darkness, to get troops to the island first, and then get them to the south side. Binh would take Third Company from the reserve and place them into the line there.

The action in the Ai Tu TOC was still frenetic, like monitoring the disparate activities at that same, never-ending round-robin, fight-to-the-death wrestling tournament. With the demise of Camp Carroll there was one less situation to cover but the remaining action at each individual point of contact with the enemy was becoming more acute. Activity at Fire Support Base (FSB) Mai Loc, where Major Jim Joy and his advisory staff along with what was left of Vietnamese Marine Brigade 147 were holding on against, like everyone else, overwhelming odds, was increasing. The Marines were actually running out of ammunition even though there had been heroic efforts at resupply. It was about to become a decision of hold and die or make a fighting withdrawal with what forces there were and plan to regroup at some later point to fight again on more favorable terms.

Improving weather made it possible for American airpower to finally begin to become a factor in the battle. The added challenges and stresses of coordinating all of that airpower would further burden the already thinly stretched resources in the TOC. The allies also would soon see the full measure of what the Communists had in their anti-aircraft weapons inventory in addition to the earlier use of the SA-7.

Lieutenant Colonel Camper, during his helicopter extract from Camp Carroll just a few hours earlier, had demonstrated the presence of mind to call into the TOC and speak to Major Brookbank. He advised that a retaliatory strike on the abandoned position be worked up as the twenty-two artillery pieces had been left behind without being spiked. (The act of "spiking" an artillery piece is something all artillerymen are schooled in.

Rarely do they ponder actually having to do the deed for real. In the event of imminent defeat, surrender, or when a unit is about to be overrun, to keep the enemy from using the captured weapons as anything but a trophy or very large paperweight, procedure calls for the destruction of the artillery piece in question. That is accomplished by closing the breech and placing an ignited thermite grenade down the tube. The resulting high temperatures melt and seal the tube and breech together, rendering the weapon completely useless.) And by the time a response could be generated the firebase would be crawling with enemy soldiers as well. The air strike against the area around Camp Carroll would be the first major effort of the day.

After nearly four days of full-scale invasion in Quang Tri Province, from both the north and west, the major attacks MACV had predicted to take place in the central and southern portions of the country had yet to materialize. The regiments constituting the Third ARVN Division had essentially failed in their duties. The 57th had fled at Dong Ha, the 56th had surrendered at Camp Carroll and the Second was a nebulous, hodge-podge assortment still in the general vicinity of Cam Lo. One of the Second's three infantry battalions could not be accounted for. At Camp Carroll it was believed that the NVA had captured, intact, most if not all of the twenty-two artillery pieces positioned there. Except for the actions of the two Vietnamese Marine brigades, allied forces had so far essentially been swept from the field of battle by the enemy in Quang Tri Province.

The first major break, the closing off of Highway One with the Dong Ha Bridge's destruction, meant that the NVA's offensive effort would necessarily shift to the bridge at Cam Lo. Naval gunfire would continue to be used against those forces within range. Joel Eisenstein and the ANGLICO people in the TOC continued to remind Gerry Turley that the commanders onboard the various destroyers were breaking every rule in the book; coming in as close to shore as they could, violating what was called the "five-fathom curve" (Ships need a certain depth beneath their keels to operate safely. By operating in waters judged to be too shallow they risk damage to their hulls and especially to the sonar domes in their bows.) to milk every last inch of range from their guns, and pour steel on the enemy. For the American Navy, and for those counting on their support, it was a very good thing that there was no local submarine threat.

Marine Brigade 258 commander Colonel Dinh and his advisor Lieutenant Colonel Turley would have to figure a way to deny access to the Cam Lo Bridge as well. With Turley slated to head south in the morning, the man to assume his duties while he was in Saigon would be Major Jon Easley, the next senior American Marine there in the TOC. (Major Easley was actually the senior brigade advisor to Colonel Dinh and Brigade 258.) Until he departed, though, Turley would remain in charge. Like all the others, he had not slept nor had he had a decent meal in days. And he still had to deal with the diarrhea that continued to plague him. At least he could look forward to bringing all that allied airpower to bear on the NVA. With so much equipment and literally tens of thousands of troops massed and in the open, northern Quang Tri Province was the richest, juiciest target-rich environment Turley had ever witnessed. It was payback time, and with twelve hours or more until he might leave, there was much combat left to prosecute.

BRIGADE 369 HEADS NORTH

Brigade 369 was going north. The attachments included all the Marines of the First Artillery Battalion, the unit Captain George Philip was assigned to. With the introduction of this last brigade, the entire Vietnamese Marine Corps, every single infantry battalion and all their critical support units, would now be committed to the fight in Quang Tri Province.

The Tan Son Nhut flight line was crowded with what seemed to be row upon row of USAF C-130s; more Hercs than Philip had ever seen in one place at one time. It was an odd set of circumstances in that George Philip, who had left Vietnam just prior to the initiation of this offensive and only an hour earlier returned from a Hawaii R&R, was reentering an entirely new war.

The closest dozen planes all had props turning, their aft ramps lowered, and were already taking on the lead elements of

Brigade 369. The flights north to Phu Bai were crammed with men and material; everything the Vietnamese Marines would need to fight and kill NVA with except this time they left the pigs and chickens behind. At least for now.

Bat-21...the Shoot down
Quang Tri Province
April 2, 1972 1650 hrs

All the Vietnamese Marine officers serving in the Ai Tu TOC had fought in Tet '68, and every other major offensive that anyone cared to identify, for that matter. The conventional battle Americans had long spoiled and pined for—and got in Tet '68— was opportunity to kill the enemy in great quantity with very traditional Western methods in addition to Yankee technological know-how and precision. And they did. Even though that battle would ultimately be lost in the American media and on college campuses from sea to shining sea, the streets and buildings in the cities and towns, and the trails and rice paddies in the Vietnamese *hinterlands* ran thick with Communist blood; as there were what seemed like unlimited targets to eliminate. Especially among the more serious and seasoned professional officers and men of the RVN military, there was great delight in the killing of so many of the red devils in 1968.

As bad as things had been, as poorly as the three infantry regiments of the Third ARVN Division had so far performed, there was some upside to this enemy invasion. The battlefields of northern Quang Tri Province were just about now shaping up in a manner similar to Tet of '68; maybe on an even grander scale. In fact, never before in the experience of any of those currently present, Vietnamese or American, had so much enemy force and firepower been placed before them. Out in the open. With the ongoing, incremental improvements in the weather, Turley and his crew were looking for the airpower turkey shoot to begin, to "Cry havoc and let slip the dogs of war" on General Giap's multitudes.

The package of USAF aircraft assembled for the first ARCLIGHT mission to come on station after Ripley's destroying of the Dong Ha Bridge was small but impressive. Intending to attack ground targets in the vicinity of Camp Carroll, the three-plane cell of B-52s (call signs Copper 1, 2 and 3) were properly supported to meet myriad and as yet unknown enemy threats. Mission planners had tasked two F-4s (call signs Cain 1 and 2) to deal with a potential MiG threat, two F-105Gs (call signs Coy 1 and 2) armed with missiles designed to take out enemy surface-to-air missile (SAM) radars and sites, and two EB-66s (call signs Bat 21 and 22. Bat 21 was an EB-66C and Bat 22 was an EB-66E.) to assist with electronic counter measures (ECM) against SAMs launched at the American force.[1]

The shootdown of the EB-66C, known by call sign Bat 21, took place at about 1650 local time. The plane was hit by one of the many SAM-2 missiles fired at the entire group of aircraft involved in the ARCLIGHT strike from mobile launchers the NVA had brought to the front. Of the nine planes involved in this particular mission, Bat 21 was the only one lost to enemy fire. Of the six men in Bat 21's crew—a pilot, co-pilot, and four electronic warfare officers (EWO)—there was only one survivor.

Lieutenant Colonel Iceal Hambleton, at the grand old age of fifty-three, was the senior navigator in his squadron and took a spot in his plane among the EWOs.[2] As the only man who managed to safely eject from Bat 21 and as soon as his deployed parachute deposited him on *terra firma*, within two kilometers to the northeast of the bridge at Cam Lo, he would probably become the oldest ground combatant on the allied side. Hambleton's bird's-eye view of the world beneath him, as he slowly descended under canopy to the wrong side of the Cua Viet River, might have made him wonder how fortunate he was to have survived his plane's explosion. Where he was about to land was smack-dab in the middle of what looked like thousands and thousands of advancing enemy troops.

As he continued his parachute descent (from the altitude at which he ejected, his descent took several minutes), other air force planes in the vicinity tracked his progress and, in accordance with well-established standard operating procedures, immediately began preparing Hambleton's search-and-rescue (SAR) effort. His presence in close proximity to the Cam Lo Bridge would change, radically change, the fire support challenges facing RVN forces under pressure all across northeastern Quang Tri Province.

MEDEVAC AND SAR

The American sense of and commitment to basic goodness, loyalty, and chivalry was never more clearly demonstrated in war, in modern times especially, than in the serious resources dedicated to the search and rescue of downed air crews, attempts to extract or reinforce units in extreme peril or about to be overrun, or simply the near routine daily heroics of those personnel involved in all aspects of medevac and emergency helicopter extraction operations.

The American notion for placing high value on human life, along with the rescue and saving of downed comrades, was as much a part of their cultural proclivities as anything else. Dedication to recovering the wounded, leaving no one behind—in most cases— was also partly a function of the country's relative wealth. When Americans went to war they brought with them an entire infrastructure to care for the wounded. They invested tremendous resources into the expeditious treatment of battlefield casualties to ensure the highest possibility of survival.

The men slugging it out in Vietnam's jungles and rice paddies had strong confidence that if they were hit and required medevac, heaven and earth would be moved and many brave men unknown to them personally would risk incredible odds to get them out of harm's way. The near round-the-clock pervasiveness of helicopters throughout the four corps regions of Vietnam often ensured that even if a specific medevac bird was not available for immediate tasking, other helicopters nearby might well be able to assist. The "Cavalry," the Good Guys, the White Hats, whoever they were, it seemed like there was always someone around—above—to swoop in and attempt to save the day no matter the risks or consequences.

In the specific mission of recovering downed aircrews and those special operations forces working behind enemy lines, there was a whole other level of additional combat power that only a nation with near unlimited resources could attempt to bring to the battlefield.

VIETNAMESE MEDEVAC

For the Vietnamese the issue of medevac was an entirely different story. ARVN and Vietnamese Marine unit commanders were routinely forced to make life-and-death decisions involving their own troops far beyond those made by their American contemporaries. Solely a function of the resources available to them, or not available to them, the combat medevac realities for the average ARVN or TQLC infantryman offered considerably fewer chances for survival if he was seriously wounded in action.

John Ripley, in his role as an advisor to Third Battalion and experiencing everything the men of the Soi Bien experienced during his many months in the field with them, was witness to action the folks at home in America, even those who had served in combat wholly apart from their allies in Vietnam, would have had great difficulty in processing let alone sympathizing with. As the operational tempo intensified during the Nguyen Hue Offensive, he gained further insight into the mental and emotional toughness men like Binh were routinely required to demonstrate as they applied very limited battlefield resources in their effort to defeat a tenacious foe.

So ingrained for Americans was the concept of decent medical treatment and of expeditious medevac once a man was wounded, it was difficult to imagine any other option. And yet, for the Vietnamese soldier or Marine who was severely wounded during heavy action to the point that he was non ambulatory and his side was, at least for the time being, on the disadvantaged end of things, the options were quite limited. It would probably have been the Viet Cong or the NVA, organizations likewise resource-challenged in similar ways, who would have had more empathy for the heartrending decisions South Vietnamese commanders and those men having to be left behind were often forced to make.

The process for dealing with those to be left behind was rather basic. Ripley had witnessed it just a few times prior to the beginning of this offensive. He would, unfortunately, be witness to it again before the current offensive concluded. The Vietnamese, relative to their American brothers-in-arms, had few helicopters of their own. What helicopters there were available were used primarily for command and control purposes or as weapons platforms. The medevac mission ranked below those in importance. Helicopters were far too precious to be risked in such a manner. American advisors, if there was American helicopter support nearby, would often call in what they could for medevac for their allies. By early 1972 however, with the ongoing drawdown and Vietnamization of the war, that capability was rapidly diminishing.

When a position needed to be abandoned those men to be left behind were identified and set aside. Even though it was probably not standard enough to have been written down, Ripley surmised that this was the way it was likely done in other RVN units in the most extreme situations. The process he witnessed was dignified, respectful, and in its own way, as tender as it could be. The wounded were made to be as comfortable as possible. There was usually some sort of a last rites exchange between parting comrades. Identity cards and important papers, letters and pictures, always kept in a man's left breast pocket, were taken so that they might later go to next of kin.

For Ripley the Occidental, it was interesting to note that the men were divided up by their faith, Buddhists and Catholics. Each man was given a hand grenade. Buddhists were given the grenades with the pins still in them (The cotter pins that held the spoon in place were bent in, made straight and were thus easier to pull as the wounded may not have had the strength to pull a "normal" pin.) so that they would have the option to sometime later take their own lives rather than fall into the hands of the advancing NVA who might torture before killing them anyway.

For the Catholic troops, the suicide option was obviated by taking grenades with the pins already pulled and placing them under the back of their head, in the nape of the neck, with the spoon down so that there was sufficient pressure to keep the grenade from going off. As long as there was pressure on the spoon, the grenade would not explode. Once a man lost consciousness or died his head would likely turn to the side and the grenade would then be activated.

Most Americans would never understand. To the Vietnamese this battle, every battle, was battle for survival. The decision to leave men behind, to implicitly expect them to blow themselves up rather than face an even more painful ending if captured, was not taken lightly. What other choices, what other options were there? The responsibility for the mission given and for the lives of those still able to fight rested squarely on the man in command. If one might step back one might see some compassion; certainly dignity in this sole option. Even behind that veil of stern decisiveness, of outward inscrutability, Ripley knew Binh's heart, and how he cared for his Marines. He could only begin to imagine how much that decision would forever weigh in upon him. In risking his own life countless times and in the extreme, Ripley was thankful that he did not also have to make those calls.

ATTEMPTS TO RESCUE BAT 21

The near-instantaneously begun rescue effort for Iceal Hambleton, now referred to almost exclusively and only as "Bat 21," got very ugly very early.

Whenever American attack and bomber aircraft were launched for a strike like the kind just run near Camp Carroll, a Search and Rescue (SAR) package was an integral part of the mission plan. When Bat 21 was hit, there were several dedicated SAR aircraft in the vicinity in addition to a number of nearby U.S. Army helicopters conducting other support.

The first two aircraft to respond and attempt pickup of Bat 21 was an army Huey, call sign Blueghost 39, and an AH-1 Cobra gunship for fire support, call sign Blueghost 28. Neither aircraft were officially part of the dedicated SAR. Like so many of the other helicopter crews the Marine *covans* had come to depend on, Blueghosts 39 and 28 were just two more crews willing to go anywhere and do anything for comrades in need. As they approached the area for extract, Blueghost 39 was quickly shot down. Three of its four-man crew were instantly KIA. The fourth crew member would turn up later in Hanoi as a POW. Blueghost 28 was also hit by ground fire, forced to retire from the area, but was able to crash land near the coast without loss of life. The Cobra was a complete loss. The SAR effort for Hambleton would only devolve from there.[3]

Another aspect of "typical" SAR operations was that they were almost always conducted in remote areas; areas away from where other allied forces were involved in ground combat. Given those circumstances, it was entirely reasonable and practical that the air force then control all air power and fire support within the area of the intended rescue. This was done to minimize the chances of friendly forces being hit by friendly ordnance. The Americans called it "Big sky, little bullet." That became routine standard operating procedure. No problem. No problem unless there was a battlefield covered with enemy troops and equipment all in the attack and arrayed as perfect targets. There was initially very poor and ineffective communication between the airborne SAR forces and the Ai Tu TOC. Had there been proper discussion, the people on the ground would have strongly advised against the attempted helicopter extract.

The matter of Bat 21's rescue should have become just one more issue the staff in the Ai Tu TOC had to contend with as the NVA onslaught continued. The allies knew Hambleton's exact location within one hundred meters thanks to the standard rescue radio he had which was carried by all aircrew. His position to the northeast of the Cam Lo Bridge put him solidly in enemy territory. After his landing, a number of SAR aircraft had laced the ground around his position with "area denial" weapons to discourage the enemy from attempting capture. To Turley and crew the world around them, the shrinking world around them, was much, much bigger than just Bat 21. With so many targets now revealing themselves it was finally about time to apply the full measure of air support to kill bad guys.

It came as a complete shock to the personnel in the Ai Tu TOC when, at about 2115 on Easter night, word came that the Seventh Air Force was about to undertake a massive SAR for Bat 21. The first thing they did was establish a twenty-seven-kilometer no-fire ring around Hambleton's *known* position. Twenty-seven kilometers. Twenty-seven kilometers in every direction. An area that size included virtually the entire battlefield. Any reasonable person could see, without even looking at the map, that this was foolish, crazy, downright idiotic. Turley needed to destroy the Cam Lo Bridge. He needed to bring whatever fire power to bear on targets that were everywhere across the northern I Corps landscape. Instead they were virtually sending an invitation to the NVA to continue their invasion almost unopposed. Someone up the chain of command would surely agree.

There was certainly furor and gnashing of teeth when all fire support was terminated to accommodate air force SAR procedure. The Vietnamese officers in the TOC were stunned. Their American advisors alongside them there were stunned as well. And angry. Colonel Dinh, the Brigade 258 commander, who had been around, experienced enough of war's strangeness, witnessed the subtle and not so subtle differences between the Oriental and the Occidental, stood next to Turley. He raised his left index finger, looked at his friend, and speaking with stoic resignation and equanimity simply asked: "Just one?" In his face and voice Gerry could, at once, sense both calm understanding and total incredulity; acceptance for the American quixotic beliefs and bitter frustration for the complete lack of prudence these actions would have on everyone else who was not an American, as well as the few U.S. advisors there with him.[4]

Turley was not so accepting. Neither was his air liaison officer, USAF Major Dave Brookbank. Together they and the others in the TOC furiously began to work the system of phones and radios calling back to Danang and Saigon to change the fire support situation. It was to no avail, at least initially.

The unfortunate remarks attributed to an air force general in Danang were probably an accurate reflection of how most regular Americans felt by April 1972. The general spoke initially under the assumption that there were two survivors rather than one: "I would rather lose two ARVN divisions than those two U.S. Air Force crewmen."[5] Who could blame him or most Americans for those feelings? After so much time, so much blood and treasure invested...and for what? As far as the American effort in Vietnam was concerned, there was little that anyone could point to that was tangible and positive. And yet the general's remarks also reflected the attitude of Americans who came to Vietnam, gave everything they had, and somehow missed the kind of personal connections Gerry Turley, John Ripley, George Philip, and most of the others who served in the advisory capacity had eventually made very late in the war with Vietnamese citizens fully committed to keeping their country free of Communist domination. Along with that, the Vietnamese had no natural constituency among the American population sympathetic to their cause—like Israel did with millions of Jewish Americans—and fewer and fewer powerful politicians willing to stick their necks out to support a situation growing increasingly unpopular.

Gerry Turley and Dave Brookbank worked the radios and phones feverishly to get someone in authority to come to their senses. To his front, Turley still faced several divisions of NVA still bent on the destruction of the Third ARVN Division—which was almost already accomplished—and the two still stubbornly holding on Marine brigades. To his rear was all of the MACV staff and whoever else there was still sniping and challenging his very legitimacy.

The only fire support Turley's small group could muster was what remaining ARVN and Vietnamese Marine artillery there was left, which was not very much. Bending the rules, he and his American Marine advisors instead placed a six-kilometer ring around Bat 21, assumed responsibility for his safety, and fired what missions they could. Because naval gunfire could not possibly reach Bat 21's position, Gerry ensured that Joel Eisenstein and his crew continued to apply those resources whenever possible. It was all he could do, all they could do, as Easter was coming to an unceremonious end in northern Quang Tri Province.

Turley needed to get some rest before he presented himself to a MACV staff he was certain would happily crucify him for crimes he was not yet sure he had committed. As he tried to begin to back off, to prepare to get a few hours of sleep—his first in four days—he ate several bites of a c-ration meal but did not have the appetite to finish it. Taking his field jacket to use as a pillow, Gerry found a spot on the floor in the most remote portion of the bunker. As exhausted as he was, sleep did not come easily. Even with his body essentially inert, his mind still raced. He wondered, almost wistfully, as he painfully willed himself to slow down, what else he might do to assure survival and what else could go wrong short of their being overrun. He would have that question answered soon enough.

The no-fire zone around Bat 21 would eventually be reduced to a still substantial but more manageable area. Lieutenant Colonel Iceal Hambleton would ultimately be rescued eleven days later. It was a rescue made possible by the ingenuity, tenacity, blood, and sweat of countless very brave men, both American and Vietnamese. By the time his recovery was completed his SAR effort would be the most expensive in the history of the Vietnam War. Eleven Americans were killed and one became a POW as a direct result of the Bat 21 SAR effort. In addition to the American human cost, several aircraft were lost and many, many others incurred heavy damage from anti-aircraft fire. The greatest tragedy, the greatest unknown of the entire Bat 21 saga however, would be the unquantifiable price paid by Vietnamese civilians and RVN troops lost as a result of firepower *not* used against enemy forces when it could have and should have been, and how events might have turned had allied efforts to stop the NVA not been so egregiously hampered during that period.

BACK TO THE BATTLE FOR DONG HA

For the Nguyen-Hue Offensive's participants, Easter Sunday 1972 was a day seemingly without end. Near the site of the still burning Dong Ha Bridge (the bridge structure would burn for several days) the battle resumed in a way different than it had been before John Ripley was able to destroy it. The downing of the VNAF aircraft by some sort of new, never-before-seen weapon and subsequent capture of the pilot by the NVA diminished the satisfaction Binh's men had temporarily enjoyed.

The NVA spearhead's momentum had clearly been blunted by the destruction of the Dong Ha Bridge. Action on the north side of the river had slowed significantly, almost completely, once the bridge had been blown. It was obvious to both Ripley and Binh that the enemy unit commanders were probably huddling up and discussing their other options or, more likely, awaiting further instruction from somewhere higher up the ponderous Communist chain of command.

To Ripley the enemy appeared to have temporarily lost interest in the fight. Perhaps they had been ordered to finally conserve ammunition. The NVA tanks did not have, right near the bridge area, too many targets worthy of their main guns anyway as Binh's men were dispersed and well dug in. None of the T-54s had line of sight shots at the few ARVN M-48s still mixed in with the Marines near the river. Even though there was a significant amount of enemy force arrayed against the Marines right there at the bridgehead, the bulk of the NVA forces were still lined up, backed up thanks to the bridge being destroyed, on Highway One or on positions immediately adjacent to it extending way back up the road. They were a perfect north-south linear target for an air strike had there been one; anti-aircraft threat notwithstanding.

The enemy now really had only two tactical choices. They could wait until it got dark and attempt to send groups of infantrymen across the river in rafts, small boats or whatever other craft they might have; or simply head west to Cam Lo.

Where he could not get to immediately in person, Binh used his radios and foot messengers in continuing to direct the tactical actions of his companies. He also maintained ongoing contact with Colonel Dinh in the TOC. Binh and Ripley began discussing possible displacement of some units to meet the likely changes in case the NVA shifted their effort towards the west of town. The old railroad bridge, approximately two kilometers upstream, still stood and was capable of handling light traffic. The railroad bridge was too far inland for naval gunfire to hit. And with the apparent new and extremely formidable anti-aircraft capability, it was unlikely the men of the Soi Bien would be receiving much in the way of any future air support. The railroad bridge was also too far away from the current action to send an independent company or even the Bravo Command Group at this stage of the battle. Even though Binh's battalion would soon go back to the routine practice of splitting forces into Alpha and Bravo groups, he currently needed to concentrate what force he could in and around Dong Ha.

Second Company maintained the Soi Bien's western flank several hundred meters west of the bridge. Binh moved Third Company from the reserve position into the line a few hundred meters upstream from the burning bridge. He placed them near the river's edge immediately opposite the sandbar-island in the event the NVA tried to cross from the north bank to the island and then to the south bank. It was an obvious move as the sandbar's vegetation masked the view from either side of the river. First and Fourth Companies remained at their previous positions, although Binh had them each extend their open flanks to cover a broader area, and to also defend against the predictable night crossing.

Binh still had a hold on the ARVN tank battalion commander who continued to cooperate with less than complete enthusiasm. Most of the tanks were redeployed into the built-up areas of Dong Ha where they could observe and shoot on enemy targets from behind what cover and rubble there was. The logistical requirements for maintaining all of that armor assured that resupply and medevac for Binh's Marines was better than it would otherwise have been.

Second Lieutenant Nguyen Luong and his men were ordered to remain in place for the evening in their blocking position across the road a few hundred meters back from the bridge. As Binh had spread the First and Fourth Companies over a broader, longer front at the river, Luong's platoon now had responsibility for the real estate to his immediate north, which included the approaches to the burning Dong Ha Bridge. Even without being told, it was obvious to Luong that the NVA would likely try to cross near the bridge when darkness fell. It is what he would have ordered if he was one of the NVA leaders. It gave the new platoon commander, who had witnessed more than his share of the day's action but had yet to engage or lead his men in battle from his location just back from the bridge, an added sense of confidence that one of the M-48s had taken up a night position adjacent to his own tiny command post near to what was now the "old" tire shop.

No one would have ever accused the NVA forces in the assault at Dong Ha of having a lack of zeal. No one would question their tenacity or focus on victory; the casualties they had inflicted on all of the innocent civilians turned refugees who had already fled the area or lay dead where they were slaughtered were proof of that. The Communists wanted Dong Ha. Dong Ha was the key to the rest of Quang Tri Province. If they could capture and control Dong Ha, they could likely capture the city of Quang Tri, and after Quang Tri they would again attempt to retake Hue. At this stage of their offensive it was essential to take the northernmost portion of the country for a whole number of reasons; all of them political, all of them psychological.

At this stage of the enemy offensive it was essential that the few remaining southern defenders hold onto the northernmost province of their country for a whole number of reasons; all of them political, all of them psychological. The main difference between the two sides, as darkness crossed the landscape in northern I Corps, was that the Saigon government had far fewer people defending it at the point of contact than did the invaders trying to capture it.

Depending on one's point of view, the NVA were either to be admired for their focus on capturing Dong Ha, or castigated for the uncreative ways in which their leadership cavalierly poured men into battle at the point of contact where the odds were momentarily not in their favor. Perhaps it was due to the Communists' slavish devotion to following whatever was the current party line, the inability to deviate from a pre-established plan and risk the criticism of superiors. Their plan called for taking Dong Ha *at* Dong Ha. With the bridge now gone, that was more of a challenge. Even so, they continued with their frontal assault mentality rather than initially attempt to go around, or go to some alternate plan. The near relentless, near suicidal night attacks right into the teeth of the dug in Soi Bien were ineffective; like crazed red ants attacking some inanimate object dropped onto their nest by kids enjoying the view of the creatures' frenzied, meaningless response.

While few would speak ill of the bravery of the individual NVA soldiers who continued to follow orders, there were no doubt many fathers and mothers somewhere up north without a voice to complain of the senseless manner in which their sons were slaughtered. For the men of the Soi Bien who spent the night of April 2, 1972 near the edge of the Cua Viet, there would be little or no sleep but no small amount of satisfaction in knowing they had gotten the better of their hated foe. At least for now.

The fighting had died down some after the destruction of the Dong Ha Bridge. As Binh and his trusted advisor worked to ensure that their four rifle companies were reprovisioned and positioned best to repel those invaders who were sure to come in the night, there continued to be a slow but steady exchange of rifle and machine gun fire between the invaders and defenders. Nothing heavier.

The men of the Soi Bien did not have long to wait after dark in having to repel the enemy. Even though it was apparent that the NVA could get men across the river at the old railroad bridge, and they did, they seemed unable to resist the notion of going directly against the defenses Third Battalion had placed in front of them. They were in fact able to get men over to the tiny island in the middle of the Cua Viet River who then attempted to cross the shorter distance to the south side. They were also able to get men across at or near the Dong Ha Bridge.

For the Marines of First and Fourth Companies near the bridge, and the Marines of Third Company across from the island, the evening allowed little rest. It would not be until the next morning's early light that they would realize what a "turkey shoot" they had been involved in. They would never know for sure how many of the red devils they killed as so many of the dead and wounded NVA were ultimately swept out to sea by the fairly fast running waters of the Cua Viet River right there in Dong Ha. The Marines would find few whole bodies; instead mostly parts of enemy soldiers literally blown to bits from the nighttime *melee*.

Luong's initial legitimate action occurred that night. With the benefit of some very crude but sufficient night vision binoculars from the tank adjacent to his position, Luong and his men spied the arrival of what was probably a reconnaissance squad. Taking them under fire with several M-79 grenade launchers once they made it up onto level ground after leaving the minor safety of the river bank, the enemy soldiers who were killed were killed within the first few seconds of being taken under fire. Luong was not sure but his men thought that the few survivors, if any, retreated back into the river. Luong had finally drawn first blood against his sworn enemy.

Simultaneous to the NVA attempts to sneak units of infantry across the river at various places opposite the town of Dong Ha, they also began shifting some portion of their armor forces to the west towards Cam Lo. The road that ran west on the north bank of the Cua Viet and parallel to the river, at least the portion capable of supporting the massive T-54s, was not wide at all. It was really nothing more than a rice paddy dike, in most places barely wide enough for one tank to traverse.

Ripley could hear the clanking sounds of enemy armor from across the river. On the first shot of his first naval gunfire fire mission of the night, they miraculously scored a direct hit on a westward-moving tank. The road itself was perfectly aligned for the ships off shore so that they could easily fire longitudinally along its east-west running axis. The burning tank lit up the surrounding area, making it easier for Ripley to see and adjust subsequent rounds onto other targets. The naval gunfire ships again breeched the five fathom curve to give the Marines as much protection and support as they could. The targets they were currently scoring hits on were at or very near the absolute maximum range of the ships' guns. Ripley wanted every last yard or meter of range that he could get; and got them.

In addition to the especially effective naval gunfire, a B-52 ARCLIGHT mission was run against the area to the north of the river. The bombs happened to impact within moments of the naval gunfire strikes. The hundreds and hundreds of bombs hit numerous NVA vehicles and personnel. Ripley, Binh, and all the men of the Soi Bien on the south side of the river were able to hear the subsequent mournful cries of the wounded and dying. Ground combat action would continue, intermittently but at times with extreme intensity, throughout the night.

With all that was taking place, Ripley and Binh were actually able to stabilize the battalion lines and try to get some rest. Binh rightly had great confidence in his company commanders and the Marines of the Soi Bien. He and Ripley had done all they could to prepare the battalion for whatever might take place during the night.

CHAPTER TWENTY-NINE

"We're about to be Bombed!"

T*he ARVN 20th Tank Battalion* had established a nighttime command post (CP) of sorts in some dried rice paddies just off of Highway One several hundred meters south of the river. From a communications and security standpoint it made sense for Binh to place his headquarters element together with the more substantial resources of the tankers. From a command and control standpoint they were further back than either Binh or Ripley preferred, but again, the companies were well run and prepared for the night. Binh and Ripley both needed some rest.

It was approaching midnight when Binh and Ripley finally had gotten things to the point where they were willing to take a break. As exhausted as Dai Uy Ripley was, he could not help but smile broadly at his "younger brother" and trusted radio operator. For all his Oriental stoicism and reticence Nha, especially when he was tired, was an open book. Obliquely but obviously he communicated his need for sleep to his "elder brother" Ripley who chuckled approvingly, and with friendly reassurance told Nha in pidgin Vietnamese and an odd assortment of universal hand signals: "Don't worry. We sleep."

Settling down on a piece of dried rice paddy, not too far from one of the several M-113 Armored Personnel Carriers (APC) which was part of the mobile CP for 20th Tanks, they placed Nha's radio between them as they had consistently done on every one of the many nights they had already had together in the bush. As tired as they constantly were, their senses were reliably keen enough, acute enough, to be roused from whatever level of sleep they were in whenever the radio was keyed.

Ripley intended to use his helmet for a pillow, like always. He unsnapped his chin strap, placed the helmet behind him, arranged his weapon and 782 gear adjacent to his body so that he might latch onto them in an instant if needed.

It was almost exactly midnight when Ripley finally reclined his head and back towards his helmet, hoping for a bit of sleep. He would have sworn that the very act of his touching his head to the helmet somehow flipped a switch or completed a strange circuit that caused the entire northern skyline, from the west to the east, to near instantaneously ignite in flame.

No one among the men of the Soi Bien or the ARVN 20th Tank Battalion had ever seen what was taking place. It was as if they were all of a sudden living inside some low-budget science fiction movie. From four or five or six spots north of the river and spread out all across the horizon the sky had been lit up; night briefly became day. They correctly assumed it came from some other new weapon the men on the battlefield had never seen. What they had just witnessed was the coordinated launching of an entire battery of SA-2 anti-aircraft missiles. No allied ground forces had ever seen them launched from this close by before. In case the Marines had been hoping for further close air support, even after the earlier shoot down of the T-28, those hopes seemed to rapidly slip away as the missiles just now fired soared heavenward toward some unseen targets.

The multiple missile launches scared everyone a lot, even Ripley. But neither Ripley nor Binh nor Nha nor any of the other Marines in the headquarters group were so scared that they were not able to finally grab a few hours sleep while the men at the river carried on with their tenacious defense of Dong Ha.

BRIGADE 369 ARRIVES IN PHU BAI

The late evening flight from Saigon to Phu Bai for Captain Philip was far different than his earlier-in-the-day flight from Honolulu. While returning from the islands, George had had time to sleep although he was not really able to, time to eat, and too much time to ponder the unpleasant ground situation he was returning to.

There was no one to communicate with except an occasional, bored stewardess with whom he could only make small talk. It was an especially strange sensation to be returning to war on a virtually empty jetliner. That he was the plane's sole passenger was not lost on the young captain. It seemed to symbolize his country's effort to forget about and move beyond Vietnam.

The C-130 George and Bob Sheridan were on was, like all the others currently supporting this mission, crammed full of men and material. Passenger comfort, if it had ever been a consideration, was well down the list of concerns. During most of the flight the two *covans* discussed, at a volume well above normal because of the interior cabin noise, what little they knew and how much they needed to find out. They were anxious to learn the disposition of the various Vietnamese Marine units and what had happened to all their American advisor friends spread across northwestern Quang Tri Province.

At this stage of the enemy offensive, chaos still reigned and communications were shoddy. A complete picture of the ground situation had not yet been made available to the reinforcing units. The first order of business was to get the Vietnamese Marines of Brigade 369 into the fight where they were needed most. Detailed plans for their employment would evidently follow, or so Major Sheridan and Captain Philip surmised.

It was just past midnight when the C-130s that included Major Sheridan and Captain Philip as passengers began to land, one after another after another at four- or five-minute intervals, and do their engines running offload there at the Phu Bai airstrip. Once the troops and all their gear were hurriedly pushed out and on the ground, each plane would power up and take off so that the next C-130 could land. The presence of Brigade 369 and all of the other units attached would have been an impressive, reassuring sight if this had all taken place during daylight and if they had all staged together. Two of Brigade 369's three infantry battalions, the Second and the Fifth, had landed ahead of Sheridan and Philip, and had immediately pressed forward, somewhere toward the town of Quang Tri. The two *covans* were not able to determine their location but would hope to find them at daylight. The third and final infantry battalion, the Ninth, would be up in the morning along with Colonel Chung, the brigade commander.

The enemy invasion was still well to the north of Phu Bai and things were quiet locally, although from time to time the sound of rifle fire in or near surrounding villages could be heard. The Marines who were with the two American advisors put out security to ring the airfield. With that done, most of the men were able to get several hours of sleep that night.

It was essentially an uneventful night, compared to what the Soi Bien or Turley and crew had been engaged in. Even though he was not yet back in heavy combat, he was back in Vietnam—almost— "as far as the east was from the west." Situated next to Bob Sheridan, Captain Philip could not resist the inevitable thought as he drifted off to sleep atop 81mm mortar ammo crates serving as their field-expedient cots: "Not more than twenty-four hours ago I was in Hawaii where the greatest risk was getting sunburned." In the morning they would head north, and back into the cauldron.

"WE'RE ABOUT TO BE BOMBED!"

The sleep that Gerry Turley so desperately needed was long in coming but was not of any quality. There was no way to relax, and even though he had finally drifted off into a sleep that was more than he had had for the last four days and was grateful for the break, it was very rudely and shortly interrupted.

Turley had essentially turned over operations to Major Jon Easley, the American Marine who would head up the advisory effort in the TOC while Gerry was in Saigon. It was about 2345 local time when Gerry last looked at his watch before drifting off to a marginal slumber.

It was at approximately 0240, not quite three hours later, when Gerry was shaken awake by Major Regan Wright; one of the American Marine artillery advisors working in the Ai Tu TOC. "Get up, Colonel! We're about to be bombed!"

Like before, just as it had been when those strange Saigon colonels had arrived to visit as if coming from some mystical Never-Never Land, Turley had to remind himself that he was not hallucinating. He wished he were just having some sort of bad dream. But no. He was now awake and Major Wright was not joking. This entire thing was "Hu's on First?," the Keystone Cops, and *Candid Camera* combined and to the extreme. He could at least now stop worrying about what else might go wrong.

"Major Wright, what the hell is going on?"

"They're gonna bahhhm us!"

"Wait a minute, Regan. Say that again …"

"They're gonna bomb us. The B-52s are gonna bomb us."

"Oh, shit. Now tell me …"

"Dave Brookbank just got the word that we should get our heads down. They're gonna bomb Ai Tu."

"They can't do that. We're still here."

"They don't know that."

"When are we supposed to get hit?"

"Twenty minutes!"

So much for trying to get a little rest before meeting the executioner. Maybe Turley might be spared whatever indignity that awaited him at MACV, and he would instead be blown to bits by his own air force. As it turned out, the fog of war had never lifted; never diminished. When the army colonel advising General Giai had moved his division headquarters south to Quang Tri City he had informed Saigon. What he had not told Saigon was that he had left his fire support people in Ai Tu. The decision makers in Saigon were left with the impression that *all* of Ai Tu was abandoned and currently crawling with Communists. No one thought to check with anyone and now someone somewhere, probably in Saigon, had decided it wise to conduct an ARCLIGHT on Ai Tu.

Turley was back in the operations center portion of the TOC in a flash. Dave Brookbank and the others there with him were continuing to try to get Saigon to intervene; to divert or abort the mission. They were having no luck. Between the spotty radio and telephone communications it appeared as if the planes were inbound and only moments from "bombs away."

Of the many things the U.S. Air Force prided itself on was a zealous and fastidious devotion to getting bombs on target as meticulously planned. Getting bombs on target at the precisely orchestrated moment was a major portion of the organization's Holy Grail. Acts of or intervention by God Himself were the only things that could cause change to be considered, and only begrudgingly.

In the communications section of the TOC the Americans had the emergency frequencies for the B-52 radios. They were referred to as GUARD. Since they could not get higher headquarters to intervene on their behalf, the only option left was to attempt to contact the inbound aircraft directly, via GUARD. Even though they might come up on those frequencies, no one in the TOC had a way to truly authenticate to the men up there listening who they were on the ground. As if taken from a warped scene from the movie *Dr Strangelove*, Major Brookbank was like Peter Sellers playing the visiting Royal Air Force officer trying to recall a rogue-launched strike on the Soviet Union by the crazed American, General Jack D. Ripper. The difference was that Brookbank's action was not satire. There was no humor.

Brookbank did not have the authority or the codes to abort or recall the mission. The crews of the B-52s would be professional enough to question his authenticity. Would the men in those crews not think it possible that enemy linguists were doing the talking, or that maybe they had been able to coerce American POWs to help in this ruse? The people in the TOC could only pray, and most of them had already begun to, that the men above would somehow believe them.

As he entered this portion of the bunker Gerry could see Brookbank already working to do what he could do. Gerry advised him anyway: "Dave, go up on GUARD and tell 'em we're still here. Tell 'em what squadron you were in. Tell them where you trained. Give them the names of squadron mates and old commanding officers. Tell them where you went to flight school, when you went to flight school…just keep talking …"

Major Brookbank started talking into the radio, with those around him also excitedly chiming in, telling him what else to say, what to add. He started talking, and for the next several minutes did not stop. (Due to the way the system worked there was no exchange on this frequency, no acknowledgment of message received. The men in the TOC could only assume—and keep praying—that they were being heard by the men in the lumbering bombers.) The only way they would know if they had been heard, and believed, would be whether they got blown to bits or not.

Major Brookbank kept talking, passing more personal information about himself, anything to make him sound like a real, live, breathing American Air Force officer fifty thousand feet below them square in the cross-hairs of their bomb sites. There was no acknowledgement from the aircraft somewhere nine miles above them. No one was exactly certain when the planes would be at their weapons release point. As Brookbank continued to speak, the men there in the TOC continued to look up into the ceiling a few feet above them as if they would somehow be able to get a glimpse of the bombs falling onto the Ai Tu TOC and witness their impact the micro-second before they would all be vaporized.

The tension in the Ai Tu TOC had never been higher than it now was. After all they had been through in these last days, after all they had been able to coordinate, salvage and accomplish, what a horrible, nasty twist of fate to have the end come by mistake, and be destroyed by your own side.

Major Brookbank kept talking. He gave them the TOC's grid coordinates. He gave them his wife's name and where she currently lived. He just kept talking into the microphone hoping it was being transmitted into the ether and being received, via GUARD, by crews in the B-52s way up there who would understand that all these Americans and their Vietnamese allies really were down there in Ai Tu.

From fifty thousand feet, when bombs are dropped, the time to impact is several minutes. Brookbank kept talking. The clock slowly ticked away, and Brookbank kept talking.

As the clock ticked down to the moment of expected bomb impact, the tension inside the TOC increased. The men kept looking up into the ceiling of the bunker. Brookbank kept talking. The second hand of the main clock on the wall of the TOC near the main situation map swept past the moment of planned impact. Nothing. The tension did not diminish. The clock was not synchronized to those aboard the bombers. A minute passed.

Brookbank kept talking. The tension remained high. Another minute ended without their destruction. Brookbank kept talking. Another minute was gone; and then another. Five minutes down and they were still breathing, even though in a very tense manner.

The United States Air Force always bombed on time. In particular, the vaunted Strategic Air Command which owned all B-52s, the creation and pride and joy of General Curtis LeMay—"Bomber" LeMay—the man whose strategic thinking included the horribly effective firebombing of Japanese cities, perhaps the single most powerful American military personality of the Cold War, would have surely then blown a gasket to know *his* boys in *his* bombers had been diverted or failed to release on time. Six minutes passed, then seven...ten minutes. There was never an acknowledgement from the airborne B-52s. At twenty minutes the danger was probably gone. The tension subsided. They began to breathe easier, but had been worn down further by the extra excitement and adrenalin expenditures. The men in the bombers must have believed Dave Brookbank, the current man of the hour, at least in the Ai Tu TOC.

With that danger diminished they could now go back to focus solely on working to stop the ever-advancing red hordes with the ever-diminishing ground resources available. Not surprisingly, Gerry Turley never even tried to go back to sleep during the remainder of the night.

Enroute to Phu Bai
Early Monday morning April 3, 1972

When Lieutenant Colonel Gerry Turley departed the Ai Tu TOC on early Monday morning he was unclear if he was coming back or not. He left his appointed place of duty believing he had done everything he could have to fight the good fight. He had given 100 percent from the moment he had been informally but formally and legally but illegally placed in charge. And now he was headed south to be judged by people he was certain would not be at all amenable to his opinions or perspectives, or empathetic to the circumstances to which he had been forced to respond.

Gerry Turley had just concluded four nonstop days of coordinating the most intense combat he had yet experienced against a determined and numerically superior Communist foe. Now he was headed in a different direction to shore up his rear with a MACV staff which he believed considered him to be, at best, a serious nuisance or at worst, as some sort of enemy. He would much rather have continued on in the TOC against the NVA. That would have been the simpler task.

The agglomeration of Vietnamese and American military officers who, under Turley's leadership, had melded together during the most unfavorable conditions, into a proactive, productive team were stretched and tired but still functioning; and giving the enemy far more trouble than anyone would have expected.

In the last twenty-four hours the ground combat situation had improved. The Dong Ha Bridge's destruction had slowed the heretofore unstoppable NVA *juggernaut*. The bridge's destruction bought response time for the allies that, to Turley and his mates in the TOC, was being partially squandered by the seemingly futile attempt to save Bat 21 because of the restrictions being placed on critical fire support. The Vietnamese Marines, horribly outnumbered all across the map, were still managing to exact a tremendous blood price from the NVA at every point of contact.

Sunday evening had been anything but calm in Dong Ha. The defense of the southern shore of the Cua Viet continued throughout the night and into the early morning, almost all of it right at the shoreline. When it was light enough Binh and Ripley, who had both actually finally been able to sleep for three or four hours, inspected their company's positions. What they found were a number of horribly mangled bodies of NVA soldiers who had somehow made it to the south bank of the river into the combined, withering fire of the Marines and their tanker allies. The men of the Soi Bien were convinced that these bodies represented a small percentage of the enemy forces who had attempted the in-vain continuous night crossing under fire. The rest—however many there were—never even made it out of the fast-moving Cua Viet and their bodies were carried down river and ultimately into the South China Sea.

As the sun rose over all of northern I Corps the men of the Soi Bien, incredibly outnumbered, were still solidly in control of Dong Ha. It was apparent to all that the enemy had, under cover of darkness, begun the shifting of forces, at least partially, a bit upstream toward Cam Lo.

Aside from the Soi Bien at Dong Ha, the only viable allied ground forces in northern Quang Tri Province still capable of fighting were the Marines of Brigades 147 and 258. (Brigade 258 was Third Battalion's current parent unit.) Wherever there were Vietnamese Marines the NVA had to pour men and resources into the battle at rates above what must have been planned for.

The fighting at Mai Loc had grown particularly brutal. In the same period that saw Third Battalion involved at the river and bridge areas in Dong Ha, the Marines of Brigade 147 at Fire Support Base (FSB) Mai Loc were likewise facing similar odds against vastly superior NVA forces. With unrelenting enemy pressure it was evident that the FSB would probably soon become untenable. Even prior to Camp Carroll's surprise surrender, the Brigade 147 commander, Colonel Bao, and his senior American Marine advisor, Major Jim Joy, had discussed such an eventuality and developed plans for a fighting withdrawal.

By 1800 on Sunday evening, Brigade 147 had lost most of its communications capabilities as the NVA artillery barrages had destroyed every antenna capable of long-range transmission. With the brigade's artillery pieces having shot nearly all of their ammunition, the order to "spike" the guns was issued and carried out. The various units comprising Brigade 147 then made their fighting withdrawal off the position under extremely intense enemy artillery and infantry pressure. That they were able to pull it off and maintain unit integrity was testament to the superior training, *élan*, and leadership at every level of the TQLC. The American Marine advisors likewise played key roles in assisting in the retrograde operation; among them Jim Joy and Andy De Bona. The collective actions of the Vietnamese and Americans would save the brigade and most of its forces to get back into the fight on more favorable terms in the coming days and weeks.

Prior to leaving the TOC bunker, Turley thought to take with him one of the tactical maps they had used to plot the advance of the NVA. The map itself was laminated and wall-mounted much like a painted canvas was stretched beneath an elaborate frame. To remove this map from the frame Turley took his K-Bar fighting knife and effectively carved it out. Every firebase and position lost to the enemy had been boldly crossed off using a red grease pencil with the date and time of loss noted. The "X" marks spread across the map that was northern I Corps told a vivid story requiring little explanation. Gerry meticulously folded the map and placed it in one of his trouser cargo pockets. He would use the map in his report to MACV.

It was just getting light when Gerry "officially" turned over his portion of the operation in the TOC to Jon Easley. A salty-looking Vietnamese Marine sergeant was assigned as his jeep driver for the eighty-kilometer trip from Ai Tu to Phu Bai. That there was even a remaining, functioning vehicle at all, in light of the continuous artillery pounding the entire area had taken these last ninety-six hours, seemed a miracle in itself.

Under circumstances other than those now in place, with a motivated Marine as one's jeep driver, the ride should have taken a bit more than an hour, ninety minutes max. Except to relieve himself every so many hours on the general's lawn next to the blown up jeep or to briefly take a look at what was going on around Ai Tu from the bunker entrance, Turley had not been outside for the entire period of the siege. The sights, the sounds, the smells, the sheer and utter destruction he witnessed upon emerging from the bunker for his first legitimate time outside of it nearly overwhelmed him.

When they set off for Phu Bai heading south on Highway One they were at once in the thick of all the personal horror visited upon the local population. The roads going away from Ai Tu and nearly as far south as Quang Tri, approximately six kilometers, were still choked with civilians fleeing the northern portions of Quang Tri Province and the incessant, indiscriminate but very discriminating enemy shelling. During that portion of the trip on Highway One Gerry's driver was forced to motor along at a speed barely faster than the civilians on foot they were passing. He leaned on the weak-sounding jeep's horn with little effect as was common for most drivers in Turley's Asian experience.

Gerry tried not to stare, to remain clinical, aloof and impassive, but it was not humanly possible to escape the enormity of the suffering going on right there in front of him, on his left and right, and to his rear. Gerry's crusty and probably long-serving sergeant—Turley could not adequately guess his age—spoke no English. Turley, who had not attended any Vietnamese language training but had expanded his vocabulary in the last few days, endured the ride in near complete silence.

They passed a sea of humanity: thousands and thousands of men, women, children, old people, infirm people; some moving as obvious families, others appearing dazed and shell-shocked from the horror, but always moving south. With them the people carried whatever was most precious; infants on their mothers' backs, older siblings carrying younger ones, and what meager possessions or food stuffs they could haul on strong shoulders or upon what wheeled contraptions there were. Boys no older than Gerry's sons Bob and Chris were managing water buffaloes, herding them along like seasoned pros.

Upon departing Ai Tu and for the first few kilometers Gerry could see burned-out vehicles, blown-apart bicycles, overturned ox carts. Animal carcasses and a few human corpses were left to rot where NVA artillery had cut them down. Everywhere there was the smell of flesh and other things burning. As they moved further south, outside of the current NVA artillery fan, the amount of roadside destruction diminished. The evidences of the nascent free market economy he had observed not one full week ago on his helicopter ride in with Jim Joy were now gone.

Of the Western authors writing about Asia whom Turley had read, this current episode he was living in somehow seemed like the most disturbing parts of a Pearl Buck novel come to life. Buck had a way of framing, dissecting and then expressing in simple terms the complicated relationships of Asian culture. More than anyone else Turley knew of, Buck had the ability to empathetically and respectfully describe the suffering long endured by Asia's multitudes. That suffering was visited upon all, but especially upon the average peasants who constituted most of the population in any Asian country. In Buck's writings suffering was tied mainly to the earth's cycles; to famine and drought, flood and pestilence. The human pain was tied to the universal experience, with an oriental twist, of fidelity and infidelity, avarice, lust, and revenge. Included were the orderly but complex relationships between men and women, fathers and sons, mothers and daughters.

Buck captured well, and reduced to words so Westerners might comprehend, the near stoic acceptance of life's harshness these people now come to life all around Gerry Turley were enduring. He felt as if he was moving inside of a slightly more modern version of what she had not so long ago written about. If she had been there with him, if she had been riding in the back seat of the jeep or walking beside them as they inched along near Quang Tri, she would have been able to express the misery and pain; place it in historical context and compare it to what had earlier been. And really, in all the wars fought before, in the more than two thousand years of Vietnamese history where strife and struggle were ubiquitous, with invasion after invasion and the constant resistance to foreign subjugation or local oppression; the only difference now was the more modern manner in which the current misery was inflicted upon those now experiencing that misery. Life managed to go on.

As Gerry's assigned driver deftly maneuvered their jeep through the multitudes in and around Quang Tri, the crowds began to thin to the south of town. As unpleasant as all of this adversity and pain was to witness, Turley also sensed what lay in store for him at MACV and was certainly in no hurry to appear at his own Saigon execution. Between taking in the human tragedy all about them and the relative comfort of his jeep seat, he settled back, dozing in and out of consciousness for a portion of the ride. As exhausted as he was, he remained alert and found his thoughts shifting from what was reality on the ground for these unfortunate civilians and what might await him down at MACV. Seeing so many women and children, innocent victims of this current invasion, who might have been the same age as his dear

Bunny and five kids, weighed especially heavy on his heart and made him more homesick than he otherwise would have felt.

Within twenty kilometers of Phu Bai they spied the first evidence of friendly reinforcements. Short convoys of jeeps and trucks laden with Marines recently flown into Phu Bai, and pulling trailers with war fighting material or 105mm cannons were wending their way north, into the breach. They waved as they passed and both Gerry and his driver waved back. Once they were within ten kilometers of the airfield they could see ahead and above them a number of planes, obviously C-130s, stacked up in a pattern awaiting the chance to land and offload their cargo of men and weapons. Every few minutes they would also see the single C-130, climbing straight out from the field so another could come in, clawing for altitude and heading south to pick up more Marines and ARVN reinforcements.

When they got to the airstrip, Gerry gave his driver hand signals to get as close as he could to the lead C-130 at the northern end of the field. The Marines and equipment were just about completely unloaded as Turley approached the nose of the bird whose engines were turning but not yet at maximum power for takeoff, weapon and gear in hand. There were two or three other C-130s still in various stages of unloading backed up behind the forward plane. Like a kid on any American road or freeway, but looking more like some sort of ramshackle hobo with his four days growth of beard and unkempt appearance, he put out his thumb. He was the only American there, and of course the pilot or co-pilot signaled him to come aboard.

Gerry Turley, aside from the C-130's crew, was the plane's only passenger for the two-hour flight back to Tan Son Nhut. The crew chief did not think to check the weapon belonging to a rather tough-looking American Marine lieutenant colonel even though the magazine was still in and there was a round in the chamber; an egregious safety violation. Turley had originally come north with not much more than a rucksack and weapon. Carrying only the most basic necessities, he had also served as mail courier, a duty he successfully completed. The one item he failed to deliver was a bottle of cognac for Captain Ray Smith whom he had been unable to link up with. Gerry had forgotten that he still had Smith's booze.

Gerry Turley never drank hard liquor. He was not a teetotaller, he would drink a beer or two at the officers' club or sip a glass of wine when he and Bunny went to dinner. Surprised that he still had Ray Smith's package and uncertain if he would ever see Ray again, he unwrapped it, unscrewed it, offered his new Air Force friends a sip—which they politely declined—and then took a single swig for himself. That done, he replaced the cap, put it back in his rucksack, stretched out on the nylon-web seating along the bird's starboard bulkhead, and promptly fell asleep. He did not wake up until the crew chief gently nudged him as they taxied to a halt on the Tan Son Nhut tarmac.

CHAPTER THIRTY

Lonely Bull

Going to MACV
Early Monday afternoon, April 3, 1972

Gerry Turley *was respectfully shaken awake* by the C-130 crew chief as he was sprawled out on the loosely configured web seating of the plane's cavernous interior just as the bird came to a halt at Tan Son Nhut. The seemingly endless stream of C-130s were cycling through Saigon as they returned empty to refuel and take up fresh loads of Vietnamese Marines and ARVN Rangers to Phu Bai. Turley was reasonably certain that Captain Ray Smith would not have begrudged his having taken a swig of the cognac he was unable to deliver to him. The two-hour, liquor-induced nap was the first real, uninterrupted sleep he had had in more than four days.

While airborne and enroute to Tan Son Nhut, the C-130's crew had radioed ahead that Turley was aboard. Upon landing, Gerry headed first to a bank of phones in the military terminal and called over to the Marine Advisory Unit (MAU). Speaking with an American Marine, a junior admin officer there who briefed him in on the local situation, it was the first time Gerry was made aware of a series of messages—officially called "Naval Messages"—that he had allegedly authored. These missives were, in fact, developed aboard the naval gunfire ships offshore during a period of maximum confusion in the battle, and were sent to higher naval headquarters as well as MACV. The information shared with him by the admin officer, delivered with a great deal of exuberance and nervous energy, hit him hard. And he hadn't even learned about *all* the messages. Turley began to understand now why he was being treated by everyone in the army chain of command away from northern Quang Tri Province as if he had the Black Plague. Not only were the messages error-filled, erroneous, inflated and controversial, they appeared to usurp and undercut—and therefore embarrass—MACV. That was considered a mortal sin.

After calling the MAU, Gerry next phoned Lieutenant Colonel Pete Hilgartner, a Marine officer who was part of the joint (meaning composed of men from the various military services) operations staff over at MACV. Gerry and Pete were long-time friends and had served together as company commanders on Okinawa back in 1959.

The stiff, formal, stand-offish manner in which Pete spoke to his slightly junior friend was the second blow landed after the stunner from the admin officer moments earlier. This near dressing down from his comrade was far more difficult to parry or absorb. There were no pleasantries, no working up to the issues at hand, no chitchat about the wives and kids. Pete Hilgartner was direct and to the point, going right to the heart of the matter. He questioned Gerry about what everyone at MACV had been referring to as the "Land the Landing Force" *communiqué*, which he read to him over the phone.

Turley was beside himself with incredulity. How could he have known *anything* about these things? Because he had not issued any of those messages he knew nothing, and up until these last few moments was at least "happily ignorant," like having some sort of cancer he did not yet know he had. He could barely believe what he was hearing. Hilgartner continued. There were other messages which were, if true, equally damning, equally controversial. Like a methodical prosecuting attorney, Lieutenant Colonel Hilgartner, beginning with the "Land the Landing Force" message, read aloud naval message after naval message. If this stuff could be proven to be accurate, MACV would sentence Turley for some as-yet-unspecified crime and have him permanently assigned to somewhere just this side of Hades.

After a moment or two of listening to things he found so far outside of anything he might ever have contemplated no matter how grave the ground situation in Quang Tri Province, Gerry

414

found an opening. One of the messages he had allegedly authored had claimed that the NVA, with tanks, was in control of Quang Tri airfield, which was several kilometers to the immediate south of Dong Ha on Highway One. He could point out that with the bridge at Dong Ha destroyed it would have been physically impossible for the NVA to get armor forces there that quickly. He would never have sent such a ridiculous or inaccurate message. Hilgartner grudgingly conceded that point. He began to relent, but not much. The call concluded with the strong counsel that Turley head straight to NavForV to meet with the admiral before going to MACV. It seemed as friendly a welcome to Saigon as the Germans gave the allies when they stormed ashore at Normandy.

Gerry was met outside the military terminal by Ha Si Chow, the cheery Vietnamese Marine corporal assigned as his driver prior to his trip north. He was still reeling from the shock of the earlier revelations. It was all so bizarre, almost surreal.

At the same time that Gerry was trying his best to intellectually process what he had just heard, the stark contrasts between Saigon and northern I Corps, along with the difference between his own personal appearance and that of everyone else, were made apparent to him long before his jeep cleared the gate at Tan Son Nhut.

It was important for Gerry that he maintain the sense of urgency he had left Phu Bai with (The divulgences from the admin officer at the MAU and then from Pete Hilgartner ensured that Turley would feel anything but relaxed and comfortable for the near future.) and not be lulled into the complacency and genuine sense of well-being he observed everywhere on the avenues of Saigon. The normal tempo of business and commerce betrayed not a hint that there was a war on anywhere nearby. He reminded himself that as he motored to his first destination, Headquarters Naval Forces Vietnam (HQNavForV), three hundred miles away the NVA were likewise driving south and east at every critical point all across northern I Corps. The enemy was currently being slowed only by the efforts of a small number of Vietnamese Marines and even fewer ARVN troops. No one with authority in

Saigon seemed to really understand or grasp just how critical the current ground situation in Quang Tri Province really was.

Ripley Home
Blacksburg, Virginia
0100 EST March 3, 1972 (12 hours behind Vietnam)

Moline Ripley had experienced as good an Easter as she could have given that her husband was half a world away doing only God knew what. The children had consumed their share of goodies and participated in egg hunts at both sets of grandparents' homes. For Moline's in-laws holidays were particularly challenging. As much as Bud and Verna Ripley reveled in having children and grandchildren in abundance and attendance, the combination of son Mike's recent death, George's serving on Okinawa, and John's being in Vietnam—probably in the thick of what combat had begun in earnest as minimally reported in the press—made the mood less ebullient than it might have been. All of the Ripley boys were sorely missed. Still the Blaylocks (Moline's parents) and the greater Ripley clan gave thanks for their many blessings; celebrating the Resurrection and the presence of what family there was.

Moline had driven the short hop back from Radford to Blacksburg, gotten her children to bed, and watched some of the evening news before going to sleep. What news there was about Vietnam was not encouraging, but it was not specific enough yet for her to invest significant energy in worrying about her husband more than she normally did. She had prayed her prayers and fallen asleep before midnight.

When the telephone rang sometime shortly after 1 a.m., her first thought was not of John. Moline Ripley had been a Marine Corps wife for almost eight years—nearly the entire time America had been at war in Vietnam. From personal experience when John was wounded in 1967 and from what far too many of their friends had likewise dealt with, she knew that notifications for serious casualties were not done by phone. Casualty calls, whether a man was KIA or WIA, were made in person. The Corps did not shirk that duty. When the call came this late, her first concern was for her folks, John's folks, maybe her sister's family; something bad had probably happened to someone she cared about.

The very cordial, professional, and almost clinical sounding voice on the other end of the phone recognized that Mrs. Ripley was at a disadvantage. He identified himself twice, apologizing for the time of the call and immediately began assuring her that the nature of the call was not to deliver bad news. It took Moline only a few seconds to be instantly alert and focused to process disconcerting information.

The colonel told Mrs. Ripley that her husband had personally destroyed, in the face of incredible enemy opposition, a key bridge in some forlorn, far-flung place neither she nor anyone in the Ripley family at home had heard of. Captain Ripley had performed something big and heroic, something quite meaningful, and his name was on the lips of everyone at the Pentagon.

Moline was trying to make sense of the information shared with her, attempting to place her actions and whereabouts here at home during the period her husband had been doing whatever it was he did that warranted this call. Colonel So-and-so, by the time they had concluded the call, had assured her that John was alive and well. At least he was however many hours ago. Mrs. Ripley was told that the story of Captain Ripley was about to be on all the major news networks. What he did was a big deal.

"Keep watching the news, Mrs. Ripley. Any station. He'll be on every channel."

As soon as she hung up, Moline called her in laws and then her parents. Her father-in-law, she knew, would be stressed but extremely proud. She also knew that she needed to get some rest before her children woke up. None of them would be able to understand their daddy's actions and they would, as usual, require the full measure of her attention. She was unable to sleep, even though she tried. She tossed and turned, prayed, worried a bit, and cat-napped. She did what she could to suppress her feelings of worry, but still decent sleep escaped her. She knew her husband, at this very moment was most likely still in maximum danger, and even though she understood that he would not want her to worry, and as seasoned as she was as the wife of Lima Six Actual, she worried just a bit more, a lot more than normal.

Moline Ripley began her new day as mother to her three children significantly sleep deprived. She was at least grateful to know that she and her children were far from the physical dangers facing their father.

Turley Home
Oceanside, California
2200 PST March 2, 1972 (15 hours behind Vietnam)

Just as Gerry Turley traveled from Tan Son Nhut to Headquarters Naval Forces Vietnam (HQ NavForV) in downtown Saigon, not too far from Military Advisory Command Vietnam (MACV), for what he expected to be his summary execution, he allowed himself the minor luxury of a few moments to think of Easter at home.

Bunny and their four youngest children—oldest daughter Anne was currently away at nursing school—would likely have just a few hours ago wrapped up Easter with Gerry's parents down in San Diego. They would have all attended Sunday services at St. Vincent de Paul Church, the same church they had been married in back in the early summer of 1950, right before the beginning of the Korean War, now almost twenty-two years ago. Gerry could at least know that many people, probably folks he had not even met, had been praying for him that very day. He would need the benefit of those prayers, he thought.

Bunny Turley was a seasoned Marine Corps wife. This was her third combat tour, and compared to the other two this one seemed like it would be the least dangerous for her husband. The best part about this tour at this time, when compared to his earlier ones in both 1951 and 1966, was that American combat involvement had been far more intense then than things were now in the spring of 1972. On top of that, her husband was relatively senior and was not out in the field at the point of contact leading troops, or so she surmised. Military families especially were aware that at this stage of the war very few Americans were being killed. Those who were at greatest risk were pilots and air crews. To her knowledge Gerry

Turley was "flying" a desk in Saigon. Bunny Turley, like Moline Ripley whom she did not yet know, and so many other military wives tried not to worry about those things over which they had no control. And like so many military wives, she had four children and a household to honcho. There was little time to spend worrying and for that she was quite grateful.

Bunny was also aware, from reading what snippets of information there were in the *San Diego Union* and on television, that there was new action way up in the northern portion of South Vietnam but did not yet think to place her husband in it. Mercifully, the last letter he had written to her from Saigon, which told of the routine trip he was taking to visit the Vietnamese Marines and his advisors in Quang Tri, was yet to arrive. The California Turleys could enjoy their Easter celebration without the added worries of the real challenges Gerry was facing.

Cam Banh
Home of Le Ba Sach (Binh's father)
Tan Dinh Saigon
April 3, 1972

What many would identify as the "Vietnam Experience" for Americans was radically different than the "World War II Experience'" of their parents' generation. Far fewer citizens shared the burden of transacting this war or were exposed to similar risk of loss. Instead of celebrating its participants for their sacrifices, the unpopularity of the· Vietnam War seemed to isolate rather than elevate those who disproportionately carried the load. Certainly by 1972, with the bulk of American combat forces gone from Southeast Asia, except mostly for air crews, the level of interest by the general population in the day-to-day activities of the war was greatly reduced. Such was not the case for the citizens of the Republic of Vietnam; all of whom had a major stake in the war's outcome.

Since the American Civil War the nation had experienced no serious combat on its own shores, except for what there was left to conquer and settle in the Wild West. In every conflict subsequent to the Civil War, American boys and men went *away* to fight, and worried little for the personal risks facing their loved ones at home. For every single citizen of the Republic of Vietnam, whether they had a son or brother or husband or father directly involved in the combat, the situation was completely different than what Americans currently living had ever faced.

The Vietnamese experience with the unending war in their country was beyond anything Americans could genuinely relate to. For the generation of young Vietnamese adults who came of age—like Le Ba Binh and Cam Banh—from the 1950s and into the 1970s, conflict was *all* they knew. "Peace," "stability," "security," and "normal" were all relative, transitory terms with meanings far outside of what Americans had ability to empathize with.

Cam Banh's stake in the conflict, nowhere near unique among her family, friends, or neighbors, was still significant. Not only was her husband currently at the absolute tip of the spear of the Republic of Vietnam's efforts to keep the red devils at bay, both of her younger brothers currently wore the uniform of their country. Her oldest younger brother had finished university in 1968, and like many patriotic young Vietnamese men after witnessing firsthand the atrocities of the Communists during that year's Tet Offensive, volunteered for combat duty. By 1972 he was a captain in the Vietnamese Airborne Division and had seen significant action. (The Vietnamese Airborne Division was viewed as the co-equal to the TQLC in terms of military prowess and political reliability. The two divisions together constituted the nation's strategic reserve. They were the country's "Fire Brigades.") Cam's baby brother had enlisted into the Air Force in 1969 and was now a sergeant serving as a helicopter mechanic.

As much as life was "normal" in Saigon, as much as regular business could be transacted without the incipient inflation that always accompanied a panic, and no one was being shot at locally, there was still an underlying tension for all citizens remotely related to any young soldier or Marine now being sent north. With the early recall of Brigade 369 and all of its supporting elements, the entire Vietnamese Marine Corps was now committed to this particular fight. A man or woman did not need to understand Clausewitz or Sun Tzu to sense the situational gravity. At a time like this it was particularly important for Cam Banh, as the senior wife of the Soi Bien and to best honor her husband and serve their country, to maintain her calm and equanimity, to be available to assist the other wives and families, to fill in where and when she would be needed. In the meantime she continued in her role at the home of Le Ba Sach, helping to manage the household with her mother-in-law.

Headquarters Naval Forces Vietnam (NavForV)
Monday afternoon April 3, 1972

When Gerry Turley first left the Ai Tu TOC to begin the process of heading south to Saigon and had a moment to ponder the situation, his situation *vis-à-vis* all the people lined up as his opponents at MACV (And quite possibly now at NavForV as well.), he expected bad things to happen to him. Now that he had arrived in Saigon, now that he had spoken with the admin officer over at the Marine Advisory Unit and more especially Pete Hilgartner, he expected *very* bad things to happen to him. He was not quite sure how the end would come, or exactly what the end would consist of. Turley was a professional, though, and would go in with his head held high and receive whatever justice was to be meted out to him like the professional Marine officer he was. But before going down he would do his level best, just like Paul Revere, to make sure the decision makers in the rear knew what was going on in northern I Corps. The *Red Coats* really were coming.

Ha Si Chow cheerfully and deferentially deposited his passenger at the main entrance to NavForV in downtown Saigon. Already uncomfortable with his own personal appearance and hygiene, there was nothing Lieutenant Colonel Gerry Turley could do about it for the moment. The sentries who checked his ID and cleared him into the building were professional as well, but Turley knew that once he passed they were certain to comment about his unkemptness and assuredly discuss how ripe he must have smelled to them. Their impressions of him were the least of his worries.

The assault on Gerry Turley's emotional and psychological well-being that had nebulously begun with the initiation of the artillery attacks at the end of lunch on March 30 continued, but in even more ungraspable, incomprehensible ways. As much as Turley was the veritable odd man out, the peculiar fellow in this aggregation of regular people, it was he who thought that everyone around him might not be sane. As out of place, as uncouth and unwashed as he appeared in this relative sea of gentility and civility to those around him, it was he who could barely process the reality in the halls of NavForV. Just as the jeep ride in from Tan Son Nhut had betrayed not a hint of danger, the operational tempo inside the generously constructed French-built edifice that served as the headquarters building there for Naval Forces Vietnam was routine. Had it not been for the uniforms, flags and marginally military *décor*, along with a few weapons, he might as well have been in a regular office building to transact a business deal or execute a contract. While those who saw him must have thought his appearance a bit out of place, Turley was trying to keep it all together. *"Am I really still in Vietnam?" "Don't these guys know what is going on?"* The American naval officers were wearing uniforms so white, so bleachingly white, it hurt his eyes. And they were wearing Bermuda shorts. Bermuda shorts. There was a war on and these guys were wearing Bermuda shorts, for crying out loud!

The indifference and odd stares from the disinterested masses of American and Vietnamese personnel he passed by as he headed to the admiral's office transitioned to cold reception and downright hostility when he reported in to those senior American naval officers he needed to see.

By the time he had arrived at NavForV Gerry Turley was tired; more tired than he had ever been. He had hours and hours ago concluded that he was expendable. He realized and had sufficient perspective to understand that this was not about *him*, and so what happened to him did not really matter in the grand scheme of things. He had already begun to believe, especially after the exchange with Pete Hilgartner, that somehow his career as a Marine was washed up, finished, *caput*. His primary concern was to tell the truth, the complete story of what had recently and was right now taking place up in northern I Corps. In doing that he hoped not to bring any discredit to the Marine Corps.

Far more important than the attacks up north being outside of what MACV had expected was what it all meant about Vietnamization. After the ARVN's, at best, marginal performance less than a year earlier during *Lam Son 719*—at least as reported in the Western media—and all the public doubt over the south's abilities to fight the north on its own, the utter collapse of the Third ARVN Division appeared as another nail in the struggling republic's coffin. Gerry Turley was only the messenger, but his physical presence was a most unpleasant reminder that Vietnamization was not working; that was something far outside the party line at both MACV and NavForV. If what Turley was saying was true, then the program's future did not look too bright. Messengers delivering unpleasant news sometimes became expendable.

The blatant contempt in which Gerry Turley was already held became apparent to him as he entered the admiral's outer office. Un-shouldering his weapon and rucksack as he cleared the hatch, he placed them on a standard, generic-looking, vinyl-covered, government-issue couch. A few feet away he spied the chief of staff at his desk. A navy captain (the same rank as full colonel in the other three services), he was clad in an extremely bright, starched, and pressed white dress uniform. Although Gerry could not see his legs, he was sure the captain, like all the others, was wearing Bermuda shorts. Turley was certain his entrance had been observed. It would have been impossible not to have noticed his appearance, or smell his arrival.

The chief of staff pretended to keep working, face buried in paperwork, as Turley formally approached his desk, centering himself in front of him with Marine Corps boot camp precision. Turley could see already that he was *persona non grata*. His story, his egregious disregard for MACV protocol (from the MACV perspective), his very existence were contrary to the preconceived and universally subscribed to party line at MACV that Vietnamization was working and the NVA, when their offensive began, would initiate the action in the central and southern portions of the country, not up north in Quang Tri Province. The put-down was anything but subtle as he stood there silent, the chief of staff refusing to look up and acknowledge him. Finally Gerry spoke.

"Lieutenant Colonel Turley reporting to see the admiral as ordered, sir!"

"Yea...sure Colonel...I bet you are...Wait one ..." was the terse, churlish response. The chief of staff knew of Turley only by his recently acquired reputation—the rogue Marine lieutenant colonel from somewhere near the DMZ—the man who was the boy crying "Wolf!"

The navy captain did not invite Turley to stand at ease but left him rigid there while he retreated into the admiral's office. Gerry was fatigued and still battling diarrhea. For a moment he stood there ramrod straight and eyeballed the office as he waited. Gerry mulled the irony and the completely eccentric circumstances for which he was at ground zero. Only hours ago he had been controlling and coordinating—for four very full days—more firepower, along with all the attendant responsibilities, than he ever would again unless he were a Marine division commander in World War III battling the Soviets in combination conventional and nuclear combat. Now he was standing tall like some errant private awaiting his company commander's punishment after having gotten into trouble on liberty.

Standing there, as tired as he was, a thousand thoughts flooded through his mind. A lesser man might have gone mad. He continued to attempt to assimilate his surroundings. Compared to where he had come from he may as well have been on a completely different planet. This navy office was spotless, efficient, orderly. He could smell coffee brewing somewhere. There was a Filipino steward standing by waiting to serve the admiral and his staff. It was *so* Navy.

Gerry continued to wait; but finally began to relax. He turned to the steward, who appeared sympathetic, and asked for a cup of coffee. It was his first taste of civilization in some time. He retired, without being invited, to the couch upon which he had earlier placed his weapon and rucksack. As he sipped the navy brew he somehow drifted off just a bit; probably for five or ten minutes before the chief of staff returned.

"The admiral will see you now."

Lieutenant Colonel Gerry Turley put down his coffee cup and semi-marched, from the outer office to the inner sanctum, directly to the spot that was front and center in front of the admiral's desk. He presented himself respectfully and professionally, halfway expecting the personal digs at his leadership and conduct to continue. He was not shocked by the greeting. "Been sending any naval messages lately, Colonel?" was the opening salvo he received from the commanding officer of Naval Forces Vietnam.

"No, sir. I have not written or released *any* messages."

Turley was frustrated, angry, but kept his composure. The admiral, puzzled at the response, appeared unconvinced. Gerry requested permission to explain his story, which the admiral granted. With that, he pulled from his trouser pocket the folded-up map—the one he had carved off the wall in the TOC—and tried to spread it out on the desk before him but there was too much clutter so he placed it on the floor behind the admiral's position, got down on his hands and knees, and began to explain the chronology of events in northern Quang Tri Province from lunchtime of March 30th on.

It was the strangest scene, but it fit perfectly into this bizarre tale Turley had been a part of now for five days. If he had been a member of a television audience watching what was taking place he would have sworn this was simply bad comedy. Here he was, on all fours on the floor behind the admiral's desk, smelling to high heaven, trying to seriously explain the odd set of circumstances in Quang Tri Province. The admiral, knobby knees, hairy legs, white ankle socks, and all was bent over in his swivel chair, at nearly eyeball level with Turley, watching as this stenchy Marine pointed out places on the map absorbed by the advancing Communist invasion. There was no humor. None.

Turley began to explain, and a rush of energy, nervous energy, erupted out of him even though he was exhausted and between bouts of diarrhea. He spoke at a volume far above necessary but could not control himself. The chief of staff was behind them and was also looking on. Turley continued. He swore as he spoke, even though he had no intention to. It simply came out.

Meticulously, Gerry began to explain the sequence of events, from the moment the first artillery barrages began. He could tell by their facial expressions that this was the first time the admiral and his chief of staff had heard this information. Turley kept going. And then, all of a sudden, he was overcome by the physical need to run to the head, again. It was so embarrassing, but there was nothing else he could do. He went to the bathroom, did what he needed to and washed his face, for the first time in awhile feeling once more a bit like a human being. He returned to the admiral's office and pressed on with the story.

Gerry Turley was spent, enervated. The demands of his duties—emotional, psychological, and physical—had depleted him to the point of near complete exhaustion. The recurring diarrhea had left his insides empty, his physical presence and strength diminished. Still he would allow himself no rest. There was too much at stake, too many lives to consider. Maximum effort was his only option. As wound up as he was, and as loudly and coarsely as he spoke—expletives and all—Turley stayed on task; methodically and chronologically describing event after event, including the relatively shabby performance of the Third ARVN Division's units, the heroic stands put up by the Marine brigades' constituent battalions, firebase after firebase lost, position after position overrun by the steadily advancing NVA.

The red grease pencil markings on the well-worn map which was now spread out on the deck so the admiral could have a better sense of the heretofore unbelieved story Turley was relating. The big "X" marks signifying the loss of so much critical terrain at so many points all across Quang Tri Province was the picture worth a thousand words. When he got to the part about being ordered, against his will, to take over command in the Ai Ti TOC by the army colonel, the admiral stopped him.

"What did you just say, Colonel?" Gerry told him again.

"Would you repeat that one more time, Colonel?" Turley complied. The admiral and his chief of staff exchanged puzzled looks. Turley went on to explain how he had even taken down the colonel's Social Security number as a form of crude insurance; proof that this action was not his idea, and that he had not appropriated the power on his own. The mood in the inner sanctum began to change ever so slightly; Gerry could feel it. He continued with his story.

Gerry Turley, wiped out as he was, still had the presence of mind to appreciate his audience. It was no exaggeration to describe, in great detail, the criticality of the naval gunfire support received by the forces in and around Dong Ha. Where these senior naval officers might not fully understand the nature of the ground combat, they knew naval gunfire. Turley was effusive in his praise of the ships' captains who had run their vessels almost aground to ensure continual coverage and maximum range inland. The Marines at Dong Ha could not have held on without naval gunfire. He had them hooked. The navy had finally taken some ownership of this "Turley Situation."

When Turley had finished the impromptu briefing the admiral thanked him. It was the first time he actually called him by his name. Gerry was beginning to feel just a bit more like a human. The admiral was not finished, though. He asked Turley to stand by and in a few minutes two more admirals showed up. Turley was told to give the same brief again. And so he did.

Once the briefing for the admirals concluded, Turley knew he would have to head to MACV. But first he wanted to clean up. He felt just like he thought he smelled. He considered his appearance unprofessional and less than dignified. The wise old admiral believed differently. "No Turley, go now. Go right now. Go as you are."

Gerry was not happy about it but did the proper thing: "Aye, aye, sir."

The admiral knew his contrasting appearance would have more impact, give his story added credibility. The admiral guessed Turley would need every edge he could get over at MACV. Gerry grabbed his gear, headed back to the building's entrance, found Ha Si Chow snoozing in his jeep while he waited under what appeared to be a manicured Frangipani tree, also known as plumeria in Hawaii, there on the NavForV grounds, and moved on down the road to MACV.

CHAPTER THIRTY-ONE

Turley Faces MACV

Third Marine Battalion
Dong Ha
Late Monday afternoon

All of Dong Ha, from the north side of the Cua Viet, was well within range of every artillery piece—including the ubiquitous 82mm mortars—the NVA had brought down from the DMZ with abundance never before experienced in this war by allied forces. After John Ripley had blown the bridge, after an evening of the Soi Bien thwarting every local attempt at crossing in front of their dispersed and one-Marine-chest-width deep lines, and after beginning to shift their armor forces westward toward Cam Lo and its intact bridge, the enemy continued to pour men and material against Dong Ha. No one had ordered them to do otherwise. Even without the bridge to cross, even with the major break in momentum its destruction had caused, they still possessed most of the battlefield advantage; in spite of near continuous naval gunfire support near the coast.

The BAT-21 shoot down, with the current restrictions imposed on the use of airpower, had given the NVA almost free reign of the northern I Corps battlefield inland from the coast for the time being. In what was perhaps the most target-rich environment of the entire war, Americans were holding back for fear of endangering one downed pilot awaiting rescue. The enemy was taking full advantage of these opportunities to continue their assault.

At Dong Ha, Binh's Third Battalion, now consisting of fewer than seven hundred Marines, was facing nearly twenty thousand

NVA soldiers along with a still indeterminate number, but likely far more than earlier estimated, of tanks and artillery. The defenders, as tenaciously as they were resisting, simply did not have enough ammunition and spare parts, or men, to hold on forever. It was evident to both Binh and Ripley that this was the enemy's maximum effort; and to them victory, this victory, final victory, was worth spending so much human capital to attain. To prevent that outcome both men were aware that they would be required to hold their ground at all costs. For Third Battalion at Dong Ha all meant *all*.

In addition to shifting a good portion of their armor towards the west at Cam Lo, the hungry for victory and relentless NVA also began to send a significant number of infantry and light support units across the river upstream from Dong Ha at the Old French Railroad Bridge. (The Old French Railroad Bridge was beyond the range of naval gunfire.) These forces became a menacing threat as Binh was unable to shift any of his rifle companies or the still attached tanks from the ARVN tank battalion away to directly block that particular crossing. He simply had too much territory in Dong Ha proper to cover with very limited resources.

The morning's lull did not last long. The growing threat from NVA forces able to cross the river at the Old French Bridge, even though they did not have their own armor support currently with them, would soon require Binh to realign his rifle companies. The enemy numbers were staggering and were, for the moment, out of naval gunfire range. And since there was currently no allied air support going, the NVA crossed there at will.

Binh would communicate by both radio and messenger with his company commanders; checking their status, ensuring they had sufficient ammunition, making sure they understood their commander's intent. They did.

The allies were still receiving reasonable replenishment up on Highway One and were able to evacuate the most seriously wounded chaps who could no longer add combat value with their presence when resupply vehicles would go back south empty. When time and the situation allowed, Binh and Ripley would walk the lines of the strategically placed rifle companies. Ripley was struck by the tenacity and undiminished fighting spirit he saw in nearly every Marine. They needed little encouragement to do what they were continuing to do. As he observed this he wished he could have had a few correspondents in tow. Really there was nothing too complicated in what was going on. These Marines were defending *their* country. John Ripley liked to think that given the same set of circumstances Americans would respond this way as well. The shooting and the shelling and the fighting continued on into the late afternoon, with the NVA numbers on the upstream south bank of the Cua Viet steadily increasing. There would be little rest again this evening.

As it was for the men of the Soi Bien at Dong Ha, so it was for the other battalions of Vietnamese Marines; all under the same unremitting pressure and in continuous contact with a materially and numerically superior foe across the remaining contested northern I Corps battlefield.

Headquarters MACV
Monday April 3, 1972
Afternoon

The ride from Headquarters Naval Forces Vietnam (NavForV) back to Tan Son Nhut where Headquarters Military Advisory Command Vietnam (MACV) was located was of insufficient time for Gerry to consider too many disparate thoughts beyond what he had already been thinking, except for one. It was evident by what the admirals asked that they really did not have an understanding of the ground situation and the attendant implications. Or maybe they did; but to Gerry their concerns seemed more political than winning the actual battle. Perhaps he was wrong in that assessment. He hoped he was. Those issues were way above his pay grade anyway.

Turley was exhausted. And he was still battling diarrhea. At NavForV he had been able to freshen up ever so slightly but believed his physical appearance was embarrassingly less than professional and that he probably still smelled to high heaven. This pending "performance" at MACV might well be the single

431

final act of his entire career. Turley suffered no illusions and, while not a pessimist at all by nature, was not expecting a positive outcome from this situation that had become both a political Gordian knot and would become, if not expeditiously addressed, a serious military defeat.

Pete Hilgartner was there to meet Gerry when he arrived at MACV. Before they were to go upstairs to see the senior MACV commanders and their closest staff he advised his friend: "You better go down to the COC." Unlike the relatively large but stuffy bunker Turley had left up in Ai Tu, the MACV COC was the picture of American military-industrial might and organizational efficiency. The COC, along with being populated by dozens of mid and high-level officers conducting business, also housed the very latest electronic gizmos to track what was taking place throughout the country. Gerry could have fit the northern bunker in one small corner of the room he was about to enter. As soon as he stepped inside, Turley would have sworn he heard several dozen eyeballs click as they all focused on him. He would have further sworn he heard most every army officer, *sotto voce*, say something like: "Hey, there's *that* a—hole from up north."

Lieutenant Colonel Turley's arrival into the COC was, in fact, announced by another Marine officer there in attendance. The room, normally abuzz with activity, suddenly became quiet, almost suspenseful. Everyone there, every single one of them, was focused on him. Without hesitation Turley stepped forward and began to speak: "Gentlemen, my name is Lieutenant Colonel Gerry Turley. Many of you may already know who I am. Now I'm not sure what is going to happen to me, whether I'm going to jail, whether I'm gonna be sent home. I don't know. But you folks here in the COC need to know what is going on right now …" And for the next several minutes he told them, in great detail, just what had taken place and what the current situation was. He held nothing back. Although he could not be certain—he was very tired and may have misread his audience—he finished his unofficial presentation with the belief that he left the MACV COC having dispersed a great deal of the battlefield fog that had so far clouded MACV's collective, institutional judgment of events in northern

Quang Tri Province. The next stop was the office of MACV's deputy commander, General Frederick Weyand.

The office belonging to General Frederick Weyand, Deputy Commander MACV and shortly to assume command of MACV, was up two floors from the COC. His office was across the hall from that of General Creighton Abrams, MACV's current commanding officer. The job of commanding officer for the Military Advisory Command Vietnam was a big one. General Abrams' predecessor had been William C. Westmoreland; a name known to nearly every American—and probably every person in the world—who in the last few years had read a newspaper, listened to the radio, or had access to some sort of television news. The top job at MACV, while not the single most critical or senior job in the American military was, while the nation still had significant resources invested in Southeast Asia, clearly the most high-profile one as far as the public was concerned.

Turley was not surprised when he entered General Weyand's office to find a half dozen other general officers and at least as many full colonels waiting for him. The contrasts with his own personal appearance were again not lost on Gerry. He momentarily harkened back to that mysterious visit in Ai Tu from those six Saigon army colonels who had come and gone under the most bizarre conditions. While only a few days earlier, due to all the unconventional circumstances, it now seemed an eternity ago. Just like those six earlier apparitions, this group, this inner circle of MACV power now surrounding him and awaiting his brief, appeared as a manifestation out of the same Westmoreland mold: tall, lean, and distinguished fellows with that salt-and-pepper, close-cropped soldierly look to them. This would be a different briefing than the one he had just given to all the operations people in the large COC downstairs.

Gerry Turley scanned the faces of the men who surrounded him. Except for Pete Hilgartner there were none who could have been called friends, and except for Hilgartner he was certain that even the designated "coffee boys" there were senior to him. Turley commenced with the presentation almost perfunctorily, as he had already given it twice to the admirals and once to the crew in the MACV COC. Modifying it slightly for the now weightier, more upscale audience, he began at the beginning.

It started routinely enough, with Turley explaining the reason for his trip north, and the odd set of circumstances which had placed him in the Ai Tu bunker when the new enemy offensive began. His audience, cool to him initially at best and probably making every effort to effectively size him up, began to show obvious discomfort once Turley discussed how he had been forced, quite literally conscripted, into serving as the man in charge of operations in the Team 155 bunker by the senior U.S. Army colonel advising General Giai. His audience's body language along with the muffled grunts and groans told him that issues of turf and blame and responsibilities for things no one wanted responsibility for were coming to the surface. When Turley, in great detail, began to very specifically describe how he had been given authority, one of the generals who did not believe him challenged: "Now wait a minute ..." It was precisely at that moment that Gerry reached into his pocket and produced the small slip of paper with the army colonel's Social Security number along with the time the event took place. The proof was incontrovertible.

Before Gerry could continue, one of the Westmoreland look-a-likes came up to him, pointed at the piece of paper and said: "Let me have that."

Turley was tired but he was not intimidated. His flat, firm response was "No." The room was quiet until some other colonel also demanded the paper. Turley refused a second time. "I just want to reproduce it." "No." More silence. Awkward, painful silence.

It was Pete Hilgartner, friend to Turley and member of the MACV operations staff known to all the others in the room, who stepped into the breach as arbiter. "Let me have it, Gerry. I'll make a copy and get it back to you."

"Okay, Pete..."

And that was that. Lieutenant Colonel Hilgartner took the piece of paper from his friend and left the room to make a photocopy of it. While he was gone the odd silence continued with only minor small talk. Turley said nothing.

When Pete Hilgartner returned, he handed the paper to Gerry who placed it back in his trouser pocket. The copied piece of paper was passed around for all to see. Suddenly there was proof, the undeniable proof, that Turley was not the mad man they had wanted to believe he was. Maybe the world really was coming apart up in northern I Corps.

Gerry then continued with his briefing. He went on to describe the call he received from the general granting authority to direct air power, the shameful surrender of Camp Carroll, John Ripley's heroic demolition of the Dong Ha Bridge, the criticality of the naval gunfire support to those friendly units closest to the coast, everything; everything up until the time he had left the bunker in Ai Tu to come to this meeting.

As it was wrapping up, the flag officers retired to General Weyand's inner office for discussion while the rest waited in the outer office or went on with other business. When the senior officers concluded, one of them came out to talk with Turley. Thanking him briefly for his input, the general asked him what he wanted to do. "They need me up north, sir. I'd like to get back to my duty."

"Fine, Colonel. There's a plane leaving at 1800." There was sufficient time for Ha Si Chow to run Gerry back to his Saigon quarters, take a serious shower, shave, and don a fresh, clean uniform before flying out.

Just as Lieutenant Colonel Turley was gathering his pack and weapon to leave, General Weyand himself emerged from the inner office. Throughout the course of the briefing he had moments ago delivered, Gerry had been taken by the professionalism and non-parochial, above-the-fray nature of General Weyand's comments and questions. Addressing him by name, General Weyand reached to shake his hand, sincerely thanking him for his selfless service and for having done all that he had done under such horrible circumstances. Although he was near complete exhaustion, Turley was deeply moved by the general's unexpected magnanimity.

THE OFFENSIVE EXPANDS AND SO DOES THE DEFENSE...FINALLY

Ha Si Chow was able to get his passenger over to his Saigon quarters for that critical shave and shower, fresh uniform and then out to Tan Son Nhut in time for the flight that got him as far north as Danang for the evening. Gerry had even had a moment to call Bunny and the kids, to tell them he loved them and that he was okay, to find out that she and the kids were all doing fine, and yes that they all loved him too. In Danang Gerry ran into a few of the army people in the COC there who had been part of the "Turley is a Mad Man Club" from the previous days. While it was uncomfortable, it turned out to be no big deal. Stuck in Danang for the evening, Gerry was actually able to get a reasonable night's sleep in a real bed. He hoped to somehow shuttle north the following morning.

The fighting in northern I Corps continued from Monday on into Tuesday without relent. Naval gunfire remained on station shooting the missions the ships were able to while airpower continued to be limited in its full range of options by the no-fire ring around Bat 21. The people in Saigon kept a more focused, informed watch on the action in Quang Tri Province. RVN forces engaged in the defense of the area, now mostly just the Vietnamese Marine battalions still occupying key terrain, gave ground only grudgingly.

If the enemy had been looking for locals to rise up and support their offensive, it had yet to happen. There were, in fact, few locals remaining in northern Quang Tri Province at all. They were all moving south; away from the incessant, indiscriminate shelling. In addition, the local Viet Cong infrastructure had yet to reconstitute itself. This was actually a problem for the NVA all over the country. The local Communist forces had been so thoroughly decimated during Tet '68 and subsequent operations that the Nguyen-Hue Offensive was shaping up entirely as an outside invasion.[1]

The general NVA offensive allied intelligence had called for, at places other than Quang Tri Province, was finally initiated on the morning of Wednesday April 5, 1972. Moving out of eastern Cambodia, approximately one hundred kilometers northwest of Saigon, the initial thrusts cut Highway 13 between An Loc and the capital city. The assault towards An Loc, if successful, would put close, direct pressure on Saigon and cause broader panic than the attacks up near the DMZ.

The current air campaign that was locally hampered by bad weather and targeting issues with the presence of Bat 21 near Cam Lo would soon expand to levels not before seen during the entire American portion of the war. As much as many poorly informed citizens outside of Asia may have been led to believe that the hapless, helpless, peace-loving regular civilian peasants of the Democratic Republic of Vietnam (DRV) were victims who had bravely endured the cruel and barbaric punishment meted out by U.S. Air Force and Navy bombers for years and years, such was not the case.

The bombing campaigns conducted earlier in the war had been the product of flawed and *naïve* strategic thinking. Influenced by the surprise mass Chinese entry into the Korean War in November of 1950, President Johnson's planners worked to ensure that there would be no grounds or provocation for a repeat of that experience by restricting and severely limiting the targets American forces could strike in the DRV.

While B-52s were seen by those opposed to America's effort in Southeast Asia as a contrasting symbol of military-industrial oppression versus the enlightened forces of liberation, they had yet to be used at all against targets in and around Hanoi and Haiphong. All of the prior bombing had been conducted by tactical attack aircraft such as the Air Force's F-105, known as the "Thud," Navy carrier-based aircraft, and what USMC aircraft were available. With self-imposed rules of engagement that were so restrictive and counterintuitive as to at times be almost suicidal, it was an amazing testimony to the professionalism of the air crews who flew those missions that there was not some effort towards mutiny or mass refusals to execute their orders. Targets which directly threatened air crews were often restricted due to proximity of civilian population or it was believed by Johnson's war managers that such targeting might somehow send too inflammatory a message to the Soviets or Chinese. For a long period of time U.S. forces could not directly strike enemy airfields or shoot down enemy fighters when they were landing or taking off. The Communists were wise in their refusal to return the American's sense of chivalrous idiocy. They were concerned only with winning. American aircrews paid an unnecessarily heavy price in following these and other orders which risked their lives for little gain.

The United States had unilaterally ceased the bombing of North Vietnam above the 20th Parallel in November of 1968 as a measure of goodwill towards what it thought was a workable peace process. The Communists wisely used the cessation of air operations to rebuild their defenses with the latest in Soviet anti-aircraft missile technology and also were able to redirect assets closer to the South Vietnamese battlefields. The Communists were interested only in winning.

Complicating the issues of massive retaliatory response with American strategic and tactical airpower was the delicately evolving diplomacy President Nixon was working on with the Russians and the Chinese. Fortunately for the Vietnamese and Americans on the ground, Nixon pressed ahead with the air strikes.

On April 6, 1972, the United States initiated Operation Freedom Trail which became the first sustained bombing effort north of the DMZ since November of 1968.[2] Sorties concentrated on targets mostly south of the 20th Parallel while a few hit further north. Freedom Trail would continue into early May to be replaced by Operation Linebacker which sent American forces north of the 20th Parallel *en masse* and saw, for the first time in the war, the use of B-52s against strategic targets in the Hanoi and Haiphong areas. The earlier targeting restrictions would be significantly reduced although the obvious avoidance of civilian targets such as schools, hospitals, etc remained in effect. As part of Linebacker U.S. naval aircraft would mine the harbor entrances to every single DRV port. Further inland, bridges and rail connections with China were also targeted for destruction. Even with American forces facing the most sophisticated anti-aircraft defenses in the world, the introduction of first and second generation precision weapons allowed for greater target destruction while minimizing collateral damage to civilians who, in Communist propaganda stories, always seemed to be living next to whatever military targets the Americans struck.[3]

CHAPTER THIRTY-TWO

Ongoing Action at Dong Ha

Thursday April 6, 1972
Early morning

T*he main highway bridge at Dong Ha* was destroyed, but action in the immediate area was such that Binh and his advisor believed it best to maintain the preponderance of Third Battalion's strength right there. Since early Easter Sunday when John Ripley had blown the bridge the fighting had been near constant. With so much combat power—at least two NVA divisions—still clustered just north of the Cua Viet adjacent to Highway One, although an unknown percentage of enemy armor had shifted west toward Cam Lo, the men of the Soi Bien had their hands full.

THE COMMANDANT SENDS A MESSAGE

Lieutenant General Le Nguyen Khang, *commandant* of the Vietnamese Marine Corps, had also come north with the last of his brigades to be closer to the action. Unfortunately for Khang, he would be required to spend too much of his time fighting internecine service squabbles with a number of senior ARVN generals also now serving in I Corps whose dislike for the TQLC seemed only a bit less than their antipathy for the Communists.

General Khang had been a junior officer in the Soi Bien in the early days of the republic. It was a young Major Khang who had spotted and recruited an even younger, untried but very promising Second Lieutenant Le Ba Binh into Third Battalion. It was well-known, even though he was the consummate professional, that Khang had a special place in his heart for his old battalion. The men of the Soi Bien likewise had a special reverence for their *commandant*. They considered him to be one of them.

During the day on April 4, while the rifle companies of Third Battalion were spread out in and around Dong Ha, their *commandant* had a small plane drop leaflets, congratulating them for their heroic service and exhorting them to continue the fight. The leaflets came fluttering down, like manna from the heavens, and the message was eagerly absorbed by Binh's Marines. Binh translated the wording for his *covan*. As tired and worn out as he was, Ripley the Realist was still also Ripley the Romantic, and found himself stirred, just as his friends in the Soi Bien genuinely were, by General Khang's rich prose.

The message was generous with praise but not overdone. Because the Marines were culturally and organizationally sparing with compliments the *commandant's* remarks were especially impacting. It was not at all like the verbose Communist propaganda Ripley had read translations of which were so riddled with meaningless terms and falsehoods as to become boring. Ripley had fought in and through the battles General Khang was now praising his Marines for. That praise chronicled what Ripley had experienced alongside Binh's men. The *commandant* told his Marines of the great affection the nation had for them, of how all freedom-loving Vietnamese were aware of their gallant stand at Dong Ha along with the tremendous sacrifices they were making. His message had a powerful ending; reminding his Marines that *he* was proud of them, that they should forever remember to look out for the people, to treat them with kindness and respect, and finally to honor their Corps and to continue the fight against the hated Communist invaders.

Even though he could not read too much Vietnamese, Ripley snatched up and placed a few copies of the message in his personal effects; and then like all the others, got back into the fight.*

---

* General Khang's admonition "to always look out for the people" was institutional counsel never taken lightly. On occasions too numerous to count John Ripley had observed Marines of the Soi Bien, many of them as cold-blooded in their hatred of the invaders as was humanly possible,

For the Marines of Third Battalion, and all units closest to the coast on April 6, naval gunfire remained the only reliable supporting arms available. The NVA were sophisticated enough to know the ships' range limitations. The railroad bridge upstream, while partially destroyed and not capable of supporting armor or large vehicles, could handle foot traffic; and was just outside the naval gunfire fan. There had been no local air support since the shoot down of the VNAF attack aircraft above the Dong Ha action by the SA-7 Strela missile on Sunday afternoon; and ARVN artillery batteries had been abandoned or surrendered.

With only the four increasingly under-strength rifle companies of Third Battalion and the remaining M-48s of the ARVN 20th Tank Battalion to defend the entire Dong Ha area, and the most critical position was right at the blown bridge, friendly forces were stretched thin. The Marines and their less enthusiastic tanker allies could not be everywhere at once and so NVA infantry were able to cross the railroad bridge essentially unchallenged.

---

display behavior that bordered on outright tenderness when it came to dealing with the regular people it was their duty to defend. Conversely, the men of the Soi Bien were equally zealous in eliminating those who abused innocents; NVA or otherwise. It was the day after the leaflets were dropped when Ripley witnessed another instance of the zeal for which Binh's Marines took their mission to protect the people to extreme completion.

On the early morning of the 5th, an ARVN truck approached a position near to where Binh, Ripley, and the Alpha Command Group were located. The vehicle was driven by a fellow who was very obviously an ex-ARVN soldier. He did not have a weapon or any of his regular gear. His uniform had been stripped of name and unit tags. It was one of Binh's corporals who stopped him, ordering him out of the vehicle that was trying to head south. Pulling back the tarpaulin that covered the rear bed, the corporal discovered a treasure trove of booty obviously looted from the homes of local civilians. Ripley, who had experienced a tremendous amount of action with the Soi Bien, rarely saw Binh lose his composure or display his anger. This incident became one of those exceptions. When it was made apparent to the commanding officer of the Soi Bien that this ex-ARVN soldier had so egregiously violated the public trust, there was only one possible outcome. The perpetrator was expeditiously lined up against his vehicle and summarily executed. Several of the Marines a moment later observed that they had just wasted a perfectly good vehicle, one that they could have put to good use, in the process.

Binh knew his Marines would soon be required to meet the enemy buildup on the south side of the river to their immediate west. His westernmost rifle company had already conducted a number of squad-sized patrols to recon enemy dispositions nearest to them. He expected that he would deal with them beginning today. Still he needed to maintain the position at the bridge.

Well aware of the burgeoning NVA threat upstream Binh, with Ripley's input, at first light ordered the displacement from the bridge area of one rifle company, his entire Alpha Command Group headquarters section and the headquarters section of the tank battalion to a position roughly one kilometer south on Highway One near the intersection with Route 9; the highway that ran all the way out to Khe Sanh and on into Laos. A few hundred meters west of Highway One, on the north side of Route 9 Binh had his men and their attached armored personnel carriers set up a temporary command post adjacent to a pagoda that had obviously been there a very long time.

This late in the battle, Ripley had observed that the entire area was devoid of its regular population. There were no living civilians, not one, within his view except for Binh's Marines and what NVA soldiers he was able to occasionally eyeball. The innocent, unburied dead remained; their bodies bloated and distended in death, rotting and stinking in the heat. It would have been merciful to call in a napalm strike now, if there had been air power available, simply to eliminate the millions of flies feasting on their Communist-supplied spoils of war.

Across the road from the pagoda, on the south side of Route 9, Ripley could not help but notice that there was a cemetery. In his experience it seemed large by Vietnamese standards. Even the long-buried dead, probably several generations of ancestors of the families now fleeing south, were similarly allowed no peace as the NVA artillery and rocket fire had churned up giant sections of this formerly sacred ground.

While Binh's Marines and their armor attachments were holding on to their assigned real estate, their situation was not improving. Even though Highway One south of Dong Ha was still in friendly hands, resupply and replenishment, especially for the maintenance heavy, diesel chugging, ammunition consuming M-48s was slow in coming. The tanks were running out of ammo for their main guns. They were also in need of routine maintenance which was a monumental challenge to perform. For the Marines the difficulties posed by the current situation were equally significant. Even though the wounded and dead were still being evacuated, there had been no replacements yet for the men lost to Third Battalion during the fight for Dong Ha. The tactical challenge for Binh and his *covan* was in figuring how best to defend the area and execute their orders with the continually diminishing pool of combat-capable men.

Binh had maneuvered his forces to counter, as best he could, the growing NVA threat now on the south side of the Cua Viet to his immediate west. Moving the designated Marines and tankers back from the bridge area prior to first light on April 6, they were in position and set up around the pagoda before the sun had climbed too much off the eastern horizon. The terrain adjacent to the pagoda was wooded enough to provide good concealment but poor overhead cover.

For Binh and Ripley there was no choice but to remain in Dong Ha until they were KIA or ordered to withdraw. Even though the commanding officer of the 20th Tank Battalion had stayed and kept his unit in the fight so far, the influence of Jim Smock as his advisor could not be overstated to that end. But if the remaining tanks and support vehicles were not reprovisioned soon they would become useless to the allies.

John Ripley had certainly lived through more than his share of strange situations and odd moments. Life as a Marine and living with Marines, American and Vietnamese, especially during wartime, provided an unending supply of material for personal amusement and for stories he might later tell that would be believed only because the listeners had confidence in the storyteller's veracity.

The arrival of a number of press correspondents to Third Battalion's new headquarters position near the pagoda off of Route 9 at approximately 0730 on Thursday morning reminded Ripley, yet again, just how unbelievable combat circumstances were. Some of the events, many of the events, that took place were simply too bizarre to have imagined beforehand.

To the extent that there were automobiles in Vietnam, Saigon in particular, the very humble-looking, utilitarian French-made Citroen was preeminent, ubiquitous. Small by American standards, the common model would never have made the cut for American families who required interior room and power. It was a shock for all the Marines there spread out around the pagoda to watch the jerky approach and rapid halt of the very much out-of-place Citroen on the road just south of their positions.

As strange as the car seemed to Americans arriving in Saigon who, by 1972, were used to bigger size and certainly—by their own standards—more gracious styling to their own vehicles, to see such a small contrivance out of which poured too many people to have reasonably fit inside seemed to Ripley like some odd fraternity stunt. *"How do they get so many people inside?"* he thought to himself. The Citroen was almost the kind of car one would see driven by Shriners clowns at some other than serious event. Ripley could imagine Peter Sellers as Inspector Clouseau emerging to add his own special breed of insanity to the scene. The last man out was carrying one of those ponderous-looking, large, reel-to-reel cameras, the kind that looked like a set of over-sized Mickey Mouse ears. John had always associated those contraptions with the newsreels he grew up watching whenever he went to the local picture show as a boy in Radford all those years ago.

Spotting Ripley from the road, the tiny mob rapidly rushed towards the now-acknowledged American Marine hero, humping tape recorders, still cameras, and of course the large newsreel machine. Even before they reached the man who had destroyed the Dong Ha Bridge they began to shout out questions. The men with microphones had their arms extended long before they could have recorded his response. Surrounding him immediately they repeated the questions they had braved so much discomfort on the long ride up from wherever they had come from to have answered. This brief little interlude might have been a jovial moment for Ripley had it not been for the NVA infantry coming out of the wood line to the northwest who made their presence known within seconds of the correspondents' arrival.

The cacophony of a half-dozen frantic reporters all speaking volubly to Ripley at once, asking pretty much the same question, in no way masked the unforgettably unique sounds that made every fighting man's blood run cold. The "thunk, thunk, thunk" of what had to be enemy 82mm mortar rounds leaving their tubes not very far away were followed quickly, too quickly, by the rapid explosions from impact all around.

What saved John Ripley was the human sandbag wall of correspondents in a tight 360 around him. Jim Smock had been a few meters away, atop one of the armored personnel carriers (APC), looking with binoculars toward the wood line and the advancing NVA. He had taken shrapnel to his back in the first volley. Ripley's radio operator, his "Younger Brother," the very faithful, resolute, and resourceful Nha was killed instantly. The same shrapnel burst that took his life also sheared the antenna from the radio he had just been using. In fact, except for Ripley who was shielded by the hapless reporters, every Marine and soldier who was not inside an APC or under significant cover in the immediate vicinity was hit by shrapnel.

Binh's Marines at the pagoda had just deployed to meet the advancing NVA. Even before the mortar barrage Binh was under cover talking on the net with his rifle company commanders and his weapons company, attempting to respond to the new local threat. The number of enemy troops to their front was significant. Within moments it was obvious that the Marines attached to Binh were again vastly outnumbered, had a major fire fight on their hands, and it was all infantry versus infantry.

The fighting was particularly brutal, and it was evident within the first few minutes that the outnumbered Marines around the pagoda would need to pull back to the better cover afforded by a large ditch running east to west on the south side of Route 9. With Binh busily coordinating the action, Ripley focused on getting the exposed-to-enemy-fire wounded closest to him to safety. He was also in need of a replacement antenna for the radio

Nha had been carrying so that he might talk on the *covan* net in order that he could call in naval gunfire.

While Binh was engaged in coordinating the movement and firepower of all of Third Battalion, Ripley concerned himself with shuttling the wounded correspondents and what Marines were in his immediate vicinity to the ditch on the south side of Route 9. Once he had gotten that accomplished, Ripley turned his attentions to entreating the crew of one of the APCs from the ARVN tank battalion to lend him assistance in moving the non-ambulatory wounded. The one he approached was completely buttoned up—all hatches closed to minimize the risk to the crew snug inside. Ripley took the butt of his CAR-15 and wrapped it on the rear hatch of the M-113 until finally a young ARVN trooper cracked it open just a shade. The soldier's eyes were wide with fear. It took Ripley a bit of quick convincing but he was able to momentarily enlist the help of the APC and its crew in accepting a few of the wounded aboard.

The NVA were nowhere near as logistically challenged as Binh's Marines. The fighting in the vicinity of the pagoda carried on with the enemy continuing to feed troops into the action; and it was quite evident that if the Marines remained in place they would be overrun. Binh's decision to move his remaining forces to the south side of Route 9 was made while Ripley had been tending the wounded.

There was no sugar-coating it. The allied ground situation appeared grim; even grimmer than it had these last few days. With Major Jim Smock wounded and in the process of being medevaced out, whatever positive influence he had so far had for the eight days of the enemy invasion on the man he was advising was instantaneously gone. Before Binh could get the men of Third Battalion all to the south side of Route 9, the remaining tanks and APCs of the 20th Tank Battalion began to, on their own, bug out from the area surrounding the pagoda, without picking up their own dead or fully accounting for all their wounded.

Ripley had placed the last of the wounded Marines, including Smock, inside the one APC he had momentary, nominal control over, and then went looking for Nha. The APC, in trace of the others, then rapidly left the area. Right where he had earlier delicately placed his corpse, he realized that he and his radio operator were now alone. He reached down and almost gingerly slung the lifeless body of his "Younger Brother" up onto his shoulders.

The fog of war was thickest nearest the point of contact right there at the pagoda. A mix of battlefield chaos and the strange, daily morning mist common to many places in I Corps pervaded the area. To his rear, and not very far, just as he had shouldered his dear friend, Ripley spied what had to be a squad of NVA infantry slowly advancing towards them. Expecting to be shot in the back at any moment, Ripley stepped southward; toward where he thought the men of the Soi Bien might be, resigned to whatever might happen. He was not about to leave Nha.

Blowing him away would have been a certainty at this range. Somehow the NVA soldiers failed to engage as Ripley continued on. Soon, he was hailed by Binh and the unflappable, ferocious Jack who had come back to find him. They then together headed for the relative cover and safety on the south side of the road.

Thieu Ta (Major) Le Ba Binh, Captain John Walter Ripley, and the remainder of Third Battalion were ordered out of Dong Ha on April 7th, walking the five kilometers back to Ai Tu where they rejoined Brigade 258. Binh had entered Dong Ha on March 30th with seven hundred troops. When they arrived at Ai Tu nine days later the Soi Bien mustered barely two hundred combat-effective Marines. The other TQLC battalions during the same period had likewise been fully engaged against the tenacious NVA all over northern Quang Tri Province.[1]

The "Big Picture" view of the action across most of South Vietnam was hardly encouraging at the close of business on April 8th. The NVA by now had launched all three of the major thrusts of their Nguyen Hue Offensive. In the central portion of the country they were focused on driving east along Route 19 towards Pleiku and Kontum, with the intent of dividing the country in half. Further south, the enemy had also just captured Loc Ninh and surrounded An Loc northwest of Saigon.

While not terribly cheery, the ground situation in northern I Corps at the end of the day on April 8th was significantly better than at other places on the map where the NVA had attacked. The rapid reintroduction of Brigade 369 back into theater was having salutary impact on morale and battlefield performance.

With Brigade 369 now in the fight, the entire Vietnamese Marine Corps was up against the NVA all across northern Quang Tri Province. Even though they remained outnumbered, and were generally still being forced back, their stubborn defense at every point of contact was disrupting the enemy timetable for victory. During the next several days there would be glimmers of hope, even victory, where tenacious Marines refused to give ground. (ARVN conduct in northern I Corps—limited to the actions of Third Division—thus far ranged from abysmal to traitorous. Fortunately for the stretched-to-the-limit Marines, Saigon had also begun to reinforce ARVN units with the First Division and a number of Ranger battalions whose battlefield conduct would be far more in keeping with the Ranger tradition; as understood by Americans.)

George Philip with First Artillery Battalion
April 7, 1972
Early afternoon

From Phu Bai north and back into the fight George had returned to action with First Artillery Battalion in support of Brigade 369. After linking up with old comrades he had learned that one of his friends, Dai Uy (Captain) Nguyen Tam, a true warrior and professional from Philip's experience, and the 105mm artillery battery he had commanded, had been caught out at Camp Carroll. Even though they were located adjacent to them, the Marines were *not* part of the 56th Regiment's perfidious and shameful surrender. But they had been overwhelmed and overrun.

Well aware by this late in his tour of the cultural differences between Americans and Vietnamese, George was given the clearest example so far of "face" and saving it at lunchtime on April 7th. Reflecting more the French influence and gentility than the obviously boorish, less-than-palatable American manner of staying fueled by eating c-rations on the run—which Captain Philip usually appreciated—the artillery battalion commander,

Doan Trong Cao, and his entire command element properly broke for their noon meal just off of Highway One.

With clean, unrolled straw mats placed and set, and with perhaps a dozen in attendance, they had just begun eating when an enemy artillery round impacted, George guessed, maybe five hundred meters beyond them. The battalion commander and his entire staff maintained poker faces, sitting formally cross-legged as they always did at meals while George experienced a bit of increasing pucker factor. Taking their cues from Lieutenant Colonel Cao, the staff continued eating. No big deal.

A few moments later, a second, single round landed beyond them, this time about three hundred meters long. George was now reasonably certain they were under enemy observation. Unshaken, his Vietnamese friends continued with their meal. Philip had learned that NVA artillery crews were generally quite competent but often a bit slower than American and VNMC crews in making adjustments—thankfully. George expected there would soon be another round.

Sure enough, the third single round landed, this time long by what seemed like not quite two hundred meters. George's insides were churning now but his hosts were nonplussed. The American advisor no longer had an appetite.

In what seemed to Philip like an eternity, the fourth round finally came—this time short by a few hundred meters. The bad guys had established the necessary bracket. Halfway decent forward observers and the gun crews they controlled would have the next rounds right on the money. Lieutenant Colonel Cao was no fool. With the bracket established, he knew the next adjustment would be "fire for effect" executed by multiple guns with lots of rounds expended for that mission.

Without breaking a sweat and with complete calm in his voice, after putting his chopsticks and rice bowl down, he spoke in understated English for George to hear: "We go now." And so they did.

April 8th
Macroview continued

As bad as the ground combat situation in northern Quang Tri Province had been since the beginning of the Communist Nguyen Hue Offensive at lunchtime on March 30th, things certainly could have been far worse. In spite of the Americans' self-imposed no-fire ring around Bat 21 which had unnecessarily left countless targets free from air and artillery attack, (therefore causing an indeterminate number of additional RVN casualties) and allowed the NVA to capture the Cam Lo Bridge intact, the enemy inexplicably had kept back at least two full divisions north of the DMZ as part of their strategic reserve.

Whether this was part of the original plan or not would remain unclear to the allies who benefited by the inordinate fear the Communist leadership had of the American Marine forces floating offshore. The arrival on April 1st of amphibious forces just over the horizon had not gone unnoticed by the enemy. By April 8th the entire Ninth Marine Amphibious Brigade was steaming in the Tonkin Gulf. The NVA had very sophisticated radio intercept capabilities and may have been listening to the open conversations Turley, Ripley, and all of the others had earlier had with the naval gunfire ships offshore. Those broadcasts from the gunfire line to Turley that "his brothers" were out there simply awaiting an invite to come ashore, and the "Land the Landing Force" message of mysterious origin for which he had known nothing but was nearly drawn and quartered by the MACV staff, may have served greater purposes than anyone might then have appreciated or realized.

From the NVA perspective, the long coast which could be assaulted by the Marines if they decided to attack, from the mouth of the Cua Viet to north of the DMZ all the way up towards Vinh, well inside the Democratic Republic of Vietnam, was a serious contingency they believed they needed to have forces available to contend with. Showing a temporary lapse of political acumen and familiarity with the current American political climate—although it might have been a strategic blow to strike the NVA with American Marines in their very exposed and heretofore never-attacked rear areas it would have been political suicide for President Nixon to recommit American ground combat forces back into Vietnam, especially North Vietnam—this probably unintended amphibious demonstration may well have slowed significantly the enemy's advance. (In Marine Corps parlance an "amphibious demonstration" is meant to serve as a strategic deception to the enemy by making them think you may come ashore at any given place, or not. By doing this the enemy is required to invest forces defending greater areas and thus spreading out or tying up resources which would then not be available to fight elsewhere.)

Had the enemy's additional two divisions been fed into the battle in northern Quang Tri Province more expeditiously, Ripley's destruction of the Dong Ha Bridge notwithstanding, it is doubtful that the thinly spread Vietnamese Marine forces could have held as they did.[2]

TURLEY RETURNS

Gerry Turley had returned to the Ai Tu COC late on the morning of April 4th, following his evening hiatus in Danang. It felt almost almost like "coming home" after his MACV ordeal. Curiously, in his absence and during the period of his trip south, Turley had missed the return of his American Marine boss, Colonel Josh Dorsey, in passing. Colonel Dorsey, who had long ago scheduled a short Easter holiday interlude with his wife in the Philippines, had come back as quickly as he could have and, like all of his Marines and the people they advised, headed straight north. Colonel Dorsey arrived in Quang Tri Province with Gerry down south and not fully dialed in on the then still developing "Turley situation." The Colonel was enough of a professional and had seen enough to keep from getting too riled before his junior mate briefed him in fully on the battlefield circumstances which had gone so awry.

When they linked back up, Colonel Dorsey naturally assumed his duties as the senior Marine advisor which suited Gerry just fine. With the ever-expanding battle and increasing number of

TQLC units to track, there was no end of action to keep Turley fully engaged, although not at quite the same intensity as before.

The complete unfolding of the enemy's Nguyen Hue Offensive presented an overwhelmingly target-rich environment throughout South Vietnam, even with the Bat 21 restrictions in northern Quang Tri Province. American tactical and strategic (B-52s) bombers were initially required to come to the aid of RVN forces in the central and southern portions of the country that, in many cases, were surrounded or cut off from reinforcement by the invaders.

As more American airpower was daily being brought back into Southeast Asia, assets could be directed against targets north of the DMZ. Whether the Communists were surprised by the American response is doubtful. They were well prepared and presented the latest in Soviet-supplied anti-aircraft defenses. The best news for the American aircrews was that they were now at least flying against high-value, meaningful targets. In private conversation with his advisors President Nixon was succinct: "The bastards have never been bombed like they are going to be bombed this time."[3]

On April 10, B-52s attacked targets near Vinh. It was to be the first such strike that far north since November 1968. On April 16 B-52s struck key locations in Hanoi and Haiphong for the very *first* time in the war. Communist propaganda reported that the Stratofortresses had accomplished nothing other than the killing of innocent civilians. The bombing of the DRV would continue at an intensity not yet seen in the war.[4]

Second Lieutenant Nguyen Luong

First Platoon, Fourth Company, Third Battalion
Somewhere slightly northwest of Ai Tu
April 12, 1972
Early evening

When *the Soi Bien* was pulled back to Ai Tu from Dong Ha, the battalion was infused with its first group of replacement troops since the enemy invasion had begun. Most of the new Marines were fresh-faced young men who had only recently completed their initial boot camp training down south. The Vietnamese Marine Corps did not now have the luxury of allowing any of its nine infantry battalions to stand down following difficult duty. After the meat grinder at Dong Ha and the subsequent withdrawal further south, the lightest duty Third Battalion's brigade commander could give them was to assist First Battalion in providing for the active defense of Ai Tu.

Second Lieutenant Nguyen Luong had arrived for service at the dawn of the new year with Third Battalion's Fourth Company and in the first two weeks of April experienced combat as intense as experienced by any of the Soi Bien's longest-serving members. The learning curve for new infantry platoon commanders in every fighting organization was always steep. None steeper than what the TQLC in northern Quang Tri Province were now facing.

Third Battalion, since Ripley had blown the Dong Ha Bridge on Easter Sunday, had again been operating with both an Alpha

Command Group (ACG) and a Bravo Command Group (BCG). Binh and his advisor were with the ACG which included First and Third Companies along with most of the Weapons Company and the main elements of the battalion headquarters. The slightly smaller Bravo Command Group was led by Third Battalion's executive officer and included Second and Fourth Companies. The BCG for Third Battalion currently had no American advisor attached to it.

Fourth Company had been covering the battalion's western flank, away from Ai Tu. By this late in the battle, and even with the enemy not able to cross the Cua Viet River right at Dong Ha, they were able to get troops across upstream at the Old French Railroad Bridge, and armor further west at Cam Lo. Unfortunately for the Vietnamese Marines, what allied airpower there now was did not keep the NVA from maintaining a decided manpower advantage on the battlefield, even as far east as Ai Tu.

Luong's platoon, First Platoon of Fourth Company, was the westernmost platoon in his company's area of responsibility. All day they had engaged the NVA who enjoyed considerable local firepower superiority as they were locked in contact so near as to nullify the benefits of American naval gunfire; but not the impact of the ubiquitous 82mm mortars the Communists were so adept at using in close quarters.

Nearing the end of his second week of combat command, Luong had assimilated and learned what he could from these brief but extremely intense experiences. As it was just getting dark the enemy to his front and left flank again launched an infantry assault supported by 82mm mortars against Luong's intended overnight position. The overwhelming volume of fire and number of NVA made it evident to the young platoon commander that he needed to consolidate his position and pullback closer to his company's other platoons. With the enemy advancing at a fairly rapid clip, Luong sent the lead elements of First Platoon back towards the rest of the company in reasonably orderly fashion. He made certain his three squads and the extra Marines assigned to him from Weapons Company were safe, away from the line of fire before he ordered his own small platoon command element to begin moving.

With Luong were three other Marines: his radio operator Ha Si (Corporal) Thanh, his attendant or "cowboy" Ha Si Duoc, and another young Marine named Loi. They were all about to step off into the gathering darkness, in trace of the rest of their mates, when a particularly heavy barrage of mortar rounds impacted on and around them. In an instant two of Luong's three Marines were dead. Ha Si Duoc was wounded but would shortly succumb. Luong reached over to his radio operator to find that the PRC-25 radio which he had been humping had also taken shrapnel, rendering it useless. There was so much fire and so much impact that Luong dove for cover not realizing that he too was hit. Without keeping track of the time, he guessed it had been a few moments before he felt the warm stickiness of his own blood from the wound in his left leg.

The shelling continued. For some reason the NVA infantry did not at that moment advance against what was a position now occupied by only four Marines, three of them dead. Luong could tell the enemy was close. He could hear them, smell them, even sense their presence. Unable to get up because of the wound, he dared not move for fear of drawing their attention. Luong had been partially covered by dirt and dust from the ongoing shelling his position received. He was alone while the rest of his platoon, he hoped, had escaped the mortar fire and was under cover somewhere not too far to his east.

Luong was stuck and alone in the dark. He knew his men would come looking for him when they could. Until then he would stay put, with the lifeless bodies of his dead comrades haphazardly arranged around and near to him. Luong expected the enemy to advance into his position at any minute. He snatched a grenade from the cartridge belt of his cowboy, pulled the pin, keeping the spoon firmly covered. If the NVA wanted him they would pay for the privilege. All he could do now was wait, and so he did.

Two weeks was long enough for Luong to understand that battles did not always progress in linear fashion. For some reason unknown to him, the NVA had halted a few meters somewhere in front of his position. Luong remained still, palming the grenade, bleeding and breathing as slowly as he could.

Luong was not able to precisely track the time. The pain and throb from the hole in his leg, to which he had earlier quietly applied a battle dressing in order to slow the bleeding, reminded him that he was alive but in deep, deep danger. Every few minutes as one hand grew weary from the enormity of holding the live grenade he would switch it to the other one; still expecting the enemy to come and get him. Sometimes he would drift off, but then quickly regain consciousness with the fear he might involuntarily let go of the live bomb.

The NVA finally came. About a squad of them arrived an hour or two later, as if materializing out of the nothingness. Luong was silent. His breathing could not be discerned, his eyes averred. But he could still see them, sense them, make out the shapes of their pith helmets. They were carrying their AK-47s at the ready, bayonets extended and fixed. To the enemy he was a dead man like the other three.

Luong had earlier paid no attention to it but the NVA scavengers noticed: his three comrades, quite naturally, had all been carrying their backpacks. From long-term experience the Marines knew that NVA soldiers, while incredibly brave and aggressive in general as fighters, were often poor peasants, country bumpkins by the standards of their much more materially endowed southern enemies. Luong, mercifully, had been carrying no pack and was therefore not likely to yield souvenirs of food or booty or whatever else these red devils were after. For good measure they ran their bayonets through the corpses of Luong's comrades before picking through their packs and taking what treasures there were. Luong processed those unique, disturbing sounds; at the next moment expecting the same for himself. That moment never came. Maybe they never saw him. Maybe they saw him and thought not to bother. Whatever. As stealthily as they had appeared, they vanished; leaving the bleeding infantry platoon commander alive and still quietly gripping the hand grenade.

When the NVA departed his position, they must have left the area. Now Luong really was alone, or so he surmised. It was just him and his hours-ago-killed and freshly bayoneted comrades on this unmarked piece of real estate somewhere west of Ai Tu. Luong was wise enough, still had sufficient presence of mind, to not completely trust his senses or his second lieutenant intuition and so he waited, very quietly with his grenade.

His concern began to shift from whether there were enemy present or not to whether he could maintain enough lucidity to keep a firm grasp on his grenade. With the loss of blood and all the other things which had taken place, consciousness began to elude him. His bodily strength, he could tell, was waning.

The physical tension from gripping the grenade was becoming a problem. It was as if he had been squeezing a tennis ball for hours and hours. The muscles and tendons in each of his forearms and hands screamed from overuse. He forced himself to continue holding on, knowing that his strength was ebbing. Beyond the time from when he was certain the enemy was gone, for good measure, he held the grenade until finally he knew that he would soon be spent entirely. Luong, as he had earlier, again caught himself drifting in and out of consciousness but fortunately managing to still hold down the grenade's spoon. At some point he would either fall asleep and release the grenade or simply drop it from exhaustion. In either event he would manage to kill only himself and no NVA. Guessing that it was safe, he finally pitched the live grenade away from himself and the bodies of his comrades.

Luong had lost more blood than realized. His throw, from the supine position, was weaker than planned, and was inside the weapon's burst radius. When the grenade exploded, he felt the sharp sting of fragments biting into his left arm. There was no local reaction or apparent movement in response to that disturbance. He continued to slowly bleed from his old wound, and now also from the new ones.

The manner of waiting had suddenly changed. With the NVA gone from the area, Luong's survival now hinged on not bleeding to death rather than being bayoneted, shot, or blown up. Up until these past few moments he could focus his energies, when he could focus, on his flesh and blood enemies. The enemy had now changed. His enemy was no longer finite. His new enemy was time. His enemy was doubt, worry, and blood supply.

Luong had time to ponder many things: his entire life, the best parts, the parts he had long ago shuffled into his mind's recesses. He thought about his parents, his siblings, his girlfriend, his comrades, the men of his platoon. He had time to think many of the same thoughts many times. No longer concerned with worry for blowing himself up, he did have luxury to drift off now and then. There was little he could do other than to remain hopeful, to think about his service, to act like and conclude his life like a Marine, to bring honor to his unit and country. He already knew in his heart that he would have blown himself up, along with his sworn enemy, rather than being taken prisoner. No one would take that from him. He lay there alone, not knowing what would come next: death or some divine deliverance.

During the seemingly unending period that Luong was alone in the strange, anomalous quiet somewhere west of Ai Tu, in and out of consciousness, all over Vietnam the action continued at a frenetic pace. In the central and southern portions of his country ARVN troops battled furiously to beat back the advancing NVA. American airpower was being applied at every point to assist ARVN forces. In Quang Tri Province as well the fighting carried on except for where Luong now was.

One of Luong's two staff sergeants led the recovery effort that finally came back for his platoon commander's missing group. The others with Staff Sergeant Diem he could not see or hear.

Good old Diem. A month earlier the bachelor Luong had happily given him half his pay to assist with the birth of his first child for which Diem was especially grateful. To most of the men in Luong's platoon, Diem *was* the TQLC. Diem had been a Marine, it seemed to Luong, forever, even though he was no more than ten years Luong's senior. Known for his prowess as a martial artist, he was to Luong as Jack was to John Ripley; ferocious, selfless, resolute, unflappable, hard core, the Vietnamese Marine prototype for "Old Corps."

It must have been four, perhaps five in the morning, when they arrived. Luong had by now lost all track of time when he was set upon and lifted back into the world of the living by the stalwart Diem. Speaking in hushed tones only enough to brief each other in on what had happened, the powerful platoon sergeant carried his young commander, whose pain and massive blood loss were evident, back toward friendly lines.

The Vietnamese Marine Corps, and also the Army of the Republic of Vietnam (ARVN), as earlier described, were nowhere near as resource rich as their American counterparts in terms of providing expeditious battlefield medevac and close-to-the-scene extensive medical care for their combat wounded. The Vietnamese Marine Corps shared many organizational similarities with their American Marine brothers. One major difference though was that the TQLC was *not* part of the Vietnamese Navy, and, because of their country's logistical limitations had very little to do operationally with the navy. Where the U.S. Navy provided the medical support given their Marines, the TQLC was on its own. Each infantry battalion, only nine of them by the beginning of the Easter Offensive, had assigned to it one medical doctor (the same as American battalions) and a group of medical assistants. Where American Marine and army units had the same number of physicians—one—at the battalion level as did their Vietnamese allies, the number of corpsmen (medics in the army) available for critical support was nowhere near as great for the Vietnamese.

In TQLC infantry battalions the medical doctor typically traveled with the Alpha Command Group while his senior assistant maneuvered with the Bravo Command Group. What assistants there were, were generally divided equally and were sometimes attached out to companies but almost never to platoons as was common for American operations. There were simply too few trained medical assistants to go around and so they generally stayed in headquarters locations to treat and triage the wounded that got to them.

Staff Sergeant Diem mustered what strength he had left to carry his half bled-out platoon commander all the way back to the closest aid station. As much as he tried to walk evenly and minimize Luong's pain, the distance was great and the ride for the casualty less than ideal. At least he was in friendly hands, literally, and was moving in the proper direction.

Approaching the aid station after what seemed like an interminable hike, both Luong and his guardian angel were at the point of complete exhaustion. There were signs posted indicating medical treatment and evacuation. One way was for wounded officers to go to a jeep that was equipped with a stretcher. The other way, a bit closer, led to a large GMC-type ambulance for all wounded personnel.

Knowing how tired his platoon sergeant was, Luong told Diem to take him to the ambulance. Moments later both vehicles departed for the Third ARVN Division's field hospital somewhere between where they now were and Quang Tri.

The one jeep and one ambulance medical convoy had not traveled two hundred meters before being taken under fire by large-caliber enemy artillery. In the opening salvo the jeep, serving as the lead vehicle, took a direct hit, exploding right in front of the ambulance following in trace. The very scared and aroused ambulance driver continued on, steering wildly through the mayhem. Those in the vehicle's rear were tossed around like rag dolls, but at least they were still alive.

The ride to the Third Division's field hospital in between Ai Tu and Quang Tri City was not the end of the line; certainly not the end of the day's excitement for Luong. Staying faithfully by his side in transporting him to the rear, Staff Sergeant Diem had also been a passenger in the back of the ambulance that had earlier narrowly escaped the enemy's shelling. Although the Third Division field hospital was considered to be in a relatively "rear area" compared to Dong Ha and Ai Tu, the NVA by now were everywhere. Also, headquarters troops remaining as part of the barely functioning ARVN division provided the security for the hospital. Hardly elite troops.

Staff Sergeant Diem made sure that his lieutenant made it back to the Third Division field hospital. The battle-hardened platoon sergeant remained at his commander's side throughout, as if he believed the situation was not quite right. Within an hour of their arrival as Luong had been placed on a stretcher, waiting for appropriate medical help to attend to his wound, an enemy unit attacked into the hospital area itself. Diem was nimble enough to sense the danger, and again snatched up his lieutenant before the NVA troops made it to where they were. Had Diem waited any longer before taking his officer to a covered position away from the makeshift hospital, they both might have been killed. The attackers shot and bayoneted what hospital staff and patients there were before exiting the area. Order was slowly reimposed; and when it was Luong was evacuated further south to Quang Tri, with Staff Sergeant Diem still by his side.

Not that far from the front, Quang Tri was still solidly in friendly hands. It was judged safe enough for Mrs. Nguyen Van Thieu, wife of the nation's president, to visit the troops. As he again waited to be seen and have his wounds tended to, Luong and Diem were visited by the first lady who, in Vietnamese tradition, passed out small envelopes of cash to the wounded soldiers and Marines, in much the same manner American troops might be awarded Purple Hearts. The first lady, hearing Luong's story from Diem, awarded the young lieutenant ten envelopes and even gave a few to his platoon sergeant.

In the hospital at Quang Tri, Luong vaguely remembered meeting Mrs. Thieu, being looked at by a doctor, being given blood, and then being placed aboard some sort of aircraft. That was it. Mrs. Thieu must have pulled a few strings. When he woke up again he was in the TQLC hospital in Saigon.

SITUATION IN I CORPS

John Ripley's miraculous and heroic actions at the Dong Ha Bridge had purchased critical time for the allies to buck up under the initial strain and shock of the enemy invasion. The failure of the allies to follow through with the destruction of the Cam Lo Bridge, because of the Bat 21 situation, was now nearly two weeks later still plaguing the South Vietnamese and the remaining American advisors in Quang Tri Province.

Bat 21 was eventually rescued the same evening Second Lieutenant Nguyen Luong finally made it back to the rear and proper medical attention. By that time the NVA had moved significant armor and infantry forces across the Cam Lo Bridge. These legions, which would have been denied such easy entry onto the field of battle had the bridge been taken down, were now directly threatening the entire area south of the Cua Viet

River and the cities of Quang Tri and Hue. One major benefit to the conclusion of the rescue effort was that the air assets used to support the saving of "just one man"[1] could now be redirected toward the general effort against the NVA.

In the first two weeks of the Nguyen Hue Offensive, the NVA had unleashed its most massive invasion of the war, eclipsing by a fair margin the effort of Tet '68. In the first two weeks of the fighting in Quang Tri Province, the Communist advance had not gone a full twenty miles; thanks almost entirely to the tenacious defense put up by the Marines.

Unlike the very questionable performance of what was left of the Third ARVN Division in Quang Tri Province, the initial setbacks in the central and southern portions of the country were beginning to subside. A curious metamorphosis was beginning to take place. ARVN forces there were no longer everywhere falling back in full retreat. ARVN resolve was no longer everywhere crumbling. Without the American leadership and manpower crutch the Vietnamese had leaned on for so many years, ARVN leadership and those young men doing the fighting had no option other than to fight or perish. Across the three areas of operations, ARVN was starting to show signs of strength and resolve, as was the national leadership. General Abrams, the commanding general of MACV, noted a major improvement in the nation's political and military leadership even since the recent *Lam Son 719* operations of less than a year earlier.[2]

Western opponents to the war would continually point to the huge American air campaign as the sole factor in blunting the Communist invasion. Certainly tactical and strategic airpower played a major, major part. It was more than needed to balance the blank-check logistical *largesse* provided the northerners by the Russians and Chinese which received far less public acknowledgement, scrutiny, or criticism. All the American airpower there was would have mattered little, however, had ARVN forces—in addition to the efforts of the Vietnamese Marines which had all along been resolute—not begun to show the determination now becoming evident at many points of contact with the enemy.

Third Battalion stayed and fought in Ai Tu until April 22 when Brigade 258, the Soi Bien's parent unit, was replaced by Brigade 147. The reinforcement of northern I Corps by ARVN units other than the Third Division, to include several Ranger groups, was slowly beginning to have salutary impact.

The fighting in and around Ai Tu for Third Battalion, after Second Lieutenant Nguyen Luong's evacuation, continued to be extremely intense, intensely bitter, bitterly personal. Even though Binh and his company commanders maintained firm control over their daily-shrinking units, the battles were of such vigor and ferocity that it seemed as if it was all being conducted entirely at the individual and squad levels.

Jack, the ferocious, near-iconic symbol of everything martial for the Marines of Third Battalion, died as Ripley would have expected him to: in the attack, against a vastly numerically superior force. It was just about midnight the day after Luong's evacuation when Ripley and Binh observed Jack and two others rush past them, to the outside of the wire towards an enemy force of indeterminate size.

The darkness was divided only by the eerie, other-worldly light sporadically and randomly provided from the ubiquitous artillery or mortar-fired parachute flares used by the advancing NVA. Outnumbered, always outnumbered, the Marines closed with the invaders somewhere far enough away to not be seen in the void less than twenty meters from the wire. The contact was disturbingly close enough, though, to discern the particular clatter of men grappling and scraping to the death. After a time there was no movement, no sound, no nothing.

It was only when the sun came up again that those inside the wire could finally view the carnage. Three Marines, to include Jack, lay twisted and dead among perhaps two dozen NVA. The fighting knife Jack had always carried was buried up to its hilt in the chest of the enemy soldier who had shot and killed, at point-blank range, Binh's most faithful bodyguard.[3]

Since they had flown north the same day George Philip returned from his Hawaii R&R, the Marines of First Artillery Battalion had been serving in support of the three infantry battalions of Brigade 369. Having lost the one battery out at Camp

Carroll that had been adjacent to the ARVN regiment that shamefully surrendered, the remaining batteries and gun crews, down to the most junior men, understood this invasion's gravity and all that was at stake. Captain Philip took particular pride in these Marines who answered every call for artillery support with alacrity and precision.

George was always busy: assisting his Vietnamese counterparts in coordinating the calls for fire and the movement of units. The NVA artillery and rocket threat was such that the Marines were required to relocate their guns two to three times a day, which was standard procedure anyway. Aside from ensuring that the battalions they supported always had at least one battery capable of delivering fire, resupply of ammunition was critical. So far the guns had ample rounds to shoot but there was nothing to waste. Every round was meant to count; had to count. The NVA still had them outgunned, and seemed to still have more rounds to shoot although their rates of fire were not what they had been at the invasion's beginning.

Throughout April and into May George worked very closely with Lieutenant Colonel Cao, the battalion commander it was his duty to advise. The American *covan* made sure that proper procedure and safety issues were adhered to, and even though the shooting was essentially continuous, there was always opportunity to teach and improve ever so slightly what these motivated-for-revenge artillerymen were aggressively seeking to accomplish.

When George was not interfacing with the battalion commander or his staff, he was touring the gun lines, visiting with the battery commanders and their troops. He likewise spent considerable time and effort communicating with the American advisors further up the chain from him in Ai Tu or Quang Tri or wherever it was they were. He was always moving, always busy; doing whatever the man he advised asked him to do.

Supporting George throughout this effort had been his faithful cowboy, Ha Si Tuong. Just as before, Tuong kept his American Dai Uy (Captain) as well provisioned as was humanly possible in the circumstances they were daily facing. Even though George's language skills had improved significantly since his return, Tuong was old-school Vietnamese Marine Corps and so he spoke sparingly with his assigned officer. Captain Philip had tremendous admiration and respect for the selfless Tuong. He liked him a lot.

The Vietnamese Marines and their American advisors in Quang Tri Province, beginning the moment NVA artillery and rocket rounds intentionally began crashing indiscriminately into civilian homes and property, had seen no end to weeping and misery. Making the many thousands of personal tragedies spread out before him in these last few weeks easier to process and not think too much about was the fact that George had no personal connection to any of these people.

The pain and suffering outside of the small circle of warriors George had always been surrounded by in war was made more real the afternoon Lieutenant Colonel Cao called him aside to deliver disturbing news. Cao, out of respect for his *covan*, told George first. Ha Si Tuong had a son who was serving with the ARVN down south in An Loc near Saigon, where the fighting had been especially brutal. Cao had just been informed that Tuong's son was killed in action. The news hit the American harder than he might have thought it would.

Lieutenant Colonel Cao summoned Tuong to their makeshift field command post. With deep respect and dignity Tuong was given the bad news. Demonstrating a stoicism that amazed the American, Ha Si Tuong bowed his head and wept quietly. All those present were silent and deferential until he was able to compose himself. Lieutenant Colonel Cao then reached into his pocket, pulled out a large wad of Vietnamese cash and gave most of it to Ha Si Tuong. Tuong was then sent south to attend to his family's needs and given an abbreviated leave. He could not stay away for too long. During these conditions all hands were needed at the front.[*]

---

[*] As mentioned earlier in the story, the methods used to provision Vietnamese Marine units were different than those used by the Americans. The very obvious issues of resupplying war-fighting materials like weapons, ammunition, fuel, and spare parts were accomplished through military channels. Food and rations were handled in a more *laissez faire* manner. Rather than rely on a ponderous supply chain, unit commanders were instead given funds to purchase food in the local economy. The benefits were significant. Supply issues and planning challenges were reduced, the

Throughout April the NVA continued to feed men and material into the bloody battles for Quang Tri Province. An improving weather situation and the conclusion of the Bat 21 rescue allowed for more effective use of allied air power. The battlefield advantage though, remained with the invaders whose willingness to spend lives seemingly with little regard for cost and the still relatively small number of defending forces kept their momentum going.

Allied forces had continued to hold on at Dong Ha and Ai Tu much longer than might have been expected, aided tremendously by continuous naval gunfire support. Of necessity the northerners shifted their effort to where they had the advantage, and so they attacked from the east. Ultimately the Vietnamese were forced to pull back from both towns which had experienced so much carnage.

Having seen the introduction of the Soviet-built SA-7 Strela shoulder-fired anti-aircraft missile the day Ripley blew the Dong Ha Bridge, the enemy also chose to introduce the wire-guided AT-3 Sagger anti-tank rocket onto the northern I Corps battlefield. The weapon's presence initially wreaked havoc with ARVN armor. The Americans would soon rush to the field their own version, the TOW, which would also see its first action up north.

The unrelenting pressure of the NVA invasion was forcing the ARVN and TQLC forces slowly south. Issues of command and control were likewise plaguing the allied effort. The ersatz sort of patchwork structure that had been designed for the Third ARVN Division to direct the forces up north worked only on

---

local economies were boosted, and fewer troops were required in the logistical effort. On the negative side, when they were operating away from places where they could purchase food from locals, rations often got thin or the men were required to resort to American c-rations.

One not so minor material advantage artillery units had over their brother infantry units in the purchase of food was that the wooden boxes artillery rounds came packaged in were of value to civilians. In First Artillery Battalion, the funds raised by the sale of those boxes were used to supplement the men's rations. Captain Philip noted on several occasions that the standard diet the artillerymen enjoyed was just a bit better than what he observed for the infantry units.

paper and only when there was no fighting. The division commanding general, Brigadier General Vu Van Giai, as noted earlier was no coward, but his abilities to effectively drive his units and utilize his staff were left seriously wanting. Command and control of the various maneuver units was lacking and fighting withdrawals under pressure for ARVN forces pulling back to more propitious lines of defense often devolved into chaos. By early May the allies had also lost Quang Tri City. Their new line of defense would be the My Chanh River, to the north of Hue and just a bit to the south of Firebases Barbara and Nancy, the area Ripley and Binh had left before they had headed to Dong Ha at the invasion's beginning.

At the highest levels in Saigon, the Vietnamese Joint General Staff and President Thieu recognized the need for change if they hoped to expel the invaders. On May 4 the Joint General Staff replaced the MR1 (synonymous with I Corps) commanding general, General Lam with the much more aggressive and innovative Lieutenant General Ngo Quang Truong. Many senior Americans considered Truong to be ARVN's single best fighting general. Truong's ascension to leadership up north delivered near instantaneous efficacy.[†] The president issued Truong his orders. There would be no falling back from the My Chanh River.[4]

TRANSITION OVER TO THE OFFENSIVE

General Truong's assignment as the man to lead the effort to reclaim the portions of Military Region 1 (MR1) that had been lost to the advancing NVA was wisely made. His methods and manner of leadership were like an elixir to the formerly disheartened ARVN troops. His effective use of media was also a major psychological boost to the increasingly disheartened national civilian population.

[†] At the same time, Lieutenant General Khang was promoted to become Chairman of the Joint General Staff for Operations. Brigadier General Bui Te Lan, the same fellow who had assigned Second Lieutenant Luong to Third Battalion because of the amphibian nature of his name, became the new *commandant*.

While his predecessor had already begun the planning to counterattack and the push back to the north, it was Truong's superior leadership and more effective use of his staff that was the critical constituent in making things happen.

While the fighting raged all across South Vietnam at the level of the individual infantryman and villager, and more and more in the air above North Vietnam, at the highest strategic levels President Nixon and Henry Kissinger were maneuvering with the Russians, the Communist Chinese, and the North Vietnamese. Having already visited Communist China not two months earlier and initiated the beginnings of some sort of rapprochement, the American president was also looking to restore a relationship with the Soviets who were anxious to gain Most Favored Nation (MFN) status for the material and economic benefits that would bring.

By engaging the two Red behemoths on a broader scale the United States would appear to again be reasserting its position as leader of the free world with interests beyond Southeast Asia. The interaction with the Soviets and Communist Chinese was also intended to gain leverage over the DRV and use their influence to encourage them to return to the negotiating table. In between all that was taking place among the Americans, Soviets, and Communist Chinese, Henry Kissinger made time to resume his secret negotiations in Paris with officials of the DRV.

On the American side there was concern that the increasing intensity of the air war against the north, especially the outright mining of Haiphong's ports, would keep the Soviets from their meeting. The Soviet desire for MFN, at least for the moment, trumped their loyalty to the Vietnamese Communists. Nixon's Moscow meeting with Brezhnev would go forward as scheduled in late May.

Going Home

Le Huu Sanh—Hospital for Marines
Thu Duc—outside of Saigon

T*he decision to amputate Luong's left leg* above the knee was given to the young lieutenant himself by a committee of doctors at the Marine hospital in Thu Duc. The senior surgeon explained to him that his leg did not need to come off, but that it was so badly damaged the bones would never again be properly aligned. Even when it healed, he continued, there would likely be chronic pain and his leg would atrophy to some point where normal movement would be a challenge. If they amputated, Luong could at least be fitted with a prosthesis. Either way his Marine Corps career, to his extreme disappointment, was ended. This sequence of events he quietly accepted with a maturity beyond his relative youth. The war continued, now without Second Lieutenant Nguyen Luong.

Since the enemy invasion began, ARVN forces had been reinforced by more than thirty battalions in the north to include Rangers and most of the First ARVN Division, a unit of good standing and fighting reputation. Elements of the Airborne Division, the other half of Vietnam's national strategic reserve, would soon also join the fight to liberate Quang Tri Province from the invaders.

John Ripley's last action with the Soi Bien was during the brutal and inconclusive fighting out west of Ai Tu. From Ai Tu Third Battalion, which by early May looked more like a rifle company, was taken back south to Hue by armored convoy.

Hue, the old imperial capital with its massive citadel, a city with a rich history many centuries longer than America's; a place renowned in better times for its gentility, culture, and fine cuisine before it became known to Americans for the bloody fighting of Tet '68, was a beehive of activity.

Even after all he had experienced since the beginning of the enemy invasion, it came as a complete shock to Ripley to view the spectacle of mobilized humanity on the city's outskirts. He had never seen anything like it. Thousands and thousands of regular civilians; old men and old women, young women, children, and even great numbers of young men, former soldiers who had obviously been wounded in action and could no longer fight but could still dig, were together excavating trenches and fighting holes, constructing obstacles, filling sandbags. Ripley was reminded of what the Russians had accomplished at Stalingrad against the advancing Nazis. The population of Hue, increased by uncounted multitudes of those fleeing from the north, did not have to think back too far for motivation to prepare the ramparts. While the American media had made the world aware of the evils perpetrated at My Lai by the poorly led soldiers in one company of the U.S. Army's Americal Division, the local Vietnamese recalled the savagery of the last NVA invasion in 1968 when the red devils murdered and then buried in mass graves between three thousand and five thousand civilians whose only crime was that they were *not* Communists.[1]

On the early morning following their arrival, the men of the Soi Bien were mustered together on a tiny parade deck so that their *commandant* might address them, and personally thank them for their heroic service. Though Binh's battalion had started the action with seven hundred men and had been reinforced a number of times since March 30, there were exactly fifty-two men there to listen to what Lieutenant General Khang had to say. The *commandant's* speech, while similar to what was written in the leaflets earlier air-dropped to Third Battalion, was far more impacting in person. It was an experience Ripley would never forget. He was certain also, that if any of this small group of Vietnamese comrades now present survived the war, they too would forever remember being so specially addressed.

Following the *commandant's* speech, John Ripley said his final goodbyes to Third Battalion. He gave his CAR-15, the weapon carried by most *covans,* to Binh in the same manner one *samurai* might pass on his most precious sword to another warrior of equal stature. The exchange between the two friends was personal and deep. As much as he was now beginning to think about going home, Ripley left the Soi Bien with a heavy heart. The men of Third Battalion would have little time to miss their *covan.* The next day, after again being reinforced with new troops, would find them pressed back into significant action.

John Ripley was driven from Hue down to Phu Bai and then dropped off at the air strip to await pickup for extraction to Saigon in the same way Gerry Turley had been. He would wait and thumb a ride from whatever planes came in. The air field at Phu Bai, once considered among the busiest airports in the world, was at the particular moment Ripley was deposited there, like a ghost town. Without his CAR-15, the appendage he had lived with for nearly the last twelve months, he felt vulnerable and exposed. From where he was on the strip Ripley could see that up in the tower across the way there were a few people. That was it. There was no security, no ground crews, no nothing. He stood there waiting for the arrival of the next plane in, which was sure to pick him up after dropping off whatever might be dropped off. Certainly there would be an inbound plane, in the not too distant future, from down south bringing troops or supplies that would gladly take him back.

The quiet and the lack of human presence were disconcerting. Ripley had not been this alone, ever, in Vietnam. He scanned the area as he waited. He soon found that he was not alone. Over on the tarmac near the tower was a single, flag-draped casket of some young Vietnamese trooper, about to take his last trip home. The presence of that fallen warrior only magnified the quiet.

GOING HOME

John Ripley's rotation date home was essentially set in concrete. This is how it had been for virtually all American fighting men who had ever served in theater but especially now with President Nixon focused on extricating troops from the region. When

Ripley's time was up, that was it. The Americans were leaving, and nothing, not even this latest invasion, would interrupt the process.

While John Ripley as a husband and father was anxious, extremely anxious, to get home to his wife and their three children, he had conflicting emotions when it came to leaving. He was a professional, and had personally invested so much in this effort that was yet to be successfully concluded. At the same time he also understood that he had used up more lives than a dozen cats between his tenure as Lima Six Actual in 1967 and then again while serving with the Soi Bien. Surely, at some point his luck would run out. No one, especially his American Marine contemporaries or his friend Binh, would begrudge his surviving this second tour.

Ripley's efforts had mattered a great deal to the Soi Bien, actions at the Dong Ha Bridge notwithstanding. His acumen with calling in naval gunfire and the other supporting arms had hurt the NVA significantly, but the recent loss of friends like Nha and Jack, drove him to seek greater retribution. Ripley would not have the opportunity to completely sate his desire for revenge.

When he left it would not be like in the movies. John Ripley had confidence that RVN forces would prevail; eventually, so long as American material support continued. This particular battle, just one more in the unending *miasma* that was the Vietnam War, if it had been part of some odd film, was stuck in an interminable, unyielding climax scene; and Ripley was set to depart in the middle of it, without the closure and satisfaction of experiencing the job to completion. But that was the way it was. There was nothing Ripley or anybody else could do.

Just like the other *covans* whose tours were winding down, though the fighting was not, he would not be replaced. When Ripley left, the Soi Bien would be on their own. It did not concern or worry him greatly. Ripley had experienced and seen enough to have supreme confidence in Binh, his XO, the rest of his company commanders, and the men of Third Battalion. Arranging fire support would be a bit more challenging, but not a whole lot. And even though the ground situation had not completely stabilized in Quang Tri Province, the Vietnamese were now aggressively moving over to the offensive. Ripley could see the momentum and leadership beginning to move in the right direction. Outsiders and members of the press might not get it, but the professionals could sense the broad unquantifiable, intangible, positive changes slowly but discernibly gathering steam.

When it came time for Ripley to say his goodbyes to the friends he had made during all the hard fighting, most especially to Binh, whose friendship and respect he particularly valued, he believed down to his very core that the good guys were winning; and would win their fight for freedom as long as they continued to receive the material support of the Americans. The Vietnamese, and not just the Marines this time, it seemed to John Ripley, were demonstrating a broader willingness to pay the manpower price required to expel the invaders.

After departing Phu Bai, Ripley was flown to Saigon where his outbound processing took two days. It gave him opportunity to locate and pay his respects to the widow and children of his friend Jack. His "Little Brother" Nha had not been married and his parents did not live in Saigon.

From Saigon John Ripley flew first to Okinawa where he enjoyed a brief reunion with older brother George who was serving on the Third Marine Division staff. The division's commanding general, Major General Joe Fegan, had the younger Ripley brief his senior staff along with his regimental and battalion commanders on the unfolding Vietnam situation before he was allowed to press on toward home.

The America that John Ripley was coming home to, *his* America, would be one of love, affirmation, and celebration, at least initially. Just as it always had been with Moline, their kids, his folks and their extended family, the soon-to-be-promoted-to-major returning war hero really would get recognition and be accorded a bit of the glory he was due. Aside from later being awarded the Navy Cross, the nation's second highest award for combat valor, by Secretary of the Navy John Warner himself (Warner was also a Virginian and former Marine who immediately took an interest in Ripley's award upon learning about it) in a very grand, public ceremony attended by many dozens and dozens of Ripley family, friends, and fans, John was a much in-demand commodity with ranking civilians and senior military officers first at Headquarters Marine Corps and then at the Pentagon who needed to be apprised on the current and still-developing ground situation in I Corps.

Ripley was the first American Marine advisor with combat experience in the recent Communist invasion to come back to the U.S. Almost immediately upon his return and before he had even had a chance to see his children (He was mercifully allowed to at least meet with Moline.), Ripley was squired from briefing to briefing in the capacious, cavernous building answering pointed and specific questions, offering detailed insight on what he had just experienced. These meetings continued for several days. In one of the rooms he entered he was told, just before he was set to begin, by the civilian who seemed to be in charge—a man Ripley did not know—that he would do his country a great service by passing on all the information he could. Another fellow—and Ripley had never seen him, either—retorted "Jesus Christ!!! This man personally stopped the Communist invasion. He has already done his country an incredible service…"

In another meeting one of the attendees asked, not quite rhetorically, how good the Vietnamese Marines were and how they compared to U.S. Marines. After all he had already described, Ripley nearly lost his composure. With a passion and zeal that likely shocked his distinguished audience he replied: "Do I think they're as good? My God, these Marines are defending *their* country! They are fighting like Banshees …" With that same zeal he continued without relent to share example after example, from personal observation, of things he had witnessed only recently of young Marines being wounded time and time again, refusing to be medevaced until they were either killed in action or finally wounded so grievously that they could no longer function.

He spoke of individual Marines engaging enemy tanks at close range, and winning. Ripley went on and on. It became evident to the audience that the individual acts of bravery and wholesale sacrifice of the Marines Ripley had served with were, in fact, quite common among that group. The fellow who offered the original question was probably sorry he asked. But he at least gave John Ripley the forum necessary to remind these senior people that the Vietnamese stood a good chance at winning their war, of repelling the invaders, if the United States maintained its material support. It was certainly Ripley's impression, when he left Quang Tri Province, that the good guys had finally begun to turn the tide and were winning.[2]

GEORGE PHILIP AT THE MY CHANH

As the Vietnamese Marines and their ARVN allies began the consolidation and fortification of their defensive positions at the My Chanh River, and before they transitioned over into the offensive, the method of employment for the Marine artillery units had changed a bit. No longer as desperately needed at the battalion level, George was transferred, or "chopped back," to a higher headquarters job where he and a number of other *covans* were used as watch standers to ensure round-the-clock proper coordination of the American supporting arms, mostly airpower, for the various Marine and ARVN units in contact. For a couple of weeks George stood the evening watch and became close friends with Major Walt Boomer, late of the TQLC's Fourth Battalion, and another *covan* who, like John Ripley, had cheated death on too many occasions to count. The advisors worked tirelessly with American navy and air force counterparts off shore and in the skies putting ordnance where it was needed most.

Perhaps the most heart-pounding aspect of watch standing was witnessing the higher level coordination of B-52 ARCLIGHT strikes. It always made George, along with every other American and Vietnamese not on the receiving end of an ARCLIGHT, grateful not to be a Communist when a mission went in. Even from miles away the thumping, the overpressure, the earth shaking, concussive effects could be felt and heard.

In their sometimes off-beat, *macabre* humor, the *covans* in various locations would chat up on the radio net, totally violating proper communication procedures.

One late evening while George was standing watch, his friend Captain Larry Livingston was doing the same at some other location as an ARCLIGHT came on station. As the hundreds and hundreds of bombs rippled through the target area distant from either *covan's* position, they could feel and hear the destruction. Livingston radioed over to Philip: "Hey, George. They're playing our song...Over."*

Standing the evening watches was but half of Captain Philip's new duties now that he no longer served directly with First Artillery Battalion. During the days, George often flew as an airborne observer and coordinator with U.S. Army "Pink Teams."† Long before it became his pleasure to work with these helicopter pilots and crews, George had been convinced that the fellows flying army choppers were easily, as a group, the bravest and the craziest bastards he had ever observed. Flying with them for a few weeks only corroborated those earlier beliefs.

Each morning, after standing watch in the COC, Captain Philip would grab some chow, his rifle, and 782 gear and head for the Highway One rendezvous point where he was dutifully picked up by the Command and Control (C & C) Huey that was part of the Pink Team he flew with. In addition to the C & C bird, the team had two Cobras for fire support and two Light Observation Helicopters (LOH), referred to as Loaches. The Loaches worked sort of as bird dogs. It was their duty to fly low and slow, to sniff out the enemy, to *try* to draw fire so that the Cobras or other nearby aircraft awaiting the call might come in and turn the Red Devils into pink mist. Flying with the Pink Teams was never dull, and George continued to be impressed by the absolute levels of sheer bravery the army chopper pilots routinely demonstrated time and time again.

THE OTHER AMERICA

Unfortunately for John Ripley and his Vietnamese friends, the audiences he addressed at Headquarters Marine Corps and the Pentagon were far too small to have significant impact on the greater

---

* Livingston, an infantry officer serving as an advisor with the TQLC's First Battalion, would later be awarded the Navy Cross for action during the July 1972 counterattacks north. Captain Livingston would survive his *covan* tour and eventually retire from the USMC as a major general.
† Pink Teams consisted of several types of U.S. Army helicopters employed synergistically to kill the enemy.

national mood or will. The enduring images of the war in Vietnam would be a far cry from one of U.S. Marines raising Old Glory atop Mount Suribachi. By the summer of 1972 Vietnam would be remembered with pictures of self-immolating Buddhist monks protesting Diem's corruption, of the naked little girl fleeing in sheer panic from the mistaken napalming of her village by allied aircraft (South Vietnamese aircraft actually), of General Loan during Tet '68 executing a "helpless" Vietcong prisoner on a Saigon street, of the actress Jane Fonda smiling for her Communist hosts while she sat in the gunner's seat of a North Vietnamese anti-aircraft gun pretending to shoot at the evil warplanes from her own country.

As American participation in Vietnam wound down, it also concluded without producing the kind of public heroes the nation had been familiar with in the two World Wars. There was no Alvin York from World War I, immortalized in celluloid by the "aw shucks" simple goodness of the Gary Cooper portrayal. There was no Audie Murphy, self-immortalized in his own movie with the same imputed qualities of innocence, bravery, and sacrifice all Americans admired. Neither was the leadership revered. There was no Halsey or Nimitz, no Patton or Eisenhower or MacArthur. It was not because the men who fought in Vietnam were any less brave than their fathers or grandfathers, or any less well led. The war-fighting heroes and the leaders were ignored, uncelebrated. As the war and everything associated with it managed to lose public support, the only names that became widely known were those that symbolized the perversion and corruption of the American cause, like Calley at My Lai.

The cynic and the anti-hero, the Hawkeyes and Billy Jacks of the world had replaced the genuine good guy. Contemporary movies and television increasingly portrayed a recurring theme of the Vietnam veteran as mostly honorable but flawed, wary of authority, damaged and diminished by his service, a victim of the impersonal, all-consuming military-industrial complex. At best, those who served were shown as well-intentioned dupes, at worst they were drug-addicted, baby-killing crazies; either way they were irreparably harmed for having dutifully answered their nation's call. And yet, for Binh and his Marines, the war went on.

GEORGE PHILIP RETURNS

The earlier arrival of the Ninth Marine Amphibious Brigade (MAB) offshore had tied down NVA units concerned with defending their very exposed coast north of the DMZ. With every passing day it probably became more obvious to the Communists that the reintroduction of American Marines into the ground battle was not likely. But while the infantry battalions stayed aboard ship and were a threat only to the extent that they *might* be used, the Americans unhesitatingly reintroduced Marine helicopter support into the fight. On May 13, U.S. Marine CH-53 and CH-46 helicopters were used to lift two TQLC infantry battalions into landing zones north of the My Chanh. Supported by U.S. Army helicopters, the Marine lift capabilities would be further utilized and exploited to press the attack in the days and weeks and months ahead.

By the time Captain Philip left I Corps in late June, the ARVN and Vietnamese Marines had just gone over to the offensive. The ground situation for the Vietnamese had improved significantly even since John Ripley departed. George had observed an increasingly pervasive sense of confidence among the Marines. As he said his goodbyes, he was certain the invaders would be expelled.

Flying into Saigon prior to heading home, that confidence was confirmed. To him the Pearl of the Orient seemed like it did before he had originally been sent north: business as usual. George would never have known that there was or had been combat nearby had he not known about it. The particularly brutal fighting out at An Loc, the place where his cowboy Ha Si Tuong had lost his son, seemed a million miles away even though, in American terms, it was the equivalent distance of Santa Rosa to San Francisco, Oxnard to Los Angeles, Fort Collins to Denver, Fredericksburg to Washington, D.C. The now-sensitive-to-Vietnamese-culture *covan* could discern no change or impact from the nearby combat. Like all of the other Americans who understood, George Philip had tremendous respect for the resolve and resilience of the Vietnamese.

The War Goes On
June-July 1972

Not two weeks prior to Captain Philip's departure from Vietnam, on June 17 back in Washington, D.C., five men were arrested for breaking into the offices of the Democratic National Committee at the Watergate Hotel. On its own the event was just more news. The consequences though of the Watergate break in would ultimately have more impact in Vietnam than in the United States.

The ground combat in the three areas attacked by the NVA continued with massive American air support. Besides the air support in Quang Tri Province, the naval gunfire effort included upwards of twenty U.S. Navy men of war. And yet, in the meantime Henry Kissinger and Le Duc Tho resumed their Paris negotiations.

For the forces of the Republic of Vietnam, the months of June and July 1972 were spent stopping the enemy advances, stabilizing friendly lines, and then beginning the painful, arduous process of taking back the territory brutally acquired by the ruthless NVA. In northern Quang Tri Province the bitterest fighting during RVN advances back north would be experienced in the retaking of Quang Tri City itself.

BINH GETS WOUNDED — AGAIN

A few kilometers south of Quang Tri City
Mid-July 1972

Thieu Ta (Major) Le Ba Binh was selected for promotion to lieutenant colonel (Trung Ta) in May of 1972. Like most military services, the system of administration for promotions was a bit slow in moving the news along and so he was not officially advanced, to the point of actually pinning on his new rank, until a month later. The beauty of the bureaucratic inefficiency was that he was actually promoted in person by his original mentor, Lieutenant General Le Nguyen Khang, during a private and dignified ceremony in Hue.

As the Vietnamese Marines and their ARVN allies closed in on the Citadel at Quang Tri City, the fighting had grown even more bitter. The shelling and the bombing had reduced much of the built-up areas to rubble.

The Soi Bien was to be part of a multi-battalion attack against the stubbornly entrenched NVA. Before stepping off there was a great deal of planning and coordinating to do. Binh and his small staff had attended the requisite meetings to ensure every unit fully understood its mission. He had just returned to his *bivouac* area with the critical members of his staff and had retired for a few hours' sleep when an NVA artillery strike caught them. Wounded in the left arm and both legs, the best that could be said about Binh was that the shrapnel missed all of his organs. There were others in his group who were not as fortunate.

Wound number nine was serious enough that Binh could no longer command his battalion. Binh was tended to by his battalion doctor and stabilized for medevac. Mercifully there were American helicopters in the area, and it was ironic that a U.S. Marine bird responded to the call to get him to the rear.

By the summer 1972, the Vietnamese Marine Corps was as large as it had ever been. Its successes were so widely known, its reputation with the citizens of the country was so firmly established that recruiting qualified, motivated young men to replace the scores and scores of killed and wounded Marines was not a problem. At fifteen thousand strong the TQLC was still small enough so that it had not lost its familial feel, especially among those who had been a part of the organization for more than a few years.

Binh knew almost everyone who was anybody in the TQLC. *Everyone* who was anyone inside the TQLC knew Binh personally or was well versed with his record as a warrior. When word was out that the heretofore virtually indestructible leader of Third Battalion had been seriously wounded, there was a bit more than routine effort to take care of him.

Cam Banh, Binh's wife, was notified within twenty-four hours of his being wounded. She immediately called the TQLC's chief of staff in Saigon who quickly wangled a seat on a military flight north for her so that she might be by his side as he was processed back to Saigon and adequate medical care.

Binh's wounds were severe enough to keep him in the hospital for an agonizingly long two months; an eternity for the normally always moving, always active Marine officer. More than the physical pain of his wounds, it caused him tremendous grief to no longer serve with the men of his beloved Soi Bien. Binh was a much better combat commander than he was a hospital patient at Le Huu Sanh.

Liberation finally in Quang Tri City
September 16, 1972

The entire Marine Division, at various times, along with numerous ARVN units, had participated in the liberation effort for Quang Tri City from a most determined Communist enemy. Third Battalion, serving with all of its sister battalions, had continued to distinguish itself in the weeks after Binh had turned over command.

Victory had come at extremely high price. The Citadel and the surrounding buildings of the city had been reduced to ruins. Well before the battle had concluded, the fighting had been close quarter and bloody; in fact the battle for the Citadel itself had been the single most costly engagement of the Easter Offensive for the Marines to date. Since the March 30 initiation of the enemy invasion the TQLC had, out of a total force of barely fifteen thousand, suffered nearly fourteen hundred men KIA and more than fifty-five hundred men WIA. Intelligence estimates put the number of front-line NVA killed in fighting against the Marines at 10,200.[3] There were no hard figures for the number of innocent civilians killed as a result of enemy action.

On the morning of September 16 the Republic of Vietnam flag once again flew above what remained of the Quang Tri's Citadel. President Nguyen Van Thieu was there to witness the aftermath of the fighting and to personally thank those who survived the carnage for the tremendous sacrifices they and their fallen comrades had made.

The eyes of South Vietnam were upon the victors. Stories of individual and collective acts of bravery dazzled the starved-for-good-news population. The expulsion of the Communists from

Quang Tri at such high cost to the tiny republic was their equivalent to the American triumph at Iwo Jima. For the Vietnamese troops who took part in the battle, just as it was said by Admiral Nimitz of the American Marines on Iwo, "Uncommon valor was a common virtue."

In Vietnam the story was big news. Huge, miraculous news. In the United States there was little mention of it. So taken and grateful were the citizens of Vietnam by the intrepidity of their fighting men in the northern areas that the new song "Victory Flag Flying Over the Quang Tri Citadel" became the number one tune in the country.[4] It certainly received no play in the U.S. where songs like Curtis Mayfield's "Super Fly" and "Love Train" by the O'Jays were more in keeping with the current mood.

While Vietnamese Marines and soldiers were taking back the city of Quang Tri on an inch-by-inch basis and expending liberal amounts of blood and sinew to do it, Americans at home had marveled at the Olympic swimming exploits of Mark Spitz as he won a then-record seven gold medals in Munich. That joy was short-lived as the world also witnessed the horror of the "Black September" terror attacks against Israeli athletes. Perhaps another harbinger of the decline of American primacy was the ignominious and controversial first-ever loss of the basketball gold to the Soviets.

"Cease Fire"

Major Robert Sheridan
Observations Prior to Departure

Major Bob Sheridan, senior U.S. Marine advisor to Brigade 369 and George Philip's American boss, had been located right near the action on May 22, out near a place known to many as the "Street Without Joy," a bit north of the My Chanh River line, when allied forces scored their very first kill of an enemy tank with a TOW missile. In the ensuing melee the Vietnamese Marines killed an estimated two hundred to three hundred NVA and destroyed an additional thirteen tanks. The remaining baker's dozen of armor was taken out with LAAWs and by 105mm artillery pieces shooting in the *direct fire* mode; at ranges of 150 meters or less. The fighting was close and personal but very one-sided.

The seasoned American advisor observed that most of the dead and all of the prisoners taken were either young boys no more than sixteen years of age, or very old men; men who were probably grandfathers back home. He was certain the NVA had used up the cream of its youth and was close to spent entirely; an observation any reasonably experienced gunfighter would make. His assessment of current enemy capabilities proved to be correct. The NVA never breeched the My Chanh Line. When he followed Captain Philip home about a month later, he too was convinced the good guys had the necessary momentum going.[1]

Life Goes On
Three Rivers Stadium
Pittsburgh, Pennsylvania
September 30, 1972

It was not quite two weeks after Vietnamese Marines and ARVN forces recaptured Quang Tri City from the Communist invaders, and one day after Japan and the People's Republic of China normalized relations, that former Ripley's Raider Chuck Goggin registered his first hit as a major leaguer in his first at bat in a game against the New York Mets. Goggin had left the Corps more than four years earlier to resume his baseball career. The hard work and single-minded dedication was starting to pay off. Playing second base, he was the leadoff man in the day's home game; the same game in which teammate Roberto Clemente would record his three thousandth and, tragically, final hit. The Pirates topped the Mets 5-0.

Song Than
Outside of Saigon
Early October 1972

Trung Ta Binh was grateful to be leaving Le Huu Sanh. As thankful as he was to check out after two months, it pained him to see the many wards full of friends and comrades; so many very young Marines cut down in their prime, before they reached the prime of their lives. To those who had given so much and who could no longer give much more Binh felt doubly obliged to continue his fight against the Red Devils.

Not fully recovered from his wounds, it was still more painful for Binh to do nothing. When he reported for duty as the new commanding officer of the sprawling (at least by Vietnamese standards) Song Than base complex just outside of Saigon, he still required crutches to get around.

Commanding Song Than was not like leading his beloved Soi Bien. With the Soi Bien it was Binh and his Marines against the elements and the wily Communists. At Song Than he had other concerns and issues to consider, other people to answer to.

Song Than was the main base for the entire TQLC. Within its confines the *cadre* of drill instructors ran the boot camp where normal young Vietnamese boys made the unique metamorphosis to Marine Corps manhood. Song Than served as the major supply depot for the TQLC. It was also the place where most of the families of those Marines who were married lived. As the commanding officer of Song Than, Binh wore several hats. He was responsible for ensuring that all of the disparate missions of the subgroups stationed there were accomplished. He was responsible for ensuring the base defense and the safety of all the dependents living inside its walls and fences. He was commander, sheriff, and mayor rolled into one. He would much rather have been back with Third Battalion. At least he was home most nights which made Cam happy.

The recapture of Quang Tri City was a significant historical highpoint for ARVN and TQLC forces. In the months following, the fighting with the NVA continued throughout the country but at nothing like the earlier intensity. Up north the lines had essentially stabilized with the enemy largely in control of South Vietnamese territory north of the Cua Viet River up to the DMZ and out west toward Laos.

In the face of the ongoing fighting and air war, negotiations between the Americans and North Vietnamese in Paris continued. At the heart of the matter the North Vietnamese were still focused on victory, which ultimately meant domination of the south. The Americans were looking for an honorable exit. They wanted a treaty that guaranteed the sovereignty of the south, and they wanted their POWs home. President Thieu and most in his government, who were not directly involved in the negotiations, believed nothing of what the Communists were promising.

In early October 1972, with the U.S. presidential elections looming, negotiations between Henry Kissinger and Le Duc Tho appeared to reach a breakthrough. The Communists sensed the Americans were anxious to conclude a deal prior to the election. Word was even leaked that a peace agreement was near. The Communists proposed that they arrange a cease-fire with the

Americans and leave the political issues to later be decided by the Vietnamese on both sides.

For years the Communists, as a condition for peace, had insisted on the removal of the Thieu government. In their new tentative deal that wording had not been included. The wording also left out any mention of the Communists removing their troops that remained in the south. The Americans gave their implicit approval. An agreement was quickly crafted which called for a cease-fire, the release of POWs, withdrawal of U.S. forces and a process to have internationally supervised elections in the south.

Nguyen Van Thieu wanted nothing to do with these negotiations that essentially allowed NVA forces to, by treaty, remain in the south. The enmity between Thieu and Kissinger was an open secret. In Saigon the Vietnamese chief executive gave a televised speech to the nation stating that "coalition with the Communists means death" and that in order for there to be peace the Communists would have to "be killed to the last man."[2]

The Americans were going to depart Southeast Asia whether President Thieu liked it or not. American patience and generosity, at least from the perspective of many Americans, had been stretched to a point where the end was approaching. America had already lost more than fifty thousand men defending the Republic of Vietnam and had paid additionally in so many other intangible but nonetheless almost as costly ways. There was an approaching limit to what the nation would continue to suffer for very little tangible gain. As assurance to get him to go along with what was being negotiated — without his explicit input — President Nixon continually promised that once a permanent cease-fire or peace plan was in place, American air power would be there to aggressively punish the Communists for any treaty violations.

The ongoing negotiations lasted through the U.S. presidential elections, which Nixon won in an electoral landslide. The president took little solace from that victory. He would face Democrat majorities in both the Senate and House, and challenges to all funding for Vietnam in the New Year.

Henry Kissinger and Le Duc Tho would meet several more times in November and into December before the talks would be broken off on December 16 in frustration over differences neither side would compromise on. In the face of the political realities facing his country, Nguyen Van Thieu was not at all excited about negotiating an end to the war that mandated the complete withdrawal of American troops and authorized the implicit acceptance of Communist forces remaining in South Vietnam. The American response was to begin Operation Linebacker II on December 18.

"Reverse R&R"
Bunny Turley Visits Saigon
Christmas 1972

Bunny Turley's arrival at Saigon's Tan Son Nhut airport, except for her husband's very obvious glee and delight, went largely unnoticed. Coming several days after the initiation of what the press would call the "Christmas Bombing," Operation Linebacker II dwarfed even the heretofore extensive bombing campaign—Operation Linebacker, or now referred to as Operation Linebacker I—from the recent Easter Offensive.

Operation Linebacker II was President Nixon's response to perceived Communist intransigence and equivocation at the Paris negotiating table. It was also meant to be a demonstration of American resolve to President Thieu. The effort would turn into the most aggressive bombing campaign of the entire war. As always, American airpower was expressly forbidden from hitting civilian targets but the broader missions, in addition to the earlier authorized targets of the original Operation Linebacker I strikes from months ago, included radio stations, power plants, railroad yards, shipyards, communication facilities, air defense positions, and supply transshipment points.

Had the United States desired to inflict maximum damage without the use of nuclear weapons, the intricate system of irrigation dikes in the Red River delta could easily have been destroyed. Such targeting was judged, *by the Americans*, as unacceptable and inhumane. The Americans had maintained that viewpoint throughout the entire war. While the Communist invaders had been held to no standard wherever and whenever they fired their artillery or terrorized civilians in the south, the U.S. was fastidious, to the point of risking and losing aircrews to ensure it, that their air strikes minimized civilian casualties.

The B-52s did not darken the skies above the north, as the unending stream of B-17s were described as doing over Berlin not thirty years earlier. Still the round-the-clock missions for a twelve-day period from December 18-30, except for a Christmas Day break, signaled a higher intensity of attacks than had ever been experienced by the Communists. The North Vietnamese would expend virtually their entire SAM supply, shooting down fifteen of the massive bombers in the process. They ran out of missiles before the Americans ran out of crews and airplanes.[3] When the campaign concluded at the end of December, the Communists would agree to return to the Paris negotiating table in early January 1973.

Bunny Turley had flown for twenty-four hours with two intermediate stops from Los Angeles International Airport to Vietnam in order to spend Christmas with her husband. Just as they had done in 1959 prior to Captain Gerry Turley's departure for his one-year tour on Okinawa, and that was the last time the two of them had taken a vacation together as a couple, Bunny's folks had come up from San Diego to tend to the four youngest Turley children. (Oldest daughter Anne was living in Wisconsin with her husband.) In the middle of a war, Saigon was certainly a strange place for a second honeymoon.

"Reverse R&R" was a program Lieutenant Colonel Turley stumbled upon months ago. A Navy officer friend he met in Saigon who had brought his wife out to visit made him aware of it. At this late stage of the war, with the number of American men in Vietnam shrinking rapidly, not too many women took advantage of the opportunity; nor was the opportunity available to too many wives.

By Christmas of 1972, even with the initiation of Linebacker II, Gerry believed it was safe enough for his bride to join him in Saigon. She was game anyway. Bunny Turley matched her husband pound for pound, inch for inch, with a sense of adventure and willingness to experience new things. This was her very first trip outside the United States and she was anxious to see what she could of this place where her husband, so many of their friends, and her country had invested so much blood and treasure and heartache.

Gerry met Bunny at the airport and shuttled her into the forever-alive-with-action capital, playing tour guide as they drove into the center of town. Saigon was Saigon; still very much the Pearl of the Orient, and Bunny was fascinated by the routine hustle and bustle of commerce and the Vietnamese twist to life going on all around them.

From Tan Son Nhut Gerry motored, in a circuitous route so that his wife might get a better sense of the ground disposition, to his regular quarters at the Brinks Hotel. Next to the venerable Hotel Continental which dated from the late nineteenth century and the National Assembly in downtown Saigon, the Brinks was a relatively secure home to American military officers and those who worked for other government agencies. When Bunny was not with him Gerry shared his digs with a gentleman who worked for the CIA. That gentleman had graciously offered to bunk out while Bunny was in town.

FIRST NIGHT IN SAIGON

After their reunion and accounting for Bunny's jetlag, the happy couple retired for the evening before midnight. They were both sound asleep when Gerry was stirred by the far sounds of what he believed to be some sort of artillery exchange. This sort of thing was not that unusual. Gerry could tell the difference, even from a distance, between outgoing and incoming, between Soviet and American guns. He sat up and put his feet on the floor at the bedside, holding his head in his hands as he listened. Bunny was sound asleep. There were the dull, instantaneous flashes of men at war on his horizon that briefly flickered into their room.

Suddenly, for what had to be two or three seconds, the entire Saigon night became day. The darkness was interrupted by a brilliance of light nearly as strong as the noonday sun. It was as if someone had thrown a massive on switch, and then, just as if to harass everyone in view, immediately turned it back off. Several seconds after the flash came the incredibly loud rumbling sound of the explosion which had caused the daylight. Gerry knew what to expect next and was quickly proven correct. A crush of over pressure unlike anything he had ever experienced from a distance swept into the room. Bunny was still asleep.

The glass jalousies of their room were blown in by the split-second hurricane force over pressure. Had Gerry been standing up and facing outboard, instead of being still hunched over with his head lowered, he would likely have been struck in his face and body by the shards of glass sent flying all across their room.

Mercifully, the air conditioning had been on. Bunny was snuggled up under the covers. What glass there was passed harmlessly over or onto her bed with no injury to her; and hardly any to her husband. The door from their room, which led to the hallway, had been blown open by the blast of wind. Gerry was dumbfounded. Bunny finally stirred and made the comment, still mostly asleep: "What was that? I thought this went on all the time." She then turned over and tried to go back to sleep before her husband began to tell her what had just taken place.

They would soon learn that a lucky enemy artillery round had exploded inside the substantial ammunition dump out at Bien Hoa, probably eight to ten miles away, causing the thousands of tons of ordnance in the entire dump to ignite at once. It was then the single biggest explosion to rock the greater Saigon area. In true Marine Corps spouse fashion, Bunny Turley still managed a good night's sleep.

Bunny Turley's trip to Vietnam was not a complete vacation for her husband. While authorized to take a bit of time off, he was still required to work a few hours most days. Bunny Turley was the proverbial rolling stone who gathered no moss. On several of the days she was toured around by the wife of another American officer who was stationed there. They spent time at an orphanage where as soon as they walked in they were handed infant children to feed and take care of as if they were performing near-motherly duties. There was even a day when, on her own, Bunny hiked around Saigon experiencing the people, sites, smells, and unusual shopping. It was only after she returned that her husband was shocked to learn of her entering a restricted black market area. Whether she had ever been truly at risk or not, Bunny never felt unsafe, and the Vietnamese civilians she encountered on her walks seemed ever gracious to the tiny American woman who disarmed them all with her smile and the sparkle in her eyes.

Bunny and Gerry together attended the very last Christmas show put on by Bob Hope in Vietnam which included Hope's typical bevy of attractive young women. Their time together was as perfect as it could be; perhaps made more perfect by the fact that they were in such an exotic place at such an unusual time. They missed their children and yet cherished the special circumstances they were allowed to experience.

Bunny's Saigon time was actually extended a few days because of the effort to continue the drawdown of American servicemen. Bumped from a number of outbound flights so that the men might leave, neither of the Turleys complained, and the still very much in love couple enjoyed their extra time together.

Lieutenant Colonel and Mrs. Gerry Turley managed to cram a great deal of fun and memories, aside from the Bien Hoa attack, into their too-brief period of Saigon bliss. For Bunny, hers was a successful tour of duty, and from Bob Hope she could borrow his signature line and say "Thanks for the memories."

1972 SUMMARY

There were a few positive numbers for the U.S. as 1972 ended. For the entire year, the number of American servicemen killed in Vietnam totaled three hundred, the lowest since 1964. By December of 1972 there were fewer than thirty thousand Americans still in country; most of them service and support troops. For the RVN, the best thing American critics might say was that the casualty numbers had certainly been "Vietnamized." Nearly forty thousand of the combined RVN forces had been KIA in 1972; the highest number of any year so far. Allied intelligence estimated that the enemy had lost more than one hundred thousand KIA; most of those from their Nguyen Hue invasion attempt. There was no accurate count for the number of killed and displaced civilians resulting from the enemy invasion.[4]

While Bunny and Gerry Turley were enjoying their abbreviated period of bliss in Saigon, the bigger picture issue of serious negotiating was getting ready to play out. There would, in the following years, be arguments and counterarguments as to the efficacy of the twelve-day bombing campaign put on by the Americans in December of 1972. Many would claim that it was meant to demonstrate to President Thieu that the United States would stick by him in the event of treaty violations, as President Nixon had and would continue to promise. Some believed that it came close to breaking the will of the northern Communists and should have continued, along with the U.S. demanding concessions from them. The most vocal critics of the bombing condemned the actions as barbaric and inhumane, and asserted that the only result was to kill innocents. In any event, the Communists did agree to return to the negotiating table in Paris in early January of 1973.[5]

"AGREEMENT ON ENDING THE WAR AND RESTORING PEACE IN VIETNAM"

The terms and conditions of the final negotiations agreed to in January of 1973 were not radically different than those nearly agreed to in October of 1972. The meticulously crafted, exceedingly verbose legal document was intended to outline every aspect and eventuality to ensure a meaningful and enforceable peace. It would, of course, become a vehicle by which the Communists and the media could measure or limit the American response.

The agreement called for a complete cessation of hostilities throughout Vietnam at 2400 Greenwich Mean Time on January 27, 1973 (0800 on January 28 in Vietnam). The U.S. agreed to cease all military activities throughout the area as well as begin the removal and deactivation of all mines they had placed in northern ports and navigable rivers. All acts of force on the ground, sea, and air were to be prohibited. There were to be no acts of terror or reprisal. The United States agreed to withdraw its forces, except for an extremely small number of security and logistics personnel, from Vietnam within sixty days. There would also be an expeditious return of POWs.

Both Vietnams were allowed to be resupplied for the gear they already had. There was no mechanism to effectively measure what the NVA possessed, but since RVN was funded through congressional approval, keeping track of what they were sent or were not sent became very public information.

To police and enforce the cease-fire agreement, a Byzantine arrangement of several commissions was formed. The first was the Four-Party Military Commission. It consisted of representatives of the North Vietnamese and the Viet Cong on one side, and the South Vietnamese and Americans on the other. Another commission, the International Commission of Control and Supervision (ICCS), was the one meant to enforce and oversee the transition to peace. Two of the participating parties were from the Communist world and the other two were from the non-Communist world. The initial four parties were Hungary and Poland, and Canada and Indonesia.*[6]

The Americans could now leave Vietnam under cover of this hard-won agreement. President Nixon would, on January 23, 1973, proclaim "Peace with Honor" in a televised speech to the world. It would shortly become evident that there was no peace, and certainly no honor.

---

* The observer status of the communist members was quickly recognized as nothing more than a treaty-authorized method by which they could move around Vietnamese positions at will, mapping and photographing anything they desired. From February-June 1973 RVN forces watched helplessly as Hungarian military officers and NCOs carried out their flagrant spying/reconnaissance. In June it was noted that enemy sappers had destroyed at least two critical facilities—a fuel storage area at Camp Evans and an ammunition dump at Phu Bai—following visits by the Hungarians (Lam, *The Twenty-five Year Century*, 296-297).

Turley Up North the Day of the Cease Fire
The coastal village of Huong Dien—serving as the forward HQ of the
VNMC Division approximately fifty-five kilometers south of the DMZ and
twenty kilometers northeast of Hue
28 January, 1973
0745 local time

There were fifteen minutes left before the very much publicized official cease fire, the one President Nixon had described as "Peace with Honor," went into effect. The Communist invaders and the South Vietnamese both continued their struggle to control as much territory as they could before they were supposed to end hostilities. It was estimated that the Communists had control of between 15-25 percent of the country's geography and as much as 15 percent of the population, along with as many as 145,000 troops still in the south.[7] There were no RVN forces in the DRV. No reasonable Vietnamese citizen expected the Communists to abide by an agreement inked in Paris, or anywhere else for that matter.

The moment's minor irony was not lost on Lieutenant Colonel Gerry Turley. Offshore, out on the gun line, were the two or three remaining American destroyers to deliver the final calls for fire. Up until the evening before, the ships had been firing a total of thirteen hundred rounds per day. The majority of the naval *flotilla* had already retired from the area, heading back towards Subic Bay in the Philippines where young sailors might indulge in the things young men indulge in.

Among the remaining ships was the USS *Turner Joy* (DD-951). Where most average Americans might have forgotten, Turley and the others present all knew. *Turner Joy* had been one of the two U.S. Navy ships involved in the still controversial August 1964 Gulf of Tonkin incident, the action that effectively precipitated the wholesale American involvement in Vietnam.[†]

In his current position it was more or less his prerogative to call in what would be the final naval gunfire mission before the

---

[†] The other ship was the USS *Maddox* (DD-731). The *Maddox* was decommissioned in 1969 and later sold to Taiwan.

cease fire went into effect. It seemed to Turley only fitting that since *Turner Joy* had been there to start it all, she should be the one to get in the last licks. When he called out to the ships he specifically requested she shoot the final mission, which she did with very little fanfare.

The next morning Lieutenant Colonel Gerry Turley found himself alone with Brigadier General Bui Te Lan, the *commandant* of the Vietnamese Marine Corps. The silence, the complete lack of out going or incoming fire, seemed so out of place as to be almost disconcerting. At the same time Gerry could not help but notice, just as he had the day before the Easter Offensive had been launched when he had flown north with Major Jim Joy, observing all the daily life going on around him, as if there was no war at all. The perseverance and resiliency of the regular Vietnamese people continued to amaze Turley.

Walking through the tiny village which, like the countless others across Quang Tri Province and all the war-ravaged areas of the country, were doing all they could to regain the normalcy from some earlier time, the two senior warriors ambled with no particular purpose or destination but only so that they might talk as the friends they had over these last few months become. Gerry felt a genuine, deep respect for this man with the weight of the world on his shoulders. Few men in Turley's long experience had as much presence or passion for the work that remained now that the Americans were leaving.

For the Americans, the advisors about to depart, the mood was generally ebullient, upbeat. Their war was over. If they got killed now it would be only by mistake. They were going home. Far away from northern Quang Tri Province. There was no NVA in California or Virginia or Iowa or Texas. Even though there were folks opposed to the war, who might even have the temerity to say unkind things to them, no one back home was trying to kill them or invade their country. The cease fire now in effect had actually allowed the invaders to keep the northern portions of the province adjacent to the DMZ and Laos, as well as other parts of the Republic of Vietnam. Would the Americans have ceded a part of

Minnesota to Canada or San Diego to Mexico? It was a bitter, bitter pill for the Vietnamese *commandant* and his Marines to swallow.

The Americans had fought hard; given far more than what most freedom-loving Vietnamese had expected. The fight they had made was now no longer theirs, although they would be forever changed by that service. For the American Marine officers present there would be other duty, assignments in other parts of the world; the "every clime and place" stuff, jobs to broaden them out, prepare them for more responsibilities and higher command, time for family and extended leave, trips to Disneyland or the Grand Canyon. It was different for the Vietnamese.

One did not need to be the *commandant* of the TQLC to know that for the Vietnamese Marines there would only be more war— but now without American fire power.

Gerry and the *commandant* walked along, through the tiny hamlet and down a narrow road that led towards many hectares of rice paddies, and then on towards another village if they had kept going. At what would be the natural limit of their advance before turning to walk back to where the others were, the American and Vietnamese officers waiting for the two to return, it was General Lan who made the strongest statement after the gracious pleasantries had been exchanged. The *commandant* noted the contributions of his American friends from the very beginning in 1954. So many very fine men. So much magnanimous sacrifice. Turley replied by describing the growing successes of the TQLC and their record as warriors. They continued walking.

The general was a realist; he understood his enemy. He knew that the cease fire was a piece of paper only, meant to assuage the eager-for-settlement Americans. They seemed to him like Neville Chamberlain who had thirty-four years earlier boldly but *naïvely* proclaimed "Peace in our time." Turley could not disagree.

By early 1973, out of a total population of approximately 17 million citizens, the Vietnamese had well more than one million men under arms. Of those million-plus Vietnamese, there were now nearly fifteen thousand Marines. They were enough to make a difference, but not enough to make *all* the difference. As good as they were, as tenaciously as they had fought and would continue to fight, Lan knew the challenges ahead. They were about to conclude their stroll but not before the general said to his friend in his understated, matter of fact manner, and without recrimination, referring to the end of American naval gunfire and air support: "Today we have lost our right arm." He was so right, and Turley was unable to give response. Silently they walked back to the division's headquarters compound.

In accordance with the very publicly proclaimed rules of the now in effect cease-fire agreement, the American Marines would immediately need to leave the field of battle. Before flying out the Americans and their hosts gathered together for one last time as a group. General Lan presented awards to all of the *covans*, thanking each man personally when each award was pinned on. There was good cheer and fellowship among the group that was mixed with solemnity and a bit of melancholy. Later in the day all of the *covans*, except for Turley and four others, would be on a C-130 out of Phu Bai headed for Saigon. Gerry and his small team would remain for a few more days before they too would head south and ultimately home. When his group left they would close forever, write the last paragraph of the last chapter of the eighteen-year American Marine service with their brother Vietnamese Leathernecks in the grueling ground war of Southeast Asia.

Operation Homecoming

In accepting the "Agreement on Ending the War and Restoring Peace in Vietnam," the United States agreed to a number of conditions. All but a few American military personnel were required to leave Vietnam within sixty days, and the mines which had bottled up the north's harbors were to be immediately cleared. American POWs would be returned. For its part, at some later point, the U.S. would also be obligated to provide billions of dollars in financial and material aid for the reconstruction of North Vietnam.

It was apparent from Day One that the peace accords were horribly flawed. No one was surprised by the Communists' egregious treaty violations. While the actual fighting within the confines of the Republic of Vietnam diminished markedly at the outset, the Communists used the cessation of hostilities to focus on the rebuilding of the logistical infrastructure that would support their next invasion of the south. With the all-but-eliminated threat of U.S. bombing, the Ho Chi Minh Trail system was improved to the point that it virtually became a paved highway. Where gasoline and petroleum products had before been inefficiently transported in barrels aboard trucks or carts, the Communists began construction of a pipeline stretching literally to the outskirts of Saigon.

Had reasonable Americans stopped to consider that negotiations for peace in Vietnam were effectively conducted with little input or participation from the government of the Republic of Vietnam, they might have sympathized with the fears and frustrations of President Nguyen Van Thieu. Thieu had been basically dragooned into accepting terms the Americans and Communists ultimately agreed to.

The agreements included implicit allowance for the Communists to keep significant forces in the Republic of Vietnam. In order to secure his limited blessing of the accords, President Nixon gave President Thieu his personal promise that American airpower would deliver massive retaliatory response to any Communist treaty violations.[1] Thieu effectively had no choice other than to trust in what would be Nixon's fleeting assurances.

American public interest in Southeast Asia moderated significantly as the withdrawal of combat and support troops continued. The one area of growing concern, the one overarching issue for a great percentage of informed citizens was the expeditious return of the large number of POWs, mostly aircrews shot down over the DRV, some of them held there since 1964, existing in utterly cruel and barbaric conditions. The initial repatriation of the first American POWs, beginning in February of 1973, ignited a torrent of patriotic fervor not seen during the entire period of the war. When the POWs came home they were warmly received. America turned out for them almost as if to assuage its collective guilt for having ignored the hundreds of thousands of other warriors who served and returned, but received no tumultuous homecoming parades. While the revelry was genuine and heartfelt, and the POW stories of bravery, suffering, and faithfulness were difficult for the average citizen to comprehend, there seemed to be, among certain groups, more a celebration of the POWs' victimhood rather than their heroics.

LUONG GETS MEDICALLY DISCHARGED

The process by which Luong's parents and girlfriend were notified of his being wounded and arriving as a patient at Le Huu Sanh was not the typical one. An old boyhood chum from his neighborhood in Bien Hoa, now also a Marine lieutenant but not with Third Battalion, happened to have been in the bed next to him similarly recovering from combat wounds. Having arrived there earlier than Luong, he was established and receiving regular visits. When Luong showed up, his friend's parents immediately got the word back to Luong's family, obviating the need for the official notification.

The period of recovery, from the time of his amputation, therapy, and getting used to working with the prostheses was about eight months. Luong was discharged from the Vietnamese Marine Corps in January of 1973. As disappointed as he was to no longer be able to serve, Luong was grateful that he was still a whole man, physically capable of nearly everything but to lead Marines in combat.

Veterans' benefits for the disabled were not insignificant. The government of the Republic of Vietnam paid the former lieutenant a quarterly stipend of 105,000 *piasters*—approximately $260 at the current official exchange rates. In addition, any children Luong might father would be guaranteed spots in good schools.

Fortunately for Luong, his strong science and engineering background made him competitive in the hunt for a job. He was doubly blessed in that the man who hired him to work as a system operator for the Bien Hoa Power Plant was one of his old teachers who knew his work ethic and actually liked him. His monthly pay at the power plant doubled his government benefits, allowing him to live in a minor amount of comfort. He and his long-time girlfriend, his high school sweetheart, began the process of moving forward with marriage plans.

GOING IT ALONE: RVN FORCES IN THE BALANCE

As part of the U.S. effort to prepare its Vietnamese ally to go it alone, a major equipment transfer and logistical effort had taken place prior to the date of the official cease fire. The Vietnamese Air Force (VNAF), almost overnight, became the world's fourth largest air force. Hundreds and hundreds of new and used aircraft were placed in its inventories. The greatest percentages were helicopters.

What was *not* in the aircraft mix was most instructive. Even with all of its new equipment the Vietnamese lacked the critical maintenance and support infrastructure to give their forces the punch and sustainability they had grown used to from American air power. There were no B-52s. There were no high-performance fighter-bombers like the F-111, F-4, or F-105. There were no electronic counter-measure (ECM) aircraft like the EB-66 or EA-6.

The NVA gave up nothing and were increasingly supplied with the latest in Soviet anti-aircraft weaponry and brought it all to the forward edge of whatever battlefield they chose to fight on. This and the ubiquitous presence of SA-7 Strela missiles would wreak havoc with ARVN helicopter and close-air support.

The story for the Vietnamese Navy was similar to that of the VNAF. RVN troops operating close to their country's shoreline had grown used to the accuracy and heavy volume of fire provided by the U.S. Navy ships offshore. There was simply no way the Vietnamese Navy could deliver the quantity of rounds the Americans had routinely placed on target.

The American resupply effort was also inhibited by the public nature of the cease-fire agreement. Any attempt to replace equipment not authorized, or effort to use American-flown aircraft in direct support of RVN forces would have been happily reported in the press. The Communists were not at all subject to the same kind of scrutiny, and when they routinely violated the peace treaty there was no outcry or anger in the media for them to cease and desist.

The undoing of the Republic of Vietnam was still not a *fait accompli* in early 1973. In fact, there was reason to believe that the young republic just might make it. The Communist invasion of 1972 had been beaten back. While the defenders had taken tremendous casualties, the invaders had again paid a far higher price. Political conditions in the north were such that General Vo Nguyen Giap, the hitherto second only in god-like status to Ho Chi Minh, was cast aside for presiding over the tremendous losses taken.

Just as John Ripley, George Philip, and Bob Sheridan had observed from their own particular vantage points when they had departed, Lieutenant Colonel Gerry Turley felt similarly in February of 1973 that the good guys were winning. As he stepped aboard the Freedom Bird headed first for Okinawa before taking him to California, his assessment was that the Vietnamese had a good chance, a very good chance, of making it—as long as the United States continued to keep them supplied.

THE REST OF THE YEAR 1973

By spring 1973 American public interest in Vietnam began to trail off significantly, especially after the repatriation of POWs. American focus on responsibilities and obligations beyond Southeast Asia quickly filled whatever foreign policy void the Vietnam withdrawal created.

In Vietnam NVA treaty violations started on the first day of the official cease fire and continued—without American response. The Communists remained solely focused on victory, but for most of 1973 RVN forces held their own, continuing to gain back ground not yet retaken from the enemy's 1972 invasion. For the still free citizens of the Republic of Vietnam, 1973 would become a year when that freedom would be increasingly compromised more by events outside their country and beyond their abilities to influence rather than by how well their forces performed against their battlefield foe.

Whatever the collective feelings of joy and thankfulness felt by Americans from having the POWs home and remaining troops out of Vietnam were, by May 1973 they began to rapidly dissipate. Revelations of the Watergate cover-up were daily front page news and President Nixon's focus necessarily shifted from saving the world for democracy to saving his own presidency. At the same time the war's opponents in Congress continued to battle his effort to support the Thieu government, still very widely perceived as illegitimate, evil, and corrupt.

Whether or not the national mood among the citizenry was as dark and uncharitable towards the still-free-from-Communist-yoke South Vietnamese as that displayed by a fair percentage of the members of Congress could not be measured. It did not really matter. The people's elected representatives set out in the summer of 1973 to reclaim what prerogative for war power granting many believed had been gradually usurped from Congress beginning with Franklin Roosevelt. That Richard Nixon was extremely unpopular with so many did not help. Perhaps the single greatest blow to strike the citizens of the struggling Republic of Vietnam, more impacting than the Communist attacks of 1968 or 1972, came on July 1, 1973 with the passage of the Fulbright-Aiken Amendment. Set to go into effect the following month, more than anything else it signaled to the politically astute Communist Vietnamese in the north that the U.S. would never return to Southeast Asia as a fighting ally.

One short paragraph effectively neutralized every assurance President Nixon had publicly and privately given the Vietnamese that America would stand by and respond militarily in the event of treaty violations:

> Notwithstanding any other provision of the law, on or after August 15 1973, no funds herein or heretofore appropriated may be obligated or expended to finance directly or indirectly combat activities by United States military forces in or over or from off the shores of North Vietnam, South Vietnam, Laos, or Cambodia.[2]

Unless Nixon, or any subsequent president, was now willing to egregiously break the law to come to the aid of the Vietnamese, the Communists in the north were essentially given a free pass for another invasion. It was already underway.

The Vietnamese cause in America was without a native or any other sort of active constituency. The Vietnamese, at least the ones in the south, had very few American friends with political clout still willing to advocate on their behalf. As events developed in the Middle East during the fall of 1973, that lack of support was made even more obvious. The unintended consequences of what became known to the world as the Yom Kippur War and the subsequent oil price increases instigated by OPEC would end up having a particularly deleterious impact on the Republic of Vietnam's effort to remain free.

Lieutenant Colonel Gerry Turley's next assignment was not meant to be nearly as stimulating as the one he had just come from. The title was generic enough—"Joint Planning Officer"—and he worked a desk at Headquarters Marine Corps. The "Joint" part in the title meant that Lieutenant Colonel Turley was to work at whatever he was assigned to do with the three other U.S. military services as directed by the Joint Chiefs of Staff or the secretary of defense. With the pullback from Vietnam, nearly everything going forward was for training operations and contingencies in the event of future conflict. Eight to five type stuff or a bit longer on some days during peacetime.

MEANWHILE, ELSEWHERE IN ASIA

Consumed largely by whatever they were then directly involved in, a great many Americans since the end of the Second World War had grown used to seeing their country as leader and policeman of the free world. For far too many, their solipsistic view of the globe was such that the universe outside the U.S. existed only if and when they considered or were directly involved in it. Americans had come to believe, without really thinking about it, that freedom was somehow a uniquely American concept, and not the natural yearning of the human spirit. Many viewed the world as divided up with the U.S., its Western allies, and Japan in one corner against a surging, aggressive, irresistible Soviet bloc which included an axis of cohorts throughout Asia, Africa, central Europe, and everywhere else people could be convinced they were oppressed.

The line credited to Chairman Mao that "political power grows out of the barrel of a gun" stopped many barely perceptive people from understanding the very obvious concept that *all* people everywhere want freedom. Given the choice, they prefer more of it rather than less; and if given the opportunity to work for its blessings would. The period of excessive introspection and collective self-flagellation forced on America in the 1960s by so many of those opposed to the war in Vietnam and the issue of American "imperialism" blinded those in the West to the natural forces of human nature; Adam Smith's "invisible hand(s) of the free market," at work everywhere to undermine Communism's very unnatural restraints to the human condition. All of this managed to take place without the nefarious involvement or assistance of the CIA.

Among the Eastern elites it was never polite to mention the obvious and point out that there were few, if any, recorded attempts then being made by sane people risking life and limb to break *into* any of the totalitarian paradises. With more than fifty thousand of its young men killed, tens of billions of dollars of the nation's wealth seemingly squandered, the societal fabric stretched and in some instances torn, the American perspective of the war was far from positive when limited only to the American experience.

Yet throughout Asia there were indications, hints, tiny signs of incipient freedom and capitalism, however imperfect, that were starting to blossom. The Association of Southeast Asian Nations, known by the acronym ASEAN, came into being in 1967.[3] Originally comprised of the countries of Thailand, Singapore, Malaysia, Indonesia, and the Philippines, ASEAN was designed to be an "association of states engaged in nation building." ASEAN was meant to promote peace, economic growth, and social harmony in ways free of Communist domination and unwanted influence from outside any of the member nations' borders.

In fact, across Asia, from the Republic of Korea and Japan in the north, continuing south to Taiwan and through the ASEAN countries, capitalism was taking hold with a vengeance, often in the face of only recent defeats to insurgent, local Communist forces. Americans would recall the bloody fight for Korea in 1950–1953 along with the subsequent permanent stationing of forces there to ensure a tenuous peace. Japan by the early 1960s was well on the road to prosperity. Only the most erudite would recall that recently there had also been significant gains made against Communists in Indonesia, Malaysia, and the Philippines. While the American effort appeared to yield mostly a bitter harvest in Vietnam, throughout the region, on the eastern and southern peripheries of the Soviet Union and China, Communists were *not* gaining influence.

THE ARAB-ISRAELI WAR OF 1973 AND OTHER CHALLENGES

It was probably a merciful thing for the United States that it was no longer involved militarily in Vietnam by October 1973. While still having to meet its global commitments and provide deterrence against the Soviet Union, the American military was struggling with how best to deal with the internal challenges of race and drugs. Domestically, President Nixon, his administration, and the nation were becoming fully consumed by the Watergate scandal.

On October 10, Vice President Spiro Agnew was forced to resign from office; later to be replaced by Gerald Ford.

As the United States tried to shed itself of the quagmire that was the Vietnam entanglement, another was birthed with the hostilities between Israel and the entire Arab world. The ongoing Arab-Israeli enmity, known by its 1973 eruptive episode as the Yom Kippur War, was not a repeat of the swift victory enjoyed by the Israelis in 1967. While the war's outcome would actually bolster the U.S. position in the Middle East *vis-à-vis* the Soviets, those gains came at high price. The new power of OPEC, with its grip on a fair share of the world's oil production coupled with a strong distaste for Israel, was exercised by imposing a 400 percent increase in the price of the black gold. The size of the increase caused a massive jolt to the world economy, producing a raging inflation and global recession.

Unlike the Six-Day War of 1967 when the Israelis caught their Arab enemies by surprise, the tables were partially turned in 1973. Hostilities began on October 6, 1973: Yom Kippur. Given that Yom Kippur was the holiest day on the Jewish calendar, by attacking then the Arabs caught their enemy largely unawares. Initial Israeli casualties were high with resulting loss of territory and equipment. In the beginning, things were so grave for the Israelis that there was even a hint that they might resort to using the nuclear weapons they fiercely denied having but which everyone seemed to know they possessed.

The U.S. logistical response to Israeli cries for assistance was at first rather subdued and lethargic. It would shortly become a torrent, a smorgasbord of top-line American military gear and resupply.

As a part of the U.S. effort to get a handle on the military situation, the secretary of defense, on October 12, dispatched an eclectic team of officers from the four services to better assess what was going on and what could be done to assist. From his desk assignment at Headquarters Marine Corps, Lieutenant Colonel Gerry Turley was picked to be a part of this small group of experts. Of the fifteen total officers—five from the Air Force, five from the Army and four from the Navy—Gerry was the only Marine and the only infantry officer. The others were sent to deal mostly with aviation and logistical issues. Turley, with his recent experience facing enemy armor in northern Quang Tri Province, was highly qualified to serve in the short-term capacity he was tasked with.

Where Gerry Turley had genuinely developed a rapport and outright friendship with a great many of his Vietnamese allies, the American Marine made no new friends on this trip. To be fair to the Israelis, they were facing an immediate crisis and the potential threat of annihilation. Their concern was survival, and their first goal was getting the most out of their American benefactors as possible. The Israelis also had the confidence in knowing that their powerful and wealthy cohorts in the U.S. would be unlikely to let them down. The difference between American support for Israel with its incredible breadth of confederates in Congress and that for Vietnam was made apparent within days. In a three-*week* timeframe the Israelis were given $2.1 billion in direct military aid versus $2.2 billion for Vietnam for *all* of Fiscal Year 1973. A total of forty brand new F-4 Phantoms were transferred to the Israeli Air Force.[4] Those Phantoms would be up against the same sophisticated Soviet anti-aircraft weaponry which the Vietnamese were daily facing with mostly propeller-driven aircraft and helicopters.

The American team of observers and experts arrived in Israel on October 12, 1973. Their Israeli Defense Force (IDF) hosts hurriedly and perfunctorily shuttled them to the various battlefields to witness the carnage and destruction. Several days into the war, the Israelis had already lost hundreds of tanks; a fact they were not happy to share other than to use their massive losses as a plea to gain more immediate and substantial aid.

Most of the American observers were content to remain in their vehicles and simply drive by whatever there was to see. Gerry Turley was not. Ever the infantry officer, he made his driver and host stop at place after place so that he might walk the ground in order to gain a better sense for what had transpired. Armed with both a still and movie camera, Lieutenant Colonel Turley shot roll after roll, reel after reel of film to the painful chagrin of the very private, security-conscious IDF personnel.

Gerry's hosts were not subtle in hiding their displeasure with the American Marine's probing questions and continued picture taking. They felt no obligation to cooperate with his prying thoroughness. Several times they asked him, demanded really, that he cease his cinematic endeavors; admonishing him to turn over the film to them. Turley was not intimidated, and just as bluntly told them where to put it. The IDF were not in his chain of command, and so he pressed on. His hosts grew more unpleasant, more petulant. Turley was still not intimidated. The tension was palpable. He did not care, and kept on doing what he had been assigned by the secretary of defense.

It was lunchtime on day three of Gerry Turley's journey with his IDF guides. They had just stopped at the north end of the Suez Canal near the Mediterranean. As everyone was lining up to go through the chow line, one of the Israeli officers invited the American Marine to go first. "Here, Colonel Turley, this is for you…" Gerry had not been paying close attention. Usually USMC officers ate after their troops. His host insisted. Turley gave in, thinking "when in Rome…"

The meal was some sort of turkey sandwich. Turley had eaten military food for nearly a quarter century. He had certainly eaten worse, and did not see it coming. He should have known, or so he would think, chastising himself less than an hour later when whatever was in that sandwich caused him to double over in pain. Between alternate bouts of diarrhea and vomiting Turley became a casualty no longer capable of doing the observing he needed to observe.

Not quite one hundred percent certain the Israelis had not tried to kill him rather than make him violently ill, Gerry was of no further value on the battlefield. He was taken back to his hotel for the remainder of his Israel time so that he might vomit and move his bowels in the privacy of his room. Score one for the IDF.

Gerry Turley would get the last laugh. For the next three days, during his conscious moments between sitting on or leaning over the commode in his hotel room, he composed meticulous notes on all that he had observed; something he never would have had the time or privacy to do had he remained in the field. To ensure that those notes and undeveloped rolls of film made it back to the

U.S.—he figured his IDF friends would somehow go through his gear or confiscate them upon departure—he gave them to a trusted contact at the American Embassy with very simple instructions: "Deliver these to the *commandant* of the Marine Corps."

When Turley returned to Washington he was a hot commodity. The man who had come close to being sacrificed for conduct construed as borderline crazy in Quang Tri Province was now briefing the Joint Chiefs of Staff, the Secretary of Defense, Secretary of State, and Vice President Ford. When Gerry briefed Henry Kissinger, the Secretary of State, who had no idea who Turley was, first looked at the pictures he had taken and asked him who he was and what he did. After Gerry explained, Kissinger gave him an understated compliment. "Colonel Turley, these pictures are so good, I thought maybe you were a professional photographer."

To the extent that there really was a broad, amorphous funk sweeping America with the continued societal upheaval from the mid-1960s, along with the overall denigration of tradition and respect for authority, the economic discordance could be more tangibly measured. Arthur Okun, an economic advisor to President Johnson, had developed something he termed the "U.S. Misery Index." Okun's index was simply the sum of the inflation rate and the unemployment rate.[5] For calendar year 1973 the Misery Index gave its highest reading since 1951 at 11.02. What that number represented, in addition to the unraveling of the Nixon presidency, and the fact that the Dow Jones Industrial Average lost more than 13 percent of its value as a result of the oil crisis, kept many Americans in a sour mood.

Song Than
December 1973

Most of the fighting in 1973, conducted after the phony cease fire, was not at the scale or level of the grand engagements during the Easter Offensive. Still there was no shortage of combat and the casualty numbers reflected that continuous action. While RVN forces still predominated on the battlefield, they did so at significant cost. For all of 1973 RVN forces suffered 27,901 men killed; behind only 1972 and 1968 in total KIAs.[6] Those casualty figures, though, painted a very incomplete picture.

The greater, cumulative problems of population displacement and a now chronic inflation were cause for an overall despondency that began to creep into the national psyche. The country's still crude physical infrastructure was being stretched beyond its limited capacity. As more and more refugees were forced into the cities, unemployment, crime, and social unrest increased. The Thieu government, heretofore concerned mostly with defeating the Communist invaders, would necessarily begin to divert resources to dealing with these other increasingly serious challenges. If there could have been a similar misery index for the Republic of Vietnam, it would have been five to ten times that of the United States.

Compared to all he had experienced while leading Third Battalion, duty as the commanding officer of Song Than was relatively quiet, although certainly not uneventful. For Binh, the fighting he was directly responsible for leading was security in and around Song Than. The local Viet Cong were not suicidal and generally gave the Marines there a wide berth. This allowed Binh to focus his energies on his other duties and responsibilities. The best news for Binh and Cam as they headed into the end of the year was that Cam was pregnant with their first child and was expected to deliver sometime in late June or early July of 1974.

PREPARING FOR THE END

At about the time of Turley's departure from Vietnam, the United States Marine Corps began to invest considerable planning and training resources for what would be the final evacuations out of Phnom Penh and Saigon if the situation deteriorated to that point. The passage of the Fulbright-Aiken Amendment in the late summer of 1973, aside from signaling the Communist leadership in the north to press ahead with further plans for invasion, was a harbinger for American military leaders and those responsible for contingency planning that the chances of those plans eventually needing to be executed would become reality.

From mid-1973 through the beginning of 1975, several rotations of middle- and senior-level officers who passed through their assigned service on Okinawa had worked with their sister service counterparts to make plans, revise those plans, and then revise them again when it came to figuring on how best to get Americans and what friendly allies they could out who might need saving from advancing Communist forces. Infantry battalions stationed on Okinawa and the helicopter squadrons that supported them rehearsed their expected missions, were put on alert for those missions, and spent time at sea aboard amphibious shipping awaiting the call for those missions.

For the Communists bent on consuming the south at any price, time and the oddest set of worldwide circumstances continued to work in their favor. The unraveling of the Nixon presidency from late 1973 and into 1974 severely limited the President's ability to honor the personal commitments he had made to Nguyen Van Thieu. Congress was feeling no charity when it came to authorizing aid to Vietnam. From $2.2 billion given in fiscal year 1973, aid was cut to $1.5 billion in fiscal year 1974.[7] The percentage decline was actually far more injurious than the 32 percent cut from fiscal year 1973. The price of fuel was up 400 percent. The cost of ammunition and other war-fighting essentials had likewise skyrocketed. The real purchasing power of aid to RVN had shrunk precipitously. The ability of RVN forces to function in the field began to be severely degraded.[8]

At the same time, the Soviets, who had been denied Most Favored Nation status over their treatment of Jewish dissidents, removed from Hanoi the restraints they had earlier placed in an effort to accommodate the Americans. Where RVN support was more than cut in half, aid to the DRV was ramped up considerably, perhaps even doubling.

In the face of, and in addition to, all the bad news out of Washington, the leadership in the Republic of Vietnam failed to adjust to the harshly imposed new logistical realities. President Thieu and many around him could not, or refused to, comprehend that the United States was no longer going to ride to the rescue or keep open the floodgates of material support. For too great a time period Thieu continued to try and fight the war as if nothing had changed. Thieu's intransigence and inflexibility were marginally codified into something referred to as the "Four Nos." They included: no negotiations with the enemy, no Communist activity inside the Republic of Vietnam, no coalition government, and—most important—no surrender of territory to the enemy.[9]

President Thieu's obsession with keeping all territory within the confines of the Republic of Vietnam free of Communist control or influence would ultimately be his country's undoing; or at least speed the process. While his generals made every attempt to comply with his orders, Thieu's insistence on defending everywhere, even the most remote and strategically insignificant territory, again ceded the battlefield initiative always to the flush with Soviet equipment NVA. Stretched thin and seriously hampered by their own logistical constraints, to defend everywhere in reality meant to lose almost everywhere.

BINH AND THE VIETNAMESE MARINE CORPS CULTURE

About the only thing Le Ba Binh genuinely appreciated in his assignment to Song Than was that he was present for the birth of his daughter on July 4, 1974. Le Mong Ngoc was born in a private hospital in Gia Dinh, near the home of Binh's parents. In keeping with Vietnamese tradition, Binh and his mother-in-law were present with Cam for the delivery. Ngoc was a healthy little girl, and her parents were both grateful for her arrival.

In his job as the commanding officer of the Song Than base, Binh experienced a frustration and angst he had never known while serving with Third Battalion. At Song Than his disparate duties, which had little to do with directly disposing of the enemy, taxed him in ways that leading Marines in combat had not. He understood that he had to adjust, that the missions they performed there were entirely critical, and did his best. Still he believed his greatest strength and contribution to his country was to lead Marines against the red devils.

Through 1974 and into 1975, when U.S. financial and material aid was cut yet again by nearly 50 percent, the Vietnamese Marine

Corps (TQLC) remained mostly free of the problems endemic to the Army of the Republic of Vietnam (ARVN). From the *commandant* on down, the entire organization remained zealous in taking care of the families of Marines so that the warriors could focus on fighting their wily and crafty enemy. It was understood by all that when a Marine knew that his wife and children were safe and well fed, as they were at Song Than, he could fight with a happy heart. If the wives of Marines raised a clamor, and the complaints were legitimate, action was swiftly taken. TQLC leadership spared no effort to ensure that the families at Song Than had ample supplies of food and that the base was as much a haven as it could be made to be. Binh was pleased that he could help provide a safe place for the families of all Marines. He still would much rather have been leading Marines up north.

The newer system of resupply in the "post-American" world of the RVN military was different for the Vietnamese Marines than it was for the much larger Army of the Republic of Vietnam (ARVN). Because they were so widely regarded as warriors by all in political power, the Vietnamese Marine Corps was spared the most when it came to cutting back on the assignment of war fighting supplies. In addition the TQLC, still about fifteen thousand strong, was reprovisioned directly by the U.S. Navy without going through whatever corrupt, perfidious hands there were currently at work in Saigon. With that small an organization the logistical effort was reasonably efficient. There were fewer problems getting all the gear to those units most in need.

As a much larger organization with nowhere near the uniformity in quality as the TQLC, ARVN logistical challenges became a major theme of Western media reports. With the increase in enemy action from late 1974 into 1975, stories of corruption and outright treason, stories of troops having to pay for fire support or their own medevac were made to seem common. Tales of the scandalous acts of unscrupulous generals and public officials selling critical supplies on the black market aside, it was true that a genuine lack of fuel, spare parts, and proper maintenance was keeping planes from flying, vehicles from moving, and weapons from firing. The NVA seemed to have as much or more destructive firepower than ever, and was as willing as ever to employ it against any and all targets, military or civilian.

It was a rare situation indeed when TQLC units ran low on critical ammunition or spare parts, as the political and military leadership at every level knew those resources dedicated for use by Marines would never be squandered. The only problem with the TQLC, and the few other truly reliable ARVN units, was that there were simply not enough of them to make enough of a difference in the war's ultimate outcome; which was still not absolutely certain to everyone, especially President Thieu, in the south going into the end of 1974 who believed that the United States might still, somehow, find a way to ride to the rescue.

In November of 1974 Binh finally got his wish to return to action. Leaving Cam and Ngoc in Saigon, he was given command of Sixth Battalion, known as *"Than-Ung,"* which translated roughly as "Sacred Bird," and was back in Quang Tri Province leading Marines in combat. He would remain with the Sixth Battalion until the mid-morning of April 30, 1975.

CHAPTER THIRTY-SEVEN

Operation Frequent Wind

A *nother nail in the coffin* of the struggling Republic of Vietnam was added on August 8, 1974, with the resignation of the horribly politically wounded Richard Nixon. While President Ford immediately signaled to a rightfully concerned President Thieu that nothing had changed, the astute observers in Hanoi knew better. In fact nothing really had changed. For more than a year the Communists had been routinely violating the Paris accords and Nixon had done nothing. Would an even weaker Nixon replacement be any different? Preparations for a new, larger offensive were in process but the most cautious members of the Politburo wanted more assurance the Americans would not return with their B-52s.

The official *malaise* in the United States continued into the end of the year. For 1974 Okun's Misery Index would post a reading of 16.6 (unemployment of 5.6 percent plus inflation at 11 percent). For the year the Dow Jones Industrial Average gave up an additional 23.1 percent. Americans were feeling anything but charitable towards their Vietnamese ally.

With what would turn out to be the final offensive well underway in late 1974, with ARVN morale showing few signs of hope or resiliency, and with the American material spigot virtually shut off, the North Vietnamese wanted one more sign that the United States would leave its ally to twist in the wind. The January 1975 all-out assault against Phuoc Long, about seventy-five miles north of Saigon, without any hint of American response was the final signal to even the most wary, conservative politburo members that it was now completely safe to press ahead for total victory.

THE END OF THE REPUBLIC OF VIETNAM

The end came fairly quickly, at least by the outward indicators. Then again, given the pervasive hopelessness apparent to outsiders, the Republic of Vietnam took a long time to die. Back in Fortress America, interest in Vietnam had continued to ebb. As it is always almost impossible for regular folks to process the enormity of suffering done far outside their experience or existence, the stories of the tens of thousands, soon to be hundreds of thousands and then millions of displaced persons fleeing before the advancing Communist tide meant very little. They were simply more stories in the news that to most meant nothing. Americans were emotionally enervated by the Vietnam experience; even though for most it was a vicarious experience. That the Communists continued to routinely target innocents in their advance to power was something few now cared about. For most Americans it was time to move on, turn the channel, close this particular book. The Vietnamese, for whom the war had been anything but vicarious, were likewise war weary and certainly anxious for peace, but for those who would be stuck in the nightmare the Americans were soon about to exit, it would be a peace without freedom. It would be peace with retribution. Peace with payback. Peace with subjugation. Peace with hunger. Peace with maximum pain.

For the politically astute and wary-of-American-response Politburo members, the success of their effort at Phuoc Luong was cause for celebration. From the northernmost provinces of Quang Tri and Thua Tien all the way down to Saigon, it was full speed ahead. RVN leadership failed miserably with any sort of strategic defensive plan, although TQLC and certain ARVN units fought tenaciously and bravely as they were usually outnumbered and always outgunned. President Thieu clung stubbornly to the notion of ceding the enemy no territory, and the lugubrious hope that the Americans might somehow still come through. Where there might have been opportunity to inflict maximum cost on the advancing

NVA had a more cogent defensive plan been implemented, RVN forces were instead employed with minimal strategic effect. The NVA continued to roll on towards Saigon.

With defeat a virtual certainty, hopelessness prevailed. As the Lunar New Year came and went, in all but the very best military units, morale collapsed and army units melted into nothingness; the troops now focused on their own and their families' survival. It was only a matter of time. The end became a self-fulfilling outcome.

Accompanying the pending demise of the Republic of Vietnam were the societal issues: the huge population displacement, the fear, the anger, the shame, the horror, the financial panics, the hoarding, the hyper inflation, the efforts to leave, to cover up one's past or at least best prepare for the "new boss," and a million other things, none of them positive.

BINH WITH SIXTH BATTALION

There was little time for transition from what Binh had experienced, the relative calm at Song Than, back to the complete intensity of the full-on, all-out fighting in Quang Tri, Thua Thien, and Quang Nam Provinces in Military Region I. Binh's Marines fought as he expected, giving ground at high price to the numerically and materially superior enemy, and this time without benefit of American naval gunfire or air support. Making the combat even more chaotic were the changing, conflicting, and contradicting orders issued from Saigon by President Thieu and his closest advisors. As a part of Brigade 369, Binh's battalion fought their way back to the coast, after the New Year, to defend Danang which was said to have upward of one million desperate refugees fleeing the Communist invasion.

After two weeks in Danang, and recognizing that the situation up north was lost, the Marines were put aboard ship and sent south to Cam Ranh. Even though the end seemed imminent, and the Marines had taken huge casualties, being reduced from twelve thousand to roughly four thousand, discipline within the Marine Brigade remained ironclad.[1] No one deserted. From Cam Ranh, the Marines moved to Vung Tau where they reorganized all remaining forces and set out in mid-April for Bien Hoa. Bien Hoa would be the place of their final stand; their Alamo. Jim Bowie and Davy Crockett would have recognized the ground situation and felt at home.

Operation Baby Lift was an effort many Americans at home would still relate to even this close to the war's unfortunate conclusion. The war in Vietnam had created thousands and thousands of orphans. Many of those to be left behind were the product of American fathers and Vietnamese mothers. They would face particular discrimination in a society that did not necessarily, at this point in time especially, appreciate the mixing of blood, nor the reminder that foreigners had come and left their mark.

In March and early April 1975, there were those intrepid Americans who hoped to get as many of the unclaimed and helpless orphans out; get them to America where there would be no shortage of families anxious to adopt and take in these children of Vietnamese and mixed ethnicity.

On April 4, the first flight of orphans was going to the U.S. along with a number of volunteers who had worked selflessly and tirelessly on behalf of these children. The C-5A Galaxy aircraft that was to be their freedom bird experienced serious malfunctions just as it was lifting off from Tan Son Nhut and crashed moments later, killing more than one hundred of the children and volunteers. Although there were survivors, the tragedy in this story seemed to signal to the war-weary Americans that even in trying to do good, very little about Vietnam was turning positive.

EPIC BATTLE AT XUAN LOC, PRESIDENT THIEU RESIGNS

During the period of April 8-21, the ARVN 18th Division, reinforced by a regiment from the ARVN Fifth Division and a brigade from the Airborne Division put up a mighty, last-ditch defense at Xuan Loc. Just over sixty kilometers from the heart of downtown Saigon, it was truly ARVN's ultimate stand before the invaders were at the city's outskirts. The tenacity of the ARVN defenders surprised those in the Western media. Just prior to and up until the time of the battle, General Frederick Weyand, currently serving as the Army chief of staff and who had been the last commander of MACV (and who as deputy commander of MACV had thanked Gerry Turley for his service during the craziest days of the Easter Offensive), had concluded a fact-finding trip to Vietnam and had gone back to Washington in hopes of convincing members of Congress to spring for emergency funds to shore up the Vietnamese. His pleas fell on deaf ears. All that the defenders of Xuan Loc bought with their blood sacrifices was additional time for many of their countrymen to begin to organize their own departures from the dying republic.

The ultimate defeat of ARVN forces at Xuan Loc, at tremendous cost to the NVA, was the final act of President Thieu's term in office. Extremely bitter at the obvious outcome, his televised three-hour April 21 resignation speech transferred power to Vice President Tran Van Huong. (Tran Van Huong would a few days later transfer that authority to General Duong Van Minh.) In that very long, rambling tirade Thieu was generous with blame towards the United States. "The United States has not respected its promises. It is inhumane. It is not trustworthy. It is irresponsible." Thieu and his family left the country the next day for Taiwan.[2]

The remaining Marines of Sixth Battalion fought the Communists out near Bien Hoa, to the bitter end, and would have continued to fight to the last man and the last bullet, until they were ordered to lay down their arms at approximately 10:30 a.m. on April 30th. Their brigade commander, Colonel Tri, had finally passed the word that it was now the most prudent thing for his men to go home and take care of their families as best they could. Many of the Marines wanted to continue fighting, pleading with their commanders not to surrender. There was a great gnashing of teeth, much rancor, but what else, what more could they do? Those were the orders issued from on high. The Marines were professionals; so they obeyed without joy or gladness. Reluctantly, and undefeated, they put down their arms and tried to go back to homes which no longer really existed.

To spare Cam and Ngoc potential retribution, Binh believed it wise to spend the first few days of the "new order" at the home of his aunt near Bien Hoa. He was concerned that the new turncoats, the new collaborators and quislings, the "April 30th Communists," whoever they would turn out to be, might somehow seek favor with their new masters in turning over a senior Marine for capture.

As of the late morning on April 30, 1975, the Vietnamese Marine Corps, after nearly twenty-one years of continuous combat, no longer existed except in the hearts and minds of those who had belonged. The official history of their individual and collective sacrifices, their bravery and loyalty to each other and the country they had bled so much for would be twisted, expunged, eliminated by the spiteful invaders. It was well known that the victors have the privilege of writing history. No one expected charity or truth from the Red Devils. Everyone who held that belief would soon be proven correct.

BUGGING OUT—OPERATION FREQUENT WIND

April 29, 1975

For Marines the word "retreat" is *anathema*, downright hateful. It is not a part of their official lexicon. With liberal euphemism, very liberal euphemism, the final evacuation of remaining American personnel and their unfortunate Vietnamese allies from Saigon could have been called a "retrograde operation."

During the Korean War, Major General O.P. Smith, commanding the First Marine Division—and the fellow who later observed a young, hard-core Sergeant Gerry Turley personally put down a riot with little more than a two-by-four and his bare knuckles in the open-air brig at Camp Pendleton before enthusiastically endorsing his application for a direct officer's commission—was widely quoted as he led his Marines out of the Chosin Reservoir: "We're not retreating. Hell! We're just attacking in a different direction!" The American Marines were *not* retreating with so many Chinese Communists all around them. They were, just as their commander had said, quite simply, attacking in a different direction. And they did...all the way to the sea.

In Southeast Asia in late April 1975 the United States was not attacking in a different direction. The great assemblage of American naval might—nearly the entire Seventh Fleet—along with embarked Marines and numerous chartered merchant vessels, were gathered to execute what would turn into one of the largest humanitarian evacuations ever conducted under pressure in such a short period.

American military personnel taking part in what was officially known as Operation Frequent Wind, the final evacuation of the dying Republic of Vietnam, would not leave their theater of operations with the satisfaction of at least, one more time, destroying great numbers of the now drunk-with-victory NVA legions. While the American forces involved in Operation Frequent Wind (OFW) executed their duties heroically and professionally, the greater national and international implications for the United States were far less positive. American primacy, particularly throughout the greater Pacific Ocean areas, had been eclipsed by the seemingly ascendant Soviet Bear, China, and their Communist surrogates. In South Vietnam the light of freedom was being simply but brutally snuffed out.

Aboard the USS Okinawa *(LPH-3)*
Somewhere off the coast of Vietnam near Vung Tau in the South China Sea
Mid morning April 29, 1975

Captain John Webster Bowman, Jr. USMC, Princeton Class of 1966, had gotten little sleep the previous evening, or in the last several days for that matter. He had not expected to, and it really did not matter anyway. The tension and excitement, the seriousness of all that would take place in the following hours would ensure his heightened state of alert and that his blood would be pumping as he piloted his AH-1J Sea Cobra gunship through the skies above Saigon providing attack helicopter escort for the Marine troop-transport helicopters shuttling an unending supply of Americans and Vietnamese to the ships of the Seventh Fleet steaming in circles twenty miles out to sea.

Very much like George Philip's family, the Bowman clan was also patrician of sorts. They were not patrician in the sense of great material wealth but in the generational concentration of men who had disproportionately served the nation in the profession of arms. In the most contemporary generations, his mother's father, Smith

523

Hempstone, was a Navy captain with a distinguished career that included service in World War I, Haiti, and with the fabled Yangtze River Patrol in China during the pre-World War II years. His mother's brother, Smith Hempstone, Jr., had served as a Marine artillery lieutenant in the Korean War. Upon leaving the Corps, Uncle Smith became a distinguished journalist with several newspapers to include the Chicago *Daily News*. (Hempstone, a noted expert on African affairs, had also authored several books, and had been awarded a prestigious Neiman Fellowship at Harvard.) Bowman's father, John W., Senior, was U.S. Naval Academy Class of 1943. The Annapolis Class of 1943, due to the exigencies of the war, had graduated a year early. The senior John W., upon commissioning as a Marine, became a communications officer and reached the Pacific in time to see combat on Roi Namur, Tinian, Saipan, and Iwo Jima. Colonel Bowman graciously retired from active duty, as his son would often joke, to spare the Corps the challenge of dealing with two of them, the same day the junior Bowman pinned on his gold bars.

From Princeton and then Basic School in Quantico, Second Lieutenant Bowman was assigned to flight school in Pensacola, Florida, where he earned his naval aviator wings as a helicopter pilot. Due to the length and nature of flight school, and promoted while a student there, First Lieutenant John Bowman arrived in country months and months after the fellows in his Basic School class who had become infantry officers had had ample opportunities to die for their country. Many of them did, especially since most of them had gotten there in time to participate in Tet of 1968. The newly-trained pilots from Bowman's particular TBS class began to arrive in Southeast Asia in late 1968.

Assigned as a UH-34D Seahorse pilot with the "Ugly Angels" of HMM-362, John's flying life centered on the transporting of troops into and out of both hot and cold landing zones, routine and emergency medevac missions, the insertion and extraction of reconnaissance teams, and an occasional milk run. In its time, the UH-34 was a workhorse helicopter. Now it was being largely supplanted and replaced by the newer, more capable CH-46 Sea Knight. The old Seahorse was capable of carrying up to five fully-equipped infantrymen, depending on weather and atmospheric conditions. (Air density impacted lift capability.) The CH-46 could carry more than three times the load.

Aboard the USS Kirk *(DE-1087)*
Early morning April 29, 1975

Petty Officer Second Class Jim Bongaard had joined the Navy two years out of high school in 1971. Like so many young men of his age group, he had joined the Navy rather than be drafted into the Army. Known as "Bon" to his shipmates, Jim had graduated high school in Florida and attended two years of junior college in Broward County. His hand was forced in 1971 when President Nixon ended college deferments. And like many of the young men in that age group who served in Southeast Asia after the major American withdrawals had taken place, they would mercifully be spared the intensity of combat experienced by those fellows who had preceded them by several years.

After boot camp in Orlando, Florida Jim went to further schooling to become what was called an "Operations Specialist." Aboard the *Kirk*, Bon's duty station kept him in the Combat Information Center; "CIC" for short. Everyone referred to the CIC as "Combat." "Combat" was the nerve center for all offensive and defensive operations. The inside of the CIC was always kept dark so that the group of Operations Specialists who needed to monitor the various air and surface radar scopes would have maximum visual acuity. Bon spent most of his time in Combat watching these scopes.

To those familiar with old *Victory at Sea* documentaries or war movies about naval operations the actions in *Kirk's* CIC would seem familiar. The relatively large space was crammed with men and electronic gear. There were those men who, like Bon, constantly watched the radar scopes, and more junior lads who stood behind the plexiglass information screens transmitting and receiving info over sound-powered head phones they were required to monitor, and with grease pencils wrote backwards onto the clear panes so the decision makers on the interior of the arrayed screens could rightfully be apprised of the ever

525

developing, always changing air and sea situation. And there was the constant sound of messages being transmitted and received, of orders being given and acknowledged. Aboard the *Kirk*, and most ships of the line, Combat was always the most exciting place to be.

The USS *Kirk* had entered service with the fleet in 1972 and Bon was one of her original crew members. Members of a ship's first crew were called "plank owners." In April of 1975 approximately half of the *Kirk's* crew were still plank owners.

The USS *Kirk* had been built at the Avondale Shipyard in Louisiana and was home ported in San Diego. Her primary role as a surface combatant was fleet protection; read as protecting aircraft carriers from surface and subsurface, mostly subsurface, threats. She had limited anti-aircraft capabilities which, in the event of hostilities, would have been provided by other ship types used in synergistic combination.

By 1973 the U.S. Navy had returned to the pre-Vietnam pattern of show-the-flag-forward deployments in the western Pacific. The *Kirk* was, like other ships of the line, an instrument of American foreign policy; out there closest to wherever the need might arise to ensure the peace or be available for war.

Kirk's first western Pacific cruise, (The area of interest and influence for "WestPac" encompassed the Indian Ocean, the northern Pacific to include Korea, Japan, and areas adjacent to the Soviet Union, down south all the way past China, Taiwan, the Philippines, Vietnam, and the critical choke point at the Strait of Malacca.) always referred to as "WestPac" by sailors, Marines and their families, saw her depart San Diego just before Christmas in 1973. From San Diego she headed to Pearl Harbor and then out to WestPac. During that six-month deployment, except for being info'd in on naval messages, there was little to no concern for events in Vietnam. *Kirk* steamed as part of an aircraft carrier task force out to the Indian Ocean as a show of support for the ill-fated Shah of Iran. They made routine, uneventful port calls in Hong Kong and other places. Her crew, especially those who had never done a WestPac, were shocked and overstimulated by the completely raucous, libidinous living in Subic Bay and the modern-day Sodom and Gomorrah village of Olongapo outside of Subic's main gate. Their first WestPac, concluded in May of 1974, was a successful, basically normal deployment.

For her second WestPac, *Kirk* was skippered by Commander Paul Jacobs. At the ripe old age of thirty-eight, he was both literally and figuratively the "Old Man." Even the ship's saltiest, most wizened chief petty officers were younger than he was. The skipper was always amazed, and a little bit in awe, of the power and responsibilities commanders and their young crews were routinely given. Prior to shoving off in San Diego he had checked all the records and the average age for his approximately 250 man crew, officers and chiefs included, was barely twenty. He was the "Old Man" alright; and this was his *third* command.

The USS *Kirk* departed San Diego for her second WestPac cruise in late March of 1975. Senior American military planners had long considered, even before the loss of Vietnam to the Communists was a certainty, the need for contingency evacuation plans from Southeast Asia. As *Kirk* steamed westward, she was ordered to close with the USS *Hancock* (CVA-19) and escort the proud but aging aircraft carrier toward WestPac. For the officers and crew of the *Kirk*, the transit was made more exciting as the operational tempo increased and activities such as underway replenishments were conducted at higher speeds. The *Hancock*, an old *Essex*-class carrier from the glory days of World War II, had offloaded her airwing and onloaded a score of Marine-heavy and medium-lift helicopters to be used for the pending evacuations of American and other personnel from Cambodia and Vietnam, if the need arose.

OPERATION EAGLE PULL — THE WITHDRAWAL FROM CAMBODIA

By March 1975, the Communist tide appeared as an unstoppable *juggernaut*, at least in Southeast Asia. While few Americans truly understood the nature of the situation in Vietnam, in terms of sheer evil, Cambodia was even more incongruous. The Ohio-sized country had the unfortunate reality of being located adjacent to Vietnam and Laos. It had strategic importance to Vietnam as the Ho Chi Minh Trail wended its way through the eastern portions of the country where NVA troops routinely took sanctuary. The rise of the merciless Khmer Rouge, whose complete ruthlessness would soon be made apparent, was lost on Americans who simply wanted out of the nightmare that was the entire Vietnam experience.

The final fall of Cambodia to Communist forces and the evacuation of American personnel, along with what allies were able to get out with them, took place in mid-April. Known as Operation Eagle Pull, the helicopter evacuation of Phnom Penh occurred on April 12, 1975. U.S. Marine and Air Force helicopters lifted out not quite three hundred Americans, Cambodians, and other foreign nationals to a small group of ships off shore in the Gulf of Thailand. In size and scope, the retrograde from Phnom Penh was far simpler than what would soon follow, but was a good training exercise for those forces involved.

John Bowman had concluded his first Vietnam tour in November of 1969. He had survived many missions where a number of his dearest friends had not. From Vietnam his duties were far more in keeping with reasonably normal operations that all Marine officers were tasked with as they progressed along in their careers and were not off fighting somewhere.

In the spring of 1974, with the Corps' return to the Okinawa deployment routine, he was sent to "The Rock" for a one-year tour; this time piloting the new AH-1J Sea Cobra attack helicopter.

Captain Bowman spent about a month on Okinawa, becoming further qualified as a Cobra driver. He was then assigned to a squadron and put to sea aboard the USS *New Orleans* (LPH-11). The United States Marine Corps, since 1775, had been America's "force in readiness." In keeping with that tradition, the Corps took quite seriously the need to meet a wide range of military needs in the most unusual situations. Like their brothers on the ground side of the house, the Marines in the air wing organized their squadrons for specific missions. Under normal circumstances, such as during home deployments, a squadron would be made up of one type of aircraft only. The squadron John went to sea with in the spring of 1974, HMH-462, was usually made up entirely of CH-53 heavy-lift helicopters (The first "H" of HMH stood for "Helicopter," the "M" stood for "Marine," and the second "H" stood for "Heavy.") As they went to sea with the mission of supporting ground Marines, the squadron was known as a "composite squadron" and was "task organized"; (Being "task organized" meant that a unit was organized for a specific mission or tasking.) with a generous blend of troop-transport aircraft—CH-53s and CH-46s, several AH-1Js for escort and fire support, and a few UH-1 Hueys to serve as command and control aircraft. As missions changed or evolved, the Marine Corps would routinely modify the composition of the ground and helicopter forces afloat.

During the course of the next year Bowman would serve on the *New Orleans* and the USS *Tripoli* (LPH-10) before moving over to the *Okinawa*. In that same period he would serve for a period as a member of HMM-164; normally a CH-46 squadron. (The second "M" stood for "Medium" as in "Medium Lift.") By April of 1975, having extended beyond his normal rotation date as he was certain there would be action which he was honor bound to participate in, he was again back with HMH-462.

Outside the U.S. Embassy
Saigon
Tuesday, April 29, 1975
Late afternoon

For the ill-fated, about-to-lose-their-freedom Vietnamese who were seeking escape, the American helicopter evacuation of Saigon was like some oversized, cruel, real-life game of musical chairs with far too few seats available and music that was just about to be turned off—permanently.

If someone had a mind for history, the completely incongruous, utterly surrealistic and psychedelic playing of Bing Crosby's "White Christmas" over Saigon radio during the late morning of Tuesday the 29th as the known-by-all signal that the evacuation was set to begin, they might have recalled the scene from *The Longest Day* where members of the French Underground received obtuse but obvious coded radio messages telling them of the pending D-Day landings. The greatest difference now for the losing side in Saigon was that there would be no joy, no liberation; only subjugation. For Vietnamese people who cherished their freedom, they were set to

529

begin their own hellish "Longest Day"—or more appropriately their longest night. The conquering, humorless Communists would never again allow the public playing of "Victory Flag Flying over the Quang Tri Citadel."

Most of the U.S. Marines shortly to land at the designated Saigon extract points were not veterans of earlier Vietnam combat. Even if they were, duty in the final days of the dying republic was thankfully outside of anything they had ever experienced. The panic and desperation of people normally reticent and in complete control of their emotions gave the air that everyone breathed a weirdness even the dullest American, if he was uninformed and new to the action, could discern.

Occidentals witnessing the hopelessness were reasonably assured of a ticket out, and could be thankful while those around them suffered all the stresses of their country and life as they knew it in a culture they loved dying an inglorious, tragic death. Ceasing to exist. The physical geography and infrastructure would remain. The mountains and the rice paddies and the rivers, even the graves of ancestors, they would all still remain; but the Vietnam everyone knew would simply vanish; consumed by the insatiable Communist totalitarian tide.

The Americans, civilians mostly, who were still there were leaving jobs and in many cases friends, perhaps some cherished memories. The Vietnamese, those hoping to get out, were leaving all that was familiar, in many cases all or a portion of their families, and uncounted generations of buried ancestors behind, everything that was dear and sacred, they were leaving, escaping so that they might not live in fear. For some Vietnamese, those who had exited the north in 1954, this was the second big move in their lives. Their long-deceased ancestors could never have fathomed so much change in a single generation.

Inbound from the USS Okinawa
1500 hours—approximate

The initial order to execute and launch what would be known as Option IV of Operation Frequent Wind was issued at about 1100 local time on April 29. The order to launch the Marines and their helicopters followed soon after. Thousands and thousands of man hours had been invested in the planning and ongoing coordination for what was now about to be implemented. The plan was incredibly complex, requiring maximum effort, professionalism, flexibility, and skill from all the people involved. A little bit of luck would help as well. The first aircraft sent aloft were the CH-53s carrying the Marines who would make up the security forces at the Defense Attache Office (DAO) compound adjacent to Tan Son Nhut, and later at the U.S. Embassy. The Cobras followed. Captain John Bowman and his co-pilot First Lieutenant Dave Androskaut were in the air soon after, in trace of the much larger troop-transport helicopters.

On his first sortie of the day, Captain Bowman and his wingman crossed the Vietnamese coast south of Vung Tau. A few minutes later, to their front, out on the western horizon, they could see the smoke which appeared, at this distance, as a single layer of dense haze above the dying city. It was not until they got closer to Saigon that they could make out the individual plumes of black, oily smoke rising from whatever it was the advancing NVA or now bands of anarchic South Vietnamese had torched.

The only good thing about all that was burning was that the NVA SA-7 men, if they were inclined to fire at the Marines, would have a harder time locking onto American aircraft; the missile's ability to track denigrated by the lack of clear sky as a target background. In the panic and confusion below, Bowman had listened in on the various radio transmissions as some pilots reported to have been shot at by the menacing Strelas. Maybe it happened. Maybe not. For many of the younger pilots, today was their first real, live action under combat-like conditions. Bowman had not personally witnessed the firing of any SA-7s, but he would be certain, on his subsequent sortie which crossed the coast north of Vung Tau, that he and his wingman had been fired upon by the no-less-deadly 57mm anti-aircraft guns the NVA had obviously brought with them as they closed in on their prize.

As a returning combat pilot, Captain Bowman did not allow himself too much time for melancholy reflection or introspection.

He had his job to do, his plane to fly. But like it always seemed to do, time had a way of slowing when things were most stressful, and he now thought with a warrior's clarity.

Staying mindful of his course, speed, altitude, fuel levels, the enemy threat somewhere down on the ground, and everything else, he could still ponder the war. The war that would not end really was about to end; at least from his own country's perspective.

In those odd moments that were really only milliseconds of reflection, Bowman recalled his earlier tour; the hundreds of missions, the faces and names of pilots and air crewmen he had flown with. He thought of his Princeton Navy ROTC buddies. To his knowledge he was, on this particular day, the only one currently in Southeast Asia. He thought about his friend and college roommate Ed Keeble.

First Lieutenant Edwin A. Keeble USMCR, had been shot down and killed near the Laotian border during Operation Dewey Canyon in February 1969. His Huey gunship had been hit by heavy-caliber machine gun fire on a mission to save seriously wounded Marines.

John Bowman could not recall, would never be able to remember all the great times that particularly special group of young men had had together. For some strange reason while he flew on into harm's way, he remembered that he had borrowed Ed Keeble's Brothers Four "B.M.O.C." (which in this example stood for "Best Music on Campus") album. He could picture the record jacket right now and its backside with "Keeble" printed above the "B" in "B.M.O.C." It was a hot album in 1960 and still popular when they were at Princeton.

The lyrics of "The Green Leaves of Summer," the first song on Side B, seemed oddly appropriate this afternoon in the smoky skies above Saigon; "… a time to be reapin', a time to be sowin', the green leaves of summer are callin' me home …" It bothered John Bowman that he had somehow not returned the album to his friend.

CHAPTER THIRTY-EIGHT

Fall of Saigon

During the period April 21-28 the U.S. Air Force, using C-141 and C-130 aircraft, had flown a total of 304 combined sorties, evacuating nearly forty-three thousand Americans and Vietnamese—mostly Vietnamese—from Tan Son Nhut. NVA rocket and artillery attacks against the facilities there on the 28th shut down that effort which ultimately pushed forward the motivation to execute Option IV of Operation Frequent Wind. The initial decision to execute Option IV was made just before 1100 on April 29.[1]

Prior to the commencement of Option IV, there had been a surge in outbound activity from shore; all sorts of boats small and large, laden with families anxious to escape the conquering tide, and hopeful that the U.S. Navy and merchant ships would provide initial respite on the journey to some new land where there were no Communists.

Since its arrival off the Vietnam coast several days earlier, the crew of the USS *Kirk* had not yet gone to General Quarters (GQ) but remained in a heightened state of alert and activity. The action in *Kirk's* Combat Information Center (CIC), since early the day before had ramped up dramatically. The tension and excitement all over the ship, but especially in Combat, was palpable.

For Petty Officer Second Class Jim Bongaard and his shipmates, the current situation gave them all a sense of purpose they had heretofore not experienced, even during the earlier evacuation from Phnom Penh. They were working twelve hours on and twelve hours off, "port and starboard." By definition the twelve off" were meant to include sleep and rest. Under current conditions, with the surface and air radar scopes in Combat tracking so much activity, with assignments to all the extra working parties these unusual events required, there was little time for sleep. It was almost an all-hands event.

What no one in the entire Seventh Fleet, from the most informed, senior admirals down to the most junior deck hands on the various ships of the line, could be sure of was whether the NVA might try to attack those fleeing subjugation or how those coming to American warships and merchant vessels might behave. It was believed that the threat of direct attack on American warships by the almost-victorious northerners was minimal. Still the Americans maintained their guard. There were few commitments the Communists had kept. Constant vigilance was the only option.

In addition to regular duties in Combat, Bon was the man responsible for tracking *Kirk's* distance from shore. The NVA had by now taken Vung Tau. On its promontory Vung Tau had shore guns— Bon believed them to have earlier belonged to the ARVNs but was not certain—that were meant to shoot out to sea. The folks in Combat had a fairly good sense for the guns' maximum range. Bon's primary duty was ensuring that *Kirk* remained outside that artillery fan. In the meantime his shipmates tracked what seemed like an increasing number, a very large number, of unknown seaborne contacts. So far, most of the airborne contacts were the waves of U.S. Marine helicopters heading in to Saigon. Soon they would be routinely crossing in both directions as the shuttle service continued in earnest. Soon they would also begin to pick up unknowns, bogeys flying toward them helter skelter that would turn out to be fleeing Vietnamese Air Force (VNAF) helicopters and even a few small propeller driven aircraft seeking friendly decks upon which to land.

ABOVE THE SKIES OF SAIGON

The missions performed by the Marines during Operation Frequent Wind were quite straightforward but incredibly complex. The infantry Marines sent to the DAO and then later also to the U.S. Embassy to beef up the security force already there were meant to provide order, stability, and intimidation so that the evacuation from Saigon might go as planned. Leadership at every level was aware that there would be issues for which they had not developed contingencies—as in sending extra Marines to man the Embassy walls. They could at least have confidence in knowing that the Marines would, at every level, demonstrate the resourcefulness to adapt to the always changing ground situation. Coordinating all of the Marine and USAF helicopters and their movement to and from ships, in the crowded skies and diminished visibility over Saigon, and then trying to somehow coordinate the uncoordinated VNAF helicopter retrograde was an entirely separate and equally challenging issue.[*]

For Captain John Bowman and co-pilot First Lieutenant Dave Androskaut, their broad mission included providing attack helicopter support for the Marine transport helos in the air and the troops on the ground. Their menacing, obvious presence in the skies above Saigon was meant to serve as deterrence to any NVA commander or soldier who might wish to be among the last to die a glorious death for Ho Chi Minh and the Revolution as their forces liberated the southern puppets from the American imperialists. In addition to the primary role of helicopter escort and deterrence as they circled the Saigon landing zones (LZs), the Cobras served as airborne command and control platforms, pathfinders, and communications beacons. Along with the obvious issues of command, control, and the possibilities of having to take fire from both the NVA and embittered southerners, the weather added to the list of hazards the air crews needed to overcome. Visibility was also degraded by the smoke. The Cobra crews and all the others were required to be fully aware, fully engaged all the time.

Under normal circumstances when completely topped off, an AH-1J Cobra carried in excess of eighteen hundred pounds of fuel. Under normal flying conditions the Cobra burned about one hundred pounds of fuel every ten minutes; giving a typical bird three hours maximum flight time although no one ever tried to

---

[*] The Marine helicopter force was augmented by eight USAF CH-53C model helicopters and two HH-53s from Thailand which had been deployed aboard the USS *Midway* (CV-41) (Dunham and Quinlan, "U.S. Marines in Vietnam: The Bitter End 1973-1975," 192).

go that long. The fuel gauges on the Cobras were sometimes known to be inaccurate when attempting to read levels near empty. The missions planned for Operation Frequent Wind were never expected to be more than two and a half hours in length.

As Bowman neared the point of requiring refueling on his initial sortie, he and his wingman were vectored back aboard the *Okinawa*. The evacuation was proceeding at a reasonably good clip, although it was evident to many that it would be just about impossible to get all the Vietnamese who needed extracting out. For brief periods John Bowman was able to ponder their fates and futures. It disturbed him greatly that America was abandoning folks who had thrown in with the U.S. only now to be essentially cast aside as inconvenient, no longer in the national interest. Where the Americans were quick to forget, Bowman knew the NVA just down the Saigon avenues would have long memories. They would never forget. They would never forgive.

Aboard the Kirk

By mid-afternoon, April 29, the exodus of outbound VNAF helicopters was becoming a torrent. In effort to aid those seeking refuge, *Kirk's* CIC transmitted on the air distress frequency, a radio channel known to all airmen, that she had an open flight deck. Most of the freedom-seeking pilots, who had packed their birds full of family and friends, had never landed on a moving ship with a heaving deck. As small as an aircraft carrier's flight deck must always appear the first time a pilot attempts to put his plane on it, especially under less than ideal conditions, attempting to put overloaded helicopters often running on fumes and vapors aboard the postage-stamp sized space afforded by a ship like the USS *Kirk*, must have seemed a near impossibility.

Necessity always trumped other considerations. Given the option of crashing into the ocean and near certain death or whatever flight deck there was, it was amazing how many of the intrepid freedom seekers succeeded in touching down.

Kirk's flight deck was built to accommodate the LAMPS helicopter she normally carried as part of her anti-submarine capability. Her flight deck could safely accommodate exactly one helicopter with turning rotor blades. While the recovery of the first helicopter seemed a novelty and was stored forward, that novelty soon wore off. When the second one came aboard it was realized that the people would stay but the helicopters would have to go; over the side. These actions were being repeated again and again on every ship afloat off the Vietnam coast with enough room to land a small helicopter. Video and still photos of helicopter after helicopter being deep sixed, sent to the bottom of Davy Jones' Locker would make the news back in Fortress America after Saigon fell; reinforcing the notion that this war, to the very end, with these many, many, too many helicopters thrown away, with millions and millions of dollars literally floating down the drain, was a huge waste of American material wealth.

The good news for the 157 Vietnamese men, women and children safely aboard *Kirk* by midnight, was that they were alive, breathing air as completely desperate but unbeaten, unconquered free people.

In all the action Bon had been operating like most of his shipmates—nonstop. As the evening grew darker, the number of VNAF helicopters tapered off and he was spelled by one of the others in Combat. Bon finally hit the rack a little before midnight. He had been up for more than twenty-four hours.

THIRD AND FINAL SORTIE FOR APRIL 29, 1975

For their second refueling Bowman and Androskaut were directed to the USS *Duluth* (LPD-6) rather than to the *Okinawa*; only because she currently had an open flight deck. The action at sea was frenetic on all the ships with flight decks. Conditions aloft had deteriorated when the sun set as the darkness increased the danger in the crowded skies. That did not matter. The helicopters continued on with their missions. Refueled, Bowman and Androskaut were soon back above the Embassy doing what they needed to.

Piloting his war bird during the night of April 29th in the skies above Saigon was like flying inside of a corked bottle filled with fog. Inbound to and outbound from the city the helos flew on instruments. Over the city, even with diminished visibility, they flew visually. The ongoing fires that littered the landscape, the arc of tracer rounds which erupted every now and then like giant neon garden hoses lazily spraying in random directions, and the occasional flash of explosions gave the place a hellish feel and look. The pervasiveness of the haze often prevented the pilots from determining up and down, where the horizon was, and where the flashes were actually coming from.

There were two ways Bowman aided his brother transport pilots. Using the onboard UHF radio's automatic direction finding capabilities to gain a bearing coming into or out of the soupy, darkened LZs was the first part. To pinpoint those darkened LZs as the inbound birds vectored towards him, Bowman flew with all lights on so that the CH-53 pilots would know that the landing zones were directly below. As much as it aided the transport pilots, flying that way was also just begging NVA gunners to take a shot at him. In fact, all during the evening they had been shot at from time to time. To protect his aircraft as they circled the Embassy, Bowman varied both his speed and his altitude. In the haze and the muck and confusion it was all but impossible to tell where the shooting was coming from. To have returned fire indiscriminately might have killed innocent civilians, and so they just kept flying.

Cobras were always employed in two-plane sections. The tactical advantages and synergies were obvious; and it was doctrine that was rarely violated. Nearing the end of the day's third sortie, Bowman, above the Embassy, heard the Cobra section flying over the DAO call low fuel and return to the *Okinawa*. Aware that there were still civilians and more than one hundred Marines on the ground requiring extract, Bowman violated doctrine for the first time that day. Ordering his wingman to cover the Embassy alone, Bowman and Androskaut flew the short distance to Tan Son Nhut and took up station above the DAO LZ. Still flying with all lights on, they circled and waited as three flights of four CH-53s each came into the DAO to take on what civilians there were left and then begin the extract of the Marine security force.

Nearing low-fuel state themselves it was time to turn their bird in the direction of the Seventh Fleet and some friendly flight deck offshore on the pitch-black eastern horizon. But the Marines below in the last flight were not yet aboard their extract helicopters. The lead elements of the NVA vanguard were literally down the street, not two kilometers from the DAO compound and the gates of Tan Son Nhut. Maybe the NVA would leave the 53s alone. So far none of the helos had been shot down. Bowman could not be sure. Bowman was like the proverbial mother hen concerned for all her chicks while the nasty, evil, ravenous fox was approaching the henhouse. He would never be able to live with himself if he left and the evening's last lift had been shot down, or became disoriented and crashed without his proper escort.

If Bowman and Androskaut stayed on station too much longer they would not have fuel to clear the coast let alone get to a friendly flight deck. The prospect of being the last Americans killed (two Marines who were part of the Marine detachment of the Embassy had been killed in an NVA rocket attack the day before near Tan Son Nhut) or becoming "guests" of the NVA held little appeal. "Dave, we're staying here until the last 53 clears the LZ."

Without objection his co-pilot rogered him and told him what he already knew. "… John, we're probably almost bingo fuel (The forward cockpit of the Cobra where the gunner/co-pilot sat did not have fuel gauges.) …"

"Roger… I know… I know…"

Saigon burned. All around the DAO and Tan Son Nhut, Saigon was on fire. Even the intermittent rain squalls could not seem to dull the flames. Bowman was thankful he knew none of the thousands, probably tens of thousands of star-crossed, and now with the evacuation near completion, literally hopeless Vietnamese who likely faced imprisonment or execution when the NVA figured out who was who. He could at least focus his energies on ensuring that these last few Marines got out.

After what seemed an eternity but was probably only a minute or two more—the grunts on the ground were just as anxious to get the heck out of there—the final flight of four 53s made radio contact, signaling that the security force Marines were all aboard. There was minimal radio discussion but everyone began to breathe just a shade easier. The massive helicopters applied power and lifted off without incident. The pucker factor would ratchet down further once they cleared the coast and were "feet wet." They would, of course, only rest completely easy when the Marines had all been fully recovered aboard ship and accounted for. The Marines Bowman had adopted for these past few moments, Marines who would never know his name or what he did, or if his Cobra's presence several hundred feet above them had really made *the* difference in their safe extract were as safe as he and Dave Androskaut could make them. It was just about midnight. Mission accomplished...

"What's our fuel look like, John?"

"Not too good, Dave..." Bowman was watching his fuel gauges. They were flying in and out of the soup. He called "feet wet" even though he really could not see the separation between coast and ocean. He assumed their Cobra to be over water when he could look down and no longer see any lights. The transmission was acknowledged, probably by the helicopter direction center (HDC) aboard *Okinawa*. *Thank God*, he thought to himself. At least if they crashed now they would not likely be captured by the NVA, or their bodies would at a minimum be recovered, if they could be recovered, by friendlies.

Somewhere between the Vietnamese coast and ships of the U.S. Seventh Fleet
Five minutes later
April 30, 1975 0005 hours

In his current low-fuel state it bothered John Bowman that he had to fly approximately thirty miles from Saigon simply to get to the coast. Seventh Fleet and the USS *Okinawa* were another thirty miles out to sea. Bowman had been flying at about one thousand feet when he went "feet wet." Slowly he began to descend, to get himself in landing pattern altitude for a carrier or LPH. Conditions aloft were marginal at best. Even with the moon out, they were continually in and out of cloud cover. When they were not in the soup all they could see above were stars. Every once in awhile they spied the white mast light of a ship below. With radio communications a challenge, Bowman was never made aware of any nearby open flight decks.

Captain Bowman had not gotten the normal TACAN navigational lock on which should have occurred with the *Okinawa* prior to his going "feet wet." The HDC aboard the LPH was able to give him a heading to follow, which he did. Finally, at about thirty miles out to sea, his helo picked up its TACAN, and it indicated another five miles to his mother ship.

As he followed the *Okinawa's* vector, he saw out in front of them a lighted gray ship; hopefully belonging to the U.S. Navy. Initially expecting it to be his LPH, he quickly realized as they closed on it that it was a small destroyer or frigate with a "clobbered" flight deck. (The last Huey which the *Kirk* had recovered in the evening had not been pushed over the side.) There was no choice but to continue in the direction of the *Okinawa*. It was in the next moment that things started to go horribly wrong.

When the AH-1J Cobra carrying Captain John Bowman and First Lieutenant David Androskaut flamed out, somewhere between the Vietnamese coast and ships of the U.S. Seventh Fleet, the fuel gauges indicated about 250 pounds—approximately twenty-five minutes of flying time—remaining.

Captain Bowman was flying mostly by instruments while Dave Androskaut, who could not see much because they were still in and out of cloud cover, focused on finding a place to land. The fuel gauge needle was not moving. It seemed stuck at 250 pounds.

As Bowman nursed his bird along at three hundred feet, just after passing the *Kirk* with the fouled flight deck, (at that moment he did not know the ship's name) the first engine began rolling down. Not a good sign. Number two engine followed shortly after.

John Bowman did it just like he had been taught to, and practiced dozens of times. In complete darkness—even though there was a moon out it was currently behind clouds—he exercised a night instrument auto-rotation. In complete darkness. Bowman maintained his heading, rapidly lowering his collective to minimize their rotor speed decay. By the book. Completely by the book.

As their tiring, dying Cobra neared the water, all forward airspeed had bled off. At seventy-five feet reading on the radar altimeter Bowman pulled the nose of the Cobra up just a shade, pulled in his collective to cushion their landing. The Cobra, with

541

zero forward airspeed, settled into a mercifully calm South China Sea. By the book, Captain Bowman rolled his aircraft to the right because the co-pilot's canopy opened to the left. It was his duty to make sure Dave Androskaut exited the aircraft first.

John Bowman's harness release lever was not where it should have been when he reached for it. Before he blew his own canopy he watched as the sea above closed over the plexiglass of his helicopter and slowly, but with an increasing momentum, began to sink into the black liquid abyss. He was still firmly attached to the now useless, inert machine. He reached for the harness release lever a second time—missing. "Come on Bows, come on Bows..." he said swearing to himself and praying to God in the next moment. The third time was the charm. After finding the release lever he quickly reached for the canopy release handle, unlocked it, took two breaths, and pulled it. The canopy exploded, and the dark waters of the South China Sea began rushing into the cockpit. With discipline and deliberation he felt all around to ensure that nothing he was wearing would tangle or get snagged and drag him to the bottom.

Whatever depth he was at, it was completely dark and there was no horizon, no bubbles, nothing. Suddenly his Princeton education kicked in. He felt the Cobra beneath his legs sliding away. "That must be down," he rightly surmised and so he kicked with all his might in the opposite direction. His earlier surfing skills from boyhood days in Hawaii were coming back to him, although there had never been a wave that took him this deep. In a literal flash, the moon above appeared after having, for what seemed another eternity, been hidden behind the clouds. He spied the shadowy figure of the treading water legs of his co-pilot above him. Dave Androskaut, who had initially believed his pilot had gone down with the Cobra and drowned, was happy to have the company, thrilled that his friend had made it, and was actually doing quite well. A moment later, as he continued to tread water, the knee board all aviators wore that was still attached to his leg came loose and before he realized it thought the odd rubbing was "something" brushing up against him.

The now Cobra-less Marine aviators treaded water for only a few moments, although just like waiting for the Marines in the DAO landing zone, that period seemed longer than it really was. *Kirk's* motor whaleboat had already been in the water prior to their approach, and made an immediate bee-line to where they thought they had observed the helo go down. In the meantime Bowman had fired off a few pencil flares and was now holding his tiny strobe light out of the water so the men in the rescue boat might see them better. Captain John Bowman USMC and First Lieutenant David Androskaut USMCR were, moments later, expeditiously plucked from the South China Sea and returned to the USS *Kirk* where they were warmly received by the captain and a good portion of her crew.

Bowman and Androskaut remained overnight as guests of the *Kirk*. In the morning the two were flown "home" to the USS *Okinawa*. Demonstrating the true class and *savoir faire* for which all Marine officers, especially Marine aviators, are known, their squadron commander sent the *Kirk* a five-gallon container of strawberry ice cream for pulling his two Cobra drivers from the drink.[†]

THE END OF THE AMERICAN WAR IN VIETNAM

April 30, 1975

Saigon's evacuation, which had been halted briefly with the last lift out of the Bowman-Androskaut-escorted sortie from the DAO LZ near midnight, was shortly resumed at the U.S. Embassy, extending into the early morning of April 30. At 0458, the CH-46, call sign "Lady Ace 09," with Ambassador Graham Martin (who

---

[†] By the close of Operation Frequent Wind the USS *Kirk* had directly recovered close to two hundred Vietnamese civilians. Prior to retiring from the area off of the Vietnamese coast and returning to Subic Bay, the *Kirk* and her intrepid crew played a key role in helping to get thirty-two ships of the now former navy of the Republic of Vietnam and approximately thirty thousand fleeing refugees safely to Subic Bay. The details of this massive humanitarian effort are widely known within the grateful American-Vietnamese community and are worthy of further reporting.

had himself lost an adopted son in Vietnam combat), the few remaining American civilians, and the flag which had recently flown over sovereign American property in downtown Saigon, lifted out of the Embassy helipad. While this was the concluding lift of civilians, the remaining Marines who were there to ensure the Ambassador's safe exit would follow soon after; finally putting to an end all official American presence in Vietnam.

In less than a twenty-four-hour period the Marine helicopter evacuation had flown 682 sorties and taken 1,373 Americans and 5,595 non-Americans out to the waiting ships.[2] For the five-thousand-plus Vietnamese spared death or imprisonment, those were intense but ultimately rewarding hours. For the uncounted Vietnamese whose lottery tickets had not been pulled, who had hoped to go but had been left behind or somehow chose to remain, their end to the day would be far from cheery.

By approximately 1200 local time on April 30, 1975, with the Seventh Fleet beginning to retire over the eastern horizon and slowly steam toward Subic Bay, the Vietnam War, at least the one sometimes described by the Communists as "the American War," came to an end, however inglorious. For nearly every American citizen, the subject of Vietnam could now be moved from "current events" to "history." For the shell-shocked citizens of the former Republic of Vietnam, their ongoing nightmare was not yet even close to climax.

PERSPECTIVE

The end in Vietnam, at least the final end to the American involvement, on April 30, 1975, gave those outside the country's Communist-controlled borders pause for reflection and introspection. There was no argument that Americans, after their bitter experience in Southeast Asia, had grown more insular, more isolationist. They would certainly, going forward, be far less interested in becoming involved in foreign entanglements requiring blood and material investment again anytime soon.

Perhaps the most astute, insightful observation of the changing world came from one outside the American orbit but certainly one of the recent conflict's intended and unintended beneficiaries. Lee Kwan Yew, the long-serving founding prime minister of an increasingly prosperous Singapore, and in many circles considered the young wise old man of the economically ascendant, non-Communist Asia, did not shrink from his opinion:

> It was the Americans who stopped the Chinese and Vietnamese Communists from spreading insurgency into Cambodia and Thailand.... Because Americans were resolutely anti-Communist and prepared to confront them, Nehru, Nasser, and Sukarno could afford to be nonaligned.[3]

American resolve, while it had lasted, purchased the time required to keep Asian dominos from falling into the Communist camp.

The American process of healing from the Vietnam War, especially for those who paid the highest prices, was a conundrum. For the warriors who had given so much, who had won *every* engagement large and small, who had done everything demanded of them, the war was still lost. There were no great homecomings, no tumultuous victory parades or grand affirmations of their sacrifices or thank yous, no proper closure like that accorded their fathers, the men who had successfully delivered the world from fascism and won an ephemeral peace in 1945.

Perhaps as galling, especially to those who had not stepped back from their duties, was that for those who had actively and intentionally avoided service, or passively and intentionally avoided service, either by going to Canada, taking measures to fail their military physicals, staying in school longer, lucked out with high lottery draft numbers, or those who simply felt no need to volunteer, there was no shame or guilt or consequence. In fact, in certain circles like the college campuses many young veterans returned to, those who served were often viewed with scorn and derision, while those who had actively avoided service were accorded moral superiority.

The pervasive sense of duty, perceived as near universal in the men and women of the generation who fought World War II, was incompletely passed on to their sons and daughters. For a great many, sense of duty, service to the country, and sacrifice had been supplanted by greater focus on self, self preservation, and the pursuit of personal pleasure. Unlike World War II when *everyone* served, and those who could not or did not probably had a good reason but still carried the guilt for not shouldering their share of freedom's load, the burden of Vietnam's cost was not equally borne. For many of those who answered the call to arms, this would be a far harder war than the one their fathers had fought from which to again take up life.

In a late April 1975 conversation in Hanoi between an NVA colonel and U.S. Army Colonel Harry G. Summers, Jr., who was there as part of an American negotiating team, what was all along obvious to the wily Communists was made bluntly so for the linear-thinking American officer.‡

> Summers: "You know you never defeated us on the battlefield."
>
> NVA Colonel: "That may be so, but it is also irrelevant."⁴

SOCIALIST PARADISE

The pain and shock of ignominious defeat was perhaps dulled and put off temporarily by the sheer weirdness of Saigon trying to absorb and adjust to its northern conquerors. To a very large degree the *bo doi*, the NVA soldiers who were the vanguard of the invasion may as well have come from another planet. So different, so uncitified, uncultured, and thoroughly propagandized were these out-of-their-element northerners, that they too had to be in a state of disconcertment, a disconcertment not as great as felt by those they had just conquered, but great nonetheless.

The ranks of the invaders were made up of three basic groups of soldiers. The first were the long-serving and battle-hardened veterans, survivors of so much combat and brutality, used to tough conditions and ultra-ascetic living. The rest were either the

---

‡ Harry Summers would go on to further distinguish himself as one of the Army's top intellects. His incisive, trenchant work "On Strategy—A Critical Analysis of the Vietnam War" was and still is required reading for U.S. military officers of every branch.

too young or the too old, as so many of the military age young men were used up, consumed pursuing the Politburo's directives. In any event, all three groups were completely unprepared and completely unfamiliar with the material wealth their misguided southern cousins had all along accumulated while they had been sacrificing themselves to liberate them from the clutches and evils of this pervasive, relative opulence none of the teaching they had been made to believe over the years had mentioned.

If the situation on the ground in Vietnam had not now been so dismal and desperate, the antics of these northerners might have been the subject for the most bizarre, *macabre* type of comedy. Stories of *bo doi* fascination with indoor plumbing, flush toilets in particular, made the rounds. So too did their apparent belief that ceiling fans were capitalist contraptions used to behead people.

The notion that even poor people in the south owned transistor radios, wrist watches that really worked, and other things that dazzled them, failed to jibe with the nearly three decades' worth of unchallenged propaganda they had been force fed. How could all these oppressed southerners, victims of the treacherous Thieu and the U.S. imperialists and the very brothers and cousins they had just shed so much blood to "liberate" and reorient, have in abundance the things which only senior party members in Hanoi might have—maybe?

There would be very little to laugh about in all that would follow. As outlandish and unfashionable in appearance as the initial wave of Ho Chi Minh's shock troops were, the power wielded by the senior *cadre* who followed in close trace would be something that would wipe the smiles from the faces of even the heartiest, most stalwart southerners.

As amateurish and ridiculous as the new masters may have looked, and as utterly nonsensical as the tripe they spouted off may have sounded to reasonable, rational people, the pain inflicted by the new order was broad and deep; and probably meticulously thought out and planned.

INITIATION TO "REEDUCATION"

Demonstrating acute cunning and sheer meanness, the Communists implemented the process of "reeducation" with genius and incremental brutality. Known in the West by its very liberal euphemism, "reeducation" or "thought reform," *"cai tao tu tuong"* in Vietnamese, was nothing more than organized revenge on a massive scale. Wasting no time after their victory, they gained rapid control of all forms of media. On May 3, 1975, the radio declared that the process of reeducation was set to begin. First to attend would be lower ranking military types: junior officers, NCOs, and minor government officials. Because they were not key people in the resistance to the Communists, their period of reeducation was set to last three days. The actual processing of these people, with their very public return to civilian life once reeducation had concluded showed a small level of good faith on the part of the Communists.[5] More senior officers would be next to go, and since their crimes were judged by the new authorities as a bit more egregious, their period of reeducation was set to be thirty days. The fact that the first group had been released as promised disarmed the skeptics. "Thirty days. How bad could that be?" When Binh and the others were summoned, they were told to bring thirty days' worth of food. Binh was also told to bring warm clothes. *"Warm clothes? What is this all about, or is it just part of the Communist plan to deceive us?"* What choice did any of those who had remained have? The Communists had the guns. To resist further would only bring more pain to their families.

The big lie worked, of course. Always the masters of the big lie, once the group the Communists really wanted—the mid-level and senior officers—had almost willingly walked into the trap, like sheep to the slaughter, there was no escape. The tragedy that would befall the family of Le Ba Binh was repeated several hundred thousand times. What pain he and Cam and Ngoc would endure, which was the same for several hundred thousand other Vietnamese families trapped and forced to live under the vengeful system of reeducation went far, far beyond the now ended American experience in Vietnam.

CHAPTER THIRTY-NINE

Reeducation

The *circumstances that spared* Second Lieutenant Nguyen Luong, medically retired from the Vietnamese Marine Corps, the horrors and deprivations of reeducation were more bureaucratic mix-up than acts of kindness on the part of the northern invaders. Luong's own abilities to bluff and articulate his case may have helped as well.

The social safety net which had been in place up until the end in late April of 1975, the one which paid disabled RVN veterans a small monthly stipend to help them along, ended with the Communist takeover. There would be no special spots in schools held open for children of the men who had sacrificed so much for the now defunct Republic of Vietnam. The new rulers felt no obligation to reward anyone for having fought against them.

Like the others told to report for reeducation in May, Luong would have been a part of the first group to go because of his rank, although there was some concern that even junior officers and NCOs from the more elite units—Marines, Rangers, Airborne— might get singled out for special retribution, might get more than the three days proclaimed by the new masters.[1]

The bureaucratic chaos which remained to be ironed out in the weeks following the fall of Saigon worked to the benefit of the young former Marine officer. When Luong reported for processing he told the low-level administrator handling the paperwork that his job at the Bien Hoa Power Plant was critical. If Luong was taken away to reeducation all of Bien Hoa might be without electricity; and that would make everyone unhappy, including the Communists.

The electric plant would have been able to run without Luong's presence, of course. But this low-level bureaucrat did not know that. He was not an engineer. And fortunately for Luong he was scared enough to not want to risk upsetting any of his superiors, or appear to this RVN Marine to have no authority. Either one would be a major loss of face.

And so Luong was spared the indignity and pain of *any* reeducation. It was that simple. Unfortunately the power plant at Bien Hoa shortly came under new leadership—Communist leadership. The new management had no room for a former Marine and Luong was not retained. He counted himself fortunate that he was soon able to get a technical position working in an ice-making plant not too far from his home in Bien Hoa. At least he had a job in the new socialist paradise. His battalion commander shared none of Luong's good fortune.

IS BINH DEAD OR ALIVE?

Binh's first stop on what would turn into an undefined, interminable period of revenge and reeducation was in Saigon at Long Khanh. This early on, Communist domination and control was not yet complete and in those first few days Cam was able to make use of friends and acquaintances that had contacts in and around where the former RVN military officers were held. Men and women working as vendors or cyclo drivers or whatever would covertly pass on information that made it back to concerned wives and family members that their men were alright.

From Long Khanh, Binh and his group were quietly taken at night to Suoi Mau near Bien Hoa. The rough translation for "*Suoi Mau*" is "Blood Stream" which for the moment seemed forebodingly named. Binh's group of former RVN officers, nearly all of them captains, majors, and lieutenant colonels, were kept there for approximately two months. Even in Suoi Mau, Cam was able, through similar use of friendly people passing information covertly, to keep loose tabs on her husband.

It was at Suoi Mau where the routine of "control by the stomach" was thoroughly introduced and established. Prisoners were less likely to cause problems, less likely to try to escape, less likely to aggressively resist if their physical strength was drained from them.

Prior to the war's end Binh had weighed in right at a trim, lean sixty kgs. Within a year of incarceration he would lose, like most of his fellow prisoners, about a third of his original body weight.

Life in and around Saigon for Cam and all the others who had not yet escaped in the second *diaspora* or been sent to reeducation was a tough, tough adjustment as May became June and then July. As the northern invaders quickly warmed to their new power and access to all material things which were now theirs for the confiscating, the normal bristle of activity of commerce and life going on had been virtually drained from the ether. Formerly average and even prosperous people were reduced to penury or near penury. To survive, regular citizens were forced to sell their belongings, all things precious to them. Saigon became, in American terms, one big yard sale with the northern masters in the best position to buy on the cheap.

The culture of paranoia endemic to all totalitarian regimes was demonstrated early on, repeatedly, and would continue. At Binh's first stop in what for him and the others was to be their "30 Day Period of Reeducation," all of the former military officers in his group were required to write detailed family biographies going back two generations.

Binh and the others were forced to listen to Communist *cadre* berate them, accuse them of all sorts of nonsensical things, in addition to having fought against the now victorious side, things only Communists could think up. Binh and the others were still somewhat in shock over the entire process which had taken their freedom from them. *"Do these people really believe all the things they are saying?"* The former RVN military officers were incredulous.

Many of the *cadre* statements and later questions of interrogation demonstrated a near complete lack of worldliness and understanding of reality; at least the reality known by the incarcerated southerners. Mao had many years earlier said and the current situation proved him to be correct: "Political power grows out of the barrel of a gun." The Communists had the guns, so theirs was the reality that counted for now. One question asked or accusation stated time and time again, in various versions and permutations was, "What did you do for the CIA?"

Everyone was accused of working for the evil, nefarious, ubiquitous, all-powerful capitalist tool. If only the American CIA had possessed the tiniest fraction of power ascribed to it by these *cadres*, the Communists would have been defeated before 1954.

Taking his time, Binh dutifully tried to put down on paper as much writing as was required but without giving too much information. No matter what he wrote, it was rejected for various reasons, none of which made sense. "Do it again...and this time include..." It was near impossible to understand what the new masters wanted, even though everyone spoke Vietnamese. Communist jargon still made no sense to any of the rational-thinking southerners. Terms like "reactionary," "decadent," "*bourgeois*," "petty *bourgeois*," "*bourgeois comprador*," "hooligan," "pseudo-pacifist," and on and on made no sense. Binh knew nothing of these terms. He would, unfortunately, along with several hundred thousand others, have time to learn.

Binh finally cleared this initial hurdle placed before him not by writing what they wanted but by writing the same thing once more, only printing so small that one almost needed a magnifying glass to read it. The exasperated *cadre* he turned it in to, waved him off with a sneer. It was Binh's first victory against his captors.

So far in Binh's or any other prisoner's experience, there was no official correspondence with family members. Had it not been for the ability to use "spies" and friendly informers at Long Khanh and Suoi Mau, Cam would have had no idea where her husband was. It was after the movement from Suoi Mau that Cam's ability to track her husband, learn even the faintest hint of information, ran into a complete stone wall.

Long known as masters of camouflage and stealthy maneuver, the Communists were equally adept in their movement of prisoners. Taken one night in complete darkness from Suoi Mau by covered truck to the coast, the prisoners were put in the sealed hold of a ship and sent north. Given minimal food and without facilities to relieve themselves, Binh and the others were always hungry but overcome more with seasickness; always thirsty, and forced to urinate and defecate right where they were kept. After three nights and two days at sea, the ship arrived in Ben Thuy near Haiphong.

From the hold of their now thoroughly fouled ship the prisoners were marched to crudely fashioned railroad boxcars that would take them to their final destination. Along that short route the locals came out to curse at them; some of them even throwing rocks. Binh was not sure if the group had appeared spontaneously or was there because of some government order. In either event, he did not let it bother him.

Except for all the participants being Vietnamese, the entire situation at the transfer point between ship and train reminded Binh of some low-budget World War II movie about Jews being sent to concentration camps; with his group playing the part of the Jews. The box cars were roughly hewn, poorly constructed of wood. Had it not been for a few pieces of planking being already broken out there would have been no ventilation for the men who were packed in like sardines. As it was, two of the men in the car Binh rode in up to the mountains of Yen Bai died of suffocation.

Yen Bai was actually an entire series of different prison camps. Located in the mountains approximately 120 kilometers to the northwest of Hanoi, it was equidistant to the border with the People's Republic of China. Binh was not sure but had heard that there were between sixty and eighty camps in the general area.[2] The camp that was to be his new "home" was home to 442 others as well. As the camp was only partially constructed when they arrived, it fell to the prisoners to finish the job.

Opportunities for successful escape were minimal at best. Prisoners were kept at near starvation levels by meager and very substandard rations, ensuring that no man had the energy to get very far. In addition, difficult terrain, a thoroughly indoctrinated local population which knew to be on the lookout for escapees, and close proximity to the other camps whose guards would happily shoot a man they believed to be on the run, stacked the odds in favor of the jailers.

There were 443 prisoners in the Yen Bai camp that was now Binh's home. All of the others were captains through lieutenant colonels, with between five and fifteen years of military service apiece. To the Communists these professional military officers were the worst kind of enemy.

Yen Bai was a military camp, meaning that the men who ran the camp were soldiers. To a limited extent there were some professional courtesies exchanged and the thinnest modicum of respect between the jailers and their charges. The troops used to run the Communist prison camps were hardly the best and brightest, certainly far from elite. Many of the guards were fourteen, fifteen, or sixteen years old. Likewise, the political *cadres* brought in to run the "reeducation" portion of the incarceration were often barely literate and seemed capable only of blaring whatever they had been told to say.

The typical day for Binh and his 442 comrades began at 0500. Prisoners were given minimal time to toilet and eat a meager breakfast before beginning their twelve-hour workday. The food provided was humble at best. If there was soup it was basically just briny, salted hot water with a few vegetables, if any at all, thrown in. Most of the rice given prisoners was said to have come from old NVA rice *caches* on the Ho Chi Minh Trail; so it was often rotten, stale, or mildewed and marginalized by time and climate. Protein was minimal and the quantity of fruit or vegetables or the more common sweet potatoes would soon depend on what the prisoners were able and allowed to grow in camps or forage for when in the forests working. Supplementing diets with what could be scrounged for became a necessity. Lizards, frogs, insects, mice, rats, snakes; all that could be caught were killed and ravenously consumed. Starvation has a way of changing a person's standards of what is palatable.

Health issues continually plagued the prisoners. Dysentery and diarrhea were common problems which could and did sometimes lead to death since the quantity of genuine medicines was close to nonexistent. Reliance on local herbal remedies sometimes sufficed. In the event a man was injured, even an injury which under non-prison circumstances and prior to the days when the Communists ran things required the most minor surgery, there was significant risk of infection and death. If a prisoner required major medical intervention, he was good as dead. There was no anesthesia anywhere, and it was known that some surgeries had actually been performed with nothing more than razor blades. Psychological issues were as bad as or worse than the physical challenges faced by the prisoners. The problems of depression and isolation could never be dealt with adequately. Many men died for reasons never diagnosed. For those who would survive, every one of them would carry the scars of their reeducation experience forever.

Depending on their daily assignment, which in Binh's Yen Bai camp usually meant working out in the forests, prisoners were issued tools and equipment for their specific work detail. At the end of the day all tools were carefully inventoried to ensure against escape attempts. If something was lost or could not be accounted for there was swift retribution. Prisoners on various work details in Yen Bai's jungle forests were often unsupervised as opportunities for escape were virtually nonexistent. It was on one of those routine four-man details that Binh and his mates experienced a rare moment of blessing and victory that kept them going during the long, torturous dry spells of pain, hunger, and monotony.

On a day which was no different than any of the countless ones preceding it during the first year at Yen Bai, Binh was part of an unsupervised four-man detail chopping wood, when a member of his group discovered the carcass of a calf that appeared to have just died. Immediately checking to see if there was anyone around who might claim it, the four starving RVN officers determined that they were now the rightful owners. Nearby was a cold running mountain stream. Quickly they hatched a scheme whereby they would stash the body of the cow beneath the water's cool surface. In this manner they could carve off slices of the precious meat and stretch the consumption over as long a period as possible. For nearly an entire month the four comrades, who kept the cow's presence a secret, returned daily to slice and consume raw hunks of meat. As ravenously hungry as they always were, it tasted as good to Binh as anything he had ever eaten those two lifetimes ago in Virginia or San Francisco.

As doltish and simplistic as were most of the guards and *cadre* in Binh's camp, they still had the guns, still had the power. Chronic hunger kept the prisoners basically compliant. Every now and then a new guard or *cadre*, one with a bit more petulance and meanness in him, would show up for duty and display the kind of cruelty which surprised none of the prisoners.

Attempting to spread division and conflict amongst the prisoners, after a day's work one *cadre* came up to a prisoner and, making a very public pronouncement said: "Prisoner So-and-So, today you have worked very hard. You are a model prisoner. We are awarding you this duck for you to eat. You must share this with the 442 others. Show us how you will do this. Report back to us ..." The duck in this example was especially scrawny. It only made Binh and the others hate the guards that much more.

While the prisoners' typical workday concluded at 1730 or so, their day was far from over. Once the tools and equipment were turned in and accounted for, there was a quick and grossly insufficient dinner. Following dinner was the daily two-hour pain and monotony of the real reeducation effort. For two hours every day the prisoners were subjected to *cadres* spoon-feeding them whatever it was they were told to say.

In every Asian culture which had not yet been savaged by Communist thought, there was still traditional respect and veneration for elders. Conversely, there was little respect accorded men who were not yet men in the eyes of their elders. It was rather nonsensical and galling to these former RVN officers, most of whom were college educated, to sit and listen to lectures given by males who sometimes really could not yet be described as men, let alone even informed youth. It was also frustrating to have to listen to things being said which they knew were not partial lies, but completely wrong, sort of white is black, day is night kind of wrong. But they had the power, they had the guns. If they wanted to eat they had to endure the pain of propaganda. The prisoners sat there and listened.

One time a *cadre* told the story of how the Vietnamese Air Force had defeated the Americans. In that tale it was apparent that the *cadre* clearly did not even understand how planes flew or how gravity worked. Often, and this was before the 1979 war with China, the *cadre* would speak of the three most powerful nations in the world as being Russia, Vietnam, and China, usually in that order. Many, many times the prisoners sitting there would give the speaking *cadre* thunderous applause and cheers; especially after making patently outrageous claims. The *cadres* were usually too dimwitted and simple to catch the slight, the cynicism; that the prisoners were actually scorning them, scorning them with passion. Those were the small victories, but victories nonetheless that kept the men sane and able to endure all the indignities heaped upon them.

A benefit incidental to living in a state of permanent semi-starvation and the resulting weakness it caused was its sometimes dulling of one's senses. If a man or woman had to focus all, or nearly all, of his or her energies simply on surviving, there was less energy left or time allowed to ponder all that was lost, or the separation from loved ones. Sometimes. Every day was a battle to survive. Every day's survival was a victory over a man's jailers. Still there were those quiet moments that belonged only to Binh and no one else during which he could think about his beautiful wife and sweet little daughter. As tired and weak as he would ever become, Binh never gave up hope that he would someday be reunited with them. He would never give up. The Communists had not beaten him in regular battle. They would not defeat him now. Binh would never give up hope. Never.

BACK IN SAIGON

Once Binh had been taken away, and even before Cam had lost complete track of him, life had taken a definite turn for the worse. Like nearly every one of the other hundreds of thousands of wives whose husbands were now mysteriously gone, it fell to the women to provide for their children and families. Like many of the wives of former RVN officers, Cam along with Ngoc was turned out of their house by northern soldiers. Mercifully she was able to move in with her mother.

Even prior to being turned out of her home Cam had begun the process of selling the things which had been theirs. All the things. All the things except for the few family photo albums that were critical in proving that they had really existed before, that Binh had existed even though he was now gone. Cam sold everything, nearly all the possessions they had, to buyers who paid next to nothing for them. Many of the buyers, most of the buyers, were starry-eyed northerners unused to even the simplest conveniences. It pained Cam greatly to sell their clothes, their kitchen utensils and pots and pans, their furniture, everything. But she and Ngoc had to eat. It was the same for her neighbors. "Where would these northerners take this stuff?" The answer was simple. It was all shipped back to the north. While the shock and pain of their new circumstances prevented them from thinking it initially, the dispossessed southerners would one day ponder that the northerners were at least being forced to recognize the big lie of the revolution. The south of Vietnam, relatively speaking, was awash in material abundance while the north had little. Communism had delivered nothing in their years of sacrifice except for what they could now essentially steal from those who had worked for what they had.

Once she had moved in with her mother, Cam would take care of her daughter and work seven days a week making and selling rice cakes, or retailing what items she could purchase in one place and selling them somewhere else on the street for meager markup. Every day. In the mornings, afternoons and evenings. Thousands and thousands, hundreds of thousands of other women were forced into similar existences. Grandparents watched grandchildren so that the mothers could do what needed to be done.

In the evenings when Cam had time with Ngoc she would hold her and they would sit together to review the pictures in their family albums. Every night Cam would amuse and delight her daughter with stories of her father as they slowly turned the too few pages of magnificent memories that Ngoc, especially in the first few years of Binh's absence, had no concept or recollection of. But it was important to Cam that Ngoc understand that she did have a father who loved her; even though Cam was not sure if Ngoc's father was dead or alive.

MACRO VIEW IN SAIGON AND AROUND VIETNAM ...

The real northern conquest of the south began after the official fighting had ceased on April 30, 1975. The Communists instantly proved that they were far more capable soldiers than government and societal administrators. While the ongoing confiscation of public and personal property which had belonged to those in the south continued without relent and the goods were hurriedly shipped north to people who would not be able to fathom the vastness of the south's wealth which was now theirs, and those sent to reeducation had yet to be heard from, new government policies were put in place which further increased the pain and suffering.

In the twinkling of an eye, everything was now government property. If farmers had goods to sell grown on land which was no longer really theirs, they were supposed to sell them to the government. If people wanted to buy things—officially—they were supposed to buy them from the government in government controlled stores. Everything for sale had an "official" price and everyone who worked earned an "official" wage. Everything critical to Vietnamese life was now rationed. All that this setup assured was that there were guaranteed shortages for everything of value, and that a thriving black market arose to meet the needs of hungry and dispossessed citizens. If misery loved company, it had plenty.

Proving further that the recent conquest was more invasion than liberation, even the southern Communists, old members of the National Liberation Front (NLF) and former Viet Cong, were cast aside as second rate and undesirable. Some were even included in the groups sent to reeducation. All the people in the south who had constituted the active opposition to the Thieu government, whether Communists or simply anti-government folks who had done so much to undermine and speed the demise of their own country, were treated with near the same derision as were those who had all along either been loyal to Saigon or indifferent. The biggest change this time was that there were now no press reporters or photographers to chronicle the new violations of their rights; which they no longer had anyway. For the resolute citizens of the south who had remained steadfast in their opposition to the Communists this was their bitter, Pyrrhic victory and very minor vindication.[3]

In order to make their conquest more complete, but under the auspices of punishing speculators and those who would hoard goods, the government in September 1975 instituted a currency exchange. People were allowed to exchange only limited amounts of their old money for the northern currency. Anything above what the government allowed would essentially become worthless. For citizens who had any savings, at least in the old currency, above and beyond the minimal amount allowed to be exchanged, that money was now worthless. To have had too much of the old currency also identified a person as an exploiting, rapacious, evil capitalist. Hit particularly hard by this first currency exchange were the local Chinese who for years and years had dominated southern commerce.[4]

Along with currency reform, the new government began the forced relocation of citizens mostly from overcrowded Saigon, in true Communist fashion, to what were called New Economic Zones (NEZ). People sent to the NEZs included the unemployed, underemployed, and those judged as undesirable by the new masters. Some of the NEZs were areas with heavy exposure to Agent Orange. The deleterious impact on the health of those people would immediately begin to show up as would the increase in the number of birth defects from children born to those people. In areas where there were high concentrations of unexploded ordnance, it was not unusual for workers to be forced to clear mines and bombs with their bare hands. The other NEZs were often vast swaths of land which had heretofore not been used for much because they were long ago judged marginal and of little economic value. Since price, practicality, and free market forces no longer were part of the decision making process, the unfortunate citizens coerced into the NEZs would be the ones expected to cut down forests and plant rice where rice was not meant to grow, to make silk from a sow's ear, to turn dirty water into wine.

At the same time as the Communists were attempting to impose their new order, thousands and thousands and thousands of citizens began the process of leaving the country. While the second *diaspora* had begun well before April 30, and the U.S. Navy had rescued upwards of thirty thousand Vietnamese in that late April and early May period, a new term would soon be known to the rest of the world: "Boat People."

The "Boat People" phenomenon, which saw citizens leaving the country from before the end of the war into the late 1980s and early 1990s, would strip the nation of a high percentage of its most talented citizens, certainly many of its most intrepid citizens. Those who would choose to leave the country of their birth, once they had successfully skulked and bribed their way clear of their ancestral homeland, were then forced to brave the challenges of open ocean sailing, potential rape, murder, and pillaging from the ubiquitous pirates waiting off the coast, and a host of other unknowns. There would never be any truly accurate numbers for those who perished in their attempts to live free of Communism, but it was believed that more than two million people made it to freedom. The greatest percentage of those who left would ultimately end up in the United States. That so many people were willing and eager to risk so much to leave the land of their ancestors was a sign that things were especially bad. The societal loss, the brain and manpower drain, the real "opportunity cost" to what remained of Vietnam would be incalculable.

REUNIFICATION MADE OFFICIAL

The April 1976 sham elections made the reunification of the two Vietnams official, even though it was reunification made permanent solely by firepower. The unified country was renamed the Socialist Republic of Vietnam (SRV). As if to further rub salt and broken glass into the wounds of the subjugated southerners, Saigon was renamed "Ho Chi Minh City" in June of the same year.[5]

Relations with both the Soviet Union and the People's Republic of China took on new meaning and importance once the American portion of the war concluded. While both Communist behemoths had provided critical material aid and technical advice during the war, old enmities with the Chinese began to reassert themselves to the Soviet advantage.

In America, the need to move on included the cathartic expunging of all things Nixon. The new openness which Americans found themselves seeming to now want was expressed by the fellow who would defeat President Ford in the 1976 elections. In the

561

November 1976 issue of *Playboy*, which hit the newsstands in early October, Georgia Governor Jimmy Carter made the public confession that in his heart he had lusted after women other than his wife. President Ford, the man who had pardoned the disgraced and reviled Nixon, had made no similar confession. Americans appeared to appreciate that openness and elected Carter as the nation's thirty-ninth president.

Meanwhile, as Americans pondered the strange observations and confessions of the man who would be their new leader, Binh and the hundreds of thousands of other prisoners stuck inside of their bamboo gulag were lusting as well: lusting for food, any kind of food to free them of their chronic and painful hunger, food to fill the constant empty spaces in their stomachs; forget about sex.

WAR WITH KAMPUCHEA, WAR WITH CHINA

Attempting to comprehend American interests in Southeast Asia prior to April 30, 1975, had insightfully been described by some as like trying to peel an onion; layer by layer, expecting at some inner point to come to a core of enlightenment and understanding. The problem, of course, was that in removing each ring and getting down to the last one, there was nothing, and the entire exercise was simply one in maximum futility. If gaining insight and understanding on Vietnam was a single onion, attempting to fathom what was taking place next door in Cambodia in the post-American time period was an entire bushel.

The kind of evil that was slowly being found out about in Cambodia, now Kampuchea, was so bizarre, so irrational, so outrageous, it robbed Vietnam and its luckless subjects whose rights were routinely being egregiously violated of most of the international public scrutiny which might have been applied had things not been so bad a few miles to the west. Pol Pot, the maniacal Khmer Rouge leader made Hitler, Stalin, and Mao seem mild in comparison. Even to the ruthless Vietnamese Communists who obviously thought nothing of executing those many, many thousands of folks killed immediately after taking over without due process, and subsequently shipping off hundreds of thousands of RVN military officers and former government officials to reeducation for what ultimately would be indeterminate years of revenge and punishment, the scale of the Khmer Rouge purge and the manner in which that purge was carried out—on their *very own people*—many of them avowed Communists, boggled everyone's minds. Only the coldest-hearted among the Communist *cadre* in Vietnam could relate to the line attributed to Khmers Rouges soldiers speaking to those they wished to intimidate: "*If we kill you we lose nothing. If we let you live we gain nothing.*"

Events in Cambodia still mattered for Vietnam for a number of reasons. There was a sizable Vietnamese minority population living inside of Cambodia. The Khmers Rouges were generally very broad-brushed in applying brutality, but were especially aggressive against ethnic groups perceived as contrary to the interests of the new *Angkar*. The ultra-paranoid Khmers Rouges, who mistrusted literally everyone, had a special paranoia for the unwelcome Vietnamese residents, as well as a centuries-old, almost genetic cultural hatred of their eastern neighbors.

Demonstrating further the paranoia and complete lack of reason and rational behavior by which the world was coming to know them, it was actually the far smaller and materially inferior Khmers Rouges whose repeated and deliberate actions over a period of many months precipitated the first legitimate war that was recognized by the world as a war between Communist countries. (Soviet invasions or the putting down of popular uprisings in Hungary in 1956 and Czechoslovakia in 1968 did not count.)

The old David and Goliath analogy was not analogy enough to describe the relative differences in quantitative and qualitative military capabilities between the two countries. Unless every Khmer Rouge soldier could kill thirty Vietnamese, it was a physical impossibility for them to gain victory. And if this truly was to be a David versus Goliath encounter, the God which neither the Khmers Rouges nor the Vietnamese Communists believed in would have had to intervene on behalf of the more evil Khmers Rouges. He did not.

There had been fighting between Vietnamese and Khmers Rouges troops for quite some time before Cambodia suspended relations with its neighbor in late December of 1977. Vietnamese political leadership decided in the spring of 1978 to launch a late year offensive in attempt to rid the region of Pol Pot. The offensive began on December 22, 1978, and in less than three weeks the Vietnamese Army genuinely liberated Phnom Penh. The Vietnamese did not capture or kill the Khmers Rouges leadership but rather forced them from power and installed a government friendly to them. Vietnamese troops officially remained in Cambodia until 1989, placing even greater strain on the limited resources needed for rebuilding in their own country.[6]

CHAPTER FORTY

Binh Survives the Bamboo Gulag

ar costlier in terms of men killed and equipment lost, Vietnam's brief and bloody war with China was a direct result of the latter's foray into Cambodia. The PRC had been the main supporters of the Khmers Rouges, and their quick defeat was a loss of face for the Chinese. In addition there were other reasons why Chinese-Vietnamese relations had recently soured. The draconian measures taken in Vietnam to thwart capitalism—the currency exchanges, movement of people to the NEZs, etc.—were seen by the Chinese as not so subtle methods of singling out the substantial and disproportionately successful Chinese minority living there. Along with the current issues, the historical enmity between Vietnamese and their northern neighbor ran far deeper than the hatred for the Cambodians.

The Soviet Union would be the immediate beneficiary of the strain in Sino-Vietnamese relations. For the price of rather substantial financial and continued military aid, the Soviet navy would gain unfettered access to the superior, American-constructed facilities at Cam Ranh Bay. Considered by many to be the finest deep-water port in the region, Soviet naval operations in the western Pacific and their ability to project power so far from home became an increasing concern for the United States at a time when it was still attempting to pull back from obligations in Asia.

The Chinese would call it the "1979 Punitive War," and though they initiated the action, in pure Communist double speak it was termed a "self-defensive counterattack." Short and intense, both sides would, again in pure Communist propaganda fashion, claim victory. Both sides were believed to have lost approximately thirty thousand men killed in a three-week period. When the fighting concluded, the Chinese withdrew their troops pretty much to the original border areas.[1]

Due to Yen Bai's proximity to the Chinese border, the Vietnamese chose to relocate the prisoners to areas where they would not be at risk of being set free by advancing Chinese soldiers if the military situation devolved to that. There had been talk that some of the prisoners had offered their services to the government in exchange for having their sentences commuted. Those offers were refused. To Binh's knowledge none of the Marine officers he knew had been made offers to assist. Binh gave his captors credit for understanding that had they issued weapons to any of the Marine officers, they would have been immediately turned against their captors.

From Yen Bai, Binh was moved to Nam Ha, which was out of the mountains and closer to the coast, southeast of Hanoi. It was prior to his departure for Nam Ha, at the end of year three of his reeducation period that Binh was finally allowed to write a letter to his wife. Although not instructed on what to say, Binh understood that the letter would be read by *cadre* before making it to his wife. Binh wrote a letter which could have been described as routine, perfunctory. He knew Cam would understand. Binh made mention that he was well, that the reeducation was going alright, and asked the obligatory questions like "How are you doing?" and "How is our daughter?" and on and on.

Cam, of course, was overjoyed, relieved, elated, ecstatic when she received the letter in the mail. Binh was alive, for sure. She had been praying all this time and was never quite certain. She understood her husband was a warrior. She understood that he was considered an absolute tiger in the old TQLC, and because of that he might have done something to cause his execution or tried to do something that would have enraged his captors. That Binh was alive was the very best news Cam had received since the fall of their country.

The initial correspondence between prisoners and families opened the door for further communication, as well as authorization for a possible future visit. In a sense it was almost merciful that Cam had not earlier been allowed to visit her husband. In the first few years she could not have afforded it; could not have come up with funds to pay all the bribes necessary to allow for travel so far away, let alone acquire all she would later be able to purchase and deliver to her husband.

In the new Vietnam, the only things there were no shortages of were pain and misery and hunger. Never having had too much extra of anything anyway, except during the period she had worked for the Americans and was able to help pay the costs of educating her brothers, Cam knew how to save. Every citizen of the SRV, if they had not learned before the Communists imposed their brand of economic justice on the southern portion of the country, of necessity learned to save, to stretch, to make things last, to fashion ersatz meals and feasts out of what paltry resources there were available in the new Socialist Paradise.

The process was hard but simple. Every day Cam would try to live on less than she made so that there were cash savings. Those cash savings she would quickly turn into other things tangible, things which would not lose value, things she might later use to trade for other items of superior importance or value to her.

Few citizens had confidence in the Communist currency, especially after what had happened in 1975. On the black market it was better to trade in dollars (and not get caught) or gold or simply to barter with hard goods; so much rice for a chicken, so much this for that. While the *dong* were certainly not quite like Reichmarks of the 1920s, if you used the currency with Ho Chi Minh's picture on it you needed a lot of it. And that confidence only weakened when the government again replaced the currency, again for largely the same reasons—to punish rapacious, wanton speculation and capitalism—in May of 1978.

While Cam and hundreds of thousands of other wives in similar situations scraped and battled to provide for their children and that tiniest margin to collect and accumulate for the pending annual visits with their incarcerated husbands, their men were stuck wherever they were; in the first few years especially, mostly in the northern gulags, fantasizing about food, wondering what their children now looked like, if they even remembered them, and trusting that their wives had remained faithful. The psychological and emotional impact to families, husbands and wives, the relationships between fathers and their children would forever be harmed in ways that could never be fully described or completely healed. The challenges could only be suffered through and somehow endured.

By the late 1970s the first of those who had left Vietnam as part of the second *diaspora* were becoming established in their new homelands. The first order of business for nearly every filial Vietnamese man and woman was to get resources back to those still stuck behind the Bamboo Curtain, to those whose suffering was still a certainty. In the United States, France, Canada, Australia, and other places the initial wave of freedom seekers had landed, the intrepid newcomers seized opportunities wherever and whenever they appeared. No matter what they did, no matter how much they did or did not earn, they dutifully sent generous amounts back to spouses, parents, brothers, sisters, aunts, uncles, cousins, and other family members.

Cam's sister and her six children had gone to Canada in 1975, while her husband was stuck in a reeducation camp somewhere in the north of Vietnam like Binh. (He would remain there for more than ten years before he was able to leave the country.) By 1977 Cam's sister was routinely mailing packages of items quite unremarkable for people in Canada or the United States but considered as near treasure by those, like her sister, who received them in Vietnam. While it was not always safe to trust the mail, most of the packages actually got through.

A typical package usually included toiletries like toothpaste, articles of clothing, and food. Of the food items, candies, anything sweet and chocolatey, were like gold. They were far too valuable to consume. Cam's sister faithfully sent package after package, completely understanding their commercial value. It was a rare occasion that Cam would allow herself the pleasure of consuming any but would usually indulge Ngoc just a bit. Most of what was received became inventory for Cam to sell or trade, to turn into other merchandise to later trade or sell. Once Cam had reestablished communications with her husband and would need those extra resources to visit him and supply him, her business acumen became that much more important.

While the reestablishment of communication between Binh and Cam was a high point, a significant event, it was their one joy in two very small worlds; Binh's in his camp and Cam's in Saigon of simply trying to survive. Each of them might separately recall that song from long ago, the one which told of the soldier far away and his lover at home, both seeing the same moon at the same time and because of that they were somehow together, of one spirit even though physically distant. Like "Victory Flag Flying over the Quang Tri Citadel," that song had been expunged from the records and would never again be played over the airwaves. Binh was not authorized to write things like that in the letters he would send home. The Communist *cadre* would not have allowed for such *bourgeois* foolishness and sentimentality. But they could not stop him or his wife from thinking that.

In the meantime Binh's every day was spent turning large rocks into small rocks and then every night having to listen to the continual drivel of Communist propaganda. Six days a week, with time off on Sundays to mostly listen to more propaganda. For Cam it was just a bit more varied. She could at least have the pleasure of motherhood in those moments she was not working at whatever she was required to do so that there might be rice, vegetables, and maybe a little fish for her daughter, mother, and herself to eat. If she really pushed, there might be funds remaining to save towards her visit to see her husband. The entire family joined in the effort and pooled resources so that Cam, Ngoc, and all their supplies might go north to see Binh.

FIRST VISIT TO NAM HA

Ngoc's first personal encounter with her father, at least the one she would finally be old enough to remember, was under less than ideal conditions. Not quite one year old when he was sent away for his indefinite period of Communist revenge and reeducation, her father was made real for her by her mother who daily regaled her with story after story of his exploits as a Marine and telling her over and over how much he loved her. Ngoc never tired of looking at all of the pictures in the remaining family albums, one of the few things they had not sold for food, or listening to her mother's animated descriptions of this handsome, mythical man who was somewhere far away.

As much as Ngoc could enjoy life in Saigon, she did. The circumstances for her family, which were all she had experienced and was too young anyway to fully appreciate, were the same for most of the other folks they knew. Many, many thousands of children in Saigon were growing up without the benefit of their fathers' physical touch and presence.

The three-day train ride from Saigon to where they needed to catch the final ride to Nam Ha was anything but pleasant. There was very little sleep, no privacy, and minimal comfort. Cam began the journey with approximately 250 kilograms of food, medicines and sundries; a portion of which she expected to sell to people further north who were crazy to buy anything from the south, especially some of the food dishes she was able to bring along. Moving 250 kgs of stuff—six times her body weight—and shepherding her daughter as well was a logistical challenge, a major logistical challenge not for the faint of heart or spirit. In expecting to sell or barter approximately fifty kgs worth of her *cache*, some of that would be used as payment for getting porters to assist them. What was left would be for her husband to consume or trade as he saw fit. When she and Ngoc returned to Saigon, the trip would be less logistically demanding.

By 1979 the Communists had at least gotten the train which ran the entire length of the country to run on a fairly regular schedule. The ascetic, utilitarian Communists allowed comfort only for the most senior party members on the train. Regular folks shared the collective misery of riding in the crudely constructed passenger cars with wooden seats that were overcrowded and essentially open to the outside. The coal-fired locomotive belched out black smoke and soot that in the sticky humidity and breeze of forward motion blew back into the exposed passengers. By the time they arrived at the end of the railroad portion of the journey, and even though Cam the merchant had successfully retailed what food and goods she had hoped to, all of the long-suffering passengers; men, women, small children, everyone except the tiniest infants covered up with blankets, looked like diminutive and odd Vietnamese caricatures of Al Jolson; masked in coal soot. As much as Cam tried to scrub Ngoc and herself off in a nearby stream before they boarded the vehicle that would deliver them closer to Nam Ha, as much as she wanted them both to be at their prettiest, she knew that Binh would be thrilled to see and touch them no matter how they looked. She was right.

After they departed the train, Cam would need to hire two porters to help her and Ngoc lug all the food and sundries they had brought along to Nam Ha. Cam was also expeditiously able to "hire" a small truck loaded with firewood going in their direction. And so Binh's wife and daughter, their two temporary employees, and approximately two hundred remaining kgs of rice, salt, sugar, dried beef sticks (sort of the Vietnamese equivalent to beef jerky), cans of sweet condensed milk—the same stuff Binh's bodyguard "Three-Finger Jack" lovingly fed to an exhausted John Ripley after he blew up the Dong Ha Bridge—a few other food items, some medicines, and toiletries rode atop a truckload of charcoal to the front gate of Nam Ha.

Upon arrival with all their supplies, the items were inspected and then a female *cadre* searched Cam and Ngoc to ensure they carried no contraband. After that, they were allowed inside the camp. The two porters were dismissed.

The *twenty-minute* visit they were granted included the presence, always included the presence, of a political *cadre* in the room with them. They were allowed to sit at a table with Binh across from his wife, and the *cadre* at the head. Twenty minutes was a privilege, not a right. Take it or leave it.

From the time Binh had left up until the day they departed Saigon for their first trip, Cam had wisely and faithfully, on a daily basis, showed her impressionable daughter pictures of the now mythical man who was her father. "This is your father. He loves you very much," was Cam's standard line as they both seemed to enjoy looking at the pictures of the dashing Marine in uniform standing with both of them or alone in the few pictures remaining. Cam would tell her daughter stories of her father in a gallant attempt to keep his memory alive.

When they finally reached Nam Ha and were able to glimpse Binh for the very first time in more than four years, the initial meeting between father and daughter was not a happy one; not like in the movies or in a cheery fairy tale. The man before Ngoc was not *her* father, at least not the father from all the pictures shown her everyday by her mother. This man, this very skinny man with the smile but foul-smelling breath and body odor was dirty. This man was so skinny. This man who reached out and took hold of her reminded her of the garbage men she had seen in Saigon. This man scared her. And then suddenly their twenty minutes had expired.

The challenges of the first reunion were, compared to the shock for their daughter, minor for Binh and Cam. For both of them, even with their daughter tenuous towards her father, it was a joyous, albeit too short time. For Ngoc the reality of her father's situation, although far from unique among people her family knew, was difficult, nearly impossible for a five-year-old girl to process, make sense of, and feel comfortable about. There was genuine trauma caused by all she had just now experienced, and it would take a long, long time to heal and to understand all that was going on.

Ngoc's consternation was exacerbated by the return trip. To get back to where they needed to pick up the train, the same route they had come up on, was difficult as there were no vehicles going in the opposite direction and so the two women who mattered most to Binh were forced to walk ten or so kilometers of unpaved, dark, and scary jungly roads before they again reached an area where they were able to get a ride to the train station. To see and touch Binh, to talk with him face to face and know that he was alive and in reasonably decent health was reassuring. Now they could start the clock for another trip next year if the Communists allowed it. Like her husband, Cam would suffer the pain, but would never give up hope for the future. *Their* future.

The three-day trip home was at least a bit simpler logistically. No longer strapped with managing 250 kgs of goods, the primary burden was emotional; for both Cam and Ngoc. Would her husband survive another year? Would the Communists be so generous and allow her to visit again? How long would it take for five-year old Ngoc to have a genuine understanding for what was really going on?

Cam's additional *raison d'être*, along with caring for her daughter, would be the scraping and saving and plotting for the return trip. And she did it again in 1980, 1981, 1982, and 1983. Twenty minutes each time. In five years of visits there was not quite enough cumulative time to watch *To Hell and Back*—the movie that could have been played twice during the time John Ripley was under the Dong Ha Bridge rigging it with explosives—once. During that time Binh and Cam had both gone there. They had yet to return. At this point in their lives it did not yet look like they ever would.

Ngoc would not make the subsequent visits to Nam Ha as it was too expensive and the emotional challenges too severe. She would be watched by her grandmother while her mother spent a week away, traveling both ways for the twenty-minute visit she was magnanimously granted. As the years began to pass Ngoc came to understand that the "garbage man" was indeed her father, and the trauma diminished a bit. It had to. Take it or leave it. There was no other option for the families of these unconvicted criminals. In between each visit were nearly four hundred days of drudgery and monotony and pain. Take it or leave it.

LIFE IN NAM HA FOR BINH AND THE OTHERS

Nam Ha was different from Yen Bai in a number of ways. Closer to the coast and out of the mountains, it was much warmer during both the days and evenings; although still cool at night. At least when there was water for bathing one did not freeze in order to get clean, or in actuality simply less filthy.

Binh's duties at Nam Ha centered on making rock aggregate—turning big rocks into small rocks—as the particular camp he was in made concrete for various projects nearby. He would do the same thing every day. Every single day that he was at Nam Ha, he did the same thing.

Nam Ha was also different from Yen Bai in that it was a prison run by police and not the military. To the extent that some professional courtesies and a modicum of respect existed between adversaries at Yen Bai, that was gone at Nam Ha. Perhaps the police who ran Nam Ha felt intimidated for not being soldiers. Whatever it was; whether there was some sort of institutional inferiority complex or not, Binh noticed that the leadership and guards were generally just plain meaner and more corrupt. At least the guards and jailers could be bribed and bought off to a certain extent. Once the family visits for prisoners were initiated, life began to improve ever so slightly.

Between the small packages Cam sent to her husband in the mail, and what she brought during their fully supervised twenty-minute annual visits, Binh was able to eat better although his weight remained low as the work demands and still meager regular rations kept all prisoners significantly undernourished. In the circle of friends which most prisoners developed, the deliveries of food and toiletries were generally shared to everyone's benefit.

It was not uncommon while goods for prisoners were being received in for guards or *cadres* to randomly claim that such and such an item was unauthorized and take it for themselves. If money was given to the prisoners and the guards found out, they would make them exchange it for tokens to be used at the prison canteen. The prison canteen was set up for staff to purchase things. The prisoners were only able to purchase leftover items no one else wanted; which usually meant things like crackers which had ossified on the shelves and would break teeth if bitten into. Wives were required to become a bit more creative in the smuggling in of cash for their husbands; which they did.

The one item most prized by prisoners when wives came was sugar. Plain, raw, granulated sugar. With their ultra bland, meager rations of soup, vegetables, minimal rice, and protein, there was *never* anything sweet. Even for regular, non-incarcerated citizens there was very little sugar to go around. For the prisoners it was that much dearer. For every prisoner "sugar was more precious than diamonds." And far more pleasurable. So ravenous and starved for anything sweet were all the prisoners, that when given plain, raw sugar, their first response always was to wolf it down right away. Sugar and candy were not as happily shared, even among friends, as was rice and toothpaste.

Over time, with each successive visit by the wife and family of a prisoner, Binh and his mates would accumulate small amounts of money and other items for barter. Virtually everything they had was the result of their wives' back-breaking labor and steadfast loyalty. At Nam Ha one of the prisoners had somehow been able to procure a transistor radio. For security reasons it was always kept in several component pieces. When they were able to gather together in the prison yard each holder of a component piece would cleverly pass it to another fellow who would quickly reassemble the radio and they would huddle together, trying not to draw too much attention and listen to what they could from the BBC or VOA (Voice of America). What they were able to listen to would then be told and retold to prisoners who had not heard the news directly.

The prisoners knew more about the outside world than every one of their *cadres*. They knew about the war with the Chinese. They knew that the Soviets had invaded Afghanistan. They knew about the space shuttle although did not know exactly what it looked like. They knew about almost everything. The former RVN military officers in Binh's small universe were especially disturbed when they learned of the attempt on the life of the strongly anti-Communist President Ronald Reagan. That he had survived his assassin's bullet was seen as a propitious omen.

It was while surreptitiously listening to the VOA broadcasts that Binh and his fellow prisoners first heard of something called the Orderly Departure Program, ODP for short. The Orderly Departure Program was instituted in 1979 as a way to expedite the immigration of Vietnamese to the United States. "ODP" became almost a magic term, a mantra which would give so many in the long-suffering but un-reeducated group new hope for their futures. It was while he was still a prisoner in Nam Ha that Le Ba Binh decided that he and his family were going to America. Eventually.

The war in Vietnam, at least the one understood by Americans who had come and participated in with so much human and material investment was still ongoing, albeit in a much less tangible, identifiable manner. The victory that eluded the American effort, the one which had never been reduced to definition or set as a goal to achieve was now being waged between Communist jailers and their enslaved new citizens.

Unlike regular combat, the kind between armed opponents with its physical and logistical limitations—you fought until you ran out of troops or bullets and then broke contact—to survive in the bamboo gulag required other skills, other strengths. The war in the camps was moved to an entirely different arena. In addition to their jailers, the new enemy was time and doubt, despair and hunger. To gain victory a man had to endure time, overcome doubt, and suppress his despair and hunger. It was that or die. Every day. The Communists had possession of their bodies and controlled their stomachs, but their hearts and minds did not necessarily follow. And the war continued on; without end.

For Binh and every man held in the daily battle for thought control and revenge and retribution, victory was reduced to a bare-bones minimum. Each new day, when it too slowly came and replaced the one too slowly ended, if a man was alive and not completely broken and given over to surrender, was a victory. Each new day when one man times however many there were remaining in the hundreds of camps all over the SRV gulag, who had not given up and gone over to the other side was a win. Every new day brought Binh one day closer to release or death, and Binh knew that either way he would leave whatever camp he was in not giving in to the lies and foolishness his jailers were trying to put into his mind.

The people who now controlled the entire geography of Vietnam had written the truth of the TQLC and ARVN out of the history books. Every copy of "Victory Flag Flying over the Quang Tri Citadel" found and confiscated by the Communists had been destroyed. The song would never again be played over free airwaves in the Socialist Republic of Vietnam. But no one could keep it from being played in the mind of Le Ba Binh or the minds of his friends and prison mates; and there was victory in that.

In the recesses of Binh's mind he could recall a conversation he heard early on in his "reeducation" experience between a prisoner he could no longer remember and a jailer he could no longer remember. "How long will you hold us?" was the prisoner's earnest question.

The reply, which at the time seemed too cruel to even imagine, was cold and matter of fact. "You will spend a year in reeducation for each year you served the puppet government." That earlier assessment would ultimately prove to be close to accurate for most of the prisoners.[*]

To simply live one more day in the face of the abjectly horrible conditions, often physically and emotionally isolated, to survive the guards and *cadres* who at best were indifferent and at worst cold-hearted and sadistic, in the filth and disease, separated from family with only the affirmation of close comrades, the occasional letter from home and now a once a year twenty-minute supervised visit, to live without adequate food and medicine, with chronic hunger, to remain cold and not be made warm at night, to remain hot and unrefreshed during the day's stultifying heat, to attempt sleep with the thoroughly annoying high-pitched drone of disease-laden mosquitoes, always in your ear and sucking at your blood because the nets they were given always had holes, day after day, to be reduced to nothingness and not give up—that was victory. And so the war continued, without end.

For the Americans who had remained in Saigon—now Ho Chi Minh City—to the bitter end, the slide into the economic abyss would have made the place near unrecognizable in the years immediately following the Communist takeover. No seeing American could have missed that before the end, there were poor people, people on the streets begging, people in need of help. And yet with all the suffering caused by the war that could be blamed by the Communists on Thieu and Nixon and Kissinger, there was still food available for purchase. The markets had teemed with produce and fish and meats and merchandise.

---

[*] It was very common for men senior to Binh, full colonels and general officers, to end up spending sixteen to seventeen years in reeducation—if they were somehow able to last that long. Those men and their families had even greater emotional and psychological challenges to face once reunified.

By 1979 the misery and lost productivity due to attempted elimination of free market forces reapportioned the pain of shortages to a far greater percentage, virtually 100 percent, of the population. By government *fiat* the laws of supply and demand had been rescinded, and yet price was still the way, via the black market, to allocate scarce resources. The care package lifeline from America and Canada and France and wherever else became a major source of goods with which to supplement what the Socialist Republic of Vietnam was no longer able to produce.[2]

CHAPTER FORTY-ONE

American Dreams

By the time Binh was transferred from Nam Ha to Ham Tan in 1983, he had been a "student" of reeducation for more than eight years. While he and most of his fellow prisoners had accepted nothing of the Communist preaching, by this late in their reorientation experience, each man had earned an honorary doctorate in hardship, pain, and suffering.

At least Ham Tan was inside his *old* country, just 150 kilometers northeast of Saigon—it would *never* become Ho Chi Minh City to any of the stalwart southerners. Ham Tan's climate was more in line with what the RVN officers, unless they were displaced northerners, had grown up with. After being in the north for so long, the old climate would take getting used to, but that would be a good thing.

Binh's duties at Ham Tan were mostly farming related. Essentially he and the others did whatever their jailers required to raise crops of rice and vegetables. A good portion of the time they spent pulling plows, the most basic things that on typical Vietnamese farms were taken care of by oxen or water buffalo.

In addition to being much closer to home—Ham Tan was a mere six-hour bus ride away—the Communists were growing positively *bourgeois* and almost sentimental. Once Binh was moved to Ham Tan, Cam was allowed to visit him once a quarter; and for an entire two-hour period. The visits were still supervised, but the closer proximity and reduced cost of coming allowed for Ngoc to resume visits with her father which was good for all involved, allowing for some of the earlier emotional trauma for Ngoc to begin healing. It was still prison, though. Binh and his comrades still lived in primitive conditions at near-subsistence levels. No one got fat, even at Ham Tan. The days and the nights were just as long, the misery and the loneliness just as intense as it always had been; and there was never a hint that there would be an end to the process. Binh would have time there to pick up his second or third honorary doctorate in pain and privation. So too did his wife.

COMING HOME, BUT STILL IN PRISON

Binh's release from Ham Tan was anticlimactic, utterly unremarkable, and certainly unlike anything which might have been done in the movies. The morning of his release was little different than the more than four thousand other days he had already endured slaving like an animal for his Communist jailers. When the men on his particular work detail fell in to begin their work day, Binh was called aside and told to remain in camp. "Today you are going home." That was it. So he handled the paperwork he needed to, got on a bus for the six-hour ride back to Saigon—now Ho Chi Minh City—and went to the home of his mother-in-law to find his wife and daughter.

The process of sending a prisoner home was actually a bit more involved than just shipping him back. Prior to his departure, contacts were made with the police in his neighborhood and with his family. Interviews were conducted. The authorities wanted assurances that everyone would act like proper citizens, and that there would be no attempts at escape. It was sort of "Yessir, yessir, three bags full"…anything to get their men home. And so while Binh was surprised to learn of his release, Cam and Ngoc knew he was coming about forty-eight hours in advance. Needless to say, it was good to be home. Certainly there were adjustments to make, but those would be mostly joyful, and far less challenging than all they had been through in the last eleven years.

Between April 1975 and August 1986 a whole lot of life had happened. Binh and Cam had been married only three years when he was taken away. His prison experience was nearly four times longer than the time they had been married, and much of that time he was off fighting Communists. During that eleven-year absence he had really only known his daughter as an infant, quarterly visits to Ham Tan notwithstanding. There was significant adjustment for everyone involved. It would be a challenge, a challenge difficult to overstate, but one they would meet together, and certainly far easier to meet than all they had recently come through.

The world beyond Vietnam had changed as well. There would be no way people on the outside, especially people who had never had their country invaded and their freedom forcefully taken from them would be able to understand or empathize with the scale of the crime and brutality of "reeducation." And yet, it was somehow endured; second by second, minute by minute, hour by hour, day by day, week by week…and on and on until the years ran on to the too impossible to comprehend. For Binh and Cam and all of the others the only option open to them was to press ahead. There was no one they could sue.

During the period the SRV exacted its revenge against Binh and Cam and the hundreds of thousands of other former RVN military officers, government officials, and their families, the United States had moved on as well. From April of 1975 and into the 1980s, from the fall of Saigon, through the Carter presidency, the failed hostage rescue attempt in Iran in April of 1980—which again seemed to underscore the end to American military supremacy—and into the Reagan years, it was a tough slog. Americans endured recessions, inflation, stagflation, stock market volatility, and disco. But no one, not one regular citizen, except for those held hostage by the Iranians for 444 days, went through what the hundreds of thousands in the Vietnamese gulags and their families burdened by the losses experienced. A bad day in America was a far cry from a bad day in Vietnam.

Normal for anyone, normal for everyone, is a particularly relative term. For Marines who have spent significant periods in combat, time after is always appreciated in ways those who have not experienced war cannot quite fathom. Especially critical for experienced warriors is the need to press ahead with new learning; to not rely solely on what was already learned, to not expect to fight the last war during the next one.

Considerable resources and effort—intellectual and material— would be invested in the post-Vietnam War world so that American forces might match the more obvious Soviet or Soviet- surrogate threats in Europe, northern Asia, or wherever else the Eagle and the Bear might come to blows.

After Vietnam it was, for American Marines, back to the "every clime and place" stuff: jungle training, desert training, cold weather training, mountain training, and on and on, and over and over. For professionals like Gerry Turley, John Ripley, and George Philip, their paths would continually cross in the small world that was the U.S. Marine Corps and they would enjoy brief periods of fellowship. Whenever Ripley and Philip met they would shout, "King Kong lives!" and then take time to explain the meaning to those in earshot.

When Saigon finally fell Gerry Turley was still assigned to duty in Washington, D.C., and tangentially working with those few Vietnamese Marine officers taking courses at Quantico. At Camp Pendleton George Philip commanded his own artillery battery before being temporarily tasked with serving in the relief effort put on right there aboard the base to house thousands of Vietnamese refugees.

As the Marine officer instructor to the Navy ROTC program at Oregon State University, John Ripley watched the collapse of Vietnam and evacuation of Saigon on television. Like so many of his friends and comrades he could not quite comprehend his country's abandonment of its commitments. He was at once furious and melancholy. There was little he could do but press on; and so he did. Unsure as to what would happen to Binh and Cam and their infant daughter, he simply expected the worst. It was a bitter pill to swallow.

What would seem remarkable to most people living outside of any military experience, even during peace time, would be routine and almost mundane for what followed Vietnam for Gerry Turley, John Ripley, George Philip, and every other professional officer moving ahead in their careers. Going from posting to posting, from job to job; jobs as commanders, jobs as members of staffs, and time spent as students in various rank-appropriate schools kept them busy and moving ahead in a world which kept them focused mostly on the ubiquitous Soviet threat.

The best part of life after Vietnam, especially for Turley and Ripley, was that they were able to attempt to make up for lost time, to focus more on their wives and children. George Philip would pursue life and career as a maturing but still carefree bachelor.

There was no way for Turley, Ripley, Philip, or any of their former *covan* buddies to track those Vietnamese who had not been able to escape. Vietnam itself was like a black hole from which came no good news. While they secretly hoped and would continue to pray for their friends, that men like Binh were even still alive was beyond logical expectation.

Chuck Goggin, whose first hit as a major leaguer had been in Roberto Clemente's last game, continued playing through September of 1974 and then went on to manage in the minors for five more years. After four years in the private sector, he was appointed the U.S. Marshall for the middle district of Tennessee in 1983 by President Reagan. And life went on for the Americans.

Even though Binh was no longer in Ham Tan or Yen Bai or Nam Ha, he was still not free. As a former Marine officer, he would never be, could never be trusted. Upon his release in August of 1986 Binh was on what people in the west would call "parole" for the next year. Binh and Cam and Ngoc were visited frequently by the police during the following twelve months to ensure his proper thinking and citizenship.

Living at bare subsistence levels Binh was fortunate to find a job, through friendly connections, working in a small factory that produced Chinese seasoning sauce, called *"xi dau"* and not to be confused with the ubiquitous and traditional Vietnamese *"nuoc mam."* (Had Binh not found a job he would likely have been sent to one of the NEZs.) Once there, the people in charge recognized Binh's leadership and management skills. Before long he was effectively running most of the operation. It was not a difficult job for Binh. There had been significant wage and price inflation during the time he had been stuck in the gulags. His pay, as a manager, was a whopping one thousand *dong* per month. On the black market Binh would have to shell out three hundred *dong* for a single fresh egg.

The one critical benefit to working in the seasoning sauce factory was that they at least provided a rather hearty—compared to what he recalled from all the camps he had lived in—free lunch for employees. When he was not working there he was collecting trash items for recycling. Cam continued with the work she did while her husband was away although she no longer had to save for prison visits.

The dream hatched in Binh's mind the first time he had heard that Voice of America broadcast talking about the Orderly Departure Program all those years ago in the prison yard at Nam Ha had never dulled, never left his consciousness. Once he was able to communicate with his wife without the benefit of political *cadre* in attendance, Binh shared his dream of going to America. Cam was solidly behind the notion. They would tell Ngoc later when the time was right. It was not yet safe for her to know about it in the event she shared information with the wrong people at school.

Their new savings effort would be for paying the needed bribes to move the ODP process along. They would wait two years before they initiated the paperwork. Once begun, the actual bureaucratic process would take three more years. But what was that time after more than eleven years in the gulags?

Even though officially out of reeducation, Binh and his family were still *in* prison. All of the SRV, to them, was a prison. They were always being watched, Binh especially. The one major joy they could now appreciate was that they were a family again. The daily struggle to put food on the table and save a bit to accumulate for the bribes and everything else could at least be done as a family. They would work towards the other benefits of hard labor once they got to America.

The Communist masters in Vietnam were sparing in their charity toward anyone judged as an enemy of the revolution. The cruel treatment of prisoners proved that point. Families of those in the gulags, while not themselves held behind barbed wire, were nevertheless ostracized, denigrated, marginalized by those in power. Cam would note that over the entire period of Binh's being in prison nearly all the southerners she had contact with, many of whom shared similar circumstances, were kind and empathetic. That was not the case with the new leadership and rush of northerners brought to Saigon to fill the leadership voids. By the carpetbagging northerners moved down to run the new territory, families of prisoners were considered as enemies of the state. Children of men in prison were likewise punished for the sins of their fathers.

It was not at all uncommon for the children of prisoners to be ostracized and placed in separate classes at school, apart from the other children, as if they had some contagious disease, and were made to feel guilty and inferior. The psychological and emotional damage caused to children was not insignificant.

The Communists were big on the indoctrination of young boys and girls from an early age. There was no Western equivalent to the "Young Pioneers." The closest thing might have been scouting, but that was a huge stretch. At about ten years of age children joined the Young Pioneers and whatever indoctrination they had already been given in school was dramatically reinforced. It also ran contrary to most things taught and learned in traditional Vietnamese households. With conflicting pressure on them from their teachers and families, it was tough for children to make choices, to pick sides in the loyalty battle for their souls at so young an age.

The Communists were at least kind enough to allow children of most prisoners to complete high school. Resources for university education were an entirely different matter, and could not be wasted on people whose loyalty and citizenship were the least bit suspect. There was absolutely no upward mobility for children whose parents would always be enemies of the state. If Binh chose to remain in Vietnam, the opportunities for his daughter to get ahead would be virtually nonexistent.

"FOR THOSE WHO FIGHT FOR IT"

There was an adage common to American fighting men of the Vietnam era, origin unknown—one story claims it was written and seen on the sleeve of a c-ration box during the siege at Khe Sanh— which said: "For those who fight for it, freedom has a flavor the protected will never know," or words to that effect. Taking that concept a bit further, for men like Binh who had fought so hard and given so much for so long, and then had their freedom brutally stolen from them, only to then suffer again for so long, there was an almost unique, transcendent, inimitable appreciation for the true cost and real value of liberty. Few people would ever experience or comprehend what Binh and his mates endured, what Cam and her contemporaries persevered through while they waited for their men in the most unkind circumstances.

For the millions of enslaved people of the former Republic of Vietnam, the tortuous, flexuous road to freedom would take them away from everything they held dear, everything they had battled, bled, and suffered for. The liberty they had fought to gain, keep, or maintain was impossible to achieve in the new SRV. They would have to redirect their fight, change the method of battle and focus their energies in an entirely new direction. That new direction became the only viable alternative, and the only viable alternative was to leave. Leave the graves of generations of ancestors. Leave those close family members and friends unable or unwilling to make the hard journey. Leave all that were now only memories anyway, to give up most or all of their culture and embrace a foreign one, to suffer the challenge of starting over completely new, completely fresh in a strange culture with a completely dissimilar language.

REEDUCATION RECAP/LEAVING THE SRV

If the goals of the massive reeducation effort forced upon the people who died or suffered through it was to inflict maximum pain and long-term emotional trauma, the program was a huge success. In terms of gaining new, willing converts and advancing the cause of Communism or somehow enriching the nation, the program was an abject, catastrophic failure.

The nation and the people who were victims of the wholesale retribution would move on. Vietnam would advance into the future absent the individual and collective contributions those people might have made. For those who managed to survive; all of them scarred, some of them broken, and few of them given over to the new way of thinking, how they chose to deal with the remainders of their lives, whether in Vietnam or a new homeland, would be up to them.

In plotting his family's move Binh allowed himself no rest, no comfort, no complacency. The Orderly Departure Program (ODP) he had first learned of while a prisoner in Nam Ha had morphed into something now being referred to as Humanitarian Operation (HO). Whatever it was, Binh had confidence in the Americans. He had traveled to the United States all those years ago and liked it. The American Marines he had known were honorable, brave men. Even though many Vietnamese still had bad feelings over being abandoned by the Americans, Binh did not. He never did. He saw America as his family's only real hope for their future. He had confidence that if the United States said they could come, it would not change its mind.

Binh did not have that same sense of certainty about Vietnam. He was under no illusions. Somehow the Communist government might find excuse to detain him or his wife and daughter, maybe send him back for further reeducation. The Vietnamese government could do what it wanted. It already had; with him and all of his friends. They very well might do it again. Until he and his family were far, far away, where there were no secret police and the prying eyes and ears which always were on them, he would not rest easy.

It was 1989 when Binh initiated the process by which he, Cam, and Ngoc might come to America. The paperwork requirements, not surprisingly, were daunting. So too were the bribes and "gifts" needed to move things along. For three years he shelled out a little bit here, a little bit there. Sometimes the money was well spent; sometimes it went into the palms and pockets of officials without benefit. Eventually though, the wheels of progress seemed to be turning in his favor. They had long ago been accepted to come to the United States. The U.S. government had approved and Binh had sponsors; an aunt in Pennsylvania and a cousin in San Jose, California. It was left to the government in Vietnam to begrudgingly say "yes." It finally did, and in September of 1991 they were scheduled to leave.

There was great anticipation. There was also anxiety. Ngoc had just completed high school. She wanted to go to America where she might really go to college. She would have to learn English along the way. Although life for her family had always been extremely hard, she was leaving everything she knew. So too was her mother. They were nervous and excited, a little bit afraid of the unknown, but also expectant of a better future. They had been through tough times before. That was all they knew. At least in America no one would try to put any of them in prison.

Le Ba Sach, Binh's father, Vietnamese patriot and the man who had counseled his son to serve his country as a Marine so that he might participate in the eventual liberation of their northern homeland, was not well. With only months to live in the late summer of 1991, his son was aware that when he said goodbye to his father this time, it would be the final goodbye. Before they left, his father had some critical, concluding counsel. "Go...Go to America where you can be free, where my granddaughter and her children will go to school and be free, and prosper."

Binh and his father had many discussions in their last months together. His father never equivocated. "Go now. In America you do not have to worry about the government putting you in prison for no reason."

Le Ba Sach knew he would never see his son again. Everyone knew that. Binh especially knew that. "Do not be sad for me. With you in America I can have peace. I can die with a happy heart knowing that you and Cam and Ngoc are free."

Binh had suffered for too long to fully trust the government of the Socialist Republic of Vietnam. Even though he had the tickets, even though he had the paperwork in order, he developed a Plan B. He had already discussed it with Cam and Ngoc. If for some reason their emigration was denied at the last minute, he would get his wife and daughter out by boat or overland through Cambodia. He would somehow follow. Or die trying. He was *not* going back to reeducation.

Even though he knew it to be the absolute correct thing to do, leaving Vietnam was still difficult. Except for dying, he had essentially given his life, at least his youth, for his country— thirteen years of combat service from 1962 to 1975, and then "service" after his country ceased to exist for another eleven years in prison. He still loved the Vietnam which was now only a memory. Binh was realist enough, practical enough to spend little time pining for what would never be again. Whether he might return at some later point in the future or not, Binh knew he would never again see his father alive. If he did come back it would be to visit his father's grave and pay his respects. His father's encouragement and blessing mattered to Binh. But even without them he knew that moving to America was the only option for himself, Cam, and Ngoc.

REALLY LEAVING

After all he had experienced, Binh feared that somehow all their plans, all the paperwork, all the fees and bribes paid might come undone. The first leg of their journey to America was on a small Vietnam Airlines plane between Saigon and Bangkok. As the turbo-prop taxied out onto the tarmac to assume takeoff position Binh still would not allow himself to relax. Someone in the control tower might learn of his presence aboard the plane and order it back to the gate.

As the engines powered up for takeoff, as the pilot released the brakes and began their movement down the runway, Binh's edginess began to dissipate; ever so slightly. The takeoff roll seemed to take longer than it should have. "What is wrong?" he thought to himself for a second or two until finally, finally Binh's freedom bird broke its earthly bond and took to the air. He stared out the nearest window, as the aircraft climbed and banked towards the west, to have one last look at the country that once was his. Cam and Ngoc were looking out as well. After the plane reached sufficient altitude and seemed set on the proper course towards Thailand, Binh began to relax. They were on their way. Finally.

Just as it was not possible to adequately reduce to words or attempt to properly explain the extreme pain and suffering people like Binh and Cam endured through all the years of war followed by nearly as many of reeducation, it is not possible to overstate how special coming to America is for immigrants from countries where freedom is limited and abused. No song was too sentimental, no poem was too maudlin to describe how wonderful this New World, *their* New World, was.

Native-born Americans, who at birth are routinely vaccinated and immunized against a number of serious illnesses are, through probably no fault of their own, likewise inured and blinded to the too numerous to count blessings and opportunities people who have never had those blessings immediately sense and see upon arrival.

To paraphrase that Vietnam-era adage known by American fighting men, it is true that the protected are blessed in many, many ways they are unable to even fathom. For the Vietnamese men, women and children who constituted the second *diaspora*, the blessings of American liberty were very obvious, very tangible, and extremely sweet.

As their giant 747 approached touchdown in San Francisco, it would be Binh's second trip to America, but the first to his new homeland. It became his pleasure, though, to witness the wonder of seeing his new country through the eyes of his bride and daughter. Although there was trepidation and anxiety over the enormity of the adjustments before them, it was nothing compared to what they had already come through. They would learn the language. They would adjust to the culture. They would make do, and do well.

CHAPTER FORTY-TWO

Binh the American

June 1999
Hayward, California

L*e Mong Ngoc*, also known to her American friends as Caroline Le, graduated from California State University at Hayward in June of 1999 with a degree in computer information systems. She did it the way her parents had in Vietnam and the way most Vietnamese seemed to be doing it now in America: by perseverance and hard work.

After arriving in the U.S., she worked for four years, more than full-time actually, as a physician's assistant during the week and as a pharmacy technician on weekends. In 1995 Ngoc began college, still working full-time throughout her entire higher education experience. With a college textbook in one hand and her well-worn English-Vietnamese, Vietnamese-English dictionary in the other, Ngoc completed her bachelor's degree in four years.

In the audience to gleefully witness the moment of their daughter crossing the graduation dais were two extremely proud and thankful new American citizens: Le Ba Binh and Cam Banh. That Ngoc had been born on the 4th of July was something not lost on her father.

Joy
The USMC and Vietnamese Marine Corps Reunion
Washington, DC and Quantico, Virginia
August 2003

The expansive Marine Corps base at Quantico in northern Virginia, known to all Leathernecks as "The Crossroads of the Corps," holds a particularly special place in the hearts of generations of officers commissioned as second lieutenants of Marines. Home to "The Basic School" or "TBS," the quality and depth of training imparted in roughly six months of intensive, hands-on instruction there is so complete, so transformational, so impacting; the experiences delivered there run to soul deep; far beyond the learning of infantry tactics or Marine Corps drill and ceremony.

Most who later return there come back with a reverence and nostalgia beyond that felt for the good times in high school or college. The Basic School experience is the base line, starting point, ground zero for every officer; whether he serves an entire career as a professional Marine or only a single tour before returning to the civilian world. Basic School education ensures a very high minimum standard of quality for all junior officers before they are turned loose on the Fleet Marine Forces.

For nearly every Marine who passes through, it is always heartwarming, like going back to the old neighborhood, to reflect on special times, special friends and special experiences unique to Quantico. The same is true for the formerly young men of friendly foreign military services who have trained there; like so many Vietnamese Marine lieutenants did beginning in the 1950s until the war ended. And so it was entirely natural, almost obvious and unspoken, intuitively expected, that John Ripley and Le Ba Binh would together, just the two of them, after they had happily linked up, return to Quantico, to their individual and collective roots to rediscover and revisit their common experiences in their uncommon brotherhood.

The ride from Alexandria down to Quantico was long and pleasant. The traffic was moderate but far greater than anything Binh had remembered from his days there. Almost everything they drove by was new since Binh had served as a young student lieutenant nearly forty years earlier. There were few recognizable landmarks on I-95 although the surrounding woods on either side of the massive freeway, cleared back some since the early 1960s for all the development that had subsequently taken place, were familiar.

It was only when John turned off of the freeway to head first to Quantico's main entrance that it all began to come surging back...the smaller version of the Iwo Jima statue, Iron Mike, the enthusiastic salute and greeting given them by the young Marines manning the main gate at the northern end of the base, and the obligatory ride through Q-town always looking like some cross between a Rod Serling *Twilight Zone* episode and something out of the Great Depression, a place that was more black-and-white than TechniColor, with sparing, utilitarian red brick construction. This was a place that to everyone who passed through it seemed mired in more spartan times, times they had not experienced but could only imagine because of the minimalist nature of the place.

From Quantico town, Ripley gave his friend the once around the greater base. Most of the buildings were new to Binh, but the style of architecture had not changed so there was some familiarity, continuity from the past.

They then headed towards the southern gate, passing the massive PX which had been nothing but woods in Binh's day, crossed the freeway, and drove the back route up to Camp Barrett. Binh's mind was flooding with memories. He began to recall, in no particular order because it had been too long, the countless field problems and exercises, day and night, humping all that gear over Quantico's trails, his first experience with snow.

Arriving at TBS Binh observed very little from before that was the same. The Basic School facilities had gotten much larger. As they slowly drove around, an occasional Marine witnessing the officer sticker on Ripley's vehicle would offer a snappy salute. Binh felt very comfortable being there. Almost like home.

Ripley knew where to park, and so they did. Binh followed in close trace of his friend as they made their way to O'Bannon Hall. He began to remember O'Bannon and all that had gone on there; his American lieutenant friends, the noble but not entirely successful efforts made by the O'Bannon chow hall cooks to produce rice the way he and the other Vietnamese lieutenants preferred it. All of those things made him smile.

They crossed O'Bannon's main entrance and began their more serious amble down their collective memory lane. Neither Binh nor Ripley had paid close attention to the time. They were walking their old haunts inside of O'Bannon Hall, the capacious main Bachelor Officers Quarters building at Basic School. Named after First Lieutenant Presley O'Bannon who gained fame for his exploits against the Barbary pirates in the early nineteenth century, O'Bannon Hall was a hub of activity and all second lieutenants who were students at TBS, even if they were not housed there, at a minimum, ate in its chow hall, attended classes there, and drank beer in its pocket-sized and always crowded officers' club.

The "O Club" also had special significance as it was a place where bold and brash, indestructible and idealistic new officers drank pitchers of beer and proclaimed unending allegiance to their brother lieutenants and to the Corps. The tiny club itself, referred to by everyone simply as "the Hawk," was named after First Lieutenant William Hawkins. Prior to enlisting in the Marine Corps Reserve in early 1942, Hawkins had first attempted to join the Army and the Navy, but was rejected by both as physically unqualified. After service at Guadalcanal, Hawkins was instrumental in getting the action going while Marines were pinned down in their attempt to storm Betio Island during the amphibious landing on Tarawa in November of 1943. Hawkins personally initiated attacks into the withering fire of several Japanese bunkers which helped gain momentum for the Marines. When mortally wounded he refused evacuation, instead remaining to direct the actions of his men. For his heroic and selfless leadership he was posthumously awarded the Medal of Honor.

In Binh and Ripley's day, single lieutenants lived in O'Bannon Hall and drank beer in "the Hawk." Married officers lived off base or in government-supplied quarters somewhere else in Quantico, but were also welcome to drink beer in "the Hawk." (Since then, Graves Hall was also built to accommodate more unmarried officers. It was named for Terry Graves who had been a second lieutenant with Third Force Reconnaissance Company in Vietnam. He was posthumously awarded the MOH.)

It was entirely natural for Binh and Ripley, as they strolled down the corridors to this particular memory lane, which were at least weekly waxed and buffed by the student lieutenants living there, to find their old rooms in O'Bannon Hall. As it turned out, even though they had not attended TBS together, they had been housed, at different times, not five rooms apart. It was also apparent as they discussed the names of young officers they had known while serving as students there that a disproportionate number of them from this corner of O'Bannon had paid the ultimate price in Vietnam.

Binh and Ripley would walk along and then stop to look at some item or picture of interest, chat a bit, and then do it again in a way that only old friends who are completely at ease with each other could do. There was much to discuss, to catch up on, to share. As much as they talked, as little as they talked, most of the real communication was implicit; nonverbal but clear, deep, intense. Each friend was engrossed and focused in serious thought, recalling both difficult and pleasant memories until less was said; and it was completely appropriate.

The clock was running and each friend knew they would soon need to head back to Alexandria, back to the big evening banquet where all the Marines—Vietnamese and American—and their families would be gathered to commemorate and celebrate all the best of their collective sacrifices.

Tonight would be the Vietnamese and U.S. Marines official reunion with many, many hundreds in attendance; everyone who had even been remotely involved in the USMC-TQLC advisory experience between 1954-1975. Prior to this evening's get-together, most of the old *covans* had already linked up with their former Vietnamese compatriots. The stories for the Americans of which Vietnamese had survived (survived the war, reeducation, the horror of Communist retribution, and finally the challenges of coming to America), who made it out, who did not, were already making the rounds. For most it was their first reunion and for the wives and children of American Marines to finally make the acquaintance of these flesh and blood Vietnamese was distant history come to life.

Most of the Americans, retired Marine officers like Ripley, were all excited and aflutter to see their Vietnamese friends, and revel in their successes since coming to their new world. John had already seen a number of them. What made him feel the absolute best was to witness how well they had done. Ripley and all of the American officers in attendance were aware of their incredible suffering before coming to America with nothing; and then starting out on the bottom rungs of the socioeconomic ladder. Bringing with them the same tenacity and work ethic which had nearly secured their victory not thirty years prior and then sustained them through all those years of reeducation, within one generation so many of these Vietnamese were now firmly established inside of the American dream.

Horatio Alger would have been proud of their extraordinary accomplishments that were so common as to appear almost clichéd or trite. The stories of Vietnamese families who, in less than thirty years, had worked and sacrificed to get their children into the best universities and most critical professions were as good as any told of earlier immigrants who had come through Ellis Island a hundred or more years ago. John Ripley would have a wonderful time tonight for sure, but without the intimacy he was so enjoying currently with Binh.

The two friends continued going about the various places in O'Bannon Hall. Every now and then they would run into a lieutenant or two or three. The young officers in the hall or wherever else were of sufficient perspicacity to figure that these two relics were old Marines from long ago. They were always respectful, always deferential. The lieutenants would kindly greet or pass them by with a "Good afternoon, gentlemen," or "By your leave, gentlemen."

Ripley would professionally and properly answer with the customary "Granted." He would then boldly and characteristically make an additional remark; along the lines of "Carry on, Devil Dogs!" and the lieutenants would scream an "Oorah!" or something close to it. Binh just smiled. This self-guided tour went on for quite some time although neither friend had been looking at his watch.

After what seemed to be the naturally closing moments at O'Bannon Hall, after many but what for each of them were too few exchanges, and as they needed to be winding down, there was a prolonged silence which sort of signaled the end of the tour.

It was Binh who finally broke the silence: "Ripp-lee..." John Ripley, from the time they had first met way back in 1971, had always liked the way his name sounded when Binh said it. They were still ambulating gradually down one of the hallways. Slowly, with obvious thought and deliberation, Binh spoke with a voice that was barely audible. John Ripley knew his friend was about to deliver an important message. To better hear him Ripley stopped and leaned his head inboard. When Binh lowered his voice, it was a signal that something deep and difficult to say might follow. John Ripley looked squarely into his friend's eyes. "Ripp-lee, I am happy..."

Ripley heard his friend's words, paused, but obviously not long enough for Binh's liking, and replied with an answer too stock for Binh, "Yes, Thieu Ta, I am happy also."

Binh, the master of the understatement, was certain and frustrated that his friend had missed what he was attempting to convey. He tried again. Slowly and with the same deliberation he spoke one more time: "No, no, no, Ripp-lee, in here. In my heart." Binh raised his right hand, tapping his fingers loosely over the center of his chest; "In my heart, I am happy."

It hit him. It hit him right where it was supposed to. Suddenly, in the twinkling of an eye, Ripley was switched on, fully engaged and alert, his blood coursing. All of a sudden he felt like he did when he was Lima Six Actual or during the time of heaviest contact while serving as Binh's *covan*. He understood. He had received his friend's message. Binh the Reticent. Binh the Minimalist—when it came to expressive communications. With Binh, less was more, and he had just said it all. Ripley was not quite certain if it was his friend's challenge with sharing his deepest thoughts in English or simply *his* way. Perhaps it was a little bit of both.

In his own way, in his own understated way, Le Ba Binh had shared with his best warrior friend *everything* he could. Ripley got it, loud and clear. Ripley translated to himself the things Binh had said but that he was already pondering. Binh's "I am happy" statement was broad expression for so much, so many related but disparate experiences, sacrifices, so much suffering and effort. To both men, to all their brother warriors who had not backed down from their manly responsibilities, it meant: "I did my duty. I risked everything and was not found wanting." And now, with the benefit of time and age and wisdom, "I am happy" also meant that such service "gives me great personal satisfaction." Ripley was thinking all of these things and more as Binh spoke.

They had both paused now, all forward movement ceasing. They were face to face, not two feet apart, somewhere in the bowels of O'Bannon Hall. John Ripley—"Ripp-lee"—the warrior, the trusted advisor, for all time skipper to his Raiders, the man who blew the bridge at Dong Ha, husband, father, grandfather, friend, and mentor to so many, and more than anything still a Marine, stood there at near attention, smiling at his friend. Tears unashamedly streamed down both cheeks.

Binh's warm smile was returned to *his covan*. This time, before he spoke, Ripley placed his hands squarely at the side of his friend's shoulders, freezing him in his gaze. There he was. Binh, his wisest friend, *his* Thieu Ta, the man who, more than anyone he had ever met, exemplified all that was good and decent and strong, the man who, to him, had most personified the fighting spirit of the Vietnamese Marine Corps, the man who had taken all the Communists could administer, the man who suffered every indignity with incredible dignity, the man who had endured more than four thousand days of reeducation without being reeducated; leader of his vaunted Soi Bien, husband, father, grandfather, and likewise still a Marine, *always* a Marine, stood there waiting for the response, his eyes moistening as well.

John Ripley cleared his throat, a signal to Binh that what he was about to say had meaning and was difficult to deliver. Clearing his throat a second time, and with unwiped tears still flowing, he began. Slowly, very slowly, he spoke: "Yes, Thieu Ta, I understand, I understand. I am happy also." And he was.

After arriving in the U.S., getting established in a new life and working career, Binh finally retired in 2007. Now he and Cam focus most of their time and energies on assisting with the care of their two strapping grandsons, while daughter Caroline and her husband pursue professional careers. They all live together in northern California.

The post-Vietnam road traveled by the Turley clan was bittersweet. In 1976, while Gerry was the commanding officer of the Second Marine Regiment at Camp Lejeune, youngest son Chris was killed by a drunk driver.

After his assignment with Second Marines, Gerry was posted to 29 Palms in the California desert where he was a driving force behind the development of the Corps' very forward-thinking combined-arms exercise programs. Upon retirement—Gerry retired a colonel—from active duty in 1981 he penned his well-known book *The Easter Offensive: The Last American Advisors, Vietnam 1972.* In 1984 he received an appointment by President Reagan as Assistant Secretary of Defense for Readiness and Training, a job he held until 1987. Since then and up until the publishing of *Ride the Thunder*, Gerry has continued to work as a high-level consultant to senior Marine officers. In 1994, serving as a member of the Board of Directors on the Marine Corps Historical Foundation, he originated the concept for a new Marine Corps museum, which later became the National Museum of the Marine Corps at Quantico.

When not involved in USMC-related endeavors, Gerry and wife Bunny enjoy traveling, golfing, and spending time with their four children, eleven grandchildren (grandson James Bell, son of Peggy, has recently returned from his first tour in Iraq as a Marine combat engineer), and two great grandchildren. They live in northern Virginia.

George Philip retired from active duty in 1989 as a lieutenant colonel. Married a bit later in life, he and wife Fran—a senior executive with L.L. Bean—live in Maine.

Able to avoid reeducation, Nguyen Luong did not miss participating in the wholesale *malaise* of the Vietnamese reunification experience. Married after his discharge from active duty to his long-time girlfriend, they have two children—a son and a daughter—and, like Binh, were able to take advantage of the ODP. They came to the U.S. and northern California in 1991 where Luong still works.

Le Nguyen Khang was ultimately persuaded by senior American advisors and sensitive intelligence that placed him on the "shoot on sight" list of the Hanoi Communist regime to leave Vietnam during the final Saigon evacuation as it was a certainty that the invaders would have executed him and possibly his immediate family. He, his wife, and their three children moved to southern California in 1976. Khang died of lung cancer in 1996. He is survived by his wife, three children—a son and two daughters—and eight grandchildren. All three of the children are UCLA graduates. All three are professionals—an engineer, a pharmacist, and an attorney. General Khang's son married one of General Loan's daughters.

Chuck Goggin is still active in law enforcement and lives with wife Wendy—a former U.S. attorney and currently a senior official with a major U.S. government agency—in northern Virginia. They have two sons and two grandchildren.

Joel Eisenstein survived his ANGLICO tour in Vietnam and went home to finish law school. He currently practices law in St. Charles County, Missouri.

John Bowman retired from the Marine Corps in 1991 as a lieutenant colonel. He retired from his civilian career in 2007 and currently lives with his wife Grace in northern Virginia where he does volunteer work for veterans' organizations and enjoys spending time with their two sons and grandchildren.

David Androskaut—John Bowman's co-pilot on April 29, 1975, was killed while piloting an AH-1J Cobra between Tustin and Yuma, AZ a few years after returning from Vietnam. The accident was NOT pilot error.

John Ripley left active duty as a colonel in 1992 to further serve in different ways. From being president and chancellor of Southern Virginia University, president of Hargrave Military Academy, director of the USMC History & Museum Division, and a driving force behind the development of the National Museum of the Marine Corps at Quantico, John Ripley continued to operate only at full speed—and remained so until the day of his death on October 28, 2008.

Up until the day of his death John Ripley remained a presence both at the U.S. Naval Academy and within the Marine Corps. Ripley's passion for leadership training and character development were such that he was most at home interacting with young Marines and midshipmen in whom he invested great personal interest and concern. As with the undiminished passion his Raiders had for their skipper forty-plus years after he led them, he was near universally revered by those who knew him. Aside from the Corps and Naval Academy, he was only more zealous in his commitment to his faith, family, and close friends. John Ripley remained devoted to his wife Moline and their four children (sons Steve and Tom each served four years as Marine infantry officers). For his eight grandchildren John Ripley would attempt to move heaven and earth.

John Ripley's influence on the Marine Corps and all who knew him cannot be overstated. Present at his funeral were Marines of every era from World War II forward and of every rank from private to general. American Marines—a good many of them Ripley's Raiders—Royal Marines, Vietnamese Marines, Naval Academy midshipmen, and several thousand friends wept together at his passing.

AMERICANS

Philip Family

George Philip III: Graduate of U.S. Naval Academy Class of 1967, artillery advisor to TQLC's First Artillery Battalion 1971-72.

George Philip, Jr.: George's father who graduated with the U.S. Naval Academy Class of 1935, KIA during the Battle of Okinawa in 1945.

Margaret Taussig Helmer (Philip): George Philip III's mom.

Wilbur Helmer: George Philip III's stepfather, also a Marine artillery officer.

Snow Philip: George Philip III's older sister.

John, Jody, and Betsy Helmer—George Philip III's half brother and sisters.

Ripley Family

John Ripley: Graduate of U.S Naval Academy Class of 1962, advisor to Le Ba Binh's Third Battalion from 1971-72.

Moline Ripley: John Ripley's wife.

Steve, Tom, Mary, and John Michael: John and Moline Ripley's children.

Bud and Verna Ripley: John Ripley's parents.

George Ripley: John Ripley's oldest brother, also a Marine infantry officer.

Mike Ripley: Older than brother John Ripley by less than two years, served as A-4 pilot in Vietnam and was the first test pilot for the AV-8 Harrier.

CHARACTERS

Turley Family

Gerry Turley: Enlisted in the USMC Reserves in 1949, received direct officer's commission upon return from duty during the Korean War.

Bunny (Bernardine) Turley: Gerry Turley's wife.

Anne, Jeri, Peggy, Robert, and Chris Turley: Gerry and Bunny Turley's children.

American Marines

John Bowman: Cobra pilot who covered Saigon evacuation.

Charles Goggin: Infantryman and radio operator with Lima 3/3. Part of original Ripley's Raiders. Later went back to professional baseball.

Robert Sheridan: Senior American Marine advisor to TQLC Brigade 369 during 1971-72 and George Philip III's American boss during his advisor tour.

VIETNAMESE

Vietnamese names are presented in the Vietnamese culturally correct format, with the last name coming first. In America, Le Ba Binh is Binh Le.

Le Ba Binh: Vietnamese Marine officer who spent 1962-72 as a member of Third Battalion, starting as a platoon commander and finishing as battalion commander.

Cam Banh: Wife of Le Ba Binh.

Le Mon Ngoc: Daughter of Binh and Cam, born on the 4th of July 1974.

Le Ba Sach: Binh's father.

Nguyen Luong: Platoon commander in Third Battalion's Fourth Company, graduate of Vietnamese National Military Academy Class 24.

Le Nguyen Khang: First commanding officer of Third Battalion, first *commandant* of the TQLC during 1960-72, promoted to Vietnamese Joint General Staff in 1972.

Bui The Lan: Second *commandant* of the TQLC during 1972-75.

Vu Van Giai: Commanding general of Third ARVN Division during Easter Offensive.

Nguyen Van Thieu: Former ARVN general and president of RVN.

Nguyen Cao Ky: Former RVN Air Force general and president, vice president of RVN.

Nguyen Ngoc Loan: Brigadier General in ARVN who became national police chief prior to Tet '68. Made famous by photo and video of his execution of Viet Cong terrorist.

Ho Chi Minh: Communist leader aka Nguyen Sinh Cung, Nguyen Ai Quoc.

Vo Nguyen Giap: NVA general and Minister of Defense, most famous for masterminding French defeat at Dien Bien Phu in 1954. Also credited with planning Tet of 1968 and the Nguyen Hue Offensive.

Ngo Dinh Diem: RVN leader assassinated just prior to the assassination of President Kennedy.

EPIGRAPHS

1. President Theodore Roosevelt, "Citizenship in a Republic," Speech given at the Sorbonne, Paris, April 23, 1910.

2. President Richard Nixon, *No More Vietnams*, Avon Books, November 1994.

CHAPTER ONE : RED TIDE

1. Cima, *Vietnam: A Country Study*, 41.

2. Ibid., 43.

3. Ibid., 50-51.

4. Canh, *Vietnam Under Communism*, 120-123.

CHAPTER TWO: DRAWING THE BAMBOO CURTAIN

1. Canh, *Vietnam Under Communism*, 6.

2. Vo, *Vietnamese Boat People*, 37.

3. Canh, *Vietnam Under Communism*, 122.

4. Martin, *Warriors of the Sea*, 26.

5. Dunnigan, *Secrets of the Vietnam War*, 287.

6. Canh, *Vietnam Under Communism*, 10.

7. Karnow, *Vietnam: A History*, 281.

8. George Kennan to Chip Bohlen, 30 January, 1948. Accessed online at the George C. Marshall Foundation Web site, http://www.marshallfoundation.org/library/doc_strategic_background.html, May 19, 2009. The original is in the State Department records (Record Group

59 [Records of Charles E. Bohlen, Box 6]) at the U.S. National Archives and Records Administration, College Park, Maryland.

9. Whitlow, "US Marines in Vietnam: The Advisory & Combat Assistance Era 1954-1964," 50.

10. Ibid., 32.

CHAPTER FOUR: SUICIDE SQUEEZE

1. Lehrack, *No Shining Armor*, 113.

CHAPTER NINE: 1968: BEGINNING OF THE END

1. Nguyen, *Buddha's Child*, 231.

2. Ibid., 258.

3. www.lbjlib.utexas.edu/johnson/archives.

4. Shulimson, "U.S. Marines in Vietnam: The Defining Year 1968," 19.

5. Ibid., 17.

6. Lam, *The Twenty-five Year Century*, 25.

7. Ibid., 221.

8. Woodruff, *Unheralded Victory*, 301-303.

CHAPTER TEN: TET OFFENSIVE: OPENING ROUNDS

1. Nguyen, *How We Lost the Vietnam War*, 261 and Vo, *The Bamboo Gulag*, 45.

2. Nguyen, *How We Lost the Vietnam War*, 264-266 and Lam, *The Twenty-five Year Century*, 210.

3. Nguyen, *How We Lost the Vietnam War*, 265.

4. Nolan, *Battle for Hue,*184-185.

5. Shulimson, "U.S. Marines in Vietnam: The Defining Year 1968," 283.

6. Turley, *The Easter Offensive*, 10.

CHAPTER ELEVEN: HEARTS AND MINDS AT HOME

1. Karnow, *Vietnam: A History*, 547.

2. Andrew and Mitrokhin, *The World was Going Our Way*, 318.

3. Bowman, *The Vietnam War Almanac*, 200.

CHAPTER TWELVE: FORWARD OBSERVER WITH BRAVO 1/26

1. Shulimson "U.S. Marines in Vietnam: The Defining Year 1968," 585.

CHAPTER THIRTEEN: MAI LAI

1. Andrew and Mitrokhin, *The World was Going Our Way*, 305-306.

2. Ibid., 279.

3. Crozier, *The Rise and Fall of the Soviet Empire*, 266.

4. Andrew and Mitrokhin, *The World was Going Our Way*, 52.

CHAPTER FOURTEEN: BACK TO VIETNAM

1. *USMC—A Complete History*, various.

2. Melson and Arnold, "U.S. Marines in Vietnam: The War That Would Not End 1971-1973," 185.

3. Turley, *The Easter Offensive*, 14.

4. Martin, *Warriors of the Sea*, 15-19; and Binh, interview; John Ripley, interview; and Gerry Turley, interview.

5. Miller, various.

6. Miller, *The Co-Vans*, 166-186.

CHAPTER FIFTEEN: BACK IN THE STATES

1. Shaw, *The Cambodian Campaign*, 153.

2. Turley, *The Easter Offensive*, 25.

3. Miller, *The Co-Vans*, 124-125.

4. Sorley, *A Better War*, 269-271.

5. Miller, *The Co-Vans*, 50, 112.

CHAPTER SEVENTEEN: KING KONG LIVES!

1. Turley, interview.

CHAPTER EIGHTEEN: "TALK, FIGHT. TALK, FIGHT."

1. Nguyen, *How We Lost the Vietnam War*, 1-3.

CHAPTER NINETEEN: THE EASTER OFFENSIVE

1. Turley, *The Easter Offensive*, 56.

2. Gerry Turley, interview.

CHAPTER TWENTY-THREE: EASTER MORNING AT DONG HA

1. Gerry Turley, interview.

CHAPTER TWENTY-FOUR: EASTER MORNING IN SAIGON

1. Turley, *The Easter Offensive*, 145.

2. Ibid., 147.

CHAPTER TWENTY-FIVE: HIGH NOON AT DONG HA

1. Turley, *The Easter Offensive*, 156, and John Ripley, interview.

CHAPTER TWENTY-SIX: RIPLEY AT THE BRIDGE

1. John Ripley, interview.

CHAPTER TWENTY-SEVEN: A FOUR-HOUR ETERNITY

1. Lam, *The Twenty-five Year Century*, 266.

2. Turley, *The Easter Offensive*, 166-167.

3. Miller, *The Bridge at Dong Ha*, 150-159, and John Ripley, interview.

4. Gerry Turley, interview.

5. Turley, *The Easter Offensive*, 172.

6. Miller, *The Bridge at Dong Ha*, 158-159, and John Ripley, interview.

CHAPTER TWENTY-EIGHT: THE ONGOING VIEW FROM DONG HA

1. Whitcomb, *The Rescue of BAT 21*, 25-27.

2. Ibid., 30.

3. Ibid., 32-36.

4. Gerry Turley, interview.

5. Whitcomb, *The Rescue of BAT 21*, pg 43.

CHAPTER THIRTY-ONE: TURLEY FACES MACV

1. Sorley, *A Better War*, 322-323.

2. Frankum, *Like Rolling Thunder*, 156-157.

3. Ibid., 156-162.

CHAPTER THIRTY-TWO: ONGOING ACTION AT DONG HA

1. Melson and Arnold, "U.S. Marines in Vietnam: The War That Would Not End 1971-1973," 66-68; John Ripley, interview; Binh, interview.

2. Melson and Arnold, "U.S. Marines in Vietnam: The War That Would Not End 1971-1973," 285; Sorley, 323-324.

3. Summers, *On Strategy*, 134-135.

4. Bowman, *The Vietnam War Almanac*, 305-306; Frankum, *Like Rolling Thunder*, 149-163.

CHAPTER THIRTY-THREE: SECOND LIEUTENANT NGUYEN LUONG

1. As many as ninety missions per day, Melson and Arnold, "U.S. Marines in Vietnam: The War That Would Not End 1971-1973," 72.

2. Sorley, *A Better War*, 325.

3. John Ripley interview; Miller, *The Bridge at Dong Ha*, 179.

4. Melson and Arnold, "U.S. Marines in Vietnam: The War That Would Not End 1971-1973," 92.

CHAPTER THIRTY-FOUR: GOING HOME

1. Shulimson, "U.S. Marines in Vietnam—The Defining Year 1968," 214-216, and Vo, *The Bamboo Gulag*, 29-30.

2. John Ripley, interviews.

3. Melson and Arnold, "U.S. Marines in Vietnam: The War That Would Not End 1971-1973," 121, 126.

4. Tran, *History of the South Vietnamese Marine Corps*, 1168-1174.

CHAPTER THIRTY-FIVE: "CEASE FIRE"

1. Sheridan, interviews.

2. Bowman, *The Vietnam War Almanac*, 323-325.

3. Frankum, *Like Rolling Thunder*, 163-165.

4. Willbanks, *Abandoning Vietnam*, 42, 152.

5. Frankum, *Like Rolling Thunder*, 163-166.

6. Dunham and Quinlan, "U.S. Marines in Vietnam: The Bitter End 1973-1975," 2-4.

7. Bowman, *The Vietnam War Almanac*, 338.

CHAPTER THIRTY-SIX: OPERATION HOMECOMING

1. Vo, *The Bamboo Gulag*, 10, and Lam, *The Twenty-Five-Year Century*, 292.

2. Buhite, *Major Crises in Contemporary American Foreign Policy*, 324.

3. Aseansec.org.

4. Lam, *The Twenty-five Year Century*, 318, and Isaacs, *Without Honor*, 522.

5. www.miseryindex.us/customindexbyyear.

6. Willbanks, *Abandoning Vietnam*, 42.

7. Vo, *The Bamboo Gulag*, 10.

8. Willbanks, *Abandoning Vietnam*, 196.

9. Ibid., 193.

CHAPTER THIRTY-SEVEN: OPERATION FREQUENT WIND

1. Martin, *Warriors of the Sea*, 46-47.

2. Willbanks, *Abandoning Vietnam*, 270.

CHAPTER THIRTY-EIGHT: FALL OF SAIGON

1. Dunham and Quinlan, "U.S. Marines in Vietnam: The Bitter End 1973-1975," 169-171, 206.

2. Ibid., 199-202.

3. Lee, *From Third World to First*, 452.

4. Summers, *On Strategy*, page 1.

5. Vo, *The Bamboo Gulag*, 53-55.

CHAPTER THIRTY-NINE: REEDUCATION

1. Canh, *Vietnam Under Communism*, 188-196.

2. Vo, *The Bamboo Gulag*, 198-202, and Toai, *The Vietnamese Gulag* p 135, 195-197, 214-215.

3. Ibid.

4. Canh, *Vietnam Under Communism*, 37.

5. Ibid., 13.

6. Becker, *When the War Was Over*, 559-562.

CHAPTER FORTY: BINH SURVIVES THE BAMBOO GULAG

1. Chen, *China's War with Vietnam*, 105-117.

2. See tables from Canh, *Vietnam Under Communism*, 101-102.

TERMS AND ABBREVIATIONS

782 Gear: Marine term used to describe what a man carries on his body, including cartridge belt, canteens, ammunition pouches, first aid kit, etc.

AFB: Air Force Base.

ARVN: Refers to the Army of the Republic of Vietnam, which did not include the South Vietnamese Marines.

ANGLICO: Air & Naval Gunfire Liaison Company; a Marine unit used to specifically coordinate air power and naval gunfire assets.

Arclight: Term used to describe a B-52 strike mission.

CINCPAC: Refers to naval command at Pearl Harbor, Commander in Chief Pacific.

Covan: Vietnamese term used to describe advisors. Rough translation is "trusted friend."

Cowboy: Man assigned to serve as an officer's attendant or batman.

DMZ: Demilitarized Zone. The imaginary line at the 17th Parallel which separated the two Vietnams.

DRV: Democratic Republic of Vietnam, Communist North Vietnam.

Easter Offensive: The name by which the Communist invasion of 1972 became known in the West.

FAC: Forward Air Controller; an airborne fellow who coordinates air action over the battlefield.

FB: Fire Base.

FSB: Fire Support Base.

I Corps: Pronounced "Eye Corps" aka Military Region 1. The Republic of Vietnam was divided into four corps regions. I Corps was the territory closest to the DMZ, where most of the war's heaviest fighting took place.

JGS: Joint General Staff; refers to the senior South Vietnamese military leadership structure.

KIA: Killed in action.

LAAW: American answer to the RPG, rocket-propelled grenade.

M-48: The main battle tank of American design used by ARVN forces near Dong Ha during the Easter Offensive.

MACV: Military Advisory Command Vietnam.

Medevac: Medical evacuation; usually refers to the use of helicopters for the movement of the wounded from a battlefield.

MIA: Missing in action.

Nguyen Hue Offensive: The name by which the Communist invasion of the south was known in the north.

NVA: North Vietnamese Army; refers to the professionally trained and capable forces of the Communist north. Generally regarded as superior in capabilities to the Viet Cong which was usually made up of volunteers and conscripts from the south.

POW: Prisoner of war.

PT-76: Soviet-designed amphibious capable light tank, used in conjunction with other armor.

Quang Tri Province: The northernmost province in the Republic of Vietnam, also where most of the fighting in this story takes place.

RPG: Rocket propelled grenade; extremely lethal anti-tank, bunker, anti-personnel weapon of Russian origin.

R&R: Rest and relaxation; refers to any period when a man or unit is physically away from the field of battle. For Americans fighting in Vietnam it mostly meant five-day trips to Hawaii or other ports of call in the Orient.

RVN: Republic of Vietnam; non-Communist South Vietnam. In the story it is often used to describe all free forces, including units other than ARVN.

SAM: Surface to Air Missile; in this story refers mostly to the large SAM 2 and the man-packed SA-7 Strela.

SAR: Search and Rescue; refers to Allied efforts to recover downed airmen as in the case of Bat 21.

SRV: Socialist Republic of Vietnam. The name of the new country once the south had been officially absorbed into the DRV.

T-54: The main battle tank used by NVA forces in the Easter Offensive.

Team 155: Collection of mostly U.S. Army officers used to advise and coordinate action for Third ARVN Division in northern I Corps.

TOC: Tactical operations center.

TQLC: Tuy Quan Luc Chien; RVN Marines.

Viet Cong or VC: Usually refers to Communist forces from South Vietnam. Generally, but not always, less capable than NVA.

Viet Minh: Precursor to the Viet Cong and NVA.

VNMC: Vietnamese Marine Corps.

USMC RANKS (ENLISTED) LISTED IN ASCENDING ORDER

Private
Private First Class
Lance Corporal
Corporal: The ranks of corporal and sergeant are considered non-commissioned.
Sergeant: Officer, referred to as NCO.
Staff Sergeant: From the rank of staff sergeant and higher, called staff NCO.
Gunnery Sergeant
First Sergeant
Sergeant Major

Officer Ranks
Second Lieutenant
First Lieutenant
Captain
Major
Lieutenant Colonel
Colonel
Brigadier General (one star)
Major General (two stars)
Lieutenant General (three stars)
General (four stars)

VIETNAMESE MARINE RANKS

Ha Si: Corporal
Trung Si: Sergeant
Thieu Uy: Second Lieutenant
Dai Uy: Captain
Thieu Ta: Major
Trung Ta: Lieutenant Colonel
Dai Ta: Colonel

MILITARY UNITS

Lima Company, Third Battalion, Third Marines: John Ripley was the company commander to Lima 3/3 in his first combat tour 1966-67.

Third Battalion of the TQLC: Known as *Soi Bien* or "Wolves of the Sea" This was the battalion Le Ba Binh served with as a platoon commander, company commander, executive officer, and battalion commander between 1962-1972.

Third ARVN Division: The senior ARVN unit in northern I Corps during the Easter Offensive of 1972. Composed of the Second, 56th, and 57th Regiments.

VNMC Brigades: Each TQLC brigade was made up of three infantry battalions and support units. During the Easter Offensive the TQLC had three brigades.

During the Easter Offensive the senior American Marine advisors were:

Brigade 147: Major Jim Joy
Brigade 258: Major Jon Easley
Brigade 369: Major Robert Sheridan.

Andrew, Christopher and Vasili Mitrokhin. *The World Was Going Our Way: The KGB and the Battle for the Third World*. New York: Basic Books, 2005.

Ballendorf, Dirk A. and Merrill L. Bartlett. *Pete Ellis: An Amphibious Warfare Profit 1880-1923*. Annapolis: Naval Institute Press, 1997.

Becker, Elizabeth. *When the War was Over: Cambodia and the Khmer Rouge Revolution*. New York: Public Affairs, 1998.

Blackwill, Robert D. and Paul Dibb. *America's Asian Alliances*. Cambridge: MIT Press, 2000.

Blair, Clay. *The Forgotten War: America in Korea 1950-1953*. Annapolis: Naval Institute Press, 1987.

Bix, Herbert P. *Hirohito and the Making of Modern Japan*. New York: Harper Collins, 2000.

Boot, Max. *The Savage Wars of Peace: Small Wars and the Rise of American Power*. New York: Basic Books, 2002.

Bowman, John S. *The Vietnam War Almanac*. New York: World Almanac Publications, 1985.

Buck, Pearl S. *The Good Earth*. New York: John Day Company, 1931.

Buhite, Russell D. *Major Crises in Contemporary American Foreign Policy—A Documentary History*. Westport: Greenwood Press, 1997.

Butler, David. *The Fall of Saigon: Scenes From the Sudden End of a Long War*. New York: Simon & Schuster, 1985.

Canh, Nguyen Van. *Vietnam Under Communism, 1975-1982*. Stanford: Hoover Institution Press, 1983.

Cargill, Mary Terrell and Jade Quang Huynh. *Voices of Vietnamese Boat People*. Jefferson: McFarland & Company, 2000.

Catton, Philip E. *Diem's Final Failure: Prelude to America's War in Vietnam*. Lawrence: University of Kansas Press, 2002.

Chang, Iris. *The Rape of Nanking: The Forgotten Holocaust of World War Two*. New York: Penguin Books, 1997.

Chang, Jung and Jon Halliday. *Mao: The Unknown Story*. New York: Alfred A. Knopf, 2005.

Chanoff, David and Doan Van Toai. *The Vietnamese Gulag*. New York: Simon and Schuster, 1986.

-----. *Portrait of the Enemy*. New York: Random House, 1986.

Chen, King S. *China's War with Vietnam, 1979: Issues, Decisions and Implications*. Stanford: Hoover Institution Press, 1987.

Cima, Ronald J. *Vietnam: A Country Study*. Department of the Army, 1990.

Crozier, Brian. *The Rise and Fall of the Soviet Empire*. Roseville: Prima Publishing, 1999.

Cutler, Thomas J. Brown *Water, Black Berets: Coastal and Riverine Warfare in Vietnam*. Annapolis: Naval Institute Press, 1988.

Dunnigan, James F and Albert A Nofi. *Dirty Little Secrets of the Vietnam War*. New York: Thomas Dunne Books, 1999.

Fall, Bernard. *Hell in a Very Small Place: The Siege of Dien Bien Phu*. Cambridge: De Capo Press, 1966.

-----. *Street Without Joy*. New York: Schocken Books, 1972.

Fenby, Jonathan. *Chiang Kai-Shek: China's Generalissimo and the Nation He Lost*. New York: Caroll & Graf, 2003.

Frank, Richard B. *Downfall: The End of the Imperial Japanese Empire*. New York: Random House, 1999.

Frankum, Ronald B., Jr. *Like Rolling Thunder: The Air War in Vietnam 1964-1975*. Lanham: Rowman & Littlefield Publishers, Inc., 2005.

Gaddis, John Lewis. *The Cold War: A New History*. New York: Penguin Books, 2005.

Giap, General Vo Nguyen. *People's War, People's Army: The Viet Cong Insurrection Manual for Underdeveloped Countries*. Honolulu: University of Hawaii Press, 2001.

Hickey, Gerald Cannon. *Village in Vietnam*. New Haven: Yale University Press, 1964.

Hoffman, Colonel Jon T., USMCR. *Chesty: The Story of Lieutenant General Lewis B. Puller, USMC*. New York: Random House, 2001.

Isaacs, Arnold R. *Without Honor: Defeat in Vietnam and Cambodia*. Baltimore, Johns Hopkins University Press, 1983.

Karnow, Stanley. *Vietnam: A History*. New York: The Viking Press, 1983.

Kennedy, David M. *Freedom From Fear: The American People in Depression and War, 1929-1945*. New York: Oxford University Press, 1999.

Lacouture, Jean. *Vietnam: Between Two Truces*. New York: Vintage Books, 1966.

Lam, Quang Thi. *The Twenty-five Year Century: A South Vietnamese General Remembers the Indochina War to the Fall of Saigon*. Denton: University of North Texas Press, 2001.

Lee, Kuan Yew. *From Third World to First, The Singapore Story: 1965-2000*. New York, Harper Collins, 2000.

Lehrack, Otto. *No Shining Armor: The Marines at War in Vietnam, An Oral History*. Lawrence: University of Kansas Press, 1992.

Lind, Michael. *Vietnam The Necessary War*. New York: The Free Press, 1999.

McCullough, David. *Truman*. New York: Simon & Schuster, 1992.

Mahan, Captain Alfred Thayer, USN. *The Influence of Sea Power Upon History 1660-1783*. New York: Hill and Wang, 1957.

Marine Corps Association. *USMC: A Complete History*. Quantico: Marine Corps Association, 2002.

Martin, Michael. *Warriors of the Sea: Marines and the Second Indochina War*. Paducah, Kentucky: Turner Publishing Company, 2001.

Metzner, Edward P, Huynh Van Chinh, Tran Van Phuc, and Le Nguyen Binh. *Reeducation in Postwar Vietnam—Personal Postscripts to Peace*. College Station, Texas: Texas A & M University Press, 2001.

Miller, Colonel John, USMC. *The Bridge at Dong Ha*. Annapolis: Naval Institute Press, 1989.

-----. *The Co-Vans: U.S. Marine Advisors in Vietnam*. Annapolis: Naval Institute Press, 2000.

Millett, Allan R. *Semper Fidelis: The History of the United States Marine Corps*. New York: Macmillan Publishing, 1980.

Murphy, Edward F. *Vietnam Medal of Honor Heroes*. New York: Presidio Press, 1987.

Morris, Stephen J. *Why Vietnam Invaded Cambodia: Political Culture and the Causes of War*. Stanford: Stanford University Press, 1999.

Nguyen, Cao Ky with Marvin Wolf. *Buddha's Child: My Fight to Save Vietnam*. New York: St Martin's Press, 2002.

Nguyen, Cao Ky. *How We Lost the Vietnam War*. New York: Cooper Square Press, 2002.

Nolan, Keith William. *Battle for Hue: Tet 1968*. Novato: Presidio Press, 1983.

Peebles, Curtis. *Twilight Warriors: Covert Air Operations against the USSR*. Annapolis: Naval Institute Press, 2005.

Sewell, Kenneth with Clint Richmond. *Red Star Rogue: The Untold Story of a Soviet Submarine's Nuclear Strike Attempt on the U.S.* New York: Simon & Schuster, 2005.

Shaw, John. *The Cambodian Campaign: The 1970 Offensive and America's Vietnam War*. Lawrence: University Press of Kansas, 2005.

Sorley, Lewis. *A Better War: The Unexamined Victories and Final Tragedy of America's Last Years in Vietnam*. New York: Harcourt, 1999.

Shecter, Jerrold and Leona. *Sacred Secrets: How Soviet Intelligence Operations Changed American History*. Washington D.C.: Brassey's Inc, 2002.

Sheehan, Neil. *A Bright Shining Lie: John Paul Vann and America in Vietnam*. New York: Vintage Books, 1988.

Summers, Harry G., Jr. *On Strategy: A Critical Analysis of the Vietnam War*. New York: Vintage Books, 1982.

Tarling, Nicolas. *The Cambridge History of Southeast Asia Volume Two, The 19th and 20th Centuries*. Cambridge: Cambridge University Press, 1994.

Tin, Bui. *Following Ho Chi Minh: Memoirs of a North Vietnamese Colonel*. Honolulu: University of Hawaii Press, 1995.

Toland, John, *The Rising Sun: The Decline and Fall of the Japanese Empire 1936-1945*. New York: Random House, 1970.

Tran, Xuan Dung MD. *History of the South Vietnamese Marine Corps Volumes 1 & 2*. South Melbourne: Corporate Printers, 2007.

Truong, Nhu Trang. *A Viet Cong Memoir: An Inside Account of the Vietnam War and its Aftermath*. New York: Vintage Books, 1985.

Tuchman, Barbara W. *Stilwell and the American Experience in China 1911-1945*. New York: Macmillan Company, 1970.

Turley, Colonel G.H., USMCR. *The Easter Offensive: The Last American Advisors, Vietnam, 1972*. Annapolis: Naval Institute Press, 1985.

Vickery, Michael. *Cambodia 1975-1982*. Chiang Mai. Silkworm Books, 1999.

Vo, Nghia M. *The Bamboo Gulag: Political Imprisonment in Communist Vietnam*. Jefferson: McFarland & Company, 2004.

-----. *The Vietnamese Boat People: 1954 and 1975-1992*. Jefferson: McFarland & Company, 2005.

Warr, Nicholas. *Phase Line Green: The Battle for Hue, 1968*. Annapolis: Naval Institute Press, 1997.

Whitcomb, Darrel D. *The Rescue of BAT 21*. New York: Dell, 1999.

Willbanks, James H. *Abandoning Vietnam: How America Left and South Vietnam Lost Its War*. Lawrence: University of Kansas Press, 2004.

Woodruff, Mark. *Unheralded Victory: The Defeat of the Viet Cong and the North Vietnamese Army 1961-1973*. Arlington: Vandamere Press, 1999.

Zhai, Quiang. *China & the Vietnam Wars, 1950-1975*. Chapel Hill: University of North Carolina Press, 2000.

PERSONAL INTERVIEWS

Banh, Cam, various interviews with author, 2003-2008.

Bell (Turley), Peggy, various interviews with author, 2003-2008.

Binh, Le Ba, various interviews with author, 2003-2008.

Bongaard, Jim, various interviews with author, 2007-2008.

Bowman, Lieutenant Colonel John W., Jr., USMC, Ret., various interviews with author, 2007-2008.

Gilley (Turley), Anne, varioud interviews with author, 2003-2008.

Goggin, Charles, various interviews with author, 2004-2008.

Joy, Brigadier General James, USMC, Ret., various interviews with author, 2007-2008.

Luong, Nguyen, various interviews with author, 2003-2008.

McCourt, Captain Ed, USMC, Ret., various interviews with author, 2003-2006.

Philip, Lieutenant Colonel George, USMC, Ret., various interviews with author, 2003-2008.

Ripley, Colonel John W., USMC, Ret., various interviews with author, 2003-2008.

Sheridan, Lieutenant Colonel Robert, USMC, Ret., various interviews with author, 2007-2008.

Tan, Hue, various interviews with author, 2003-2008.

Turley, Bernardine (Bunny), various interviews with author, 2003-2008, various

Turley, Colonel Gerry, USMCR, Ret., various interviews with author, 2003-2008.

Wischmeyer, Colonel William, USMC, Ret., various interviews with author, 2003-2004.

U.S. GOVERNMENT DOCUMENTS

Foreign Area Studies—The American University. "Area Handbook for North Vietnam June 1967." Washington, DC: U.S. Government Printing Office, 1967.

Headquarters, Department of the Army. "Vietnam: A Country Study." Washington, DC: U.S. Government Printing Office, 1989.

United States Marine Corps. "Small Wars Manual 1940." Manhattan: Sunflower University Press, 2004.

-----. "Quantico: Crossroads of the Marine Corps." By Lieutenant Colonel Charles Fleming, Captain Robin Austin, and Captain Charles Braley, III, History and Museums Division, Headquarters, U.S. Marine Corps: Washington, DC, 1978.

-----. "US Marines in Vietnam: The Advisory & Combat Assistance Era 1954-1964." By Captain Robert H. Whitlow, History and Museums Division, Headquarters, U.S. Marine Corps: Washington, DC, 1977.

-----. "U.S. Marines in Vietnam: The Landing and the Buildup 1965." By Jack Shulimson and Major Charles Johnson, History and Museums Division, Headquarters, U.S. Marine Corps: Washington, DC, 1978.

-----. "U.S. Marines in Vietnam: An Expanding War 1966." By Jack Shulimson, History and Museums Division, Headquarters, U.S. Marine Corps: Washington, DC, 1982.

-----. "US Marines in Vietnam: Fighting the North Vietnamese 1967." By Major Gary Telfer, Lieutenant Colonel Lane Rogers, V. Keith Fleming, Jr., History and Museums Division, Headquarters, U.S. Marine Corps: Washington, DC, 1984.

-----. "U.S. Marines in Vietnam: The Defining Year 1968." By Jack Shulimson, Lieutenant Colonel Leonard Blaisol, Charles R. Smith, Captain David Dawson, History and Museums Division, Headquarters, U.S. Marine Corps: Washington, DC, 1997.

-----. "U.S. Marines in Vietnam: Vietnamization and Redeployment 1970-1971." By Graham Cosmay and Lieutenant Colonel Terrence Murray, History and Museums Division, Headquarters, U.S. Marine Corps: Washington, DC, 1986.

-----. "U.S. Marines in Vietnam: The War That Would Not End 1971-1973." By Major Charles Melson and Lieutenant Colonel Curtis Arnold, History and Museums Division, Headquarters, U.S. Marine Corps: Washington, DC, 1991.

-----. "U.S. Marines in Vietnam: The Bitter End 1973-1975." By Major George Dunham and Colonel David Quinlan, History and Museums Division, Headquarters, U.S. Marine Corps: Washington, DC, 1990

I

J

Q

R

X

Y